Frommer's®

Miami &
the Keys 2000

Here's what the critics say about Frommer's:

"Amazingly easy to use. Very portable, very complete."
—*Booklist*

♦

"The only mainstream guide to list specific prices. The Walter Cronkite of guidebooks—with all that implies."
—*Travel & Leisure*

♦

"Complete, concise, and filled with useful information."
—*New York Daily News*

♦

"Hotel information is close to encyclopedic."
—*Des Moines Sunday Register*

Other Great Guides for Your Trip:

Frommer's Florida

Frommer's Florida from $60 a Day

The Unofficial Guide to Miami and the Keys

Frommer's Walt Disney World and Orlando

The Unofficial Guide to Walt Disney World

The Complete Idiot's Travel Guide to Walt Disney World

The Complete Idiot's Travel Guide to Florida

Frommer's Florida Best-Loved Driving Tours

Frommer's® 2000

Miami & the Keys

by Victoria Pesce Elliott

with Online Directory by Michael Shapiro

MACMILLAN • USA

ABOUT THE AUTHOR

Victoria Pesce Elliott is a freelance journalist who contributes to many local and national newspapers and magazines, including *The New York Times*. A native of Miami, she returned there after nearly a decade in New York City, where she graduated from the Columbia University School of Journalism. She is a co-author of *Frommer's Florida* and *Fromer's Florida on $60 a Day.*

MACMILLAN TRAVEL

Macmillan General Reference USA, Inc.
1633 Broadway
New York, NY 10019

Find us online at **www.frommers.com**

Copyright ® 1999 by Macmillan General Reference USA Inc.
Maps copyright ® by Macmillan General Reference USA Inc.

ISBN 0-02-863233-8
ISSN 1047-790X

Editor: Bob O'Sullivan
Production Editor: Donna Wright
Photo Editor: Richard Fox
Design by Michele Laseau
Staff Cartographers: John DeCamillis and Roberta Stockwell
Additional Cartography by Raffaele DeGennaro and Ortelius Design
Page Creation by Melissa Auciello-Brogan and Bob LaRoche

SPECIAL SALES

Bulk purchases (10+ copies) of Frommer's and selected Macmillan travel guides are available to corporations, organizations, mail-order catalogs, institutions, and charities at special discounts, and can be customized to suit individual needs. For more information write to Special Sales, Macmillan General Reference, 1633 Broadway, New York, NY 10019.

Manufactured in the United States of America.

5 4 3 2 1

Contents

7   **What to See & Do in Miami   115**

8   **Driving & Strolling Around Miami   140**

9   **Miami Shopping   151**

10   **Miami After Dark   166**

List of Maps

AN INVITATION TO THE READER

In researching this book, we discovered many wonderful places—hotels, restaurants, shops, and more. We're sure you'll find others. Please tell us about them, so we can share the information with your fellow travelers in upcoming editions. If you were disappointed with a recommendation, we'd love to know that, too. Please write to:

Frommer's Miami & the Keys 2000
Macmillan Travel
1633 Broadway
New York, NY 10019

AN ADDITIONAL NOTE

Please be advised that travel information is subject to change at any time—and this is especially true of prices. We suggest, therefore, that you write or call ahead for confirmation when making your travel plans. The authors, editors, and publisher cannot be held responsible for the experiences of readers while traveling. Your safety is important to us, however, so we encourage you to stay alert and be aware of your surroundings. Keep a close eye on cameras, purses, and wallets, all favorite targets of thieves and pickpockets.

WHAT THE SYMBOLS MEAN

✪ Frommer's Favorites

Our favorite places and experiences—outstanding for quality, value, or both.

The following abbreviations are used for credit cards:

AE	American Express	EURO	Eurocard
CB	Carte Blanche	JCB	Japan Credit Bank
DC	Diners Club	MC	MasterCard
DISC	Discover	V	Visa

FIND FROMMER'S ONLINE

Arthur Frommer's *Budget Travel Online* (www.frommers.com) offers more than 6,000 pages of up-to-the-minute travel information—including the latest bargains and candid personal articles updated daily by Arthur Frommer himself. No other Web site offers such comprehensive and timely coverage of the world of travel.

The Best of Miami & South Florida

It's hard to know in which language to introduce yourself to the mini-nation of Miami. When you land at Miami International Airport, the nation's second-largest hub for international travelers, you'll hear Spanish, Portuguese, creole, French, and Italian as a matter of course. Once in Miami, you'll find a curious mix of Caribbean immigrants, orthodox Jews, retirees seeking easier winters, models, actors, artists, wealthy real estate moguls, and movie executives, as well as an already diverse crowd of long-time Floridians, black descendants of Bahamian railroad workers, Native Americans, and Hispanics. The city is a virtual mosaic of colors, sounds, and scents.

Since the Spanish first colonized the area in the 16th century, Miami has been a magnet for the masses, and it continues to grow at a rapid pace. Since 1980, Miami-Dade County's population has increased by nearly 33%. Despite the uncontrolled influx of foreigners (and partly because of it) the area has become an international tourist destination.

Through its many incarnations, two Miami characteristics have remained constant—its predictable year-round warmth and its location on a peninsula pointing emphatically toward so many other nations. Now Miami, known as "The Capital of the Americas," serves as Latin American and international headquarters for hundreds of multinational corporations.

Encompassing both the mainland and the barrier islands of Miami Beach, Greater Miami boasts about two million residents and hosts more than nine million visitors annually. They come for different reasons. Some are drawn by the sea and surf; some for the outrageous nightlife; others for the business opportunities; still others can't get enough of the natural wilderness right in the city's backyard.

Fortunately, the evolution of America's southernmost metropolitan region—from a simple playground to a vibrant cosmopolitan city—has not been achieved at the expense of the area's celebrated surf and sand. Despite Miami's quick transformation, the almost complete absence of heavy industry has left the air and water relatively unpolluted. Miami is not just a beach vacation, however—you'll also find high-quality hotels, distinctive restaurants, unusual attractions, some quality cultural offerings, incredible nightlife, and top shopping.

Florida

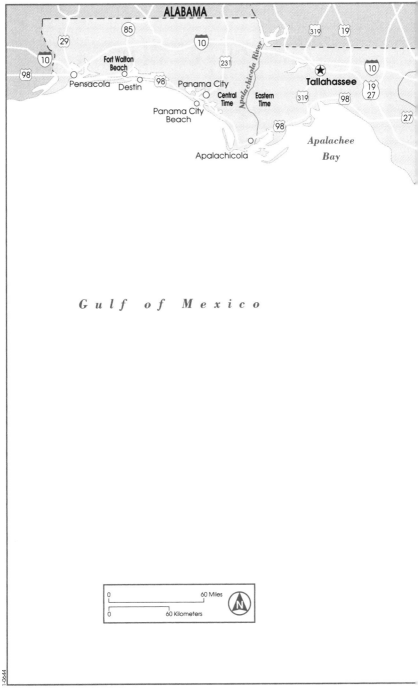

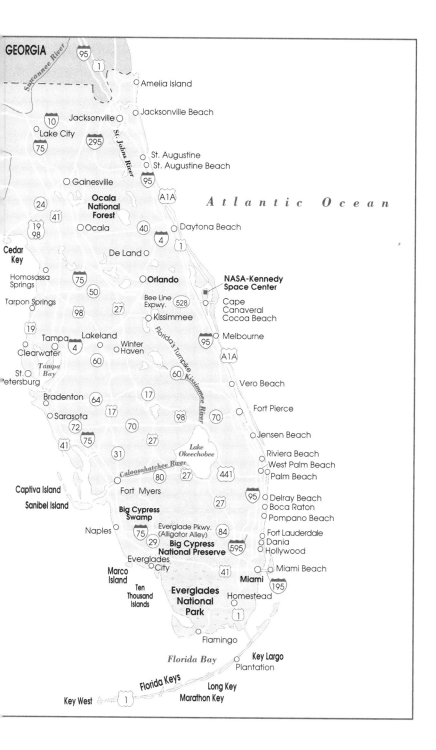

And while you're down here, why not take a day or two to escape the city and explore some of the experiences unique to the Keys and the cities of South Florida's Gold Coast? In addition to the experiences mentioned below, I've expanded this edition of the book to include coverage of Fort Lauderdale, Boca Raton, the Palm Beaches, Jupiter, and other cities and towns along this famed bit of coastline. For more information on the Florida Keys and the Gold Coast, turn to chapters 12 and 13, respectively.

1 Frommer's Favorite South Florida Experiences

- **Boating off the Coast of Miami Beach.** Jump on a party boat, take a sightseeing cruise, or rent a skiff. A boat ride off the coast of Miami Beach is the best way to see the elegant waterfront mansions, dramatic skyline, and gorgeous coastline that make Miami so alluring.
- **Shopping.** One of Miami's biggest draws is its incredible selection of stores. Many visitors from the Caribbean and Latin America come for the sole purpose of buying. From electronics to shoes and hardware to exotic grocery items, this is the place to shop. Bring the credit cards.
- **Cruising with the Top Down.** Driving in a convertible over the causeways to any of Miami's wonderful islands is one of my favorite things to do, especially in the mild winter months from December through March. Tune the radio to a Latin station, catch the warm sun on your bare shoulders, and watch the water glimmer around you.
- **Lunching in Little Havana.** Miami's Cuban center is the city's most distinctive ethnic enclave. Located just west of Downtown, Little Havana is centered around "Calle Ocho," SW 8th Street. Car-repair shops, tailors, electronics stores, and restaurants all hang signs in Spanish; salsa rhythms thump from the radios of passersby; and old men in guayaberas chain-smoke cigars over their daily games of dominoes. Stop for a big filling lunch, and top it off with a Cuban coffee to really get the day going.
- **Biking, Blading, or Walking Through the Art Deco District on Ocean Drive.** The beauty of South Beach's celebrated Art Deco District culminates on the 15-block beachfront strip known as Ocean Drive. Most of the buildings on this stretch are hotels built in the late 1930s and early 1940s. You'll appreciate the architecture and the colorful characters as you go down this street—by bike, by in-line skates, or on foot.
- **Relaxing on the Beaches.** You can choose your spot on dozens of miles of white-sand beaches, edged with coconut palms on one side and a clear turquoise ocean on the other. Each of the many area beaches boasts its own distinctive character. Don't forget your sunscreen.
- **Dancing Until Dawn.** Choose your dance floor, from salsa at the Latin clubs to techno and house at European-style places to jamming at outdoor reggae bars.
- **Enjoying New World Cuisine.** World-class chefs have discovered the richness of locally harvested ingredients, including tropical fruits and seafood. This culling of techniques and ingredients from the Cuban, Haitian, and Asian communities has created the now-famous "New World Cuisine."
- **Doing Whatever on, in, or Above the Water.** One of the best ways to appreciate South Florida is from the water—on it, in it, or above it. Options include parasailing, jet-skiing, kayaking, sailing, scuba diving, snorkeling, and windsurfing. Of course, you can always swim or ride the waves, as well.

- **Snorkeling in Biscayne National Park.** The thriving reef system at Biscayne National Park, a unique ecological preserve that's mostly underwater, attracts thousands of scuba divers and snorkelers every year.
- **Canoeing Through the Everglades.** Paddling through the unique ecosystem that is the Everglades gives you a chance to slow down and appreciate the natural beauty of South Florida. You're sure to see an alligator or two, and maybe even a manatee.
- **Strolling Las Olas Boulevard.** Fort Lauderdale's premiere shopping, eating, and people-watching promenade is fun in the day or night.
- **Bar Hopping on Duval Street.** From Mallory Square to the Atlantic Ocean you can walk or stumble (depending on how long you've been at it) to dozens of bars and clubs that line this famously wild block of Key West. From Margaritaville to Sloppy Joe's and Louie's Backyard, there are bars for all types, whether you want to watch the sunset, feel a calm breeze, or listen to Jimmy Buffet wannabes.
- **Window Shopping Along Palm Beach Worth Avenue.** It's been called "the Rodeo Drive of Palm Beach," and it's every bit as pricey. Check the Cartier display for a taste of opulence, or peek into Paper Treasures for an autograph of heroes like Amelia Earhart, Joe DiMaggio, Mickey Mantle, Andrew Jackson, and even Honest Abe Lincoln.

2   Best Hotel Bets

- **Best Historic Hotel:** The **Biltmore Hotel Coral Gables** (☎ **800/228-3000** or 305/445-1926) will soon celebrate its 75th birthday and is Miami's oldest hotel. The founder of Coral Gables, George Merrick, built this grand old hotel in a Mediterranean style, with a huge bell tower based on the Giralda tower in Seville. It's now restored to its original 1926 splendor, and rooms are large and luxurious.
- **Best for Business Travelers:** The **Hotel Inter-Continental Miami** (☎ **800/332-4246** or 305/577-1000) wins for its amenities and convenient location, near the Metrorail and only a 10-minute drive from Miami International Airport. It features an extensive variety of well-appointed meeting rooms and every imaginable executive service on sight. The dining options are also superb.

  Business travelers heading to Fort Lauderdale will be thrilled to know about the four properties opened recently by **Extended Stay America/Crossland Economy Studios** (☎ **800-EXT-STAY**). Year-round rates start as low as $49 a night and $159 per week, and long-term stays are even cheaper. The gleaming new studios include coffeemakers, irons and ironing boards, kitchens, and well-lighted desks. By dispensing with all the frills like free shampoo and daily maid service, they are able to provide exceptional value.
- **Best for a Romantic Getaway:** The ivy-covered **Hotel Place St. Michel** (☎ **800/848-HOTEL** or 305/444-1666) in Coral Gables is a small old-world–style hotel. Warm architectural details like arched doorways and teak floors covered by Oriental rugs make visitors feel as if they're staying in an Italian mansion.

Impressions

They say Miami Beach will make a comeback, and who knows, maybe it will . . . for me, Miami Beach is still one of the most beautiful places in the world.
                    —Isaac Bashevis Singer, *My Love Affair with Miami Beach* (1986)

In the Keys, **Little Palm Island** (☎ 800/343-8567 or 305/872-2524), wins this designation not only because of its remote locale (on a private 5-acre island), but also because of the elegantly rustic accommodations and super pampering service.

- **Best Trendy Hotel:** With its Alice-in-Wonderlandesque interior designed by Philip Starck, the whimsically reinvented **Delano** (☎ 800/555-5001 or 305/672-2000), on South Beach, wins the vote for Miami's trendiest spot.

- **Best Hotel Lobby for Pretending You're Rich:** At the **Ritz-Carlton Palm Beach** in Manalpan (☎ 800/241-3333 or 561/533-6000), the valets wouldn't flinch if you showed up in a head-to-toe mink walking a pedigree poodle, and carrying an armload of packages from Tiffany's. Even without all that gear, though, you're likely to get the royal treatment. Find a spot near the lushly land-scaped pool, and enjoy the opulence.

- **Best for Families:** The **Sonesta Beach Resort Key Biscayne** (☎ 800/ SONESTA or 305/361-2021) has family friendly everything: restaurants, game rooms, gym, tennis courts, and a pool. Add to that the entertaining and educational programs, and you'll find your children will be coming back with their children. It's the perfect place for the entire family.

  In Fort Lauderdale, **Lago Mar Resort and Club,** 1700 S. Ocean Lane, Fort Lauderdale (☎ 800/524-6627 or 954/523-6511), is another pricey selection, but one that guarantees a good time for the kids and parents. In addition to a game room, Ping-Pong tables, a small beach, and tennis courts, the hotel offers special events for kids during holidays. It might be a clown or an ice-cream party.

  In Palm Beach, **The Breakers** (☎ 800/833-3141 or 561/655-6611) offers supervised programs for kids year-round.

- **Best Moderately Priced Hotels:** South Beach's **Hotel Leon** (☎ 305/673-3767) is hip, gorgeous, and well appointed, and for the location you can't beat the price. Slightly north in Bay Harbor is the **Bay Harbor Inn** (☎ 405/868-4141), an antique-laden hotel in the exclusive Bal Harbour area. Its impeccable service and style make it so popular with discriminating budget-conscious travelers that it's booked a year in advance in season.

  In Key West during high season, finding a room for less than $100 a night is a challenge; finding one that is comfortable, conveniently located, with all kinds of extras like balconies and kitchenettes, and downright charming is nearly impossible. It does exist, however, in the form of **The Grand,** a two-story guest cottage less than 5 blocks from Duval Street (☎ 888/947-2630 or 305/294-0590).

- **Best Hotel Pool:** The **Fontainebleau Hilton**'s (☎ 800/HILTONS or 305/ 538-2000) dramatic grotto and waterfall make its pool one of the most interesting and fun in the area. On the other hand, the pool at the **Biltmore Hotel Coral Gables** (☎ 800/228-3000 or 305/445-1926) is the nation's largest, graced with Italian statues and columns beneath a huge Gothic tower.

- **Best Hotel Golf Courses:** In Miami, the **Biltmore** and the **Doral** share the distinction. At the Biltmore (☎ 800/228-3000 or 305/445-1926), you'll find one of South Florida's first courses with beautiful rolling hills and scenic vistas; the **Doral** (☎ 800/22-DORAL, 800/71-DORAL, or 305/592-2000), offers some of the country's most challenging including the Blue Monster, the site of the annual Doral Ryder Open.

  In Palm Beach, check out Florida's oldest 18-holer at **The Breakers** (☎ 800/ 833-3141 or 888/BREAKERS). This oceanfront, par 70 course was built in 1897.

- **Best Spas:** When you want to relax or be pampered, there's no better place to go than the world-famous **Doral Golf Resort and Spa** (☎ **800/22-DORAL,** 800/71-DORAL, or 305/592-2000). And the exclusive facilities at **Fisher Island Club** (☎ **305/535-6026**) are the most luxurious I've ever seen.

  In Fort Lauderdale, The **Wyndham Resort and Spa** (☎ **800/996-3426** or 954/389-3300) offers 23 acres of lush facilities including golf, tennis, and spa. A $10 million renovation has brought it back as one of the area's premier resorts for exercise, facials, manicures, massages, and more.

3 Best Dining Bets

- **Best Spot for a Romantic Dinner:** The **Forge Restaurant,** 432 Arthur Godfrey Rd. (at 41st Street), Miami Beach (☎ **305/538-8533**), is where everyone's parents went in the 1950s for a really elegant meal. It's still the most romantic spot in town for black-tie service, stupendous food, and private conversation. For a truly intimate experience, reserve a booth in "The Library," perfect for popping the question.
- **Best Wine Lists:** The extensive and well-chosen wine list at **Smith & Wollensky,** at South Pointe Park, South Beach (☎ **305/673-2800**), beats other Miami restaurants hands-down. The wine list at **The Forge Restaurant** (see above), a tome really, encompasses more than 3,000 vintages and 250,000 bottles from all over the world.
- **Best for Kids:** On the beach is **Van Dyke Cafe** at 846 Lincoln Rd., South Beach (☎ **305/534-3600**).

  In Hollywood, the **Deli Den,** 2889 Stirling Rd. (☎ **954/961-4070**), offers a great deal for kids under 12. Every Thursday and Monday from 4 until 8pm kids eat anything they want from the children's menu for free. Choices include chicken fingers, grilled cheese, and hot dogs.
- **Best Chinese Cuisine: Chrysanthemum,** 1248 Washington Ave., South Beach (☎ **305/531-5656**), has by far the beach's very finest Chinese food. The signature dish, chicken with crispy spinach, melts in your mouth while sparking a small flame. The Szechuan menu features lots of spicy favorites made of the very best quality ingredients.
- **Best Continental Cuisine:** The offerings at **Crystal Café,** 726 41st St., Miami Beach (☎ **305/673-8266**), have been dubbed "New Continental" by local food reviewers who rightfully consider it a shame to saddle the menu of this fantastic little spot with the pedestrian-sounding label of plain old "Continental."
- **Best Cuban Cuisine:** Cuban restaurants here range from take-out windows to diners to elegant establishments. The food comes in so many different styles that it's hard to choose a "best." If you're looking for a classic and filling Cuban meal, **Versailles,** 3555 SW 8th St., in Little Havana (☎ **305/444-0240**), is it. If you want a lighter, more expensive, nouvelle experience, **Yuca** is *el más sabroso* (the most delicious). You can find it in South Beach at 501 Lincoln Rd. (☎ **305/ 532-9822**).
- **Best Italian Cuisine:** With so many good, cheap pasta joints, it's great to see Miami also knows how to enjoy elegant Italian like they have at **Escopazzo,** 1311 Washington Ave., South Beach (☎ **305/674-9450**). Though prices are high, service and quality surpass all others.

  If you're craving Italian while in Palm Beach, try **Amici,** at 288 S. Country Rd. (☎ **561/832-0201**).

- **Best Seafood:** For all-around good seafood, including tasty stews, ceviche, and shellfish, the **Fishbone Grille**, 650 S. Miami Ave., Downtown (☎ **305/530-1915**), is the place to go. They also have a location in Coral Gables at 1450 S. Dixie Highway (☎ 305/668-3033). A bonus: The prices are downright cheap.
- **Best Steakhouse:** There are suddenly dozens of steakhouses in Miami (see box below) but none is as popular as **Shula's,** at 7601 NW 154th St., Miami Lakes (☎ **305/820-8102**), and in Miami Beach, at the Alexander Hotel, 5225 Collins Ave. (☎ 305/341-6565). Other steakhouses offer big portions. Shula's are bigger. For a really delicious prime cut at a prime price, try **The Forge,** 432 Arthur Godfrey Rd., Miami Beach (☎ **305/538-8533**).

  In Boca Raton, no one compares to **New York Prime,** 2350 Executive Center Dr. (☎ **561/998-3881**), for huge meaty cuts and decadent side dishes like chopped salad, creamed spinach, and whipped potatoes.
- **Best Late-Night Dining:** You'll find dozens of good 24-hour spots, especially on South Beach, but I say, go to Little Havana, where **Casa Juancho,** 2436 SW 8th St. (☎ **305/642-2452**), serves hearty good meals till all hours.

  Fort Lauderdale's late-night scene is best at **The Floridian Restaurant,** 1410 E. Las Olas Blvd (☎ **954/463-4041**), where everything from steaks to eggs tastes good and costs very little.
- **Best People-Watching:** Nowhere will you find better people to watch than at the **Blue Door,** at the Delano Hotel, 1685 Collins Ave., South Beach (☎ **305/674-6400**). From any seat in the house, you'll have a full parade of hipsters in view.
- **Best Pretheater Dinners:** The menu at **Kaleidoscope,** 3112 Commodore Plaza (☎ **305/446-5010**), is so reasonable all the time that they need no special fixed-price pretheater meal. It's a popular spot for those on their way to the Coconut Grove theater. For an even more elegant experience, try the $28 special at **Norman's,** 21 Almera Ave., in the Gables (☎ **305/446-6767**), offered between 5 and 7pm. Even if you don't have tickets to a show, it's a great way to eat cheap at this otherwise exorbitantly priced hot spot.
- **Best Fast Food: Mrs. Mendoza's Tacos al Carbon,** 1040 Alton Rd., South Beach (☎ **305/535-0808**), is the best fast food and the best Mexican in Miami. Time after time, this place turns out the tastiest burritos, tacos, and enchiladas with a superzingy salsa for the brave. There's another location at Doral Plaza, 9739 NW 41 St. (☎ 305/477-5119). **Pollo Tropical** ranks a close second with its superior rice and beans and roast chicken. Plus, it has drive-through windows at most locations for unbeatable speed and convenience. Locations include 1454 Alton Rd., Miami Beach (☎ **305/672-8888**); 11806 Biscayne Blvd. North Miami (☎ 305/895-0274); and 18710 S. Dixie Hwy. (at 186th Street), South Miami (☎ 305/254-0666). Check the phone book for locations throughout Dade and Broward counties.

Impressions

In so many ways, Miami represents the promise of hemispheric integration. I have been deeply moved over the last few years when I've had the opportunity to go to Miami and see the heroic efforts that people have made to build a genuine, multicultural, multiracial society that would be at the crossroads of the Americas, and therefore, at the forefront of the future.
— U.S. Pres. Bill Clinton, at the Summit of the Americas, 1994

Look Familiar?

Studded with cotton candy–colored art deco buildings, superfast racing boats, and, of course, palm trees, Miami has become a popular backdrop on the large and small screen.

One of the earliest and most famous classics set in Miami Beach during its heyday was the 1959 comedy *Hole in the Head* starring a young Frank Sinatra as a hotel owner and developer determined to build a Disneyland-like theme park in the swampland. The movie's theme song, "High Hopes," won an Oscar that year.

As Miami's financial health declined in the following decades, so did its screen image. The gritty streets of Miami from Little Havana to South Beach became familiar terrain in living rooms across America in the early '80s when *Miami Vice* was one of the top shows on TV. Cocaine and curse words defined the city after Brian De Palma's gruesome action flick *Scarface* splattered the gritty city's drug culture across theaters everywhere in 1983.

More recently, moviegoers have gotten many memorable and more appealing glimpses of the city in such films as *The Birdcage, Strip Tease, The Specialist, Out of Sight, Wild Things,* and *There's Something About Mary.* If you've missed some of these at the box office, you may want to rent one or two to get you prepped for your trip.

- **Best Brunches:** The **Biltmore Hotel Coral Gables** (☎ **305/445-1926**) features the area's very best brunch for about $40 per person. A huge wraparound terrace is loaded with food stations offering sushi, omelettes, fresh carved lamb, roast beef, fresh shellfish, caviar and vodka, plus all the mimosas you can drink. There are a Spanish guitarist and harpist on hand to entertain. Children under 12 eat free. Reservations are required.

  In Boca Raton, **Boca Raton Resort and Club** (☎ **800/327-0101** or 561/395-3000) does a superb brunch daily for hotel guests or members. The price is $18.95 and includes all the usual dishes like made-to-order omelettes, carved meats, salads, and delectable desserts.

- **Best Happy Hours:** The food at **John Martin's,** 253 Miracle Mile, in Coral Gables (☎ **305/445-3777**), tastes even better when you've had one of their single-malt scotches or a pint of ale. Professionals and Irish nationals complete the scene at this weekday gala from 5 to 7pm. Drinkers can feast on hot pizza, chicken wings, cheeses, and fruits. Well drinks are usually 50¢ to 75¢ each. You'll also find a good deal at **Monty's Bayshore Restaurant,** downstairs at 400 Alton Rd. on South Beach (☎ **305/672-1148**). Not only are drinks half price between 4 and 8pm weekdays, but you can also get great deals on shellfish and raw bar items. Stone crab claws are three for $5, and shrimps, oysters, or clams are two for $1.

  In Palm Beach, the happy hour at **E. R. Bradley's Saloon** (☎ **561/833-3520**) is an institution. On weekdays between 4:30 and 6:30pm, an extensive hot buffet with pastas, chicken wings, veggies, and more attracts a diverse crowd. It's free with the purchase of two drinks.

- **Best Ice Cream:** Nothing's better than a cool cone in the middle of a hot day at the beach. Surprisingly, there aren't a lot of places making fresh ice cream. One notable exception is **The Frieze** at 947 Lincoln Rd., South Beach

The first time I saw Miami, I experienced a series of emotions and was able to relive certain atmospheres, and breathe in the same imagination and creativity that was alive in the streets of Capri and St. Tropez' golden years. That is how I began my love affair with this city—with its people, its colors, and its surprisingly contagious vitality.
—Fashion designer Gianni Versace (1946–97)

(☎ **305/538-2028**). It offers mango, banana, guanabana, mamey, coconut, and anything else in season, plus all the usual chocolatey specialties. For store-bought treats, try *Dulce de Leche* by Häagen-Dazs. It may be a national manufacturer, but this caramelly Latin favorite is pure Miami.

Planning a Trip to Miami & South Florida

2

Although it's possible to land in Miami without an itinerary or reservations, you'll be able to see and do more with a bit of advance planning.

Of the many special events scheduled throughout the year, most take place between October and May. This reflects the close relationship between tourism and festivals, but in no way means that Miami's special events are canned tourist traps. In fact, these events are just the opposite. The inspiration and creativity that goes into them is 100% homegrown.

1 Visitor Information & Money

Note: For specific information on the Keys, Fort Lauderdale, Boca Raton, and other cities and towns on Florida's "Gold Coast," refer to chapters 12 and 13.

VISITOR INFORMATION

The best source for any kind of specialized information about the city is the **Greater Miami Convention and Visitors Bureau,** 701 Brickell Ave., Miami, FL 33131 (☎ **800/283-2707** or 305/539-3063; www.miamiandbeaches.com; e-mail: gmcvb@aol.com). Even if you don't have a specific question, call ahead to request its free magazine, *Destination Miami,* which includes several good, easy-to-use maps and other useful contact numbers. The office is open weekdays from 9am to 5pm.

For information on traveling in Florida including a calendar of events, a guide to accommodations, and a list of useful internet sites, contact **Visit Florida,** P.O. Box 1100, 66 E. Jefferson St., Tallahassee, FL 32302 (☎ **888-7-FLA-USA** or 850/488-5607). The office is open weekdays from 8am to 5pm. Europeans should note that this agency maintains an office in Great Britain at Roebuck House, Palace Street, London SW1 E 5BA (☎ **071/630-6602;** fax 071/630-7703).

In addition to information on some of South Beach's funkier hotels, the **Miami Design Preservation League,** 1234 Washington Ave., Ste. 207, Miami Beach, FL 33139 (☎ **305/672-2014**), offers an informative free guide to the Art Deco District and several books on the subject. It's open Monday through Saturday from 10am to 7pm.

Greater Miami's various chambers of commerce also send maps and information about their particular neighborhoods, including the following:

- **Coconut Grove Chamber of Commerce,** 2820 McFarlane Rd., Miami, FL 33133 (☎ **305/444-7270**).
- **Coral Gables Chamber of Commerce,** 50 Aragon Ave., Coral Gables, FL 33134 (☎ **305/446-1657**).
- **Florida Gold Coast Chamber of Commerce,** 1100 Kane Concourse (Bay Harbor Islands), Miami, FL 33154 (☎ **305/866-6020**)—this office represents Bal Harbour, Sunny Isles, Surfside, and other North Dade waterfront communities.
- **Tropical Everglades Visitor's Center,** 160 U.S. Hwy. 1, Florida City, FL 33034 (☎ **305/245-9180**); open daily 8:15am to 4:45pm.
- **Miami Beach Chamber of Commerce,** 1920 Meridian Ave., Miami Beach, FL 33139 (☎ **305/672-1270**).

The following organizations represent dues-paying hotels, restaurants, and attractions in their specific areas. These associations can provide information about accommodations and tours: **Greater Miami and the Beaches Hotel Association,** 407 Lincoln Rd., Miami Beach, FL 33139 (☎ **800/531-3553** or 305/531-3553), and **Sunny Isles Beach Resort Association,** 17100 Collins Ave., Suite 208, Sunny Isles, FL 33160 (☎ **305/947-5826**).

MONEY

You never have to carry a lot of cash in Miami. Automated-teller machines (ATMs) are located at virtually every bank in the city, and credit cards are accepted by the vast majority of Miami's hotels, restaurants, attractions, shops, and nightspots. Traveler's checks are also widely accepted for goods and services and can be exchanged for cash at banks and check-issuing offices.

First Nationwide Bank, 517 Arthur Godfrey Rd., accepts cards on Cirrus, Honor, and Metroteller networks. For the location of the nearest ATM, call

What Things Cost in Miami	U.S. $
Taxi from Miami Airport to a downtown hotel	18.00–26.00
Local telephone call	.35
Double room at the Grand Bay Hotel (expensive)	285.00
Double room at the Indian Creek Hotel (moderate)	130.00
Double room at the Suez Motel (inexpensive)	70.00
Lunch for one at the News Café (moderate)	9.00
Lunch for one at Mrs. Mendoza's (inexpensive)	6.00
Dinner for one, without wine, at Chef Allen's (very expensive)	49.00
Dinner for one, without wine, at Versailles (inexpensive)	13.00
Pint of beer	2.75
Coca-Cola in a restaurant	1.50
Cup of coffee	1.25
Roll of ASA 100 film, 36 exposures	6.50
Admission to Miami Metrozoo, adult	8.00
Movie ticket	6.50

☎ **800/424-7787** for the Cirrus network or ☎ **800/843-7587** for the Plus system. American Express cardholders can write a personal check, guaranteed against the card, for up to $1,000 in cash at any American Express office (see "Fast Facts: Miami" in chapter 4 for locations).

2 When to Go

Miami's tourist season, from December through April, is more reflective of the weather up north than it is of climatic changes in South Florida. It's always warm in Miami. No matter what time of year you visit, you'll find that indoor spaces are always air-conditioned, cafes have tables out on the sidewalk, and the beaches are busy.

The tropical temperature has always been Miami's main appeal, especially during the winter, when the rest of the country is shivering. When it's winter in Wisconsin, it's still summer in the Sunshine State.

South Florida's unique climate is extremely tropical. Hot, sometimes muggy summers are counterbalanced by wonderfully warm winters. It's not uncommon for a sudden shower to be followed by several hours of intense sunshine. For natives, "winter" is too cold for swimming; however, for many visitors, 70° January afternoons are great beach days. It isn't always perfect though—there are occasional cold snaps, and even one short tropical rain shower can ruin a day at the beach.

However, don't overlook traveling to Miami during the "off" seasons, when the weather is warm, but hotel prices are significantly lower. In addition, restaurants, stores, and highways are less crowded.

Finally, a word about Florida's tropical storms and hurricanes. Most occur between August and November, and for local property owners the tumultuous winds that sweep in from the Atlantic can be devastating. In August 1992, for example, Hurricane Andrew—one of the fiercest storms ever recorded in Florida—caused about $30 billion in damage to residential and business districts in Dade and Monroe counties. More than 250,000 people were left homeless. In 1998, one of the busiest storm seasons on record, hurricanes caused enormous damage in the Florida Keys.

For visitors, high winds and incessant rains usually mean little more than a delayed vacation. Even Hurricane Andrew caused relatively little damage to most of Miami's hotels and major tourist attractions, all of which have been rebuilt.

Meteorologists know far in advance when a storm is brewing off the Atlantic Coast and can determine pretty accurately what force it will have; the information is then broadcast nationwide. With respect to Andrew, the National Hurricane Center, located in Coral Gables, gave due warning of the storm and tracked it closely as it approached Florida, although it couldn't predict the exact spot where the storm would make landfall, leaving the inland residents in Homestead unprepared for the hit. However, if there are reports of an impending storm before you leave for Florida, you may want to postpone your trip.

Miami's Average Temperatures & Rainfall

	Jan	Feb	Mar	Apr	May	June	July	Aug	Sept	Oct	Nov	Dec
Avg. High (°F)	75	76	79	82	85	87	89	90	88	84	80	76
Avg. Low (°F)	59	60	64	68	72	75	76	77	76	72	66	61
Avg. Rain (in.)	2.0	2.0	2.3	3.6	6.3	8.6	6.7	7.2	8.6	6.9	2.9	1.9

South Florida Calendar of Events

January

- **Orange Bowl,** Miami. Two of the year's college football teams do battle at Pro Player Stadium, preceded by the King Orange Jamboree Parade (see December listing, below). Tickets are available starting March 1 of the previous year through the Orange Bowl Committee. Call ☎ **305/371-4600** for details. Usually January 1 (but note that dates of this and the other college bowl games mentioned below may vary to accommodate TV schedules).

- **Art Miami,** Miami. This annual fine art fair attracts more than 100 galleries from all over the world. International, modern, and contemporary works are featured here, attracting thousands of visitors and buyers. For information and ticket prices, call ☎ **561/220-2690.** Early January.

- **Three Kings Parade,** Miami. Since Cuban Pres. Fidel Castro outlawed this religious celebration more than 25 years ago, Cuban Americans in Little Havana have put on a bacchanalian parade winding through Calle Ocho from 4th Avenue to 27th Avenue, with horse-drawn carriages, native costumes, and marching bands. Call ☎ **305/447-1140** for the exact date during the first week of January.

- ✪ **Art Deco Weekend,** South Beach, Miami. Held along the beach between 5th and 15th streets, this festival—with bands, food stands, antique vendors, artists, tours, and other festivities—celebrates the whimsical architecture that has made South Beach one of America's most unique neighborhoods. Call ☎ **305/ 672-2014** for details. Usually held on Martin Luther King weekend.

- **Martin Luther King Day Parade,** Miami. This parade concludes a week of festivities, lectures, and concerts in honor of Dr. King's birthday. The parade takes place in Liberty City along NW 54th Street, between NW 12th and 32nd avenues. For information, call ☎ **305/636-1924.**

- ✪ **Royal Caribbean Classic,** Key Biscayne. World-renowned golfers compete for more than $1 million in prize money at Crandon Park Golf Course, formerly known as The Links. Lee Trevino has won this tournament twice. Call ☎ **305/ 374-6180** for more information. Late January.

- **Winter Antique Show,** Miami Beach. Antique glasswork, coins, jewelry, furniture, and more fills 800 booths and two halls at the mammoth Miami Beach Convention Center. Call ☎ **305/754-4931** for details. Late January to early February.

- **Taste of the Grove Food and Music Festival,** Coconut Grove. This fundraiser in the Grove's Peacock Park is an excellent chance for visitors to sample menu items from some of the city's top restaurants and sounds from international and local performers. Call ☎ **305/444-7270** for details. Mid-January.

- **The Key Biscayne Art Festival,** Key Biscayne. One of the finest in the country, this high-quality, juried fine art show, held in Cape Florida State Park, brings hundreds of artists, some crafts makers, and lots of great international food together for charity. Call ☎ **305/361-5207** for details. Last weekend in January.

- ✪ **Key West Literary Seminar.** This 3-day festival attracts the biggest names in literature. Some past participants included Joyce Carol Oates, Amy, and Jamaica Kincaid. This event sells out months in advance. Call ☎ **888/293-9291** for details or check out the Web site at www.KeyWestLiterarySeminar.org. Early to mid-January.

February

- **Homestead Rodeo.** Bucking broncos, clowns, and competition mark this family event out in horse country. Call ☎ **305/247-3515** for details. Early February (the first weekend after the Super Bowl).
- **Winter Gayla,** Ft. Lauderdale. More than 10,000 gay men and women turn out for this 10-day pride festival with parties, games, vendors, and displays. Call ☎ **954/561-2020** for details. Early February.
- ✪ **Everglades Seafood Festival,** Florida City. As many as 75,000 people show up each year for this 2-day eating festival in the quaint old town of Florida City. Florida delicacies like stone crab and gator tails are dished up from shacks and food booths on the outskirts of town. Friday night is family night where a carnival and craft fair attract the youngsters. No admission charge. Call ☎ **941/695-4100** for more details. First full weekend in February.
- ✪ **Miami Film Festival,** Miami. This 10-day festival has made an impact as an important screening opportunity for Latin American cinema and American independents. It's relatively small, well priced, and easily accessible to the general public. Contact the Film Society of Miami at ☎ **305/377-FILM.** Early February.
- ✪ **The Palm Beach International Art and Antiques Fair,** West Palm Beach. This relatively new event features top dealers from New York galleries and around the world. It has quickly gained a national reputation since its inception in 1997. For details, call ☎ **561/220-2690.**
- **Palm Beach Seafood Festival,** West Palm Beach. This festival at Currie Park features arts and crafts, kiddie rides, and of course, stone crabs, lobster, and more. Call ☎ **561/832-6397** for the word on the day's catch. Mid-February.
- ✪ **Coconut Grove Art Festival,** Coconut Grove. This is the state's largest art festival and the favorite annual event of many locals. More than 300 artists are selected from thousands of entries to show their works at this prestigious outdoor festival. Almost every medium is represented, including the culinary arts. Call ☎ **305/447-0401** for details. Presidents' Day weekend.
- ✪ **Miami International Boat Show,** Miami. This show draws almost a quarter of a million boat enthusiasts to the Miami Beach Convention Center and surrounding locations to see the megayachts, sailboats, dinghies, and accessories. It's the biggest anywhere. Call ☎ **305/531-8410** for more information and ticket prices. Mid-February.
- **Royal Caribbean Classic,** Key Biscayne. The first stop of the Senior PGA tour, this decade-old tournament attracts all the big players. For information, call ☎ **305/374-6180.** End of January or early February.
- **Doral Ryder Golf Open,** West Miami. One of the country's most prestigious annual tournaments. Call ☎ **305/477-GOLF** for more information. Late February to early March.
- **Hatusume Fair,** Delray Beach. Popular with residents and visitors alike for more than 20 years, this 2-day fair features art, music, food, plants, and martial arts performances to celebrate the first buds of spring. The elegant Morikami Japanese museum and garden hosts more than 15,000 visitors at this annual festival, which is also a great choice for families. ☎ **561/495-0233.** Last weekend of February.

March

- **Winter Party,** Miami. The Dade Human Rights Foundation hosts this gay and lesbian weekend-long party, which features several activities at clubs around town and culminates in a huge all-day dance fest on the beach on Sunday. Travel reservations can be made through Different Roads Travel—the official travel company of the event—at ☎ **888/ROADS-55,** ext. 510. For more information on specific events and ticket prices, call ☎ **305/538-5908** or check out their Web site at www.winterparty.com. Early March.

- **The Italian Renaissance Festival,** Miami. Stage plays, music, and period costumes complement Villa Vizcaya's neo-Italianate architectural style. Call ☎ **305/250-9133** for more information. Mid-March.

- **Miami Gay & Lesbian Film Festival,** Miami. A 10-day festival of short and feature-length films and videos by gay filmmakers is presented at South Beach's Colony Theater on Lincoln Road and other smaller venues. For details, call Robert Rosenberg ☎ **305/532-7256.** Mid-March.

- **Grand Prix of Miami,** Homestead. This high-purse, high-profile auto race rivals the big ones in Daytona. It attracts the top Indy car drivers and large crowds. For information and tickets, contact Homestead Motorsports Complex at ☎ **305/230-5200.** Sometime in March.

- ✪ **Calle Ocho Festival,** Miami. This salsa-filled blowout marks the end of a 10-day extravaganza called Carnival Miami. It's one of the world's biggest block parties, held along 23 blocks of Little Havana's Southwest 8th Street between 4th and 27th avenues. Call ☎ **305/644-8888** for more information. Early to mid-March.

- **Lipton Championship,** Miami. One of the world's largest tennis events is hosted at the lush Tennis Center at Crandon Park on Key Biscayne. Call ☎ **305/446-2200** for details. Mid- to late March.

- **Blues Festival,** Coral Gables. Mozart Stub restaurateur Harald Neuweg hosts this all-day street fest featuring down-home blues tunes as well as great food and lots of beer. Call ☎ **305/446-1600** for more details or see "Oktoberfest" listing below. Third weekend in March.

April

- **The Little Acorns International Kite Festival,** South Beach. Thousands of kite masters come from all over the world to display their flying works of art filling up a mile of sky from 5th to 15th street. Kids can build their own kites and scramble for candy during the candy drop at one of the country's largest festivals of its kind. Food and drinks, and of course, kites are sold to benefit this nonprofit educational organization. For more information on this free event, call ☎ **305/667-7756.** Third weekend of April.

- **PGA Seniors Golf Championship,** Palm Beach Gardens. Held at the PGA National Resort & Spa, it's the oldest and most prestigious of the senior tournaments. Call ☎ **561/624-8400** for the lineup. Mid-April.

- **World Cup Polo Tournament,** Palm Beach. Join royalty at the Palm Beach Polo and Country Club to see the best in international polo circles as the season closes. Call ☎ **561/793-1440** for details. Mid-April.

- **Sunfest,** West Palm Beach. A huge party happens on Flagler Drive in the downtown area with four stages of continuous music, a craft marketplace, a juried art show, a youth park, and fireworks. Call ☎ **561/659-5992** for details. Late April to early May.

- **Texaco Key West Classic,** Key West. Hailed as the top fishing tournament in Florida, this catch-and-release competition offers $50,000 in prizes to be divided between the top anglers in three divisions: sailfish, marlin, and light tackle. Call ☎ **305/294-4042** for more information. Late April-Mid May.

May

- **Arabian Nights Festival,** Opa-Locka. This yearly event commemorates the distinctive Moorish architecture in the heart of Opa-Locka. Historical tours, street festivals, live music, and food booths are part of the fun. For details, call ☎ **305/688-4611.** Early May.
- **Coconut Grove Bed Race,** downtown Coconut Grove. A colorful event in which local participants race hand-rigged beds to raise money for the Muscular Dystrophy Association (☎ **305/717-9937**). Usually the Sunday after Mother's Day.
- **Coconuts Dolphin Tournament,** Key Largo. This is the largest fishing tournament in the Keys, offering $5,000 and a Dodge Ram pickup truck to the person who breaks the record for the largest fish caught. The competition is fierce! Call ☎ **305/451-4107** for details. Mid-May, usually the weekend before Memorial Day.
- **The Great Sunrise Balloon Race & Festival,** Homestead. Every Memorial Day weekend, dozens of multicolored balloons rise up over Homestead Air Reserve Station as sky divers fall from the sky and other aircraft perform. The race is celebrated on the ground with a variety of food, music, arts, and crafts. For information, call ☎ **305/275-3317.**
- **Cajun/Zydeco Crawfish Festival,** Fort Lauderdale. Spend 3 days at Fort Lauderdale stadium dancing to Cajun music—if you don't know how, sign up for free lessons. Can you peel? If so, enter the crawfish-eating contest. Call the Crazee Crawfish 24-hour hot line at ☎ **954/761-5934.** Second weekend of May.
- **Shell Air and Sea Show,** Fort Lauderdale. A spectacular display of aeronautics featuring the Blue Angels and aquatic demonstrations by the navy guaranteed to evoke oohs and aahs. Call ☎ **954/527-5600** for details. Early May.

June

- **Super Boat Racing Series,** Key West. This event features 3 days of food, fun, and powerboat racing around downtown Key West. Call ☎ **305/296-6166** for details. Early June.
- ✪ **Coconut Grove Goombay Festival,** Miami. This bash, one of the country's largest black-heritage festivals, features Bahamian bacchanalia with dancing in the streets of Coconut Grove and music from the Royal Bahamian Police marching band. The food and music draw thousands to an all-day celebration of Miami's Caribbean connection. It's lots of fun—if the weather isn't scorching. Call ☎ **305/372-9966** for festival details. Early June.

July

- **Independence Day,** Miami. Celebrate July 4th on the beach, where parties, barbecues, and fireworks flare all day and night. For a weekend's worth of events on Key Biscayne, call ☎ **305/361-5207.** You can also find one of the wildest parties around—complete with fireworks and top-notch festivities—at Bayfront Park, 301 N. Biscayne Blvd. For more on this free event, call ☎ **305/358-7550.** It's a good idea, though, to check local papers for a more detailed list of events.
- **Miccosukee Everglades Festivals,** Miami. Native American rock, Razz (reservation jazz), and folk bands perform while visitors gorge themselves on exotic treats like pumpkin bread and fritters. Watch alligator wrestling and craft demonstrations. Call ☎ **305/223-8380** for prices and details. One in early and one in late July.
- ✪ **Lower Keys Underwater Music Fest,** Looe Key. At this outrageous celebration, boaters go out to the underwater reef of Looe Key Marine Sanctuary off Big Pine

Key, drop speakers into the water, and pipe in music. It's entertainment for the fish and swimmers alike! A snorkeling Elvis can usually be spotted. Call ☎ **800/872-3722** for details. Usually second Saturday of July.

☼ **Hemingway Days Festival,** Key West. After years of controversy with Hemingway's heirs, this blowout is still going strong. Topped off by a humorous look-alike contest. Call ☎ **305/294-4440** for details. Mid- to late July.

• **Wine and All That Jazz,** Boca Raton. A great way to quench your thirst on a sweltering summer day. It's one of the largest wine-tasting parties in the state; sample your choice from more than 100 wines and vintages while listening to a little live jazz. For details, call ☎ **561/395-4433.** Friday night at the end of July or beginning of August.

☼ **Fourth of July Festivities,** Delray Beach. You can attend a celebration featuring art and jazz on Atlantic Avenue and Fla. A1A and enter a sand-sculpting contest, fly a kite, and sample fare from Delray's neighborhood restaurants. Call ☎ **561/278-0424** for more information. July 4.

August

• **Miami Reggae Festival,** Miami. Jamaica's best dance-hall and reggae artists turn out for this 2-day festival. Burning Spear, Steel Pulse, Spragga Benz, and Jigsy King have participated recently. Call Jamaica Awareness at ☎ **305/891-2944** for more details. Early August.

September

• **Festival Miami,** Miami. A 4-week program of performing arts featuring local and invited musical guests. Based in the University of Miami School of Music and Maurice Gusman Concert Hall. For a schedule of events, call ☎ **305/284-4940.** Mid-September to mid-October.

☼ **Columbus Day Regatta,** Miami. Find anything that can float—from an inner tube to a 100-foot yacht—and you'll fit right in. Yes, there actually is a race, but how can you keep track when you're partying with a bunch of seminaked psychos in the middle of Biscayne Bay? It's free and it's wild. Rent a boat, jet-ski, or sailboard to get up close. Be sure to secure a vessel early, though—everyone wants to be there. Check local newspapers for exact date and time. Columbus Day weekend.

October

• **SunTrust Sunday Jazz Brunch at Riverwalk,** Fort Lauderdale. This year-long music and food gig kicks off on the banks of the historic New River, promising leisurely afternoons of great live jazz and tasty food in the company of fellow music lovers. Call ☎ **954/761-5363** for details. First Sunday of every month.

☼ **Fort Lauderdale International Boat Show.** Your chance to meet fellow boating enthusiasts and look over more than 1,400 boats and every imaginable variety of marine paraphernalia. Call ☎ **800/940-7642** for details. Late October to early November.

• **Lincoln-Mercury American Music Festival,** Fort Lauderdale. An impressive lineup of folk, country, and Native American musicians shows up for this lively show at the baseball stadium off Commercial Boulevard. Dates vary, so call ☎ **954/761-5934** for details.

• **Oktoberfest,** Miami. They close the streets for this German beer and food festival thrown by the Mozart Stub Restaurant in Coral Gables. You'll find loads of great music and dancing at this wild party. Call Harald Neuweg (☎ **305/446-1600**) to find out where and when.

☼ **Fantasy Fest,** Key West. It might feel as though the rest of the world is joining you if you're in Key West for this world-famous Halloween festival, Florida's version of Mardi Gras. Crazy costumes, wild parades, and even wilder revelers gather for an opportunity to do things Mom said not to. Definitely leave the kids at home! Call ☎ **305/296-1817.** Last week of October.

✪ **Goombay Festival,** Key West. Sample Caribbean dishes and purchase art and ethnic clothing in this celebration with a Jamaican flair that coincides with Fantasy Fest (see above).

November

- **Blues Festival at Riverwalk,** downtown Fort Lauderdale. This huge corporate-sponsored music event attracts big name performers to various venues in and around Ft. Lauderdale. Call the blues hot line ☎ **954/761-5934** for info. First weekend of November.

- **South Florida International Auto Show,** Miami Beach. An impressive collection of the latest models is on display in the vast halls of the Convention Center. For details call ☎ **305/947-5950.** Early November.

- **The Jiffy Lube Miami 300 Weekend of NASCAR,** Homestead. Here's more world-class racing at a recently constructed 344-acre motor sports complex. For information and tickets, contact Homestead Motorsports Complex, One Speedway Blvd., Homestead (☎ **305/230-5200**). Mid-November.

- **Chili Cook-Off,** Miami. Sample some of the nation's best chili as the area's "hottest" restaurants compete for the glory of being the best. For details, call ☎ **305/441-6677.** Mid-November.

✪ **Miami Book Fair International,** Miami. An event that draws hundreds of thousands of visitors, including foreign and domestic publishers and authors from around the world, with great lectures and readings by world-renowned authors. Call ☎ **305/237-3258.** Mid-November.

- **Super Boat World Championship Key West.** More than a week of high-speed fun and competition around downtown Key West. Call ☎ **305/296-6166** for details. Mid-November.

✪ **The Ramble,** Miami. Old-time Floridians love this yearly event at the Fairchild Tropical Gardens. Here you can buy antiques, exotic orchids, or vintage clothes. If you're not shopping, it's still worth strolling around the lush park where you can see an impressive array of botanical miracles. For more information, call ☎ **305/667-1651.** Mid-November.

- **Mercury Outboards Cheeca/Redbone Celebrity Tournament,** Islamorada, in the Upper Keys. Curt Gowdy from *American Sportsman* hosts this fishing tournament, the proceeds of which go to finding a cure for cystic fibrosis. The likes of Wade Boggs, actor James B. Sikking, and Gen. Norman Schwartzkopf compete most years. Call ☎ **305/664-2002** for more information. Second and third weekends of November. This event is followed by the George Bush Cheeca Lodge Bonefish Tournament. Call ☎ **305/664-4651,** ext. 556 for details.

✪ **White Party Week,** Miami. This weeklong AIDS fundraiser begins with a series of events in Miami Beach nightclubs and leads up to the Sunday night gala, where more than 10,000 gay men and women from around the country come out to celebrate at Vizcaya, the Renaissance mansion. Since the gala always sells out, make sure to buy your tickets as soon as they go on sale October 1. Call ☎ **305/667-9296** for details; www.whitepartyweek.com. Thanksgiving week.

December

- **Winterfest Boat Parade,** Fort Lauderdale waterways. For more than a quarter century this festival has showcased some of the most extravagant boats in the area. Outfitted in holiday decorations, the vessels ply the local waterways to celebrate the winter season. The best view is from the water aboard your own boat or at one of the waterfront restaurants. For details, call ☎ **954/767-0686.**

• **King Mango Strut,** Coconut Grove, Miami. This fun-filled march encourages everyone to wear wacky costumes and join the floats in a spoof of the King Orange Jamboree Parade, held the following night. Runs from Commodore Plaza to Peacock Park in Coconut Grove. Comedians and musical entertainment follow in the park. Call ☎ **305/444-7270** for details. December 30.

✪ **King Orange Jamboree Parade,** Miami. The world's largest nighttime parade is followed by a long night of festivities leading up to the Orange Bowl football game (see January listing, above). Runs along Biscayne Boulevard. For information and tickets (which cost $7.50 to $13), contact the Greater Miami Convention and Visitors Bureau at ☎ **305/539-3063.** Usually December 31.

✪ **Santa's Enchanted Forest,** west of Coral Gables. The world's largest Christmas theme park includes rides, games, and food. A family tradition for years, this seasonal event is especially popular with teenagers. For details and ticket prices, call ☎ **305/893-0090.** From late November to mid-January.

• **First Night,** Miami Beach. One of many nationwide New Year's Eve celebrations that are offered for families, this event starts in the late afternoon and offers dance, theater, art, poetry, and story reading. With no alcohol and lots of kid-friendly events, this is sure to become a big draw. Buttons for admission to all events cost $10 for New Year's 1999. Call ☎ **305/670-7005** for info.

3 Safety Concerns

Reacting to several highly publicized crimes against tourists, both local and state governments have taken steps to help protect visitors. These measures include special, highly visible police units patrolling the airport and surrounding neighborhoods, and better signs on the state's most tourist-traveled routes. Also, look for bright orange sunbursts on highway exit signs that point the way to tourist-friendly zones.

When driving around Miami, always keep a good map handy, keep the doors locked, and stay alert. Never stop on a highway—if you get a flat tire, drive to the nearest well-lighted, populated place. If you are renting a car, you may consider additional safety features in the car, such as cellular telephones or electronic maps. For short stays or trips that will be centered in one area of the city, such as South Beach, you could dispense with a rental car altogether, and just rely on taxis, which are generally safe and relatively inexpensive.

During the hurricane season, listen to radio and television broadcasts, which will describe evacuation routes. Better hotels will arrange transportation for their guests to safe areas.

Last but not least, be sure to use sunscreen, even on breezy, overcast days—the sun's rays in Miami are always powerful. There's nothing like a third-degree sunburn to ruin a trip.

4 Tips for Travelers with Special Needs

Note: Again, for specific information on the Keys and cities on the "Gold Coast," please refer to chapters 12 and 13.

FOR TRAVELERS WITH DISABILITIES   Many hotels offer special accommodations and services for wheelchair-bound visitors and travelers with disabilities, including large bathrooms, ramps, and telecommunication devices for the deaf. The

Greater Miami Convention and Visitors Bureau (see "Visitor Information," above) has the most up-to-date information.

The **City of Miami Department of Parks and Recreation,** 2600 S. Bayshore Dr. (Coconut Grove), Miami, FL 33133 (☎ **305/860-3800;** TTY 305/579-3436), maintains quite a few programs for people with disabilities at parks and beaches throughout the city. Call or write for a listing of special services. The office is open weekdays from 8am to 5pm. The **Metro-Dade County Parks & Recreation Department** also runs hundreds of programs from swimming to sailing for visitors with disabilities. For a complete listing, call the department (☎ **305/755-7848**) weekdays from 9am to 5pm. Primarily a referral service, the **Deaf Services Bureau,** 4800 W. Flagler St., Suite 213, Miami, FL 33134 (☎ **305/668-4407;** TTY 305/668-3323), may be contacted for any special concerns you have about traveling in and around Miami. They're available from 9am to 5pm. The **Division of Blind Services,** 401 NW 2nd Ave., Suite 700, Miami, FL 33128 (☎ **305/377-5339**), offers services to those with visual impairments. The office is open weekdays from 8am to 5pm.

Many of the major car-rental companies now offer hand-controlled cars for disabled drivers. **Avis** can supply such a vehicle at any of its locations in the United States with 48-hour advance notice; **Hertz** requires between 24 and 72 hours of advance reservation at most of its locations. **Wheelchair Getaways** (☎ **800/873-4973** for information, or try the Web site, www.blvd.com/wg.htm) rents specialized vans with wheelchair lifts and other features for people with disabilities throughout the United States.

FOR GAY & LESBIAN TRAVELERS   Miami, particularly South Beach, has a large gay community, supported by a wide range of services. There are many gay-oriented publications with information, up-to-date calendars, and listings of gay-friendly businesses and services. *TWN* is the only local gay newspaper in town; you'll find it in lavender boxes throughout the city and at bookstores and gay bars. Other local publications include *WIRE, Miamigo, Out Pages,* and *Scoop.*

The **Lambda Passages/Gay Community Bookstore,** 7545 Biscayne Blvd. (☎ **305/754-6900**), features quality literature, newspapers, videos, music, cards, and information on local businesses. It's open Monday to Saturday from 11am to 9pm and Sunday from noon to 6pm.

For a map and directory of gay businesses or a copy of the gay and lesbian community calendar (sponsored by the Dade Human Rights Foundation), call ☎ **305/893-5595.** For a copy of the calendar and other information, you can also log on to the foundation's Web site at www.dhrf.com.

For information of gay-friendly businesses in the area, contact the **South Beach Business Guild** at ☎ **305/534-3336.**

FOR SENIORS   Miami is well versed in catering to seniors. Ask for discounts everywhere, at hotels, movie theaters, museums, restaurants, and attractions—you'll be surprised how often you're offered reduced rates. Many restaurants offer early bird specials and honor AARP memberships.

FOR STUDENTS   A valid high school or college ID often entitles you to discounts at attractions (particularly museums) and sometimes to reduced rates at bars during "college nights." You're most likely to find these discounts at places near local colleges, in downtown Miami and Coral Gables.

You'll find lots of students at the large main campus of the **University of Miami** in south Coral Gables. In addition to the academic buildings, this campus encompasses a huge athletic field, a large lake, a museum, a hospital, and more. For general information, call the university (☎ **305/284-2211**). The school's main student building is the Whitten University Center, 1306 Stanford Dr. Social events are often scheduled here, and important information on area activities is always posted. The building houses a recreation area, a pool, a snack shop, and a Ticketmaster outlet.

For tickets to Miami Hurricanes basketball, football, and baseball home games, call the **U of M Athletic Department** (☎ **800/GO-CANES** in Florida, or 305/284-3822). See "Spectator Sports" in chapter 7, "What to See and Do in Miami," for more information.

5 Getting There

BY PLANE

Most major domestic airlines fly to and from many Florida cities, including American (☎ 800/433-7300; www.americanair.com), Continental (☎ 800/525-0280; www.flycontinental.com), Delta (☎ 800/221-1212; www.delta-air.com), Northwest/KLM (☎ 800/225-2525; www.nwa.com), TWA (☎ 800/221-2000; www.twa.com), United (☎ 800/241-6522; www.ual.com), and US Airways (☎ 800/428-4322; www.usair.com). Miami is one of American's biggest hubs.

Several so-called no-frills airlines—offering low fares but no meals or other amenities—fly to Florida. The biggest is ✪ **Southwest Airlines** (☎ **800/435-9792;** www.iflyswa.com), which has flights from many U.S. cities to Fort Lauderdale (plus Jacksonville, Orlando, and Tampa). An arm of the popular cruise line, **Carnival Air** (☎ **800/824-7386**) flies from New York and Washington, D.C., to Fort Lauderdale.

Others flying to Florida include **AirTran** (☎ 800/AIR-TRAN; www.airtran); **Delta Express,** a branch of Delta Airlines (☎ **800/ 325-5205**); **Eastwind** (☎ 800/644-3592); **MetroJet,** an arm of US Airways (☎ 800/428-4322); **Midway** (☎ 800/44-MIDWAY); **Midwest Express** (☎ **800/452-2022**); **Spirit** (☎ 800/ 722-7117); **SunJet** (☎ 800/478-6538); **Tower Air** (☎ 800/348-6937); and **Vanguard** (☎ 800/826-4827).

If you're planning to visit Florida from another country, see chapter 3, "For Foreign Visitors," for information on which international carriers serve the Miami area.

FINDING THE BEST AIRFARE

There's no shortage of **discounted and promotional fares** to Florida. November, December, and January often see fare wars that can result in savings of 50% or more. Watch for advertisements in your local newspaper and on TV, call the airlines and do some comparison shopping, or surf for bargains on the Web (see Frommer's Online Directory at the back of the book for lots of advice on how to do this).

- **Consolidators,** also known as bucket shops, are a good place to find low fares, often below even the airlines' discounted rates. There's nothing shady about the reliable ones—basically, they're just big travel agents that get discounts for buying in bulk and pass some of the savings on to you. Before you pay, however, ask for a confirmation number from the consolidator and then call the airline itself to confirm your seat. Be prepared to book your ticket with a different consolidator—there are many to choose from—if the airline can't confirm your reservation. Also be aware that consolidator tickets are usually non-refundable or come with stiff cancellation penalties.

  Small ads for consolidators usually run in the Sunday travel section at the bottom of the page. But we recommend going with one of these reliable

Money-Saving Tip

If your schedule is flexible, you can almost always secure a cheaper fare by staying over a Saturday night or by flying midweek. Many airlines won't volunteer this information, so be sure to ask.

companies: Lots of folks on our staff have gotten great deals on a number of occasions from **Cheap Tickets** (☎ **800/377-1000** or 212/570-1179; www.cheaptickets. com). **Council Travel** (☎ **800/226-8624;** www.council-travel.com) and **STA Travel** (☎ **800/781-4040;** www.sta.travel.com) cater especially to young travelers, but their bargain-basement prices are available to people of all ages. **Travel Bargains** (☎ **800/AIR-FARE;** www.1800airfare.com) was formerly owned by TWA but now offers the deepest discounts on many other airlines, with a four-day advance purchase. Other reliable consolidators include **1-800-FLY-4-LESS; Cheap Seats** (☎ **800/451-7200;** www.cheapseatstravel. com); **1-800-FLY-CHEAP** (www.1800flycheap.com); or "rebators" such as **Travel Avenue** (☎ **800/333-3335** or 312/876-1116) and the **Smart Traveller** (☎ **800/448-3338** or 305/448-3338), which rebate part of their commissions to you.

• Search the **Internet** for cheap fares—though it's still best to compare your findings with the research of a dedicated travel agent, if you're lucky enough to have one, especially when you're booking more than just a flight. See Frommer's Online Directory at the back of this book to learn how to use the Web to your best advantage.

A few of the better-respected virtual travel agents are **Travelocity** (www.travelocity.com) and **Microsoft Expedia** (www.expedia.com). Each has its own little quirks—Travelocity and Expedia both require you to register with them—but they all provide variations of the same service. Just enter the dates you want to fly and the cities you want to visit, and the computer roots out the lowest fares. Expedia's site will e-mail you the best airfare deal once a week if you so choose. Travelocity uses the SABRE computer reservations system that most travel agents use, and has a "Last Minute Deals" database that advertises really cheap fares for those who can get away at a moment's notice. Another good bet is **Arthur Frommer's Budget Travel** (www.frommers.com), which offers detailed information on 200 destinations around the world, plus ways to save on flights, hotels, car reservations, and cruises. Book an entire vacation online, or direct travel questions to Arthur himself. The newsletter is updated daily to keep you abreast of the latest breaking ways to save.

• Great last-minute deals are also available through **E-savers,** free e-mail services provided directly by the airlines. Each week, the airline sends you a list of discounted flights, usually leaving the upcoming Friday or Saturday and returning the following Monday or Tuesday. You can sign up at each airline's Web site (see above for Web addresses).

Better yet, save yourself the headache and register with **Smarter Living** (www.smarterliving.com). Every week you'll get a customized e-mail summarizing the discount fares available from your departure city. Smarter Living tracks more than 15 different airlines, so it's a worthwhile time-saver. The site also features concise lists of links to hotel, car rental, and other hot travel deals.

• No-frills airlines have reduced their price advantage, but some **charter flights** still go to Florida, especially during the winter season and particularly from

Canada, such as **Air Transat** (☎ **800/470-1011**) and **Canada 3000** (☎ **800/ 993-4378**). They often cost less than regularly scheduled flights, but they are very complicated. It's best to go to a good travel agent and ask him or her to find one for you and to explain the pros and cons.

MONEY-SAVING PACKAGE DEALS

Before you start your search for the lowest airfare, you may want to consider booking your flight as part of a travel package.

Package tours are not the same as escorted tours. They are simply a way to buy airfare and accommodations (and sometimes rental cars) at the same time. For Miami and many other destinations in Florida, a package can be a smart way to go. In many cases, one that includes airfare, hotel, and car rental will cost you less than the hotel alone would have had you booked it yourself. That's because packages are sold in bulk to tour operators, who resell them to the public at a cost that drastically undercuts standard rates.

Packages, however, vary widely. Some offer a better class of hotels than others. Some offer the same hotels for lower prices. With some packagers, your choice of accommodations and travel days may be limited. Which package is right for you depends entirely on what you want.

Here are a few tips to help you tell one from the other, and figure out which one is right for you:

- **Read this guide.** Do a little homework; read up on Miami. Compare the rack rates that we've published to the discounted rates being offered by the packagers to see what kinds of deals they're offering—if you're actually being offered a substantial savings, or if they've just gussied up the rack rates to make their offer *sound* like a deal. If you're being offered a stay in a hotel I haven't recommended, do more research to learn about it, especially if it isn't a reliable brand name like Holiday Inn or Hyatt. It's not a deal if you end up at a dump.

- **Read the fine print.** Make sure you know *exactly* what's included in the price you're being quoted, and what's not. Are hotel taxes and airport transfers included, or will you have to pay extra? Before you commit to a package, make sure you know how much flexibility you have, say, if your kid gets sick or your boss suddenly asks you to adjust your vacation schedule. Some packagers require iron-clad commitments, while others will go with the flow, charging minimal fees for changes or cancellations.

- **Use your best judgment.** Stay away from fly-by-nights and shady packagers. If a deal appears to be too good to be true, it probably is. Go with a reputable firm with a proven track record. This is where your travel agent can come in handy; he or she should be knowledgeable about different packagers, the deals they offer, and the general rate of satisfaction among their customers.

So how do you find a package deal?

The best place to start your search is the travel section of your local Sunday newspaper. Also check the ads in the back of national travel magazines like *Travel & Leisure, National Geographic Traveler,* and *Condé Nast Traveler.*

The major airlines package their flights to Florida together with accommodations. These include **America West Vacations** (☎ 800/356-6611; fax 602/3505), **American Airlines Vacations** (☎ 800/321-2121; fax 800/472-2987; www.americanair. com), **Continental Airlines Vacations** (☎ 800/634-5555; fax 954/357-4661; www.flycontinental.com), **Delta Vacations** (☎ 800/367-9112; fax 954/468-4765; www.deltavacations.com), **Midwest Express Vacations** (☎ 800/444-4479;

fax 414/351-5256), **Northwest WorldVacations** (☎ 800/727-1111; fax 800/ 655-7890; www.nwa.com), **Southwest Airlines Vacations** (☎ 800/524-6442; fax 407/857-0232; www.iflyswa.com), and **US Airways Vacations** (☎ 800/455-0123).

Another option is the old reliable **American Express Vacations** (☎ **800/ 241-1700;** fax 954/357-4682; www.leisureweb.com). Check out its **Last Minute Travel Bargains** Web site, offered in conjunction with **Continental Airlines** (www6.americanexpress.com/travel/lastminutetravel/default.asp), with deeply discounted vacations packages and reduced airline fares that differ from the E-savers bargains that Continental e-mails weekly to subscribers.

One of the biggest packagers in the Northeast, **Liberty Travel** (☎ **888/271-1584;** www.libertytravel.com) boasts a full-page ad in many Sunday papers. You won't get much in the way of service, but you will get a good deal.

For one-stop shopping on the Web, go to **www.vacationpackager.com,** a search engine that will link you to many different package-tour operators, often with a company profile summarizing the company's basic booking and cancellation terms.

In addition to these all-inclusive tours, many Florida hotels and resorts and even some motels offer **golf and tennis packages,** which bundle the cost of room, greens and court fees, and sometimes equipment into one price. These deals usually don't include airfare, but they do represent savings over paying for the room and golf or tennis separately. See the accommodations sections in the following chapters for resorts offering special packages to their guests.

BY CAR

No matter where you start your journey, chances are you'll reach Miami by way of I-95. This north-south interstate is the city's lifeline and an integral part of the region. The highway connects all of Miami's different neighborhoods, the airport, and the beach, and it connects all of South Florida to the rest of America. Unfortunately, many of Miami's road signs are completely confusing and notably absent when you need them. Take time out to study I-95's placement on the map. You will use it as a reference point time and again.

Other major highways to Florida include I-10, which originates in Los Angeles and terminates in Jacksonville, and I-75, which begins in North Michigan and runs through the center of Florida.

Before you set out on a long car trip, you might want to join the **American Automobile Association (AAA;** ☎ **800/596-2227**), which has hundreds of offices nationwide. Members receive excellent maps (they'll even help you plan an exact itinerary) and emergency road service. Other auto clubs include the **Allstate Motor Club,** 1500 Shure Dr., Arlington Heights, IL 60004 (☎ **847/253-4800**), and the **Motor Club,** P.O. Box 9046, Des Moines, IA 50369 (☎ **800/334-3300**).

BY TRAIN

Amtrak (☎ **800/USA-RAIL**) may be a good option. Two trains leave daily from New York—the Silver Meteor at 7:05pm and the Silver Star at 11:50am. They both take from 26½ to 29 hours to complete the journey to Miami. At press time, the lowest-priced round-trip ticket from New York to Miami cost $146 for a coach seat, climbing to a whopping $417 for a sleeper (based on double occupancy).

If you are planning to stay in South Florida for some time, you might consider taking your car on Amtrak's East Coast Auto Train. The 16½-hour ride, connecting Lorton, Virginia (near Washington, D.C.), with Sanford, Florida (near Orlando), has a glass-domed viewing car and includes breakfast and dinner in the ticket price. Round-trip fares are only a few dollars higher than one way—about $170 for adults,

$85 for children under 12, and $300 for your car. One-way fares are discounted as much as 50% when most traffic is going in the opposite direction.

You'll pull into Amtrak's Miami terminal at 8303 NW 37th Ave. Unfortunately, none of the major car-rental companies have an office at the train station; you'll have to go to the airport, just over 5 miles away, to rent a car.

Taxis meet each Amtrak arrival. The fare to downtown will cost about $22; the ride takes less than 20 minutes.

3

For Foreign Visitors

This chapter gives you specific suggestions about getting to the United States as economically and effortlessly as possible, plus some helpful information about how things are done in Miami—from receiving mail to making a local or long-distance telephone call.

1 Preparing for Your Trip

ENTRY REQUIREMENTS

Immigration laws are a hot political issue in the United States these days, and the following requirements may have changed somewhat by the time you plan your trip. Check at any U.S. embassy or consulate for current information and requirements.

DOCUMENT REGULATIONS Citizens of Canada and Bermuda may enter the United States without visas, but they will need to show proof of nationality, the most common and hassle-free form of which is a passport.

The U.S. State Department has a Visa Waiver Pilot Program that allows citizens of certain countries to enter the United States without a visa for stays of fewer than 90 days of vacation travel. At press time, they included Andorra, Argentina, Australia, Austria, Belgium, Brunei, Denmark, Finland, France, Germany, Iceland, Ireland, Italy, Japan, Liechtenstein, Luxembourg, Monaco, the Netherlands, New Zealand, Norway, San Marino, Spain, Sweden, Switzerland, and the United Kingdom. (The program as applied to the United Kingdom refers to British citizens who have the "unrestricted right of permanent abode in the United Kingdom," that is, citizens from England, Scotland, Wales, Northern Ireland, the Channel Islands, and the Isle of Man, and not, for example, citizens of the British Commonwealth of Pakistan.)

Citizens from these countries need only a valid passport and a round-trip air or cruise ticket in their possession upon arrival. If they first enter the United States, they may then visit Mexico, Canada, Bermuda, and/or the Caribbean islands and return to the United States without needing a visa. Further information is available from any U.S. embassy or consulate.

Citizens of countries other than those specified above, or those traveling to the United States for reasons or a length of time outside the restrictions of the Visa Waiver program, or those who require waivers of inadmissibility must have these two documents:

- A valid passport, with an expiration date at least 6 months later than the scheduled end of the visit to the United States. (Some countries are exceptions to the 6-month validity rule. Contact any U.S. embassy or consulate for complete information.)
- A tourist visa, available from the nearest U.S. consulate. To get a visa, the traveler must submit a completed application form (either in person or by mail) with a 1½-inch square photo and the required application fee. There may also be an issuance fee, depending on the type of visa and other factors.

Usually you can get a visa right away or within 24 hours, but it may take longer during the summer rush period (June to August). If you cannot go in person, contact the nearest U.S. embassy or consulate for directions on applying by mail. Your travel agent or airline office may also be able to give you visa applications and instructions. The U.S. consulate or embassy that issues your visa will determine whether you receive a multiple- or single-entry visa. The Immigration and Naturalization Service officers at the port-of-entry in the United States will make an admission decision and determine your length of stay.

MEDICAL REQUIREMENTS　No inoculations are needed to enter the United States unless you are coming from, or have stopped over, in areas known to be suffering from epidemics, particularly cholera or yellow fever.

If you have a condition requiring treatment with medications containing narcotics or drugs requiring a syringe, carry a valid signed prescription from your physician to allay any suspicions that you are smuggling drugs.

CUSTOMS REQUIREMENTS　Every adult visitor may bring in free of duty 1 liter of hard liquor, 200 cigarettes or 100 cigars (but no cigars from Cuba) or 3 pounds of smoking tobacco, and $100 worth of gifts. These exemptions are offered to travelers who spend at least 72 hours in the United States and who have not claimed them within the preceding 6 months. It is altogether forbidden to bring foodstuffs (particularly cheese, fruit, and cooked meats) and plants (vegetables, seeds, tropical plants, and so on) into the country. Foreign tourists may bring in or take out up to $10,000 in U.S. or foreign currency with no formalities; larger sums must be declared to Customs on entering or leaving.

INSURANCE

There is no national health system in the United States. Because the cost of medical care is extremely high, I strongly advise all travelers to secure health coverage before setting out.

You may want to take out a comprehensive travel policy that covers (for a relatively low premium) sickness or injury costs (medical, surgical, and hospital); loss or theft of your baggage; trip-cancellation costs; guarantee of bail in case you are arrested; and costs of accident, repatriation, or death. Automobile clubs sell packages (for example, "Europ Assistance" in Europe) at attractive rates; packages are also offered by insurance companies and travel agencies.

MONEY

CURRENCY　The U.S. monetary system has a decimal base: one American dollar ($1) = 100 cents (100¢). Dollar bills commonly come in $1 ("a buck"), $5, $10, $20, $50, and $100 denominations (the last two are not welcome when paying for small purchases and are not always accepted in taxis).

There are six coin denominations: 1¢ (one cent or "penny"), 5¢ (five cents or "nickel"), 10¢ (10 cents or "dime"), 25¢ (25 cents or "quarter"), 50¢ (50 cents or "half dollar"), and the $1 pieces (both the older, large silver dollar and the newer, small Susan B. Anthony coin).

TRAVELER'S CHECKS   It's actually cheaper and faster to get cash at an automated-teller machine (ATM) than to fuss with traveler's checks. If you do bring them, traveler's checks denominated in U.S. dollars are readily accepted at most hotels, restaurants, and large stores. Just don't bother bringing checkes in any other currency.

CREDIT CARDS   The most widely used method of payment is the credit card: Visa, MasterCard (EuroCard in Europe, Access in Britain, Diamond in Japan), American Express, Discover, Diners Club, enRoute, JCB, and Carte Blanche, in descending order of acceptance.

You can save yourself trouble by using "plastic" rather than cash or traveler's checks in 95% of all hotels, motels, restaurants, and retail stores. A credit card can also serve as a deposit for renting a car, as proof of identity, or as a "cash card," enabling you to draw money from automated-teller machines (ATMs) that accept them.

You can telegraph money or have it wired to you very quickly by using the **Western Union** system (☎ **800/325-6000**).

SAFETY

While tourist areas are generally safe, crime is a persistent problem everywhere, and U.S. urban areas tend to be less safe than those in Europe or Japan. Visitors should always stay alert. This is particularly true of large U.S. cities such as Miami. It is wise to ask the city's or area's tourist office if you're in doubt about which neighborhoods are safe. Avoid deserted areas, especially at night. Don't go into any city park at night unless there is an event that attracts crowds.

Remember also that hotels are open to the public, and in a large hotel, security may not be able to screen everyone entering. Always lock your room door—don't assume that once inside your hotel, you are automatically safe and no longer need to be aware of your surroundings.

DRIVING   Safety while driving is particularly important. Question your rental agency about personal safety or ask for a brochure of traveler safety tips. Get written directions, or a map with the route marked in red, from the agency showing how to get to your destination. Opt for any additional safety features in the car, such as cellular telephones or electronic maps. And, if possible, arrive and depart during daylight hours. If you are arriving at night, consider taking a taxi from the airport to your hotel and then having your rental car delivered.

Recently, more and more crime has involved cars and drivers. If you drive off a highway into a doubtful neighborhood, leave the area as quickly as possible. If you have an accident, even on the highway, stay in your car with the doors locked until you assess the situation or until the police arrive. If you are bumped from behind on the street or are involved in a minor accident with no injuries and the situation appears to be suspicious, motion to the other driver to follow you. Never get out of your car in such situations. Go directly to the nearest police precinct, well-lighted service station, or all-night store.

If you see someone on the road who indicates a need for help, do not stop. Take note of the location, drive into a well-lighted area, and telephone the police by dialing 911.

As we rode over the causeway, I could hardly believe my eyes. It was almost unimaginable that in Miami Beach it was 80 degrees while in New York it was 20. Everything—the buildings, the water, the pavement—had an indescribable glow to it. The palm trees especially made a great impression on me.

—Isaac Bashevis Singer, describing his first visit to Miami in 1948

Park in well-lighted, well-traveled areas if possible. Always keep your car doors locked, whether attended or unattended. Look around you before you get out of your car, and never leave any packages or valuables in sight. If someone attempts to rob you or steal your car, do not try to resist the thief/carjacker—report the incident to the police department immediately.

Reacting to several highly publicized crimes against tourists in Florida, both the local and state governments have taken steps to help protect visitors. These measures include special, highly visible police units patrolling the airport and surrounding neighborhoods and better signs on the state's most tourist-traveled routes. Still, especially in Miami, the signs can be extremely confusing. Make sure to chart your course before leaving an area. If you are staying on South Beach, you might want to consider skipping a car rental altogether, or at least for the time you are on the island. Taxis are plentiful and relatively inexpensive (see "Getting Around," in chapter 4).

2 Getting to the United States

Travelers from overseas can take advantage of the APEX (Advance Purchase Excursion) fares offered by all the major U.S. and European carriers. **British Airways** (☎ **081/897-4000** from within the U.K.) offers direct flights from London to Miami and Orlando, as does **Virgin Atlantic** (☎ **02/937-47747** from within the U.K.). Canadian readers might book flights with **Air Canada** (☎ **800/776-3000**), which offers service from Toronto and Montreal to Miami and Tampa.

Miami International Airport is a hub for flights to and from Latin America. Carriers include **Aerolineas Argentinas** (☎ 800/333-0276), **Aeromexico** (☎ 800/245-8585), **American Airlines** (☎ 800/433-7300), **Avianca** (☎ 800-284-2622), **Lan Chile Airlines** (☎ 800/735-5526), and **Varig Brazilian Airlines** (☎ 800/468-2744).

The visitor arriving by air, no matter what the port of entry, should cultivate patience and resignation before setting foot on U.S. soil. Getting through Immigration control could take as long as 2 hours on some days, especially summer weekends, so have your guidebook or something else to read handy. Add the time it takes to clear Customs, and you will see you should make a very generous allowance for delay in planning connections between international and domestic flights—figure on 2 to 3 hours at least.

In contrast, for the traveler arriving by car or by rail from Canada, the border-crossing formalities have been streamlined to the vanishing point. For the traveler by air from Canada, Bermuda, and some places in the Caribbean, you can sometimes go through Customs and Immigration at the point of departure, which is much quicker.

For further information about getting to Miami, see "Getting There" in chapter 2.

3 Getting Around the United States

BY AIR   On their transatlantic or transpacific flights, some large U.S. airlines offer special discount tickets for any of their U.S. destinations (American Airlines' Visit USA program and Delta's Discover America program, for example). The tickets or coupons are not on sale in the United States and must be purchased before you leave your point of departure. This system is the best, easiest, and fastest way to see the United States at low cost. You should get information well in advance from your travel agent or the office of the airline concerned, since the conditions attached to these discount tickets can be changed without advance notice.

BY RAIL   International visitors can also buy a USA Railpass good for 15 or 30 days of unlimited travel on **Amtrak** (☎ **800/USA-RAIL**). The pass is available through many foreign travel agents. Prices in 1999 for a 15-day pass were $285 off-peak, $425 peak; a 30-day pass was $375 off-peak, $535 peak (peak is June 17 to August 21). With a foreign passport, you can also buy passes at some Amtrak offices in the United States, including locations in San Francisco, Los Angeles, Chicago, New York, Miami, Boston, and Washington, D.C. Reservations are generally required and should be made for each part of your trip as early as possible.

Visitors should be aware of the limitations of long-distance rail travel in the United States. With a few notable exceptions (for instance, the Northeast Corridor line between Boston and Washington, D.C.), service is rarely up to European standards: Delays are common, routes are limited and often infrequently served, and fares are rarely significantly lower than discount airfares. Therefore, cross-country train travel should be approached with caution.

BY BUS   Although ticket prices for short bus trips between cities are often the most economical form of public transit, at this writing, bus passes are priced slightly higher than similar train passes. **Greyhound** (☎ **800/231-2222**), the nationwide bus line, offers an Ameripass for unlimited travel for 7 days ($199), 15 days ($299), 30 days ($399), and 60 days ($599). Bus travel in the United States can be both slow and uncomfortable, so this option is not for everyone. In addition, bus stations are often located in undesirable neighborhoods.

Fast Facts: For the Foreign Traveler

Automobile Organizations   Auto clubs will supply maps, suggested routes, guidebooks, accident and bail-bond insurance, and emergency road service. The major auto club in the United States, with 983 offices nationwide, is the American Automobile Association (AAA). Members of some foreign auto clubs have reciprocal arrangements with the AAA and enjoy its services at no charge, so inquire about AAA reciprocity before you leave. The AAA can give you an International Driving Permit validating your foreign license, although drivers with valid licenses from most home countries don't really need this permit. You may be able to join the AAA even if you are not a member of a reciprocal club. To inquire, call ☎ **800/926-4222.** In addition, some car-rental agencies now provide these services, so ask when you rent your car.

Auto Rentals   To rent a car, you need a major credit or charge card and a valid driver's license. Sometimes, a passport or international driver's license is also required if your driver's license is in a language other than English. Also, you usually need to be at least 25, although some companies do rent to younger people at a higher rate.

Business Hours   Banks are open weekdays from 9am to 3pm or later and sometimes Saturday morning. There's daily 24-hour access to the automated-teller machines (ATMs) at most banks and other outlets. Business offices are usually open weekdays from 9am to 5pm. Shops, especially department stores and those in shopping complexes, tend to stay open late—until about 9pm weekdays and until 6pm weekends.

Climate   See "When to Go" in chapter 2.

Currency   See "Money," in "Preparing for Your Trip," earlier in this chapter.

Currency Exchange   The "foreign-exchange bureaus" so common in Europe are rare in the United States.

At Miami Airport you'll find several **Miami Currency Exchanges** (☎ **305/876-0040**). The main one is at the lower level of concourse E.

Thomas Cook Currency Services offers a wide variety of services: more than 100 currencies, commission-free traveler's checks, drafts and wire transfers, and check collections. Rates are competitive and service is excellent. The Miami office is downtown at 80 N. Biscayne Blvd. between Flagler and 1st Street (☎ **305/381-9252**); it's open weekdays from 9am to 5pm. Another downtown money-changing office is **Abbot Foreign Exchange,** 230 NE 1st St. (☎ **305/374-2336**); it's open weekdays from 8am to 5pm and Saturday from 8am to 2pm.

Drinking Laws   The legal age to drink alcohol is 21.

Electricity   The United States uses 110 to 120 volts AC (60 cycles), compared to 220 to 240 volts AC (50 cycles) as in most of Europe. Besides a 100-volt converter, small appliances of non-American manufacture, such as hair dryers or shavers, will require a plug adapter, with two flat, parallel pins. The easiest solution is to purchase dual-voltage appliances that operate on both 110 and 220 volts; then, all that's required is a U.S. adapter plug.

Embassies/Consulates   All embassies are located in the national capital, Washington, D.C.; some consulates are located in Miami. Travelers from other countries can get telephone numbers for their embassies and consulates by calling **"Information"** in Washington, D.C. (☎ **202/555-1212**).

Brazil's Consulate General is in Coconut Grove at 2601 S. Bayshore Dr., Suite 800, Miami, FL 33133 (☎ 305/285-6200); the **British Consulate** is also located in Coconut Grove at the Brickell Bay Tower, Suite 2110, 1001 S. Bayshore Dr., Miami, FL 33131 (☎ 305/374-1522); a **Canadian Consulate** is at 200 S. Biscayne Blvd., Suite 1600, Miami, FL 33132 (☎ 305/579-1600); **Germany's Consulate General** is at 100 N. Biscayne Blvd., Miami, FL 33132 (☎ 305/358-0290); the **Italian Consulate** is at 1200 Brickell Ave., Miami, FL 33131 (☎ 305/374-6322); and the **Portuguese Consulate** is in Coral Gables at 1901 Ponce de León Blvd., Miami, FL (☎ 305/444-6311).

Emergencies   Call ☎ **911** for fire, police, and ambulance. If you encounter such traveler's problems as sickness, accidents, or lost or stolen baggage, call **Advocates for Victims** (☎ **305/758-2546**), an organization that specializes in helping distressed travelers.

U.S. hospitals have emergency rooms, with a special entrance where you will be admitted for quick attention. **Health South Doctors' Hospital,** 5000

University Dr., Coral Gables (☎ **305/666-2111**), is a 285-bed acute-care hospital with a 24-hour physician-staffed emergency department.

Gasoline (Petrol)   One U.S. gallon equals 3.75 liters, while 1.2 U.S. gallons equals one Imperial gallon. A gallon of unleaded "gas" (short for "gasoline"), which most rental cars require, costs about $1.30 if you fill your own tanks (it's called "self-serve"), and 10¢ more if the station attendant does it (called "full-service"). Most Miami gas stations are self-serve, with credit card processors right on the pump.

Holidays   On the following legal national holidays, banks, government offices, post offices, and many stores, restaurants, and museums are closed: **January 1** (New Year's Day); **third Monday in January** (Martin Luther King Day); **third Monday in February** (Presidents' Day, Washington's Birthday); **last Monday in May** (Memorial Day); **July 4** (Independence Day); **first Monday in September** (Labor Day); **second Monday in October** (Columbus Day); **November 11** (Veterans Day/Armistice Day); **fourth Thursday in November** (Thanksgiving); and **December 25** (Christmas). The Tuesday following the first Monday in November is **Election Day.**

Languages   Most hotels in Greater Miami have bilingual employees (Spanish and English). Unless your language is very obscure, they can usually supply a translator on request. Because more than half of Miami residents speak Spanish fluently, most signs and brochures are printed in both English and Spanish. In addition, since a large number of French, Canadian, Italian, and German tourists visit Miami, most visitor information is available in their languages.

Legal Aid   If you are stopped for a minor infraction (for example, of the highway code, such as speeding), never attempt to pay the fine directly to a police officer; you may be arrested on the much more serious charge of attempted bribery. Pay fines by mail, or directly into the hands of the clerk of the court. If accused of a more serious offense, it is best to say and do nothing before consulting a lawyer. Under U.S. law, an arrested person is allowed one telephone call to a party of his or her choice. Call your embassy or consulate.

Mail   You'll find the **Main Post Office,** 2200 Milam Dairy Rd., Miami, FL 33152 (☎ **305/639-4280**), just west of Miami International Airport. Letters addressed to you and marked "c/o General Delivery" can be picked up at 500 NW 2nd Ave., Miami, FL 33101. Mail delivery takes at least 30 days. The addressee must pick it up in person and produce proof of identity (driver's license, credit card, passport, or the like). Mailboxes are blue with a red-and-white logo, and carry the inscription "U.S. Mail."

Within the United States, it costs 20¢ to mail a standard-size postcard and 33¢ to send an oversize postcard (larger than 4¼ by 6 inches, or 10.8 by 15.4 centimeters). Letters that weigh up to 1 ounce (that's about five pages, 8½ by 11 inches, or 20.5 by 28.2 centimeters) cost 33¢, plus 22¢ for each additional ounce. A postcard to Mexico or Canada costs 40¢, a ½-ounce letter 46¢. A postcard to Europe, Australia, New Zealand, the Far East, South America, and elsewhere costs 50¢, while a ½-ounce letter is 60¢, and a 1-ounce letter is $1.

Newspapers/Magazines   The *Miami Herald* and the magazines *Newsweek* and *Time* cover world news and are available at newsstands. Most magazine racks at drugstores, airports, and hotels include a good selection of foreign periodicals, such as *Stern, The Economist,* and *Le Monde. El Herald* and *Diarios Las Americas* are Spanish-language newspapers. Spanish-language magazines are particularly abundant.

Post   See "Mail," above.

Safety   See "Safety," in "Preparing for Your Trip," above.

Taxes   In the United States, there is no VAT (value-added tax), or other indirect tax at a national level. There is a $10 Customs tax, payable on entry to the United States, and a $6 departure tax.

A 6% state sales tax (plus .5% local tax, for a total of 6.5% in Miami) is added on at the register for all goods and services purchased in Florida. These taxes are not refundable. In addition, most municipalities levy special taxes on restaurants and hotels. In Surfside, hotel taxes total 10.5%; in Bal Harbour, 9.5%; in Miami Beach (including South Beach), 11.5%; and in the rest of Dade County, a whopping 12.5%. In Miami Beach, Surfside, and Bal Harbour, the resort (hotel) tax also applies to hotel restaurants and restaurants with liquor licenses.

Telephone/Fax   Look for pay phones on street corners, as well as in bars, restaurants, public buildings, stores, and at service stations. In most areas, local calls cost 35¢. Within Miami you must dial the area code, either 305 or 786, before the seven-digit number.

For long-distance or international calls from a pay phone, it's most economical to charge the call to a telephone charge card or a credit card, or you can use a lot of change. The pay phone operator will instruct you how much to deposit and when to deposit it into the slot on the telephone box. For long distance calls, also dial 1 before the area code. 800 and 888 numbers are toll free but still require a 1 before dialing.

For local directory assistance ("information"), dial 411; for long-distance information, dial 1, then the appropriate area code, and then 555-1212.

For long-distance calls in the United States, dial 1 followed by the area code and number you want. For direct overseas calls, first dial 011, followed by the country code (Australia, 61; Republic of Ireland, 353; New Zealand, 64; United Kingdom, 44), and then by the city code (for example, 71 or 81 for London, 21 for Birmingham, 1 for Dublin) and the number of the person you wish to call.

For reversed-charge or collect calls and for person-to-person calls, dial 0 (zero, not the letter O) followed by the area code and number you want; an operator will then come on the line, and you should specify that you are calling collect, or person-to-person, or both. If your operator-assisted call is international, immediately ask to speak with an overseas operator.

Before calling from a hotel room, always ask the hotel phone operator if there are any telephone surcharges. There almost always are, often as much as 75¢ or $1, even for a local call.

In the past few years, many American companies have installed voice-mail systems. Listen carefully to the instructions (you'll probably be asked to dial 1, 2, or 3 or wait for an operator to pick up); if you can't understand, sometimes dialing zero will put you in touch with a company operator. It's frustrating even for locals!

Many car-rental companies also rent cellular phones, a wise and convenient option when traveling in unfamiliar territory.

Most hotels have fax machines available for their customers and usually charge to send or receive a facsimile. You will also see signs for public faxes in the windows of small shops.

Telephone Directory   The local phone company provides two kinds of telephone directories. The general directory, called the "white pages," lists businesses and personal residences separately, in alphabetical order. The first few pages are devoted to community-service numbers, including a guide to long-distance and international calling, complete with country codes and area codes.

The second directory, the "yellow pages," lists all local services, businesses, and industries by type, with an index at the back. The listings cover not only such obvious items as automobile repairs by make of car, or drugstores (pharmacies), often by geographical location, but also restaurants by type of cuisine and geographical location, bookstores by special subject and/or language, places of worship by religious denomination, and other information that a visitor might otherwise not readily find. The yellow pages also include city plans or detailed area maps, often showing postal ZIP codes and public transportation.

Time   The United States is divided into six time zones. Miami, like New York, is in the eastern standard time zone. America's eastern seaboard is 5 hours behind Greenwich mean time. Between April and October, eastern daylight savings time is adopted, and clocks are set 1 hour ahead. To find out what time it is, call ☎ **305/324-8811.**

Tipping   Waiters and bartenders expect a 15% tip, as do taxi drivers and hairdressers. Porters should be tipped 50¢ to $1 per bag, and parking valets should be given $1. It's nice to leave a few dollars on your pillow for the hotel maid, and lavatory attendants will appreciate whatever change you have.

Toilets   Visitors can usually find a rest room in a bar, restaurant, hotel, museum, department store, or service station—and it will probably be clean (although the last-mentioned sometimes leaves much to be desired). The cleanliness of toilets at railroad stations and bus depots may be more questionable. You'll also find toilets at many public beaches and large parks. Some public places are equipped with pay toilets, which require you to insert one or more coins into a slot on the door before it will open. Rest rooms in cafes and restaurants usually are for patrons only, but in an emergency you can just order a cup of coffee or try simply asking to use the pay phone, usually conveniently positioned beside the rest rooms.

4 Getting to Know Miami

Miami is not a terribly complicated city to negotiate, but, like all unfamiliar territories, this metropolis takes a bit of time to master.

1 Orientation

ARRIVING

Originally carved out of scrubland in 1928 by Pan American Airlines, **Miami International Airport (MIA)** has emerged as one of the busiest airports in the world. Unfortunately, as it undergoes major reconstruction to expand its capacity, the airport can feel like a maze with inadequate signage and surly employees.

The route down to the baggage-claim area is clearly marked. You can change money or use your Honor or Plus System ATM card at Barnett Bank of South Florida, located near the exit.

Like most good international airports, MIA has its fair share of boutiques, shops, and eateries. Unless you are starving or forgot to get a gift for the person picking you up, bypass these overpriced establishments. The airport is literally surrounded by restaurants and shops; if you can wait to get to them, you will save a lot of money. If you are exiting Miami on an international flight, don't miss the excellent duty-free selection in the departure lounge.

Visitor information is available 24 hours a day at the **Miami International Airport Main Visitor Counter,** Concourse E, 2nd level (☎ **305/876-7000**).

GETTING INTO TOWN

The airport is located about 6 miles west of Downtown and about 10 miles from the beaches, so it's likely you can get from the plane to your hotel room in less than half an hour. Of course, if you're arriving from an international destination, it will take more time to go through Customs and Immigration.

BY CAR   All the major car-rental firms operate off-site branches reached via shuttle from the terminals. See "Getting Around" in chapter 4 for a list of major rental companies. Signs at the airport's exit clearly point the way to various parts of the city. If you're arriving at night, I might suggest taking a taxi to your hotel and having the car-rental firm deliver a car to your hotel the next day.

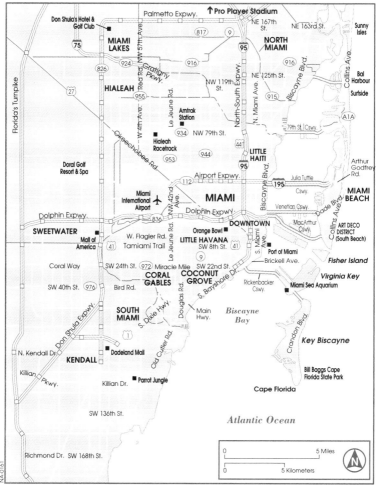

BY TAXI Taxis line up in front of a dispatcher's desk outside the airport's arrivals terminals. Most cabs are metered, though some have flat rates to popular destinations. The fare should be about $12 to Coral Gables, $18 to Downtown, and $24 to South Beach, plus tip, which should be at least 10% and more for each bag the driver handles. Depending on traffic, the ride to Coral Gables or Downtown takes about 15 to 20 minutes, and to South Beach, 20 to 25 minutes. One of the more reliable companies in the city (with an easy-to-remember number) is **Yellow Cab** (☎ **305/444-4444**).

BY LIMO OR VAN Group limousines (multipassenger vans) circle the arrivals area looking for fares. Destinations are posted on the front of each van, and a flat rate is charged for door-to-door service to the area marked.

SuperShuttle (☎ **305/871-2000**) is one of the largest airport operators, charging between $10 and $20 per person for a ride within the County. Its vans operate 24 hours a day and accept American Express, MasterCard, and Visa.

Private limousine arrangements can be made in advance through your local travel agent. A one-way meet-and-greet service should cost about $50.

BY PUBLIC TRANSPORTATION   I do not recommend taking public transportation to get from the airport to your hotel. Buses heading downtown leave the airport only once per hour (from the arrivals level), and connections are spotty at best. It could take about an hour and a half to get to South Beach. Journeys to downtown and Coral Gables are more direct. The fare is $1.25, plus an additional 25¢ for a South Beach transfer.

VISITOR INFORMATION

The best up-to-date, specialized information is provided by the **Greater Miami Convention and Visitors Bureau,** 701 Brickell Ave., Miami, FL 33131 (☎ **800/283-2707** or 305/539-3063; www.miamiandbeaches.com; e-mail: gmcvb@aol.com). Chambers of commerce in Greater Miami also send out information on their particular neighborhoods; for addresses and numbers, please see "Visitor Information & Money" in chapter 2.

When you arrive at the Miami International Airport, you can pick up visitor information at the airport's main visitor counter on the second floor of Concourse E. It's open 24 hours a day.

Always check local newspapers for special things to do during your visit. The city's only daily, the *Miami Herald*, is a good source for current-events listings, particularly the "Weekend" section in Friday's edition. Even better is the weekly giveaway, *New Times*, available in bright red boxes throughout the city.

CITY LAYOUT

Miami may seem confusing at first, but it quickly becomes easy to negotiate. The small cluster of buildings that make up the Downtown area is at the geographical heart of the city. You can see these sharp stalagmites from most anywhere, making them a good reference point. In relation to Downtown, the airport is northwest, the beaches are east, Coconut Grove is south, Coral Gables is west, and the rest of the country is north.

FINDING AN ADDRESS   Miami is divided into dozens of areas with official and unofficial boundaries. Street numbering in the city of Miami is fairly straightforward, but you must first be familiar with the numbering system. The mainland is divided into four sections—NE, NW, SE, and SW—by the intersection of Flagler Street and Miami Avenue. Street numbers (First Street, Second Street, and so forth) start from here and increase as you go further out, as do numbers of avenues, places, courts, terraces, and lanes. Streets in Hialeah are the exceptions to this pattern; they are listed separately in map indexes.

Numerical addresses are descriptive with the first digits giving the cross streets. For example, 12301 Biscayne Blvd. is located at 123rd Street and 501 Ocean Dr. is at 5th Street. It's also helpful to remember that avenues generally run north-south, while streets go east-west.

Getting around the barrier islands that make up Miami Beach is somewhat easier than moving around the mainland. Street numbering starts with First Street, near Miami Beach's southern tip, and increases to 192nd Street, in the northern part of Sunny Isles. Collins Avenue makes the entire journey from head to toe. As in the city of Miami, some streets in Miami Beach have numbers as well as names. When they are part of listings in this book, both names and numbers are given.

You should know that the numbered streets in Miami Beach are not the geographical equivalents of those on the mainland, but they are close. For example, the 79th Street Causeway runs into 71st Street on Miami Beach.

STREET MAPS   It's easy to get lost in sprawling Miami, so a reliable map is essential. If you are not planning on moving around too much, the tourist board's maps, located inside its free publication "Destination Miami," should be adequate. If you really want to get to know the city, it pays to invest in one of the large accordion-fold maps, available at most gas stations and bookstores. The Trakker Map of Miami ($2.50) is a four-color accordion map that encompasses all of Dade County.

Some maps of Miami list streets according to area, so you'll have to know which part of the city you are looking for before the street can be found. All the listings in this book include area information for just this reason.

The Neighborhoods in Brief

Much of Miami is sprawling suburbia. But every city has its charm, and aside from a fantastic tropical climate and the vast stretch of beach that lies just across its glistening Biscayne Bay, Miami's unique identity comes from extremely interesting cultural pockets within its residential communities. Here's a brief rundown of the characteristics of its diverse neighborhoods:

South Beach—The Art Deco District   In the last several years, South Beach has been the hottest area of Miami. While technically it's just 15 blocks at the southern tip of Miami Beach, South Beach has a style all its own. The thriving Art Deco District within South Beach contains the largest concentration of art deco architecture in the world. (In chapter 8, there's an in-depth walking tour of this fascinating area.)

Young investors, artists, model-types, and the usual Miami smattering of Cubans, African Americans, and Caribbeans populate this vibrant community. Hip clubs and cafes are filled with vacationing Europeans, working models, photographers, musicians, and writers who enjoy the exciting and sophisticated atmosphere.

Miami Beach   To tourists in the 1950s, Miami Beach *was* Miami. Its huge self-contained resort hotels were vacations unto themselves, providing a full day's worth of meals, activities, and entertainment. Then, in the 1960s and 1970s, people who fell in love with Miami began to buy apartments rather than rent hotel rooms. Tourism declined, and many area hotels fell into disrepair.

However, since the late 1980s, Miami Beach has experienced a tide of revitalization. Huge beach hotels are finding their niche with new, international tourist markets and are attracting large convention crowds. The **Miami Beach Convention Center,** 1901 Convention Center Dr., Miami Beach, FL 33139 (☎ **305/ 673-7311**), has more than 1 million square feet of exhibition space. New generations of Americans have discovered the qualities that originally made Miami Beach so popular, and they are finding out that the sand and surf now come with a thriving international city.

The north part of "The Beach"—**Surfside, Bal Harbour, Sunny Isles,** and other small neighborhoods—is, for the most part, an extension of the beach community below it. **Collins Avenue** crosses town lines with hardly a sign, while hotels, motels, restaurants, and beaches continue to line the strip. For visitors, it seems that—with some outstanding exceptions—the farther north one goes, the cheaper lodging becomes. All told, excellent prices, location, and facilities make Surfside and Sunny

Isles, although a little rough around the edges, attractive places to stay. To keep up with demand for beachfront property, many of the area's moderately priced hotels have been converted to condominiums, leaving fewer and fewer kitschy and affordable places to stay.

In exclusive Bal Harbour, a huge alfresco mall attracts decked-out shoppers. A few elegant hotels remain amid the many beachfront condominium towers. Fancy homes, tucked away on the bay, hide behind walls, gates, and security cameras.

Note that **North Miami Beach,** a residential area near the Dade–Broward County line, is a misnomer. It is actually northwest of Miami Beach on the mainland and has no beaches. North Miami Beach is part of North Dade County and has some of Miami's better restaurants and shops. Also, South Beach, the historic art deco district, is treated as a seperate neighborhood, see above.

Key Biscayne   Miami's forested and fancy Key Biscayne is technically one of the first islands in the Florida Keys. However, this luxurious island is nothing like its southern neighbors. Located south of Miami Beach, off the shores of Coconut Grove, Key Biscayne is protected from the troubles of the mainland by the long Rickenbacker Causeway and a $1 toll. Key Biscayne is largely an exclusive residential community with million-dollar homes and sweeping water views, although it also offers visitors great beaches, some top resort hotels, and several good restaurants. Hobie Beach, adjacent to the causeway, is the city's premier spot for sailboarding and jet-skiing (see "Water Sports" in chapter 7). On the island's southern tip, Bill Baggs State Park has great beaches, bike paths, and dense forests for picnicking and partying.

Downtown   Miami's Downtown boasts one of the world's most beautiful cityscapes. If you do nothing else in Miami, make sure you take your time studying the area's inspired architectural designs. During the day, a vibrant community of students, businesspeople, and merchants make their way through the bustling streets. Vendors sell fresh-cut pineapples and mangos while young Latin American consumers on shopping sprees lug bags and boxes. The Downtown area has its mall (Bayside Marketplace, where many cruise passengers come to browse), its culture (Metro-Dade Cultural Center), and a number of good restaurants (listed in chapter 6, "Dining").

Little Haiti   During a brief period in the late 1970s and early 1980s, almost 35,000 Haitians arrived in Miami. Most of the new refugees settled in a decaying 200-square-block area north of Downtown. Extending from 41st to 83rd streets and bordered by I-95 and Biscayne Boulevard, Little Haiti is a relatively depressed neighborhood with at least 60,000 residents, more than half of whom were born in Haiti.

On Northeast Second Avenue, Little Haiti's main thoroughfare, is the now-closed, once-colorful Caribbean Marketplace, located at the corner of 60th Street. Previously filled with bustling shops, it stands as a sad reminder of the neighborhood's economic distress.

Little Havana   Miami's Cuban center is the city's most important ethnic enclave. Referred to locally as "Calle Ocho" (pronounced *Ka*-yey *O*-choh), SW Eighth Street, just west of Downtown, is the region's main thoroughfare. Car-repair shops, tailors, electronics stores, and inexpensive restaurants all hang signs in Spanish. Salsa rhythms thump from the radios of passersby, while old men in *guayaberas* smoke cigars over their daily game of dominoes.

Coral Gables   At just over 75 years old, Coral Gables is the closest thing to "historical" that Miami has. It's also one of the prettiest parcels in the city. Created by

George Merrick in the early 1920s, the Gables was one of Miami's first planned developments. The houses here were built in a Mediterranean style along lush tree-lined streets that open onto beautifully carved plazas, many with centerpiece fountains. The best architectural examples of the era have Spanish-style tiled roofs and are built from Miami oolite, a native limestone commonly called "coral rock." Coral Gables is a stunning example of "boom" architecture on a grand scale—plus, it's a great area to explore. Some of the city's best restaurants are located here, as are top hotels and good shopping. See the appropriate chapters for listings and "Driving Tour 2," in chapter 8.

Coconut Grove   There was a time when Coconut Grove was inhabited by artists, intellectuals, hippies, and radicals, but times have changed. Gentrification has pushed most alternative types out, leaving in their place a multitude of cafes, boutiques, and nightspots. The intersection of Grand Avenue, Main Highway, and McFarlane Road pierces the area's heart, which sizzles with dozens of interesting shops and eateries. Sidewalks here are often crowded with businesspeople, high school students, and loads of foreign visitors—especially at night, when it becomes a great place to people-watch.

Coconut Grove's link to The Bahamas dates from before the turn of the century, when islanders came to the area to work in a newly opened hotel called the Peacock Inn. Bahamian-style wooden homes, built by these early settlers, still stand on Charles Street. Goombay, the lively annual Bahamian festival, celebrates the Grove's Caribbean link and has become one of the largest black-heritage street festivals in America (see "South Florida Calendar of Events," in chapter 2).

Southern Miami–Dade County   To locals, South Miami is both a specific area, southwest of Coral Gables, and a general region that encompasses all of southern Dade County and includes Kendall, Perrine, Cutler Ridge, and Homestead. For the purposes of clarity, this book has grouped all these southern suburbs under the rubric "Southern Miami–Dade County." Similar attributes unite the communities: They are heavily residential, and all are packed with shopping malls amidst a few remaining plots of farmland. Tourists don't usually stay in these parts, unless they are on their way to the Everglades or Keys, However, Southern Miami–Dade County does contain many of the city's top attractions (see chapter 7), making it likely you'll spend some time during the day here.

2 Getting Around

Officially, Dade County has opted for a "unified, multimodal transportation network," which basically means you can get around the city by train, bus, and taxi. However, in practice, the network doesn't work too well. In most cases, unless you are going from downtown Miami to a not-too-distant spot, you are better off in a rented car or a taxi.

With the exception of downtown Coconut Grove and South Beach, Miami is not a walker's city. Because it is so spread out, most attractions are too far apart to make walking between them feasible. In fact, most Miamians are so used to driving that they do so even when going just a few blocks.

BY PUBLIC TRANSPORTATION
BY RAIL   Two rail lines, operated by the **Metro-Dade Transit Agency** (☎ **305/ 638-6700** for information), run in concert with each other.

Metrorail, the city's modern high-speed commuter train, is a 21-mile elevated line that travels north-south, between downtown Miami and the southern suburbs. If you are staying in Coral Gables or Coconut Grove, you can park your car at a nearby station and ride the rails Downtown. Unfortunately for visitors, the line's usefulness is limited. There are plans to extend the system to service Miami International Airport, but until those tracks are built, these trains don't go most places tourists go. Metrorail operates daily from about 6am to midnight. The fare is $1.25.

Metromover, a 4.4-mile elevated line, connects with Metrorail at the Government Center stop and circles Downtown. Riding on rubber tires, the single-train car winds past many of the area's most important attractions and shopping and business districts. Metromover offers a fun, futuristic ride that you might want to take to complement your Downtown tour. You get a beautiful perspective from the towering height of the suspended rails. System hours are daily from about 6am to midnight. The fare is 25¢.

BY BUS Miami's suburban layout is not conducive to getting around by bus. Lines operate, and maps are available, but instead of getting to know the city, you'll find that relying on bus transportation will acquaint you only with how it feels to wait at bus stops. You can get a bus map by mail, either from the Greater Miami Convention and Visitors Bureau (see "Visitor Information" in chapter 2) or by writing the Metro-Dade Transit System, 3300 NW 32nd Ave., Miami, FL 33142. In Miami, call ☎ **305/638-6700** for public-transit information. The fare is $1.25.

BY CAR

Tales circulate about vacationers who have visited Miami without a car, but they are very few indeed. If you are counting on exploring the city, even to a modest degree, a car is essential. Miami's restaurants, attractions, and sights are far from one another, so any other form of transportation is impractical. You won't need a car, however, if you are spending your entire vacation at a resort, are traveling directly to the Port of Miami for a cruise, or are here for a short stay centered in one area of the city, such as South Beach.

When driving across a causeway or through Downtown, allow extra time to reach your destination because of frequent drawbridge openings. Some bridges open about every half hour for large sailing vessels that make their way through the wide bays and canals that crisscross the city, stalling traffic for several minutes. Don't get frustrated by the wait. It's all part of the easy pace of South Florida life.

RENTALS It seems as though every car-rental company, big and small, has at least one office in Miami. Consequently, the city is one of the cheapest places in the world to rent a car. Many firms regularly advertise prices in the neighborhood of $100 per week for their bottom-of-the-line tin can—not an unreasonable sum for 7 days of transportation in the land of sun and fun.

A minimum age, generally 25, is usually required of renters. Some rental agencies have also set maximum ages. A national car-rental broker, **A Car Rental Referral Service** (☎ **800/404-4482**), can often find companies willing to rent to drivers over the age of 21 and can also get discounts from major companies as well as some regional ones.

National car-rental companies with toll-free numbers include **Alamo** (☎ 800/327-9633), **Avis** (☎ 800/331-1212), **Budget** (☎ 800/527-0700), **Dollar** (☎ 800/800-4000 or 800/327-7607), **Hertz** (☎ 800/654-3131), **National** (☎ 800/328-4567), and **Thrifty** (☎ 800/367-2277). One excellent company that has offices in every conceivable part of town and offers extremely competitive rates is **Enterprise** (☎ **800/325-8007**). Just make sure that you call several companies and comparison shop. Car rental prices can fluctuate more than airfares.

Many companies offer cellular phones or electronic map rental. It might be wise to opt for these additional safety features, although the cost can be exorbitant; the phone especially can come in handy if you get disoriented. There is nothing worse than being lost in an unfamiliar city in a questionable area with no one to turn to.

Finally, think about splurging on a convertible. Few things in life can match the feeling of cruising along warm Florida highways with the sun smiling on your shoulders and the wind whipping through your hair. At most companies, the price is only about 20% more.

PARKING   Always keep plenty of quarters on hand to feed hungry meters. Or, on Miami Beach, stop by the Chamber of Commerce at 1920 Meridian Ave. or any Publix grocery store to buy a magnetic **parking card** in denominations of $10, $20, or $25. Parking is usually plentiful (except on South Beach and Coconut Grove), but when it's not, be careful: Fines for illegal parking can be stiff, up to $18.

In addition to parking garages, valet services are commonplace and often used. Expect to pay from $3 to $10 for parking in Coconut Grove and on South Beach's Ocean Drive on busy weekend nights.

LOCAL DRIVING RULES   Florida law allows drivers to make a right turn on a red light after a complete stop, unless otherwise indicated. In addition, all passengers are required to wear seat belts, and children under 3 must be securely fastened in government-approved car seats.

BY TAXI

If you're not planning on traveling much within the city, an occasional taxi is a good alternative to renting a car. If you plan on spending your holiday within the confines of South Beach's Art Deco District, you might also want to avoid the parking hassles that come with renting your own car. Taxi meters start at $1.50 for the first ¼ mile and 25¢ for each ⅛ mile. There are standard flat-rate charges for frequently traveled routes—for example, Miami Beach's Convention Center to Coconut Grove would cost about $16.

Major cab companies include **Metro** (☎ **305/888-8888**), **Yellow** (☎ **305/444-4444**), and, on Miami Beach, **Central** (☎ **305/532-5555**).

BY BICYCLE

Miami has several interesting areas to bike, including most of Miami Beach, where the hard-packed sand and boardwalks make it an easy and scenic route. However, unless you are a former New York City bicycle messenger, you won't want to use a bicycle as your main means of transportation.

For more information on bicycles, including where to rent the best ones, see chapter 7, "What to See & Do in Miami."

Fast Facts: Miami

Airport   See "Orientation," earlier in this chapter.

American Express   You'll find American Express offices in downtown Miami at 330 Biscayne Blvd. (☎ **305/358-7350**); 9700 Collins Ave., Bal Harbour (☎ **305/865-5959**); and 32 Miracle Mile, Coral Gables (☎ **305/446-3381**). Offices are open weekdays from 9am to 5pm and Saturday from 10am to 4pm.

The Bal Harbour office is also open on Sunday from noon to 6pm. To report lost or stolen traveler's checks, call ☎ **800/221-7282.**

Area Code   The original area code for Miami and all of Dade County was 305. That is still the code for older phone numbers, but all phone numbers assigned since July 1998 have the area code 786 (SUN). Even though the Keys still share the Dade County area code of 305, calls to there from Miami are considered long distance and must be preceded by 1-305. Within the Keys, simply dial the seven-digit number. The area code for Fort Lauderdale is 954; for Palm Beach and Boca Raton, it's 561.

Business Hours   Banking hours vary, but most banks are open weekdays from 9am to 3pm. Several stay open until 5pm or so at least 1 day during the week, and many banks feature automated-teller machines (ATMs) for 24-hour banking. Most stores are open daily from 10am to 6pm; however, there are many exceptions. Shops in the Bayside Marketplace are usually open until 9 or 10pm, as are the boutiques in Coconut Grove. Stores in Bal Harbour and other malls are usually open an extra hour one night during the week (usually Thursday). As far as business offices are concerned, Miami is generally a 9am to 5pm town.

Car Rentals   See "Getting Around," earlier in this chapter.

Climate   See "When to Go," in chapter 2.

Curfew   Although not strictly enforced, there is a curfew in effect for minors after 11pm on weeknights and midnight on weekends in all of Miami-Dade County. After those hours, children under 17 cannot be out on the streets or driving unless accompanied by a parent or on their way to work.

Dentists   The East Coast District Dental Society staffs an **Emergency Dental Referral Service** (☎ **305/285-5470**). **A&E Dental,** 11400 N. Kendall Dr., Mega Bank Building (☎ **305/271-7777**), also offers round-the-clock care and accepts MasterCard and Visa.

Doctors   In an emergency, call an ambulance by dialing 911 from any phone. The Dade County Medical Association sponsors a **Physician Referral Service** (☎ **305/324-8717**) weekdays from 9am to 5pm. **Health South Doctors' Hospital,** 5000 University Dr., Coral Gables (☎ **305/666-2111**), is a 285-bed acute-care hospital with a 24-hour physician-staffed emergency department.

Driving Rules   See "Getting Around," above.

Drugstores   See "Pharmacies," below.

Embassies/Consulates   See chapter 3, "For Foreign Visitors."

Emergencies   To reach the police, ambulance, or fire department, dial ☎ **911** from any phone. No coins are needed. Emergency hot lines include **Crisis Intervention** (☎ **305/358-HELP** or 305/358-4357) and **Poison Information Center** (☎ **800/282-3171**).

Eyeglasses   **Pearle Vision Center,** 7901 Biscayne Blvd. (☎ **305/754-5144**), in Miami, can usually fill prescriptions in about an hour.

Hospitals   See "Doctors," above.

Information   See "Visitor Information," above.

Laundry/Dry Cleaning   For dry-cleaning, self-service machines, and a wash-and-fold service by the pound call **All Laundry Service,** 5701 NW 7th St. (west of Downtown, ☎ **305/261-8175**); it's open daily from 7am to 10pm. **Clean**

Machine Laundry, 226 12th St., South Beach (☎ **305/534-9429**), is convenient to South Beach's art deco hotels; it's open 24 hours. **Coral Gables Laundry
& Dry Cleaning,** 250 Minorca Ave., Coral Gables (☎ **305/446-6458**), has
been dry-cleaning, altering, and laundering since 1930. It offers a lifesaving
same-day service and is open weekdays from 7am to 7pm and Saturday from
8am to 3pm.

Liquor Laws   Only adults 21 or older may legally purchase or consume alcohol
in the state of Florida. Minors are usually permitted in bars that serve food.
Liquor laws are strictly enforced; if you look young, carry identification. Beer and
wine are sold in most supermarkets and convenience stores. The city of Miami's
liquor stores are closed on Sunday. Liquor stores in the city of Miami Beach are
open all week.

Lost Property   If you lost it at the airport, call the **Airport Lost and Found**
office (☎ **305/876-7377**). If you lost it on the bus, Metrorail, or Metromover,
call **Metro-Dade Transit Agency** (☎ **305/638-6700**). If you lost it somewhere
else, phone the **Dade County Police Lost and Found** (☎ **305/375-3366**). You
might also want to fill out a police report for insurance purposes.

Luggage Storage/Lockers   In addition to the baggage check at Miami International Airport, most hotels offer luggage-storage facilities. If you are taking a
cruise from the Port of Miami (see "Cruises and Other Caribbean Getaways," in
chapter 11, "Side Trips from Miami"), bags can be stored in your ship's departure terminal.

Newspapers/Magazines   The *Miami Herald* is the city's only English-language
daily. It is especially known for its Latin American coverage and its excellent
Friday "Weekend" entertainment guide. There are literally dozens of specialized
Miami magazines geared toward visitors and natives alike. Many are free and can
be picked up at hotels, at restaurants, and in self-serve boxes all around town.
The most respected alternative weekly is the give-away tabloid called *New Times,*
which contains up-to-date listings and reviews of food, films, theater, music, and
whatever else is happening in town. Also free if you can find it is *Ocean Drive,* a
gorgeous oversized glossy magazine, available at a number of chic South Beach
boutiques and restaurants. It also sells on newsstands.

For a large selection of foreign-language newspapers and magazines, check
with any of the large bookstores (see chapter 9, "Shopping") or try **News Café** at
800 Ocean Dr., South Beach (☎ **305/538-6397**), or in Coconut Grove at 2901
Florida Ave. (☎ 305/774-6397); **Eddie's Normandy,** 1096 Normandy Dr.,
Miami Beach (☎ **305/866-2026**); and **Worldwide News,** 1629 NE 163rd St.,
North Miami Beach (☎ **305/940-4090**).

Pharmacies   The most ubiquitous drugstore is **Walgreens Pharmacy,** with
dozens of locations all over town, including 8550 Coral Way (☎ **305/
221-9271**), in Coral Gables; 1845 Alton Rd. (☎ 305/531-8868), in South
Beach; and 6700 Collins Ave. (☎ 305/861-6742), in Miami Beach. The branch
at 5731 Bird Rd. at SW 40th Street (☎ 305/666-0757) is open 24 hours, as is
Eckerd Drugs, 1825 Miami Gardens Dr. NE, at 185th Street, North Miami
Beach (☎ **305/932-5740**).

Photographic Needs   One of the more expensive places to have your film
developed is **One Hour Photo** in the Bayside Marketplace (☎ **305/
377-FOTO**). They charge $17 to develop and print a roll of 36 pictures, and

they're open Monday to Saturday from 10am to 10pm and Sunday from noon to 8pm. **Coconut Grove Camera,** 3317 Virginia St. (☎ **305/445-0521**), features 30-minute color processing and maintains a huge selection of cameras and equipment. It rents, too. Walgreens or Eckerd's will develop film for the next day for about $6 or $7.

Police   For emergencies, dial ☎ **911** from any phone. No coins are needed. For other matters, call ☎ **305/595-6263.**

Post Office   The **Main Post Office,** 2200 Milam Dairy Rd., Miami, FL 33152 (☎ **305/639-4280**), is located west of Miami International Airport. Letters addressed to you and marked "c/o General Delivery" can be picked up at 500 NW 2nd Ave. Conveniently located post offices include 1300 Washington Ave. (☎ **305/531-7306**), in South Beach, and 3191 Grand Ave. (☎ **305/443-0030**), in Coconut Grove.

Radio   About five dozen radio stations can be heard in the Greater Miami area. On the AM dial, 610 (WIOD), 790 (WNWS), 1230 (WJNO), and 1340 (WPBR) are all talk. There is no all-news station in town, although 940 (WINZ) does give traffic updates and headline news in between its talk shows. WDBF (1420) is a good big band station and WPBG (1290) features golden oldies. The best rock stations on the FM dial are WZTA (94.9) and the progressive-rock station WVUM (90.5). WKIS (99.9) is the top country station. Public radio can be heard either on WXEL (90.7) or WLRN (91.3). WGTR (97.3) plays easy listening. WDNA (88.9) has the best Latin jazz and multiethnic sounds.

Religious Services   Miami houses of worship are as varied as the city's population and include St. Patrick Catholic Church, 3716 Garden Ave., Miami Beach (☎ **305/531-1124**); Temple Judea, 5500 Granada Blvd., Coral Gables (☎ **305/667-5657**); Coconut Grove United Methodist, 2850 SW 27th Ave. (☎ **305/443-0880**); Christ Episcopal Church, 3481 Hibiscus St. (☎ **305/442-8542**); and Plymouth Congregational Church, 3400 Devon Rd., at Main Highway (☎ **305/444-6521**).

Rest Rooms   Stores rarely let customers use the rest rooms, and many restaurants offer their facilities for customers only. Most malls have bathrooms, as do many of the ubiquitous fast-food restaurants. Many public beaches and large parks provide toilets, though in some places you have to pay or tip an attendant. Most large hotels have clean restrooms in their lobbies.

Safety   Don't walk alone at night, and be extra wary when walking or driving though Downtown Miami and surrounding areas. It's always a good idea to stay aware of your surroundings when you're in any unfamiliar city, even in the most heavily touristed areas. Always consult a good map and know where you are going before getting in your car. Never stop on a highway—if you get a flat tire, drive to the nearest well-lighted, populated place. Keep car doors locked and stay alert.

Taxes   A 6% state sales tax (plus .5% local tax, for a total of 6.5% in Miami) is added on at the register for all goods and services purchased in Florida. In addition, most municipalities levy special taxes on restaurants and hotels. In Surfside, hotel taxes total 10.5%; in Bal Harbour, 9.5%; in Miami Beach (including South Beach), 11.5%; and in the rest of Dade County, a whopping 12.5%. In Miami Beach, Surfside, and Bal Harbour, the resort (hotel) tax also applies to hotel restaurants and restaurants with liquor licenses.

Taxis   See "Getting Around," earlier in this chapter.

Television   The local stations are Channel 6, WTVJ (NBC); Channel 4, WCIX (CBS); Channel 7, WSVN (Fox); Channel 10, WPLG (ABC); Channel 17, WLRN (PBS); Channel 23, WLTV (independent); and Channel 33, WBFS (independent).

Time Zone   Miami, like New York, is in the eastern standard time zone. Between April and October, eastern daylight savings time is adopted, and clocks are set 1 hour ahead. America's eastern seaboard is 5 hours behind Greenwich mean time. To find out what time it is, call ☎ **305/324-8811.**

Transit Information   For **Metrorail** or **Metromover** schedule information, phone ☎ **305/770-3131.**

Weather   Hurricane season runs from August through November. For an up-to-date recording of current weather conditions and forecast reports, call ☎ **305/229-4522.**

5 Miami Accommodations

The hotel district in South Beach is recognizable by the concentration of construction workers hauling supplies and operating cranes and tractors in an effort to fix up the last few properties that have not yet been redone for the burgeoning tourist market. Since the renaissance that began in the early 1980s, the Beach has turned into an upscale boomtown. In 1999, the Loews group completed an 800-room hotel on Collins Avenue (the first large-scale new hotel to be built on South Beach in more than 30 years), Marriott and Crowne Plaza both broke ground on large hotels, and dozens of other "boutique" properties have opened their doors to guests. One notable South Beach newcomer is the former Tiffany Hotel, now called simply **The Hotel,** at 801 Collins Ave. (☎ **305/531-5796**). The interior was designed by bad boy of fashion Todd Oldham, who created a sleek and funky look but kept many of the details of the original stunning 1939 hotel. Notice the terrazzo floors, porthole windows, and the exterior spire.

And it's not just the Beach that's growing. In Coconut Grove, the Ritz-Carlton is finishing up a 250-room luxury hotel due to open in late 1999. On Key Biscayne, Carnival Resorts & Casinos is planning a 250-room Grand Bay Resort for sometime in 2000. Also planned is the Miccosukee Indians' $45 million resort hotel adjacent to its 85,000-square-foot bingo and gaming complex, which is about 20 miles west of the city.

All this building means that there are more good choices than ever for travelers. Unfortunately, the popularity of this area has also made prices skyrocket. Don't despair—there are plenty of great options at bargain prices in and around the hot tourist areas. Always remember to ask about packages, since it's often possible to get a better deal than the "official" rates.

Many of the old hotels from the 1930s, 1940s, and 1950s (when most Miami resorts were constructed) have been totally overhauled, but others have survived with occasional coats of paint and new carpeting, which some owners like to call "renovation." When checking them out, be sure to ask about exactly what work has been done; especially on the ocean, sea air and years of tourist wear can result in musty, paint-peeled rooms. Also, be sure to find out if the hotel you're booking is undergoing reconstruction while you're there. There's nothing worse than the sounds of jackhammers over breakfast. I've omitted the more worn hotels and tried to list only those that have been fully upgraded recently. Exceptions are noted.

If you can't get a room after inquiring at the hotels listed in this guide (an extremely unlikely prospect), look along South Beach's Collins Avenue. There are dozens of hotels and motels on this strip—in all price categories—so there's bound to be a vacancy.

SEASONS & RATES   South Florida's tourist season is well defined, beginning in mid-November and lasting until Easter. Hotel prices escalate until about March, after which they begin to decline. During the off-season, hotel rates are typically 30% to 50% lower than their winter highs.

But timing isn't everything. In many cases, rates also depend on your hotel's proximity to the beach and how much ocean you can see from your window. Small motels a block or two from the water can be up to 40% cheaper than similar properties right on the sand. When a hotel is right on the beach, its oceanfront rooms are significantly more expensive than similar accommodations in the rear.

Most hotels allow one or two children to stay for free when they are accompanied by their parents. Most consider children to be those under the age of 16. Others cut it off at 11 or 9. Call to check on the specific policy of the accommodation you've chosen.

Rates below have been broken down into two broad categories: winter (generally, Thanksgiving through Easter) and off-season (about mid-May through August). The months in between, the shoulder season, should fall somewhere in between the highs and lows. Rates always go up on holidays. Remember too that state and city taxes can add as much as 12.5% to your bill in some parts of Miami. Some hotels, especially those in South Beach, also tack on additional service charges. And parking is pricey.

PRICE CATEGORIES   The hotels below are divided first by area, then by price, using the following guidelines: **very expensive,** over $250; **expensive,** over $180; **moderate,** $90 to $180; and **inexpensive,** below $90. Prices are based on published rates (or rack rates) for a standard double room during the high season. Check with the reservations agent since many rooms are also available above and below the category ranges listed. And always ask about packages, since it's often possible to get a better deal than these "official" rates.

LONG-TERM STAYS   If you plan to visit Miami for a month, a season, or more, think about renting a room in a long-term hotel or condominium apartment. Long-term accommodations exist in every price category, from budget to deluxe, and in general are extremely reasonable, especially during the off-season. Check with the reservation services below, or write a short note to the chamber of commerce in the area where you plan to stay. In addition, many local real estate agents also handle short-term rentals (meaning less than a year).

RESERVATION SERVICES   **Central Reservations** (☎ **800/950-0232** or 305/ 274-6832; www.reservation-services.com; e-mail: rooms@america.com) works with many of Miami's hotels and can often secure discounts of up to 40%. It also gives advice on specific locales, especially in Miami Beach and Downtown.

The **South Florida Hotel Network** (☎ **800/538-3616** or 305/538-3616) lists more than 300 hotels throughout the area, from Palm Beach to Miami and down to the Keys.

1 South Beach

Most of the art deco hotels on South Beach were built in the late 1930s, just after the Depression, in an area originally planned as an affordable destination for middle-class northeasterners. None of them were really luxurious—they just happened to be situated on one of the most beautiful strips of beach in the country. Large resorts like the Fontainebleau and Eden Roc were built later, about 20 blocks north of South Beach, to cater to celebrities and jet-setters. These were the spots where Sinatra and the rest of the Rat Pack hung out.

But after many years of transition, South Beach gained national recognition for its unique art deco architecture. The area is now South Florida's number-one tourist destination and home to many of the city's best restaurants and nightclubs.

The most expensive rooms are on Ocean Drive or Collins Avenue, just across the street from the beach. Thankfully, for at least most of South Beach, new buildings cannot be built directly on the sand and cannot exceed three stories. Remember that the art deco hotels are generally small and have tiny bathrooms and few services and facilities.

Unless I noted otherwise, most offer no-smoking rooms. Inquire before booking. One of the best chain hotel options is the **Howard Johnson Tudor Hotel** (☎ **800/446-4656** or 305/534-2934) at 1111 Collins Ave., 1 block from the beach but right in the happening South Beach nightlife area. Rates are moderate, starting at $115 a night in season. Some more reasonably priced options include the **Days Inn** (☎ **800/325-2525** or 305/538-6631) at 100 21st St. (off Collins Avenue), and the **Holiday Inn** (☎ **800/HOLIDAY** or 305/534-1511) at 2201 Collins Ave. They're right on the ocean at the north edge of the historic district, within walking distance of the nightlife scene. They both play up the tropical look and offer standard chain-hotel–style rooms for under $90, even in high season. The Holiday Inn has lushly landscaped grounds, hidden behind an Eckerd's drugstore, and lots of amenities, including a private beach, water-sports equipment rentals, and car-rental desk. The Days Inn is on a public beach and has a car rental deck, but no water-sports equipment.

VERY EXPENSIVE

✪ **Casa Grande Suite Hotel.** 834 Ocean Dr., South Beach, FL 33139. ☎ **800/OUTPOST** or 305/672-7003. Fax 305/673-3669. www.islandlife.com. 34 units. A/C MINIBAR TV TEL. Winter $275–$450 suite; $525 two-bedroom suite; $1,500 three-bedroom suite. Off-season $225–$300 double; $345 two-bedroom suite; $750 three-bedroom suite. Additional person $15 extra. AE, CB, DC, DISC, MC, V. Valet parking $14.

Europeans and vacationing celebs looking for privacy enjoy the casual elegance and thoughtful service of this hotel right on "Deco Drive." Here, you'll feel as though you're staying in a very stylish apartment, not in a cookie-cutter hotel room. Every room is outfitted in a slightly different style with fully equipped kitchenettes, beautifully tiled baths, reed rugs, mahogany beds, handmade batik prints, and antiques from all over the world, particularly Indonesia. There's no pool on the property, but considering that you can see the ocean, stock your own fridge, and veg out with a good stereo and VCR, this is one of the most desirable hotels on South Beach. Some rooms facing the ocean can be loud, especially on weekend nights.

Amenities: Room service, overnight dry cleaning and laundry, complimentary newspaper and evening turndown with chocolates, twice-daily maid service, express checkout, baby-sitting arrangements. VCRs and videos are available to rent. Full kitchens, CD/cassette stereo, conference rooms, car rental, activities desk, access to a nearby health club.

✪ **The Delano.** 1685 Collins Ave., South Beach, FL 33139. ☎ **800/555-5001** or 305/672-2000. Fax 305/532-0099. 209 units, 1 penthouse. A/C MINIBAR TV TEL. Winter $310–$415 double; $475 loft; $700 suite; $800 bungalow; $1,850 two-bedroom; $2,200

South Beach Accommodations

To Central Miami Beach

The Bass Museum of Art

Collins Park

Miami Beach Convention Center

Jackie Gleason Theater of Performing Arts

Lincoln Road Mall — Lincoln Rd.

Venetian Causeway

Belle Island

Biscayne Bay

Española Way

Miami Beach Post Office

Flamingo Park

Beach Patrol Station

Art Deco Welcome Center

Lummus Park

Atlantic Ocean

South Pointe Park

Government Cut

23rd St.
22nd St.
20th St.
19th St.
18th St.
17th St.
16th St.
15th St.
14th St.
13th St.
12th St.
11th St.
10th St.
9th St.
8th St.
7th St.
6th St.
5th St.
4th St.
3rd St.
2nd St.
1st St.
Commerce St.
Biscayne St.

Purdy Ave.
Bay Rd.
West Ave.
Alton Rd.
Lenox Ave.
Michigan Ave.
Meridian Ave.
Pennsylvania Ave.
Washington Ave.
Collins Ave.
James Ave.
Ocean Dr.
Dade Boulevard
Jefferson Ave.
Michigan Ave.
West Ave.

The Albion Hotel 6
The Avalon Hotel 20
Banana Bungalow 1
Brigham Gardens 5
Casa Grande Suite Hotel 19
Cavalier 11
Clay Hotel & Int'l Hostel 9
The Delano 5
Essex House 15
Fisher Island Club 21
The Governor Hotel 2
Hotel Astor 16
Hotel Continental Riande 3
Hotel Leon 18
The Kent 13
Loews Miami Beach Hotel 8
The Majestic Hotel 20
Marseilles Hotel 4
The Mermaid Guesthouse 17
The National Hotel 7
Park Washington Hotel 14
The Tides 12
Villa Paradiso 10

0   .125 Miles
0   .125 Kilometers

N

51

penthouse. Off-season $180–$265 double (weekend rates for double same as winter rates); all other room rates same as winter rates. Additional person $35 extra. AE, DC, DISC, MC, V. Valet parking $16.

When the Delano—pronounced like FDR's middle name—opened in 1995, it made the front page of nearly every architecture and style magazine in the country for its whimsical and elegant design. Look for a huge hedge with a simple blue arched door in its center, or look up for a rocketlike fin (an original 1947 detail) sprouting from the top of the all-white building. New York's Ian Shrager, of Studio 54 fame, brought in designer Philippe Starck, who went wild with the decor, including 40-foot sheer white curtains hanging outside, mirrors everywhere, white billowing curtains, Adirondack chairs, and fur-covered beds. The guest rooms are all white; a perfectly crisp green Granny Smith apple in each one is the only dose of color. It may sound antiseptic, but it actually comes across as sexy and sophisticated. The poolside cabanas are the most desirable rooms because of their huge size, but they can be noisy, since they're on an active poolside walkway.

Unfortunately, the model-gorgeous staff is often aloof or simply unavailable. But the location is ideal; it's just north of the Art Deco District strip of bars and restaurants, away from the noisy street traffic but close enough to walk to hopping Lincoln Road Mall. And of course, it's right on the ocean with plenty of in-house activity to keep you busy.

Dining/Diversions: An elegant bar attracts curious and beautiful people nightly. The Blue Door (owned in part by Madonna) is known as a place to be seen and for great cuisine, but the service is full of attitude. The thatched Beach Bar restaurant serves fantastic sandwiches and salads. New in 1999 is Blue Seas, an Asian seafood restaurant with communal seating offering, among other things, sushi, stone crabs, lobster, and caviar.

Amenities: Concierge, room service, same-day dry cleaning and laundry, newspaper delivery, evening turndown, in-room massage, executive business services, express checkout. VCRs, video rentals, children's movie theater and child activity programs, large outdoor pool, wide guarded beach, business center, conference rooms, rooftop solarium, extensive water-sports recreation, funky gift shop, 24-hour state-of-the-art David Barton gym with sauna. Aqua Spa is $10 for hotel guests; open for women 9am to 7pm, men 7:30 to 11pm, and closed Tuesday night. Offers facials and a plethora of massages and water treatments.

Fisher Island Club. One Fisher Island Dr., Fisher Island, FL 33190. ☎ **800/537-3708** or 305/535-6020. Fax 305/535-6003. www.fisherisland-florida.com. 60 units. A/C TV TEL. Winter $385–$625 double; $750–$1,350 suite or cottage. Off-season $330–$415 double; $525–$1,200 suite or cottage. Golf, tennis, and spa packages available seasonally. 20% gratuity added to all food and beverages. AE, DC, MC, V.

Voted one of the best places to stay in the world by *Condé Nast Traveler* in 1998, this exclusive island just off Miami Beach is the height of luxury. Luciano Pavarotti, Oprah Winfrey, and other celebrities keep condos here and many other celebs show up for R&R. To get there, visitors and residents take a private ferry, which shuttles guests to and from the mainland every 15 to 20 minutes. Attendants rinse each Mercedes and Rolls with fresh water as it glides off the docks. Don't worry if you are carless—on this exclusive island, golf carts get you anywhere you need to go.

As for location, you're only minutes from the airport, South Beach, Coral Gables, or The Grove (not counting ferry time). Still, considering the pampering you'll receive in this former Vanderbilt mansion turned resort extraordinaire, you probably won't want to leave the island. A world-class spa and club offer anything you could possibly imagine.

Dining/Diversions: The elegant Vanderbilt Club offers continental cuisine. The Beach Club and Golfer's Grill serve basic but expensive sandwiches and salads (try the club sandwich). An Italian Cafe prepares exceptional pastas and seafood. A dinner theater features live music.

Amenities: Concierge, room service (7am to 10pm), dry cleaning, laundry, national newspaper delivery, nightly turndown, twice-daily maid service, baby-sitting, secretarial service, valet parking, airport transportation, world-class spa, P. B. Dye Golf Course, 18 tennis courts, two deep-water marinas, boutiques, huge corporate board room, helipad, seaplane ramp, auto-ferry system, beach.

The National Hotel. 1677 Collins Ave., South Beach. ☎ **800/327-8370** or 305/532-2311. Fax 305/534-1426. www.nationalhotel.com. 154 units. A/C MINIBAR TV TEL. Winter $250–$320 double; $340–$385 double with a view and/or balcony; $580–$1,000 suite. Off-season from $240 double; $250–$320 double with a view and/or balcony; $420–$800 suite. AE, CB, DC, DISC, EURO, JCB, MC, V. Valet parking $16.

This elegant newcomer has joined the ranks of South Beach's particular brand of luxury resorts. Since there is so much to offer in the neighborhood, these "resorts" tend to offer limited on-site facilities and concentrate more on style and service. The National does a super job. With its towering ceilings, sultry furnishings, and massive gilded mirrors, the elegant 1940s lobby ought to be the backdrop for a gangster flick. At 11 stories, the main building stands taller than most of its neighbors and offers grand views of the beach and ocean below. Rooms in the garden wing are slightly larger and have balconies but all are comfortable and pretty spacious. The hotel is located a few doors down from the famed Delano, right on the ocean and just a few blocks from the best shopping and dining in town.

Dining/Diversions: The Oval Room is an elegant and formal dining room offering decent fare from an eclectic menu. Two outside dining spots overlook the pools and serve drinks, light meals, snacks, and sandwiches. There are three bars, including The Deco Lounge, which features a lively happy hour with live jazz in season.

Amenities: Concierge, room service (24 hours), dry-cleaning and laundry service, newspaper delivery, evening turndown, twice-daily maid service, baby-sitting, express checkout. Stereos and two TVs in suites, VCRs, video rental, two outdoor pools, large beach, small fitness room, small business center, water-sports concession (including scuba and sailing).

✪ The Tides. 1220 Ocean Dr., South Beach, FL 33139. ☎ **800/OUTPOST** or 305/604-5000. Fax 305/672-6288. www.islandlife.com. 45 units. A/C MINIBAR TV TEL. Winter $375–$450 suite; $1,000–$2,000 penthouse. Off-season $300–$375 suite; $800–$200 penthouse. Additional person $20 extra. Rates include continental breakfast. AE, CB, DC, JCB, MC, V. Valet parking $15.

Opened in late 1997 to rave reviews, this 12-story art deco masterpiece is one of the tallest buildings on the strip of Ocean Drive. It is the latest addition to the Island Outpost group, which includes the Cavalier, The Kent, Casa Grande (reviewed in this section), and others. Rooms are starkly white but luxurious. The welcoming staff and central location are its definite strong points. Also, all rooms are at least twice the size of a typical South Beach hotel room and have a view of the ocean. Although small, the freshwater pool on the rear mezzanine is a welcome plus for those who have had enough of the wild beach scene across the street.

Dining/Diversions: Twelve Twenty is the hotel's fine restaurant. It serves dinner nightly 6pm to midnight. The Terrace, a gorgeous outdoor cafe overlooking the ocean, does a fine job of breakfast and lunch. There's also a lobby lounge with live entertainment.

Amenities: Concierge, room service (24 hour), dry cleaning, laundry service, newspaper delivery, in-room massage, twice-daily maid service, baby-sitting, secretarial services, express check-out. Stereos with cassette and CD player and a selection of CDs in each room, VCRs, video rentals, heated outdoor pool, small health club and discount at large nearby health club, conference rooms.

EXPENSIVE

Albion Hotel. 1650 James Ave. (at Lincoln Rd.). ☎ **888/665-0008** or 305/913-1000. Fax 305/674-0507. www.rubellhotels.com. 100 units. A/C MINIBAR TV TEL. Winter $250–$325 double; $375–$700 suite. Off-season $150–$225 double; $299–$600 suite. AE, CB, DC, DISC, MC, V. Valet parking $17.

An architectural masterpiece originally designed in 1939 by internationally acclaimed architect Igor Polivitzky, this large streamline moderne building looks like a cruise ship with portholes, smokestack, and sleek curved lines. It was totally renovated in 1997, under the guidance of the hip New York family, the Rubells. Although you have to walk a few blocks to find beach access, you may not want to. A huge pool and artificial beach are original features at this unusual and recommendable resort. Rooms are furnished with wonderful modern furnishings custom-designed for the space. The hotel is popular with those in the music and modeling industry and often serves as the backdrop for parties and shoots.

The Rubell family owns a second hotel just around the corner, The Greenview, with rates about 40% lower. Rooms are just as comfortable but amenities are slightly more limited—you won't find a pool, restaurant, or bar, for example—but it's a great alternative if you want to save a little spending money for shopping on nearby Lincoln Road.

Dining/Diversions: An elegant Mexican restaurant and outdoor cafe, Mayya was in the works at press time. Drinks, salads, and sandwiches are available at the pool. The Fallabella bar attracts a good-looking crowd for occasional live music and happy hours.

Amenities: Concierge, room service, dry cleaning, evening turndown, in-room massage, newspaper delivery, twice-daily maid service, baby-sitting, executive business services, valet parking, airport limo service. VCRs available on request, large outdoor heated pool with adjacent artificial sand beach, work-out room, business services on request, small conference and production rooms, stereos with CD and cassette player (but no CDs), state-of-the-art phones with data port and voice mail.

✪ **Hotel Astor.** 956 Washington Ave., South Beach, FL 33139. ☎ **800/270-4981** or 305/531-8081. Fax 305/531-3193. www.hotelastor.com. 40 units. A/C MINIBAR TV TEL. Winter $145–$200 double; $275–$320 suite. Off-season $115–$190 double; $245–$290 suite. Astor suite $420–$600. Additional person $30 extra. AE, MC, V. Valet parking $14.

For the price (at least 30% less than the Delano), this is a great option for those who like intimate but terribly hip accommodations. A small but elegant and modern hotel, the Astor attracts many loyal return guests. Originally built in 1936, the renovation in 1995 greatly improved on the original design of this simple three-story gem. There is a small lap pool and a beautiful waterfall outside the sleek lobby bar area. All the details are pure luxury, like swivel stands for the large-screen TVs, Belgian linens and towels, and funky custom lighting with dimmer switches. The hotel staff is known for bending over backwards. This low-profile is definitely a place for those in the know. Unfortunately, the few moderately priced standard rooms are usually booked months in advance but the more pricey ones are well worth the expense.

Dining: Astor Place is one of Miami's best restaurants. The Florida-style menu is diverse and delicious (see listing under "South Beach" in chapter 6, "Dining"). Sunday brunch is one of the best in town.

Amenities: 24-hour concierge service, room service, dry cleaning, laundry, newspaper delivery, in-room massage, twice-daily maid service, baby-sitting, secretarial service, express checkout. VCRs available on request, video rental, outdoor pool with jet-streams, access to nearby health club, two phones in suites.

Loews Hotel. 1601 Collins Ave., South Beach, FL 33139. ☎ **800/23-LOEWS** or 305/604-1601. www.loewshotels.com. 800 units. A/C MINIBAR TV TEL. Winter from $309 double; from $600 suite; $2,500–$5,000 for the presidential suite. Off-season from $250 double. AE, DC, DISC, MC, V. Valet parking $19.

Just opened at press time, this 800-room hotel is the first new hotel to be built in South Beach for the past 30 years. It's also the largest, which is a good thing—the beach was sorely in need of a large hotel to accommodate business travelers who come to the nearby convention center. Accordingly, it features plenty of meeting rooms, ballrooms, a large health club, and seven restaurants and lounges. Like the Fontainebleau and Eden Roc 30 blocks north, the Loews is a full-service, beachfront resort. However, it has the advantage of being brand-new and situated right in the heart of the bustling Art Deco District.

Dining/Diversions: Six different restaurants and lounges offer American, Argentinean, and casual bar food. A sleek martini bar and coffee shop round out the offerings making it possible to spend your entire time in this impressive new resort.

Amenities: 24-hour concierge service, room service, dry cleaning, laundry, newspaper delivery, in-room massage, twice-daily maid service, baby-sitting, secretarial service, express checkout. VCRs available on request, video rental, outdoor pool with jet-streams, access to nearby health club, two phones in each room.

MODERATE

Avalon Majestic Hotel. 700 Ocean Dr. (at 7th St.), South Beach, FL 33139. ☎ **800/933-3306** or 305/538-0133. Fax 305/534-0258. www.southbeachhotels.com. 103 units. A/C TV TEL. Winter $120–$210 double. Off-season $65–$175 double. Rates include continental breakfast. 10% discount for stays of 7 days or more. AE, CB, DC, DISC, MC, V. Valet parking $14.

This striking hotel offers classic art deco digs right on the beach at even more attractive prices. The simple rooms, decorated in traditional 1930s style, are nothing fancy but are comfortable if a bit on the small side. The modest lobby holds a casual restaurant, best for lunch either inside or on the breezy outdoor patio.

Room service, free coffee, refreshments, and breakfast are also available. If the Avalon is full, don't hesitate to accept a room in its companion property, the South Seas on 17th and Collins.

Cavalier. 1320 Ocean Dr., South Beach, FL 33139. ☎ **800/OUTPOST** or 305/604-5000. Fax 305/531-5543. E-mail: questions@islandoutpost.com. 45 units. A/C MINIBAR TV TEL. Winter $125–$195 double; $275–$350 suite. Off-season $95–$155 double; $230–$250 suite. Additional person $15 extra. AE, DC, DISC, MC, V. Valet parking $14; self-parking $6.

The Cavalier, a hip, well-priced hotel, is kept in shape by yearly refurbishments. You can't beat its oceanfront location, adjacent to shops and restaurants. Palm trees brush the ceilings of the modest lobby, where young trendy guests make their way to their rooms. Funky prints cover the walls, which are the colors of a tequila sunrise. A young, competent staff waits on guests and offers lots of good advice about local clubs, restaurants, and shopping. Rooms come equipped with CD players and discs. You can also use a VCR and rent videos. Despite the Ocean Drive location, most rooms are relatively quiet.

Essex House. 1001 Collins Ave., South Beach, FL 33139. ☎ **800/55-ESSEX** or 305/ 534-2700. Fax 305/532-3827. www.travelbase.com/destinations. 58 units. A/C TV TEL. Winter $150–$350 double. Off-season $109–295 double. Rates include deluxe continental breakfast. Minimum stay 2 nights on weekends in season, 3 nights on holidays. AE, DC, DISC, MC, V. Valet parking $14. Nearby parking available for $4 weekdays, $6 weekends and holidays.

This art deco landmark, just a block from the ocean, is one of South Beach's architectural gems, especially since the $3 million renovation completed in 1998. The pretty Essex House is a textbook example of streamline moderne style, complete with large porthole windows, original etched glasswork, ziggurat arches, and detailed crown moldings. The solid-oak bedroom furnishings are also original and, like many other details in this special hotel, were carefully restored. Suites feature minibars, coffeemakers, and VCRs. Ask for a room with a refrigerator, since more than a dozen standard rooms do have them. The Essex also features 24-hour reception, a baby grand, self-playing piano in the lobby/lounge, and a state-of-the-art security system. This hotel is spic-and-span, almost too much like a chain, but the staff is extremely pleasant and helpful.

A very small pool is just one of the many new additions here.

The Governor Hotel. 435 21st St., Miami Beach, FL 33139. ☎ **800/542-0444** or 305/532-2100. Fax 305/532-9139. 125 units. A/C TV TEL. Winter $89–$125 double. Off-season $69–$89 double. AE, DC, DISC, MC, V. Free parking.

This reasonably priced South Beach hotel frequented by conventioneers is nothing special, but the rooms are decent and the rates are pretty cheap. However, as an example of art deco architecture, this hotel is one of the most stylish in the area. It has streamlined details, from the checkerboard floor tiles to the steel marquee and looming flagstaffs, but don't expect too much inside. A recent revamping improved the slightly tacky decor and introduced some better staff. Though you can walk, you may want to drive to the beach since it's a few long blocks through a not-so-scenic neighborhood of hotels, many of which are under construction. The Governor has a medium-size pool and a small cafe and bar.

Hotel Continental Riande. 1825 Collins Ave., South Beach, FL 33139. ☎ **800/RIANDE-1** or 305/531-3503. Fax 305/531-2803. E-mail: riande@iconnect.net. 251 units. A/C MINIBAR TV TEL. Winter $150–$280 double. Off-season $135–$260 double. Additional person $10 extra. Frommer's readers get a 20% discount. AE, DC, DISC, MC, V. Valet parking $8.

The Riande is just the ticket if you want value and convenience right on South Beach. Catering to a largely Latin and European clientele, this hotel overlooking the ocean has become quite well known. It's just 2 blocks from The Delano and the best of South Beach. The rooms and lobby areas are clean and well maintained, but not too fussy. A large outdoor pool and sundeck are just out back. There's also a restaurant/coffee shop with both buffet and menu service. Room service is available daily for breakfast and dinner.

✪ **Hotel Leon.** 841 Collins Ave., South Beach, FL 33139. ☎ **305/673-3767**. Fax 305/ 673-5866. www.hotelleon.com. 18 units. A/C TV TEL. Winter $125 double; $165–$215 suite; $375 penthouse. Off-season $100 double; $135–$185 suite; $315 penthouse. Additional person $10 extra. AE, DC, MC, V. Valet parking $14.

A true value, this stylish sliver of a property has won the loyalty of fashion industrialists and romantics alike. The very central location, 1 block from the sea and in the heart of shopping and dining, means a car isn't necessary. The spacious well-renovated rooms are sparkling clean and warmly appointed. Gleaming wood floors and simple pale furnishings are appreciated in a neighborhood where many others overdo the art deco motif. Each room has two phones, sunken oval tubs, robes, CD players, and CDs. Unfortunately, there's no pool or sundeck but the beach is only a 2-minute walk. A meeting room and business center make it a fine choice for business trips. In the standard rooms, there are no minibars or fridges, but you can order room service. In the morning, enjoy a moderately priced breakfast ($8.50) of croissants, fresh rolls, ham, cheese, and eggs cooked to order. The owners, a young German couple, have made a commitment to providing excellent service with a distinctly personal touch, and they have succeeded.

The Kent. 1131 Collins Ave., South Beach, FL 33139. ☎ **800/OUTPOST** or 305/604-5000. Fax 305/531-0720. www.islandlife.com. 54 units. A/C MINIBAR TV TEL. Winter $125–$195 double; $275 suite. Off-season $95–$155 double; $230 suite. Additional person $15 extra. AE, DC, DISC, MC, V. Valet parking $14; self-parking $6.

This is an excellent value right in South Beach's active center. Even if the other Island Outpost hotels are full, you're likely to find a spot here. The prices are the same as the group's beachside hotels, the Cavalier and the Leslie, but the rooms tend to be less noisy. The staff includes an eager-to-please group of Caribbeans, and the clientele comes largely from the fashion industry. Frequent shoots are coordinated in the lobby and conference room, where full office services are available. Thanks to a vacant lot in the backyard (for now), some rooms in the rear offer nice views of the ocean. The decor is modest but tasteful. CD players are standard, as are bright and whimsical furnishings. VCRs and video rentals are available. There's no pool or sundeck, but you're only 1 block from the beach.

Marseilles Hotel. 1741 Collins Ave., South Beach, Fl 33139. ☎ **800/327-4739** or 305/538-5711. Fax 305/673-1006. www.marseilleshotel.com. 116 units. A/C TV TEL. Winter $115–$135 double; $180 suite. Off-season $79–$99 double; $145 suite. Frommer's readers get 10% discount. AE, DC, DISC, MC, V. Self-parking $9.

With these low promotional rates, the Marseilles is one of the very best deals in this supertrendy area. It's a full-service, inexpensive, classic art deco hotel, located right on the beach and near the best of everything. The staff is pleasant, the restaurant and bar very recommendable, and the decor is thoroughly tasteful. Still, a little worn around the edges, the property seems to improve a little bit each year. Owners Lloyd and Clara Mandell make a point of being around to see that everything runs smoothly. You may meet them in the lobby where free refreshments are usually served.

  With only about 100 rooms, the Marseilles is more intimate than the larger and similarly priced Riande, a few doors away. The suites (three of which have Jacuzzis at no extra charge) are an exceptionally good deal if you want to spend a lot of time in your room. You'll find a telescope for spying on scantily clad sunbathers below. Otherwise, standard rooms are on the small side but clean and comfortable. All have small refrigerators and bottled water upon check-in. The bar and restaurant are popular with budget-seeking locals. When the Marseilles is full, the staff may suggest putting you at the nearby Dorchester. It's cheaper and decent but not nearly as recommendable.

✪ **The Mermaid Guesthouse.** 909 Collins Ave., Miami Beach, FL 33140. ☎ **305/538-5324.** 8 units. A/C TEL. Winter $105–$125 double; $275 terraced suite. Off-season $75–$95 double; $175 suite. Additional person $10 extra. Discounts available for longer stays. AE, MC, V.

There's something magical about this little hideaway tucked behind tropical gardens in the very heart of South Beach. You won't find the amenities of the larger hotels here, but the charm and hospitality at this one-story guest house keeps people coming back. Plus, it's smack in the middle of the hottest part of South Beach and less than 2 blocks from the ocean.

In 1996 the new owners, Ana and Gonzalo Torres, did a thorough clean-up, adding new brightly colored fretwork around the doors and windows and installing phones in each room. Also, the wood floors have been stripped or covered in straw matting, one of the many Caribbean touches that make this place so cheery. There are no TVs, so guests tend to congregate in the lush garden in the evenings. The owners sometimes host free impromptu dinners for their guests and friends. Ask if they've scheduled any live Latin music during your stay; you won't want to miss it.

INEXPENSIVE

Banana Bungalow. 2360 Collins Ave., Miami Beach, FL 33139. ☎ **800/7-HOSTEL** or 305/538-1951. Fax 305/531-3217. www.bananabungalow.com. 90 units. A/C TV TEL. Winter $13–$16 per person in shared units; $60–$70 single; $70–$80 double. Off-season $12–$14 per person in shared units; $40–$50 single; $50–$60 double. MC, V. Free parking.

This youth hostel-like hotel is a welcome addition to the South Beach budget scene. Across the street is a popular beach; the best shops, clubs, and restaurants are only 6 or 7 blocks away. A redone 1950s two-story newcomer surrounds a pool and deck complete with shuffleboard, a small alfresco cafe serving cheap meals, and a tiki bar where young European travelers hang out.

The best rooms face a narrow canal where motorboats and kayaks are available for a small charge. In general, rooms are clean and well kept, despite a few rusty faucets and chipped Formica furnishings. Guests in shared rooms need to bring their own towels. This is one of the only hotels in this price range with a private pool. Guests can also take advantage of free coffee and refreshments each morning, a communal kitchen, access to a nearby health club, a coin laundry, free movies, sightseeing tours, discounts at local clubs, and a great community spirit.

✪ **Brigham Gardens.** 1411 Collins Ave., South Beach, FL 33139. ☎ **305/531-1331.** Fax 305/538-9898. www.brighamgardens-mbch.com. 19 units. A/C TV TEL. Winter $85–$130 double. Off-season $60–$110 double. Additional person $5 extra. 10% discount on stays of 7 days or longer. Pets stay for $6 a night. AE, MC, V.

There's no pool or other niceties, but you'll find this funky place a homey and affordable oasis in the midst of high prices and commercialization. Also, the location is prime. Because most rooms have full kitchens, you'll find many people staying for longer than a weekend. You may, too. All rooms have microwaves and coffee makers, at least. You can barbecue in the garden.

When you enter the tropically landscaped garden, you'll hear macaws and parrots chirping and see cats and lizards running through the bougainvillea. The tiny but lush grounds are framed by quaint Mediterranean buildings—they're pleasant, although in need of some sprucing up. This happy spot is run by a mother and daughter who go out of their way to see that guests and their pets are well cared for. A warning: Like most other small properties on South Beach, parking can be a pain though there is a city lot 1 block south.

Clay Hotel & International Hostel. 1438 Washington Ave. (at Española Way), South Beach, FL 33139. ☎ **305/534-2988.** Fax 305/673-0346. www.clayhotel.com. 350 beds in singles, doubles, and dorm rms. $40–$50 single; $45–65 double; $14–$16 dorm beds. Sheets $2 extra. During the off-season, pay for 6 nights in advance and get 7th night free. JCB, MC, V.

A member of the International Youth Hostel Federation (IYHF), the Clay occupies a beautiful 1920s-style Spanish Mediterranean building at the corner of historic

Española Way. Like other IYHF members, this hostel is open to all ages and is a great place to meet people. The usual smattering of Australians, Europeans, and other budget travelers makes it Miami's best clearinghouse of "insider" travel information. Even if you don't stay here, you might want to check out the ride board or mingle with fellow travelers over a beer at the sidewalk cafe.

Although a thorough renovation in 1996 made this hostel an incredible value and a step above any others in town, don't expect nightly turndown service or chocolates. You will find a self-serve Laundromat, occasional movie nights, and a tour desk with car rental available. Reservations are essential for private rooms year-round and recommended in season. In summer, be sure to ask for a room with air-conditioning. Don't bother with a car in this congested area.

Park Washington Hotel. 1020 Washington Ave., South Beach, FL 33139. ☎ **305/532-1930.** Fax 305/672-6706. www.parkwashingtonresort.com. 36 units. A/C TV TEL. Winter $99 double; $129 suite. Off-season $79 double; $99 suite. Rates include self-serve coffee and Danish. Additional person $20 extra. AE, MC, V.

The Park Washington is a large, refurbished hotel just 2 blocks from the ocean that offers some of the best values in South Beach—good rooms at incredible prices. Designed in the 1930s by Henry Hohauser, one of the beach's most prolific architects, the Park Washington reopened in 1989. Most of the rooms have original furnishings and well-kept interiors, and some have kitchenettes. Guests also enjoy a decent-sized outdoor heated pool with a sundeck, bikes for rent, and access to a nearby health club.

The same owners run the adjacent Taft House and Kenmore hotels. All three attract a large gay clientele, and all offer privacy, lush landscaping, a great pool and sundeck, consistent quality, and a value-oriented philosophy. You can't park on the premises, but there's a public garage at 7th Street, less than 3 blocks away.

Villa Paradiso. 1415 Collins Ave., Miami Beach, FL 33139. ☎ **305/532-0616.** Fax 305/673-5874. www.sobe.com/villaparadiso. 17 units. A/C TV TEL. Winter $100–$145 apt. Off-season $69–$105 apt. Weekly rates are 10% less. Additional person $5–$10 extra. AE, DC, MC, V.

This guest house, like Brigham Gardens, is more like a cozy apartment house than a hotel. There's no elegant lobby or restaurant, but the amicable hosts, Lisa and Pascal Nicolle, are happy to give you a room key and advice on what to do. The apartments are simple, but perfect for the beach, since you'll be spending most of your time outside anyway. Plus, the spacious apartments are quiet considering their location, a few blocks from Lincoln Road and all of South Beach's best clubs. Most have full kitchens or at least a fridge, and Murphy beds or foldout couches for extra friends. Bathrooms have recently been renovated with marble tile. There are also laundry facilities on the premises and free local phone service. Parking is available at a nearby city lot for about $12 a day.

2 Miami Beach: Surfside, Bal Harbour & Sunny Isles

The area just north of South Beach encompasses Surfside, Bal Harbour, and Sunny Isles. Unrestricted by zoning codes throughout the 1950s, 1960s, and especially the 1970s, area developers went nuts, building ever-bigger and more brazen structures, especially north of 41st Street, which is now known as "Condo Canyon." Consequently, there's now a glut of medium-quality condos, with a few scattered holdouts of older hotels and motels casting shadows over the beach by afternoon.

Miami Beach, as described here, runs from 24th Street to 192nd Street, a long strip that varies slightly from end to end. Staying in the southern section, from 24th to 42nd streets, can be a good deal—it's still close to the South Beach scene but the rates are more affordable. Bal Harbour and Bay Harbor are at the center of Miami Beach and retain their exclusivity and character. The neighborhoods north and south of here, like Surfside and Sunny Isles, have nice beaches and some shops, but are a little worn around the edges.

Just north of South Beach is the **Days Inn** (☎ **800/325-2525** or 305/673-1513) at 42nd Street and Collins Avenue. It's very well kept and right on the ocean. Rates in season start at about $99. The **Howard Johnson** (☎ **800/446-4656** or 305/532-4411) at 4000 Alton Rd., just off the Julia Tuttle Causeway (I-95), is a generic eight-story building on a strip of land near a busy road, but it's convenient to the beach, by car or bike. Rooms, renovated in 1995, are clean and spacious, and some have pretty views of the city and the intracoastal waterway. Winter rates start at $100.

VERY EXPENSIVE

✪ **Alexander All-Suite Luxury Hotel.** 5225 Collins Ave., Miami Beach, FL 33140. ☎ **800/327-6121** or 305/865-6500. Fax 305/341-6553. www.alexanderhotel.com. 150 units. A/C TEL. Winter $325 one-bedroom suite; $470 two-bedroom suite. Off-season $250 one-bedroom suite; $370 two-bedroom suite. Additional person $35 extra. Packages available. AE, CB, DC, DISC, MC, V. Valet parking $16.

This stunning hotel is a great luxury option and just a few miles to happening South Beach or ritzy Bal Harbour. It's expensive, but worth it for the service and attention. The Alexander features spacious one- and two-bedroom miniapartments. Each contains a living room, a fully equipped kitchen, two bathrooms, and a balcony. The rooms are elegant without being pretentious and have every convenience you could want, including hair dryers, coffeemakers, VCRs upon request, and cable TVs. The hotel itself is well decorated, with sculptures, paintings, antiques, and tapestries, most of which were garnered from the Cornelius Vanderbilt mansion. The two oceanfront pools are surrounded by lush vegetation; one of these "lagoons" is fed by a cascading waterfall.

Dining/Diversions: A pricey steak house was opened here in 1998 by former Dolphins football coach, Don Shula. A more casual garden restaurant, a piano lounge, and a pool bar are also available.

Amenities: Concierge, room service (24 hours), dry cleaning and laundry service, newspaper delivery, evening turndown on request, in-room massage on request, twice-daily maid service, secretarial services, express checkout. Two large outdoor pools, beach, small fitness center, four Jacuzzis, sauna, business center and conference rooms, car rental through concierge, sundeck, water-sports equipment, beauty salon.

✪ **Eden Roc Resort and Spa.** 4525 Collins Ave., Miami Beach, FL 33140. ☎ **800/327-8337** or 305/531-0000. Fax 305/674-5568. www.edenrocresort.com. 350 units. A/C MINIBAR TV TEL. Winter $280–$350 double; $820–$1,700 suite. Off-season $185–$275 double; $620–$1,500 suite. Additional person $15 extra. Packages available. AE, CB, DC, DISC, MC, V. Valet parking $20–$25.

Just next door to the mammoth Fontainebleau, this flamboyant and large hotel, opened in 1956, seems almost intimate by comparison. The accommodations here are a bit gaudy, but this is Miami Beach, after all. The amenities by far make up for the ostentation. The huge, modern spa has excellent facilities and exercise classes, including yoga. The popular pool deck overlooking the ocean is a great place to spend the afternoon.

Miami Beach Accommodations

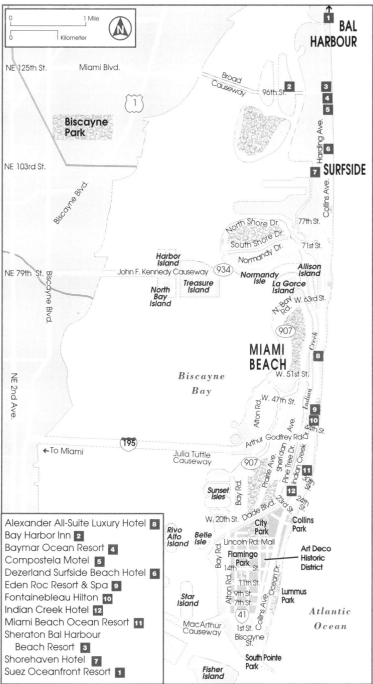

Alexander All-Suite Luxury Hotel **8**
Bay Harbor Inn **2**
Baymar Ocean Resort **4**
Compostela Motel **5**
Dezerland Surfside Beach Hotel **6**
Eden Roc Resort & Spa **9**
Fontainebleau Hilton **10**
Indian Creek Hotel **12**
Miami Beach Ocean Resort **11**
Sheraton Bal Harbour
    Beach Resort **3**
Shorehaven Hotel **7**
Suez Oceanfront Resort **1**

The big, open, and airy lobby is often full of name-tagged conventioneers. The rooms, uniformly outfitted with purple and aquatic-colored interiors and retouched 1930s furnishings, are unusually spacious. Because of the hotel's size, you should be able to negotiate a good rate unless there's a big event going on.

Dining/Diversions: The main restaurant serves northern Italian cuisine. From Jimmy Johnson's, the poolside sports bar, patrons can watch swimmers through an underwater "porthole" window. A lobby lounge and bar has occasional jazz.

Amenities: Concierge, room service, dry cleaning and laundry, newspaper delivery, in-room massage, nightly turndown, baby-sitting, secretarial services, express checkout, valet parking. Kitchenettes in suites and penthouses, VCRs for rent, two outdoor pools, beach, full-service spa and health club with sauna, business center and conference rooms, car-rental desk, sundeck, squash, racquetball and basketball courts as well as a rock-climbing arena, water-sports equipment, tour desk, beauty salon, sundries shop.

Fontainebleau Hilton. 4441 Collins Ave., Miami Beach, FL 33140. ☎ **800/HILTONS** or 305/538-2000. Fax 305/674-4607. www.fontainebleau.hilton.com. 1,206 units. A/C TV TEL. Winter $280–$360 double; $550–$850 suite. Off-season $205–$310 double; $475–$675 suite. Additional person $30 extra. Packages available. AE, CB, DC, DISC, MC, V. Overnight valet parking $13.

The most famous hotel on the Beach, the Fontainebleau (pronounced "fountain-blue") has built its reputation on garishness and excess. Its sheer size, with its full complement of restaurants, stores, and recreational facilities, plus more than 1,100 employees, makes it a perfect place for conventioneers. Unfortunately, the same recommendation cannot be extended to individual travelers. It's easy to get lost here, both physically and personally. The lobby is terminally crowded, the staff is overworked, and lines are always long. Renovations to the rooms in 1995 and 1996 did manage to freshen up the decor with new furnishings and pastel accents.

Still, this is the one and only Fontainebleau, in many ways the quintessential Miami hotel. If you don't stay here, see it as a tourist attraction; you really shouldn't miss the incredible lagoon-style pool and waterfall and the opulent lobby. Designed by famed architect Morris Lapidus, who is overseeing an expansion, this grand monolith has symbolized Miami decadence. Since its opening in 1954, the hotel has hosted presidents, pageants, and movie productions—including the James Bond thriller *Goldfinger.* This is where all the greats including Sinatra and his buddies performed in their prime.

Dining/Diversions: The Steak House serves dinner until 11pm. A continental restaurant offers a huge Sunday buffet brunch. There are five other cafes and coffee shops (including two by the pool), as well as a number of cocktail lounges, such as the Poodle Lounge, which offers live entertainment and dancing nightly. Another lounge features a Las Vegas–style floor show with dozens of performers and two orchestras.

Amenities: Concierge, room service, dry cleaning and laundry, newspaper delivery, nightly turndown on request, in-room massage, baby-sitting, secretarial services, valet parking. VCRs, two large outdoor pools, beach, large state-of-the-art health club, three whirlpool baths, sauna, game rooms, special year-round activities for children and adults, elaborate business center, conference rooms, car-rental and tour desks, sundeck, seven lighted tennis courts, water-sports equipment rental, beauty salon, boutique, large shopping arcade.

✪ **Sheraton Bal Harbour Beach Resort.** 9701 Collins Ave., Bal Harbour, FL 33154. ☎ **800/999-9898** or 305/865-7511. Fax 305/864-2601. 642 units. A/C MINIBAR TV TEL. Winter $349–$489 double; $650–$1,500 suite or villa year-round. Off-season $249–$439 double. Additional person $25 extra. Weekend and other packages and senior discounts available. Lowest rates reflect bookings made at least 14 days in advance for rooms without ocean views. AE, CB, DC, DISC, JCB, MC, V. Valet parking $12.

This hotel has the best location in Bal Harbour, on the ocean and just across from the swanky Bal Harbour Shops. Bill and Hillary Clinton have stayed here, and Bill even jogged along the beach with local fitness enthusiasts. It's one of the nicest Sheratons I've seen, with a glass-enclosed two-story atrium lobby and large, well-decorated rooms that include convenient extras like coffeemakers and hair dryers. A spectacular staircase wraps itself around a cascading fountain full of wished-on pennies. One side of the hotel caters to corporations and comes complete with ballrooms and meeting facilities, but the main sections are relatively uncongested and removed from the convention crowd.

Dining/Diversions: Guests have their choice of four restaurants and lounges. An Argentinean steak house serves good, heavy meals with live Latin music nightly. The other less formal spots serve Mediterranean-influenced beach food, pizzas, and gourmet coffees. A lounge serves good tropical drinks.

Amenities: Concierge, room service (24 hours), laundry and dry cleaning, valet, newspaper delivery, nightly turndown, in-room massage, twice-daily maid service on request, baby-sitting, secretarial services, express checkout, valet parking. VCRs in some rooms, a full complement of aquatic playthings for rent on the beach (including sailboats and jet-skis), outdoor heated pool, sundeck, large state-of-the-art fitness center and spa (with aerobics, Jacuzzi, sauna, and sundeck), two outdoor tennis courts, jogging track, games room, children's programs, large business center, conference rooms, tour desk, gift shop and shopping arcade, nearby golf course.

EXPENSIVE

Miami Beach Ocean Resort. 3025 Collins Ave., Miami Beach, FL 33140. ☎ **800/550-0505** or 305/534-0505. Fax 305/534-0515. www.mbo.com. 243 units. A/C TV TEL. Winter $170–$210, one to four people; $240–$650 suite. Off-season $150–$180, one to four people; $220–$550 suite. AE, DC, MC, V. Valet parking $6.

Popular with tour groups and Europeans, this oceanfront resort is a great choice for those who want a quiet place on the ocean in close proximity to South Beach and the mainland. It's priced like many other chains on the oceanfront, but it's got more character. The vast lobby is done up in Mexican tile, wood fretwork, and attractive furnishings. Rooms are basic but very tastefully decorated with wicker and rattan furnishings and new carpeting. Rooms also include coffeemakers and hair dryers. A huge outdoor area is landscaped with palms and hibiscus and has a large heated pool as its centerpiece. It faces a popular boardwalk for runners and strollers as well as a large beach where water-sports equipment is available.

Dining/Diversions: The recommendable restaurant serves a breakfast and dinner buffet of simple but good Caribbean and international cuisine to many who choose the meal programs. A la carte offerings and lunch are also available. A patio garden offers cake and coffee, a pool bar serves snacks and drinks, and a colorful indoor/outdoor lounge features cocktails and live music most nights.

Amenities: Concierge, room service, valet parking, laundry and dry-cleaning services, baby-sitting. Outdoor heated pool, beach, sundeck, bicycle rental, game room, self-service Laundromat, currency exchange, tour desk, conference rooms, car-rental desk, beauty salon, boutique.

MODERATE TO EXPENSIVE

✪ **Bay Harbor Inn.** 9660 E. Bay Harbor Dr., Bay Harbor Island, FL 33154. ☎ **305/868-4141.** Fax 305/867-9094. www. bayharborinn.com. 45 units. A/C MINIBAR TV TEL.

Winter $139–$229 double; $159–$279 suite. Off-season $80–$149 double; $95–$179 suite. Additional person $25 extra. Rates include continental breakfast. AE, MC, V. Free parking.

Under the management of Johnson & Wales University, this thoroughly renovated inn is just moments from the beach, fine restaurants, and Bal Harbour Shops, Miami's ritziest shopping mall (see chapter 9, "Shopping"). The inn comes in two parts. The more modern section sits squarely on a little river and overlooks a heated outdoor pool and a boat named Celeste where guests eat a complimentary breakfast buffet. On the other side of the street, "townside" is the cozier, antique-filled portion, where glass-covered bookshelves hold good beach reading. The rooms have a hodgepodge of wood furnishings (mostly Victorian replicas). Suites boast an extra half bathroom. You can at times smell the aroma of cooking from the restaurant below, but you might find that this only adds to the charm of this homey inn.

Adjacent to the hotel is The Palm, a clubby steak-and-lobster house. Students from Johnson & Wales culinary institute run a superb restaurant, The Island Cafe, and bar across the street.

Baymar Ocean Resort. 9401 Collins Ave., Miami Beach, FL 33154. ☎ **800/8-BAYMAR** or 305/866-5446. Fax 305/866-8053. www.baymar.com. 96 units. A/C TV TEL. Winter $115–$125 double; $125–$135 efficiency; $150–$235 suite. Off-season $85–$95 double; $95–$105 efficiency; $125–$185 suite. Additional person $10 extra. AE, DISC, MC, V. Parking $5.

Depending on what you're looking for, this hotel could be one of the beach's best buys. It's just south of Bal Harbour, right on the ocean, with a low-key beach that attracts few other tourists. It offers all the modern conveniences, including some kitchenettes and large closets. You won't flip over the decor, but it's pleasant enough and all brand-new. A recent renovation has done wonders. The location is close enough to walk to tennis courts, some shopping and dining and just a few minutes drive to the larger attractions. It may not be worth it to pay more for the oceanfront rooms since they tend to be smaller than the others. Rooms overlooking the large pool and sundeck area can get loud on busy days. The first-floor ocean-view rooms have a nice shared balcony space. This hotel is popular with budget travelers and conservative religious groups.

A small restaurant serving basic American fare and a tiki bar are popular with guests.

Dezerland Surfside Beach Hotel. 8701 Collins Ave., Miami Beach, FL 33154. ☎ **800/ 331-9346** in the U.S., 800/331-9347 in Canada, or 305/865-6661. Fax 305/866-2630. www. travelbase.com/destinations. 227 units. A/C TV TEL. Winter $90–$135 double. Off-season $78–$125 double. Additional person $10 extra. Special packages and group rates available. AE, CB, DC, DISC, MC, V. Free parking.

Designed by car enthusiast Michael Dezer, the Dezerland is a one-of-a-kind—part hotel and part 1950s automobile wonderland. Visitors, many of them German tourists, are welcomed by a 1959 Cadillac stationed by the front door, one of a dozen mint-condition classics around the grounds and lobby. Though not pristine, this beachfront hotel is clean and pleasant. Constant renovations improve it every year. Some rooms contain fully equipped kitchenettes. Look for the mosaic of a pink Cadillac at the bottom of its surfside pool.

Other amenities include a Jacuzzi, adjacent tennis courts and jogging track, Windsurfer and jet-ski rental, game room, laundry, car-rental and tour services desk, and an antique shop featuring 1950s memorabilia. There's also a restaurant and a lobby lounge with all-you-can-eat buffets and nightly entertainment.

Indian Creek Hotel. 2727 Indian Creek Dr. (1 block west of Collins Ave.), Miami Beach, FL 33140. ☎ **800/491-2772** or 305/531-2727. Fax 305/531-5651. www.indiancreekhotelmb.

com. 61 units. A/C TV TEL. Winter from $130–$160 double; from $220 suite. Off-season $90 double; $150 suite. Additional person $10 extra. Group packages available. Summer specials. 18% gratuity added to room service. AE, CB, DC, DISC, JCB, MC, V. Limited parking available on street.

Although there isn't much in the way of views or amenities, this small hotel just north of South Beach is pleasant and not too far from the action. Every detail of the 1936 building has been meticulously restored, from one of the beach's first operating elevators to the period steamer trunk in the lobby. The modest rooms are outfitted in art deco furnishings, with pretty tropical prints and all the modern amenities. They are used to hosting production crews and therefore provide things like data ports and voicemail in all rooms. Just one short block from a good stretch of sand, the hotel is also within walking distance to shops and inexpensive restaurants. A landscaped pool area is a great place to lounge in the sun. There's a small fitness center and conference facilities. A tiny restaurant serves continental breakfast and dinner.

INEXPENSIVE

Compostela Motel. 9040 Collins Ave., Miami Beach, FL 33154. ☎ **305/861-3083.** Fax 305/861-2996. 20 units. A/C TV TEL. Winter from $75 suite; from $65 one-bedroom apt.; $55 efficiency. Off-season from $65 suite; $55 one-bedroom apt.; $45 efficiency. Additional person $10 extra. AE, MC, V. Free parking.

At this hotel, you get a lot of space and a great location for a low price. The owners of the Compostela have recently renovated their three buildings, all within walking distance of the exclusive Bal Harbour Shops, the beaches, and many good shopping and dining areas. Although the buildings were full of run-down efficiencies for many years, the new interiors are really quite nice. All are carpeted and most have full kitchenettes. You'll find no fancy lobby, no doorman to greet you as you enter, and no amenities to speak of save an outdoor pool and laundry facilities. But you're across the street from a great beach, the area is safe, and the staff is courteous, though at some hours only Spanish speakers are available.

Shorehaven Hotel. 8505 Harding Ave. (1 block west of Collins Ave.), Miami Beach, Fl 33141. ☎ **888/775-0346** or 305/867-1906. Fax 305/867-1716. info@shorehaven.com. 15 units. A/C TV TEL. Winter $89–$129 one to three people. Off-season $69–$79 one to three people. AE, DISC, MC, V. Additional person $10 extra. Free street parking.

Located in up-and-coming North Beach, this funky one-story motel was thoroughly made over in late 1998 with style and charm by Sabrina and Scott Barnett. She is a former model who has graced the pages of major magazines, and he is a developer. The large rooms, outfitted in bright tropical prints, offer full kitchens and spacious bathrooms. Each has its own theme, like the Lemon Twist room, which has huge murals of bright yellow lemons on the walls and wood floors painted a glossy royal blue. Other rooms have romantic canopies of mosquito netting or other creative touches. All offer a real bargain just 1 block to the beach and less than a 10-minute drive to the hip and much pricier South Beach.

Suez Oceanfront Resort. 18215 Collins Ave., Sunny Isles Beach, FL 33160. ☎ **800/ 327-5278** or 305/932-0661. Fax 305/937-0058. www.suezresort.com. 200 units. A/C TV TEL. Winter $85–$99 double; $101–$118 suite. Off-season $65–$98 double; $83–$100 suite. Kitchenettes $10–$15 extra. AE, DC, MC, V. Free parking.

Guarded by an undersize replica of Egypt's famed Sphinx, the campy Suez offers newly renovated rooms on the beach, where most of the other old hotels have turned condo. Its Sunny Isles location is actually closer to Hallandale in Broward County than to South Beach but the area has got plenty to offer.

The strict orange-and-yellow motif makes the Suez look more like a Las Vegas attraction than anything in ancient Egypt. There are several convenient pluses, however, like a low-priced restaurant, fully equipped kitchenettes in some rooms, a large heated outdoor pool, a kiddie pool, an exercise room with saunas, lighted tennis courts, and a Laundromat. A kitschy but pleasant and inexpensive lounge reminds you that you are indeed in a tropical paradise. For the price, it's a great choice, and you can say you saw the pyramids.

3 Key Biscayne

There are only a couple of hotels here, not counting the superluxurious Grand Bay Resort, currently under construction. All are on the beach, and room rates are uniformly high. If you can afford it, Key Biscayne is a great place to stay. The island is far enough from the mainland to make it feel like a secluded tropical paradise, yet close enough to Downtown to take advantage of everything Miami has to offer.

Silver Sands Beach Resort. 301 Ocean Dr., Key Biscayne, FL 33149. ☎ **305/361-5441.** Fax 305/361-5477. 56 units. A/C TV TEL. Winter $149–$179 minisuite; $300 cottage; $385 oceanfront suite. Off-season $109–$129 minisuite; $200 cottage; $385 oceanfront suite. Additional person $30 extra. Weekly rates available. AE, DC, MC, V. Free parking.

If Key Biscayne is where you want to be and you don't want to pay the prices of the next-door Sonesta, consider this quaint, one-story motel. Everything is crisp and clean, and the pleasant staff will help with anything you may need, including baby-sitting. But despite the name, it's certainly no resort. Except for the beach and pool, you'll have to leave the premises for almost everything, including food. The well-appointed rooms are very beachy, sporting a tropical motif and simple furnishings; extras include microwaves, refrigerators, and coffeemakers. Oceanfront suites have the added convenience of full kitchens with stoves and pantries. You'll sit poolside with an unpretentious set of Latin American families and Europeans who have come for a long and simple vacation—and get it.

Amenities include secretarial services, twice-daily maid service, VCRs in some rooms, medium-sized outdoor pool, beach, kitchenettes, and a coin laundry.

✪ **Sonesta Beach Resort Key Biscayne.** 350 Ocean Dr., Key Biscayne, FL 33149. ☎ **800/ SONESTA** or 305/361-2021. Fax 305/361-3096. www.sonesta.com. 303 units. A/C MINIBAR TV TEL. Winter $295–$450 double; $600–$1,650 suite or villa. Off-season $160–$320 double; $525–$1,325 suite or villa. 15% gratuity added to food and beverage bills. Special packages available. AE, CB, DC, DISC, EURO, JCB, MC, V. Valet parking $12.

One of South Florida's most private and luxurious resorts, the Sonesta is an ideal retreat. From the moment the valets, clad in tropical prints, take your car, you'll know you've entered a world of no concern. Each of the nearly 300 rooms has a private balcony or terrace. Sports, from tennis to jet-skiing, are available all around you. Although you may not want to leave the lush grounds, Bill Baggs State Recreation Area and the area's best beaches are right at hand, and if you choose to venture out, you're only about 15 minutes from Miami Beach and even closer to the mainland and Coconut Grove. The vacation homes have fully equipped kitchenettes.

The hotel has four restaurants, including Purple Dolphin, for "New World" cuisine, and Two Dragons, for Chinese. There's also an excellent seafood restaurant with a terrace, and several lounges and bars. The restaurants regularly draw locals, who have few dining options on "The Key."

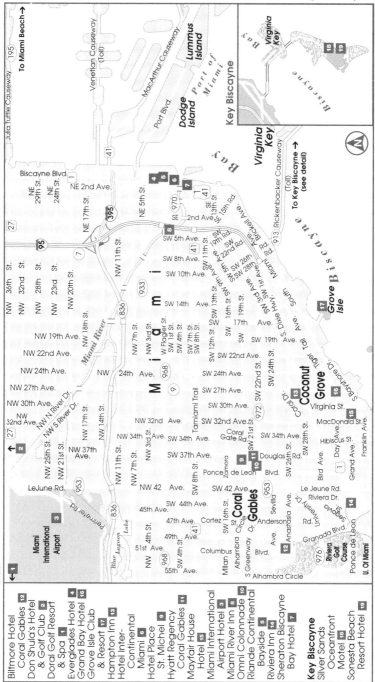

Biltmore Hotel
Coral Gables **12**
Don Shula's Hotel
& Golf Club **2**
Doral Golf Resort
& Spa **1**
Everglades Hotel **4**
Grand Bay Hotel **16**
Grove Isle Club
& Resort **17**
Hampton Inn **13**
Hotel Inter-
Continental
Miami **6**
Hotel Place
St. Michel **9**
Hyatt Regency
Coral Gables **11**
Mayfair House
Hotel **15**
Miami International
Airport Hotel **3**
Miami River Inn **8**
Omni Colonnade **10**
Riande Continental
Bayside **5**
Riviera Inn **14**
Sheraton Biscayne
Bay Hotel **7**

Key Biscayne
Silver Sands
Oceanfront
Motel **18**
Sonesta Beach
Resort Hotel **19**

NA-0164

4 Downtown

Most Downtown hotels cater primarily to business travelers, but tourists can get well-located, good-quality accommodations, too. Although business hotels are expensive, quality and service are of a high standard. Look for discounts and packages for the weekend, when offices are closed and rooms often go empty. Downtown is closest to some of Miami's best shopping. Be warned that after dark there's virtually nothing to do outside of the hotels; the streets are often deserted and crime can be a problem.

In downtown Miami, the **Wyndham** (☎ **800/WYNDHAM** or 305/374-0000), at 1601 Biscayne Blvd., above the Omni Mall, is a good option for the thrifty business traveler. It has a full business center as well as a heated rooftop pool. It's just a few minutes away from Bayside and Miami Beach. Rates are from $109 to $199.

VERY EXPENSIVE

✪ **Hotel Inter-Continental Miami.** 100 Chopin Plaza, Miami, FL 33131. ☎ **800/ 327-3005** or 305/577-1000. Fax 305/577-0384. www.interconti.com. 615 units. A/C MINIBAR TV TEL. Winter $209–$289 double; $325–$450 suite. Off-season $139–$259 double; $325–$450 suite. Additional person $20 extra. Weekend and other packages available. AE, CB, DC, DISC, MC, V. Valet parking $12.

Especially since the $5 million renovation of all its guest rooms and some common areas, the Inter-Continental is downtown's swankiest hotel. It boasts more marble than a mausoleum (both inside and out), but it's warmed by colorful, homey touches. The five-story lobby features a marble centerpiece sculpture by Henry Moore and is topped by a pleasing skylight. Plenty of plants, palm trees, and brightly colored wicker chairs also add charm and enliven the otherwise stark space. Brilliant downtown and bay views add luster to already posh rooms, outfitted with every convenience known to hotel-dom, including VCRs. Some suites have fully equipped kitchenettes.

Dining/Diversions: Three restaurants cover all price ranges and are complemented by two full-service lounges.

Amenities: Concierge, room service, dry cleaning and laundry, newspaper delivery, twice-daily maid service, express checkout, free refreshments in lobby. Olympic-size heated outdoor pool, health spa, sundeck, jogging track, large business center, 15 conference rooms, self-service Laundromat, car-rental desk, travel-agency/tour desk, beauty salon and barbershop, shopping arcade, access to nearby golf course.

MODERATE

Everglades Hotel. 244 Biscayne Blvd., Miami, FL 33132. ☎ **800/327-5700** or 305/ 379-5461. Fax 305/577-8445. www.miamigate.com/everglades. 376 units. A/C TV TEL. Year-round $92 double; $125 suite. AE, CB, DC, DISC, MC, V. Parking $7.

This hotel has been around about forever on Downtown's active Biscayne Boulevard. And it shows: The lobby and rooms border on dive quality. Many traveling business types and Latin American families stay here, however, because of its convenient, safe location, low rates, and many services, which include a bank in the building. It's also one of the only Downtown properties with a pool. The hotel is near the highways and Metrorail, and there's great shopping across the street at Bayside Marketplace.

Miami River Inn. 118 SW South River Dr., Miami, FL 33130. ☎ **305/325-0045.** Fax 305/325-9227. www.travelbase.com. A/C TV TEL. 40 units. Winter $99–$145 double.

Off-season $69–$89 double. Rates include continental breakfast. Additional person $15 extra. AE, CB, DC, DISC, MC, V. Free parking.

The Miami River is a great deal for those who want to be in a central location—close to the highway, public transportation, downtown eateries, and museums. Extras include a small outdoor pool, Jacuzzi, and complimentary coffee and wine in the lobby. Although many predict that the riverfront will soon undergo a renaissance, for now the area is still a bit seedy. Don't venture too far out of the enclave, unless you want to see the ugly underside of Miami.

Rooms are nicely furnished with a mix of antiques from all eras and gentle wallpaper prints. In the common area is a collection of books about old Miami, with histories of this land's former owners: Julia Tuttle, William Brickell, and Henry Flagler. The low year-round rates make this hotel an attractive option for those who appreciate old things. There's a small outdoor pool on the premises and a Jacuzzi.

Riande Continental Bayside. 146 Biscayne Blvd., Miami, FL 33132. ☎ **800/RIANDE-1** or 305/358-4555. Fax 305/371-5253. 250 units. A/C MINIBAR TV TEL. Winter $115–$175 double. Off-season $85–$155 double. Frommer's readers get a 20% discount year-round. AE, DC, MC, V. Parking $7.50.

Like its sister hotel in South Beach, this Riande caters to a Latin American crowd that descends on Downtown in droves to shop for clothes and electronics. The location is ideal, only steps away from a Bayside shopping center, many great ethnic restaurants, and a Metrorail stop. The reasonable prices and helpful staff are reason enough to consider staying here, if you want to be right in downtown Miami.

Sheraton Biscayne Bay Hotel. 495 Brickell Ave., Miami, FL 33131. ☎ **800/325-3535** or 305/373-6000. Fax 305/374-2279. www.sheraton.com. 598 units. A/C TV TEL. Winter $149–$189 double; $225–$305 suite. Off-season $99–$175 double; $200–$250 suite. Additional person $10 extra. Senior discounts and weekend and other packages available. AE, CB, DC, DISC, MC, V. Parking $11.

This Downtown hotel's waterfront location is its greatest asset. Nestled between Brickell Park and Biscayne Bay, the Sheraton is set back from the main road and surrounded by a pleasant bay-front walkway. Since a recent $14 million renovation, this Sheraton is especially recommendable. Its identical rooms are well furnished and comfortable. There isn't much to do in the area, but you're within a short drive to anything Miami has to offer.

The Regatta Bar and Grille serves American cuisine and a buffet with made-to-order pastas too. A huge bar has happy hours and occasional live music.

5 West Miami/Airport Area

As Miami continues to grow at its rapid pace, expansion has begun westward, where land is plentiful. Several resorts have taken advantage of the space to build world-class tennis and golf courses. While there's no sea to swim in, a plethora of facilities makes up for the lack of an ocean view.

If you've got an early morning flight to catch, by all means stay near the airport. If not, why not spend a few dollars to get to the beach, less than 10 miles away. You'll have a lot more options and will get a better value for your money.

If you must stay near the airport, consider any of the dozens of moderately priced chain hotels. You'll find one of the cheapest and most recommendable options at either **Days Inn** at 7250 NW 11th St. or 4767 NW 36th St. (☎ **800/329-7466** or 305/888-3661), each about 2 miles from the airport.

The larger property on 36th Street offers slightly cheaper rates with singles starting as low as $49. The 11th Street locale may charge more for weekends, but prices usually start at $70. Prices include free transportation from the airport.

A more luxurious option is the **Wyndham** at 3900 NW 21st St. (☎ **800/ 933-1100**) with rates from $100 to $225.

Don Shula's Hotel and Golf Club. Main St., Miami Lakes, FL 33014. ☎ **800/24-SHULA** or 305/821-1150. Fax 305/820-8190. 330 units. A/C TV TEL. Winter from $159 double; $279 suite. Off-season $99–$139 double; $189–$209 suite. Additional person $10 extra. Business packages available. AE, DC, MC, V.

Guests come to Shula's mostly for the golf, but there's plenty here to keep non-golfers busy, too. Opened in 1992 to much fanfare from the sports and business community, Shula's resort is an all-encompassing oasis in the middle of a highly planned residential neighborhood, complete with a Main Street and nearby shopping facilities—a good thing, since the site is more than a 20-minute drive on the highways from anything. The guest rooms, located in the main building or surrounding the golf course, are plain but pretty, and come with VCRs (on request).

The award-winning Shula's Steak House and the more casual Steak House Two rank in the top 10 nationwide. They serve huge Angus beef steaks and seafood. Another restaurant on the premises serves natural food.

✪ **Doral Golf Resort and Spa.** 4400 NW 87th Ave., Miami, FL 33178. ☎ **800/ 22-DORAL,** 800/71-DORAL, or 305/592-2000. Fax 305/594-4682. www.doralgolf.com. 623 units (plus an additional 58 suites at the spa). A/C MINIBAR TV TEL. Winter $225–$315 double; $315–$945 suite; $350–$1,280 spa suite. Off-season $95–$275 double; $175–$380 golf suite; $350–$825 spa suite. Additional person $35 extra. 18% service charge added. Golf and spa packages available. AE, CB, DC, DISC, MC, V. Valet parking $8.50.

The Doral epitomizes the luxury resort in Florida. While the pamperings in the spa attract worldwide attention, the next-door golf resort hosts world-class tournaments and is home to the Blue Monster Course—rated one of the top 25 in the country. The season is booked well in advance by those who have been here before or have just read about the fantastic offerings on this 650-acre, fully self-contained resort. It's just moments from the Miami airport.

The spacious lobbies and dining areas shimmer with polished marble, mirrors, and gold. The rooms, too, are luxuriously large and tastefully decorated; big windows allow views of the tropical gardens or golf courses below. The resort is surrounded by warehouses and office buildings.

The Spa restaurant serves delicious low-fat cuisine, including reduced-calorie desserts. Other options include a cafe with super Italian sandwiches, salads, and pasta. A sports bar at the golf club offers excellent club fare.

Miami International Airport Hotel. P.O. Box 997510. NW 20th St. and LeJeune Rd., Airport Terminal Concourse E., Miami, FL 33299-7510. ☎ **800/327-1276** or 305/871-4100. Fax 305/871-0800. www.miahotel.com. 260 units. A/C TV TEL. Winter $159–$179 double; $275–$650 suite. Off-season $145–$165 double; $250–$270 suite. Additional person $10 extra. AE, CB, DC, EURO, JCB, MC, V. Parking $9.

If you need to be at the airport and want excellent service, this is your best bet. I don't know of a nicer airport hotel, and you can't beat the convenience—it's actually in the airport at Concourse E. You'll find every amenity of a first-class tourist hotel here, including a large rooftop pool, health club, Jacuzzi, sauna, sundeck, racquetball courts, jogging track, small business center, conference room, beauty salon, tour desk, boutiques, and several cocktail lounges and restaurants. The rooms are modern, clean, and spacious, with industrial-grade carpeting. The furnishings are nondescript but tasteful. You might think you'd be deafened by the roar of the planes, but all of the rooms have been soundproofed and actually allow very little noise. In addition, the hotel has modern security systems and is extremely safe. The restaurants are decent, but many of Miami's best are just a short cab drive away.

6 North Dade

✪ **Turnberry Isle Resort and Club.** 19999 W. Country Club Dr., Aventura, FL 33180. ☎ **800/327-7028** or 305/932-6200. Fax 305/933-6550. www.turnberryisle.com. 340 units. A/C MINIBAR TV TEL. Winter $395–$800 resort room or suite; $315–$500 yacht club room or suite. Off-season $215–$600 resort room or suite; $170–$300 yacht club room or suite. AE, DC, DISC, MC, V. Valet parking $8; free self-parking.

A top-rated resort, this gorgeous 300-acre compound has every possible facility for active guests, particularly golfers. You'll pay a lot to stay here—but it's worth it. The main attractions are two newly renovated Trent Jones courses, available only to members and guests of the hotel. Impeccable service from check-in to checkout brings loyal fans back for more. The North Miami Beach location is about halfway between Fort Lauderdale and Miami, but you'll find excellent shopping and some of the best dining in Miami right in the neighborhood.

Unless you're into boating, the higher-priced resort rooms are where you'll want to stay. Here, you're steps from perfect spa facilities and the renowned Veranda restaurant. The well-proportioned rooms are gorgeously tiled to match the Mediterranean-style architecture. The bathrooms even have a color TV mounted within reach of the whirlpool bathtubs. Video rental is available.

There are six restaurants, including the Veranda, which serves healthful and tropical New World cuisine in an elegant dining room. The several bars and lounges, including a popular disco, also have enough entertainment and local flavor to keep anyone busy for weeks.

7 Coral Gables

Coconut Grove eases into Coral Gables, which extends north toward Miami International Airport. "The Gables," as it's affectionately known, was one of Miami's original planned communities and is still among the city's prettiest neighborhoods. It's close to the shops along the Miracle Mile and the University of Miami. Two popular and well-priced chain hotels are a **Holiday Inn** (☎ **800/327-5476** or 305/667-5611), at 1350 S. Dixie Hwy., with rates between $75 and $125, and a **Howard Johnson** (☎ **800/446-4656** or 305/665-7501) at 1430 S. Dixie Hwy. Rates range from $65 to $95. Both are located directly across the street from the University of Miami and are popular with families and friends of students.

VERY EXPENSIVE

✪ **Biltmore Hotel Coral Gables.** 1200 Anastasia Ave., Coral Gables, FL 33134. ☎ **800/727-1926,** 305/445-1926, or Westin at 800/228-3000. Fax 305/442-9496. www.biltmorehotel.com. 275 units. A/C TV TEL. Winter from $319 double; $379–$479 suite. Off-season from $239 double; $309–389 suite. Additional person $20 extra. Special packages available. AE, CB, DC, DISC, MC, V. Valet parking $9.

The Biltmore, which was built in 1926, is the oldest Coral Gables hotel and a city landmark. It was granted national recognition as an official National Historical Landmark in 1996—one of only two operating hotels in Florida to receive the designation. It's also one of the only four-star rated hotels in the area. Always a pop-ular destination for golfers, including President Clinton, the Biltmore is situated on a lush rolling 18-hole course that is as challenging as it is beautiful. The hotel is sur-rounded by a pretty residential area, 5 minutes from the airport and excellent dining and shopping selections, and about 20 minutes from Miami Beach. It is a wonderful option for those seeking a luxurious getaway in a quiet setting. I espe-cially recommend a visit to the huge, beautiful spa.

Now under the management of the Westin Hotel group, the hotel boasts large rooms decorated with tasteful period reproductions and some high-tech amenities. The enormous lobby, with its 45-foot ceilings, serves as an entry point for hundreds of weddings and business meetings each year. Rising above the Spanish-style estate is a majestic 300-foot copper-clad tower, modeled after the Giralda bell tower in Seville and visible throughout the city. Over the years, the Biltmore has passed through many incarnations (for example, it was used as a VA hospital after World War II), but is now back to its original 1926 splendor.

Dining/Diversions: An elegant European restaurant serves excellent French/Italian cuisine nightly and champagne brunch on Sunday. An impressive wine cellar and cigar room are popular with local connoisseurs. The more casual Courtyard Café and Poolside Grille both serve three meals daily. There's also a lounge and piano bar where drinks are accompanied by live music nightly.

Amenities: Concierge, room service (24 hours), laundry and dry cleaning, news-paper delivery, nightly turndown on request, twice-daily maid service, baby-sitting, secretarial services, express checkout. Kitchenettes in tower suite, VCR and video rentals, 21,000-square-foot swimming pool surrounded by arched walkways and classical sculptures, state-of-the-art health club, full-service spa, sauna, 18-hole golf course, elaborate business center, conference rooms, car rental through concierge, sundeck, 10 lighted tennis courts, beauty salon, boutiques.

Hyatt Regency Coral Gables. 50 Alhambra Plaza, Coral Gables, FL 33134. ☎ **800/233-1234** or 305/441-1234. Fax 305/441-0520. www.hyatt.com. 242 units. A/C MINIBAR TV TEL. Winter $260 double; $299–$1,800 suite. Off-season from $120 double; $175–$1,800 suite. Additional person $25 extra. Packages and senior discounts available. AE, CB, DC, DISC, MC, V. Valet parking $10; self-parking $9.

High on style, comfort, and price, this Hyatt is part of Coral Gables' Alhambra, an office-hotel complex with a Mediterranean motif. The building itself is gorgeous, designed with pink stone, arched entrances, grand courtyards, and tile roofs. Inside you'll find overstuffed chairs on marble floors, surrounded by opulent antiques and chandeliers. The hotel opened in 1987, but like many historical buildings in the neighborhood, the Alhambra attempts to mimic something much older and much farther away.

The good-size rooms are outfitted with everything you'd expect from a top hotel—terry robes and all. Most furnishings are antique.

Dining/Diversions: A good New World cuisine restaurant serves a varied menu with many local specialties. Alcazaba is a fun Latin-style dance spot (see "Latin Clubs," in chapter 10).

Amenities: Full concierge services, room service (6am to midnight), same-day laundry and dry-cleaning services, newspaper delivery, nightly turndown on request, in-room massage, baby-sitting arrangements available, secretarial services, express checkout, valet parking. Large outdoor heated pool, health club with Nau-tilus equipment, Jacuzzi, two saunas, nearby golf course, basic business center, con-ference rooms, small gift shop.

EXPENSIVE

✪ **Hotel Place St. Michel.** 162 Alcazar Ave., Coral Gables, FL 33134. ☎ **800/848-HOTEL** or 305/444-1666. Fax 305/529-0074. www.hotelplacestmichel.com. 27 units. A/C TV TEL. Winter (including continental breakfast) $165–$175 double; $200–$220 suite. Off-season $125–$140 double; $160–$180 suite. Additional person $10 extra. AE, DC, MC, V. Parking $7.

This unusual little hotel in the heart of Coral Gables is one of the city's most romantic options. The accommodations and hospitality are straight out of old-world Europe, complete with dark wood-paneled walls, cozy beds, beautiful antiques, and a quiet elegance that seems startlingly out of place in trendy Miami. Everything here is charming—from the parquet floors to the paddle fans. One-of-a-kind furnishings make each room special. Guests are treated to fresh fruit baskets upon arrival and enjoy every imaginable service throughout their stay.

Dining/Diversions: The Restaurant St. Michel is a very romantic and elegant dining choice. A lounge and deli complete the hotel options.

Amenities: Concierge, room service, laundry and dry cleaning, newspaper delivery, evening turndown, in-room massage, twice-daily maid service, complimentary continental breakfast.

The Omni Colonnade Hotel. 180 Aragon Ave. (at Ponce de León and Miracle Mile), Coral Gables, FL 33134. ☎ **800/THE-OMNI** or 305/441-2600. Fax 305/445-3929. 157 units. A/C MINIBAR TV TEL. Winter $195–$265 double; $405 suite. Off-season $105–$225 double; $365 suite. Packages available. AE, CB, DC, DISC, MC, V. Valet parking $10.

The Colonnade occupies part of a large historic building, originally built by Coral Gables's founder George Merrick in 1926. Faithful to its original style, the hotel is a successful amalgam of new and old, with an emphasis on modern conveniences. The structure stands 14 elegant stories high, although guest rooms occupy only four floors. It's popular with business travelers.

The oversized rooms are worthy of the hotel's rates. They feature sitting areas, historic photographs, marble counters, gold-finished faucets, and solid wood furnishings. Thoughtful extras include complimentary shoe-shines and champagne upon arrival.

Diversions: Doc Dammers Saloon is a good happy hour for the 30-something crowd. There's live entertainment on weekends.

Amenities: 24-hour concierge and room service, same-day laundry and dry-cleaning service, newspaper delivery, evening turndown on request, in-room massage, twice-daily maid service on request, baby-sitting, express checkout, valet parking, free morning coffee and tea in the lobby. Heated outdoor pool on rooftop, small modern rooftop fitness center, Jacuzzi, sundeck, large conference centers and meeting rooms, Laundromat, car-rental and tour desks, gift shop and shopping arcade.

INEXPENSIVE

Riviera Court Motel. 5100 Riviera Dr. (on U.S. 1), Coral Gables, FL 33146. ☎ **800/368-8602** or 305/665-3528. 30 units. A/C TV TEL. Winter from $68 double; $78 efficiencies. Off-season from $55 double; $78 efficiencies. 10% discount for seniors and AAA members. AE, CB, DC, DISC, MC, V.

Besides the newly renovated Holiday Inn down the road, this family owned motel is the best discount option in the area. The comfortable and clean two-story property, dating from 1954, has a small pool and is set back from the road, so that the rooms are all relatively quiet. Vending machines are the only choice for refreshments, but guests are near many great dining spots. You can also choose to stay in one of the efficiencies, which all have fully stocked kitchens.

8 Coconut Grove

This intimate enclave hugs the shores of Biscayne Bay, just south of U.S. 1 and about 10 minutes from the beaches. The Grove is a great place to stay, offering ample nightlife, excellent restaurants, and beautiful surroundings, and the hotel rates are reflective of the high style of living found here.

VERY EXPENSIVE

Grand Bay Hotel. 2669 S. Bayshore Dr., Coconut Grove, FL 33133. ☎ **800/327-2788** or 305/858-9600. Fax 305/859-2026. www.grandbay.com. 178 units. A/C MINIBAR TV TEL. Winter from $345 double. Off-season $205 double. Year-round $350–$1,500 suite. Additional person $20 extra. Packages available. AE, CB, DC, MC, V. Valet parking $13.

The Grand Bay opened in 1983 and immediately won praise as one of the most elegant hotels in the world. This stunning pyramid-shaped hotel is a masterpiece both inside and out. The rooms are luxurious, each featuring high-quality linens, comfortable overstuffed love seats and chairs, a large writing desk, and all the amenities you'd expect in deluxe accommodations, including VCRs and video rentals. It has recently added ironing boards, irons, and voice mail to all rooms as well. Original art and armfuls of fresh flowers are generously displayed throughout.

The Grand Bay consistently attracts wealthy, high-profile people, and it basks in its image as a rendezvous for royalty, socialites, and superstars. Guests come here to be pampered and to see and be seen.

Dining/Diversions: Opened in late 1998, the hotel's main restaurant, **Bice** (pronounced *Bee*-chey) serves classic northern Italian cuisine in an elegant setting. Drinks are served in the Ciga Bar, and the Lobby Lounge offers a traditional afternoon tea.

Amenities: Concierge, room service (24 hours), same-day laundry and dry cleaning, newspaper delivery, evening turndown, masseuse on call, twice-daily maid service, baby-sitting, secretarial services, express checkout, courtesy limousine service to Cocowalk, free refreshments in the lobby. Heated indoor pool, small health club, access to nearby health club, Jacuzzi, sauna, VCR and video rentals, sundeck, water-sports equipment rental, bicycle rental, good-sized business center, conference rooms, car-rental and activities desks, beauty salon, gift shop, nearby golf course.

Grove Isle Club and Resort. Four Grove Isle Dr., Coconut Grove, FL 33133. ☎ **800/88-GROVE** or 305/858-8300. Fax 305/854-6702. 49 units. A/C TV TEL. Winter $245–$325 double; $475 suite. Off-season $195–$295 double; $475 suite. Rates include breakfast. Additional person $20 extra. AE, DC, MC, V. Free valet parking.

A 1994 renovation has turned Grove Isle into one of the nicest spots to stay in Coconut Grove. Its location is stunning. From the lobby and many rooms, guests look out onto glimmering Biscayne Bay, where sailboats drift lazily about and dolphins sometimes leap circles in the clear blue water. You'd almost think the property is on an island; actually, it's only a few minutes from Coconut Grove's business district.

Grove Isle feels like a country club. Everyone dresses in white and pastels, and if they're not on their way to a set of tennis, they're not in a rush to get anywhere. Rooms are nicely furnished, as is the elegant but uncluttered lobby.

Dining: Baleen's, an elegant continental restaurant, serves fresh seafood and other regional specialties.

Amenities: Concierge service, room service (6:30am to 10pm), laundry and dry-cleaning services, newspaper delivery, nightly turndown, in-room massage, twice-daily maid service, baby-sitting, secretarial services, express checkout, valet parking, free coffee in the lobby. VCRs, movie channels, video rental delivered to room ($5), large heated outdoor pool, deluxe fitness facilities, 12 outdoor tennis courts, water-sports equipment rental available, jogging track, nature trails, conference rooms, beauty salon.

Mayfair House Hotel. 3000 Florida Ave., Coconut Grove, FL 33133. ☎ **800/433-4555** or 305/441-0000. Fax 305/441-1647. www.hotelbook.com/live/welcome. 179 units. A/C MINIBAR TV TEL. Winter $249–$649 suite; $450 penthouse. Off-season $220–$440 suite; $450 penthouse. Packages available. AE, DC, DISC, MC, V. Valet parking $15; self-parking $6.

If you want to be in the Grove, this hotel is a great choice. Though very expensive and more than 20 minutes from the beach, it is situated inside the posh Mayfair Shops complex, the all-suite Mayfair House is about as centrally located as you can get. Each guest unit has been individually designed and renovated in 1998. All have terraces and are extremely comfortable. Some suites are downright opulent and include a private, outdoor, Japanese-style hot tub. The top-floor terraces offer good views, and all are hidden from the street by leaves and latticework. Since the lobby is in a shopping mall, recreation is confined to the roof, where you'll find a small pool, sauna, and snack bar.

Dining/Diversions: The Mayfair Grill serves a varied menu with particularly good steaks and seafood. There's also a rooftop snack bar for poolside snacks and a private nightclub open late.

Amenities: Concierge and room service (24 hours), dry cleaning, newspaper delivery, nightly turndown, twice-daily maid service, secretarial services, express checkout. VCRs and video rentals, outdoor pool, access to nearby health club, Jacuzzi, elaborate business center, conference rooms.

MODERATE

Hampton Inn. 2800 SW 28th Terrace (at U.S. 1 and SW 27th Ave.), Coconut Grove, FL 33133. ☎ **888/287-3390** or 305/448-2800. Fax 305/442-8655. www.travelbase.com/destinations. 179 units. A/C TV TEL. Winter $119–$139 double. Off-season $79–$119 double. Rates include continental breakfast buffet. AE, DC, DISC, MC, V.

This very standard chain hotel is a welcome reprieve in an area otherwise known for having only very pricey accommodations. The rooms are nothing exciting, but the freebies, like local phone calls, parking, in-room movies, breakfast buffet, and hot drinks around the clock make this a real steal. Although there is no restaurant or bar, it is close to lots of both—only about half a mile to the heart of the Grove's shopping and retail area and about as far from Coral Gables. Rooms are brand new and have large televisions, voice mail phones, and refrigerators and microwaves upon request. A workout room, large outdoor pool, and Jacuzzi are added bonuses in this generic but recommendable hotel.

6

Miami Dining

Florida cooking, with its Caribbean and Asian influences and an abundance of tropical ingredients, has made a splash that has been heard around the globe. One of the area's premier chefs, Norman van Aken of Norman's restaurant in Coral Gables, received the prestigious James Beard award as Best American Chef in the Southeast in 1997, following in the footsteps of Allen Susser of Chef Allen's who took the award in 1994. *Esquire* magazine cited Johnny Vinczencz, then of Astor Place and Johnny V's as a "Chef To Keep Your Eye On," and a few years ago named Jonathan Eismann's Pacific Time the best new restaurant. These chefs, like so many visitors, are attracted to the energetic environment of Miami, where produce grows in backyards and fish are so fresh they're still flapping on the prep lines.

No longer do chefs get their start here with hopes of moving on to New York or Los Angeles. Quite the contrary. There are literally hundreds of successful restaurants that have opened first in the Northeast and then have opted to join the other successful outlets in sunny South Florida. They bring with them recipes and distinctive ideas about food that add even more variety to this hodgepodge of regional cuisine known as "New World."

This regional style of cooking is hard to define. It encompasses the varied tastes of the Caribbean, especially Cuba, as well as an old-Floridian and California nouvelle influence. The idea is to use locally available tropical ingredients, such as mango, papaya, avocado, jicama, coconut, snapper, lobster, and stone crab. Though at times it can be more than a bit overwhelming, in general, the results are deliciously exciting. Think of mango-infused oils over jerk tuna with jicama slaw served in a cracked coconut with yuca fries. You may need a translator. Welcome to the new world.

In addition to the exciting inventions of native chefs, you can always find the exotic foods of almost every ethnicity—from Cuban to Haitian to Jamaican to Vietnamese.

Many restaurants keep extended hours in season (roughly December to April), and may close for lunch and/or dinner on Monday, when the traffic is slower. Call for updated schedules. If you want to picnic on the beach or pick up some dessert, check out the gourmet food shops, green markets, and bakeries listed in chapter 9, "Shopping."

1 Restaurants by Cuisine

AMERICAN

Biscayne Miracle Mile Cafeteria
(Coral Gables, *I*)
Blue Door (South Beach, *VE*)
Christy's (Coral Gables, *VE*)
Curry's (Miami Beach, *I*)
The Forge Restaurant (Miami
Beach, *VE*)
Gables Diner (Coral Gables, *M*)
Here Comes the Sun (North Dade, *I*)
Joe Allen's (South Beach, *M*)
Kaleidoscope (Coconut Grove, *M*)
News Café (South Beach, *I*)
News Café in the Grove (Coconut
Grove, *I*)
S & S Restaurant (Downtown, *I*)
Sergio's (Coral Gables, *I*)
Sheldon's Drugs (Miami Beach, *I*)
Sundays on the Bay
(Key Biscayne, *E*)
Tony Roma's Famous For Ribs (West
Dade, *M*)
Van Dyke Cafe (South Beach, *I*)

ASIAN

Lucky Cheng's (South Beach, *E*)
NOA (Noodles of Asia) (South
Beach, *M*)
Pacific Time (South Beach, *VE*)
P. F. Chang's China Bistro (North
Dade, *M*)

BARBECUE

Shorty's (South Miami, *I*)
Tony Roma's (West Dade, *M*)

BISTRO

Jeffrey's (South Beach, *M*)

CANTONESE

The Red Lantern (Coconut
Grove, *M*)

COLOMBIAN

Mama Vieja (South Beach, *M*)

CONTINENTAL

Cafe Hammock (South Miami, *M*)
Crystal Café (Miami Beach, *E*)
Green Street Cafe (Coconut
Grove, *M*)
Hamilton's (Downtown, *E*)
Jeffrey's (South Beach, *M*)
The Lagoon (North Dade, *M*)
The Palm (Miami Beach, *E*)
Rusty Pelican (Key Biscayne, *E*)

CREPES

The Crepe Maker Cafe (South
Miami, *I*)

CUBAN/SPANISH

Casa Juancho (Little Havana, *M*)
La Carreta (Little Havana, *I*)
La Cibeles Cafe (Downtown, *I*)
Larios on the Beach (South
Beach, *M*)
The Oasis (Key Biscayne, *I*)
Pollo Tropical (South Miami, *I*)
Puerto Sagua (South Beach, I)
Sergio's (Coral Gables, *I*)
Versailles (Little Havana, *I*)
Victor's Cafe (Little Havana, *VE*)
Yuca (South Beach, *VE*)

DELI

Bagel Factory (South Beach, *I*)
Stephan's Gourmet Market & Cafe
(South Beach, *I*)
Wolfie Cohen's Rascal House (Miami
Beach, *M*)

DINER FARE

S & S Restaurant (Downtown, *I*)

ENGLISH TEA

The Tea Room (South Miami, *I*)

FAST FOOD

Johnny V's Kitchen (South Beach, *M*)
Mrs. Mendoza's Tacos al Carbon
(South Beach, *I*)
Pollo Tropical (South Miami, *I*)
Raja's (Downtown, *I*)

Key to Abbreviations: *E* = Expensive; *I* = Inexpensive; *M* = Moderate; *VE* = Very Expensive

FONDUE

The Melting Pot (North Dade, *M*)

FRENCH

Brasserie Les Halles (Coral
Gables, *M*)
The Crepe Maker Cafe (South
Miami, *I*)
La Boulangerie (Key Biscayne, *I*)
La Sandwicherie (South Beach, *I*)
Le Festival (Coral Gables, *E*)
L'Entrecote de Paris (South
Beach, *M*)
The Gourmet Diner (North
Dade, *M*)
Lemon Twist (Miami Beach, *M*)

GREEK

The Daily Bread Marketplace (Coral
Gables, *I*)
The Greek Place (Miami Beach, *I*)

HAITIAN

Tap Tap (South Beach, *M*)

HEALTH FOOD

Amos' Juice Bar (North Dade, *I*)
Here Comes the Sun (North Dade, *I*)

INDIAN

House of India (Coral Gables, *I*)
Raja's (Downtown, *I*)

INTERNATIONAL

Balans (South Beach, *M*)
Cafe Tu Tu Tango (Coconut
Grove, *I*)
The Globe (Coral Gables, *M*)
Norma's (South Beach, *E*)

IRISH PUB

John Martin's (Coral Gables, *M*)

ITALIAN

Anacapri (South Miami, *M*)
Bocca di Rosa (Coconut Grove, *E*)
Cafe Prima Pasta (Miami Beach, *M*)
Cafe Ragazzi (Miami Beach, *M*)
Caffe Abbracci (Coral Gables, *E*)
Carpaccio (Miami Beach, *E*)
Escopazzo (South Beach, *VE*)
Laurenzo's Cafe (North Dade, *I*)
Miami Beach Place (Miami Beach, *I*)

Oggi Caffe (Miami Beach, *M*)
Osteria del Teatro (South Beach, *VE*)
Perricone's Marketplace
(Downtown, *I*)
Sport Cafe (South Beach, *I*)
Stefano's (Key Biscayne, *E*)
Stephan's Gourmet Market & Cafe
(South Beach, *I*)

JAMAICAN

Caribbean Delite (Downtown, *I*)
Norma's (South Beach, *E*)

JAPANESE

Toni's (South Beach, *M*)

MEXICAN

Mrs. Mendoza's Tacos al Carbon
(South Beach, *I*)
Señor Frogs (Coconut Grove, *M*)

NEW WORLD CUISINE

Astor Place in the Astor Hotel (South
Beach, *VE*)
Blue Door (South Beach, *VE*)
Chef Allen's (North Dade, *VE*)
China Grill (South Beach, *VE*)
Crystal Café (Miami Beach, *E*)
Nemo's (South Beach, *E*)
Norman's (Coral Gables, *VE*)
Pacific Time (South Beach, *VE*)

PIZZA

Miami Beach Place (Miami Beach, *I*)

SEAFOOD

Bayside Seafood Restaurant and
Hidden Cove Bar (Key Biscayne, *I*)
East Coast Fisheries (Downtown, *M*)
Fishbone Grille (Downtown, *M*)
Grillfish (South Beach, *M*)
Joe's Stone Crab Restaurant (South
Beach, *VE*)
The Lagoon (North Dade, *M*)
Monty's Bayshore Restaurant
(Coconut Grove, *M*)
Monty's Stone Crab/Seafood House
(South Beach, *E*)

SPANISH

Cafe Tu Tu Tango (Coconut
Grove, *I*)
Casa Juancho (Little Havana, *M*)

Macarena (South Beach, *M*)
Puerto Sagua (South Beach, *I*)

STEAK HOUSE
Shula's Steak House (West Dade and
    Miami Beach, *VE*)
Smith & Wollensky (South
    Beach, *VE*)

SUSHI
Toni's (South Beach, *M*)
World Resources (South Beach, *I*)

SZECHUAN/PEKINESE
Chrysanthemum (South Beach, *M*)

THAI
Thai House South Beach (South
    Beach, *M*)
World Resources (South Beach, *I*)

VIETNAMESE
Hy-Vong (Little Havana, *I*)

WRAPS
Wrapido (South Miami, *M/I*)

2 South Beach

The renaissance of South Beach has spawned dozens of first-rate restaurants. In
fact, big names from across the country have decided to capitalize on South Beach's
international appeal and have begun to open branches here with great success. A
few old standbys remain from the *Miami Vice* days, but the flock of newcomers
dominates the scene, with places going in and out of style as quickly as the tides.
The listings below represent the restaurants that have quickly gained national attention or should.

The Lincoln Road area is packed with places offering good food and great atmosphere. Since it's impossible to list them all, I recommend strolling and browsing.
Most restaurants post a copy of their menu outside, and staff are happy to chat with
curious passersby.

With very few exceptions, the places on Ocean Drive are crowded with tourists
and priced accordingly. You'll do better to venture a little farther into the pedestrian-friendly streets just west of Ocean Drive.

VERY EXPENSIVE

✪ **Astor Place in the Astor Hotel.** 956 Washington Ave. South Beach. ☎ **305/
672-7217.** Reservations recommended. Main courses $15–$30. AE, DC, MC, V. Daily 7am–
2:30pm; Sun–Thurs 7–11pm; Fri–Sat 6pm–midnight. NEW WORLD CUISINE.

The Astor Hotel not only has a great bar, but perhaps the very best restaurant on
the beach. Favorites include corn-crusted yellowtail snapper with lemon boniato
(like a sweet potato, but white) mash and roasted corn sauce and sushi salad (a concoction of curry, fresh tuna, ginger shrimp, caviar, wasabi, and smoked salmon
dressed in an orange sesame vinaigrette). A stack of portobello mushrooms is served
pancake style with balsamic syrup and sun-dried tomato butter. Nightly specials
consistently sell out and are always worth a try. Another hot seller is the decadent
lobster pot pie with shrimp and vegetables. If it's available, order it.

The sleek dining room, with low-level lighting, a glass-enclosed atrium, and
marble floors, is romantic in an ultra-modern way. Well-dressed hipsters flock to
the restaurant, especially on weekend nights. A sophisticated family crowd shows
up for the Sunday jazz brunch, which features all kinds of eggs and luscious sandwiches on crisp homemade bread. There are also Italian rice dishes, salads, and
soups.

Blue Door. At the Delano Hotel, 1685 Collins Ave., South Beach. ☎ **305/674-6400.** Reservations recommended for dinner. Main courses $19–$34; soups and salads $6–$12.
AE, DC, MC, V. Daily 7am–1am. AMERICAN.

The Blue Door's setting—with plump circular booths, billowy white curtains, and polished oak accents—could be a backdrop for a 1930s movie. Celebrity sightings are almost guaranteed; with Madonna as a part owner, you would expect no less. The problem is that everyone, including your server, thinks he's the next big star. In the dining room, a steady stream of beautiful people parades through a center corridor on their way to the Alice-in-Wonderlandesque pool deck, where more people are posing on the luxurious furnishings. You'll want to sit on the patio if the weather is nice.

If your server deigns to take your order, try the delicate crab cakes, two to an order, served on a peppery fennel and tomato salad. On a recent visit, the stone crab claws were badly cracked, making the experience frustrating. The fish options, on the other hand, were fresh and prepared in a simple but elegant style. The choices include sea bass with a mashed combination of acorn squash and fennel, grilled lobster, salmon, and sautéed mahimahi in a sweet vinegar sauce.

China Grill. 404 Washington Ave. (at the corner of Fifth St.), South Beach. ☎ **305/534-2211.** Reservations recommended. Main courses $19–$30. AE, DC, MC, V. Mon–Fri 11:45am–5pm; Sun–Thurs 6pm–midnight; Fri–Sat 6pm–1am. NEW WORLD CUISINE.

Imported from New York, like so many other Miami institutions, China Grill took Miami Beach by storm when it opened in late 1995. Unfortunately, the attitude and prices are so up there that it tends to attract mostly the aging beautiful people and a few hangers-on. It's worth going to the bar for a drink to soak up some atmosphere and to people-watch. But be warned—the food sounds better than it is in this nightclub pretending to be a restaurant.

The menu and management explain that the prices are so high because the dishes are meant to be shared; however, when we tried that approach, we were left hungry. Some have complained that the service is slow and the food inconsistent. That being said, I could get addicted to the Confucius Chicken Salad, which has crispy fried noodles and a perfect blend of sesame and soy in the vinaigrette.

✪ **Escopazzo.** 1311 Washington Ave., South Beach. ☎ **305/674-9450.** Reservations required. Pastas $12–$18; main courses $18–$28. AE MC V. Mon, Tues, Thurs 6pm–midnight; Fri–Sat 6pm–12:30am and Sun 6–11pm. ITALIAN.

Owned by a personable Roman called Pino Bodoni who comes from a family of restaurateurs, this South Beach gem has been a favorite of locals for years. Thankfully, the formerly tiny space doubled in size this year, and can now accommodate the many who could never get in before. Once inside, you can choose from some stupendous hand-crafted dishes like risotto with fresh seafood, pappardelle with wild game and mushroom ragout, and braised leg of lamb with juniper berries, rosemary, and fennel. Service and style in this romantic setting are always top-rate.

Joe's Stone Crab Restaurant. 11 Washington Ave. (at Biscayne St., just south of 1st St.), South Beach. ☎ **305/673-0365.** Takeout ☎ 305/653-4611. Reservations not accepted. Market price varies but averages $42 for a serving of jumbo crab claws, $30 for large claws. AE, CB, DC, DISC, MC, V. Tues–Sat 11:30am–2pm; Sun–Thurs 5–10pm; Fri–Sat 5–11pm. Closed mid-May to mid-Oct. SEAFOOD.

Open since 1913 and steeped in tradition, this restaurant is famous in Florida and beyond, as evidenced by the ubiquitous long lines waiting to get in. A full menu is available, but to order anything but stone crabs is unthinkable, and the servers will let you know it. Service tends to be brusque and pushy.

Even after a $5 million renovation, which more than doubled the size of the place, the lines are still ridiculously long. Too many locals claim they "know someone" at the door, which usually means they were introduced through their

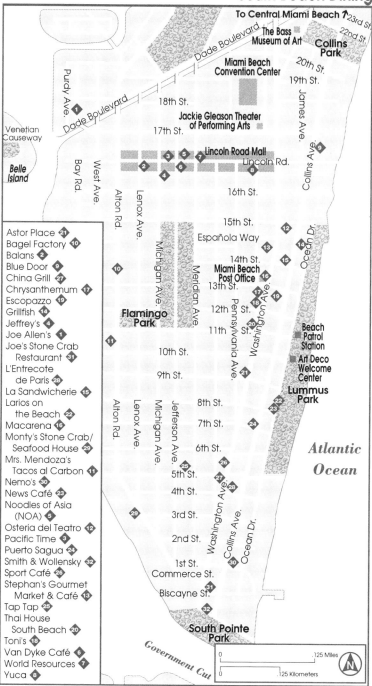

Astor Place 21
Bagel Factory 10
Balans 2
Blue Door 9
China Grill 27
Chrysanthemum 17
Escopazzo 19
Grillfish 14
Jeffrey's 4
Joe Allen's 1
Joe's Stone Crab
    Restaurant 31
L'Entrecote
    de Paris 28
La Sandwicherie 15
Larios on
    the Beach 22
Macarena 16
Monty's Stone Crab/
    Seafood House 29
Mrs. Mendoza's
    Tacos al Carbon 11
Nemo's 30
News Café 23
Noodles of Asia
    (NOA) 5
Osteria del Teatro 12
Pacific Time 3
Puerto Sagua 24
Smith & Wollensky 32
Sport Café 26
Stephan's Gourmet
    Market & Café 13
Tap Tap 25
Thai House
    South Beach 20
Toni's 18
Van Dyke Café 6
World Resources 7
Yuca 8

mutual friend, Ben Franklin. Even after heavy tipping, the wait can exceed an hour on weekend nights. If you have to say you were there, brave it and enjoy the wait in the stunning oak bar. Otherwise, try the takeout bar next door for the same price and less hassle. The claws here are the best, but also pricier than at other local restaurants. Remember, you're paying for history.

✪ **Osteria del Teatro.** 1443 Washington Ave. (at Española Way), South Beach. ☎ **305/ 538-7850.** Reservations recommended. Main courses $21–$32. AE, CB, DC, JCB, MC, V. Wed–Mon 6–11pm; Fri–Sat 6pm–midnight. Closed for 3 weeks in Sept. ITALIAN.

The curved entryway of this well-established enclave of reliable, if slightly over-priced, Italian cuisine is abuzz nightly. Reams of locals and tourists wait for a seat at one of the small tables. Move the fresh orchid aside to make room for a big basket of lightly toasted chunks of real Italian bread and then wait for your very knowl-edgeable server to recommend a daily special.

Start with any of the grilled vegetables, such as portobello mushrooms with fontina or the garlic-infused peppers. All the pastas are handmade and done to per-fection. The risotto al'aragosta is a creamy rice dish with a decadent lobster and shrimp sauce full of tasty morsels of seafood. Of the five or so entrees offered nightly, usually at least three are seafood. The tuna loin is served with a rich mush-room sauce with just a hint of rosemary. The duck breast, doused in a sweet bal-samic honey sauce and fanned over a bed of wilted radicchio leaves, is rightfully very popular. Each slice of duck is perfectly seared on the outside and tender throughout without even a hint of gamey flavor.

Pacific Time and Pacific Time Next Door. 915 Lincoln Rd. (between Jefferson and Michigan aves.), South Beach. ☎ **305/534-5979.** Reservations recommended. Main courses $19.50–$29. AE, CB, DC, MC, V. Sun–Thurs 6–11pm; Fri–Sat 6pm–midnight.; Next Door cafe Daily 11am–midnight. ASIAN/NEW WORLD CUISINE.

This exciting Lincoln Road restaurant has received accolades from the *Miami Herald, Esquire* magazine, and *Bon Appétit*. Chef and co-owner Jonathan Eismann puts out some of the funkiest dishes ever spotted this side of the equator. One of the best for meat-eaters is the Mongolian lamb salad, which has a lightly sweet, earthy taste with a crunchy kick of onion. For a main course, the ever-changing menu offers many locally caught fish specialties, including grouper served on a bed of shredded shallots and ginger with a sweet sake-infused sauce and tempura-dunked sweet potato slivers on the side. Under the midnight-blue sky ceiling and against the pale yellow distressed walls, you'll probably see stars. The famous choco-late bomb is every bit as decadent as they've said, with hot bittersweet chocolate bursting from the cupcakelike center. Some folks are put off by the exotic dishes, but more adventurous eaters return over and over again for a chance to experience this stunning Pacific-inspired meteor. New in 1998 was a more casual (and not as recommendable) outdoor cafe serving lunch and dinner with a more conventional menu and cheaper prices.

✪ **Smith & Wollensky.** 1 Washington Ave. (in South Pointe Park), South Beach. ☎ **305/ 673-2800.** Reservations suggested. Main courses $20–$30. DC, DISC, MC, V. Daily noon–midnight. The Grill open 5pm–2am. STEAK HOUSE.

This pricey New York import opened its doors in late 1997 and was packed from the start. The handsome clubby atmosphere is enhanced by views of the intercoastal waterway that leads to the Port of Miami. The menu as well as the setting is basic, almost austere, with a few chicken and fish choices and beef served about a dozen ways. The classic is the sirloin seared lightly and served naked. Also good is the thick and buttery filet mignon. Delicious side dishes such as asparagus, baked potato, onion rings, creamed spinach, and hash browns are sold à la carte. Ask for advice from the wine steward, since the vast and impressive menu can be overwhelming. Service here, unlike so many other South Beach restaurants, is usually professional and polite. Desserts are superb, too. Just hope someone else is paying.

To avoid the clanking bustle of the main dining rooms, ask for a seat upstairs or, better yet, in The Grill, where you can order from a more casual and less expensive menu. You'll find meat entrees at about 30% less than in the regular restaurant. Portions in here are a bit smaller, too, eliminating the need for doggie bags.

✪ **Yuca.** 501 Lincoln Rd. (corner of Drexel), South Beach. ☎ **305/532-9822.** Reservations required. Main courses $19–$32. AE, DC, DISC, MC, V. Sun–Thurs noon–4pm and 6–11pm; Fri–Sat noon–4pm and 6pm–midnight. Closed summer for weekday lunches. CUBAN.

This is the place to take out-of-towners you want to impress with a dose of upscale Latin culture. The menu is large and exotic. Unfortunately, it's also badly translated, so don't be shy about asking for a waiter who is proficient in English (most are) if you don't *habla español*. By the way, don't give yourself away as a gringo by pronouncing it "Yucca." It's "*Yoo*-ka," and is a play on words, being the name of a staple root vegetable and an acronym for young upscale Cuban Americans.

To enjoy your meal, insist on being seated in the front of the restaurant, facing Lincoln Road; otherwise, you'll be in the hectic path of the kitchen and too close to the very talented but loud salsa band that plays on weekends. Start with the lobster medallions with sautéed spinach and a portobello mushroom stuffed with vegetarian paella. The pieces of lobster tail are expertly grilled, with a touch of oil over just-wilted greens. The mushrooms are good, but the paella can be a bit pasty. For a main course, the pork tenderloin is a favorite—I thought it must have marinated for days, because I could cut it with a butter knife. The hearty *congrí*, a mash of red beans and rice, and a green apple and mango salsa make a perfect balance. The veal loin, the menu's most expensive entree, has a rich meaty flavor but can be a bit dry. A full selection of traditional and exotic dessert choices is available, as well as some of the best coffee in town.

Go on the weekend for a late dinner and then head upstairs for live music. If Cuban diva Albita is playing, you're in for a real experience. It's pricey but well worth it.

EXPENSIVE

✪ **Monty's Stone Crab/Seafood House.** 300 Alton Rd., South Beach. ☎ **305/673-3444.** Reservations recommended. Main courses $20–$37. AE, DC, MC, V. Sun–Thurs 5:30–11pm; Fri–Sat 5:30pm–midnight. SEAFOOD.

Seafood fans have long been enamored of Monty's various menus in the Grove and in Boca. Now Monty's has moved in to South Beach, burnished the rustic oak floor, set up a raw bar outside around a large swimming pool, and opened the doors for business. The best deal in town is still the all-you-can-eat stone crabs—about $40 for the large ones and $35 for the mediums. That's about the same price that Joe's, located 2 blocks away, charges for just three or four claws. (But don't order stone crabs in summer—they aren't as fresh.) Enjoy the incredible views and off-season fish specialties, including the Maryland she-crab soup, rich and creamy without too much thickener. Year-round, you can enjoy the saffron and tomato-based bouillabaisse, and the Key lime pie is the real deal.

✪ **Nemo's.** 100 Collins Ave., South Beach. ☎ **305/532-4550.** Reservations recommended. Main courses $17–$20; sandwiches and platters $4–$12; Sun brunch $19. AE, MC, V. Mon–Sat noon–3pm and 7pm–midnight; Sun noon–3pm and 6–11pm. NEW WORLD CUISINE.

This dark and superstylish hotspot is an oasis in a hip area of South Beach below 5th Street. Here models and celebrities rub elbows—literally, since the tables are so close together. Ask to be seated in the more private back room, which has a pleasant garden and is the only place where you can hear your dining companions or your server. In the main dining room, the din is unbearable. The staff here is professional, personable, and efficient—the best on the beach.

The menu offers many fish dishes. One of the most popular is the charred salmon. The flash-cooking in a wok gives it a unique flavor, slightly blackened outside and tender and sweet inside. If you're in the mood for something light, try the grilled portobello mushroom appetizer, served with a rich, creamy garlic polenta. The spicy Vietnamese beef salad is indeed very spicy, but it's too small a portion. You can never go wrong choosing one of the daily specials. An exotic and delicious choice for dessert is the California figs soaked in port syrup and surrounded with balls of tamarind (said to be an aphrodisiac) ice cream.

✪ **Norma's.** 646 Lincoln Rd., South Beach. ☎ **305/532-2809.** Reservations recommended. Main courses $12–$24. AE, DC, MC, V. Tues–Thurs noon–11pm; Fri–Sat noon–midnight; Sun noon–10pm. INTERNATIONAL/JAMAICAN.

This tiny jewel on Lincoln Road sparkles with its eclectic mix of classical and Caribbean cooking. The multilingual staff is polite if sometimes slightly flustered. The daily specials are always good, but you may want to call in advance to reserve whatever sounds best, because they sell out quickly.

For starters, try the smoked marlin platter with cucumbers, capers, and onion, plus a spicy pepper salsa and a creamy dipping sauce. Tender filets are flown in weekly from Montego Bay. The seared jerk tuna has a kick (like all the jerk-seasoned dishes) and is one of the Beach's best. If you prefer something milder, the *rasta pasta* is a good bet. To top it off, try the refreshing mango or guava mousse served with fresh tropical berries, melons, or tropical fruits. *Warning:* Don't drive after you've had the Appleton Rum cake and rum whipped cream.

MODERATE

Balans. 1022 Lincoln Rd. (between Lenox and Michigan), South Beach. ☎ **305/534-9191.** Reservations not accepted. Main courses $9–$17; pastas and noodles $8–$10. AE, DC, DISC, MC, V. Daily 8am–1am. INTERNATIONAL.

This well-run sidewalk cafe, a London import, is a good value, especially when the weather is right. It's a favorite hangout for the gay community, and is right at home on fabulous Lincoln Road. Dinners here are a bargain, with winning entrees like a hearty lobster club sandwich served with bacon, lettuce, and tomato on toasted onion bread, and a *hoisin Port* fillet nestled over baby *bok choy* and crisp leek spring rolls. The tempting starters are relatively small, so you can try a few. Try Thai soup, as well as the concoction of goat, cheese, and lightly breaded fried mushrooms. A large herb salad with a mix of more than five types of baby greens is a great way to start any meal. The tahini chicken salad, however, is sadly lacking in spice. The menu, with lots of healthful salads and sandwiches, seems to please a wide audience.

✪ **Chrysanthemum.** 1256 Washington Ave., South Beach. ☎ **305/531-5656.** Main courses $11–$20. AE, CB, DC, MC, V. Tues–Thurs and Sun 6–10:30pm; Fri–Sat 6pm–midnight. SZECHUAN/PEKINESE.

At first, the unpretentious atmosphere may be a surprise in glitzy South Beach, but after you've tried the tasty dishes in Chrysanthemum, the best Chinese restaurant in Miami, you'll want to come back. Count on the service to be prompt but not solicitous. The many vegetarian specialties include spicy eggplant strips in a rich balsamic vinegar sauce and black mushrooms sautéed with tiny Shanghai lettuce hearts. Start with the Chinese salad, which comes heaped with a fresh mix of greens, vermicelli, bean sprouts, and coriander. The steamed whole fish is best with the ginger and scallions. It comes with bones, but ask the waiter to remove them; he will gladly and expertly oblige.

Grillfish. 1444 Collins Ave. (corner of Española Way), South Beach. ☎ **305/538-9908.** Reservations recommended on weekends. Main courses $8–$15. AE, DISC, DC, MC, V. In season daily 6pm–midnight; off-season daily 6–11pm. SEAFOOD.

From the beautiful Byzantine-style mural and the gleaming oak bar, you'd think you were eating in a much more expensive restaurant. Grillfish manages to pay the exorbitant South Beach rent because the restaurant has a loyal following of locals who come for fresh, simple seafood in a relaxed but upscale atmosphere. As the name implies, fish, fish, and fish is what you'll get.

The servers are friendly and know the menu well. The barroom seafood chowder is full of chunks of shellfish, as well as some fresh white fish fillets in a tomato broth. The small ear of corn, included with each entree, is about as close as you'll get to any type of vegetable offering besides the pedestrian salad. Still, at these prices, it's worth a visit to try some local fare including mako shark, swordfish, tuna, marlin, and wahoo (they'll either grill or sauté it). Also, I recommend the spicy red pasta sauce as a great complement to this rustic, Italian-inspired seafood fare.

Jeffrey's. 1629 Michigan Ave. (half block south of Lincoln Rd.), South Beach. ☎ **305/673-0690.** Full meals $16–$21, pastas with salads $11–$17. AE, CB, DC, MC, V. Tues–Sat 6–11pm; Sun 5–10pm. CONTINENTAL/BISTRO.

Jeffrey's is a real find on South Beach—the genuinely concerned and doting owner, Jeffrey Landsman, treats everyone as a regular and calls grandmothers and children alike "kids." Some say this is the most romantic restaurant on the beach, and South Beach's gay crowd certainly seems to agree. Old-fashioned lace curtains and candlelight are a welcome repast from the glitz and chrome of the rest of the island.

You can choose a succulent ¾-pound burger or try a hearty chicken breast marinated in a balsamic sauce served with freshly mashed sweet potatoes over spinach on white lace tablecloths. Some of the better seafood options include the conch fritters and the crab cakes. Jeffrey's is known for its perfectly dressed Caesar salad, which could use some more anchovies for my taste, but is nonetheless delicious. Most desserts are tasty, but the homemade tarte Tatin, a caramelly deep-dish apple tart, is superb. Go early before it sells out.

Joe Allen's. 1787 Purdy Ave. (2 blocks west of Alton Rd.), South Beach. ☎ **305/531-7007.** Reservation recommended, especially on weekends. Main courses $13–$19. Weekdays 11:30am–midnight; weekends noon–11:45pm. MC, V. AMERICAN.

A lively bar scene and a classic comfort food menu make this rather plain looking box of a restaurant a popular neighborhood hangout. The food, which ranges from old-fashioned meat loaf to rigatoni with goat cheese, is reliably good. The service can be a bit sluggish, especially when the place is busy. Especially good here are the many inventive pizzas and salads.

Larios on the Beach. 820 Ocean Dr., South Beach. ☎ **305/532-9577.** Reservations recommended. Main courses $8–$15. AE, MC, V. Sun–Thurs 11:30am–midnight; Fri–Sat 11:30am–2am. CUBAN.

Gloria and Emilio Estefan brought their favorite chef to create this ultra-stylish restaurant in the heart of the South Beach hustle. Enjoy a few appetizers at the handsome chrome and wood bar while you wait for a seat amid the sea of Spanish-speaking regulars.

Portions are large and prices are reasonable. The menu runs the gamut, from diner-style *medianoches* (Cuban sandwiches with pork and cheese) to a tangy and tender *serrucho en escabeche* (pickled kingfish) with just enough citrus to mellow the fishiness but not enough to cause a pucker. You could get away with ordering three or four *aperitivos* and *ensaladas* (appetizers and salads) for two people. If you're still hungry, try the *camarones al ajillo* (shrimp in garlic sauce), *fabada asturiana* (hearty soup of black beans and sausage), or *palomilla* (thinly sliced beef served with onions and parsley). Save room for the rich custard desserts, which include a few stunning variations on the standard flan. A spoonful of pumpkin or coffee-accented custard with a cup of cortadito (espresso-style coffee with milk and sugar) will get you prepped for a full night of dancing.

L'Entrecote de Paris. 413 Washington Ave., South Beach. ☎ **305/673-1002.** Reservations suggested on weekends. Fixed-price dinner $14–18 (includes potatoes and salad). DC, MC, V. Daily 6pm–1am. FRENCH.

Everything in this classy little bistro is simple. For dinner, you choose between salmon or steak, and beyond a few salads, that's it—but both are great. The salmon looks like spa cuisine, served with a pile of bald steamed potatoes and a salad with pedestrian greens and an unmatchable vinaigrette. The steak, on the other hand, is the stuff cravings are made of, even if you're not a die-hard carnivore. Its salty sharp sauce is rich but not thick and full of the beef's natural flavor. The slices are served on top of your own little hibachi, which also keeps the accompanying fries warm.

Most diners are very Euro and pack a petit attitude. Tables and booths are squeezed tight together. On the other hand, the servers are superquick and professional, and almost friendly in a French kind of way. The short and very French wine list includes several well-priced bottles for under $20. Even if you are on a diet or have forsaken chocolate, try the *profiteroles au chocolat,* a perfect puff pastry filled with vanilla ice-cream and topped with a dark bittersweet chocolate sauce.

✪ **Macarena.** 1334 Washington Ave. South Beach. ☎ **305/531-3440.** Reservations suggested on weekends. Tapas $3–$6; main courses $11–$18. AE, DC, MC, V. Mon–Fri noon–3pm; Daily 8pm–midnight (later on Fri–Sat) SPANISH.

Despite its unfortunate name, this South Beach gem is a great place to eat and enjoy. It's looked after by a young crew of Spanish imports whose families own several popular restaurants in Madrid. If you're a non-latino, you'll probably show up before 10pm, when you're sure to get a table. After that time, especially on weekends, it's standing room only.

The gorgeous Euro crowd shows up for foot-stomping flamenco (every Wednesday, Friday, and Saturday) and an outrageous selection of tapas, as well as Miami's very best paella. Order a large portion and share it among at least four people. The garlic shrimp is tasty and aromatic, and the yellow squash stuffed with seafood and cheese is especially delicious. All the seafood, such as mussels in marinara sauce and clams in green sauce, is worth sampling. With such reasonable prices, you can taste lots of dishes and leave satisfied. Try some of the terrific sangria made with slices of fresh fruit and a subtle tinge of sweet soda.

NOA (Noodles of Asia). 801 Lincoln Rd, South Beach. ☎ **305/925-0050.** Noodles $10–$15. Sun–Thurs noon–midnight; Fri–Sat until 1am. AE MC V. ASIAN.

Another newcomer to Lincoln Road and the latest outpost in China Grill's growing empire, this Asian-inspired noodle shop attracts a trendy, good-looking crowd that comes for a variety of noodle dishes served in a stylish but uncomfortable setting. The appetizers, especially the delicate pork dumplings and the sautéed vegetables, are first-rate. Some main courses still need fine-tuning. Prices are not outrageous, but a bit high for what you get. With some work, the place could become a favorite hangout, especially thanks to an extensive and exotic selection of drinks and outrageous desserts.

Tap Tap. 819 Fifth St. (between Jefferson and Meridian aves., next to the Shell station), South Beach. ☎ **305/672-2898.** Reservations recommended in season and for special events. Main courses $8–$15. AE, DC, MC, V. Sun–Thurs 6pm–midnight; Fri–Sat 6pm–2am. HAITIAN.

The whole place looks like an overgrown tap tap, a brightly painted jitney common in Haiti. Every inch of the place is painted a neon blue, pink, or purple and every color in between, and the atmosphere is always fun. It's where the Haiti-philes and Haitians, from journalists to politicians, hang out. Even Manno Charlemagne, the mayor of Port-au-Prince, shows up when he has the time to play his brand of protest music and drink some Rhum Barbancourt.

On crowded nights, the service is impossible. I recommend going for appetizers and drinks. The *Lanbi nan citron,* a tart, marinated conch salad, is perfect with a tall tropical drink and maybe some lightly grilled goat tidbits, which are served in a savory brown sauce and are less stringy than a typical goat dish. Another supersatisfying choice is the pumpkin soup, a rich brick-colored puree of subtly seasoned pumpkin with a dash of pepper. An excellent salad of avocado, mango, and watercress is a great finish. Even if you don't stay for a full meal, try the pumpkin flan with coconut caramel sauce, an ultra-Caribbean sweet treat.

Thai House South Beach. 1137 Washington Ave., South Beach. ☎ **305/531-4841.** Reservations recommended on weekends. Main courses $7–$13 ($15–$18 for fish). AE, MC, V. Mon–Fri noon–3pm; daily 5pm–midnight. THAI.

The third in a series of successful Thai Houses in Miami, this most recent addition has perhaps the most complete and inspired menu. A whole page of tofu options for vegetarians includes massaman tofu with sweet potato, snow peas, and pineapple in a curry-based sauce. The pad Thai is nearly perfect, with a hint of fish and just a tinge of sweetness. The shrimp are few and small, but the peanut flavor and the scallions provide the required bulk. As a side, try the Thai fries, strips of *boniato* (a sweet potato-like root) dunked in coconut meat and deep fried.

The service in this quaint little storefront is spotty at best, but pleasant nonetheless. For a taste of South Beach with your meal, sit in the sidewalk area, which overlooks hectic Washington Avenue, where club-hoppers and teeny-boppers perform nightly. You'll find other Thai Houses at 715 East 9th St., Hialeah, and 2250 NE 163rd St., North Miami Beach. Try Thai Toni's across the street for a more upscale experience.

✪ **Toni's Sushi.** 1208 Washington Ave., South Beach. ☎ **305/673-9368.** Reservations recommended. Main courses $11–$22; rolls $3.50–$8.50. AE, MC, V. Daily 6pm–midnight; Fri–Sat 6pm–1am. JAPANESE/SUSHI.

One of Washington Avenue's first tenants, Toni's has withstood the test of time on fickle South Beach. By serving local fish caught daily and some imports from the Pacific and beyond, Toni has created a vast menu with options from teriyaki to hand rolls. The atmosphere is comfortable and even allows for quiet conversation—a rarity in this neighborhood. The hundreds of appetizers and rolls you can order make it a fun place to go with a group.

Consider the seaweed salad, a crunchy, salty green plant dressed with a light sesame sauce. The miso soup is hearty and a bit sweet. A good appetizer from the sushi bar is Miami Heat, which contains slabs of tuna with bits of scallion in a peppery sesame oil. I suggest skipping the entrees unless you are somehow still hungry after all the warm-ups. Many of the main dishes are good, however, like the lobster teriyaki in a dark sweet sauce over white rice.

INEXPENSIVE

Bagel Factory. 1427 Alton Rd., South Beach. ☎ **305/674-1577.** Sandwiches $1–$7. No credit cards. Mon–Sat 5:30am–5pm; Sun 5:30am–3:30pm. DELI.

There are bagel joints all over South Beach, but this narrow storefront on Alton Road is one of the best. The Rishty family makes the city's finest hand-rolled bagels in every imaginable flavor, from sunflower to banana raisin to sun-dried tomato. The bagels are deliciously chewy, but not too doughy. Add to that the phenomenal salads, including a range of decent fat-free options, and you'll understand why every weekend, the line of customers snakes out the door. Grab a spot at one of the three small inside tables or take the order to go, as most loyal patrons do.

✪ **La Sandwicherie.** 229 14th St. (behind the Amoco station), South Beach. ☎ **305/ 532-8934.** Sandwiches and salads $4.50–$7. No credit cards. Daily 9:30am–5am. Delivery 9:30am–10pm. FRENCH.

For the most incredible gourmet sandwich you've ever tasted, stop by the green-and-white awning that hides this fabulously French lunch counter. Choose pâté, saucisson, salami, prosciutto, turkey, tuna, ham, roast beef, or any of the perfect cheeses (Swiss, mozzarella, cheddar, or provolone). Vegetarians can make a meal out of the optional sandwich toppings, which include black olives, pickles, cucumbers, lettuce, onions, green or hot peppers, or tomatoes. You can have your sandwich made on delicious fresh French bread or on a relatively uninspired croissant.

If the six or so wooden stools are all taken, don't despair; you can stand and watch the tattoo artist do his work through the glass wall next door. Or douse your creation with the light tangy vinaigrette and bring lunch to the beach—that is, if you can make it 2 blocks without eating the whole thing. In addition to the cans and bottles of teas, sodas, juices, and waters, you can get coffees, fresh juices, and smoothies here.

✪ **Mrs. Mendoza's Tacos al Carbon.** 1040 Alton Rd., South Beach. ☎ **305/535-0808.** Main courses $3–$5; side dishes 79¢–$3. No credit cards. Mon–Thurs 11am–10pm; Fri–Sat 11am–11pm; Sun noon–10pm. FAST FOOD/MEXICAN.

This hard-to-spot storefront is a godsend—it's the only fresh California-style Mexican place around. The steak and chicken are grilled as you wait and then stuffed into homemade flour or corn wrappings. You order at the tile counter and pick up your dish on a plastic tray in minutes. This is a popular spot for locals.

The vegetarian offerings are huge and hearty. One of my favorites is the veggie burrito, which includes rice, black beans, cheese, lettuce, and guacamole doused in tomato salsa. They offer three types of salsa, from mild to super hot. You can see the fresh-cut cilantro and taste the superhot chiles. The chips are hand cut and flavorful, but a bit too coarse. Skip them and enjoy an order of the rich chunky guacamole with a fork.

There's another location at Doral Plaza, 9739 NW 41st St.

News Café. 800 Ocean Dr., South Beach. ☎ **305/538-6397.** Salads $4–$8; sandwiches $5–$7. AE, MC, V. Daily 24 hours. AMERICAN.

Of all the chic spots around trendy South Beach, News Café has been around the longest. Inexpensive breakfasts and cafe fare are served at about 20 perpetually congested tables. Most of the seating is outdoors, and terrace tables are most coveted.

Ocean Drive's multitude of fashion photography crews and their models meet here regularly to get the international newspapers and magazines.

The food isn't remarkable, but the people-watching is. The menu is heavy on health-oriented dishes, and includes yogurt with fruit salad, various green salads, imported cheese and meat sandwiches, and a choice of quiches.

Puerto Sagua. 700 Collins Ave., South Beach. ☎ **305/673-1115.** Main courses $8–$19; sandwiches and salads $3–$9. AE, DC, MC, V. Daily 7:30am–2am. CUBAN/SPANISH.

This dingy, brown-walled diner is one of the only old hold-outs on South Beach. Its steady stream of regulars range from *abuelitos* (little old grandfathers) to hipsters who stop in after clubbing. It has endured because the food is good, if a little greasy. Some of the less heavy dishes are a superchunky fish soup with pieces of whole flaky grouper, the chicken and seafood paella, or the marinated kingfish. Also good are most of the shrimp dishes, especially the shrimp in garlic sauce served with white rice and salad.

This is one of the most reasonably priced places left on the beach for simple, hearty fare. Don't be intimidated by the hunched older waiters in their white button shirts and black pants. Even if you don't speak Spanish, they're usually willing to do charades. Anyway, the extensive menu, which ranges from BLTs to grilled lobsters to yummy fried plantains, is translated into English. Hurry, before another boutique goes up in its place.

Sport Cafe. 560 Washington Ave., South Beach. ☎ **305/674-9700.** Reservations accepted for four or more. Main courses $8–$12; sandwiches and pizzas $4.50–$8. AE, MC, V. Daily noon–1am; sometimes earlier for coffee. ITALIAN.

Don't expect to see the latest football or baseball games at this Sports Cafe; instead, you're more likely to find a soccer match or bicycle race on the television. The Sport Cafe's owners, brothers Tonino and Paolo Doino, hail from Rome. They've put together an authentic Italian menu, listing only half a dozen entrees and a few pizzas. It can be a challenge placing your order, but definitely request a plate of fresh crushed garlic when they bring your bread and oil. I recommend asking for the day's specials and ordering one of them. Always good is the perfectly al dente penne with salmon served with a pink sauce. The eggplant parmigiano, almost always available though not on the menu, is the best in the county. For dessert, try the tiramisu, which, unlike the more common cake or pudding style, is served partially frozen, like an ice cream.

The atmosphere is rustic and young and the prices so reasonable that on some nights you may have to wait for a seat, especially for sidewalk tables.

Stephan's Gourmet Market & Cafe. 1430 Washington Ave. (at Española Way), South Beach. ☎ **305/674-1760.** Main courses $6–$12; dinner special for two with salad and a bottle of wine $24.95. AE, MC, V. Sun–Thurs 8am–midnight; Fri–Sat 8am–2am; dinner special served daily 5:30–11pm. DELI/ITALIAN.

This deli, which could be in New York's Little Italy, sells a huge assortment of fresh pastas, breads, and salads as well as cold cuts, cheeses, and grocery items. Upstairs, however, in a tiny loft used to store wine bottles, you'll find a cozy dining room with space for about 10 couples. Dinner is also served out on the sidewalk or delivered to your hotel.

A chalkboard displays the chef's special, usually a pasta dish with some kind of chicken or fish. One of my favorites is the linguini Alfredo with tender pieces of chicken breast mixed into the light cheesy sauce. While you wait, you'll want to eat baskets and baskets of the very garlicky garlic bread and get started on the bottle of wine that comes with the daily special. The red is an excellent full-bodied Italian

Merlot. (The pinot grigio, however, I found undrinkable.) If the special doesn't strike you, consider any of the other moderately priced dishes, such as rotisserie chicken with potatoes and vegetables, ziti, sausage and peppers, or eggplant parmigiano. Choose whatever looks good to you from the glass case downstairs or see what else the chef is dishing out. Other locations: 2 NE 40th St. (☎ 305/571-4070) and 19495 Biscayne Blvd. (One Turnberry Pl.; ☎ 305/932-8885).

✪ **Van Dyke Cafe.** 846 Lincoln Rd., South Beach. ☎ **305/534-3600.** Reservations recommended for evenings. Main courses $6–$11. AE, DC, MC, V. Daily 8am–1am; Fri–Sat 8am–3am. AMERICAN.

Owned by the same group that owns the successful News Café, the Van Dyke has used the same formula to guarantee its longevity on Lincoln Road. The smart,

Steak Is No Longer So Rare

Miami's always had more than its share of pricey fish houses, and don't forget the huddle of trendy restaurants serving "New World" cuisine, pasta joints, Cuban cafeterias, and fast-food drive-throughs. In this multicultural metropolis you can find cuisine from Delhi, Honduras, or Peking. But a good old-fashioned steak? It wasn't always so easy.

The old standbys like **Christy's** in Coral Gables (☎ **305/446-1400**), **Ruth's Chris** in North Miami Beach (☎ **305/949-0199**), and **The Palm** in Bay Harbor Islands (☎ **305/868-7256**) were the lonely mainstays for years. When Don Shula's took over the old Legends steakhouse in Miami Lakes in 1989 and renamed it **Shula's Steak House** (☎ **305/820-8102**), it became so popular—even in its remote location—that over the years five more branches have opened around the country. One of the latest Shula's (☎ **305/341-6565**) opened in the luxurious Alexander Hotel on Miami Beach.

And who could forget **The Forge** in Miami Beach (☎ **305/604-9798**), one of the premier dining spots in town? Its steak was voted number one in America by *Wine Spectator* in 1996. However, that was before the stampede of new restaurants came to town to capitalize on a renewed desire for flesh.

The National Cattlemen's Association reported a 41.6% increase of restaurant traffic at both casual and upscale steakhouses between 1993 and 1996. Following that trend, Miami has seen a glut of new steakhouses opening up over the years. From the **Argentine La Fusta** in Sunny Isles (☎ **305/949-0888**) to downtown's **Brazilian Porcao** (☎ **305/373-2777**) and the more upscale **Capital Grille** (☎ **305/374-4500**), it seems that every month a new one jumps in the fire.

In late 1997, New York's **Smith & Wollensky** expanded with its first restaurant outside Manhattan. This clubby elegant haven for beef lovers now occupies a scenic spot in South Pointe Park on South Beach (☎ **305/673-2800**). The venerable **Morton's of Chicago** turned up the heat in December 1997 with a luxurious spot in Downtown Miami (☎ **305/400-9990**). Another superb newcomer is the French **Brasserie Les Halles** in Coral Gables (☎ **305/461-1099**).

So far, it seems each of the establishments has found its niche and is serving up its own kind of beef in all price ranges. Less expensive spots around town include **Houston's** in North (☎ **305/947-2000**) and three **Outback Steak Houses** (☎ **305/531-1338**) in Kendall, Miami Beach, and Sunny Isles. Don Shula's also has a more casual spot in Miami Lakes called **Shula's Steak 2** (☎ **305/820-8047**).

upscale decor inside and the European sidewalk cafe outside are always crowded because of the dinerlike prices and fast, friendly service.

There is nothing too ambitious on the menu, which offers basic sandwiches, salads and, best of all, breakfast all day long. The pastas are decent, although not too exciting. House specialties include an excellent smoked salmon on thick black bread and a smooth, lemony hummus with pita chips. Also, since you're in Miami Beach, you may want to consider a nice hot bowl of cure-all chicken soup with matzo balls. In the evenings, the sounds of a talented jazz band waft down from the dark elegant club upstairs.

✪ **World Resources.** 719 Lincoln Rd., South Beach. ☎ **305/535-8987.** Main courses $6–$8; sushi hand rolls $3–$4. AE, DC, MC, V. Daily noon–midnight. SUSHI/THAI.

World Resources is an excellent little cafe and sushi bar masquerading as an Indonesian furniture and bric-a-brac store. Local hippie types and hipsters frequent this downright cheap hangout instead of cooking at home. Offerings include some of the freshest, most innovative sushi in Miami, plus many Thai specialties. The portions are generous and the cooking simple. The basil chicken, for example, is a tasty combination of white meat sautéed in a coconut sauce with subtle hints of basil and garlic. The Thai salad is heaped with fresh vegetables. Although you can get better Thai at a number of spots on the beach, you can't beat the atmosphere here, which includes dozens of outside tables surrounding a tiny pond and a stage where World Beat musicians perform nightly. From African drumming to Indian sitar playing, there is always some action at this standout on the Road. It also offers a vast selection of coffees, teas, wines, beers, and cigarettes from around the world.

3 Miami Beach: Surfside, Bal Harbour & Sunny Isles

The area north of the Art Deco District—from about 21st Street to 163rd Street—had its heyday in the 1950s when its huge hotels and gambling halls blocked the view of the ocean. Now, many of the old hotels have been converted into condos or budget lodgings and the bay-front mansions renovated by and for wealthy entrepreneurs, families, and speculators. The area now has many more residents, albeit seasonal, than visitors. On the culinary front, the result is a handful of super-expensive, traditional restaurants and a number of value-oriented spots.

VERY EXPENSIVE

✪ **The Forge Restaurant.** 432 Arthur Godfrey Rd. (41st St.), Miami Beach. ☎ **305/538-8533.** Reservations required. Main courses $19–$30. AE, DC, MC, V. Sun–Thurs 6pm–midnight; Fri–Sat 6pm–1am. AMERICAN.

English oak paneling and Tiffany glass suggest high prices and haute cuisine, and that's exactly what you get from The Forge. Each elegant dining room possesses its own character and features high ceilings, ornate chandeliers, and high-quality European artwork. The most intimate room is the library in the back. The Forge attracts a mix of young, moneyed Miamians, well-dressed Euros, and Saudi royalty. The atmosphere is elegant but not too stuffy, especially on Wednesday night, when the singles scene shows up for mingling at the bar and dancing next door at Jimmy's.

Like the rest of the menu, appetizers are mostly classics, from Beluga caviar to baked onion soup to shrimp cocktail and escargot. When they're in season, order the stone crabs. For the main course, any of the seafood, chicken, or veal dishes are recommendable, but The Forge is especially known for its steaks. In fact, in 1996, *Wine Spectator* magazine voted the Super Steak the Best in America. Finally, The Forge still has one of Miami's best wine lists and an extensive cellar. Ask for a tour.

EXPENSIVE

Carpaccio. 9700 Collins Ave (97th St., in Bal Harbour shops), Bal Harbour, ☎ **305/867-7777.** Reservations suggested. Main courses $15–$20; Pastas $12–$15. AE MC V. Daily 11:30am–11pm. ITALIAN.

Serving up some of the best northern Italian cuisine in Miami's ritziest shopping mall, this pricey and elegant cafe packs them in for elegant handmade pastas, pizzas and, of course, carpaccio in a dozen variations. Service is better than at most area restaurants, though when its really busy, you'll find it hard to attract the attention of the friendly waiters who are scurrying amid the crowds. The feel is casual though diners tend to dress in designer outfits. Some of them actually deign to wait in line on the sidewalk for a table—imagine that!

✪ **Crystal Café.** 726 41st St., Miami Beach. ☎ **305/673-8266.** Reservations recommended on weekends. Main courses $11–$25. AE, DC, DISC, MC, V. Tues–Thurs 5–10pm; Fri–Sat 5–11pm. CONTINENTAL/NEW WORLD.

The setting is sparse, with Lucite salt and pepper grinders and a bottle of wine as the only centerpiece on each of the 15 or so tables. I promise you won't need the seasoning. Chef Klime has done it all with the help of his affable wife and a superb wait staff. Enjoy his unique sparkle at this little-known hideaway, which attracts stars like Julio Iglesias and other discriminating guests.

With approximately 30 entrees, including a few nightly specials, I can't figure out how each appears so perfectly prepared and beautifully presented. The shrimp-cake appetizer, for example, is the size of a bread plate and rests on top of a small mound of lightly sautéed watercress and mushrooms. Surrounding the delicately breaded disc are concentric circles of beautiful sauces. The veal marsala is served in a luscious brown sauce thickened not with heavy cream or flour but with delicate vegetable broth and a hearty mix of mushrooms. Most main courses come with a choice of three side dishes, such as zucchini, carrots, mashed potatoes, or pasta. The osso buco is a masterpiece.

The Palm. 9650 E. Bay Harbor Dr., Bay Harbor Island. ☎ **305/868-7256.** Reservations highly recommended. Main courses $17–$29. AE, CB, DC, MC, V. Daily 5–11pm. From Collins Ave., turn west onto 96th St.; at Bal Harbour Shops, go over a small bridge, and turn right onto East Bay Harbor Dr. The restaurant is half a block down on the left. CONTINENTAL.

You feel like you're in New York in this dark clubby steakhouse known for enormous sirloins and jumbo Maine lobsters. The same celebrity caricatures and photos adorn the walls as in the other Palms in Los Angeles and New York. There are currently more than a dozen branches throughout the country, all known for pleasing a demanding corporate and tourist clientele.

You can't go wrong with the limited, simple menu filled with old standbys, such as Caesar salad, shrimp cocktail, clams oreganata, salmon, broiled chicken, and veal. A selection of steak ranges from chopped to filet mignon. The prices are as big as the portions. You'll find more martini drinkers than health-conscious types here.

MODERATE

Cafe Prima Pasta. 414 71st St. (half a block east of the Byron movie theater), Miami Beach. ☎ **305/867-0106.** Reservations not accepted. Main courses $12–$14; pastas $7–$9. No credit cards. Mon–Thurs noon–midnight; Fri noon–1am; Sat 1pm–1am. Sun 5pm–midnight. ITALIAN.

Here's another tiny pasta joint that serves phenomenal homemade noodles with good old Italian sauces, such as carbonara, dioliva, putanesca, and pomodoro. There are only 30 seats, so you might feel a bit cramped, but the crowd is generally a

Miami Beach Dining

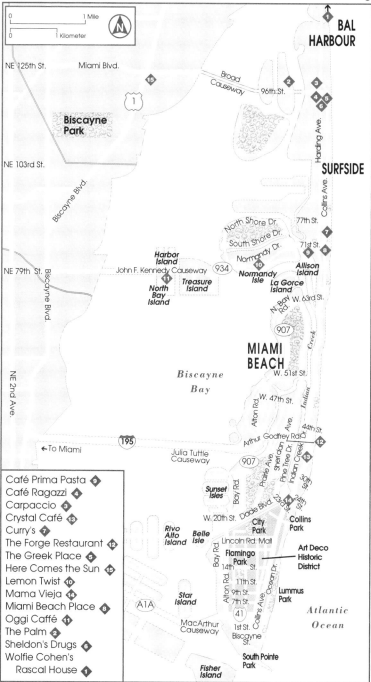

BAL HARBOUR

SURFSIDE

NE 125th St.　Miami Blvd.

Biscayne Park

NE 103rd St.

Broad Causeway

96th St.

Harding Ave.

Collins Ave.

77th St.

North Shore Dr.

South Shore Dr.

Normandy Dr.

71st St.

Harbor Island

John F. Kennedy Causeway

NE 79th St.

Biscayne Blvd.

Treasure Island

North Bay Island

Normandy Isle

Allison Island

La Gorce Island

N. Bay Rd.

W. 63rd St.

MIAMI BEACH

Indian Creek

W. 51st St.

Biscayne Bay

W. 47th St.

Alton Rd.

Sheridan Ave.

Pine Tree Dr.

Indian Creek Dr.

44th St.

Arthur Godfrey Rd.

30th St.

24th St.

23rd St.

NE 2nd Ave.

To Miami

Julia Tuttle Causeway

Sunset Isles

Bay Rd.

Prairie Ave.

Dade Blvd.

Rivo Alto Island

Belle Isle

W. 20th St.

Lincoln Rd. Mall

City Park

Collins Park

Flamingo Park

14th St.

11th St.

9th St.

7th St.

Art Deco Historic District

Lummus Park

Bay Rd.

Alton Rd.

Collins Ave.

Ocean Dr.

Star Island

Atlantic Ocean

A1A

MacArthur Causeway

1st St.

Biscayne St.

South Pointe Park

Fisher Island

Café Prima Pasta 9
Café Ragazzi 4
Carpaccio 3
Crystal Café 13
Curry's 7
The Forge Restaurant 12
The Greek Place 5
Here Comes the Sun 15
Lemon Twist 10
Mama Vieja 14
Miami Beach Place 8
Oggi Caffé 11
The Palm 2
Sheldon's Drugs 6
Wolfie Cohen's
　Rascal House 1

pleasant, young, laid-back set. The stuffed agnolotti with either tomato or pesto, spinach, and ricotta are so delicate and flavorful that you'll think you're eating dessert. Speaking of which, you'll want to try the apple tart with a pale golden caramel sauce. Ask for it à la mode and plan to come back again for more.

Its location, closer to Collins Avenue, makes this place more popular than the superior Oggi just a few miles west. Be prepared to stand in line.

Cafe Ragazzi. 9500 Harding Ave. (on corner of 95th St.), Surfside. ☎ **305/866-4495.** Reservations accepted for four or more. Main courses $11–$15; MC, V. Mon–Fri 11:30am–3pm and 5:30–11pm; Sat–Sun 5:30–11pm. ITALIAN.

A relative newcomer in a neighborhood of old-time delis and diners, this little Italian cafe, with its rustic decor and a handsome wait staff, enjoys great success for its tasty simple pastas. The spicy putanesca sauce with a subtle hint of fish is perfectly prepared, with just enough bits of tomato to give it some weight. Also recommended is the salmon with radicchio. You can choose from many decent salads and carpacci, too. Lunch specials are a real steal at $7, including soup, salad, and daily pasta. The mostly Italian/Argentinean staff is efficient, although sometimes limited in their ability to communicate. Expect a wait on weekend nights.

Lemon Twist. 908 71st St. (on 79th St. Causeway), Miami Beach/Normandy Isle. ☎ **305/868-2075.** Reservations suggested on weekends. Main courses $8–$18; pastas $7–$9.50. AE, MC, V. In season, daily 6pm–midnight; off-season Tues–Sun 6pm–midnight. FRENCH.

This hip little French bar and restaurant in a burgeoning neighborhood is certainly worth a visit. The house specialties are salads and seafood. Both are quite good, but even better is the cozy atmosphere both inside and on the outside patio. The lamb shank and the chicken with lemon and cream sauce are two of the tastier dishes, and my favorite salad here features a mound of herbed goat cheese in a puff pastry shell over a bed of fresh baby greens dressed in a delicate but spicy vinaigrette. The pastas, on the other hand, are not even worth a try—most are overcooked and others underseasoned. An original touch: Complimentary lemon vodka shots are offered after each meal.

✪ **Mama Vieja.** 235 23rd St. (just west of Collins Ave.), South Beach. ☎ **305/538-2400.** Reservations accepted, but not necessary. $7–$18 main courses. AE, CB, DC, DISC, MC, V. Daily noon–midnight. COLOMBIAN.

This funky Colombian hangout is a real find. It serves supremely fresh national specialties in a setting that might well be the backdrop for a Latin American spaghetti Western. Brightly painted walls and elevated porches look out onto a large-screen TV showing music videos from the old country. The walls and ceilings are decorated with hundreds of hats that have been donated by customers and signed in exchanged for a free meal. Bring in an interesting hat and mention it to the server before placing your order so they can bring you to the attention of the owner.

Start with an avocado salad and rich meat-filled empanadas served with spicy sauce or a creamy fish soup and green plantains stuffed with mixed seafood with large chunks of shellfish and fresh filets. The best dishes are seafood selections—one outrageous dish is called *Pargo Rojo Estofado a la Mama Vieja,* a red snapper stuffed with a super creamy and delicate seafood sauce in a rice base. It's made for two ($29.95), but if you order the *Corvina a la Mama Vieja* for one ($12.95), you can try the same rich stuffing in a slightly smaller fish for much less money. All the dishes here are worth trying and so reasonably priced it's easy to order a lot. Try to save room for the milky sweet desserts and a good strong coffee—you'll need it if you want to dance all night. Next door is a popular disco and nightclub, Studio 23 (see chapter 10, "Miami After Dark").

✪ **Oggi Caffe.** 1740 79th St. Causeway (in the White Star shopping center next to the Bagel Cafe), North Bay Village. ☎ **305/866-1238.** Reservations accepted. Main courses $12–$20; pastas $8–$10. AE, CB, DC, MC, V. Mon–Fri 11:30am–2:30pm; daily 6–11pm. ITALIAN.

Tucked away in a tiny strip mall on the 79th Street Causeway, this neighborhood favorite makes fresh pastas daily. Each one, from the agnolotti stuffed with fresh spinach and ricotta to the wire-thin spaghettini, is tender and tasty. A hearty *pasta e fagiola* is filled with beans and vegetables and could almost be a meal. I also recommend the daily soups, especially the creamy spinach soup, when it's on the menu. Though you could fill up on the starters, the entrees, especially the grilled dishes, are superb. The salmon is served on a bed of spinach with a light lemon-butter sauce. The place is small and a bit rushed, but it's well worth the slight discomfort for this authentic, moderately priced food.

Wolfie Cohen's Rascal House. 17190 Collins Ave., Sunny Isles. ☎ **305/947-4581.** Omelettes and sandwiches $4–$13; other dishes $5–$14. AE, MC, V. Open 24 hours. DELI.

Open since 1954 and still going strong, this historic, nostalgic culinary extravaganza is one of Miami Beach's greatest traditions. Simple tables and booths as well as plenty of patrons fill the airy 425-seat dining room. The menu is as huge as the portions; try the corned beef, schmaltz herring, brisket, kreplach, chicken soup, or other authentic Jewish staples. Take-out service is available.

INEXPENSIVE

Curry's. 7433 Collins Ave., Miami Beach. ☎ **305/866-1571.** Reservations accepted. $8–$17, including appetizer, main course, dessert, and coffee. MC, V. Daily 4–10pm. AMERICAN.

Established in 1937, this large dining room on the ocean side of Collins Avenue is one of Miami Beach's oldest restaurants. Neither the restaurant's name nor the Polynesian wall decorations are indicative of its offerings, which are straightforwardly American and reminiscent of the area's heyday. Broiled and fried fish dishes are available, but the best selections, including steak, chicken, and ribs, come off the open charcoal grill perched by the front window. Prices are incredibly reasonable here, and all include an appetizer, soup, or salad, as well as a potato or vegetable, dessert, and coffee or tea.

✪ **The Greek Place.** 233 95th St. (between Collins and Harding aves.), Surfside. ☎ **305/866-9628.** Main courses $5–$6. No credit cards. Mon–Fri 10am–6pm. GREEK.

The only drawback of this tiny hole in the wall is that it's open only on weekdays. It's a little diner with sparkling white walls and about 10 wooden stools that serves fantastic Greek and American diner-style food. Daily specials like pastitsio, chicken alcyone, and roast turkey with all the fixings are big lunchtime draws for locals working in the area. Typical Greek dishes like shish kebab, souvlakis, and gyros are cooked to perfection as you wait. Even the hamburger, prime ground beef delicately spiced and fresh grilled, is exemplary.

Miami Beach Place. 6954 Collins Ave., Miami Beach. ☎ **305/866-8661.** Main courses (served with spaghetti, vegetables, or rice and garlic rolls) $10–$13; pizzas and pastas $7–$16. MC, V. Sun–Fri 6pm–midnight; Sat 1pm–midnight. ITALIAN/PIZZA.

This Brazilian-owned pizza parlor is full most weekends, not only because of its good inexpensive pastas and pizzas, but also because of the fun Brazilian bands that play most weekend nights after 9pm. By midnight, the place is packed with Portuguese-speaking dancers who enjoy a late-night buffet and lots of wine and beer. I think the light garlicky rolls wrapped in golden twists are addictive. While the pizza tends to be too cheesy for my taste, its toppings are fresh instead of the canned variety offered at other places. If you've never tasted the ubiquitous Brazilian soda, Guaraná, I suggest trying a sip; it's like a rich ginger ale with not as much zing.

Sheldon's Drugs. 9501 Harding Ave., Surfside. ☎ **305/866-6251.** Main courses $4.50–$5; soups and sandwiches $2–$5. AE, DISC, MC, V. Mon–Sat 7am–9pm; Sun 7am–4pm. AMERICAN.

This typical old-fashioned drugstore counter was a favorite breakfast spot of Isaac Bashevis Singer. Consider stopping into this historic site for a good piece of pie and a side of history. According to legend, he was sitting at Sheldon's, eating a bagel and eggs, when his wife got the call in 1978 that he had won the Nobel Prize for Literature. The menu hasn't changed much since then. You can get eggs and oatmeal and a good tuna melt. A blue-plate special might be generic spaghetti and meatballs or grilled frankfurters. The food is pretty basic, but you can't beat the prices.

4 Key Biscayne

Key Biscayne has some of the world's nicest beaches, hotels, and parks, yet it's not known for great food. Most visitors eat at the island's largest hotel, where the food is reliable if not outstanding. Locals, or "Key rats" as they're known, tend to go off-island for meals or take-out, but here are some of the best on-the-island choices.

EXPENSIVE

Rusty Pelican. 3201 Rickenbacker Causeway, Key Biscayne. ☎ **305/361-3818.** Reservations recommended. Main courses $16–$20. AE, CB, DC, MC, V. Daily 11:30am–4pm; Sun–Thurs 5–11pm; Fri–Sat 5pm–midnight. CONTINENTAL.

The Pelican's private tropical walkway leads over a lush waterfall into one of the most romantic dining rooms in the city, located right on beautiful blue-green Biscayne Bay. The restaurant's windows look out over the water onto the sparkling stalagmites of Miami's magnificent downtown. Inside, quiet wicker paddle fans whirl overhead and saltwater fish swim in pretty tableside aquariums.

The restaurant's surf-and-turf menu features conservatively prepared prime steaks, veal, shrimp, and lobster. The food is good, but the atmosphere is even better, especially at sunset, when the view over the city is magical.

Stefano's. 24 Crandon Blvd., Key Biscayne. ☎ **305/361-7007.** Reservations recommended on weekends. Main courses $15–$23; pastas $11–$15. AE, DC, MC, V. Mon–Fri 11:30am–2:30pm; Sun–Thurs 6–11pm; Fri–Sat 6pm–12:30am. Disco open later. ITALIAN.

For retro-elegance, Stefano's has no match. Its restaurant and disco share the same strobe-lit atmosphere. Food is traditional and reliable, if a little pricey. You'll find an older country club crowd here in the evenings enjoying steaks, pastas, and seafood. One of the best entrees is the Delfino Livornese, a dolphin (not Flipper—a type of saltwater fish) sautéed with a spicy sauce of tomato, olives, capers, and onions. Stefano's also serves some rare game, such as guinea hen in wine sauce and quail wrapped in pancetta. I recommend sticking with the pastas and fish.

After 7:30pm, the band starts playing American pop and Latin favorites. Some nights you feel as if you accidentally happened upon your long-lost cousin's wedding,

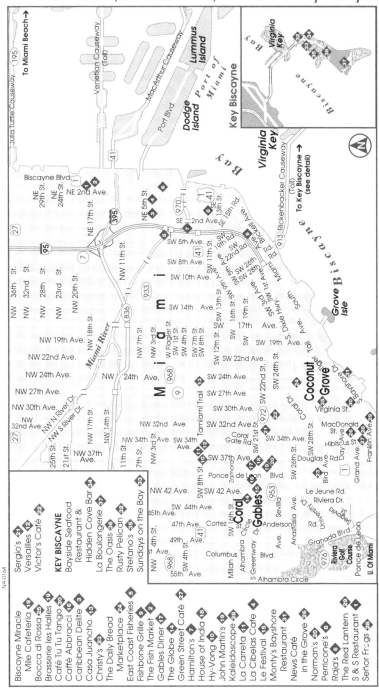

To Miami Beach→

Julia Tuttle Causeway (195)

Venetian Causeway (Toll)

MacArthur Causeway

Lummus Island

Port of Miami

Dodge Island

Port Blvd

Virginia Key

Biscayne Bay

Key Biscayne

To Key Biscayne → (see detail)

Rickenbacker Causeway (Toll)

Biscayne Bay

Grove Isle

Coconut Grove

Biscayne Blvd.

NE 29th St. NE 24th St.
NE 2nd Ave.

NE 17th St.

NE 5th St.

395

SE 2nd Ave.

SW 5th Ave.

SW 8th Ave.

SW 10th Ave.

SW 14th Ave.

SW 17th Ave.

SW 19th Ave.

SW 22nd Ave.

SW 24th Ave.

SW 27th Ave.

SW 30th Ave.

SW 32nd Ave.

SW 34th Ave.

SW 37th Ave

Ponce de Leon Blvd.

Coral Gate Rd.

Virginia St.

MacDonald St.

Hibiscus St.

Douglas Rd.

Grand Ave.

Franklin Ave.

Bird Ave.

Le Jeune Rd.

Riviera Dr.

Coral Gables

Granada Blvd.

Ponce de Leon

Riviera Golf Course

U. of Miami

Tamiami Trail

Coral Dr.

Bayshore Dr.

Miami River

NW 18th St.

NW 19th Ave.

NW 22nd Ave.

NW 24th Ave.

NW 27th Ave.

NW 30th Ave.

NW 32nd Ave.

NW 37th Ave.

NW 42 Ave.

SW 42 Ave.

SW 44th Ave.

47th Ave.

49th Ave.

Columbus Blvd.

55th Ave.

Miami

NW 36th St. NW 32nd St. NW 28th St. NW 23rd St. NW 20th St.

KEY BISCAYNE	
Sergio's	42
Versailles	12
Victor's Café	22
Bayside Seafood Restaurant & Hidden Cove Bar	34
La Boulangerie	32
The Oasis	35
Rusty Pelican	42
Stefano's	45
Sundays on the Bay	37

Biscayne Miracle Mile Cafeteria	19
Bocca di Rossa	25
Brasserie les Halles	19
Café Tu Tu Tango	40
Caffé Abbracci	16
Caribbean Delite	3
Casa Juancho	13
Christy's	43
The Daily Bread Marketplace	24
East Coast Fisheries	5
Fishbone Grille	9
The Fish Market	2
The Globe	11
Green Street Café	27
Hamilton's	4
House of India	18
Hy-Vong	10
John Martin's	19
Kaleidoscope	28
La Carreta	4
La Cibelas Cafe	4
Le Festival	14
Monty's Bayshore Restaurant	45
News Café in the Grove	20
Norman's	8
Perricone's	6
Raja's	6
The Red Lantern	23
S & S Restaurant	1
Señor Frog's	28

NA-0164

97

as you watch the parade of taffeta dresses and tipsy uncles. Stefano's has continued to do well over time because of its dependable service and kitchen.

Sundays on the Bay. 5420 Crandon Blvd., Key Biscayne. ☎ **305/361-6777.** Reservations accepted; recommended for Sun brunch. Main courses $15–$24; Sun brunch $18.95. AE, CB, DC, MC, V. Daily 11:30am–11:45pm; Sun brunch 11am–4pm. AMERICAN.

Although its food is fine, Sundays is really a fun tropical bar that features an unbeatable view of Downtown, Coconut Grove, and the Sunday's marina. The menu features local favorites—grouper, tuna, snapper, and good shellfish in season. Competent renditions of such classic dishes as oysters Rockefeller, shrimp scampi, and lobster fra diablo are recommendable. Particularly popular is the Sunday brunch, when a buffet the size of Bimini attracts the city's in-crowd.

The lively bar stays open all week until midnight and weekends until 2am, with a DJ spinning most nights from 9pm.

INEXPENSIVE

✪ **Bayside Seafood Restaurant and Hidden Cove Bar.** 3501 Rickenbacker Causeway, Key Biscayne. ☎ **305/361-0808.** Reservations accepted for 15 or more. Appetizers, salads, and sandwiches $4.50–$6; platters $7–$13. AE, MC, V. Sun–Thurs 11:30am–10:30pm; Fri–Sat 11:30am–midnight; disco on weekends ($5 cover) 11pm–4am. SEAFOOD.

Known by locals as "the Hut," this ramshackle restaurant and bar is a laid-back outdoor tiki hut and terrace that serves pretty good sandwiches and fish platters on paper plates. A blackboard lists the latest catches, which can be prepared blackened, fried, broiled, or in a garlic sauce. I prefer the blackened, which is supercrusty, spicy, and dark. The fish dip is wonderfully smoky and moist, if a little heavy on mayonnaise. Lately, the Hut has been offering happy hours on weekday evenings with open bar and snacks for $25 per person—a great deal if you'll be having more than a couple of cocktails.

But if you come here, bring bug spray or ask the servers for some (they usually keep packets behind the bar). For some reason, this place is plagued by mosquitoes even when the rest of town is not. Local fishers and yacht owners share this rustic outpost with equal enthusiasm and loyalty.

✪ **La Boulangerie.** 328 Crandon Blvd. (in Eckerd's shopping mall), Key Biscayne. ☎ **305/ 361-0281.** Sandwiches and salads $5–$7. MC, V. Mon–Sat 7:30am–8pm; Sun 7:30am–6pm. FRENCH.

Beware. You'll stop into this inconspicuous French bakery for a loaf of bread and find yourself walking out with an armload of the freshest sandwiches, salads, groceries, and pastries anywhere. You can also sit and enjoy a great breakfast, lunch, or early dinner with the jet-set in their designer sweatsuits. There are about 15 tables inside where diners enjoy vegetarian omelets, gourmet sandwiches, and dangerous desserts. The prosciutto and goat cheese sandwich on crusty French bread is unbeatable—there must be something in the mustard.

The friendly proprietors behind the counter will no doubt talk you into a heavenly fruit tart, like the pointy-tipped apricot tart with plump fruit halves painted with a thin layer of sweet glaze. Try any of the cakes or rustic breads, too.

The Oasis. 19 Harbor Dr. (on corner of Crandon), Key Biscayne. ☎ **305/361-5709.** Main courses $4–$12; sandwiches $3–$4. No credit cards. Daily 6am–9pm. CUBAN.

Everyone, from the city's mayor to the local handymen, meet for delicious paella and Cuban sandwiches at this little shack. They gather around the little window or inside at the few tables for superpowerful *cafesitos* and rich *croquetas*. It's slightly dingy, but the food is good and cheap.

5 Downtown

Downtown Miami is a large sprawling area divided by the Brickell bridge into two distinct areas: Brickell Avenue and the bay-front area near Biscayne Boulevard. You shouldn't walk from one to the other—it's quite a distance and unsafe at night. Convenient Metromover stops do adjoin the areas, so for a quarter, it's better to hop on the scenic sky-tram (closed after midnight).

EXPENSIVE

Hamilton's. 400 SE 2nd Ave. (in the Hyatt Regency Hotel), Miami. ☎ **305/381-6160.** Reservations recommended. Main courses $17–$28. AE, MC, V. Mon–Fri 11am–3pm and Mon–Thurs 6–11pm; Fri–Sat until midnight. CONTINENTAL

A plush dining room outfitted with mahogany and leopard prints, professional service, and elegant food raises hotel dining to a new level. Hamilton's (as in George) gives visitors everything they could ask for—at a price. From the coconut prawns with horseradish orange marmalade to the herb-crusted rack of lamb and prosciutto-wrapped tuna, each dish is superb. Of course, since the tan man has his own brand of cigars, you'd also expect a cigar bar and you won't be disappointed. Nightly jazz and a great selection of martinis enhances the experience.

MODERATE

✪ **East Coast Fisheries.** 360 W. Flagler St., Downtown (south). ☎ **305/372-1300.** Reservations recommended. Main courses $9–$25. AE, MC, V. Daily 11am–10pm. From I-95 South, exit at NW 8th St. (Exit 5A). Drive straight to NW 3rd St. and turn right. The next block is North River Dr. Turn left, and you'll see the restaurant 3 blocks down on the right side. SEAFOOD.

East Coast Fisheries is a no-nonsense retail market and restaurant offering a terrific variety of the freshest fish available. The dozen or so plain wood tables are surrounded by refrigerated glass cases filled with snapper, salmon, mahimahi, trout, tuna, crabs, oysters, lobsters, and the like. The absolutely huge menu features every fish imaginable, cooked the way you want it—grilled, fried, stuffed, Cajun-style, Florentine, hollandaise, or blackened. However, the smell of frying grease detracts from the otherwise quaint old Miami feel right on the riverfront. Service is fast, but good prices and good food can mean long lines on weekends.

✪ **Fishbone Grille.** 650 S. Miami Ave. (SW 7th Ave., next to Tobacco Rd.), Downtown. ☎ **305/530-1915.** Reservations recommended for 6 or more. Entrees $8–$18; pizzas and pastas $9–$20. AE, CB, DC, DISC, MC, V. Mon–Thurs 11:30am–10pm; Fri 11:30am–11pm; Sat 5–11pm. SEAFOOD.

This is by far Miami's best and most reasonably priced seafood restaurant. Located in a small strip mall it shares with Tobacco Road, this sensational fish shop prepares dozens of outstanding specials daily. The atmosphere is nothing to speak of, although at one cool table you can stare into a fish tank.

Try the excellent seviche, which has just enough spice to give it a zing, yet doesn't overwhelm the fresh fish flavor. The stews, crab cakes, and all the starters are superb. If you like a nice Caribbean flavor, try the *jerk Covina* (the Biblical fish) or one of the excellent dolphin specialties. There's another Fishbone Grille in Coral Gables at 1450 S. Dixie Highway (☎ 305/668-3033).

INEXPENSIVE

✪ **Caribbean Delite.** 236 NE First Ave. (across the street from Miami Dade Community College), Downtown. ☎ **305/381-9254.** Menu items $5.50–$9; full meals $4–$7. AE, MC, V. Mon–Sat 8:30am–7pm; Sun 8:30am–4pm. JAMAICAN.

You'd never spot this tiny storefront diner if you weren't looking for it, but you might smell it from the sidewalk. The aroma of succulent jerk chicken or pork beckons regulars back over and over again. Try the Jamaican specialties, such as the oxtail stew or the curried goat, tender tasty pieces of meat on the bone in a spicy yellow sauce. The kitchen can be stingy with its spectacular sauces, leaving the dishes a bit dry, so ask for an extra helping on the side, and they are happy to oblige. Also, if you come early in the day, you can get a taste of Jamaica's national dish, salt fish and ackee (usually served for breakfast). Ask chef-owner Carol Whyte to tell you the story of the National dish of her homeland made with "brain fruit" or quiz one of the many Jamaicans who stop in while they are in port off the cruise ships a few blocks away.

La Cibeles Cafe. 105 NE 3rd Ave. (1 block west of Biscayne Blvd.), Downtown. ☎ **305/ 577-3454.** Main courses $5–$9. No credit cards. Mon–Sat 7:30am–7:30pm. CUBAN.

This typical Latin diner serves some of the best food in town. Just by looking at the line that runs out the door every afternoon between noon and 2pm, you can see that you're not the first to discover it. For about $5, you can have a huge and filling meal. Pay attention to the daily lunch specials and go with them. A pounded, tender chicken breast (*pechuga*) is smothered in sautéed onions and served with rice and beans and a salad. The trout and the roast pork are both very good. When available, try the *ropa vieja,* a shredded beef dish delicately spiced and served with peas and rice.

Perricone's Marketplace. 15 SE 10th St. (corner of S. Miami Ave.), Downtown. ☎ **305/ 374-9693.** Sandwiches $5.50–$7; pastas $10–$15. AE MC V. Daily 7:30am–around midnight (closing depends on customer demand). ITALIAN.

A large selection of groceries and wine, plus an outdoor porch for dining makes this one of the most welcoming spots downtown. Sundays offer buffet brunches and all-you-can-eat dinners, too. But, it's most popular weekdays at noon when the suit-types show up for delectable sandwiches, quick and delicious pastas, and hearty salads.

Raja's. 243 E. Flagler St. (in the Galeria International mall), Downtown. ☎ **305/539-9551.** Menu items $3–$6; specials, including salad, rice, and vegetable side dishes $5. No credit cards. Thurs–Tues 9am–6:30pm; Sun 9am–4:30pm. INDIAN/FAST FOOD.

Nearly impossible to find, this tiny counter in the hustling Downtown food court serves some of the feistiest chicken stews and vegetarian dishes in Miami. It's surrounded by mostly Brazilian fast-food places packed with tour groups on shopping sprees.

If you like it spicy, try the rich Masala Spicy Chili Chicken. For vegetarians, the heaping platters of dal, cauliflower, eggplant, broccoli, and chickpeas are a valuable find. For those who know to request them, there are half a dozen tasty condiments, including lemon chutney with fresh orange rinds, bright green cilantro sauce, and glistening gold mango chutney that will complement the rough stews and tasty soups. The *Masala Dosa* (rice crepes stuffed with vegetable mash) is a filling lunch or dinner made to order.

S & S Restaurant. 1757 NE Second Ave., Downtown. ☎ **305/373-4291.** Main courses $5–$11. No credit cards. Mon–Fri 6am–4pm; Sat–Sun 6am–2 or 2:30pm (later on Heat game nights). AMERICAN/DINER FARE.

This tiny chrome-and-linoleum-counter restaurant in the middle of Downtown looks like a truck stop. But locals have been coming back since it opened in 1938. Expect a wait at lunchtime while the mostly male clientele, from lawyers to linemen, wait patiently for huge quantities of old-fashioned fast food.

You'll get a slice of Miami history along with your pie at S & S. Although the neighborhood has become pretty undesirable, the food—basic diner fare with some excellent stews and soups—hasn't changed in years. It's one of the only places in town I know that serves creamed chicken on toast. Also good when it's on the specials board is the stuffed cabbage roll in a pale brown sauce. In addition to cheap breakfasts, the diner serves up some of the most comfortable comfort food in Miami.

6 Little Havana

The main artery of Little Havana is a busy commercial strip called Southwest 8th Street, or Calle Ocho. Auto body shops, cigar factories, and furniture stores line this street, and on every corner there seems to be a pass-through window serving superstrong Cuban coffee and snacks. In addition, many of the Cuban, Dominican, Nicaraguan, Peruvian, and Latin American immigrants have opened full-scale restaurants ranging from intimate candlelit establishments to bustling stand-up lunch counters.

VERY EXPENSIVE

Victor's Cafe. 2340 SW 32nd Ave. (1 block south of Coral Way), Little Havana. ☎ **305/ 445-1313.** Reservations recommended. Main courses $19–$32. AE, DC, MC, V. Sun–Thurs noon–midnight; Fri–Sat noon–1am. CUBAN.

At Victor's, you'll get good food in an upscale setting—it's a place for tourists and celebrations. Locals say it's overpriced. Strolling guitarists add an air of romance to this kitschy old Havana-style restaurant. Lively salsa music wafts through the regal dining room where attentive waiters look after most details. Stick around for the wild cabaret most nights after 11pm. Ask to sit on El Patio where oversized umbrellas shade you from the sun and create a private little cocoon overlooking the lush courtyard.

The cooking takes liberties with Cuban classics with generally good results. Some of the best dishes are the fish and shrimp plates, all served with rice and beans. My favorite appetizer is the *snapper ceviche* marinated in Cachucha pepper and lime juice. The beef dishes are also good. The *bistec alo Victor con tamal en balsa* is a tender oak-grilled top sirloin served with Cuban-style polenta.

MODERATE

✪ **Casa Juancho.** 2436 SW 8th St. (just east of SW 27 Ave.), Little Havana. ☎ **305/ 642-2452.** Reservations recommended, but not accepted Fri–Sat after 8pm. Tapas $6–$8; main courses $15–$34. AE, CB, DC, DISC, MC, V. Sun–Thurs noon–midnight; Fri–Sat noon–1am. SPANISH.

One of Miami's finest Hispanic restaurants, Casa Juancho offers an ambitious menu of excellently prepared main dishes and tapas. The several dining rooms are decorated with traditional Spanish furnishings and enlivened nightly by strolling Spanish musicians. Try not to be frustrated with the older staff that don't speak English or respond quickly to your subtle glance. They are used to an aggressive clientele.

I suggest ordering lots of *tapas,* small dishes of Spanish "finger food." Some of the best include mixed seafood vinaigrette, fresh shrimp in hot garlic sauce, and fried calamari rings. A few entrees stand out, like roast suckling pig, baby eels in garlic and olive oil, and Iberian-style snapper.

INEXPENSIVE

✪ **Hy-Vong.** 3458 SW 8th St. (between 34th and 35th aves.), Little Havana. ☎ **305/ 446-3674.** Reservations not accepted. Main courses $8–$15. No credit cards. Wed–Sun 6–11pm. Closed 2 weeks in Aug. VIETNAMESE.

Cuban Coffee

Despite the fact that a dozen Starbucks have descended on the city in 1999, locals still rely on the many Cuban cafeterias for their daily fix.

Cuban coffee is a long-standing tradition in Miami. You'll find it served from the take-out windows of hundreds of *cafeterías* or *luncherías* around town, especially in Little Havana, Downtown, Hialeah, and the beaches. Depending on where you are and what you want, you'll spend between 40¢ and $1.50 per cup.

The best *café cubano* has a rich layer of foam on top formed when the hot espresso shoots from the machine into the sugar below. The result is the caramelly, sweet, potent concoction that's a favorite of locals of all nationalities.

To partake, you've just got to learn how to ask for it *en español.*

The most commonly ordered take-out coffee is the *colada.* This large cup of sweet black coffee is served in a Styrofoam cup with five or six thimble-size plastic cups on top, meant to be shared with friends or co-workers.

If you're alone, you'll probably want a *café* or *cafecito,* a thimble-size cup of the same thick black espresso with lots of sugar. It's usually swallowed in one quick gulp. Unless you ask for it to go (*para llevar*), you'll probably get it in a miniature ceramic cup and saucer. Don't be fooled by the small size. With regard to caffeine, one shot of this stuff is equal to two or three mugs of the American version.

For the less brave, there is the *cortado* or *cortadito,* the same dose of strong coffee cut with a bit of steamed milk.

Even more mild is the *café con leche,* a large cup of steamed milk with a single shot of coffee. You can ask for it *oscuro* (dark) or *claro* (light), but count on it being sweet. This coffee is especially popular at breakfast, when it often accompanies *pan tostada,* a long hunk of grilled, flattened, and buttered bread that you dunk in the cup, donut style.

To avoid the sweetness, order your coffee *sin azúcar,* without sugar, or con *poco azúcar,* with a little sugar—but even then, you'll have to be vigilant. The person behind the counter has probably heaped thousands of spoons of sugar over the years. It's an automatic motion. Ask twice and watch closely. If you want artificial sweetener, ask for *azúcar de dieta.*

You can even find decaffeinated coffee, *café descafeínado,* in some shops. Café Bustelo, the most ubiquitous brand of Cuban coffee, began marketing a neutered version of its famous espresso several years ago. It's not bad, but it certainly doesn't have the same effect as the real stuff. Low-fat or skim milk is harder to find. But just say skim and they'll give it to you if they've got it.

Finally, if you insist, you can usually get a cup of American coffee, *café americano,* in a Latin restaurant, although I wouldn't advise it. It was probably brewed hours ago. Locals sometimes call it *agua sucia,* dirty water, and that's most likely what it will taste like. It's worse than airline coffee; I wouldn't recommend it. Stick with the real stuff, but watch out—it can be habit-forming. Remember, you're supposed to relax in Miami.

Expect to wait hours for a table, and don't even think of mumbling a complaint—despite the poor service, it's worth it. Vietnamese cuisine combines the best of Asian and French cooking with spectacular results. Food at Hy-Vong is elegantly simple and superspicy. Appetizers include small, tightly packed Vietnamese spring rolls, and kimchee, a spicy, fermented cabbage. Star entrees include pastry-enclosed chicken with watercress cream-cheese sauce and fish in tangy mango sauce.

Enjoy the wait with a traditional Vietnamese beer and lots of company. Outside this tiny storefront restaurant, you'll meet interesting students, musicians, and foodies who come for the large delicious portions.

La Carreta. 3632 SW 8th St., Little Havana. ☎ **305/444-7501.** Main courses $4–$19. AE, CB, DISC, DC, MC, V. Daily 24 hours. CUBAN.

This cavernous family-style restaurant is filled with relics of an old farm and college kids eating *medianoches* (midnight sandwiches with ham, cheese, and pickles) after partying all night. Waitresses are brusque but efficient and will help Anglos along who may not know all the lingo. The menu is vast and very authentic. Try the *sopa de pollo,* a rich golden stock loaded with chunks of chicken and fresh vegetables or the ropa vieja, a shredded beef stew in a thick brown sauce.

Because of its immense popularity and low prices, La Carreta has opened several branches throughout Miami, including a counter in the Miami airport. Check the white pages for other locations.

✪ **Versailles.** 3555 SW 8th St., Little Havana. ☎ **305/444-0240.** Soup and salad $2–$10; main courses $5–$8. DC, DISC, MC, V. Mon–Thurs 8am–2am; Fri 8am–3:30am; Sat 8am–4:30am; Sun 9am–2am. CUBAN.

Versailles is the meeting place of Miami's Cuban power brokers, who meet daily over *café con leche* to discuss the future of the exiles' fate. A glorified diner, the place sparkles with glass, chandeliers, murals, and mirrors meant to evoke the French palace. There's nothing fancy here—nothing French, either—just straightforward food from the home country. The menu is a veritable survey of Cuban cooking and includes specialties such as *Moors and Christians* (flavorful black beans with white rice), ropa vieja, and fried whole fish.

7 West Dade

As all of South Florida expands westward, good restaurants will follow as well. So far, however, only a few have distinguished themselves, and they are reviewed here.

VERY EXPENSIVE

✪ **Shula's Steak House.** 7601 NW 154th St. (Don Shula's Golf Club off the Palmetto Expressway), Miami Lakes. ☎ **305/820-8102.** Reservations recommended. Main courses $18–$58. AE, CB, DC, MC, V. In season Mon–Fri 6:30am–2:30pm and 6–11pm; Sat–Sun 7–11am and 6–11pm; call for hours off-season (May–Nov). STEAK HOUSE.

This is the place to get huge slabs of red meat cooked however you like. A limited à la carte menu lists entrees by weight. You could start with the petite 12-ounce filet mignon, so tender and juicy you could almost cut it with your fork. Linebackers might consider the 48-ounce porterhouse. I haven't tried it myself, but am told it's one of the best. Potatoes and a few vegetables are available, but don't bring your vegetarian friends here—they'll go hungry.

Retired Miami Dolphin coach Don Shula is said to be spending more time around this shrine to his old team as he puts the final touches on his new location in the Alexander Hotel in Miami Beach.

MODERATE

Tony Roma's Famous For Ribs. 6728 Main St. (at Ludlum Rd.), Miami Lakes. ☎ **305/558-7427.** Reservations not accepted. Main courses $9–$14; sandwiches $6. AE, CB, DC, DISC, MC, V. Mon–Thurs 11am–11pm; Fri–Sat 11am–1am. AMERICAN/BARBECUE.

Rib lovers rave over this Miami-based chain that now has more than a dozen locations in South Florida. In Miami Lakes, the place is packed with regulars who order

From Ceviche to Picadillo: Latin Cuisine at a Glance

In Little Havana and wondering what to eat? Many restaurants list menu items in English for the benefit of *norteamericano* diners. In case you're wondering what to eat, though, here are translations and suggestions for filling and delicious meals:

Arroz con pollo   Roast chicken served with saffron-seasoned yellow rice and diced vegetables.

Café cubano   Very strong black coffee, served in thimble-size cups with lots of sugar. It's a real eye-opener.

Camarones   Shrimp.

Ceviche   Raw fish seasoned with spice and vegetables and marinated in vinegar and citrus to "cook" it.

Croquetas   Golden-fried croquettes of ham, chicken, or fish.

Paella   A Spanish dish of chicken, sausage, seafood, and pork mixed with saffron rice and peas.

Palomilla   Thinly sliced beef, similar to American minute steak, usually served with onions, parsley, and a mountain of french fries.

Pan cubano   Long, white crusty Cuban bread. Ask for it tostada, toasted and flattened on a grill with lots of butter.

Picadillo   A rich stew of ground meat, brown gravy, peas, pimientos, raisins, and olives.

Plátano   A deep-fried, soft, mildly sweet banana.

Pollo asado   Roasted chicken with onions and a crispy skin.

Ropa vieja   A delicious shredded beef stew, whose name literally means "old clothes."

Sopa de pollo   Chicken soup, usually with noodles or rice.

Tapas   A general name for Spanish-style hors d'oeuvres, served in grazing-size portions.

full slabs of thick meaty pork with the usual side dishes, such as coleslaw and a crispy onion loaf. You can't beat the prices, and the dark woody atmosphere makes you feel like you're in a much more upscale place.

Other locations include 15700 Biscayne Blvd., North Miami (☎ **305/949-2214**); 18050 Collins Ave., Miami Beach (☎ **305/932-7907**); and 2665 SW 37th Ave., Coral Gables (☎ **305/443-6626**).

8 North Dade

Although there aren't many hotels in North Dade, the population in the winter months explodes due to the onslaught of seasonal residents from the Northeast. A number of exclusive condominiums and country clubs, including William's Island, Turnberry, and The Jockey Club, breed a demanding clientele, many of whom dine out nightly. That's good news for visitors who can find superior service and cuisine at value prices.

VERY EXPENSIVE

✪ **Chef Allen's.** 19088 NE 29th Ave. (at Biscayne Blvd.), North Miami Beach. ☎ **305/ 935-2900.** Reservations suggested. Main courses $26–$31. AE, DC, MC, V. Sun–Thurs 6–10:30pm; Fri–Sat 6–11pm. NEW WORLD CUISINE.

For one of South Florida's finest dining experiences, Chef Allen's is a must. There simply isn't better food to be found in the county. Owner-chef Allen Susser, of New York's *Le Cirque* fame, has built a classy yet relaxed restaurant with art deco furnishings, a glass-enclosed kitchen, and a hot-pink swirl of neon surrounding the dining room's ceiling. It's more than a little kitschy, but this is Miami, after all. In a town of flash-in-the-pan restaurants, this 14-year-old spot has become an institution, helped by a young, energetic staff.

Appetizers are alluring and may include lobster-and-crab cakes served with strawberry-ginger chutneys, or baked brie with spinach, sun-dried tomatoes, and pine nuts. Favorite main dishes include crisp roast duck with cranberry sauce, and mesquite-grilled Norwegian salmon with champagne grapes, green onions, and basil spaetzle. Local fish dishes, in various delectable guises, and homemade pastas are always on the menu. The extensive wine list is well chosen and features several good buys. Handmade desserts are works of art and sinfully delicious.

MODERATE

The Gourmet Diner. 13951 Biscayne Blvd. (between NE 139th and 140th sts.), North Miami Beach. ☎ **305/947-2255.** Reservations not accepted. Main courses $10–$17. MC, V. Mon–Fri 11am–11pm; Sat 8am–11:30pm; Sun 8am–10:30pm. FRENCH.

This retro 1950s-style diner serves plain old French fare without pretensions. The atmosphere is a bit brash, and the lines are often out the door. You'll want to get there early anyway to taste some of the house specialties, such as beef Burgundy, the trout amandine, and frog legs Provençale—these dishes tend to sell out quickly.

Check the blackboard, which, depending on where you are seated, can be hard to see. The salads and soups are all prepared to order. Even a simple hearts of palm becomes a gourmet treat under the basic, tangy vinaigrette. A well-rounded wine list with reasonable prices makes this place a standout and a great deal. The homemade pastries are also delicious.

The Lagoon. 488 Sunny Isles Blvd. (163rd St.), North Miami Beach. ☎ **305/947-6661.** Reservations accepted. Main courses $12–$22; lobster special $22.95. AE, CB, MC, V. Daily 4:30–11pm; early bird dinner 4:30–6pm. SEAFOOD/CONTINENTAL.

This old bay-front fish house has been around since 1936. Major road construction nearby should have guaranteed its doom years ago, but the excellent view and incredible specials make it a worthwhile stop. If you can disregard the somewhat dirty bathrooms and nonchalant service, you'll find the best-priced juicy Maine lobsters around.

Yes, it's true! Lobster lovers can get two 1¼ pounders for $22.95. Try them broiled with a light buttery seasoned coating. This dish is not only inexpensive but incredibly succulent, too. Side dishes include fresh vegetables, like broccoli or asparagus, as well as a huge baked potato, stuffed or plain. The salads are good but come with too much commercial-tasting dressing. To be safe, ask for oil and vinegar on the side, or, better yet, skip all the accouterments to save room for the lobster.

The Melting Pot. 3143 NE 163rd St. (between U.S. 1 and Collins Ave., in Sunny Isles Plaza shopping center), North Miami Beach. ☎ **305/947-2228.** Reservations recommended on weekends. Main courses $9–$11 for cheese fondue; $11–$18 for meat and fish fondues. AE, DISC, MC, V. Sun–Thurs 5:30–10:30pm; Fri–Sat 5:30pm–midnight. FONDUE.

Traditional fondue is supplemented by combination meat-and-fish dinners, which are served with one of almost a dozen different sauces. The place, with its lace curtains and cozy booths, was voted most romantic restaurant in the local alternative paper several years ago.

As more diners become health conscious, the owners have introduced a more healthful version of fondue, in which you cook vegetables and meats in a low-fat broth. It tastes good, although this version is less fun than watching drippy cheese flow from the hot pot. Best of all, perhaps, is dessert: chunks of pineapple, bananas, apples, and cherries you dip into a creamy chocolate fondue. No liquor is served here, but the wine list is extensive, and beer is available.

A second Melting Pot is located at 9835 SW 72nd St. (Sunset Drive) in Kendall (☎ 305/279-8816).

P. F. Chang's China Bistro. 17455 Biscayne Blvd., Aventura/North Miami Beach. ☎ **305/957-1966.** Reservations not accepted. Main courses $8–$13; salads $5–$10. AE, MC, V. Sun–Thurs 11:30am–11pm; Fri–Sat until midnight. ASIAN.

This chain is spreading around the country and is worth a taste. An open kitchen turning out fantastically fresh cuisine and a modern, casual decor make it quite a popular place. Classic Chinese dishes from around the continent are Americanized enough to make them attractive but also authentic enough to make them interesting. In other words, you won't find chopped chicken feet, but will find luscious warm duck salad and a variety of noodle dishes with fresh stir-fried veggies and meats. The best part is you'll find the prices moderate and the servers relatively informed. For a quick lunch or dinner, this is an excellent choice. Another P. F. Chang's is located in the Fall's Shopping Center at 8888 SW 136th St. (☎ **305/234-2338**).

INEXPENSIVE

Amos' Juice Bar. 18315 W. Dixie Hwy. (1 block west of Biscayne Blvd.), North Miami Beach. ☎ 305/935-9544. Sandwiches and salads $4–$6. No credit cards. Mon–Sat 8:30am–6:30pm. HEALTH FOOD.

This brightly painted stand in the middle of a busy road attracts a varied crowd, from young pony-tailed Europeans to bikers. If you don't mind a bit of car exhaust with your snapper sandwich, consider this landmark in North Dade.

The food is made on the premises and includes one of the most unusual tuna salads I've ever run across, served in a pita with tons of crisp vegetables, including alfalfa sprouts, tomato, and lettuce. The hummus is also superb, although garlic lovers might want a hint more spark. You can also get a fresh smoothie or vegetable juice made on the spot.

Here Comes the Sun. 2188 NE 123rd St. (west of the Broad Causeway), North Miami. ☎ 305/893-5711. Reservations recommended in season. Main courses $10–$14; early bird special $7.95; sandwiches and salads $5–$7.50. AE, DC, DISC, MC, V. Mon–Sat 11am–8:30pm. AMERICAN/HEALTH FOOD.

One of Miami's first health-food spots, this bustling grocery-store-turned-diner serves hundreds of plates a night, mostly to blue-haired locals. It's noisy and hectic but worth it. In season, all types pack the place for a $7.95 special, served between 4 and 6:30pm, which includes one of more than 20 choices of entrees, soup or salad, coffee or tea, and a small frozen yogurt. Fresh grilled fish and chicken entrees are reliable and served with a nice array of vegetables. The miso burgers with "sun sauce" are a vegetarian's dream.

⚑ Family-Friendly Restaurants

The Crepe Maker Cafe *(see p. 113)*   This little French café lets you and the kids create your own crepe concoctions. You can even get ice cream crepes for dessert. Afterwards, the kids can entertain themselves in a small play area.

Señor Frogs *(see p. 112)*   This Coconut Grove restaurant, with its lively atmosphere and universally appealing Mexican dishes, plus margaritas for the adults, is a good choice for the entire family. The service is generally efficient, and the food is reasonably priced. If you ask for half portions of some of the more popular dishes, such as the quesadilla, the kitchen will happily oblige. High chairs and booster chairs are available.

Van Dyke Cafe *(see p. 90)*   One of South Beach's only family friendly sit-down restaurants, Van Dyke is a large indoor/outdoor cafe whose whole menu is for children. From PB and Js to grilled cheese to burgers, this is the spot for kids of all ages.

Versailles *(see p. 103)*   This quirky, bustling Cuban diner is great for kids. Although there's no specific children's menu, the place is used to catering to patrons of all ages. You'll find *abuelitos* and *niños*, little old grandparents and children, as well as high-powered politicians and teenage revelers. The prices are cheap, and there are plenty of choices for even the most finicky eater. Try croquetas of ham, chicken, or fish, or a Cuban sandwich.

Laurenzo's Cafe. 16385 West Dixie Hwy. (at the corner of 163rd St.), North Miami Beach. ☎ **305/945-6381.** Main courses $4–$12; salads $2–$5. No credit cards. Mon–Sat 11am–7pm; Sun 11am–4pm. ITALIAN.

This little lunch counter in the middle of a chaotic grocery store has been serving delicious buffet lunches to the *paesanos* for years. A meeting place for the growing Italian population in Miami, the store has been open for more than 40 years. Daily specials usually include a lasagna or eggplant parmigiano and two or three salad options. Also good are the rustic pizzas.

Choose a wine from the vast selection and take your meal to go or sit in the trellis-covered seating area amid busy shoppers buying their evening's groceries. You'll get to eavesdrop on some great conversations over your plastic tray of real southern Italian–style cooking.

9 Coral Gables & Environs

VERY EXPENSIVE

Christy's. 3101 Ponce de León Blvd., Coral Gables. ☎ **305/446-1400.** Reservations recommended. Main courses $17–$30. AE, CB, DC, MC, V. Mon–Thurs 11:30am–4pm; Fri 4–11pm; Sat 5–11pm; Sun 5–10pm. AMERICAN.

Arrive famished. One of the Gables' most expensive and elegant establishments, Christy's is known primarily for its generous cuts of thick, juicy steaks and ribs, despite its demure Victorian style. Some say it's one of the most romantic spots in Miami. I say it's just fine for serious carnivores.

The prime rib is so thick that even a small cut weighs about a pound. New York strip, filet mignon, and chateaubriand are all on the menu here, and all steaks are fully aged without chemicals or freezing. Each entree is served with a jumbo Caesar salad and a baked potato. Seafood, veal, and chicken dishes are also available; however, ordering anything but a steak at this pricey little candlelit spot would be a disappointment.

✪ **Norman's.** 21 Almeria Ave. (between Douglas and Ponce de León), Coral Gables. ☎ **305/446-6767.** Reservations highly recommended. Main courses $25–$32. AE, DC, MC, V. Mon–Thurs noon–2pm and 6–10:30pm; Fri noon–2pm and 6–11pm; Sat 6–11pm. NEW WORLD CUISINE.

Master chef Norman Van Aken, one of the originators of New World Cuisine, reemerged after a 2-year break from restauranting to open what he has called his "culmination." The result is an open kitchen, surrounded by well-dressed diners, where a handful of silent industrious chefs prepare Asian- and Caribbean-inspired dishes.

The food is the main focus of attention. Some think the exotic-sounding menu is pretentious or overwrought. I think there's plenty to enjoy, like pizzas and pastas with a good glass of wine and a hunk of bread. The fish, too, is out of this world. The *Rhum*-and-pepper-painted grouper on mango-Habanero Mojo is an exotic-tasting dark-fleshed fish with an explosion of sauces to complement its heavy flavor.

The staff is adoring and professional and the atmosphere tasteful without being too formal. The portions are realistic, but still, be careful not to overdo it. You'll want to try some of the wacky desserts, such as mango ice cream served with Asian pears and crushed red pepper (the pepper really just adds color to the plate).

EXPENSIVE

✪ **Caffe Abbracci.** 318 Aragon Ave. (between LeJeune Rd. and Miracle Mile), Coral Gables. ☎ **305/441-0700.** Reservations recommended for dinner. Main courses $16–$24; pasta $14–$20. AE, CB, DC, MC, V. Mon–Fri 11:30am–3pm; Sun–Thurs 6–11pm; Fri–Sat 6pm–midnight. ITALIAN.

You'll be greeted with a hug by the owner and maître d' Nino, who oversees this remarkable spot as only an Italian could. The food is remarkable, yet the restaurant is not known to many outside of the Gables. Still, it's packed on weekends by those in the know. You are guaranteed perfect service in a pretty wood and marble setting, with the only drawback being the unfortunately loud dining room.

It's hard to get beyond the appetizers here, which are all so good that you could order a few and be satisfied. My favorite is the shrimp with a bright pesto sauce that has just enough garlic to give it a kick, but not so much you won't get a kiss later. The excellent risottos are served in half portions so that you'll have room for the indescribable fish dishes.

Le Festival. 2120 Salzedo St. (5 blocks north of Miracle Mile), Coral Gables. ☎ **305/442-8545.** Reservations required for dinner. Main courses $16–$25. AE, CB, DC, DISC, MC, V. Mon–Fri 11:45am–2:30pm; Mon–Thurs 6–10:30pm; Fri–Sat 6–11pm. FRENCH.

Le Festival's contemporary pink awning hangs over one of Miami's most traditional Spanish-style buildings, hinting at the unusual combination of cuisine and decor that awaits inside. The modern dining rooms, enlivened with New French features and furnishings, belie the traditional highlights of a well-planned menu.

Shrimp and crab cocktails, fresh pâtés, and an unusual cheese soufflé are star starters. Both meat and fish are either simply seared with herbs and spices or doused in wine and cream sauces. Dessert can be a delight if you plan ahead: Grand Marnier and chocolate soufflés are individually prepared and must be ordered at the same time as the entrees. There's also a wide selection of other homemade sweets.

MODERATE

Brasserie Les Halles. 2415 Ponce de León Blvd. (at Miracle Mile), Coral Gables. ☎ **305/ 461-1099.** Reservations suggested on weekends. Main courses $14.50–$21.50. AE, DC, DISC, MC, V. Daily 11:30am–midnight. FRENCH.

Known especially for its fine steaks and delicious salads, this very welcome addition to the Coral Gables dining scene became popular as soon as it opened in 1997 and has since continued to do a brisk business. The modest and moderately priced menu is particularly welcome in an area of overpriced, stuffy restaurants. For starters, try the mussels in white wine sauce and the escargot. For a main course, the duck confit is an unusual and rich choice. Pieces of duck meat wrapped in duck fat are slow-cooked and served on salad frissé and baby potatoes with garlic. Service by the young French staff is polite but a bit slow. The tables tend to be a little too close, although there is a lovely private balcony space overlooking the long thin dining room where large groups can gather.

Gables Diner. 2320 Galiano Dr. (between Ponce de León Blvd. and 37th Ave.), Coral Gables. ☎ **305/567-0330.** Main courses $9–$16; pasta $10–$12; burgers and sandwiches $7–$9; salads $8–$10. AE, DC, DISC, MC, V. Daily 8am–10pm; Fri–Sat until 10:30pm. AMERICAN.

This upscale diner serves an eclectic mix of comfort food and nouvelle health food. From meat loaf to Chinese chicken salad, there are moderately priced options for everyone. My favorite is the chicken pot pie, a flaky homemade crust filled with big chunks of white meat, pearl onions, peas, and mushrooms. Also good are the large burgers with every imaginable condiment. Vegetarians can find a few good choices, including pastas, bean soups, pizzas, a vegetable stir-fry, and some hearty salads. All the ingredients are fresh and crisp. No need to dress up here, although the clean, almost romantic setting is as appropriate for first dates as it is for families.

✪ **The Globe.** 377 Alhambra Circle (just off Le Jeune Rd.), Coral Gables. ☎ **305/ 445-3555.** Reservations for 6 or more. Main courses $9–$19; salads $4–$10; pizzas and sandwiches $7–$11. AE, DISC, MC, V. Mon–Fri 11:30am–midnight; Sat 6:30pm–2am; Sun 10:30am–10:30pm. INTERNATIONAL.

This funky coffee shop/travel agency is an odd and welcome addition to a neighborhood dominated by fancy eateries and hotels. Take advantage of the hip surroundings and enjoy the quite decent food. Especially good are the salads and pizzas, particularly the chicken and blue cheese pizza, my favorite. In addition to an extensive list of wines and specialty beers, there are many interesting non-alcoholic choices. More important, sample some of the excellent live music every weekend.

✪ **John Martin's.** 253 Miracle Mile, Coral Gables. ☎ **305/445-3777.** Reservations recommended on weekends. Main courses $12–$20; sandwiches and salads $4–$8. AE, DC, DISC, MC, V. Mon–Thurs 11:30am–midnight; Fri–Sat 11:30am–1am; Sun noon–10pm. IRISH PUB.

Food at this Irish pub is a step above average. The basic menu is loaded with fried bar snacks as well as some Irish specialties, such as bangers and mash and shepherd's pie.

Of course to wash it down, you'll want to try one of the ales on tap or one of the more than 20 single-malt scotches. The crowd is upscale and chatty, as is the young wait staff. Check out happy hour on weeknights, plus the Sunday brunch with loads of hand-carved meats and seafood.

INEXPENSIVE

Biscayne Miracle Mile Cafeteria. 147 Miracle Mile, Coral Gables. ☎ **305/444-9005.** Main courses $3–$4. MC, V. Mon–Sat 11am–2:15pm and 4–8pm; Sun 11am–8pm. AMERICAN.

Here, you'll find no bar, no music, and no flowers on the tables—just great Southern-style cooking at unbelievably low prices. The menu changes, but roast beef, baked fish, and barbecued ribs are typical entrees, few of which exceed $5.

Food is picked up cafeteria-style and brought to one of the many unadorned Formica tables. The restaurant is always busy. The kitschy 1950s decor is an asset in this last of the old-fashioned cafeterias, where the gold-clad staff is proud and attentive. Enjoy it while it lasts.

The Daily Bread Marketplace. 2400 SW 27th St. (off U.S. 1 under the monorail), Coral Gables. ☎ **305/856-0363** or 305/856-0366. Sandwiches and salads $3–$6. MC, V. Mon–Sat 8am–8pm; Sun 11am–5pm. GREEK.

Not only is there great take-out food and homemade breads, but also backgammon boards and water pipes are for sale. The falafel and gyro sandwiches are large, fresh, and filling. Spinach pie for less than $1 is also recommended, though short on spinach and heavy on pastry. Salads, including luscious tabouli, hummus, and eggplant are also worth a go. To take in or eat out, the Middle Eastern fare here is a real treat, especially in an area so filled with fancy French and Cuban fare. Plus, you can pick up hard-to-find groceries like grape leaves, fresh olives, couscous, fresh nuts, and pita bread.

House of India. 22 Merrick Way, Coral Gables (near Douglas and Coral Way, a block north of Miracle Mile). ☎ **305/444-2348.** Reservations accepted. Main courses $7–$10. AE, DC, DISC, MC, V. Daily 11:30am–3pm; Sun–Thurs 5–10pm; Fri–Sat 5–11pm. INDIAN.

House of India's curries, kormas, and kebabs are very good, but the restaurant's well-priced all-you-can-eat lunch buffet is unsurpassed. All the favorites are on display, including tandoori chicken, naan bread, various meat and vegetarian curries, as well as rice and dal (lentils). This place isn't fancy and could use a good scrub-down (in fact, I've heard it described as a "greasy spoon"), but it is nicely decorated with hanging batik prints.

Sergio's. 3252 Coral Way, Coral Gables. ☎ **305/529-0047.** Reservations not accepted. Main courses $5–$7. AE, DC, MC, V. Sun–Thurs 6am–midnight; Fri–Sat 24 hours. AMERICAN/CUBAN.

Located across from Coral Gables' Paseos Mall, Sergio's stands out like a Latin-inspired International House of Pancakes, with red-clothed tables, neon signs in the windows, and video games along the back wall. The family style restaurant serves everything from ham-and-eggs breakfasts to grilled steak sandwich lunches and dinners, but it specializes in native Cuban-style dishes, as well as grilled chicken, fajitas, and a variety of sandwiches. Low prices and late-night dining keep it popular with locals.

10 Coconut Grove

Coconut Grove was long known as the artists' haven of Miami, but the rush of developers trying to cash in on the laid-back charm of this old settlement has turned it into something of an overgrown mall. Still, there are several great dining spots both in and out of the confines of Mayfair or Cocowalk.

EXPENSIVE

Bocca di Rosa. 2833 Bird Ave. (between SW 27th and Virginia sts.), Coconut Grove. ☎ **305/444-4222.** Reservations suggested. Main courses $16–$24; pastas $11–$17. AE, DC, DISC, MC, V. Sun–Thurs 6–11pm; Fri–Sat 6pm–midnight. ITALIAN.

This elegant restaurant is nestled in a cozy corner of the Grove, but from the smells and tastes here you might as well be in Roma or Sicily. With dishes like *coniglio all contadina* (rabbit stew with white beans and polenta) and *penne cons salsa di sarde* (a sardine and fennel pasta), the menu touches all points on "the boot." On any day, there may be as many as 15 specials. The remarkably fresh seafood is especially recommended. My favorites are a savory bowl of steamed mussels in a white wine broth and a delicately seared swordfish. Frankly, whatever Chef Giorgio is cooking up is bound to be good.

✪ **Monty's Bayshore Restaurant.** 2550 S. Bayshore Dr., Coconut Grove. ☎ **305/858-1431.** Reservations recommended upstairs on weekends. Main courses $20–$37; sandwiches $6–$8; platters $7–$10. AE, CB, DC, MC, V. Daily (downstairs) 11:30am–2am. SEAFOOD.

This place comes in three parts: a lounge, a raw bar, and a restaurant. Among them, Monty's serves everything from steak and seafood to munchies such as nachos, potato skins, and Buffalo chicken wings. At the outdoor, dockside bar, there's live music nightly, as well as all day on weekends. This is a fun kind of place, usually with more revelers and drinkers than diners. Upstairs, an upscale dining room serves one of the city's best Caesar salads, fantastic she-crab soup, and respectable stone crab claws in season. Be sure, however, not to order the claws from May until October, since they'll serve you some imported version that simply doesn't compare.

MODERATE

Green Street Cafe. 3110 Commodore Plaza, Coconut Grove. ☎ **305/567-0662.** Reservations not accepted. Main courses $6–$16. AE, MC, V. Sun–Thurs 7am–11:30pm; Fri–Sat 7am–1am. CONTINENTAL.

Green Street is located at the "100% corner," the Coconut Grove intersection of Main Highway and Commodore Plaza that 100% of all tourists visit. The location and the loads of outdoor seating (great for people-watching) relieve the pressure on Green Street to turn out fine meals, but the food is still well above average. Continental-style breakfasts include fresh croissants and rolls, cinnamon toast, and cereal. Heartier American-style offerings include eggs and omelettes, pancakes, waffles, and French toast. Soup, salad, and sandwich lunches are overstuffed chicken, turkey, and tuna-based meals. Dinners are more elaborate, with several decent pasta entrees as well as fresh fish, chicken, and burgers, including one made of lamb.

✪ **Kaleidoscope.** 3112 Commodore Plaza (intersects Grand Ave. and 32nd St.), Coconut Grove. ☎ **305/446-5010.** Reservations recommended. Main courses $12–$15 for pasta; $14–$20 for meat and fish. AE, CB, DC, MC, V. Mon–Fri 11:30am–3pm; Mon–Sat 6–11pm; Sun 5:30–10:30pm. AMERICAN.

I'd recommend Kaleidoscope, in the heart of Coconut Grove, even if it were located somewhere less exciting. The atmosphere is relaxed, with low-key, attentive service, comfortable seating, and a terrace overlooking the busy sidewalks below. Dishes are well prepared, and pastas, topped with sauces like seafood and fresh basil or pesto with grilled yellowfin tuna, are especially tasty. The linguini with salmon and fresh dill is prepared to perfection.

Although there is no special pretheater dinner, many locals stop into this reliable and reasonable second-floor spot for an elegant meal before a show down the street at The Coconut Grove Playhouse.

The Red Lantern. 3176 Commodore Plaza (Grand Ave.), Coconut Grove. ☎ **305/529-9998.** Main courses $9–$20. AE, MC, V. Mon–Thurs 11:30am–11pm; Fri 11:30am–midnight; Sat 4pm–midnight; Sun 4–11pm. CANTONESE.

This popular Chinese spot is better than most. Specialties include shark's fin with chicken and steamed whole snapper with black-bean sauce. There's also an assortment of vegetarian dishes and some excellent soups. My favorite is the clay-pot stew of chicken in a ginger broth. Although the atmosphere is nothing to speak of, the varied menu and interesting preparation keep locals happy and make a meal here worthwhile.

Señor Frogs. 3480 Main Hwy., Coconut Grove. ☎ **305/448-0999.** Reservations not accepted. Main courses $9–$15. AE, CB, DC, DISC, MC, V. Mon–Sat 11:30am–2am; Sun 11:30am–1am. MEXICAN.

Filled with a college-student crowd, this restaurant is known for a raucous good time, its mariachi band, and especially its powerful margaritas. The food at this rocking cantina is a bit too cheesy, but tasty, if not exactly authentic. The mole enchiladas, with 14 different kinds of mild chiles mixed with chocolate, is as flavorful as any I've tasted. Almost everything is served with rice and beans in quantities so large that few diners are able to finish.

INEXPENSIVE

Cafe Tu Tu Tango. 3015 Grand Ave. (on the second floor of CocoWalk), Coconut Grove. ☎ **305/529-2222.** Reservations not accepted. Main courses $4–$8. AE, MC, V. Sun–Wed 11:30am–midnight; Thurs 11:30am–1am; Fri–Sat 11:30am–2am. SPANISH/INTERNATIONAL.

This second-floor restaurant in the bustling CocoWalk is designed to look like a disheveled artist's loft. Dozens of original paintings—some only half-finished—hang on the walls and studio easels. Seating at sturdy wooden tables and chairs is either inside, on wooden floors among the clutter, or outdoors, overlooking the Grove's main drag.

Flamenco and other Latin-inspired tunes complement a menu with a decidedly Spanish flare. Hummus spread on rosemary flat bread and baked goat cheese in marinara sauce are two good starters. Entrees include roast duck with dried cranberries, toasted pine nuts, and goat cheese, plus Cajun chicken egg rolls filled with corn, cheddar cheese, and tomato salsa. Pastas, ribs, fish, and pizzas round out the eclectic offerings, and several visits have proved each consistently good. Try the sweet, potent sangria and enjoy the warm lively atmosphere from a seat with a view. Especially when the rest of the Grove has shut down, Tu Tu Tango is an oasis.

Another Cafe Tu Tu Tango is located at 19501 Biscayne Blvd., (in Aventura Mall), 2nd Floor, Aventura. (☎ **305/932-2222**).

News Cafe in the Grove. 2901 Florida Ave. (behind Mayfair), Coconut Grove. ☎ **305/774-6397.** Main courses $6–$16. AE, DC, MC, V. Daily 24 hours. AMERICAN.

Like its predecessor in South Beach, this big modern diner offers everything from Caesar salads to hummus to burgers to omelets to ice cream sundaes. The food is predictably good and the service lively and pleasant. The best part is that it's open around the clock to serve the after-movie crowd from CocoWalk and Mayfair as well as the real late-night club-goers.

11 South Miami

This mostly residential area has some very good dining spots scattered mostly along U.S. 1.

MODERATE/INEXPENSIVE

✪ **Anacapri.** 12669 S. Dixie Hwy. (in the South Park Center at 128th St. and U.S. 1), South Miami. ☎ **305/232-8001.** Main courses $8–$16. AE, DC, DISC, MC, V. Daily 11:30am–2:30pm; Mon–Thurs 5–10:30pm; Fri–Sat 5–11:30pm; Sun 5–9pm. ITALIAN.

Neighborhood fans wait in line here happily with a glass of wine and pleasant company for somewhat heavy but flavorful Italian cuisine. Prices are reasonable and everyone is treated like a member of the family. If you're in the area, check it out. Stick with the basics, such as pastas with red sauce, which are all flavorful, although a bit heavy on the garlic and oil. An antipasto with thinly cut meats and cheeses and some good green peppers is a great start to a hearty meal.

Cafe Hammock. 500 SW 177th Ave. (in the Miccosukee Indian Gaming site on Krome Ave. and Tamiami Trail), South Miami. ☎ **305/222-4600.** Reservations accepted. Main courses $10–$22; dinner specials $5–$6. DISC, MC, V. Daily 24 hours. CONTINENTAL.

In the clanging environs of the Native American gaming village way down south, you can dine on stone crab claws and decent steak for a few bucks while overlooking hundreds of fanatical bingo players. If you can keep away from the dealers and slots and don't mind a bit of smoke, you'll be amazed at the excellent service and phenomenal specials it runs to entice gamblers to this bizarre outpost. Don't expect Native Americans in native dress; you'll find servers from New Jersey and California before you see a Miccosukee serving burgers here.

The Crepe Maker Cafe. 8269 SW 124th St., South Miami. ☎ **305/233-4458** or 305/233-1113. Crepes $3–$7.50. No credit cards. Mon–Sat 11am–8pm; Sun noon–6pm. CREPES/FRENCH.

Create your own delicious crepes at this little French cafe. You can choose from ham, tuna, black olives, red peppers, capers, artichoke hearts, and pine nuts. Some of the best combinations include a Philly cheese steak with mushrooms and a classic cordon bleu. Delicious desert crepes have ice cream, strawberries, peaches, walnuts, and pineapples. Enjoy your crepe fresh off the griddle at the counter or on a bar stool. The soups are also delicious. Kids can run around in a small play area, too.

✪ **Pollo Tropical.** 18700 SW 40th St., South Miami. ☎ **305/225-7858.** Main courses $3–$6. No credit cards. Sun–Thurs 11am–10pm; Fri–Sat 11am–11pm. CUBAN/FAST FOOD.

This Miami-based chain is putting up new terra-cotta–arched, fast-food places so fast you can hardly finish your meal before another one has taken root.

This is lucky for Miamians and the Southeast, where dozens of these restaurants provide hot tender chicken with a variety of healthful side dishes, such as fresh chunks of carrots, onions, zucchini, and squash on wooden skewers and a variety of salads. The chicken is marinated in a seriously secret sauce and served with well-seasoned black beans and rice. The menu, although Latin inspired, is clearly spelled out in English. Pollo Tropical is a good place to get an education in Latin *sabor* (taste).

Other locations include 1454 Alton Rd., Miami Beach (☎ **305/672-8888**), and 11806 Biscayne Blvd., North Miami (☎ **305/895-0274**). Check the phone book for others.

✪ **Shorty's.** 9200 S. Dixie Hwy. (between U.S. 1 and Dadeland Blvd.), South Miami. ☎ **305/670-7732.** Main courses $5–$9. DISC, MC, V. Mon–Thurs 11am–10pm; Fri–Sat 11am–11pm. BARBECUE.

A Miami tradition since 1951, this hokey log cabin is still serving some of the best ribs and chicken in South Florida. People line up for the smoke-flavored, slow-cooked meat that's so tender it seems to jump off the bone into your mouth. The secret, however, is to ask for your order with sweet sauce. The regular stuff tastes bland and bottled. All the side dishes, including cole slaw, corn on the cob, and baked beans, look commercial but are necessary to complete the experience. This is Barbecue, with a neon capital *B*.

A second Shorty's is located in Davie at 5989 S. University Dr. (☎ **305/ 944-0348**).

The Tea Room. 12310 SW 224th St. (at Cauley Square), South Miami. ☎ **305/258-0044.** Sandwiches and salads $6–$7; soups $3–$4. AE, DISC, MC, V. Mon–Sat 11am–4pm. ENGLISH TEA.

Do stop in for a spot of tea at this recently rebuilt tea room in historic Cauley Square off U.S. 1. The little lace-curtained room is an unusual site in this heavily industrial area better known for its warehouses than its doilies.

Sample some simple sandwiches, such as the turkey club with potato salad and a small lettuce garnish or an onion soup full of rich brown broth and stringy cheese. Daily specials, like spinach-and-mushroom quiche, and delectable desserts are a must before beginning your explorations of the old antiques and art shops in this little enclave of civility down south.

Wrapido. 5812 Sunset Dr. (near 58th St.), South Miami. ☎ **305/662-7999.** Wraps and salads $5–$6. AE, MC, V. Mon–Fri 10:30am–10pm Sat–Sun until 11pm. WRAPS.

This trendy, fast-paced shop sells an impressive variety of wraps from Thai chicken to teriyaki tofu. All ingredients are super fresh and the sauces are fantastic, too. The sides reflect the ethnic mix of the city, with choices like black beans and rice, sweet plantains, or tortillas with guacamole and salsa. More than a dozen smoothies make choosing difficult, though I like the Maui Dream with peach juice, passion fruit, strawberries, bananas, coconut, and frozen yogurt.

Another location is in Coral Gables at 2334 Ponce De León Blvd. (☎ **305/ 443-1884**).

What to See & Do in Miami

More and more visitors are coming to Miami each year—around 10 million in 1998—to get a taste of the incredibly diverse offerings scattered throughout this sprawling metropolis. Also, Miami's population, especially in the winter months when the "snow birds" descend, is exploding and developers are keeping pace with the rapid growth by building ever more attractions, entertainment complexes, and shopping malls.

The best things down here are still the treasures nature put there, such as the Everglades National Park and the sea and the wide sandy beaches, but don't discount the human-made attractions altogether. The city was, and still is, designed to court visitors (and their dollars) from around the world, and many of these efforts make for fantastic entertainment. Nearly destroyed in the early '80s by developers' wrecking balls, the Art Deco District in South Beach is now by far the area's most popular tourist site. It's here amid the cotton candy–colored architecture that locals and visitors skate, stroll, shop, play, dance, and dine beneath palm trees and neon lights.

Also worth your time are many of the city's older attractions, such as Monkey Jungle, Parrot Jungle, Coral Castle, and the Seaquarium. Historical buildings such as Villa Vizcaya, Venetian Pools, and The Spanish Monastery are also not to be missed.

Take your pick from the many suggestions below. There is plenty to keep you busy for a day or a month.

1 Miami's Beaches

Perhaps Miami's most popular attraction is its incredible stretch of beachfront which runs more than 35 miles long from the tip of South Beach north to Sunny Isles and circles Key Biscayne and the numerous other pristine islands dotted throughout the Atlantic. The characteristics of Miami's many beaches are as varied as the city's population. Some are shaded by towering palm trees, while others are darkened by huge condominiums. Some attract families or old-timers, others a gay singles scene, but basically, there are two distinct beach alternatives: Miami Beach and Key Biscayne.

MIAMI BEACH'S BEACHES   Collins Avenue fronts more than a dozen miles of white-sand beach and blue-green waters from 1st to 192nd streets. Although most of this stretch is lined with a solid

Miami Area Attractions & Beaches

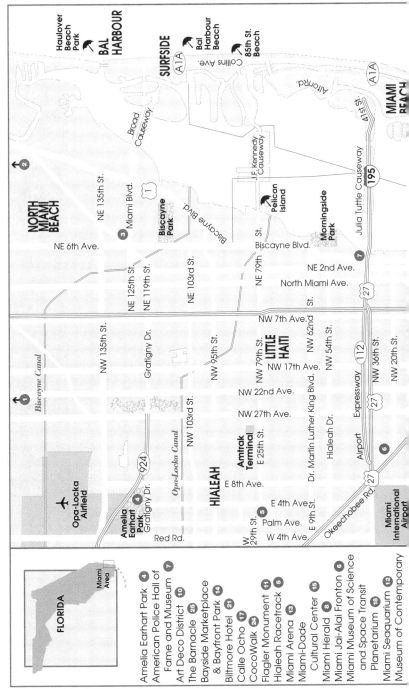

Amelia Earhart Park ❹
American Police Hall of
  Fame and Museum ❼
Art Deco District ㉕
The Barnacle ㉕
Bayside Marketplace
  & Bayfront Park ⑭
Biltmore Hotel ㉑
Calle Ocho ⑰
CocoWalk ㉔
Flagler Monument ⑪
Hialeah Racetrack ❺
Miami Arena ⑬
Miami-Dade
  Cultural Center ⑮
Miami Herald ❽
Miami Jai-Alai Fronton ❻
Miami Museum of Science
  and Space Transit
  Planetarium ⑱
Miami Seaquarium ⑫
Museum of Contemporary

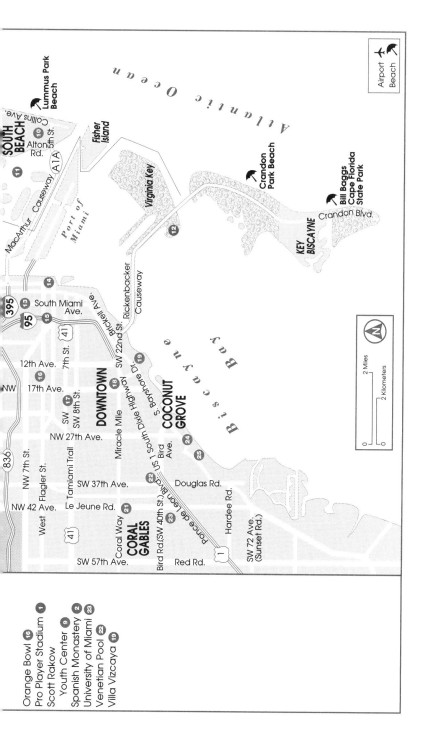

Atlantic Ocean

Lummus Park Beach

SOUTH BEACH

Collins Ave. 5th St.

Alton Rd.

MacArthur Causeway (A1A)

Port of Miami

Fisher Island

Virginia Key

Crandon Park Beach

Bill Baggs Cape Florida State Park

Crandon Blvd.

KEY BISCAYNE

Rickenbacker Causeway

Brickell Ave.

SW 22nd St.

395

95

41

South Miami Ave.

12th Ave.

17th Ave.

NW

7th St.

836

NW 7th St.

NW Flagler St.

Tamiami Trail

West

NW 27th Ave.

SW 37th Ave.

NW 42 Ave.   Le Jeune Rd.

41

SW 57th Ave.

CORAL GABLES

Coral Way

Bird Rd.(SW 40th St.)

US 1 South Dixie Highway

Ponce de Leon Blvd.

Red Rd.

Douglas Rd.

Hardee Rd.

1

SW 72 Ave. (Sunset Rd.)

DOWNTOWN

Miracle Mile

SW 8th St.

SW 7th St.

S. Bayshore Dr.

Bird Ave.

COCONUT GROVE

Biscayne Bay

N

0   2 Miles

0   2 Kilometers

Airport ✈

Beach 🏖

Orange Bowl 16
Pro Player Stadium 1
Scott Rakow Youth Center 9
Spanish Monastery 23
University of Miami 22
Venetian Pool 23
Villa Vizcaya 19

wall of hotels and condos, beach access is plentiful. There are lots of public beaches here, wide and well maintained, complete with lifeguards, toilet facilities, concession stands, and metered parking (bring lots of quarters). Except for a thin strip close to the water, most of the sand here is hard-packed—the result of a $10 million Army Corps of Engineers Beach Rebuilding Project meant to protect buildings from the effects of eroding sand.

In general, the beaches on this barrier island become less crowded the farther north you go. A wooden boardwalk runs along the hotel side of the beach from 21st to 46th streets—about 1½ miles—offering a terrific sun-and-surf experience without getting sand in your shoes. Aside from "The Best Beaches," listed below, Miami Beach's lifeguard-protected public beaches include 21st Street, at the beginning of the boardwalk; 35th Street, popular with an older crowd; 46th Street, next to the Fontainebleau Hilton; 53rd Street, a narrower, more sedate beach; 64th Street, one of the quietest strips around; and 72nd Street, a local old-timers' spot.

KEY BISCAYNE'S BEACHES   If Miami Beach is not private enough for you, try Virginia Key and Key Biscayne. Crossing Rickenbacker Causeway ($1 toll) is almost like crossing into The Bahamas. The 5 miles of public beach here are blessed with softer sand and are less developed and more laid-back than the hotel-laden strips to the north.

THE BEST BEACHES

Here are my picks:

- **Best Party Beach:** In Key Biscayne, **Crandon Park Beach,** on Crandon Boulevard, has 3 miles of oceanfront beach, 493 acres of park, 75 grills, three parking lots, several soccer and softball fields, and a public 18-hole championship golf course. The beach is particularly wide and the water is usually so clear you can see the bottom. Admission is $2 per vehicle. It's open daily from 8am to sunset. Many locals prefer the stretch of beach just past the toll booth under the causeway. The beach is narrower but admission is free and there's always salsa and merengue blaring from stereos for those who like to dance.

- **Best Beach for People-Watching:** The ultra-chic **Lummus Park Beach,** which runs along Ocean Drive from about 6th to 14th streets in South Beach, is the best place to go if you're seeking entertainment as well as a great tan. On any day of the week, you might spy models primping for a photo shoot, nearly naked sun-worshippers avoiding tan lines, and the best abs anywhere.

- **Best Swimming Beach:** The **85th Street Beach,** along Collins Avenue, is the best place to swim away from the maddening crowds. It's one of Miami's only stretches of sand with no condos or hotels looming over sunbathers. Lifeguards patrol the area throughout the day.

- **Best Windsurfing Beach: Hobie Beach,** on the right side of the causeway leading to Key Biscayne, is not really a beach, but an inlet with predictable winds and a number of places where you can rent Windsurfers.

- **Best Shell-Hunting Beach:** You'll find plenty of colorful shells at **Bal Harbour Beach,** Collins Avenue at 96th Street, just a few yards north of Surfside Beach. There's also an exercise course and good shade—but no lifeguards.

- **Best (Ahem) All-Around Tanning Beach:** Although the state has been trying to pass ordinances to outlaw nudity, several regional nude beaches are thriving. In Miami-Dade County, **Haulover Beach,** just north of the Bal Harbour border, attracts nudists from around the world and has created quite a boom for area businesses that cater to them.

In case you want to see the world.

At American Express, we're here to make your journey a smooth one. So we have over 1,700 travel service locations in over 130 countries ready to help. What else would you expect from the world's largest travel agency?

do more

Travel

In case you want to be welcomed there.

We're here to see that you're always welcomed at establishments everywhere. That's why millions of people carry the American Express® Card – for peace of mind, confidence, and security, around the world or just around the corner.

do more

Cards

In case you're running low.

We're here to help with more than 190,000 Express Cash locations around the world. In order to enroll, just call American Express at 1 800 CASH-NOW before you start your vacation.

do more

Express Cash

And in case you'd rather be safe than sorry.

We're here with American Express® Travelers Cheques. They're the safe way to carry money on your vacation, because if they're ever lost or stolen you can get a refund, practically anywhere or anytime. To find the nearest place to buy Travelers Cheques, call 1 800 495-1153. Another way we help you do more.

do more AMERICAN EXPRESS

Travelers Cheques

- **Best Surfing Beach: Haulover Beach/Harbor House,** just north of Miami Beach, seems to get Miami's biggest swells. Go early to avoid the rush of young locals prepping for Maui.

2 The Art Deco District

The best single attraction in Miami is not a museum or an amusement park, but a piece of the city itself. Located in South Beach, the Art Deco District is a whole community made up of outrageous and fanciful 1920s and 1930s architecture. The district is roughly bounded by the Atlantic Ocean on the east, Alton Road on the west, 6th Street to the south, and Dade Boulevard (along the Collins Canal) to the north. In chapter 8, you'll find a map of the neighborhood (page 149) as well as a detailed walking tour.

Most of the finest examples of the whimsical art deco style are concentrated along three parallel streets—Ocean Drive, Collins Avenue, and Washington Avenue—from about 6th to 23rd streets.

After years of neglect and calls for the wholesale demolition of its buildings, South Beach got a new lease on life in 1979. Under the leadership of Barbara Baer Capitman, a dedicated crusader for the art deco region and the Miami Design Preservation League, an area made up of an estimated 800 buildings was granted a listing on the National Register of Historic Places. Designers then began high-lighting long-lost architectural details with soft sherbet shades of peach, periwinkle, turquoise, and purple. Developers soon moved in, and the full-scale refurbishment of the area's hotels was under way.

Today, hundreds of new hotels, restaurants, and nightclubs have been renovated or are in the process, and South Beach is on the cutting edge of Miami's cultural and nightlife scene.

EXPLORING THE AREA

If you're touring this unique neighborhood on your own, start at the **Art Deco Welcome Center,** 1001 Ocean Dr. (☎ **305/531-3484**), the only beachside building across from the Clevelander Hotel and bar. They give away lots of informational material including maps and pamphlets. Art deco books (including *The Art Deco Guide,* an informative compendium of all the buildings here), T-shirts, postcards, mugs, and other paraphernalia are for sale. It's open Monday to Saturday from 9am to 6pm, sometimes later.

Take a stroll along **Ocean Drive** for the best view of sidewalk cafes, bars, colorful hotels, and even more colorful people. Another great place for a walk is **Lincoln Road,** which is lined with galleries, cafes, and funky art and antique stores. The Community Church, at the corner of Lincoln Road and Drexel Avenue, is the neighborhood's first church and one of its oldest surviving buildings, dating from 1921.

For details on self-guided tours of the area, see chapter 8, "Driving & Strolling Around Miami," or for guided tours read "Sightseeing Cruises & Organized Tours," below.

3 Animal Parks

Kids of all ages will enjoy Miami's animal parks, which feature everything from dolphins to lions to parrots. Of course, there are plenty of alligators, too. Call to inquire about discount packages or coupons which may be offered at area retail stores or in local papers.

✪ **Miami Metrozoo.** 12400 SW 152nd St., South Miami. ☎ **305/251-0400.** Admission $8 adults, $4 children 3–12. Daily 9:30am–5:30pm (ticket booth closes at 4pm). From U.S. 1 south, turn right on SW 152nd St. and follow signs about 3 miles to the entrance.

This impressive 290-acre complex is completely cageless—animals are kept at bay by cleverly designed moats. Especially if you're with children, it's worth it. Mufasa and Simba (of Disney fame) were modeled on a couple of Metrozoo's lions, still in residence. Plus, there are two rare white Bengal tigers, a Komodo dragon, rare koala bears, a monorail "safari," and a petting zoo. You can even ride an elephant. The facilities are always improving and adding new exhibits.

✪ **Miami Seaquarium.** 4400 Rickenbacker Causeway (south side), en route to Key Biscayne. ☎ **305/361-5705.** Admission $22 adults, $17 children 3–9. Daily 9:30am–6pm (ticket booth closes at 4:30pm).

You'll want to arrive early to experience this fun and educational attraction. You'll need at least 3 hours to tour the 35-acre oceanarium and see all four daily shows starring these talented ocean mammals, although you can do it in about 2 if you're on a tight schedule. Trained dolphins, killer whales, and frolicking sea lions play with trainers and visitors. New in 1999 is a program that allows visitors to touch, swim, and even smooch with dolphins. The cost is $125 per person and is offered twice daily Wednesday through Sunday. Children must be at least 52 inches tall to participate. Call ☎ 305/365-2501 in advance for reservations.

Monkey Jungle. 14805 SW 216th St., South Miami. ☎ **305/235-1611.** Admission $11.50 adults, $9.50 seniors and active-duty military, $6 children 4–12. Daily 9:30am–5pm (tickets sold until 4pm). Take U.S. 1 south to SW 216th St. or from Florida Turnpike, take Exit 11 and follow the signs.

See rare Brazilian golden lion tamarins. Watch the "skin-diving" Asian macaques. Yes, it's primate paradise! There are no cages to restrain the antics of the monkeys as they swing, chatter, and play their way into your heart. Screened-in trails wind through acres of "jungle," and daily shows feature the talents of the park's most progressive pupils. Slight warning: You've got to love primates to get over the heavy smell of the jungle; it's been here for more than 60 years.

Parrot Jungle and Gardens. 11000 SW 57th Ave., Southern Miami–Dade County. ☎ **305/666-7834.** Admission $13.95 adults, $12.95 Seniors, $8.95 children 3–10. Daily 9:30am–6pm. Cafe opens at 8am. Take U.S. 1 south, turn left at SW 57th Ave. or exit Kendall Dr. from the Florida Turnpike and turn right on U.S. 1.

It's loud and silly, but it's fun. Not just parrots, but hundreds of magnificent macaws, peacocks, cockatoos, and flamingos occupy this 22-acre park. Continuous shows in the Parrot Bowl Theater star roller-skating cockatoos, card-playing macaws, and more stunt-happy parrots than you ever thought possible. There are also alligators, tortoises, and iguanas on exhibit. Other attractions include a wildlife show focusing on indigenous Florida animals, an area called "Primate Experience," a children's playground, and a petting zoo. It's worth the extra $3.25 to buy the jungle adventure key, which allows you access to taped trivia about the park and its inhabitants.

Important note: After more than 50 years at this location, Parrot Jungle is planning to move to its own island midway between downtown Miami and the beaches; the relocation is in the works.

4 Miami's Museum & Art Scene

Miami's museum scene has always been quirky, interesting, and inconsistent at best. Though several exhibition spaces have made forays into collecting nationally acclaimed work, limited support and political infighting have made it a difficult proposition. Recently, with the reinvention of the Wolfsonian, the reincarnation of MOCA, and the increased daring of the Miami Art Museum, the scene has improved dramatically. It's now safe to say that world-class exhibitions start here. Listed below is an excellent cross-section of the valuable treasures that have become a part of the city's cultural heritage, and as such, are as diverse as the city itself.

For gallery lovers, see "Specialized Tours," below, for scheduled gallery walks, and chapter 9, "Shopping," for a highlight of a few of the best.

IN SOUTH BEACH

Bass Museum of Art. 2121 Park Ave. (1 block west of Collins Ave.), South Beach. ☎ **305/ 673-7530.** Admission $5 adults, $3 students and seniors, free for children 6 and under; second and fourth Wed of the month by donation from 5–9pm. Tues–Sat 10am–5pm; Sun 1–5pm (every second and fourth Wed open 1–9pm). Closed major holidays.

An important and growing visual arts museum in Miami Beach, Bass displays European paintings, sculptures, and tapestries from the Renaissance, baroque, rococo, and modern periods as part of their small permanent collection. Temporary exhibitions alternate between traveling shows and rotations of the Bass's stock, with themes ranging from 17th-century Dutch art to contemporary architecture.

Built from coral rock in 1930, the Bass sits in the middle of more than a dozen tree-topped, landscaped acres. Under construction at press time, the museum will soon have double the gallery space.

The Wolfsonian. 1001 Washington Ave., South Beach. ☎ **305/531-1001.** Admission $5 adults; $3.50 senior citizens, students, and children 6–12; $5 tour-group members; free on Thurs evenings. Members, children under 6, and students or faculty of Florida Universities are admitted free. Mon, Tues, Fri–Sat 11am–6pm; Thurs 11am–9pm; Sun noon–5pm.

Mitchell Wolfson Jr., an eccentric collector of late 19th- and 20th-century art and other paraphernalia, was spending so much money storing his booty that he decided to buy the warehouse that was housing it. It ultimately held more than 70,000 of his items, including glass, ceramics, sculptures, paintings, and photographs. He's given this incredibly diverse and controversial collection to Florida International University. The former storage facility has been retrofitted with such painstaking detail that it's the envy of curators around the world.

✪ **Holocaust Memorial.** 1933 Meridian Ave. (at Dade Blvd.), South Beach. ☎ **305/ 538-1663.** Free admission. Daily 9am–9pm.

This heart-wrenching memorial is hard to miss and would be a shame to overlook. The powerful centerpiece is a bronze statue by Kenneth Treister that depicts thousands of victims crawling into an open hand to freedom. You can walk through an open hallway lined with photographs and the names of concentration camps and their victims. From the street, you'll see the outstretched arm, but do stop and tour the sculpture at ground level—what's hidden behind the beautiful stone facade is extremely moving.

IN & NEAR DOWNTOWN

Florida Museum of Hispanic and Latin American Art. 4006 Aurora St. (between Altara St and Bird Rd.), Coral Gables. ☎ **305/444-7060.** Free admission. Tues–Fri 11am–5pm; Sat 11am–4pm. Closed Aug and major holidays.

In addition to the permanent collection of contemporary artists from Spain and Latin America, this 3,500-square-foot museum hosts monthly exhibitions of works from Latin America and the Caribbean Basin. Usually, the exhibitions focus on a

A Secret Stash of Contemporary Art

Art aficionados always find their way to major art exhibitions in the cities and towns they visit, but nothing can be more exciting and more unusual than being invited to tour a private collection.

Next time you're in Miami for a weekend, consider yourself on the guest list. Your hosts are four New Yorkers, Mera and Don Rubell and their adult children, Jennifer and Jason, who together have opened two hip hotels on South Beach (The Albion and the Greenview). They have also brought with them their price-less collection of more than a thousand works of contemporary art, by the likes of Paul McCarthy, Keith Haring, Jean-Michel Basquiat, Charles Ray, and Cindy Sherman. These pieces are now on view in a former Drug Enforcement Agency warehouse in downtown Miami.

"I'm jealous," says David A. Ross, director of the San Francisco Museum of Modern Art. "There are few collections of its equal anywhere in the world."

The works, many of which are too big or too daring for your average museum, reveal the Rubells' taste for the strange, humorous, and irreverent. They include McCarthy's Cultural Gothic (1992–93), a motorized sculpture of a man coaxing a young boy into an act of bestiality, and Beverly Semme's Blue Gowns (1993), three giant gowns flowing from a neck-craning height onto the floor.

If you don't know these names, you should probably skip this stop. There's no avoiding nudity, erotica, and themes some may find offensive; bring the kids at your discretion. The collection is open from 11am to 4pm Friday through Sunday and is located at 95 NW 29th St., near the Design District (☎ **305/ 573-6090**).

theme, such as international women or surrealism. It's not a major attraction, but definitely worth a stop if you're an art lover. On the same block, you'll find great design stores and a few other galleries.

✪ **Miami Art Museum at the Miami-Dade Cultural Center.** 101 W. Flagler St., Miami. ☎ **305/375-3000.** Admission $5 adults, $2.50 senior and students, free for children under 12, by contribution on Tues. Tues–Fri 10am–5pm; third Thurs of each month 10am–9pm; Sat–Sun noon–5pm. Closed major holidays. From I-95 south, exit at Orange Bowl–NW 8th St. and continue south to NW 2nd St.; turn left at NW 2nd St. and go 1½ blocks to NW 2nd Ave.; turn right.

The Miami Art Museum (MAM) features an eclectic mix of modern and contemporary works by such artists as Eric Fischl, Max Beckman, Jim Dine, and Stuart Davis. Rotating exhibitions span the ages and styles and often focus on Latin American or Caribbean artists. The shows are almost always superbly curated and installed, and sometimes subject to controversy from the ultrapolitical Cuban community.

The Miami-Dade Cultural Center, where the museum is housed, is an oasis for those seeking cultural enrichment during their trip to Miami. In addition to the acclaimed Miami Art Museum, the center houses the main branch of the Miami-Dade Public Library, which sometimes features art and cultural exhibits, and the Historical Museum of Southern Florida, which highlights the fascinating history of the area.

American Police Hall of Fame and Museum. 3801 Biscayne Blvd., Miami. ☎ **305/ 573-0070.** Admission $6 adults, $4 seniors over 61, $3 children 11 and under, $1 police officers. 50% off coupons often available from hotel racks. Daily 10am–5:30pm. Drive north on U.S. 1 from downtown until you see the building with the police car affixed to its side.

This strange museum appeals mostly to those fascinated by police and their gadgetry. Once inside, you'll find a combination of reality and fantasy that's part thoughtful tribute, part Hollywood-style drama. Just past the car featured in the motion picture *Blade Runner* is a mock prison cell, in which visitors can take pictures of themselves pretending they're doing 5 to 10. Also on hand are execution devices, including a guillotine and an electric chair. In the entry is a touching memorial to the more than 3,000 police officers who have lost their lives in the line of duty.

✪ **Museum of Contemporary Art (MOCA).** 770 NE 125th St., North Miami. ☎ **305/893-6211.** Admission $4 adults, $2 seniors and students with ID, free for children 12 and under. Tues–Sat 11am–5pm; Sun noon–5pm. Closed major holidays.

MOCA recently acquired a new 23,000-square-foot space in which to display its impressive collection of internationally acclaimed art with a local flavor. You can see works by Jasper Johns, Roy Lichtenstein, Larry Rivers, Duane Michaels, and Claes Oldenberg. Guided tours are offered in English, Spanish, French, Creole, Portuguese, German, and Italian.

An impressive screening facility allows for film presentations to complement the exhibitions. Although the $3.75 million project was built in an area otherwise avoided by tourists, MOCA is worth a drive to view important contemporary art in South Florida.

IN CORAL GABLES & COCONUT GROVE

Miami Museum of Science and Space Transit Planetarium. 3280 S. Miami Ave. (just south of the Rickenbacker Causeway), Coconut Grove. ☎ **305/854-4247** for general information, 305/854-2222 for planetarium show times. $9 adults, $7 students, seniors and children 3–12, free for children 2 and under. Planetarium, $5 adults, $2.50 children and seniors. Combination ticket, $9 adults, $5.50 children and seniors. Half price 4:30–6pm weekdays. Museum of Science, daily 10am–6pm; call for planetarium show times. 25% discount for AAA members.

The Museum of Science features more than 140 hands-on exhibits that explore the mysteries of the universe. Live demonstrations and collections of rare natural history specimens make a visit here fun and informative. Two or three major traveling exhibits are usually on display as well.

The adjacent Space Transit Planetarium projects astronomy and laser shows as well as interactive demonstrations of upcoming computer technology and cyberspace features. Plan to spend at least 3 or 4 hours exploring the fascinating exhibits and displays here.

Weeks Air Museum. 14710 SW 28th St. (south of 120th St. and west of the Florida Turnpike at the Kendall-Tamiami Airport), Miami. ☎ **305/233-5197.** Admission $6.95 adults, $5.95 seniors, $4.95 children under 12. Daily 10am–5pm.

This well-maintained museum is a must-see for aeronautic buffs who will enjoy talking with the thoroughly dedicated staff who are always eager to answer questions from fellow enthusiasts. Exhibitions include a dramatic portrait of the Tuskeegee Airmen who tell of their experiences on video. Also on display are dozens of airplanes dating from the turn of the century and an intriguing display of planes damaged by Hurricane Andrew in 1992. Other highlights include a collection of propellers throughout the ages; a J47 jet engine; an aerobatic plane, the "Little Stinker" Soviet bombers; and lots of war memorabilia.

5 Fantastic Feats of Architecture

Not all the great buildings in Miami are in South Beach's Art Deco district. You'll also find many exciting enclaves filled with Mediterranean gems and eclectic wonders, especially in Coral Gables. Even if you aren't staying there, check out the Biltmore Hotel (see chapter 5, "Miami Accommodations") and the stunning Congregational Church across the street.

Villa Vizcaya. 3251 S. Miami Ave. (just south of Rickenbacker Causeway), North Coconut Grove. ☎ **305/250-9133.** Admission $10 adults, $5 children 6–12, free for children 5 and under. Villa daily 9:30am–5pm (ticket booth closes at 4:30pm); gardens daily 9:30am–5:30pm.

Sometimes referred to as the "Hearst Castle of the East," this magnificent villa is the setting for many society weddings and galas. It was built in 1916 as a winter retreat for James Deering, cofounder and former vice president of International Harvester. The industrialist was fascinated by 16th-century art and architecture, and his ornate mansion—which took 1,000 artisans 5 years to build—became a celebration of that period. Most of the original furnishings, including dishes and paintings, are still intact.

The spectacularly opulent villa wraps itself around a central courtyard. Outside, lush formal gardens, accented with statuary, balustrades, and decorative urns, front an enormous swath of Biscayne Bay, near the homes of Sylvester Stallone and Madonna.

The Barnacle State Historic Site. 3485 Main Hwy. (1 block south of Commodore Plaza), Coconut Grove. ☎ **305/448-9445.** Admission $1. Tours Fri–Sun at 10am, 11:30am, 1pm, and 2:30pm. Group tours Mon–Thurs with 2-week advance reservations. From downtown Miami, take U.S. 1 south to 27th Ave., make a left, and continue to South Bayshore Dr.; then make a right, follow to the intersection of Main Hwy. and turn left.

The former home of naval architect and early settler Ralph Middleton Munroe is now a museum in the heart of Coconut Grove. The house's quiet surroundings, wide porches, and period furnishings illustrate how Miami's privileged class lived in the days before skyscrapers and luxury hotels. Enthusiastic and knowledgeable state park employees offer a wealth of historical information to those interested in quiet, low-tech attractions like this one. Call for details on monthly moonlight concerts during which folk, blues, or classical music are presented. Cost is $5 per person, free for children under 10.

Coral Castle. 28655 S. Dixie Hwy., Homestead. ☎ **305/248-6344.** Admission $7.75 adults, $6.50 seniors, $5 children 7–12. Daily 9am–6pm. Take U.S. 1 south to SW 286th St.

There's plenty of competition, but Coral Castle is probably the strangest attraction in Florida. In 1923, the story goes, a crazed Latvian, suffering from unrequited love, immigrated to South Miami and spent the next 25 years of his life carving huge boulders into a prehistoric-looking, roofless "castle." It seems impossible that one rather short man could have done all this, but there are scores of affidavits on display from neighbors who swear it happened. Apparently, experts have studied this phenomenon to help figure out how the Great Pyramids and Stonehenge were built.

Listen to the audio tour to learn about this bizarre spot, now in the National Register of Historic Places. The commentary lasts about 25 minutes and is available in four languages. Although Coral Castle is overpriced and undermaintained, it's worth a visit when in the area.

✪ **Spanish Monastery Cloisters.** 16711 W. Dixie Hwy. (at NE 167th St.), North Miami Beach. ☎ **305/945-1461.** Admission $4.50 adults, $2.50 seniors, $1 children 11 and under. Mon–Sat 10am–4pm; Sun noon–4pm.

Did you know that the oldest building in the western hemisphere dates from 1141 and is located in Miami? The Spanish Monastery Cloisters were first erected in Segovia, Spain. Centuries later, newspaper magnate William Randolph Hearst purchased and brought them to America in pieces. The carefully numbered stones were quarantined for years until they were finally reassembled on the present site in 1954. Visitors are free to explore; you'll want to spend about an hour touring the cold, ancient structure, the beautiful grounds, and the gift shop.

Venetian Pool. 2701 DeSoto Blvd. (at Toledo St.), Coral Gables. ☎ **305/460-5356.** Admission and hours vary seasonally. Nov–Mar, $5 13 and older, $2 children under 13; April–Oct, $8 13 and older, $4 under 13. Children under 36 months not allowed in the facilities. Call for hours.

Miami's most beautiful and unusual swimming pool, dating from 1924, is hidden behind pastel stucco walls and is honored with a listing in the National Register of Historic Places. Underground artesian wells feed the free-form lagoon, which is shaded by three-story Spanish porticos and features both fountains and waterfalls. It can be cold in the winter months. During summer, the pool's 800,000 gallons of water are drained and refilled nightly, ensuring a cool, clean swim. Visitors are free to swim and sunbathe here, just as Esther Williams and Johnny Weissmuller did decades ago. For a modest fee, you or your children can learn to swim during special summer programs.

6 Nature Preserves, Parks & Gardens

The Miami area is a great place for outdoors-minded visitors, with beaches, parks, and gardens galore. Plus, South Florida has two national parks; see chapter 11 for coverage of the Everglades and Biscayne National Park.

BOTANICAL GARDENS & A SPICE PARK

In Miami, the **Fairchild Tropical Gardens,** 10901 Old Cutler Rd. (☎ **305/667-1651**), features a veritable rain forest of both rare and exotic plants on 83 acres. Palmettos, vine pergola, palm glades, and other unique species create a scenic, lush environment. It's well worth taking the free hourly tram to learn what you always wanted to know about the various flowers and trees during a 30-minute narrated tour. There is also a museum, cafe, and gift shop with fantastic books on gardening and cooking and edible gifts.

Admission is $8 for adults, and free for children 12 and under accompanied by an adult. Open daily from 9:30am to 4:30pm. Take I-95 south to U.S. 1, turn left onto Le Jeune Road, and follow it straight to the traffic circle; from there, take Old Cutler Road 2 miles to the park.

A testament to Miami's unusual climate, the **Preston B. Bird and Mary Heinlein Fruit and Spice Park,** 24801 SW 187th Ave., Homestead (☎ **305/247-5727**), harbors rare fruit trees that cannot survive elsewhere in the country.

Definitely ask for a guide. If a volunteer is available, you'll learn some fascinating things about this 30-acre living plant museum where the most exotic varieties of fruits and spices, including ackee, mango, ugly fruits, carambola, and breadfruit, grow on strange-looking trees with unpronounceable names.

The best part? You're free to take anything that falls to the ground. You'll also find samples of interesting fruits and jellies made from the park's bounty in the gift store.

Cooks who like to experiment must visit the park store, which carries a number of exotic ingredients and cookbooks.

Admission to the spice park is $3.50 for adults and $1 for children under 12, and is open daily from 10am to 5pm; closed major holidays. Tours are included in the price of admission and are offered 11am, 1pm, and 2:30pm. Take U.S. 1 south, turn right on SW 248th Street, and go straight for 5 miles to SW 187th Avenue.

MORE MIAMI PARKS

The **Amelia Earhart Park,** 401 E. 65th St., Hialeah (☎ **305/685-8389**), has five lakes stocked with bass and brim for fishing; playgrounds; picnic facilities; and a big red barn that houses cows, sheep, and goats for petting and ponies for riding. There's also a country store and dozens of old-time farm activities like horseshoeing, sugarcane processing, and more. Parking is free on weekdays and $3.50 per car on weekends. Open daily from 9am to sunset. To drive here, take I-95 north to the NW 103rd Street exit, go west to East 4th Avenue, and then turn right. Parking is 1½ miles down the street.

At the historic **Bill Baggs Cape Florida State Recreation Area,** 1200 Crandon Blvd. (☎ **305/361-5811**), at the tip of Key Biscayne, you can explore the unfettered wilds and enjoy some of the most secluded beaches in Miami. There's also a recently reopened lighthouse. A rental shack rents bikes, hydrobikes, kayaks, and many more water toys. It's a great place to picnic, and a newly constructed restaurant serves homemade Latin food, including great fish soups and sandwiches. Just be careful that the raccoons don't get your lunch, because the furry black-eyed beasts are everywhere. Admission is $4 per car with up to eight people. Open daily from 8am to sunset. Tours of the recently renovated lighthouse are available every day except Tuesday and Wednesday, at 10am and 1pm. Arrive at least half an hour early to sign up—there is only room for 10 people on each.

Tropical Park, 7900 SW 40th St. (☎ **305/226-8315**), has it all. Enjoy a game of tennis and racquetball for a minimal fee, or swim and sun yourself on the secluded little lake. You can use the fishing pond for free, and they'll even supply you with the rods and bait. If you catch anything, however, you're on your own. Open daily from sunrise to sunset.

Named after the now deceased champion of the Everglades, **Marjory Stoneman Douglas Biscayne Nature Center** offers hands-on marine exploration, hikes through coastal hammocks, bike trips and beach walks. Local environmentalists and historians lead intriguing trips through the local habitat. Be sure to wear comfortable closed-toe shoes for hikes through wet or rocky terrain. The center is located in Crandon Park in Key Biscayne. Call (☎ **305/642-9600**) for tour schedules and prices.

7 Especially for Kids

The **Scott Rakow Youth Center,** 2700 Sheridan Ave. (☎ **305/673-7767**), is a hidden treasure on Miami Beach. This two-story facility boasts an ice-skating rink, bowling alleys, a basketball court, gymnasium equipment, and full-time supervision for kids. Call for a complete schedule of organized events. The only drag is that it's not open to adults (except on Sunday which is family day). Admission is $1.50 per day for visiting children 9 to 17. Open daily from 2 to 8:30pm.

The following is a roundup of other attractions kids will especially enjoy. Details on each one can be found earlier in the chapter.

To Central Miami Beach ↑

23rd St.

The Bass Museum of Art

22nd St.

Collins Park

Dade Boulevard

Miami Beach Convention Center

20th St.

19th St.

Purdy Ave.

18th St.

Dade Boulevard

Venetian Causeway

17th St.

James Ave.

Belle Island

Bay Rd.

Lincoln Road Mall

Lincoln Rd.

Collins Ave.

West Ave.

Alton Rd.

Lenox Ave.

Historic Art Deco District

16th St.

15th St.

Española Way

14th St.

Miami Beach Post Office

13th St.

Ocean Dr.

Biscayne Bay

Michigan Ave.

Meridian Ave.

12th St.

11th St.

Pennsylvania Ave.

Washington Ave.

Flamingo Park

10th St.

9th St.

Beach Patrol Station

Art Deco Welcome Center

Lummus Park

West Ave.

8th St.

7th St.

6th St.

Atlantic Ocean

Michigan Ave.

Jefferson Ave.

5th St.

4th St.

3rd St.

Washington Ave.

Collins Ave.

Ocean Dr.

South Beach Attractions
Bass Museum of Art ②
Bayshore Golf Course ①
Holocaust Memorial ⑤
Sanford L. Ziff Jewish Museum
   of Florida ⑮
The Wolfsonian ⑬
Bike & Blade Rentals
Fritz's Skate Shop ⑩
Miami Beach Bicycle Center ⑭
Skate 2000 ⑪
Gym
Crunch ⑫
Art Spaces
Colony Theater ⑨
Jackie Gleason Theater of
   Performing Arts ⑦
Lincoln Theatre ⑧
Miami City Ballet Studio ③
Performing Arts Network
   Building ⑥
Information
Miami Beach Chamber
   of Commerce ④

2nd St.

1st St.

Commerce St.

Biscayne St.

South Pointe Park

Government Cut

0   .125 Miles

0   .125 Kilometers

N

AMELIA EARHART PARK (see page 126)   This is the best park in Miami for kids. They'll like the petting zoos, pony rides, and private island with hidden tunnels.

MARJORY STONEMAN DOUGLAS BISCAYNE NATURE CENTER (see page 126)   Kids seem to enjoy touching slimy marine animals and spotting unusual creatures out at sea. This brand-new exhibit and tour center offers lots of educational and fun programs.

MIAMI METROZOO (see page 120)   This completely cageless zoo offers such star attractions as a monorail "safari" and a petting zoo. Kids love the elephant rides.

MIAMI MUSEUM OF SCIENCE & SPACE TRANSIT PLANETARIUM (see page 123)   At the Planetarium, kids can learn about space and science by watching entertaining films and cosmic shows. The space museum also offers child-friendly explanations for natural occurrences.

MIAMI SEAQUARIUM (see page 120)   Kids can get a kiss from a dolphin and watch exciting performances.

8 Game Parks & Entertainment Centers

✪ **Game Works.** 5701 Sunset Dr. South Miami. ☎ **305/740-9091.** Mon–Fri 11am–2am, Sat 10am–2am, Sun 10am–midnight. Games 50¢–$5.

The biggest thing to hit Miami in years, Steven Spielberg's SEGA Gameworks in the Shops of Sunset Place made its debut in early 1999 and quickly became the place for young adults to play. You'll see kids, Gen-Xers, and Baby Boomers fighting off dinosaurs from Jurassic Park, racing in the Indy 500, swooshing down a snowy ski trail, throwing darts, and shooting pool in this sleek, multilevel playground. The young at heart will find the perfect combination of vintage arcade games, high-tech videos, virtual reality arenas, pool tables, food, and cocktails in this playground occupying more than 33,000 square feet.

IMAX Theatre at Sunset Place. 5701 Sunset Dr. South Miami. ☎ **305/663-4629.** Shows daily from 11am–11pm. IMAX: Adults $7.50 seniors and students $6.50, children under 12 $5.50. 3-D theater: adults $9, seniors and students $8, children under 12 $7. Call for exact schedules and prices.

Using high-tech film techniques, six-story-high screens, and wraparound digital sound, this unique movie experience really makes you feel like you're part of the action. At press time, the incredible story of Everest was showing. This 50-minute documentary style film captured the terrifying experience of the mountain climbers in the Himalayas in all its frigid, blinding wonder. Also available is a 3-D theater that really tempts you to reach out and touch the images.

For other nearby arcades and game parks see chapter 13, "The Gold Coast."

9 Sightseeing Cruises & Organized Tours

BOAT & CRUISE-SHIP TOURS

Gondola Adventures. Docked at Biscayne Bay Marina, 1633 N. Bayshore Dr. (behind the Marriott Hotel), Miami. ☎ **305/358-6400.** Rates from $5 per person (minimum 4 people).

A real gondola in Miami? Well, it may not be the canals of Venice, but with a little imagination, the Biscayne Bay will do. You can go on a simple ride around Bayside, or splurge on your own private champagne cruise for $99.

Attractions in South Miami-Dade County

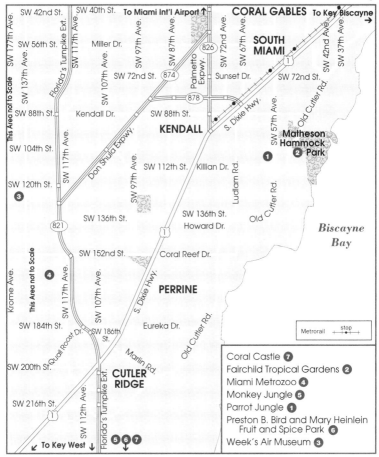

Heritage Miami II Topsail Schooner. Bayside Marketplace Marina, 401 Biscayne Blvd., Downtown. ☎ **305/442-9697.** Tickets $15 adults, $10 children 12 and under. Sept–May only. Tours leave daily at 1:30, 4, and 6:30pm, and on Fri, Sat, and Sun also at 9, 10, and 11pm.

More adventure than tour, this relaxing ride aboard Miami's only tall ship is a fun way to see the city. The 2-hour cruises pass by Villa Vizcaya, Coconut Grove, and Key Biscayne and put you in sight of Miami's spectacular skyline. Call to make sure the ship is running on schedule. On Friday, Saturday, and Sunday evenings, there are 1-hour tours to see the lights of the city.

A SIGHTSEEING TOUR

There are literally hundreds of tour operators in Miami and the Beaches. Check with your hotel's concierge to see which they recommend, or try the following company.

Miami Nice Excursion Travel and Service. 18430 Collins Ave., Miami Beach. ☎ **305/949-9180.** Admission $29–$55 adults, $25 children. Daily 7am–10pm. Call ahead for directions to various pickup areas.

Pick your destination. The Miami Nice tours will take you to the Everglades, Fort Lauderdale, the Seaquarium, Key West, Cape Canaveral, or wherever you desire. Included in most Miami trips is a fairly comprehensive city tour narrated by a knowledgeable guide. The company is one of the oldest in town.

SPECIALIZED TOURS

Besides those listed below, a great option for seeing the city is to take a tour led by Dr. Paul George. Dr. George is a history teacher at Miami-Dade Community College and a historian at the Historical Museum of Southern Florida—he also happens to be "Mr. Miami." There's a set calendar of tours, but all of them are fascinating to South Florida buffs. Tours focus on neighborhoods, such as Little Havana, Brickell Avenue, or Key Biscayne, and on themes, such as Miami cemeteries. The often long-winded discussions can be a bit much for those who just want a quick look-around, but Dr. George certainly knows his stuff. The cost is $15 to $25; reservations are required (☎ 305/375-1492). Tours leave from the Historical Museum at 101 W. Flagler St., Downtown.

Miami Design Preservation League. The Art Deco Welcome Center, 1001 Ocean Dr., South Beach. ☎ **305/672-2014.** Walking tours $10 per person. Tours leave Sat at 10:30am and Thurs at 6:30pm. Self-guided audio tours also available 7 days a week for $5. Call ahead for updated schedules.

On Thursday evenings and Saturday mornings, the Design Preservation League sponsors walking tours that offer a fascinating inside look at the city's historic Art Deco District. Tour-goers meet for a 1½-hour walk through some of America's most exuberantly "architectured" buildings. The league led the fight to designate this area a National Historic District and is proud to share the splendid results with visitors.

Art Deco Cycling Tour. 601 5th St., South Beach. ☎ **305/674-0150.** $10 per person, plus $6 for bike rental. Tours depart every other Sun at 10am from the Miami Beach Bicycle Center.

If you'd rather bike or in-line skate than walk, catch this fun and interesting Sunday morning tour. The bicycle is the most efficient mode of transportation through the streets of South Beach, and one of the best ways to see the historic Art Deco District. Call to reserve a spot.

Biltmore Hotel Tour. 1200 Anastasia Ave., Coral Gables. ☎ **305/445-1926.** Free admission. Tours depart on Sun at 1:30, 2:30, and 3:30pm.

Take advantage of these free walking tours offered on Sunday to enjoy the hotel's beautiful grounds. The Biltmore is chock-full of history and mystery, including a few ghosts; go out there and see for yourself.

Coral Gables Art and Gallery Tour. Various locations in Coral Gables. Free. For more information, call Elite Fine Art (☎ **305/448-3800**) or stop by any of the galleries in the area. First Fri of the month from 7–10pm.

On this tour, art lovers are shuttled to 20 galleries that participate in Gables Night in the gallery section of Coral Gables. Viewers can sip wine as they gaze at American folk art; African, Native American, and Latin art; and photography. Most galleries are on Ponce de León Boulevard, between SW 40th and SW 24th streets. The vans run continuously from 7 to 10pm.

Lincoln Road Gallery Walk at the Art Center. 800 Lincoln Rd. (at the corner of Meridian Ave.). ☎ **305/674-8278.** Free. Tour given second Sat of every month from 7–11pm.

Join a knowledgeable guide for a tour of artists' studios on the second Saturday of every month. Or, feel free to wander through the more than 50 studios housed in this cooperative art complex on your own. You can also walk through the pedestrian mall to catch a look at the works on display in other galleries (if you're lucky, you'll wander into one that serves wine and appetizers).

10 Water Sports

BOATING

Private rental outfits include **Beach Boat Rentals,** 2400 Collins Ave., Miami Beach (☎ **305/534-4307**), where 50-horsepower, 18-foot powerboats rent for some of the best prices on the beach. Rates are $61.25 for an hour, $165.15 for 4 hours, and $225.70 for 8 hours. All rates include taxes and gas. A $250 cash or credit-card deposit is required. Cruising is permitted only in and around Biscayne Bay—ocean access is prohibited. Renters must be over 21. The rental office is at 23rd Street, on the inland waterway in Miami Beach. It's open from 9am to 6pm (weather permitting) during the high season and 9am to 8pm during the summer.

   Club Nautico of Coconut Grove, 2560 S. Bayshore Dr., Coconut Grove (☎ **305/858-6258**), rents high-quality powerboats for fishing, waterskiing, diving, and cruising in the bay or ocean. All boats are Coast Guard equipped, with VHF radios and safety gear. Rates range from $199 for 4 hours and $299 for 8 hours to as much as $419 on weekends. Club Nautico is open daily from 9am to 5pm (weather permitting). Other locations include the Crandon Park Marina, 4000 Crandon Blvd., Key Biscayne (☎ **305/361-9217**), with the same rates and hours as the Coconut Grove location; and the Miami Beach Marina, Pier E, 300 Alton Rd., South Beach (☎ **305/673-2502**), where rates are $229 for 4 hours and $299 for 8 hours for a 20-foot boat; and $259 for 4 hours and $359 for 8 hours for a 24-footer. Nautico on Miami Beach is open daily from 9am to 5pm.

SAILING

You can rent sailboats and catamarans through the beachfront concessions desk of several top resorts, such as the Doral Ocean Beach Resort, Sheraton Bal Harbour Beach Resort, and Dezerland Surfside Beach Hotel (see chapter 5, "Accommodations").

   Sailboats of **Key Biscayne Rentals and Sailing School,** in the Crandon Marina (next to Sundays on the Bay), 4000 Crandon Blvd., Key Biscayne (☎ **305/ 361-0328** days, 305/279-7424 evenings), can also get you out on the water. A 22-foot sailboat rents for $27 an hour, or $81 for a half day. A Cat-25 or J24 is available for $35 an hour or $110 for a half day. If you've always had a dream to win the America's Cup but can't sail, the able teachers at Sailboats will get you started. It offers a 10-hour course over 5 days for $250 for one person or $350 for you and a buddy, $50 for each additional person.

   Shake-a-Leg, 2600 Bayshore Dr., Coconut Grove (☎ **305/858-5550**), is a unique sailing program for disabled and able-bodied people alike. The program pairs up sailors for day and evening cruises and offers sailing lessons as well. Consider a moonlight cruise (offered monthly) or a race clinic. Shake-a-Leg members also welcome able-bodied volunteers for activities on and off the water. It costs $60 for nonmembers to rent a boat for 3 hours; free for volunteers. Open on Wednesday through Sunday from 9am to 5pm.

JET-SKIS/WAVE RUNNERS

Don't miss a chance to tour the islands on the back of your own powerful watercraft. Many beachfront concessionaires rent a variety of these popular (and loud) water scooters. The latest models are fast and smooth. Try **Tony's Jet Ski Rentals,** 3601 Rickenbacker Causeway, Key Biscayne (☎ **305/361-8280**), one of the city's largest rental shops, located on a private beach in the Miami Marine Stadium lagoon. Jet-skis rent for about $38 for a half hour and $64 for an hour. Wave Runners for two rent for $45 for a half hour and $70 for an hour. Tony's is open daily from 10:30am to 6:30pm.

KAYAKING

The laid-back **Urban Trails Kayak Company** rents boats at 10800 Collins Ave. (☎ **305/947-1302**). It offers scenic routes through rivers with mangroves and islands as your destination. Most of the kayaks are sit-on-tops and most are plastic, although there are some fiberglass models available. Rates are $8 an hour, $20 for up to 4 hours, and $25 for over 4 hours. Tandems are $12 an hour, $30 for up to 4 hours, and $35 for the day. Open daily from 9am to 5pm.

The outfitters here give interested explorers a map to take with them and quick instructions on how to work the paddles and boats. If you have at least four people, you can get a guided tour for $35 per person for half a day. This is a fun way to experience some of Miami's unspoiled wildlife, and it's good exercise, too.

SCUBA DIVING

In 1981, the government began a wide-scale project designed to increase the number of habitats available to marine organisms. One of the program's major accomplishments has been the creation of nearby artificial reefs, which have attracted all kinds of tropical plants, fish, and animals. In addition, Biscayne National Park (see chapter 11, "Side Trips from Miami") offers a protected marine environment just south of Downtown.

Several dive shops around the city offer organized weekend outings, either to the reefs or to one of over a dozen old shipwrecks around Miami's shores. Check "Divers" in the Yellow Pages for rental equipment and for a full list of undersea tour operators.

Divers Paradise of Key Biscayne, 4000 Crandon Blvd. (☎ **305/361-3483**), offers two dive expeditions daily to the more than 30 wrecks and artificial reefs off the coast of Miami Beach and Key Biscayne. You can take a 3-day certification course for $399, which includes all the dives and gear. If you already have your C-card, a dive trip costs about $90 if you need equipment and only $35 if you bring your own gear. It's open Monday to Friday from 10am to 6pm and Saturday and Sunday from 8am to 6pm. Call ahead for times and locations of dives.

WINDSURFING

Many hotels rent Windsurfers to their guests, but if yours doesn't have a watersports concession stand, head for Key Biscayne.

Sailboards Miami, Rickenbacker Causeway, Key Biscayne (☎ **305/361-SAIL**), operates out of big yellow trucks on Hobie Beach, the most popular windsurfing spot in the city. For those who've never ridden a board but want to try it, they offer a 2-hour lesson for $39 that's guaranteed to turn you into a wave warrior or you get your money back. After that, you can rent a board for $20 an hour or $37 for 2 hours. If you want to make a day of it, a 10-hour card costs $130. Open daily from 10am to 5:30pm. Make your first right after the toll booth to find the outfitters.

11 More Ways to Play, Both Indoors & Out

CYCLING

The cement promenade on the southern tip of the island is a great place to ride. Cycling up the beach is great for surf, sun, sand, exercise, and people-watching.

Seasonal Pleasures: Pick Your Own Produce

There is a singular pleasure in getting your fingers stained red by berry juice while friends up north shovel snow. But as South Florida's farm region gets gobbled up by tract homes and shopping malls, the area's self-pick farms are disappearing, too. Some of the remaining berry fields offer ambitious pickers a chance to find their own treasures beneath the trailing vines of strawberry rows for about $2.25 a pound.

If you don't feel like waking up early to pick the juicy red jewels, at least stop by to buy a few boxes of South Florida's winter bounty. Nothing tastes like just-picked berries. They usually bloom between January and April. At other times, you may find vegetables and herbs, including cayenne, jalapeño, orange peppers, eggplant, zucchini, lettuce, cabbage, and broccoli.

On your way to any of the sites in South Dade, just look around for the bright-red "U-Pic" signs pointing the way to a nearby farm.

Also look for farm-fresh snack stands in South Dade.

Burr's Berry Farms, 12741 SW 216th St., in Goulds (☎ **305/235-0513**), makes outrageous fruit milk shakes and ice creams. To get to Burr's, drive south on U.S. 1 and turn right on SW 216th Street. The fruit stand is about 1 mile west of U.S. 1 on the same road as the Monkey Jungle. It's open daily from 9am to 5:30pm.

Go early to snatch up some of the fast-selling pastries, tarts, and jams at **Knaus Berry Farm,** 15980 SW 248th St., in Redland (☎ **305/247-0668**). At all hours, a line of anxious ice-cream lovers wait for fresh fruit treats from a little white window. You'll also find flowers, herbs, and other seasonal vegetables. They are most famous, though, for their fresh-from-the-oven cinnamon rolls. Buy one or buy a dozen—they freeze well. Knaus is slightly further south on U.S. 1. Turn right on 248th Street, and the stand is about 2½ miles down on the left-hand side. It's open Monday to Saturday from 8am to 5:30pm.

Most of the big beach hotels rent bicycles, as does the **Miami Beach Bicycle Center,** 601 5th St., South Beach (☎ **305/674-0150**), which charges $5 per hour or $14 per day. It's open Monday to Saturday from 10am to 7pm and Sunday from 10am to 5pm.

Cyclists can also enjoy more than 130 miles of paved paths throughout Miami. The beautiful and quiet streets of Coral Gables and Coconut Grove are great for bicyclists. Old trees form canopies over wide, flat roads lined with grand homes and quaint street markers. Several bicycle trails are spread throughout these neighborhoods, including one that begins at the doorstep of **Dade Cycle,** 3216 Grand Ave., Coconut Grove (☎ **305/444-5997**); it's open Monday to Saturday from 9:30am to 5:30pm, Sunday from 10:30am to 5:30pm.

The terrain in Key Biscayne is perfect for cycling, especially along the park and beach roads. If you don't mind the sound of cars whooshing by, **Rickenbacker Causeway** is also fantastic since it is one of the only bikeable inclines in Miami from which you get fantastic elevated views of the city and waterways. **Key Cycling,** 61 Harbor Dr., Key Biscayne (☎ **305/361-0061**), rents mountain bikes for $5 an hour or $15 a day. It's open Monday through Friday from 10am to 7pm, Saturday from 10am to 6pm, and Sunday from 11am to 4pm.

Intra Mark, off the Rickenbacker Bridge across from the Rusty Pelican, Hobie Beach (☎ **305/365-0502**), rents scooters for $20 an hour or $35 for 2 hours, and bicycles for $5 an hour or $10 for 4 hours. The ecominded staff directs cyclists to the best paths for nature-watching.

If you want to avoid the traffic altogether, head out to **Shark Valley** in the Everglades National Park—one of South Florida's most scenic bicycle trails and a favorite haunt of city-weary locals. See chapter 11 for more details.

Biking note: Children under the age of 16 are required by Florida law to wear a helmet, which can be purchased at any bike store or retail outlet selling cycling supplies.

FISHING

Bridge fishing is popular in Miami; you'll see people with poles over almost every waterway.

Some of the best surf casting in the city can be had at **Haulover Beach Park** at Collins Avenue and 105th Street, where there's a bait-and-tackle shop right on the pier. **South Pointe Park,** at the southern tip of Miami Beach, is another popular fishing spot and features a long pier, comfortable benches, and a great view of the ships passing through Government Cut.

You can also choose to do some deep-sea fishing. One bargain outfitter, the **Kelley Fishing Fleet,** at the Haulover Marina, 10800 Collins Ave. (at 108th Street), Miami Beach (☎ **305/945-3801**), has half-day, full-day, and night fishing

---

Fishing in Miami

The humongous tarpon swam lazily between the dock pilings at the marina, mocking us. He was immense, at least 120 pounds, and had no interest in any of the fancy lures we offered him; even if he did, he would have snapped the line on the dock and been on his way. Fortunately, the Biscayne Bay area is prime tarpon fishing country, so we liked our chances of bagging another one. Actually, it's a pretty good spot for a lot of other trophy sportfish: snook, bonefish, dolphin, and sailfish.

Scores of anglers pass through Miami International Airport every day and keep moving right on down to the Florida Keys, never realizing that incredible fishing can be found just a short cab ride away. For a fee, local guides are happy to show you the hot spots and make sure you hook up.

Our guide, Captain David Parsons (☎ **305/264-8346**), took us out in his 28' boat *Hakuna Matada,* on a nighttime quest for some "silver king." As we pulled away from the dock, I yelled back at our tormenter, "I'll be back for you later, fatty."

Capt. Parsons brought us into **Government Cut,** the inlet that joins Biscayne Bay to the Atlantic Ocean. The frenetic lights of downtown Miami backlit our boat ride as we dodged commercial freighters and the Fisher Island Ferry. We drifted through the Cut in the neon glow of South Beach. On our third cast, BOOM! A 60-pound tarpon. It leaped out of the water and splashed down like a cinder block, then did it over and over again. The aerial acrobatics lasted 20 minutes. We all but forgot about the hog back at the dock; his little brother proved a sufficient challenge.

—Pete McDonald

aboard diesel-powered "party boats." The fleet's emphasis on drifting is geared toward trolling and bottom fishing for snapper, sailfish, and mackerel, but it also schedules 2- and 3-day trips to The Bahamas. Half-day and night fishing trips are $21 for adults and $14.50 for children; full-day trips are $33 for adults and $26.50 for children; rod and reel rental is $5. Daily departures are scheduled at 9am, 1:45pm, and 8pm; reservations are recommended.

Also at the Haulover Marina is the charter boat *Helen C,* 10800 Collins Ave., Haulover (☎ **305/947-4081**). Although there's no shortage of private charter boats here, Capt. Dawn Mergelsberg is a good pick, since she puts individuals together to get a full boat. Her *Helen* is a twin-engine 55-footer, equipped for big-game "monster" fish like marlin, tuna, dolphin, shark, and sailfish. The cost is $70 per person. Sailings are scheduled for 8am to noon and 1 to 5pm daily; call for reservations. Private charters and transportation are also available. Children are welcome.

Key Biscayne offers deep-sea fishing to those willing to get their hands dirty and pay a bundle. The competition among the boats is fierce, but the prices are basically the same no matter which you choose. The going rate is about $400 to $450 for a half day and $600 to $700 for a full day of fishing. These rates are usually for a party of up to six, and the boats supply you with rods and bait as well as instruction for first-timers. Some will take you out to Key Biscayne and even out to the Upper Keys if the fish aren't biting in Miami.

You might consider the following boats, all of which sail out of the Key Biscayne marina: *Sunny Boy III* (☎ **305/361-2217**), *Queen B* (☎ **305/361-2528**), and *L & H* (☎ **305/361-9318**). Call them for reservations.

GAMING

Although gambling is technically illegal in Miami, there are plenty of loopholes which allow all kinds of wagering. Gamblers can try their luck at offshore casinos, bingo, jai alai, card rooms, horse tracks, and dog races.

Especially popular is the huge outpost west of Miami, **Miccosukee Indian Gaming,** 500 SW 177th Ave. (off S.R. 41), (☎ **800/741-4600** or 305/222-4600). This glitzy casino isn't Vegas, but you can play slots, high-speed bingo, and even poker (with a $10 maximum pot). With more than 85,000 square feet of playing space, the complex even offers overnight accommodations for those who can't get enough of the thrill.

One of the most popular gambling "cruises to nowhere" is the **Europa Sea Kruz.** It departs every afternoon and evening from Dock A, 1280 5th St., South Beach. (☎ **800/688-PLAY** or 305/538-8300). Tickets are $10 to $15. A reasonably priced à la carte menu offers basic American fare from hamburgers to grilled chicken and salads. Most evenings, you'll hear live music on board. You and a few hundred other passengers can play blackjack or the slots. The biggest drawback—if you're losing big or just get bored, you're stuck at sea for 4½ hours.

A newer and more elegant option is the **Casino Princesa,** which docks behind the Hard Rock Cafe in Bayside Marketplace. This 200-foot, $15 million yacht has more than 200 slot machines, 32 tables, a restaurant and four lounges in 10,000 square-feet of gaming space on two decks. Prices range from $13 to $18 and includes meals. Ships sail twice daily on weekdays and three times on weekends. Call ☎ **305/379-5825** for updated schedules.

GOLF

There are more than 50 private and public golf courses in the Greater Miami area. Contact the **Greater Miami Convention and Visitors Bureau** (☎ **800/283-2707**

> ### Fore!
>
> You can get information about most Florida courses, including current greens fees, and reserve tee times through **Tee Times USA**, P.O. Box 641, Flagler Beach, FL 32136 (☎ **800/374-8633,** 888/465-3567, or 904/439-0001; fax 904/439-0099). This company also publishes a vacation guide that includes many stay-and-play golf packages.

---

or 305/539-3063) for a list of more courses and costs. Some of the area's best and most expensive are at the big resorts, many of which allow nonguests to play, such as the Doral Blue Course at the Doral Resort and Spa in West Miami; Don Shula's Hotel and Golf Club, also in West Miami; and the Biltmore in Coral Gables. See chapter 5 for more details.

Otherwise, the following represent some of the area's best public courses. **Crandon Park Golf Course,** formerly known as The Links, 6700 Crandon Blvd., Key Biscayne (☎ **305/361-9129**), is the number-one ranked municipal course in the state and one of the top five in the country. The park is situated on 200 bay-front acres and offers a pro shop, rentals, lessons, carts, and a lighted driving range. The course is open daily from dawn to dusk; greens fees (including cart) are $86 per person during the winter and $45 per person during the summer. Special twi-light rates are available.

One of the most popular courses among real enthusiasts is the **Doral Park Golf and Country Club,** 5001 NW 104th Ave., West Miami (☎ **305/591-8800**); it's not related to the Doral Hotel or spa. Call to book in advance since this challenging 18-holer is so popular with locals. The course is open from 6:30am to 6pm during the winter and until 7pm during the summer. Cart and green fees vary, so call ☎ **305/594-0954** for information.

Known as one of the best in the city, the **Golf Club of Miami,** 6801 Miami Gardens Dr., at NW 68th Avenue (☎ **305/829-8456**), has three 18-hole courses of varying degrees of difficulty. You'll encounter lush fairways, rolling greens, and some history to boot. The west course, designed in 1961 by Robert Trent Jones and updated in the 1990s by the PGA, was where Jack Nicklaus played his first profes-sional tournament and Lee Trevino won his first professional championship. The course is open daily from 6:30am to sunset. Cart and greens fees are $45 to $75 per person during the winter, and $20 to $34 per person during the summer. Special twilight rates are available.

Golfers looking for some cheap practice time will appreciate **Haulover Park,** 10800 Collins Ave., Miami Beach (☎ **305/940-6719**), in a pretty bay-side loca-tion. The longest hole on this par-27 course is 125 yards. It's open daily from 7:30am to 5:30pm during the winter, and to 7:30pm during the summer. Greens fees are $5 per person during the winter, and $4 per person during the summer. Hand carts cost $1.40.

HEALTH CLUBS

Although many of Miami's full-service hotels have fitness centers, you can't count on them in less upscale establishments or in the small Art Deco District hotels. Sev-eral health clubs around the city will take in nonmembers on a daily basis. If you're already a member at the megahealth club chain **Bally's Total Fitness,** dial ☎ **800/ 777-1117** to find the clubs in the area. There are no outlets on the beaches; most are in South Miami.

One of the most popular clubs, which welcomes walk-in guests, is **Crunch,** 1253 Washington Ave., South Beach (☎ 305/674-8222), where you might work out with Cindy Crawford, Madonna, or any of a number of supermodels when they're in town. This club offers star appeal and top-of-the-line equipment. Use of the facility is $18 daily or $65 weekly. It keeps late hours, especially in season, when it's often open until midnight.

IN-LINE SKATING

Miami's consistently flat terrain makes in-line skating easy. The heavy traffic and construction, however, make it tough to find long routes. Remember to keep a pair of sandals or sneakers with you, since many area shops won't allow you inside with skates on.

Because of the popularity of blading and skateboarding, the city has passed a law prohibiting skating on the west side (the cafe-lined strip) of Ocean Drive in the evenings. In addition, the city has passed a law that all bladers must skate slowly and safely. You wouldn't want to mow down an elderly stroller. You can still have fun, though, and the following rental outfits can help chart an interesting course for you and supply you with all the necessary gear.

In Coral Gables, **Extreme Skate & Sport,** 7876 SW 40th St. (☎ 305/261-6699), is one of South Florida's largest in-line skate dealers. Even if you know nothing about the sport, they have a knowledgeable sales staff to help you.

In South Beach, **Fritz's Skate Shop,** 726 Lincoln Rd. Mall (☎ 305/532-1954), rents top-quality skates, including safety pads, for $8 per hour, $24 per day, and $34 overnight. If you're an in-line skate virgin, an instructor will hold your hand for $25 an hour. The shop also stocks lots of gear and clothing.

SWIMMING

There is no shortage of water here. See "Best Beaches" and also the Venetian Pool under "Fantastic Feats of Architecture," above, for descriptions of good swimming options.

TENNIS

Hundreds of tennis courts in South Florida are open to the public for a minimal fee. Most courts operate on a first-come, first-served basis, and are open from sunrise to sunset. For information and directions, call the **City of Miami Beach Recreation, Culture, and Parks Department** (☎ 305/673-7730), or the **City of Miami Parks and Recreation Department** (☎ 305/575-5256).

The three hard courts and seven clay courts at the **Key Biscayne Tennis Association,** 6702 Crandon Blvd. (☎ 305/361-5263), get crowded on weekends since they're some of Miami's most beautiful. You'll play on the same courts as Lendl, Graf, Evert, McEnroe, and other greats; this is the venue for one of the world's biggest annual tennis events, the Lipton Championship (see "Miami Calendar of Events," in chapter 2). There's a pleasant, if limited, pro shop, plus many good pros. Only four courts are lit at night, but if you reserve at least 48 hours in advance, you can usually take your pick. They cost $5 per person per hour. The courts are open daily from 8am to 9pm.

12 Spectator Sports

Check the *Miami Herald's* sports section for a daily listing of local events and the paper's Friday "Weekend" section for comprehensive coverage and in-depth reports.

For last-minute tickets, call the venue directly, since many season ticket holders sell singles and return unused tickets. Expensive tickets are available from brokers or individuals, listed in the classified sections of the local papers. Some tickets are also available through **Ticketmaster** (☎ **305/358-5885**).

BASEBALL

The **Florida Marlins** shocked the sports world in 1997 when they became the youngest expansion team to win a World Series, but then floundered as their star players were sold off by former owner Wayne Huizenga. If you're interested in catching a game, be warned the summer heat in Miami can be unbearable, even in the evenings. As long as the rebuilding process continues and the Marlins continue to struggle, tickets are easy to come by.

Home games are held at the **Pro Player Stadium,** 2267 NW 199th St., North Miami Beach (☎ **305/626-7426**). Tickets are $4 to $30. Box office hours are Monday to Friday from 8:30am to 6pm, Saturday from 8:30am to 4pm, and before games; tickets are also available through Ticketmaster. The team currently holds spring training in Melbourne, Florida.

BASKETBALL

The **Miami Heat** (☎ **305/577-HEAT** or 305/835-7000), now led by celebrity coach Pat Riley, made their NBA debut in November 1988 and their games remain one of Miami's hottest tickets. The season lasts from October to April, with most games beginning at 7:30pm. They'll play the 1999/2000 season in a brand-new waterfront arena downtown on Biscayne Blvd. Tickets are $14 to $50. Box office hours are Monday to Friday from 10am to 4pm (until 8pm on game nights); tickets are also available through Ticketmaster.

FOOTBALL

Miami's golden boys are the **Miami Dolphins,** the city's most recognizable team, followed by thousands of "dolfans." Coached by Jimmy Johnson, the team plays at least eight home games during the season, between September and December, at **Pro Player Stadium,** 2267 NW 199th St., North Miami Beach (☎ **305/620-2578**). Tickets cost between $20 and $40. The box office is open Monday to Friday from 8:30am to 5:30pm; tickets are also available through **Ticketmaster** (☎ **305/350-5050**).

HORSE RACING

Wrapped around an artificial lake, **Gulfstream Park,** at U.S. 1 and Hallandale Beach Boulevard, Hallandale (☎ **305/931-7223**), is both pretty and popular. Large purses and important races are commonplace at this suburban course, and the track is often crowded. Call for schedules. Admission is $3 to the grandstand, and $3 to the clubhouse; free parking. From January through March, post times are Wednesday to Monday at 1pm. Many weekends feature live concerts by well-known musicians.

You might remember the pink flamingos at **Hialeah Park,** 2200 E. 4th Ave., Hialeah (☎ **305/885-8000**), from *Miami Vice.* This famous colony is the largest of its kind. The track, listed on the National Register of Historic Places, is one of the most beautiful in the world, featuring old-fashioned stands and acres of immaculately manicured grounds. Admission is $1 to the grandstand and $2 to the clubhouse on weekdays, and $2 and $4, respectively, on weekends. Children 17 and under enter free with an adult. Parking starts at $2. Races are held mid-March to mid-May, but the course is open year-round for sightseeing Monday to Saturday from 9am to 5pm. Call for post times.

ICE HOCKEY

The young **Florida Panthers** (☎ **954/835-7000**) have already made history. In the 1994–95 season, they played in the Stanley Cup finals, and they have amassed a legion of fans who love them. Much to the disappointment of Miamians, they moved to a new venue in Sunrise the next county north of Miami-Dade. Call for directions and ticket information.

JAI ALAI

Jai alai, sort of a Spanish-style indoor lacrosse, was introduced to Miami in 1924 and is regularly played in two Miami-area frontons. Although the sport has roots stemming from ancient Egypt, the game as it's now played was invented by Basque peasants in the Pyrenees mountains during the 17th century.

Players use woven baskets, called *cestas,* to hurl balls—pelotas—at speeds that sometimes exceed 170 miles per hour. Spectators, who are protected behind a wall of glass, place bets on the evening's players.

The **Miami Jai Alai Fronton,** 3500 NW 37th Ave., at NW 35th Street (☎ **305/ 633-6400**), is America's oldest fronton, dating from 1926. It schedules 13 games per night. Admission is $1 to the grandstand, $5 to the clubhouse. It's open year-round. There are games Monday and Wednesday to Saturday at 7pm, and matinees on Monday, Wednesday, and Saturday at noon.

8 Driving & Strolling Around Miami

Miami is made up of many small neighborhoods, some of which are more car-friendly than others. If you're Downtown or in Coral Gables without a car, then you may as well plan to sit by the pool or in front of a television for your whole vacation. In these neighborhoods, attractions, restaurants, and shopping are spread out over many miles, and people simply aren't seen much on the streets after business hours. Public transportation is equally elusive. To explore the Greater Miami area and the beaches, you'll need wheels. However, if you're staying in South Beach, you'll find a car superfluous, possibly annoying. Valet rates can be as high as $20 a day, traffic can be maddening, and metered spots are hard to come by.

The two driving tours below highlight Miami's architectural, cultural, and ethnic diversity. And when you're set to stroll South Beach's Art Deco district, the walking tour will show you the highlights while giving you a chance to stretch your legs.

Driving Tour 1—Miami Panorama: The Beaches & Waterways

Start: Joe's Stone Crab Restaurant, 227 Biscayne St. (at Washington Avenue), South Beach.

Finish: Lincoln Road at Van Dyke Cafe, 826 Lincoln Rd. (at Jefferson Avenue), South Beach.

Time: Approximately 1 hour, excluding stops and allowing for light traffic.

Best Times: Weekday mornings between 10am and noon or late afternoons from 2 to 4pm.

Worst Times: Weekday rush hours, from 8 to 9am and 4 to 6pm and late night weekends.

A Word of Warning: This driving tour goes through an area that is dense with pedestrian and car traffic. During weekends and holidays, negotiating the narrow streets can be frustrating. If you notice back-ups on South Beach, consider seeing the sights on foot or saving the tour for another day. Then again, if you can get yourself a convertible and the weather is sunny, enjoy the delay and luxuriate in the warmth.

Driving Tour 1—Miami Panorama: The Beaches & Waterways

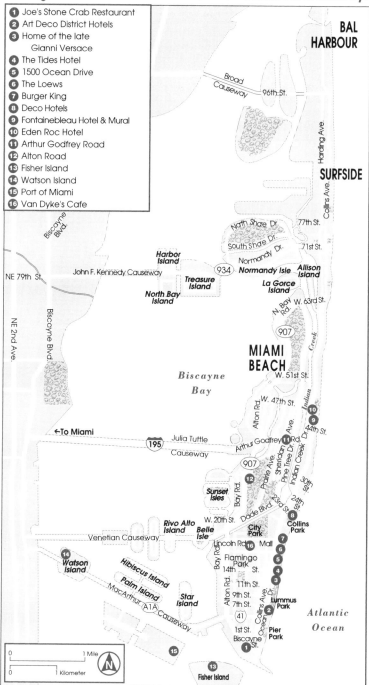

1. Joe's Stone Crab Restaurant
2. Art Deco District Hotels
3. Home of the late
   Gianni Versace
4. The Tides Hotel
5. 1500 Ocean Drive
6. The Loews
7. Burger King
8. Deco Hotels
9. Fontainebleau Hotel & Mural
10. Eden Roc Hotel
11. Arthur Godfrey Road
12. Alton Road
13. Fisher Island
14. Watson Island
15. Port of Miami
16. Van Dyke's Cafe

You'll drive through Miami Beach's varied neighborhoods, from the Art Deco District to condo-laden North Beach, and then over the causeway and back to South Beach's central section.

Start at:

1. **Joe's Stone Crab Restaurant,** 227 Biscayne St. This Miami Beach institution has served its inimitable stone crab claws to millions of customers since 1913. It's open 7 months a year (roughly October 15 through May 15), and it's always packed. Just below Joe's in South Pointe Park is a controversial building, South Beach's first megahigh-rise, Portofino Towers, which stands more than 46 stories. The pink and turquoise luxury condo was built in 1996 by German developer Thomas Kramer despite fierce public opposition to its huge shadow-casting bulk.

   Head east toward the beach and turn left onto Ocean Drive, where you'll be in the southern fringe of:

2. The **historic Art Deco district.** Drive north along Ocean Drive, also known as Deco Drive. On the right and left, you'll notice construction of several new large beachfront hotels like the Marriott and several condos. This area has yet to experience the large scale rehabilitation that has gone on slightly north. Notice the mosaic-tiled lampposts and columns done by a neighborhood artist, Daniel Sierra, despite the outcry of public officials who consider it graffiti. Once past 5th Street, on the left you'll see some of the classic examples of Art Deco hotels from the 1930s and 1940s, including the Park Central at 640 Ocean Dr. and the Avalon at 700 Ocean Dr. On the right is famous Lummus Park, graced with a long boardwalk and hundreds of palm trees. At 10th Street, dubbed Barbara Capitman Way in honor of the woman who championed the preservation of this unique area, you'll see a popular bar and hotel, The Clevelander. For a more detailed tour, see "A Walking Tour," below or call the **Miami Design Preservation League** (☎ **305/672-2014**), which runs a very informative walking tour on Thursday evenings and Saturday mornings.

   On the Northwest corner of 11th Street is the palatial:

3. **home of the late Gianni Versace,** where he was gunned down by a spree killer in 1997. Currently offered for sale by his heirs, this Italianate mansion remains one of the only private residences on Ocean Drive.

   On the next block is:

4. **The Tides,** 1220 Ocean Dr. Built in 1936, it is the largest original art deco hotel on the strip.

   Continue north and notice the newer condominiums and retail stores on the right. Straight ahead is:

5. **1500 Ocean Dr.,** a retail complex and condominium designed by famed New York architect Michael Graves. These are the first beachside residences to be built in the historic district (between 5th and 15th streets). Behind this building, you'll see a wide white spire and the St. Moritz hotel, which are part of the new Loews hotel.

   At 15th Street, you will be forced to turn left. Then make a quick right onto Collins Avenue, and look right to see a head-on view of the:

6. **Loews Miami Beach Hotel,** 1601 Collins Ave. Opened to the public in early 1999, it's South Beach's only brand-new hotel and the largest to be built here in more than 30 years. The Loews company invested more than $135 million to build this 800-room megastructure, designed to handle visiting conventioneers. Continue heading north along Collins Avenue, where you can get a good perspective on the diversity of the area. Look left and you'll see:

7. **Burger King,** at Lincoln Road. This is Miami's only art deco fast-food outlet, complete with a blue-and-yellow tropical exterior, neon lights, and trademark art deco curves. On the opposite corner is a Denny's, with equally impressive architecture.

   As you continue north, look to your right and take time to admire more:

8. **Deco hotels,** like the **National** (no. 1677), the **Delano** (no. 1685), the **Ritz Plaza** (no. 1701), and the **Raleigh** (no. 1777). These hotels are some of the region's classic deco "skyscrapers."

   Continue north, past some more art deco hotels and lots of construction. At 21st Street, notice Wolfie's famous restaurant, the public library and The Bass Museum. In another few miles, look straight ahead. You'll see a large curved blue-and-white hotel and rock waterfall behind huge Roman-style columns. This impressive site is just an illusion; it's really the:

9. **Fontainebleau Mural,** at Collins Avenue and 44th Street. The lagoon and waterfalls pictured actually exist behind the wall in the rear of the famous Fontainebleau Hilton (4441 Collins Ave.) built by Morris Lapidus in 1954. In this hotel's grand nightclub, all the big stars of the era, such as Frank Sinatra, Sammy Davis Jr., Judy Garland, Ann Margaret, Liberace, and even Elvis Presley, performed. Plans are in the works for a major expansion that will demolish the old mural and add hundreds of rooms to the already mammoth resort.

   Veer left and then right to continue on Collins Avenue.

   Next door to the mammoth Fontainebleau, you will pass the:

10. **Eden Roc,** 4525 Collins Ave., with a small fountain in front, another famous but smaller hotel, also garishly dressed in turquoise and white.

    As you continue north, you are entering an area known as Condo Canyon, a huge wall of condominiums built mostly in the 1950s and '60s that block the ocean view and shade the roads.

    Make a U-turn in front of the Wyndham Hotel and the Blue and Green Diamond skyscrapers at 48th Street, and continue until you turn right onto:

11. **Arthur Godfrey Road.** Named after the famous radio host whose shows remained popular from the 1930s though the '60s when he housed his shows on Miami Beach, this commercial strip is now a popular area for the resident Hasidic Jews to stroll and shop at the many kosher restaurants and markets. Continue straight and prepare to turn left before the causeway (SR195) onto:

12. **Alton Road.** Merge with southbound traffic and head past the Bayshore Golf course and on the right gorgeous Art Deco and Mediterranean Revival homes dating from the 1920s. Continue south on Alton Road until 5th Street, where you'll turn right to head west over the MacArthur Causeway. Look right to see the area's most exclusive private islands:

13. **Palm Island, Hibiscus Island, and Star Island.** Many of Miami's elite live here, including Gloria Estefan and her husband Emilio. Leona Helmsley also owns a home here.

    To the left is:

14. **Fisher Island,** where Oprah Winfrey, Anne Bancroft and Mel Brooks, and Luciano Pavarotti spend their winters.

    Keep alert for signs pointing to the Pan Am Clipper Sea Plane and Helicopter tours. Turn left into:

15. **Watson Island,** where many local fishers sell their catches. Stop and take a stretch at the water's edge where you can get a beautiful view of the Miami skyline. The Spanish-style peach and cream colored building is the Freedom Tower, once used as a processing center for many of the Cuban refugees who landed on

Miami's shores and now privately owned by a Cuban exile family. The brand-new stadium is a centerpiece of the skyline on the shores of Biscayne Bay. The large mirrored building with graduated steps to the left is the Nation's Bank/BankAmerica Building

Make your way back to the MacArthur Causeway (S.R. 395) heading back east toward the beach.

Look right and you can see the sprawling:

16. Port of Miami, the world's busiest cruise-ship port, where all the biggest lines dock.

Continue straight along 5th Street and turn left onto Meridian Avenue. There are many beautifully renovated Art Deco apartment houses along this tree-lined street. When you reach Lincoln Road, look for a parking spot at a meter or across from Burdine's in a metered lot. Walk back to Lincoln Road pedestrian mall for the area's best shopping, dining, and people watching.

WINDING DOWN   Head 1 block west toward the only tall building on Lincoln Road, and choose a seat at **Van Dyke Cafe,** 846 Lincoln Rd., South Beach (☎ **305/534-3600**). Open until 2am, this lively and reasonably priced sidewalk cafe is always happening. (See chapter 6, "Miami Dining").

Driving Tour 2—Downtown, Coconut Grove & Coral Gables

Start and Finish: Bayside Marketplace, 401 Biscayne Blvd. (Downtown).
Time: Approximately 1½ hours, excluding stops.
Best Times: Just before sunset, when the city will be breathtakingly illuminated or between 1 and 3pm.
Worst Times: Weekday morning rush hour, from 8 to 9:30am.

This tour takes you through Downtown to two of Miami's oldest and best-known neighborhoods: Coconut Grove and Coral Gables.

Coconut Grove, annexed by the City of Miami in 1925, was established by northeastern artists and writers. It has a reputation as being an "in" spot for bohemians and intellectuals. The first hotel in the area was built in 1880.

Coral Gables, one of Miami's first planned developments, was created by developer George Merrick in the early 1920s. Many houses were built in a Mediterranean style along lush tree-lined streets that open onto beautifully carved plazas. The best architectural examples of the era have Spanish-style tiled roofs and are built from Miami oolite, a native limestone, commonly called "coral rock."

Start at the:

1. Bayside Marketplace, 401 Biscayne Blvd. at NE 4th Street, and drive south along Biscayne Boulevard in the lanes farthest away from the water. Looking south you'll see a gorgeous Spanish Mediterranean peach colored building called the Freedom tower where thousands of Cuban immigrants were processed on their way into the United States. Now owned by the family of the late Jorge Mas Canosa, the building may become a museum.

Up ahead on the right you'll see:

2. First Union Financial Center, 200 S. Biscayne Blvd. This 55-story steel-and-glass tower was once the tallest building east of Dallas and south of Manhattan.

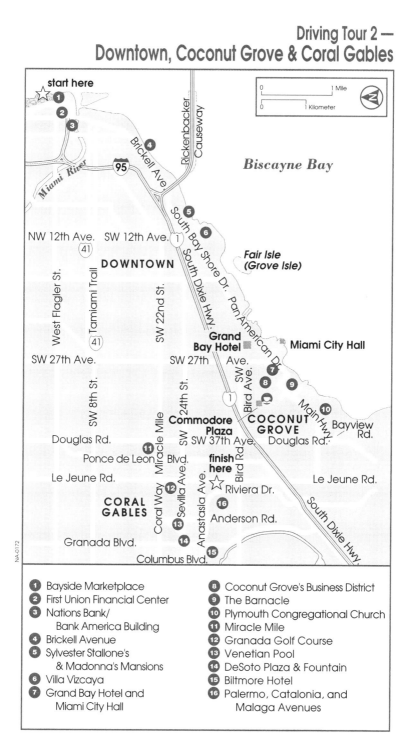

start here

Rickenbacker Causeway

Brickell Ave.

95

Miami River

Biscayne Bay

NW 12th Ave.   SW 12th Ave.

(41)

South Bay Shore Dr.

South Dixie Hwy.

DOWNTOWN

Fair Isle
(Grove Isle)

West Flagler St.

Tamiami Trail

(41)

SW 22nd St.

Pan American Dr.

SW 27th Ave.

Grand
Bay Hotel

Miami City Hall

SW 27th   Ave.

SW Bird Ave.

Main Hwy.

SW 8th St.

SW 24th St.

Commodore
Plaza

COCONUT
GROVE

Bayview
Rd.

Douglas Rd.

Miracle Mile

SW 37th Ave.

Douglas Rd.

Ponce de Leon Blvd.

Coral Way

Sevilla Ave.

Anastasia Ave.

Bird Rd.

finish
here

Le Jeune Rd.

Le Jeune Rd.

Riviera Dr.

CORAL
GABLES

Anderson Rd.

South Dixie Hwy.

Granada Blvd.

Columbus Blvd.

NA-0172

① Bayside Marketplace
② First Union Financial Center
③ Nations Bank/
    Bank America Building
④ Brickell Avenue
⑤ Sylvester Stallone's
    & Madonna's Mansions
⑥ Villa Vizcaya
⑦ Grand Bay Hotel and
    Miami City Hall

⑧ Coconut Grove's Business District
⑨ The Barnacle
⑩ Plymouth Congregational Church
⑪ Miracle Mile
⑫ Granada Golf Course
⑬ Venetian Pool
⑭ DeSoto Plaza & Fountain
⑮ Biltmore Hotel
⑯ Palermo, Catalonia, and
    Malaga Avenues

On the left is Miami Center and Citibank, a tall waterside beige building. Pass under the overpass. At the end of Biscayne Boulevard veer right and see:

3. **Nation's Bank/BankAmerica Building,** 100 SE First St. Formerly owned by the ruined Centrust Bank, this spectacular wedge-shaped building, designed by the celebrated I. M. Pei & Partners, is illuminated nightly at a cost of more than $100,000 a year. For Independence Day, the night lights are red, white, and blue; for Deco Weekend, it's done in pastels.

Stay in the left lane and turn left onto U.S. 1 toward Brickell Avenue; cross the drawbridge over the Miami River where you'll see a stunning 10-story bronze column with a 17-foot-tall bronze statue of a Tequesta Indian warrior shooting an arrow, with a woman and a baby at his feet by sculptor Manuel Carbonell. Be patient—the bridge regularly opens to let tugboats and barges through. You are now on:

4. **Brickell Avenue,** home to the largest concentration of international banks in the United States. Drive slowly. Each one of these architectural masterpieces deserves attention.

South of SE 15th Street, Brickell Avenue becomes residential, and an equally extraordinary block of condominiums rises up along the avenue's east side, including **The Palace** (1541 Brickell Ave.), **The Imperial** (1617 Brickell Ave.), and **The Atlantis** (2025 Brickell Ave.), all designed by Arquitectonica, Miami's world-famous architectural firm. The mirrored Atlantis has a square hole in its center sporting a red spiral staircase and a lone palm tree. **Villa Regina** (1581 Brickell Ave.) would be almost plain-looking if it were not for its spectacular rainbow-colored exterior, painted by Israeli artist Yacov Agam. The **Santa Maria** (1643 Brickell Ave.), completed in 1998, is the tallest residential building south of Manhattan. Note the spectacular glass atrium on its top.

Just past the turn-off toward Key Biscayne, you will come to a second set of traffic lights. At SE 26th Road, bear right and then turn left onto South Miami Avenue, which quickly becomes South Bayshore Drive. This two-lane road runs along Biscayne Bay, on the southern edge of Coconut Grove. At SE 32nd Road, just before the sign to the Villa Vizcaya, turn left and drive around the large cul-de-sac. On the right, you'll see the former:

5. **home of Sylvester Stallone,** a bay-front mansion now on the market, with a huge coral-colored gate. Keep following the road and look right to find Madonna's mansion heavily gated in black.

You may want to leave your car and stroll around **Alice Wainwright Park** (2845 Brickell Ave), a pocket-size park on the waterfront. This lovely public park, open from 7am until 7pm, has basketball courts and clean rest rooms. After you've driven around the cul-de-sac, return the way you came and turn left onto South Miami Avenue. Immediately look out on your left for the entrance to:

6. **Villa Vizcaya,** 3251 S. Miami Ave. (☎ **305/250-9133**), the elegant and opulent estate of International Harvester pioneer James Deering. The magnificent house and grounds are well worth wandering. The house is open daily from 9:30am to 5pm; the gardens, to 5:30pm. (See "Fantastic Feats of Architecture" in chapter 7.)

South Miami Avenue turns into South Bayshore Drive. Continue down this tree-lined street, passing Mercy Hospital, and in about a mile Monty's Bayshore restaurant. Look right to see:

7. **Grand Bay Hotel,** 2669 S. Bayshore Dr., and **Miami City Hall,** at the end of Pan American Drive, on your left.

At its end, South Bayshore Drive turns right, into McFarlane Road, a short street bordering a tree-lined park that terminates at Coconut Grove's most popular intersection where Cocowalk and The Shops of Mayfair are home to dozens of shops, movie theaters, and restaurants. Make a sharp left onto Main Highway and cruise slowly. This is the heart of the:

8. Grove's business district.

☕ **TAKE A BREAK**   For a light snack or a long lunch, there are plenty of places to choose from. The **Green Street Cafe,** 3110 Commodore Plaza (☎ **305/567-0662**), is located at the intersection of Main Highway and Commodore Plaza. Despite the busy street, the cafe is a relaxed place, serving breakfast, lunch, and dinner to loungers who linger at the sidewalk tables. (See the listing in chapter 6, "Dining").

Two blocks south of Commodore Plaza, you'll see the entrance to:

9. The Barnacle, 3485 Main Hwy. This former home of naval architect and early settler Ralph Middleton Munroe is now a museum open to the public (☎ **305/448-9445**). (See "Fantastic Feats of Architecture" in chapter 7.)

On the next block, on your right, is the **Coconut Grove Playhouse** (3500 Main Hwy.). Built as a movie theater in 1926, it is one of Miami's oldest showplaces. (See "The Performing Arts" in chapter 10.)

Farther along Main Highway at the intersection of Devon Road is:

10. The Plymouth Congregational Church. Founded in 1897, it's one of Miami's oldest.

Main Highway ends at Douglas Road (SW 37th Avenue). Turn right, drive north about 2 miles, and make a left onto Coral Way (SW 22nd Street). This stretch between Main Highway and U.S. 1 is a bit seedy. Depending on your comfort level, you may not want to go through here at night. You are now entering Coral Gables via the village's most famous thoroughfare, dubbed the:

11. Miracle Mile. This stretch of shops and eateries dates from the development's earliest days and is the heart of downtown Coral Gables. To your right, on the corner of Ponce de León Boulevard, stands the **Colonnade Building** (133–169 Miracle Mile), a structure that once housed George Merrick's sales offices and has since been rebuilt into a top hotel, the Omni Colonnade (see chapter 5, "Accommodations"). **Coral Gables City Hall** (405 Biltmore Way), with its trademark columned rotunda, is at the end of the Miracle Mile.

Follow Coral Way to the right of City Hall and past the:

12. Granada Golf Course, one of two public courses in Coral Gables. After 4 blocks, turn left onto DeSoto Boulevard and look for the:

13. Venetian Pool, 2701 DeSoto Blvd. on your left. This is Miami's most unusual swimming pool, dating from 1924 and listed on the National Register of Historic Places. It's hidden behind pastel stucco walls and shaded by three-story Spanish porticos. (See "Fantastic Feats of Architecture," in chapter 7.)

One block farther along DeSoto Boulevard is the:

14. DeSoto Plaza and Fountain, one of the most famous traffic circles in Coral Gables. Designed by Denman Fink in the early 1920s, the structure consists of a column-topped fountain surrounded by a footed basin that catches water flowing from four sculpted faces.

DeSoto Boulevard picks up again on the other side of the fountain and continues for about 4 blocks to its end at Anastasia Avenue, in front of the:

15. Biltmore Hotel, 1200 Anastasia Ave. This grand hotel is one of Miami's oldest and prettiest properties. The enormous cost of operating the Biltmore has forced it through many hands in recent years. It once served as a veterans hospital and even a dorm for students of nearby University of Miami. Bankruptcy shut the hotel in 1990, but the Biltmore is once again open, now under the management of the Westin chain. Its 26-story tower is a replica of the Giralda Bell Tower in Seville, Spain. Go inside and marvel at the ornate marble-and-tile interior, outfitted with mahogany furniture and a medieval fireplace.

Out back, the hotel's enormous swimming pool is the largest of its kind in North America. Just beyond is the challenging and beautiful Biltmore Golf Course. The fastest way back to downtown Miami is to continue east to the end of Anastasia Avenue, and then turn right on LeJeune Road, and then left onto U.S. 1.

Take a detour on your way home to sightsee on:

16. Palermo, Catalonia, Malaga, and other interesting tree-lined avenues. Here, you'll see many of Miami's historic homes, built in the 1920s and 1930s in Spanish and Mediterranean styles.

A Walking Tour—South Beach Highlights

Start: Art Deco Welcome Center, 1001 Ocean Dr. (South Beach).

Finish: Clevelander Hotel, 1020 Ocean Dr.

Time: Allow approximately 45 minutes, not including browsing in shops and galleries.

Best Times: Any day between 11am and 7pm.

Worst Times: Nights and Sundays, when some galleries and shops are closed.

The Art Deco District in South Beach is roughly bounded by the Atlantic Ocean on the east, Alton Road on the west, Sixth Street on the south, and Dade Boulevard (along the Collins Canal) to the north. This approximately 1-square-mile area is listed on the National Register of Historic Places. There will certainly be plenty of people to watch while you're strolling around, and amazing architecture to admire as well. This tour takes you past the Deco District's highlights. If you want more details, consider taking the 90-minute Art Deco walking tour (see chapter 7, "What to See & Do in Miami") led by the Preservation Society.

Start at the:

1. Art Deco Welcome Center, 1001 Ocean Dr. This ocean-side storefront offers free maps and Art Deco architecture information. You can also buy art deco books, T-shirts, postcards, clocks, statues, and collectibles. It's open Monday to Saturday from 11am to 6pm, and usually until 9pm depending on volunteers' availability.

Just across the street is the:

2. Clevelander Hotel, 1020 Ocean Dr., one of the few hotels in the area with an original swimming pool and deco-style sun deck area. The huge outdoor stage, located behind the pool, hosts live rock and reggae bands or deejays every night, when the Clevelander becomes one of the liveliest locales on the beach.

Walk north on Ocean Drive to the late:

3. Gianni Versace's home (on the northwest corner of 11th Street). The only privately owned residence on South Beach's Ocean Drive, this outrageously decadent mansion is where the Italian fashion designer was gunned down. It's now owned by his heirs and has an uncertain future.

Walking Tour—South Beach Highlights

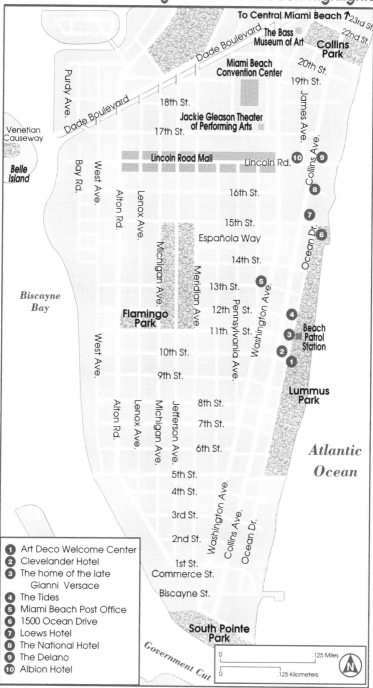

To Central Miami Beach ↑ 23rd St.

22nd St.

Dade Boulevard

The Bass Museum of Art

Collins Park

20th St.

Miami Beach Convention Center

19th St.

Purdy Ave.

Dade Boulevard

18th St.

James Ave.

Venetian Causeway

Jackie Gleason Theater of Performing Arts

17th St.

Belle Island

Bay Rd.

Lincoln Road Mall

Lincoln Rd.

10 **9**

Collins Ave.

8

16th St.

7

West Ave.

Alton Rd.

Lenox Ave.

15th St.

Española Way

6

Ocean Dr.

14th St.

Michigan Ave.

Meridian Ave.

13th St.

5

Biscayne Bay

12th St.

Washington Ave.

4

Flamingo Park

Pennsylvania Ave.

11th St.

3

Beach Patrol Station

2

10th St.

1

West Ave.

9th St.

Lummus Park

8th St.

Alton Rd.

Lenox Ave.

Michigan Ave.

Jefferson Ave.

7th St.

6th St.

Atlantic Ocean

5th St.

4th St.

3rd St.

Washington Ave.

Collins Ave.

Ocean Dr.

2nd St.

1 Art Deco Welcome Center
2 Clevelander Hotel
3 The home of the late Gianni Versace
4 The Tides
5 Miami Beach Post Office
6 1500 Ocean Drive
7 Loews Hotel
8 The National Hotel
9 The Delano
10 Albion Hotel

1st St.

Commerce St.

Biscayne St.

South Pointe Park

Government Cut

0 .125 Miles

0 .125 Kilometers

N

Continue north to:

4. The Tides, 1220 Ocean Dr., one of Ocean Drive's oldest and tallest deco buildings. Renovated in 1997 by Island Outpost, this is also perhaps the city's most elegant rehab.

Turn west (left) onto 13th Street and make your way to Washington Avenue. Across the street, you'll see the magnificent:

5. Miami Beach Post Office, 1300 Washington Ave., completed in 1938 and designed by Howard L. Cheney in the Depression moderne style as part of a Work Projects Administration (WPA) project. Step into the skylit-domed lobby, where you'll see a turret with a lantern finial and gleaming gold post boxes beneath a classic WPA mural depicting Ponce de León landing in Florida and fighting with the Native Americans.

Head north on Washington Avenue. Observe the similar art deco features on the simple buildings along the way. Many have been repainted in brighter colors than the originals to highlight the unusual features. Cross the street and turn right on 15th Street to see:

6. 1500 Ocean Drive. Designed by Michael Graves and completed in 1999, this magnificent ocean-side residential and retail complex is one of the priciest and most luxurious private buildings on South Beach.

Turn north (left) on Collins Avenue and look right to see the mammoth:

7. Loews hotel, 1601 Collins Ave., completed in early 1999, is the first new hotel to be built on the beach in 30 years.

Also on the right is:

8. The National Hotel, 1687 Collins Ave. Built in 1940, this stunning structure is now one of the beach's most beautiful hangouts.

A few doors down is:

9. The Delano, 1685 Collins. Originally built in 1947 and renovated half a century later by Phillipe Stark and Ian Schrager, this hotel epitomizes the success of South Beach's renaissance. Note the futuristic fins on top of this 12-story super-sexy hotel.

The next block is Lincoln Road where you will notice the curved corners on all the buildings, a typical deco detail that softens the cityscape. Turn left and walk half a block until you see the:

10. Albion Hotel on the right. This stunning hotel was originally built in 1939 by famed architect Igor Polivitsky and renovated by the Rubell family in 1997. This was one of the first hotels to incorporate retail stores and restaurants in a hotel structure. Note the original bas-relief of Neptune pointing the way to the ocean on the Lincoln Road entry to the Albion.

Continue straight ahead and stroll along this pretty tree-lined pedestrian mall and find dozens of upscale galleries, boutiques, restaurants, and cafes. There are dozens of establishments to choose from for a quick coffee, beer, or snack. For a reasonably priced meal, see The Van Dyke Cafe above.

Miami Shopping

9

Miami has earned a worldwide reputation as a shopping capital, especially among visitors from Latin America and the Caribbean. Take a quick glance around the airport, and you'll see more than a few departing passengers lugging refrigerator-sized cardboard boxes and bulging suitcases. From exotic tropical fruits to high-tech electronics, fine art and art deco collectibles, Latin music and hand-rolled cigars, Miami has something for everyone.

And shopping is big business. According to surveys, Latin American shoppers spend more than $1 billion annually in Miami-Dade County.

To accommodate the more than 10 million visitors from all over the world who pass through Miami each year, there are strip malls and shops everywhere. The city is blanketed with strip centers, chain stores, boutiques, and malls. And there are many more in the works.

Under construction in 1999 were two megamalls south of the city center with a combined square footage of more than 2 million square feet. Both introduced a range of dining and entertainment opportunities to keep shoppers spending long after they tire of looking for just the right pair of jeans. In this chapter, I've listed some of my favorite places to shop, but rest assured there are many more.

You may want to order the Greater Miami Convention and Visitors Bureau's "*Shop Miami: A Guide to a Tropical Shopping Adventure.*" Although it is limited to details on the bureau's paying members, it provides some good advice and otherwise unpublished discount offers. The glossy little pamphlet is printed in English, Spanish, and Portuguese and provides information about transportation from hotels, translation services, and shipping. Call ☎ **800/283-2707** or 305/539-3063.

1 The Shopping Scene

Below I've described some of the popular retail areas, where many stores are concentrated for easy browsing.

As a general rule, shop hours are Monday through Saturday from 10am to 6pm and Sunday from noon to 5pm. Many stores stay open late (until 9pm or so) 1 night of the week (usually Thursday). Shops in trendy Coconut Grove are open until 9pm Sunday through Thursday and even later on Friday and Saturday nights.

Department stores and shopping malls also keep longer hours, with most staying open from 10am to 9 or 10pm Monday to Saturday and noon to 6pm on Sunday.

The 6.5% state and local sales tax is added to the price of all nonfood purchases.

Most Miami stores can wrap your purchase and ship it anywhere in the world via the United Parcel Service (UPS). If they can't, you can send it yourself, either through UPS (☎ **800/742-5877**) or through the U.S. Mail (see "Fast Facts: Miami," in chapter 4).

SHOPPING AREAS

Most of Miami's shopping happens at its many megamalls scattered from one end of the county to the other; however, there is also some excellent boutique shopping and browsing to be done in the following areas: See "City Layout" in chapter 4 for more information about these areas.

AVENTURA   Biscayne Blvd between Miami Gardens Drive and the county line is a 2-mile stretch of huge retail stores including Best Buys, Borders, Circuit City, Linens N' Things, Marshall's, Sports Authority, and more. Also here is Loehmann's Plaza, a small one-level open shopping mall with several good shoe stores and Loehmann's, the discount clothing store (See "Fashion," below).

CALLE OCHO   For a taste of "Little Havana," take a walk down 8th Street between SW 27th Avenue and 12th Avenue where you'll find some lively street life and many shops selling cigars, baked goods, shoes, furniture, and record stores specializing in Latin music. Be sure to take your Spanish dictionary if you need it.

COCONUT GROVE   Downtown Coconut Grove, centered on Main Highway and Grand Avenue and branching onto the adjoining streets, is one of Miami's most pedestrian-friendly zones. The Grove's wide sidewalks, lined with cafes and boutiques, provide hours of browsing pleasure. Coconut Grove is best known for its dozens of avant-garde clothing stores, funky import shops, and excellent sidewalk cafes centered around Cocowalk and The Streets of Mayfair.

CORAL GABLES—MIRACLE MILE   Actually only a half-mile long, this central shopping street was an integral part of George Merrick's original city plan. Today, the strip still enjoys popularity especially for its bridal stores, ladies' shops, haberdashers, and gift shops. Recently, newer "chain" stores, like Barnes and Noble, Old Navy, and Starbucks, have been appearing on the Mile. It also features several excellent restaurants before it terminates at the City Hall rotunda (see chapter 6, "Dining").

DOWNTOWN MIAMI   If you're looking for discounts on all types of goods— especially watches, fabric, buttons, lace, shoes, luggage, and leather—Flagler Street just west of Biscayne Boulevard is the best place to start. Be prepared for some hustling and haggling. Most signs are printed in English, Spanish, and Portuguese; however, many shopkeepers may not be entirely fluent in English.

✪ **SOUTH BEACH—LINCOLN ROAD**   This luxurious pedestrian mall, originally designed in 1957 by Morris Lapidus, recently underwent a multimillion-dollar renovation restoring it to its former glory. Here, shoppers can find an array of clothing and art and a menagerie of South Beach's finest sidewalk cafes flanked on one end by a multiplex movie theater and at the other, the Atlantic Ocean. Monthly gallery tours, periodic jazz concerts, and a weekly farmer's market are just a few of the offerings on "The Road."

COLLINS & WASHINGTON AVENUES (between 6th Street & 9th Street)
For the hippest clothing boutiques including A/X Armani, Versace, Benneton, The Gap, Todd Oldham, Kenneth Cole, and Nicole Miller, stroll along this pretty strip of the deco district.

2 Shopping A to Z

ANTIQUES/COLLECTIBLES
Miami's antique shops are scattered in small pockets around the city. Many that feature lower-priced furniture can be found in North Miami, in the 1600 block of Northeast 123rd Street near West Dixie Highway. About a dozen shops sell china, silver, glass, furniture, and paintings. But you'll find the bulk of the better antiques in Coral Gables and in Southwest Miami along Bird Road between 64th and 66th avenues and between 72nd and 74th avenues. There are dozens of shops with eclectic offerings. For international collections from Bali to France, check out the burgeoning scene in the Design District centered on Northeast 40th Street west of 1st Avenue. Miami also hosts several large antique shows each year. In October and November are the most prestigious ones at the **Miami Beach Convention Center** (☎ **305/754-4931**). Exhibitors from all over come to display their wares, including jewelry. There's also a decent monthly show at the **Coconut Grove Convention Center** (☎ **305/444-8454**). Miami's huge concentration of deco buildings from the '20s and '30s makes this place to find the best selections of deco furnishings and decorations.

✪ **Architectural Antiques.** 2500 SW 28th Lane (just west of U.S. 1), Miami. ☎ **305/285-1330.**

A great place to browse—if you don't mind a little dust—this huge warehouse has an impressive stash of ironwork, bronzes, paintings, lamps, furniture, and sculptures, which have been salvaged from estates worldwide. Don't be surprised to find odd items too, like an old British phone booth or a pair of gargoyles off an ancient church.

Dietel's Antiques. 6572 Bird Rd., South Miami. ☎ **305/666-0724.**

An active trade business here means lots of different styles are revolving constantly. You'll find baubles of every assortment in this stocked shop located near Coral Gables' quaint antiques district.

Modernism. 1622 Ponce de León Blvd., Coral Gables. ☎ **305/442-8743.**

Specializing in 20th-century furnishings, this gorgeous shop has some of the most beautiful examples of deco goods from France and the United States.

Miami Twice. 6562 SW 40th St., South Miami. ☎ **305/666-0127.**

While they are not technically antiques yet, the Old Florida furniture and decorations from the '30s, '40s, and '50s are great fun (and collectible). In addition to loads of deco memorabilia, there are vintage clothes, shoes, and jewelry.

ART GALLERIES
Miami's finest art galleries are located within walking distance of one another in Coral Gables along Ponce de León Boulevard, extending from U.S. 1 to Bird Road. Still others are clustered in Bal Harbour's ritzy shopping district. And finally, South

Beach's Lincoln Road, which once had dozens of galleries, now has only a few—a result of soaring rents.

Also, check out the burgeoning art scene in the design district north of downtown just west of Biscayne Boulevard around 40th Street. Listed below is a selection of galleries both in and out of these areas.

If you happen to be in town on the first Friday of a month, you should take the free trolley tour of the Coral Gables art district. The tour runs from 7 to 10pm; meet at Elite (listed below) or any of the other participating galleries in the area.

On the second Saturday of the month, you can actually meet artists and see them working during the **Lincoln Road Gallery Walk at the Art Center,** 924 and 1035 Lincoln Rd. (☎ **305/674-8278**), from 7 until 11pm. Join a knowledgeable guide for a tour of more than 50 artists' studios.

See chapter 7, "What to See & Do in Miami" for more details on these walking tours and others.

Ambrosino Gallery. 3095 SW 39th Ave. (1 block south of Bird Rd.), Miami. ☎ **305/445-2211.**

This well-respected gallery shows works by contemporary artists and stages performance art and installations. Closed for Christmas holidays.

Elite Fine Art. 3140 Ponce de León Blvd., Coral Gables. ☎ **305/448-3800.**

Touted as one of the finest galleries in Miami, Elite features modern and contemporary Latin American painters and sculptors.

✪ **Evelyn S. Poole Ltd.** 3925 N. Miami Ave., Miami. ☎ **305/573-7463.**

Known as the most fine of the fine antiques collections, the Poole assortment of European 17th-, 18th-, and 19th-century decorative furniture and accessories is housed in 5,000 square feet of space in the newly revived Decorator's Row. Celebrity clients shop for that special "statement piece" in these vast museumlike galleries.

Gallery Antigua. 5130 Biscayne Blvd. (in the Boulevard Plaza Building), Miami. ☎ **305/759-5355.**

This frame shop and gallery in one is dedicated to showing works by African American and Caribbean artists. Gallery Antigua boasts a vast collection of prints and reproductions, as well as masks and sculptures.

Meza Fine Art. 275 Giralda Ave., Coral Gables. ☎ **305/461-2723.**

This gallery specializes in Latin American artists, including Carlos Betancourt, Javier Marin, and Gloria Lorenzo.

COSMETICS, FRAGRANCES & BEAUTY PRODUCTS
✪ **Browne's & Co.** 841 Lincoln Rd. South Beach. ☎ **305-532-8703.**

Designed to look like an old-fashioned apothecary, this beauty emporium combines the city's best selection of make-up and hair products—MAC, Shu Uemura, Kiehl's, Stila, and Dr. Hauschka just to name a few—with lots of delicious smelling bath and body stuff, plus a full service beauty salon.

Perfumania. 332 Lincoln Road. ☎ **305/538-8553,** and more than a dozen locations in Miami. Check the phone book for details.

This huge chain has many popular fragrances for men and women at discount prices. They also sell make-up and skin-care products. It's a great place to pick up a gift basket.

BOOKS

Barnes and Noble Booksellers. 152 Miracle Mile, Coral Gables. ☎ **305/446-4152** and more than six locations in Miami. Check the phone book for details.

With half a dozen outlets in the area and more on the way, this huge chain offers anything readers could ask for including a comfortable cafe, a large children's section, and tons of magazines. Plus, you'll get a 10% discount on all best-sellers and incredible close-out specials. They often schedule readings with noted authors, too.

✪ **Books & Books.** 296 Aragon Ave., Coral Gables. ☎ **305/442-4408.** Another location at 933 Lincoln Rd., South Beach (☎ 305/532-3222).

A dedicated following turns out to browse at this warm and wonderful little independent shop. Enjoy the upstairs antiquarian room, which specializes in art books and first-edition literature. If that's not enough intellectual stimulation for you, the shop hosts free lectures from noted authors and experts almost nightly.

At the Lincoln Road location, you'll rub elbows with tanned and buffed South Beach bookworms sipping cappuccinos at the Russian Bear Cafe inside the store. They stock a large selection of gay literature.

Cuba Art and Books. 2317 Le Jeune Rd., Coral Gables. ☎ **305/567-1640.**

This beautiful unpretentious shop sells old Cuban books about the island nation, and also has some prints and paintings by Cuban artists. Most titles are in Spanish and focus on art and politics.

Grove Antiquarian. 3318 Virginia St., Coconut Grove. ☎ **305/444-5362.**

One of very few out-of-print bookstores in Miami, Coco Grove Antiquarian specializes in books about Florida and the Caribbean, but also boasts a large selection of out-of-print cookbooks, sci-fi, and first editions.

Kafka's Cyberkafe. 1464 Washington Ave., South Beach. ☎ **305/673-9669.**

Check your e-mail and surf the Net while you sip a latte or snack on a sandwich or pastry with friendly neighborhood regulars. This popular used bookstore also stocks a wide range of foreign and domestic magazines.

CIGARS & CIGARETTES

Although it is illegal to bring Cuban cigars into this country, somehow Cohibas show up at every dinner party and nightclub in town. Not that I condone it, but if you hang around the cigar smokers in town, no doubt one will be able to tell you where you can get some of the highly prized contraband. Be careful, however, of counterfeits.

The stores listed below sell excellent hand-rolled cigars made with domestic and foreign-grown tobacco. Many of the *viejos* (old men) got their training in Cuba working for the government-owned factories in the heyday of Cuban cigars.

✪ **La Gloria Cubana.** 1106 SW 8th St., Little Havana. ☎ **305/858-4162.**

This tiny storefront shop employs about 45 veteran Cuban rollers who sit all day rolling the very popular torpedoes and other critically acclaimed blends. They've got backorders until next Christmas, but it's worth stopping in. They will sell you a box and show you around.

Miccosukee Tobacco Shop. 850 SW 177th Ave. (Krome Ave. and Tamiami Trail), Miami. ☎ **305/226-2701.**

At this remote Native American–owned outpost, you are spared the state cigarette tax—national brands are available for $14 a carton, generics from $8 to $13.

Mike's Cigars. 1030 Kane Concourse (at 96th St.), Bay Harbor Island. ☎ **305/866-2277.**

Mike's recently moved to this location, but it's one of the oldest smoke shops in town. Since 1950, Mike's has been selling the best from Honduras, the Dominican Republic, and Jamaica, as well as the very hot local brand La Gloria Cubana. Most say it has the best prices, too.

ELECTRONICS

The Sharper Image. 401 Biscayne Blvd. (in the Bayside Marketplace). ☎ **305/374-8539.** Another location in the Dadeland Mall, at 7507 N. Kendall Dr., South Miami (☎ 305/667-9970).

Electronics nuts will love this store. It tends to be high-end, both in merchandise and price, but it's free just to look and touch (yes, you're allowed), so even if you're not buying, visit the store to see what's new in the high-tech world.

Sound Advice. 12200 N. Kendall Dr., Kendall. ☎ **305/273-1225.** Other locations at 17641 Biscayne Blvd., Aventura (☎ 305/933-4434), and 1222 S. Dixie Hwy., Coral Gables (☎ 305/665-4434).

An audio junkie's candy store, Sound Advice features the latest in high-end stereo equipment, as well as TVs, VCRs, and telephone equipment. Techno-minded, but sometimes pushy, salespeople are on hand to help.

Spy Shops International Inc. 280 NE 4th St. ☎ **305/374-4779.**

This store is perfect for James Bond wanna-bes looking to buy electronic-surveillance equipment, day and night optical devices, stun guns, minisafes, doorknob alarms, and other anticrime gadgets.

FASHION

For the best quality designer clothes, Bal Harbour Shops is your best bet. See "Malls," below.

On the other end of the spectrum, you may want to try the popular Loehmann's (see below) for designer clothing, shoes, and accessories at deeply discounted prices. Or, consider hunting the thrift stores and resale shops (see below).

Island Trading. 1332 Ocean Dr., South Beach. ☎ **305/673-6300.**

One more part of music mogul Chris Blackwell's empire, Island sells everything you'll need to wear in the tropical resort town, like batik sarongs, sandals, sundresses, bathing suits, cropped tops, and more. Many of the unique styles are created on the premises by a team of young and innovative designers.

✪ **Loehmann's.** 18701 Biscayne Blvd. (Fashion Island), North Miami Beach. ☎ **305/932-4207.**

Loehmann's has added men's clothing and shoes to its huge stock of women's wear. This discount mecca is the place to find designer clothes at bargain prices. But, you've got to hunt. If you don't mind communal dressing rooms and hordes of zealous shoppers, look here for great deals on everything from bathing suits to evening wear.

MEN'S

Brooks Brothers. 9700 Collins Ave. (in the Bal Harbour Shops), Miami Beach. ☎ **305/865-8686.** Other location at 8888 Howard Dr. (in The Falls shopping complex), Kendall (☎ 305/259-7870).

If you need a new navy blazer or some khaki trousers to roll up for an oceanfront stroll, shop here for the classics.

Giorgio's. 208 Miracle Mile, Coral Gables. ☎ **305/448-4302.**

One of the finest custom men's stores, Giorgio's features an extensive line of Italian suits and all the latest by Canelli.

Hugo Boss. 9700 Collins Ave., Miami Beach. ☎ **305/864-7753.**

One of many men's stores in Bal Harbour, this one appeals to hipsters and businessmen alike who are willing to pay big money for the latest styles.

WOMEN'S

A B S Clothing Collection. 226 8th St., South Beach. ☎ **305/672-8887.**

This California-based chain store fits right into South Beach. You'll find both trendy and professional stuff for women here, from zebra-print minis to tailored pantsuits.

Alice's Day Off. 5900 SW 72nd St., South Miami. ☎ **305/284-0301.** Also at the Miami International Mall, 1477 NW 107th Ave, Miami (☎ 305/477-0393).

For beachwear, Alice's is the place. It comes out season after season with pretty and flattering floral patterns and many flashy bikinis. If an itsy-bitsy bikini is not your style, Alice's has a range of more modest cuts for those not shaped like a *Baywatch* babe.

Betsey Johnson. 805 Washington Ave., South Beach. ☎ **305/673-0023.**

This New York based shop sells slightly wild, faddish clothes for the young and young at heart, made of stretchy materials, velvet, knits, and more.

Therapy. 1065 Kane Concourse. Bay Harbor Islands. ☎ **305/861-6900.**

Opened by Ellen Lansburgh who ran successful shops in Aspen and New York, which catered to a famous clientele, including Cher and Goldie Hawn, this intimate boutique has one-of-a-kind pieces. The clothes, made of the most luxurious fabrics like silk, taffeta, and tulle, are elegant and comfortable.

CHILDREN'S

Most department stores have extensive children's sections. But if you don't find what you are looking for consider one of the many Baby Gaps or Gap Kids outlets around town or one of the specialty boutiques listed here.

French Kids Inc. 5829 Sunset Dr. South Miami. ☎ **305/667-5880.**

This fashionable boutique imports beautiful (and expensive) clothes for newborns to teenagers.

Roland Children's Wear. 450 41st St., Miami Beach. ☎ **305/531-0130.**

Find a unique assortment of kid's clothes for dress-up or for playtime. They specialize in cute, funky stuff.

LINGERIE

Belinda's. 827 Washington Ave., South Beach. ☎ **305/532-0068.**

This German designer makes some of the most beautiful and intricate teddies, nightgowns, and wedding dresses. The styles are a little too Stevie Nicks for me to actually consider wearing in public, but the creations are absolutely worth admiring. The prices are appropriately up there.

Caro Cuore. 642 Collins Ave., South Beach. ☎ **305/534-6494.**

This small store stocks good-quality lingerie from its private label. Most garments are made with fancy European lace, but the store also carries a wide variety of your basic cotton.

Corset Corner. 300 Miracle Mile, Coral Gables. ☎ **305/444-6643.**

As the name suggests, this little old store on Miracle Mile sells the basic, good old-fashioned gear.

La Perla. 9700 Collins Ave. (in the Bal Harbour Shops), Bal Harbour. ☎ **305/864-2070.**

The only store in Florida that specializes in this superluxurious Italian intimate apparel. Of course, you could fly to Milan for the price of a few bras and a night-gown, but you can't find better quality. Also in Bal Harbour see Flash Lingerie (☎ 305/868-7732), which carries a diverse selection of imports.

Victoria's Secret. 3015 Grand Ave., Coconut Grove. ☎ **305/443-2365.** Other locations at 401 Biscayne Blvd., Miami (☎ 305/374-8030), and Aventura Mall (☎ 305/932-0150).

You've seen the sexy catalogs—now see the goods up close. The many shops in town stock the basic undergarments in shimmery rayons and polys as well as a few Chinese silk robes and undies. You'll find one of the largest selections of thongs anywhere.

FOOD

There are dozens of ethnic markets in Miami from Cuban bodegas to Jamaican import shops and Guyanese produce stands. Check the phone book under grocers for listings. I've listed a few of the biggest and best markets in town that sell pre-pared foods as well as staple items. On Saturday mornings, vendors set up stands loaded with papayas, melons, tomatoes and citrus, as well as cookies, ice creams, and sandwiches on South Beach's Lincoln Road. Also on Saturday is the Green Market in Coconut Grove along Grand Avenue specializing in organic fruits, veg-etables, and homemade treats.

Biga Bakery. 1080 Alton Rd., South Beach. ☎ **305/535-1008.** Also at 305 Alcazar, Coral Gables (☎ 305/446-2111). Check directory for other locations.

You'll be happy to pay upwards of $6 a loaf when you sink your teeth into these inimitable old-world–style breads. Also, most of the locations have a to-die-for pre-pared food counter serving up everything from chicken curry salad to hummus and pot pies. Pastries and cakes are as gorgeous as they are delicious.

East Coast Fisheries. 330 W. Flagler St., Downtown. ☎ **305/577-3000.**

This retail market and restaurant (see the review in chapter 6, "Dining"), has sent millions of pounds of seafood worldwide from its own fishing fleet. Order 5- or 10-pound packages of stone-crab claws, Florida lobsters, Florida Bay pompano, fresh Key West shrimp, and a variety of other local delicacies to be shipped via overnight delivery.

Epicure. 1656 Alton Rd., Miami Beach. ☎ **305/672-1861.**

Here, you'll find not only fine wines, cheeses, meats, fish, and juices, but some of the best produce, such as portobello mushrooms the size of a yarmulke. This neigh-borhood landmark is best known for supplying the Jewish residents of the Beach with all the Jewish favorites like matzo ball soup, gefilte fish, and deli items. Prices are steep, but generally worth it.

Gardner's Market. 7301 Red Rd., South Miami. ☎ **305/667-9953.**

Anything a gourmet or novice cook could desire can be found here. One of the oldest and best grocery stores in Miami, Gardner's now has three locations all of which offer great take-out and the freshest produce.

Joe's Stone Crab. 227 Biscayne St., South Beach. ☎ **800/780-CRAB** or 305/673-0365.

If you've never tasted Florida's favorite seafood, you must. And once you do, you'll want more. Or you may want to send some to very dear friends at home (they are pricier than lobster). Joe's, Miami's most famous restaurant (see the review in chapter 6), ships stone crabs anywhere in the country, but only during the season, which runs from mid-October through mid-May.

La Boulangerie. 328 Crandon Blvd., Key Biscayne. ☎ **305/361-0281.**

Stop here for delicious sandwiches and fruit tarts (see review in chapter 6).

La Brioche Doree. 4017 Prairie Ave., Miami Beach. ☎ **305/538-4770.**

This tiny storefront off of 41st Street is packed most mornings with French expatriates and visitors who crave the real thing. There are luscious pastries and breads plus soup and sandwiches at lunch. No one makes a better croissant anywhere. Period.

Laurenzo's Italian Supermarket and Farmer's Market. 16385 and 16445 W. Dixie Hwy. North Miami Beach. ☎ **305/945-6381** and 305/944-5052.

Anything Italian you want—from homemade ravioli to hand-cut imported Romano cheese to smoked salmon to fresh fish and ground pork—can be found here. Be sure to see the neighboring store full of just-picked herbs, salad greens, and every type of vegetable from around the world. Incredible daily specials, such as 10 Indian River pink grapefruits for 99¢, lure thrifty shoppers from all over the city (see review of cafe in chapter 6).

Publix. 1045 Dade Blvd., South Beach. ☎ **305/534-4621.**

The largest supermarket chain in Florida keeps getting bigger. There are already more than 50 in Miami-Dade County. The latest addition on South Beach is worth at least driving by. It was designed by well-known architect Carlos Zapata and boasts 47,000 square feet plus a moving walkway to whisk shoppers and their carts to and from the aboveground parking lot. In addition to valet parking, take-out sushi, a bakery, deli, cafe, and pharmacy, there is a large selection of exotic fruits.

Todd's Fruit Shippers. ☎ **305/448-5215.**

Order grapefruits, oranges or other local produce by the bushel or basket. This longtime Florida shipper takes phone orders only.

HOUSEWARES/HARDWARE

Farrey's Decorative Hardware & Lighting. 1850 NE 146th St. (just east of West Dixie Hwy). North Miami. ☎ **305/947-5451.** Another location at 4101 Ponce de León Blvd., Coral Gables (☎ 305/445-2244).

Opened since 1924, this huge warehouse stocks elegant lighting, bathroom fixtures, and furnishings. From drawer pulls to chandeliers, plus a collection of eclectic furniture, you'll find something you absolutely must have.

Linge de Maison Veronique. 305 Alcazar Ave., Coral Gables. ☎ **305/461-3466.**

Fussy Coral Gables housewives flock here for beautiful wares, including custom and hand-embroidered linens, layettes, bed and bath accessories, and tableware to match their china patterns.

A Taste of Old Florida

Old-fashioned smokehouses used to dot U.S. 1 and Biscayne Boulevard, but as Miami grew, they were driven out of business. As popular as they were, the old shacks couldn't generate enough money from smoked fish to compete with condominiums and shopping centers.

One that remains is **Jimbo's** on Virginia Key. There's no real street address, since as Dan, an employee, likes to say: "We're out in the boonies."

Most days, depending on the seasons and the tides and who feels like shopping, Jimbo's sells marlin and salmon. Really, its primary business is selling bait shrimp to fishermen, but there is always some odoriferous fish splayed out for the pungent smoke.

If you can find your way there, you'll see the old crew of Italians playing bocce, smoking, and drinking out on the bay, in a tiny sliver of backwater life tucked away from civilization. It's worth it. They're there most days if the sun is shining, and they stay until it sets.

To get to Jimbo's, drive over the Rickenbacker Causeway en route to Key Biscayne. After you've passed the second light on Crandon Boulevard, just past the MAST Academy, turn left. Drive about a mile until you see some old wooden fishing shacks (they're used as movie props). To ask about what they're smoking, call ☎ **305/361-7026.**

Pratesi Linens Inc. 9700 Collins Ave. (in the Bal Harbour Shops), Bal Harbour. ☎ **305/861-5677.**

The quality of the Italian linen here is unmatchable, but you could buy a car with what you'll pay for a full set of king-size hand-embroidered sheets.

real.life.basic. 643 Lincoln Rd., South Beach. ☎ **305/604-1984.**

Offering cool stuff for the kitchen and cooking demonstrations too, this ultrasleek split-level shop has become a hangout for foodies. Those who work in the industry get discounts, too.

JEWELRY

For the name designers like Gucci and Tiffany & Co., go to the Bal Harbour Shops (see "Malls," below).

The International Jeweler's Exchange. 18861 Biscayne Blvd. (in the Fashion Island), North Miami Beach. ☎ **305/931-7032.** Closed Mon.

At least 50 jewelers hustle their wares from individual counters at one of the city's most active jewelry centers. Haggle your brains out for excellent prices on timeless antiques from Tiffany's, Cartier, or Bulgari or on unique designs you can create yourself.

The Seybold Building. 36 NE 1st St., Downtown. ☎ **305/374-7922.**

Jewelers of every assortment gather here daily to sell their diamonds and gold. The glare is blinding as you enter this multilevel retail marketplace. You'll see handsome and up-to-date designs, but note that there aren't too many bargains to be had here.

MALLS

There are so many malls in Miami and more being built that it would be impossible to mention them all. What follows is a list of the biggest and most popular.

You can find any number of nationally known department stores including Saks Fifth Avenue, Macy's, Lord & Taylor, Sears, and JC Penney in the Miami malls listed below, but Miami's own is **Burdines,** at 22 E. Flagler St., Downtown (☎ **305/835-5151**), and 1675 Meridian Ave. (just off Lincoln Rd.) in South Beach (☎ 305/674-6311). One of the oldest and largest department stores in Florida, Burdines specializes in good quality home furnishings and fashions.

Aventura Mall. 19501 Biscayne Blvd. (at 197th St. near the Dade-Broward County line), Aventura. ☎ **305/935-1110.**

Once this mall attracted only retirees and snow-birds. It's spruced up its image over the last few years and increased in size to over 2.3 million square feet. More than 200 specialty stores are complemented by the megastores J. C. Penney, Lord & Taylor, Macy's, Bloomingdale's, and Sears. Parking is free.

✪ **Bal Harbour Shops.** 9700 Collins Ave. (on 97th St., opposite the Sheraton Bal Harbour Hotel), Bal Harbour. ☎ **305/866-0311.**

One of the most prestigious fashion meccas in the country, Bal Harbour offers the best-quality goods from the finest names. Giorgio Armani, Dolce & Gabbana, Christian Dior, Fendi, Joan & David, Krizia, Rodier, Gucci, Brooks Brothers, Waterford, Cartier, H. Stern, Tourneau—the list goes on and on. With Neiman-Marcus at one end and a newly expanded Saks Fifth Avenue at the other, this mall hardly deserves to be called by such a pedestrian title. It's like Rodeo Drive with elevators. Well-dressed shoppers stroll in a pleasant open-air emporium, featuring several good cafes, covered walkways, and lush greenery. Parking costs $1 an hour with a validated ticket. You can stamp your own at the entrance to Saks Fifth Avenue even if you don't make a purchase.

Bayside Marketplace. 401 Biscayne Blvd., Downtown. ☎ **305/577-3344.**

A popular stop for cruise-ship passengers, this gorgeous waterfront marketplace is filled with lively and exciting shops in the heart of downtown Miami. Downstairs, about 100 shops and carts sell everything from Caribbean trinkets to high-tech electronics (some of the specialty shops are listed separately below). The upstairs eating arcade is stocked with dozens of fast-food choices and some fun bars. Most of the restaurants stay open later than the stores, which close at 11pm Monday to Saturday and 8pm on Sunday. Parking is $1 per hour.

✪ **Dadeland Mall.** 7535 N. Kendall Dr. (intersection of U.S. 1 and SW 88th St., 15 minutes south of Downtown), Kendall. ☎ **305/665-6226.**

One of the county's most profitable malls, Dadeland features more than 175 specialty shops, anchored by four large department stores—Burdines, JC Penney, Lord & Taylor, and Saks Fifth Avenue. Sixteen restaurants serve from the adjacent Treats Food Court. And the area is growing. Look for new retail stores surrounding this granddaddy of Miami's suburban mall. Parking is free.

Dolphin Mall. Florida Turnpike at S.R. 836, West Miami.

Under construction at press time, this megamall and amusement park is expected to rival Sawgrass Mills in Broward County. With outlet shops, movies, and a roller coaster, this 1.4 million-square-foot project is expected to cost $250 million and open in time for the new millennium.

The Falls Shopping Center. 8888 Howard Dr. (at the intersection of U.S. 1 and 136th St., about 3 miles south of Dadeland Mall), Kendall. ☎ **305/255-4570.**

Tropical waterfalls are the setting for this outdoor shopping center with dozens of moderately priced, slightly upscale shops. Miami's first Bloomingdale's is here, as are Polo, Ralph Lauren, Caswell-Massey, and more than 60 other specialty shops. After a recent renovation, The Falls became the quintessential shopping experience. Macy's, Crate & Barrel, Brooks Brothers, and Pottery Barn are among the newest additions. If you are planning to visit any of the nearby attractions, which include Metro Zoo, Parrot Jungle, and Monkey Jungle, check with customer service for information on discount packages. Parking is free.

Miami International Mall. 1455 NW 107th Ave., Miami. ☎ **305/593-1775.**

More than 150 specialty stores and several well-known department stores including a Burdines, JC Penney, and Sears, this popular mall is close to Miami airport and filled with foreign shoppers.

Sawgrass Mills. 12801 W. Sunrise Blvd., Sunrise (west of Fort Lauderdale). ☎ **954/846-2300.**

Although this mammoth mall is actually located in Broward County, it is a phenomenon worth mentioning since thousands of tourists and locals trek there for bargains and fun. (See chapter 13, "The Gold Coast," for more details.)

From Miami, buses run three times daily; the trip takes just under an hour. Call **Coach USA** (☎ 305/887-6223) for exact pick-up points at major hotels. The price is $10 for a round-trip ticket. If you are driving, take I-95 north to 595 west until Flamingo Road. Exit and turn right, driving 2 miles until Sunrise Boulevard. You can't miss this monster on the left. Parking is free, but don't forget where you parked your car or you might spend a day looking for it.

The Shops of Sunset Place. 5701 Sunset Dr. (at 57th Ave. and U.S. 1, near Red Rd.), South Miami. ☎ **305/663-9110.**

Completed in early 1999 at a cost of over $140 million, this sprawling "mall of the future" offers more than just shopping. Visitors will experience high-tech special effects like daily tropical storms (minus the rain) and the electronic chatter of birds and crickets. In addition to a 24-screen movie complex and an IMAX theater, there's a Gameworks, Steven Spielberg's Disney-esque playground for adults, a Virgin Records store, and a Niketown.

The Streets of Mayfair. 2911 Grand Ave. (just east of Commodore Plaza), Coconut Grove. ☎ **305/448-1700.**

Recently revamped, this small and labyrinthine complex conceals a movie theater, several top-quality shops, restaurants, art galleries, and nightclubs. The emphasis is on boutiques and entertainment. Self-parking is available for $1 per hour; there is a flat rate of $6 after 6pm.

MUSIC & MUSICAL EQUIPMENT

Blue Note Records. 16401 NE 15th Ave., North Miami Beach. ☎ **305/940-3394.**

Here for more than 15 years, Blue Note has hard-to-find progressive and underground music. There are new, used, and discounted CDs and old vinyl, too. Call to find out about performances. Some great names show up occasionally.

Casino Records Inc. 1208 SW 8th St., Little Havana. ☎ **305/856-6888.**

The young, hip salespeople speak English and tend to be music buffs themselves. Here, you'll find the largest selection of Latin music in Miami, including pop icons such as Willy Chirino, Gloria Estefan, Albita, and local boy Nil Lara. Their slogan translates to, "If we don't have it, forget it." Believe me, they've got it.

CD Warehouse. 13150 Biscayne Blvd., North Miami. ☎ **305/892-1048.** Also at 1590 S. Dixie Hwy., Coral Gables (☎ 305/662-7100).

Buy, sell, or trade your old CDs at this eclectic music hut.

Mars (Music and Recording Superstore). 12115 Biscayne Blvd., North Miami. ☎ **305/893-0191.**

You could spend a week here. With 35,000 square feet of space, MARS offers everything from musical instruments to sheet music, plus a recording studio, live stage, and repair center.

Revolution Records and CDs. 1620 Alton Rd., Miami Beach. ☎ **305/673-6464.**

Here you'll find a quaint and fairly well-organized collection of CDs, from hard-to-find jazz to original recordings of Buddy Rich. They'll search for anything and let you hear whatever you like.

Specs Music. 501 Collins Ave., South Beach. ☎ **305/534-6533.** Another location is at 12451 Biscayne Blvd., North Miami Beach (☎ 305/899-0994).

In addition to a great collection of multicultural sounds, you'll find a lively scene most weekends at this multilevel music mall. Other stores carry an impressive collection of all types of music.

Virgin Records. 5701 Sunset Place (at the Shops of Sunset), South Miami. ☎ **305/665-4445.**

Under construction at press time, this enormous music store (33,000 square feet) promises to indulge shoppers with listening booths and an "in-store radio station." They stock a huge collection of CDs, cassettes, and videos.

SPORTS EQUIPMENT

From golf to tennis, scuba to fishing, South Florida is a virtual playground. And, of course, you can find all the toys to outfit yourself nearby. One of the area's largest chains is the Sports Authority with at least six locations throughout the county. Check the white pages for details.

Alf's Golf Shop. 524 Arthur Godfrey Rd., Miami Beach. ☎ **305/673-6568.** Also at 15369 S. Dixie Hwy., Miami (☎ 305/378-6086).

The best pro shop around, Alf's can sell you balls, clubs, gloves, and instructional videos. The knowledgeable staff has equipment for golfers of every level, and the neighboring golf course offers discounts to Alf's clients.

Bass Pro Shops Outdoor World. 200 Gulf Stream Way, Dania. **954/929-7710.**

Fishing enthusiasts and sports enthusiasts must head north to Broward County to see the huge retail complex that offers demonstrations in fly-fishing, archery, and pistol ranges, classes in marine safety, and every conceivable gadget you could ask for. (See "The Gold Coast," chapter 13, for more details.)

Bird's Surf Shop. 250 Sunny Isles Blvd., North Miami Beach. ☎ **305/940-0929.**

If you're a hard-core surfer or just want to look like one, head to Bird's Surf Shop. Although Miami doesn't regularly get huge swells, if you're here during the winter and one should happen to hit, you'll be ready. The shop carries more than 150 boards. Call its surf line (☎ 305/947-7170) to find the best waves from South Beach to Cape Hatteras and even The Bahamas and Florida's West Coast.

Edwin Watts Golf Shops. 15100 N. Biscayne Blvd., North Miami Beach. ☎ **305/ 944-2925.**

> One of 30 Edwin Watts shops throughout the Southeast, this full-service golf retail shop is one of the most popular in Miami. You can find it all, including clothing, pro-line equipment, gloves, bags, balls, videos, and books. Plus, you can get coupons for discounted greens fees on many courses.

Island Water Sports. 16231 Biscayne Blvd. ☎ **305/944-0104.**

> You'll find everything from booties to gloves to baggies and tanks. Check in here before you rent that Wave Runner or Windsurfer.

Nevada Bob's. 7930 NW 36th Ave. (near the airport), Miami. ☎ **305/593-2999.**

> This chain store guarantees the lowest prices on golf equipment and accessories. There's more than 6,000 square feet of store here; you can even practice your swing at an indoor driving range with a radar gun to clock your speed.

X-Isle Surf Shop. 437 Washington Ave., South Beach. ☎ **305/673-5900.** Free surf report at ☎ 305/534-7873.

> Prices are slightly higher at this beach location, but you'll find the hottest styles and equipment. They also offer surfboard rental.

THRIFT STORES/RESALE SHOPS

The Children's Exchange. 1415 Sunset Dr., Coral Gables. ☎ **305/666-6235.**

> Selling everything from layettes to overalls, this pleasant little shop is chock-full of good Florida-style stuff for kids to wear to the beach and in the heat.

Douglas Gardens Jewish Home and Hospital Thrift Shops. 5713 NW 27th Ave., North Miami Beach. ☎ **305/638-1900.**

> Lately, they have gotten smart and started to raise prices. Still, for housewares and books, you can do all right. Call to see if they are offering any specials for seniors or students.

Rags to Riches. 12577 Biscayne Blvd., North Miami. ☎ **305/891-8981.**

> This is an old-time consignment shop in the thrift-store row. You might find some decent rags, and maybe even some riches. Not as upscale as it used to be, this place is still a good spot for costume jewelry and shoes.

Red White & Blue. 12640 NE 6th Ave., North Miami. ☎ **305/893-1104.**

> Miami's very best secret is this mammoth thrift store that is meticulously organized and well stocked. You've got to search for great stuff but it is there. There are especially good deals on children's clothes and housewares.

WINES & SPIRITS

Most gourmet stores carry wines and beers. See "Food," above.

Crown Liquors. 6751 Red Rd., Coral Gables. ☎ **305/669-0225.** Another location at 1255 Biscayne Blvd., North Miami. (☎ 305/892-WINE).

> This liquor store offers one of the most diverse selections in Miami. Its ever-rotating stock comes from estate sales around the country and worldwide distributors. And since there are several stores in the chain, the owners get to buy in bulk, which results in lower prices for oenophiles. If you want one of the tastiest and most affordable champagnes ever, try its exclusive import, Billecarte Salmon.

The Estate Wines & Gourmet Foods. 92 Miracle Mile (at Douglas and Galiano), Coral Gables. ☎ **305/442-9915.**

This exceedingly friendly storefront in the middle of Coral Gables' main shopping street offers a small but well-chosen selection of vintages from around the world. It also sells a great array of gourmet cheeses, pâtés, salads, and sandwiches.

Laurenzo's. 16385 and 16445 W. Dixie Hwy., North Miami Beach. ☎ **305/945-6381** and 305/944-5052.

Laurenzo's dedicates a few small aisles to its superb wine collection. A full-time expert can help you choose a bottle. But beware, you'll get an attitude if you're a novice.

Sunny Isles Liquors. 18180 Collins Ave., Sunny Isles Beach. ☎ **305/932-5782.**

This well-located store has on hand hundreds of brands of imported beer and hard-to-find liquor. It will also search and find decanters and minis for your collection. There's also a fine selection of imported cigarettes and cigars.

10 Miami After Dark

Miami's nightlife is as varied as its population.

One of the most surprising aspects of the city is the recent growth of its cultural scene. While none of it would rank as world class, Miami does have a talented symphony, a few notable fine art galleries, a decent opera company, some fine theater, a well-respected ballet company, and occasionally great concerts.

Then again, most travelers probably don't come to Miami in order to expand their cultural horizons. After the sun goes down, the club scene is Miami's biggest attraction, and most of the action can be found in South Beach.

Unfortunately, Miami seems to have trouble sustaining consistently good live music. In the past few years, Miami has watched more than a dozen music clubs shut their doors. Some blame the lack of community support; others say it's Miami's remote geographic location, too far a drive for bands to include on their circuit; still others claim promoters in town don't work hard enough to entice good musicians to venture down here. That being said, there are still some excellent venues for live music, especially popular spots for jazz and Latin music.

Cuban and Caribbean rhythms fit the bill for this sultry town. The beat makes dancing irresistible, as do some of the world's best deejays who show up during the season, like David Padilla, JoJo Odyssey, Junior Vazquez, and David Knapp.

For up-to-date entertainment listings, check the *Miami Herald*'s "Weekend" section, which runs on Fridays, or the more comprehensive listings in *New Times,* Miami's free alternative weekly, available each Wednesday. This award-winning paper prints articles, reviews, and advertisements on upcoming local events. Several telephone hot lines, many operated by local radio stations, give free recorded information on current events in the city. They include the **Planet Radio Stuff To Do Hotline** (☎ 305/770-2513), the **Zeta Concert Hotline** (☎ 305/770-2515), and the **UM Concert Hotline** (☎ 305/284-6477). Other information lines are listed under the appropriate headings below.

Tickets for many performances are handled by **TicketMaster;** call ☎ **305/358-5885** to charge tickets. For hard-to-get seats, try a ticket broker. Fran at **Sold-Out Events** (☎ **305/534-2021**) can usually find what you need. Otherwise, call **Ultimate Travel & Entertainment** (☎ **305/444-8499**).

South Beach After Dark

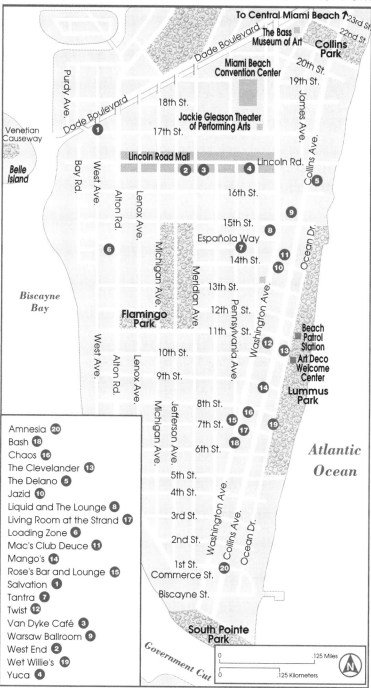

To Central Miami Beach
23rd St.
22nd St.

The Bass Museum of Art

Collins Park

Miami Beach Convention Center

20th St.
19th St.

Dade Boulevard

Jackie Gleason Theater of Performing Arts

18th St.
17th St.

James Ave.

Collins Ave.

Purdy Ave.

Dade Boulevard

Venetian Causeway

Belle Island

Lincoln Road Mall

Lincoln Rd.

Bay Rd.

West Ave.

Alton Rd.

Lenox Ave.

16th St.
15th St.
14th St.
13th St.
12th St.
11th St.
10th St.
9th St.

Española Way

Biscayne Bay

Michigan Ave.

Meridian Ave.

Pennsylvania Ave.

Washington Ave.

Ocean Dr.

Flamingo Park

Beach Patrol Station

Art Deco Welcome Center

Lummus Park

8th St.
7th St.
6th St.
5th St.
4th St.
3rd St.
2nd St.
1st St.

Jefferson Ave.

Michigan Ave.

Commerce St.
Biscayne St.

Atlantic Ocean

South Pointe Park

Government Cut

Washington Ave.

Collins Ave.

Ocean Dr.

Amnesia 20
Bash 18
Chaos 16
The Clevelander 13
The Delano 5
Jazid 10
Liquid and The Lounge 8
Living Room at the Strand 17
Loading Zone 6
Mac's Club Deuce 11
Mango's 14
Rose's Bar and Lounge 15
Salvation 1
Tantra 7
Twist 12
Van Dyke Café 3
Warsaw Ballroom 9
West End 2
Wet Willie's 19
Yuca 4

0   .125 Miles
0   .125 Kilometers

N

167

1 Bars

There are countless bars in and around Miami with the highest concentration on trendy South Beach. Keeping track of them all would be a full-time job—and not a bad one at that! The selection listed below is a mere sample. Keep in mind that many of the popular bars are in hotels. On the beach, you'd do best to walk along Ocean Drive and Washington Avenue to see what's hot. In Coconut Grove, check out CocoWalk and Mayfair next door. Unless mentioned, the bars listed below generally don't charge a cover. Most require proof that you are over 21 to enter, though some allow patrons over 18 to enter but not drink.

The Clevelander. 1020 Ocean Dr., South Beach. ☎ **305/531-3485.**

This old standby on one of Ocean Drive's busiest and most spacious corners is always crowded. You'll find mostly preppy types gathered around the large outdoor pool area up until 5am. Cheap drinks in plastic cups complete the beachy atmosphere in this casual, spring-breaky bar.

The Delano. 1685 Collins Ave., South Beach. ☎ **305/672-2000.**

I'm surprised they haven't started charging admission to this spectacular attraction. In the lobby is the Rose Bar, one of the best spots in South Beach to see beautiful people decked out in trendy splendor. Lounge on a cushy sofa or in any of the plump beds casually arranged throughout the lobby and backyard, and grab an expensive drink.

Firehouse Four. 1000 S, Miami Ave. ☎ **305/371-3473.** Cover varies from none to $10.

Renowned for its raucous weekday happy hours, this old favorite had closed for several years only to resurface in late 1998 to the thrill of its former downtown corporate patrons. Well, the ties come off after 5pm and nobody works as hard as the deejays who keep the place rocking. Each night attracts a slightly different crowd depending on the music. Thursday night is old Havana night. Call for a schedule.

The Forge. 432 41st St., Miami Beach. ☎ **305/538-8533.**

Step back in time at this ultra-elegant restaurant and bar, where Wednesday night is the night to hang with dolled-up Eurosingles and New Yorkers. Call well in advance if you want to watch the parade of characters from your dinner table (see chapter 6, "Dining"). An elegant nightclub called Jimmy'z, a spin-off of Regine's, is adjacent. They say it's a private club, but if you dine at the restaurant or know someone, you can get in. Rumored to open soon is a spin-off of the popular Latin hotspot Club Nostalgia (See "Latin Clubs," below).

Howl at the Moon Saloon. 3015 Grand Ave. (CocoWalk), Coconut Grove. ☎ **305/442-8300.** Cover $5–$10.

Drink specials are a regular fixture at night throughout the week, except Monday, when the Moon is dark. On Sunday, beers are $1.75 a pop. On Thursday night, 19- and 20-year-olds are let in, and those over 21 with a college ID can skip the cover and simply enjoy cheap buckets of beer.

Impressions

Party in the city where the heat is on, all night on the beach til the break of dawn. Welcome to Miami. Bienvenido a Miami.

—Will Smith, 1999

Mac's Club Deuce. 222 14th St., South Beach. ☎ **305/673-9537.**

Housed in a squat, neon-covered art deco building, this dive is popular with bikers, barflies, and pool players who love the dark and smoky scene. It's a real local's favorite for those who like to slum it. Here, you'll no doubt catch a great conversation, some old tunes on the juke box, or a good scene out the front picture window that faces a busy all-night tattoo parlor. Mac's is open daily from 8am to 5am. Yes, that's 5*am!*

Molly Malone's. 166 Sunny Isles Blvd. (just west of Collins Ave.), Sunny Isles Beach. ☎ **305/948-3512.**

Open all day and into the next, Molly's is a divey Irish pub, popular with young and old drinkers and folk lovers alike. There's a pool table and darts, occasional Irish rock or acoustic music, and, of course, a selection of good ales and lagers.

Murphy's Law Irish Pub. 2977 McFarlane Dr., Coconut Grove. ☎ **305/446-9956.**

This wood and brass-decorated Irish pub is for those who want to escape the more antiseptic night scene at CocoWalk down the road. Weekends offer live music, Irish or otherwise. A big-screen TV shows sports events, but this place is really about sharing a pint or two at the bar with old-timers, grungers, and young professionals.

✪ **Tantra.** 1445 Pennsylvania Ave. (at Española Way), South Beach. ☎ **305/672-4765.**

This supersexy restaurant/lounge continues to be the place for the beautiful-in-black crowd. It looks like some luxurious opium den in Marrakech from the minute you step into a small entryway covered with real grass. Continue into the lounge, where you'll find a stone waterfall, huge Indian sculptures, smoky lanterns, and low curtained tables. Plus, the food (said to have aphrodisiacal properties) includes pricey lobsters, oysters and spicy Indian meats, and love potions made of various herbs and alcohol. Dinner reservations are hard to get, and a spot at the bar is even tougher, especially after 11pm.

Wet Willie's. 760 Ocean Dr., South Beach. ☎ **305/532-5650.**

The upstairs deck overlooking Ocean Drive is one of the prime spots for watching the hectic parade that defines South Beach craziness. From up here, you can see the ocean as well as the spectacle of folks who walk the strip night and day. After just one Wet Willie's frozen concoction, you may not be able to see much of anything. Watch out: They taste like soda pop but bite like a mad dog.

There's another Wet Willie's in Coconut Grove at 3390 Mary St. (☎ **305/443-5060**) on the third level of Mayfair.

2 The Club & Music Scene

LIVE MUSIC

Despite the spotty success of local music, Latin musicians like Cuban diva Albita, Nil Lara, Willy Chirino, and, of course, Gloria Estefan got their start here. Julio Iglesias plays occasionally and Arturo Sandoval just moved here after defecting from Cuba.

South Florida's jazz scene is also very much alive with traditional and contemporary performers. Keep an eye out for guitarist Randy Bernsen, vibraphonist Tom Toyama, Melton Mustafah, and the flutist Nestor Torres, and many young performers who lead local ensembles. Many come out of the **University of Miami's** well-respected jazz studies program (☎ **305/284-6477**), which often schedules low- and no-cost recitals. Additionally, many area hotels feature live music of every description. Schedules are listed in the newspaper entertainment sections.

Churchill's Hideaway. 5501 NE Second Ave., Miami. ☎ **305/757-1807.** Cover depends on the band (up to $5).

It's a dive in a pretty rough neighborhood, but if you want to sample Miami's local music scene, Churchill's is the place to go. You might even see a fledgling band before it makes it big. At this British pub (hence the name Churchill's), you can snack on rustic shepherd's pie and good English brew. And for those homesick Brits craving a good game of rugby, Churchill's is probably the only place that broadcasts English sports via satellite. Call ahead—there has been talk of this place shutting its doors.

The Globe. 377 Alhambra Circle (at LeJeune), Coral Gables. ☎ **305/445-3555.**

This odd little cafe is attached to a travel agency. On weekends, a red curtain transforms a corner into a stage, where you'll find decent jazz and good food too. (See "Where to Dine," chapter 6.)

The Hungry Sailor. 3426 Main Hwy., Coconut Grove. ☎ **305/444-9359.** Cover Fri–Sat $5–$10. Closed Mon.

This small English-style pub has Watney's, Bass, and Guinness, and reggae regularly on tap. This place attracts an extremely mixed crowd. Sunday is dancehall reggae night and Wednesday it's ska. On other nights, you might find other live music or dance music provided by a deejay.

Jazid. 1342 Washington Ave., South Beach. ☎ **305/673-9372.** Nightly 9pm–2am.

This split-level jazz club is an unlikely spot to find on South Beach. It's warm, welcoming, cheap and even has a pool table. Music ranges from classic jazz to blues and often includes talented locals.

Luna Star Cafe. 775 NE 125th ST., North Miami. ☎ **305/892-8522.**

One of the only venues for folk musicians, this cozy little club sponsors several open mike nights. Be warned; there are a lot of uninhibited amateurs out there. But hey, it's better than karaoke, and occasionally you hear some fantastic stuff.

Power Studios. 3701 NE 2nd Ave., Miami. ☎ **305/573-8042.** Cover varies.

Opened in an up-and-coming (seedy) area just north of downtown known as "the Design District," this large warehousey club features live music on Fridays and Saturdays—mostly jazz and blues. There's plenty of room to dance.

Rose's Bar and Lounge. 754 Washington Ave., South Beach. ☎ **305/532-0228.** Cover $3–$15 Tues–Sun, depending on show.

This hip South Beach bar features local music—live rock, jazz, or whatever else strikes your fancy or theirs—almost every night on its tiny stage. Get there early to

Rock 'n Bowl

The latest fad to hit Miami is "Rave" bowling. **Cloverleaf Lanes** at 17601 NW 2nd Ave., North Dade (☎ **305/652-4197**) sets up glow-in-the-dark pins, turns the lights low and the music high every Friday and Saturday nights from 8:30pm until 3am. Games are $4.50 each. Shoes and balls are an extra $2. It's become especially popular with teens who are too young to get into the clubs.

beat the crowds and claim a spot among the sparse seating. Open every night from 5pm to 5am.

Taurus. 3540 Main Hwy., Coconut Grove. ☎ **305/448-0633.**

This rustic old favorite survived the gentrification of the surrounding area and still feels like the Grove used to. It's funky and grungy and full of great characters. Hear old rock and roll and soak up some local color. Open until midnight.

✪ **Tobacco Road.** 626 S. Miami Ave. (over the Miami Ave. Bridge near Brickell Ave.), Downtown. ☎ **305/374-1198.** Cover from none to $8.

This Miami institution is a must-see. It's been around since 1912 doing more in the back room than just dancing. These days, you'll find a good bar menu along with the best live music anywhere—blues, zydeco, brass, jazz, and more. Regular performers include The Dirty Dozen Brass band from New Orleans, which plays a mean mix of zydeco and blues with an actual dozen brass players; Bill Warton and the Ingredients, who make a pot of gumbo while up on stage; Monkey Meet; Iko Iko; Chubby Carrier and his band; and many more. Escape the smoke and sweat in the backyard patio where air is a welcome commodity. The downright cheap nightly specials, such as the $10 lobster on Tuesday, are quite good and served until 2am. The club is open until 5am.

Van Dyke Cafe. 846 Lincoln Rd., Miami Beach. ☎ **305/534-3600.** Cover varies from $3 to $6.

Enjoy live jazz 7 nights a week until midnight in an elegant upstairs lounge that features the likes of Eddie Higgins, Mike Renzi, and locals such as Don Wilner who play strictly jazz for a well-dressed crowd of enthusiasts. You can have a drink or two at the pristine oak bar or enjoy some snacks from the bustling patio seats below.

DANCE CLUBS

In addition to quiet cafes and progressive poolside bars, Miami Beach pulsates with one of the liveliest night scenes in the city. Also check out "Latin Clubs" listings, later in this chapter for more places to dance.

A popular trend in Miami's club scene are "one-off" nights—events organized by a promoter and held in established venues on irregular schedules. Word of mouth, local advertising, and listings in the free weekly *New Times* are the best ways to find out about these hot events. You can also try asking a cool-looking waiter or waitress at some South Beach eatery.

And just for the record: No, Madonna, the original Material Girl, does not own a nightclub in South Beach. The club that uses her name on its oversized billboard on Washington Avenue is a strip joint, one of a handful in South Beach.

Bash. 655 Washington Ave., South Beach. ☎ **305/538-2274.** Cover $15 weeknights and $20 weekends.

This place has been around longer than most and is still pretty hot. Bash gets going late and features an eclectic mix of music, including Eurodance, disco, and funk as well as special events, such as occasional funky fashion shows. The crowd is incredibly Eurohip and supertrendy. On weekends the back patio is open and plays World Beat music. Open every night but Monday from 10pm to 5am.

Bermuda Bar and Grill. 3509 NE 163rd St., North Miami. ☎ **305/945-0196.** Cover from none to $10. No cover before 9pm.

This huge suburban danceteria specializes in ladies' nights (Wednesday and Thursday). Plus, it hosts cash-prize contests for women who wear the skimpiest

Breaking Through the Velvet Ropes

In Miami, there are certain clued-in people who seem to know everyone on the club scene—they always look fabulous and never fret when they spy a mob at the door of the hippest spot in town. You've seen them kissing each other on both cheeks. Unless you're one of them, you may want to check out these basic rules regarding club admission etiquette:

- Never ever wear blue jeans, shorts, or sneakers. Most clubs with a discretionary door policy see only black or shades of gray—the hipper the better.
- Bring women. At the risk of sounding sexist, there is a direct mathematical relationship between the number of attractive females in your group and likelihood of getting into a hot club. Half a dozen guys without dates might as well look for the nearest frat party or pool hall.
- Call ahead to request a VIP table. You'll spend more than a couple of hundred dollars for overpriced bottles of Dom Perignon or Absolut, but at least you're guaranteed to get in.
- Call a day or two in advance and get phone-friendly with someone whose name you can drop at the door.
- Fax a guest list early in the day and wait for a confirmation number.
- Don't ever flash cash at a doorman. You're better off tipping the concierge at your hotel who can make arrangements to get on a guest list.
- Check your attitude at the sidewalk. "Don't you know who I am?" doesn't work. Be polite and positive; screaming and yelling doesn't work.
- Arrive before midnight. The later it gets, the less likely you'll get in—no matter who you are. When a club gets too full, the fire marshals show up and even Donald Trump gets the cold shoulder.
- Know when to give up. If you've been hanging out for more than 20 or 30 minutes and have been looked over by the dude with the clipboard, you have probably already been pegged as a "no-way." There are plenty of other hot spots in town, so try elsewhere.
- As a last resort, tag on to a hip crowd (this only works for one or two). When you see a good-looking crew get the nod, grab the hand of the last one in line and follow along as if you know what you're doing.

outfits. Still, everybody loves the high-energy music that packs the dance floor. Thursday is Latin night and Friday features happy hour from 5 to 8pm. Saturday is the biggest night, when all the goings-on are broadcast live on a local radio station. Good pizzas and grilled foods are available, too. It's usually open until the sun comes up. Closed Monday, Tuesday, and Sunday.

Cafe Iguana. 8505 Mills Dr. (Town & Country Mall on the corner of 88th St. and 117th Ave.), Kendall. ☎ **305/274-4948.** Cover from none to $10.

This tropical-themed bar and dance club is a bit much for low-key club-goers, but for those looking for a high-energy party, it's the place to be. Everything from male and female hot-body contests to a raging Latin night are incorporated into this nightspot.

Chaos. 743 Washington Ave., South Beach ☎ **305/674-7350.** Cover usually $20.

Miami's club of the moment, this is where Oliver Stone, Harrison Ford, and other celebs spend their nights when on the beach. Don't expect easy entry, since the number of people waiting on the sidewalk often outnumber the truly fabulous inside. Music in this intimate enclave ranges from Eurohouse to retro, but is always danceable. Open Wednesday through Saturday from 11pm to 5am.

Club St. Croix. 3015 Grand Ave., Coconut Grove (CocoWalk). ☎ **305/446-4999.** Cover from none to $15.

How many bodies can fit in one club? Club St. Croix has made it its mission to find out. If you're not blinded by the pulsating disco lights and shocking Caribbean decor, and you love loud dance music and scantily clad bodies, you'll enjoy this sub-urban bar scene. The club normally opens at 9pm and closes at 5am except on Thursday and Friday, when the party starts at 4pm for happy hour. Open Wednesday to Sunday.

Groove Jet. 323 23rd St. (1 block west of Collins Ave.), South Beach. ☎ **305/532-5150.** Cover $10–$20.

This fantastic hidden spot north of the South Beach scene has been through many incarnations. Its most recent, Groove Jet, has three distinct areas playing totally dif-ferent music. Deep house, jungle, and trance tunes are usually heard in the front room with more experimental music in the back rooms. A very hip young crowd hangs in this out-of-the-way scene, which doesn't really get going until after hours (usually after 2am), Thursday to Sunday 11pm to 5am.

Liquid and The Lounge. 1439 Washington Ave., South Beach. ☎ **305/532-9154** for information, or 305/532-8899 for table reservations. Cover $10–$20.

Liquid is reminiscent of the 1980s New York club scene, so you can expect to wait at the ropes until a disdainful bouncer chooses you. Don't dare to wear the usual casual South Beach attire; they are looking for "casual chic." Once inside, you'll find a pulsing, cavernous space with up-to-the-minute dance music and half a dozen packed bars, VIP seating in a cozy back area, a hip-hop side room, and a downstairs lounge playing jazz and funk. Sunday night is gay. The club opens doors at 11pm but the action starts late (around 2am).

Living Room at the Strand. 671 Washington Ave., South Beach. ☎ **305/532-2340.** Cover $5–$15.

This very Euro hot spot is the place to mix and mingle with South Beach's beautiful crowd. Models and moguls alike converge here to drink and relive the art of con-versation, until the music gets loud after about 10pm.

THE GAY & LESBIAN SCENE

The gay and lesbian scene in Miami is outrageous, especially on South Beach.

Much to the shock of tourists who haven't been around, gay men and women are often seen hugging, kissing, or just holding hands in clubs and bars or walking down the street. Still, most of the gay clubs welcome hetero visitors, too. And many of the normally "straight" clubs also have gay nights. Miami Beach is one of the major stops for circuit parties around the United States.

Amnesia. 136 Collins Ave., South Beach ☎ **305/531-5535.**

This huge indoor-outdoor favorite hosts tea dances where buffed boys parade around in minuscule outfits while dance music plays in the background.

Loading Zone. 1426 Alton Rd., Miami Beach. ☎ **305/531-5623.**

The town's only leather bar, complete with hot men, sexy videos, and, in case you forgot something, a leather shop in back.

Salvation. 1771 West Ave., Miami Beach. ☎ **305/673-6508.** Cover varies.

Probably the largest gay dance party in the state, with pumping dance music and some of South Beach's most recognized, and wildest, drag queens. It's a weekly party at a huge place and it goes on until the sun comes up.

Twist. 1057 Washington Ave., South Beach. ☎ **305/53-TWIST.**

One of the beach's most popular cruise bars, Twist attracts mostly male clientele but has an open-door policy. Open daily from 1pm to 5am.

Warsaw Ballroom. 1450 Collins Ave., South Beach. ☎ **305/531-4555.** Cover $10–$15.

One of Miami's oldest and most fun nightclubs, Warsaw hosts various theme nights (Wednesday is the amateur strip contest) and some of the best dance music in town. After all these years, regulars still line up out the door, waiting to get in and dance until 5am.

West End. 942 Lincoln Rd., South Beach. ☎ **305/538-9378.**

A mellow bar and pool hall on weekdays, this Lincoln Road standby gets funky on the weekends when a deejay takes over. It's is a favorite hangout for women and men. Enjoy a relaxed atmosphere and a good happy hour. Open 2pm to 5am on weekdays and noon to 5am on weekends.

LATIN CLUBS

Considering that Hispanics make up the majority of Miami's population and that there's a huge influx of Spanish-speaking visitors, it's no surprise that there are some great Latin nightclubs in the city.

Plus, with the meteoric rise of the international music scene based in Miami, many international stars come through the offices of MTV Latino, SONY International, and a multitude of Latin TV studios based in Miami—and they're all looking for a good club scene on weekends. Most of the Anglo clubs reserve at least one night a week for Latin rhythms.

Alcazaba. 50 Alhambra Plaza (in the Hyatt Regency Coral Gables), Coral Gables. ☎ **305/441-1234.**

The Hyatt's Top-40 lounge plays an eclectic mix of music but exudes a decidedly Mediterranean atmosphere that mixes fantasy with reality. Chill out with some tropical drinks and authentic tapas between songs. Happy hour—Wednesday and Friday from 5 to 7pm and Saturday from 9 to 11pm—offers half-price beer, wine, and drinks, plus a free buffet.

✪ **Cafe Nostalgia.** 2212 SW 8th St. (Calle Ocho), Miami. ☎ **305/541-2631.** Cover $10 on Thurs–Sun nights.

As the name implies, Cafe Nostalgia is dedicated to reminiscing about old Cuba. After watching a Celia Cruz film, you can dance to the hot sounds of Afro-Cuban jazz. With pictures of old and young Cuban stars smiling down on you and a live band celebrating Cuban heritage, Cafe Nostalgia sounds like a bit much; it's more than that. Be prepared—it's packed after midnight and dance space is mostly between the tables. Open Thursday to Sunday from 9pm to 4am. Films are shown from 10pm to midnight, followed by live music. Another branch is set to open on Miami Beach in late 1999.

Where to Learn to Salsa

Are you feeling shy about hitting a Latin club because you fear your two left feet will step out? Then take a few lessons before tripping the light fantastic. Here are the names of several dance companies and dance teachers around the city who offer individual and group lessons to dancers of any origin who are willing to learn. These folks have made it their mission to teach merengue and flamenco to the non-Latinos and Latino left-foots.

You'll have a blast at **Starfish** (1427 West Ave., South Beach; ☎ **305/ 673-1717**), on Friday nights when it's "Strictly Salsa."

The cover is $5 and is well worth it for a chance to see some of the best (and worst) dancers in town. Learn the moves on Monday and Wednesday nights when group lessons cost only $8.

At Ballet **Flamenco La Rosa** (in the PAN building, 555 17th St., South Beach; ☎ **305/672-0552**), you can learn to flamenco, salsa, or merengue with the best of them. They are the only professional flamenco company in the area, so you'll hear those castanets going. If you're feeling shy, $50 will buy you a private lesson; otherwise, $10 an hour will allow you to learn the art of the dance with a group of other beginners.

Nobody salsas like **Luz Pinto** (☎ **305/868-9418**), and she also knows how to teach the basics with patience and humor. She charges between $45 and $50 for a private lesson for up to four people and $10 per person for a group lesson. A good introduction is her multilevel group class at 7pm Sunday evenings at the PAN building. Although she teaches everything from ballroom to merengue, her specialty is Casino-style salsa, popularized in the 1950s in Cuba, Luz's homeland. A mix between disco and country square dancing, Casino-style salsa is all the rage in Latin clubs in town. If you are a very good student, you may be able to talk Luz into chaperoning a trip to a nightclub to show off your moves. She'll work out a fee based on the number of participants and their ability.

Angel Arroyo has been teaching salsa to the clueless out of his home at 16467 NE 27th Ave., North Miami Beach (☎ **305/949-7799**), for the past 10 years. Just $10 will buy you an hour's time in his "school." He traditionally teaches Monday and Wednesday nights, but call ahead to check for any schedule changes.

Casa Panza. 1620 SW 8th St. (Calle Ocho), Miami. ☎ **305/643-5343.**

Clap your hands or your castanets if you have them. Every Tuesday and Thursday night, Casa Panza, in the heart of Little Havana, becomes the House of Flamenco, with shows at 8 and 11pm. You can either enjoy a flamenco show or strap on your own dancing shoes and participate in the celebration. Enjoy a fantastic Spanish meal before the show, or just have a drink or two before you start stomping.

Mango's. 900 Ocean Dr., South Beach. ☎ **305/673-4422.** Cover $6–$15; varies by performer.

If you want to dance to a funky, loud Brazilian beat till you drop, check out Mango's on the beach. It features nightly live Brazilian and other Latin music on a little patio bar. When you need refreshment, you can choose from a wildly eclectic menu of Caribbean, Mexican, vegetarian, and Cuban specialties. Open daily from 11am to 5:30pm.

Studio 23. 247 23rd St. (1 block west of Collins Ave.), South Beach. ☎ **305/538-1196.** Cover $5–$10.

You've heard of *son?* Hear it here—along with salsa, cumbia, merengue, vallenato, and house music. This neighborhood Latin disco and nightclub gets going after hours with a wild strobe-lit atmosphere. If you don't know how to do it, just wait. You'll have plenty of willing teachers on hand. Open Friday to Sunday from 8pm to 4am.

Yuca. 501 Lincoln Rd., South Beach. ☎ **305/532-9822.** Cover $25, plus two-drink minimum for the Albita performance Fri–Sat nights at 11pm.

One of the city's best restaurants (see chapter 6) also serves up hot music in an upstairs club. If Albita is playing, don't miss her. The prices are ridiculous and you'll be squeezed into a table no bigger than a cocktail napkin, but it's worth it for the high-energy dance music, including traditional sol, salsa, and son from the old country. If you don't speak Spanish, sign language works here, too.

3 The Performing Arts

THEATER

In Miami, an active and varied selection of dramas and musicals are presented throughout the year. Thanks to the support of many loyal theater aficionados, especially an older crowd of New York transplants, season subscriptions are common and allow the theaters to survive, even when every show is not a hit. Some traveling Broadway shows make it to town, as well as revivals by big-name playwrights, such as Tennessee Williams, David Mamet, Neil Simon, and Israel Horowitz. The best way to find out what's playing is to check the local paper or call the theaters directly.

The **Actors' Playhouse,** at the newly restored Miracle Theater in Coral Gables (☎ 305/444-9293), is a grand 1948 art deco movie palace with a 600-seat main theater as well as a smaller theater/rehearsal hall where a number of excellent musicals for children are put on throughout the year. In addition to these two rooms, the Playhouse recently added a 300-seat children's balcony theater. Tickets run from $26 to $50.

The **Coconut Grove Playhouse,** 3500 Main Highway in Coconut Grove (☎ 305/442-4000), was also a former movie house, built in 1927 in an ornate Spanish rococo style. Today, this respected venue is known for its original and innovative staging of both international and local dramas and musicals. The house's second, more intimate Encore Room is well suited to alternative and experimental productions. Tickets run from $37 to $42.

The **Gables Stage,** on Anastasia Avenue in Coral Gables at the Biltmore Hotel (☎ 305/445-1119), stages at least one Shakespeare play, one classic, and one contemporary piece a year. This well-regarded theater usually tries to secure the rights to a national or local premiere as well. Tickets cost $22 and $28; $10 and $17 for students and seniors.

The **Jerry Herman Ring Theatre** is on the main campus of the University of Miami in Coral Gables (☎ 305/284-3355). The University's Department of Theater Arts uses this stage for advanced-student productions of comedies, dramas, and musicals. Faculty and guest actors are regularly featured, as are contemporary works by local playwrights. Performances are usually scheduled Tuesday through Saturday during the academic year. In the summer, don't miss "Summer Shorts," a selection of superb one-acts. Tickets sell for $5 to $20.

The **New Theater,** 65 Almeria Ave., in Coral Gables (☎ **305/443-5909**), prides itself on showing world-renowned works from America and Europe. As the name implies, you'll find mostly contemporary plays, with a few classics thrown in for variety. Performances are staged Thursday to Sunday year-round. Tickets are $20 on weekdays, and $25 weekends. If tickets are available, students pay half price.

ACTING COMPANIES

Miami's two well-known acting companies have suffered from poor financing and real-estate woes. Luckily, both have the support of a loyal crew of theater fans who overlook budget sets, inconsistent acting, and occasional bad taste. Call for schedules and locales.

The **Acme Acting Company** (☎ **305/576-7500**) performs Wednesday to Saturday at 8pm, and Sunday at 7pm. They usually present offbeat contemporary plays to critical acclaim. Tickets are $15 to $25 depending on the venue; students and seniors pay $10 to $20.

The award-winning **Area Stage Company** (☎ **305/673-8002**) has won respect from local and national audiences for their dramatic work in all manner of contemporary theater.

CLASSICAL MUSIC

In addition to a number of local orchestras and operas, which regularly offer quality music and world-renowned guest artists, each year brings a slew of special events and touring artists. One of the most important and longest-running series is produced by the **Concert Association of Florida (CAF),** 555 17th St., South Beach (☎ **305/532-3491**). Known for more than a quarter of a century for its high-caliber, star-packed schedules, CAF regularly arranges the best "serious" music concerts for the city. Season after season, the schedules are punctuated by world-renowned dance companies and seasoned virtuosi like Itzhak Perlman, Andre Watts, and Kathleen Battle. Since CAF does not have its own space, performances are usually scheduled in either the Dade County Auditorium or the Jackie Gleason Theater of the Performing Arts (see below). The season lasts from October through April, and ticket prices range from $20 to $70.

Florida Philharmonic Orchestra. 1243 University Dr., Miami. ☎ **800/226-1812** or 305/476-1234. Tickets $15–$60. When extra tickets are available, students are admitted free on day of performance.

South Florida's premier symphony orchestra, under the direction of James Judd, presents a full season of classical and pops programs interspersed with several children's and contemporary popular music dates. The Philharmonic performs downtown in the Gusman Center for the Performing Arts and at the Dade County Auditorium.

Miami Chamber Symphony. 5690 N. Kendall Dr., Kendall. ☎ **305/858-3500.** Tickets $12–$30.

This professional orchestra is an inexpensive alternative to the high-priced classical venues. Renowned international soloists perform regularly. The season runs October to May, and most concerts are held in the Gusman Concert Hall, on the University of Miami campus.

✪ **The New World Symphony.** 541 Lincoln Rd., South Beach. ☎ **305/673-3331.** www.nws.org. E-mail: ticketsnws.org. Tickets free to $43. Student discounts available on day of show.

This organization, led by artistic director Michael Tilson Thomas, is a stepping stone for gifted young musicians seeking professional careers. The orchestra specializes in ambitious, innovative, energetic performances and often features renowned guest soloists and conductors. The symphony's season lasts from October to May during which time there are many free concerts.

OPERA

✪ **Florida Grand Opera.** 1200 Coral Way, Miami. ☎ **800/741-1010** or 305/854-1643. Tickets $18–$100. Student discounts available.

Nearing its 60th birthday, this company regularly features singers from top houses in both America and Europe. All productions are sung in their original language and staged with projected English supertitles. Tickets become scarce when Placido Domingo or Luciano Pavarotti (who made his American debut here in 1965) come to town. The opera's season runs roughly from November to April, with five performances each week.

DANCE

Several local dance companies train and perform in the Greater Miami area. In addition, top traveling troupes regularly stop at the venues listed above. Keep your eyes open for special events and guest artists.

✪ **Ballet Flamenco La Rosa.** ☎ **305/672-0552** or 305/757-8475. Tickets $25 at door, $20 in advance, $18 for students and seniors.

For a taste of local Latin flavor, see this lively troupe perform impressive flamenco and other styles of dance on Miami stages.

✪ **Miami City Ballet.** Lincoln Road Mall at Jefferson Ave., South Beach. ☎ **305/532-4880.** Box office ☎ 305/532-7713. Tickets $17–$50.

The artistically acclaimed and innovative company, directed by Edward Villella, features a repertoire of more than 60 ballets, many by George Balanchine, and more than 20 world premieres. Stop by to watch rehearsals through the large storefront window before the company moves to their new space near the Bass museum on Collins and 22nd Street. The City Ballet season runs from September to April, with performances at the Jackie Gleason Theater of the Performing Arts (see below).

MAJOR VENUES

After years of decay and a $1 million facelift, the **Colony Theater,** on Lincoln Road, South Beach (☎ **305/674-1026**), has become an architectural showpiece of the Art Deco District. This multipurpose 465-seat theater stages performances by the Miami City Ballet and the Ballet Flamenco La Rosa, as well as off-Broadway shows and other special events.

At the **Dade County Auditorium,** West Flagler Street at 29th Avenue, Miami (☎ **305/547-5414**), performers gripe about the lack of space, but for patrons, this 2,430-seat auditorium is comfortable and intimate. It's home to the city's Greater Miami Opera and also stages productions by the Concert Association of Florida, many Spanish programs, and a variety of other shows.

At the 1,700-seat **Gusman Center for the Performing Arts,** 174 E. Flagler Street in Downtown Miami (☎ **305/372-0925**), seating is tight, and so is funding, but the sound is superb. In addition to producing a regular stage for the Philharmonic Orchestra of Florida and The Miami Film Festival, the elegant Gusman Center features pop concerts, plays, film-festival screenings, and special events. The auditorium was built as the Olympia Theater in 1926, and its ornate palace interior is typical of that era, complete with fancy columns, a huge pipe organ, and twinkling "stars" on the ceiling.

Not to be confused with the Gusman Center (above), the **Gusman Concert Hall,** 1314 Miller Dr., at 14th Street in Coral Gables (☎ **305/284-6477**), is a roomy 600-seat hall that gives a stage to the Miami Chamber Symphony and a varied program of university recitals.

The elegant **Jackie Gleason Theater of the Performing Arts (TOPA),** Washington Avenue at 17th Street, South Beach (☎ **305/673-7300**), is the home of the Miami City Ballet as well as the Miami Beach Broadway Series, which recently presented Rent, Phantom of the Opera, and Les Misérables. This 2,705-seat hall also hosts other big-budget Broadway shows, classical music concerts, opera, and dance performances.

4 Movies & More

CINEMAS

In addition to the annual Miami Film Festival in February and other, smaller film events (See "Miami Calendar of Events," in chapter 2), Miami is lucky to have some wonderful art cinemas showing a range of films from *Fresa y Chocolate* to *Crumb.*

The **Alliance Cinema** (☎ **305/531-8504**) is tucked behind a little tropical walkway just next to Books & Books at 927 Lincoln Rd., Suite 119, in South Beach. This old hideaway shows art films, Latin American features, and lots of gay films, too. You may want to bring a pillow; the seats are old and rickety. Tickets cost $6.

Astor Art Cinema, 4120 Laguna St. (☎ **305/443-6777**), is an oasis in the midst of a desert of Cineplex Odeons and AMCs in Coral Gables. This quaint double theater hosts foreign, classic, independent, and art films and serves decent popcorn, too. Tickets are $5, $3 for seniors.

Absinthe Cinemateque, 235 Alcazar Ave., Coral Gables (☎ **305/446-7144**), is a small one-screen theater, which shows good movies, often Spanish-language films, without the hustle and bustle of the crowded multiplexes. The Alcazar shows the more artsy of the major films as well as some obscure independents. Tickets are $6.

The **Bill Cosford Cinema** at the University of Miami, on the second floor of the memorial building off Campo Sano Avenue (☎ **305/284-4861**), is named after the deceased *Herald* film critic. This well-endowed little theater was recently revamped and boasts high-tech projectors, new air-conditioning, and new decor. It sponsors independent films as well as lectures by visiting filmmakers and movie stars. Andy Garcia and Antonio Banderas are a few of the big names this little theater has attracted. It also hosts the African American Film Festival and a Student Film Festival, plus collaborations with the Fort Lauderdale Festival. Admission is $5.

THE LITERARY SCENE

Books & Books, in Coral Gables at 296 Aragon Ave., and in Miami Beach at 933 Lincoln Rd., hosts readings almost every night and is known for attracting top authors, such as Colleen McCullough, Jamaica Kincaid, and Paul Levine. For details on the free readings, call ☎ **305/442-4408.**

To hear more about what's happening in Miami's literary scene, tune into the "Cover to Cover" show, broadcast at 8pm on Monday on the public radio station WLRN (91.3 FM).

5 Late-Night Bites

Although some dining spots in Miami stop serving at 10pm, many are open very late or even around the clock, especially on weekends. So, if it's 4am and you need a quick bite after clubbing, don't fret. There are a vast number of pizza places lining Washington Avenue in South Beach that are open past 6am. Especially good is **Pucci's,** with several locations, including one at 651 Washington Ave. **La Sandwicherie,** 229 14th St. (behind the Amoco station; ☎ **305/532-8934**), serves up a great late-night sandwich until 5am. Another place of note for night owls is the **News Café,** 800 Ocean Dr. (☎ **305/538-6397**), a trendy and well-priced cafe with an enormous menu offering great all-day breakfasts, Middle Eastern platters, fruit bowls, or steak and potatoes 24 hours. In Coconut Grove, there's another crowded News Cafe, 2901 Florida Ave. (behind Mayfair; ☎ 305/774-6397), serving up the same fresh food around the clock.

If your night out was at one of the Latin clubs around town, stop in at **Versailles,** 3555 SW 8th St. (☎ **305/444-0240**), in Little Havana. What else but a Cuban *medianoche* (midnight sandwich) will do? It's not open all night, but its hours extend well past midnight—usually until 3 or 4am on weekends—to cater to gangs of revelers, both young and old.

Side Trips from Miami 11

As varied as Miami and its beaches are, many people like to use this centrally located spot as a jumping-off point for other destinations including the two nearby national parks. Whether you'd like to tour the underwater treasures of Biscayne National Park or explore the swampy Everglades or hop over to the Florida Keys, all are easily accessible from here. See chapter 12 for more details on the Upper, Middle, Lower Keys, and Key West. Also convenient to Miami by boat or plane are the islands of The Bahamas, which I've highlighted below.

1 A Glimpse of Everglades National Park— The Southeast Portion

35 miles SW of Miami

Marjory Stoneman Douglas, who fought tirelessly to save this fragile resource until her death in 1998 at the age of 108, might well be called the Mother of the Everglades. This vast and unusual ecosystem is actually a shallow, 40-mile-wide, slow-moving river. Rarely more than knee-deep, the water is the lifeblood of this wilderness. Subtle shifts in water level dictate the life cycle of plants and animals. Most folks viewed it as a worthless swamp until Douglas focused attention on the area with her moving and insightful book *The Everglades: River of Grass,* published in 1947.

It was that same year that 1.5 million acres—less than 20% of Everglades wilderness—were established as Everglades National Park. At that time few lawmakers understood how neighboring ecosystems relate to each other: You can't just chop off a chunk of a much larger wilderness and expect it to survive. The land is intertwined with its surroundings, at the butt end of every environmental insult that occurs upstream.

Recently, environmental activists have succeeded in persuading politicians to enact some legislation to clean up the pollution that has threatened this unusual ecosystem ever since the days when heavy industry—most notably the sugar industry—first moved into the area. There has been a marked decrease in the indigenous wildlife here, but it remains one of the few places where you can see dozens of endangered species in their natural habitat, including the swallowtail butterfly, American crocodile, leatherback turtle, southern bald eagle, West Indian manatee, and Florida panther.

Everglades National Park

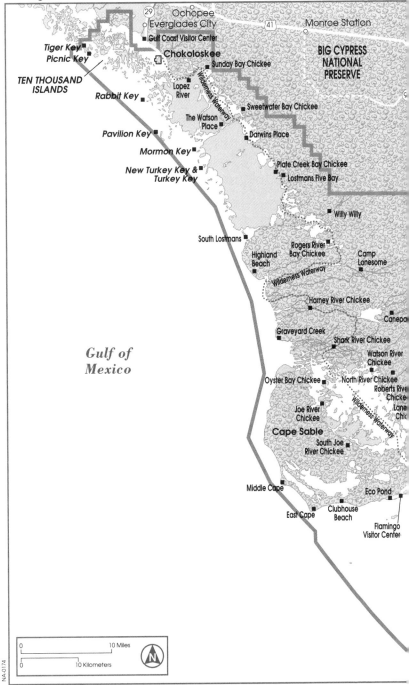

Ochopee
29 Everglades City
Gulf Coast Visitor Center
Monroe Station
41

Tiger Key
Picnic Key

BIG CYPRESS
NATIONAL
PRESERVE

Chokoloskee
Sunday Bay Chickee

TEN THOUSAND
ISLANDS

Lopez
River

Rabbit Key

Sweetwater Bay Chickee

The Watson
Place

Pavilion Key

Darwins Place

Mormon Key

New Turkey Key &
Turkey Key

Plate Creek Bay Chickee
Lostmans Five Bay

Willy Willy

South Lostmans

Rogers River
Bay Chickee

Highland
Beach

Camp
Lonesome

Wilderness Waterway

Harney River Chickee

Graveyard Creek

Canepa

Shark River Chickee

Watson River
Chickee

Gulf of
Mexico

Oyster Bay Chickee

North River Chickee
Roberts River
Chickee

Joe River
Chickee

Lane
Chic

Wilderness Waterway

Cape Sable
South Joe
River Chickee

Middle Cape

Eco Pond

East Cape

Clubhouse
Beach

Flamingo
Visitor Center

0   10 Miles
0   10 Kilometers
N

NA-0174

182

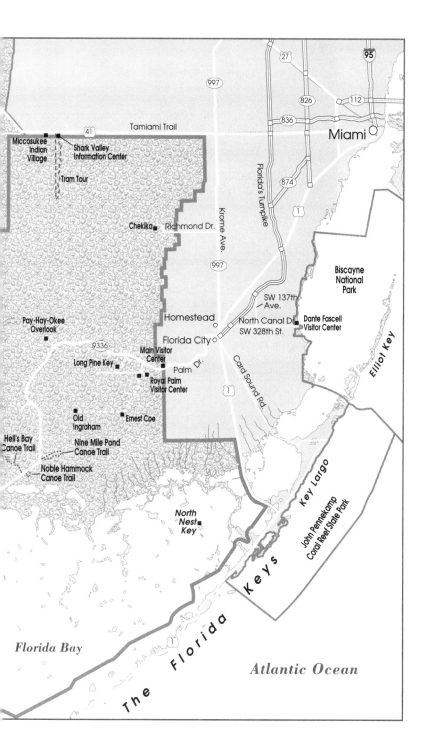

Miccosukee Indian Village
Shark Valley Information Center
Tram Tour

Tamiami Trail

41

997

27

95

826

112

836

Miami

874

Florida's Turnpike

1

Chekika   Richmond Dr.

Krone Ave.

997

Biscayne National Park

SW 137th Ave.

Pay-Hay-Okee Overlook

Homestead

North Canal Dr.
SW 328th St.

Dante Fascell Visitor Center

Elliot Key

Florida City

9336

Main Visitor Center

Long Pine Key

Palm Dr.

Card Sound Rd.

Royal Palm Visitor Center

1

Old Ingraham   Ernest Coe

Hell's Bay Canoe Trail

Nine Mile Pond Canoe Trail

Noble Hammock Canoe Trail

Key Largo

John Pennekamp Coral Reef State Park

North Nest Key

The Florida Keys

Florida Bay

1

Atlantic Ocean

183

There are no other Everglades in the world. They are, they have always been, one of the unique regions of the earth, remote, never wholly known. Nothing anywhere else is like them: their vast glittering openness, wider than the enormous visible round of the horizon, the racing free saltiness and sweetness of their massive winds, under the dazzling blue heights of space.
                                              —Marjory Stoneman Douglas, *The Everglades: River of Grass*, 1947

It takes a month for one gallon of water to move through the park, and I recommend a similar pace for you to fully experience the Everglades' grandeur. Take your time on the trails, and a hypnotic beauty begins to unfold. Follow the rustling of a bush, and you might see a small green tree frog or tiny brown anole lizard, with its bright-red spotted throat. Crane your head around a bend and discover a delicate, brightly painted mule-ear orchid.

The slow and subtle splendor of this exotic land may not be immediately appealing to kids raised on video games and rapid-fire commercials, but they'll certainly remember the experience and no doubt thank you for it later. Meanwhile, you'll find plenty of dramatic fun around the park, like airboat rides, alligator wrestling, and biking to keep the kids satisfied for at least a day.

In the 1800s, before the southern Everglades were designated a national park, the only inhabited piece of this wilderness was a quiet fishing village called Flamingo. Accessible only by boat and leveled every few years by hurricanes, the mosquito-infested town never grew very popular. When the 38-mile road from Florida City was completed in 1922, many of those who did live here fled to someplace either more or less remote. Today, Flamingo is a center for visitor activities and the main jumping-off point for backcountry camping and exploration. Flamingo is now home to National Park Service and concessionaire employees and their families.

Some 1,400 residents still live in the small enclave in the eastern section of the park although the local agency governing the area has recently begun a buy out program to remove them so that the area can be returned to its original state.

Everglades National Park's northern Shark Valley entrance and the eastern approaches described in this section are the most accessible from Miami and the rest of Florida's east coast. You'll find great amenities along the way, like Indian villages, alligator farms, and boat rides. An excellent tram tour goes deep into the park along a trail that's also terrific for biking. This is also the best way to reach the park's only accommodation (and full-service outfitters), the Flamingo Lodge.

For thorough information on Everglades City, the "western gateway" to Everglades National Park and Big Cypress Preserve pick up a copy of *Frommer's Florida*.

JUST THE FACTS

GETTING THERE & ACCESS POINTS   Everglades National Park has four entrances. The following three are the most popular and the ones most convenient to visitors from Florida's east coast, including Miami. No matter which part of Miami you are starting in, the drive should take no longer than an hour (unless of course you are traveling during rush hour: between 8 and 9:30am or from 4 until 6pm. Then, the roads, especially S.R. 836, will be backed up, and your driving time could be doubled).

The main entrance, in Homestead on the park's east side, is located 10 miles southwest of Florida City. From Miami, take S.R. 836 west to the Florida Turnpike south until it ends in Florida City. Signs will point you southwest onto the road that leads into the park, S.R. 9336. The main entrance's Park Ranger Station is open 24 hours.

The Shark Valley entrance, on the park's north side, is located on the Tamiami Trail (U.S. 41), about 35 miles west of downtown Miami. From Miami, take S.R. 836 west to the Florida Turnpike south; exit on Tamiami Trail (U.S. 41), and go west for approximately 30 miles. The park will be on your left side. Shark Valley is known for its 15-mile trail loop that's used for an excellent interpretive tram tour, bicycling, and walking. This entrance is open daily from 8:30am to 5:30pm, with some seasonal variation. Call ahead.

Chekika, popular with day visitors, picnickers, and campers, is located halfway between the two entrances above in the northeast section of the park. Chekika can be reached from Miami as if going to Shark Valley (see above). After exiting on Tamiami Trail (Highway 41), head west 5 miles to Krome Avenue (177th Avenue); turn left, then proceed to SW 168th Street (Richmond Avenue) and head west (left) until you reach a stop sign. Turn right; the entrance will be on the left side. There are picnic facilities and a 20-site campground. You can enter Chekika from 8:30am until sundown.

VISITOR CENTERS & INFORMATION   General inquiries and specific questions should be directed to **Everglades National Park Headquarters,** 40001 S.R. 9336, Homestead, FL 33034 (☎ **305/242-7700**). Ask for a copy of *Parks and Preserves,* a free newspaper that's filled with up-to-date information on goings-on in the Everglades. Headquarters is staffed by helpful phone operators daily from 8:30am until 4:30pm.

Note that all hours listed are for the high season, generally November through May. During the slow summer months, many offices and outfitters keep abbreviated hours.

The **Flamingo Lodge, Marina and Outpost Resort,** in Flamingo (☎ **800/ 600-3813** or 941/695-3101), is the one-stop clearinghouse—and the only option—for in-park accommodations, equipment rentals, and tours.

Especially since its recent expansion, the **Ernest F. Coe Visitor Center,** located at the park's main entrance, is the best place to stop to gather information for your trip. In addition to free brochures outlining trails, wildlife and activities, and information on tours and boat rentals, you will also find state-of-the-art educational displays, films, and interactive exhibits. A gift shop sells postcards, film, unusual gift items, the best selection of books about the Everglades, and a selection of your most important gear—insect repellent. It is open from 8am until 5pm daily.

The **Royal Palm Visitor Center,** a small nature museum located 3 miles past the park's main entrance, is a smaller information center at the head of the popular Anhinga and Gumbo-Limbo trails and is open daily from 8am until 4pm.

The Shark Valley Information Center at the park's northern entrance and the Flamingo Visitor Center are also staffed by knowledgeable rangers who provide brochures and personal insight into the goings-on in the park. They are open from 8:30am until 5pm.

ENTRANCE FEES, PERMITS & REGULATIONS   Permits and passes can be purchased either at the main park entrance, the Chekika entrance, or the Shark Valley entrance stations only.

Even if you are just visiting the park for an afternoon, you'll need to buy a 7-day permit, which costs $10 per vehicle. Pedestrians and cyclists are charged $5 each and $4 at Shark Valley.

An Everglades Park Pass, valid for a year's worth of unlimited entrances, is available for $20. U.S. citizens may purchase a 12-month Golden Eagle Passport for $50, which is valid for entrance into any U.S. national park. U.S. citizens aged 62 and older pay only $10 for a Golden Age Passport—that's valid for life. A Golden Access Passport is available free to U.S. citizens with disabilities.

Permits are required for campers to stay overnight either in the backcountry or in primitive campsites. See Camping, in "Where to Stay," below.

Those who want to fish without a charter captain must obtain a standard State of Florida saltwater fishing license. These are available in the park at Flamingo Lodge or any tackle shop or sporting goods store nearby. Nonresidents will pay $17 for a 7-day license or $7 for 3 days. Florida residents can get a fishing license good for the whole year for $14. Snook and crawfish licenses must be purchased separately at a cost of $2.

Charter captains carry vessel licenses that cover all paying passengers, but ask to be sure. Freshwater fishing licenses are available at various bait and tackle shops outside the park at the same rates. A good one nearby is **Don's Bait & Tackle** located at 30710 S. Federal Hwy. in Homestead right on U.S. 1. (☎ **305/ 247-6616**). Most of the area's freshwater fishing, limited to murky canals and artificial lakes near housing developments, is hardly worth the trouble when so much good saltwater fishing is available.

Firearms are not allowed anywhere in the park.

SEASONS   There are two distinct seasons in the Everglades: high season and mosquito season. High season is also dry season, and lasts from late November to May. Despite the bizarre cold and wet weather patterns that El Niño brought in 1998, most winters here are warm, sunny, and breezy—a good combination to keep the bugs away. This is the best time to visit, as low water levels attract the largest variety of wading birds and their predators. As the dry season wanes, wildlife follows the receding water, and by the end of May, the only living things you are sure to spot will cause you to itch. The worst, called "no-see-ums," are not even swattable. If you choose to visit during the buggy season, be sure to be vigilant in applying bug spray.

Also, realize that many establishments and operators either close or curtail offerings in the summer, so always call ahead to check schedules.

RANGER PROGRAMS   More than 50 ranger programs, free with admission, are offered each month during high season and give visitors an opportunity to gain an expert's perspective. Some programs occur regularly, such as Glade Glimpses, a walking tour during which rangers point out flora and fauna and discuss issues affecting the Everglade's survival. These tours are scheduled at 10:15am, noon, and 3:30pm daily. The Anhinga Ambles, a similar program that takes place on the Anhinga Trail, starts at 10:30am, 1:30pm, and 4pm.

Park rangers tend to be helpful, well informed, good-humored, and happy to answer questions. Since times, programs, and locations vary from month to month, check a schedule, available at any of the visitor centers (see above).

SAFETY   There are dangers inherent in this vast wilderness area. Always let someone know your itinerary before you set out on an extended hike. It's mandatory that you file an itinerary when camping overnight in the backcountry. When on the water, watch for weather changes; severe thunderstorms and high winds often develop very rapidly. Swimming is not recommended because of the presence of alligators, sharks, and barracudas. Watch out for the region's four indigenous poisonous snakes: diamondback and pygmy rattlesnakes, coral snakes (identifiable by their colorful rings), and water moccasins (which swim on the surface of the water). Again, bring insect repellent to ward off mosquitoes and biting flies.

First aid is available from park rangers. The nearest hospital is in Homestead, 10 miles from the park's main entrance.

SEEING THE HIGHLIGHTS

Shark Valley provides a fine introduction to the wonder of the Everglades, but don't plan on spending more than a few hours here. Bicycling or taking a guided tram tour can be a satisfying experience, but neither fully captures the wonders of the park.

If you want to see a greater array of plant and animal life, make sure that you venture into the park through the main entrance, pick up a trail map, and dedicate at least a day to exploring from there.

Stop first along the Anhinga and Gumbo-Limbo trails, which start right next to one another, 3 miles from the park's main entrance. These trails provide a thorough introduction to Everglades flora and fauna and are highly recommended to first-time visitors. There's more water and wildlife here than in most parts of the Everglades, especially during dry season. Alligators, turtles, river otters, herons, egrets, and other animals abound, making this one of the best trails for seeing wildlife. Arrive early to spot the widest selection of exotic birds; like the Anhinga Trail's namesake, a large black fishing bird that is so used to humans, many of these birds build their nests in plain view. Others travel deeper into the park during daylight hours. Take your time—at least an hour is recommended. If you treat the trails and modern boardwalk as pathways to get through quickly, rather than destinations to experience and savor slowly, you'll miss out on the still beauty and hidden treasures that await.

Also, it's worth climbing the observation tower at the end of the quarter-mile-long Pa-hay-okee Trail. The panoramic view of undulating grass and seemingly endless vistas gives the impression of a semiaquatic Serengeti. Flocks of tropical and semitropical birds traverse the landscape, alligators and fish stir the surface of the water, small grottoes of trees thrust up from the sea of grass marking higher ground, and the vastness of the hidden world you've entered seems unparalleled.

If you want to get closer to nature, a few hours in a canoe along any of the trails allows paddlers the chance to sense the park's fluid motion, and to become a part of the ecosphere. Visitors who choose this option end up feeling more like explorers than merely observers. (See "Sports & Outdoor Activities," below.)

No matter which option you choose (and there are many), I strongly recommend staying for the 7pm program, available during high season at the Long Pine Key Amphitheater. This talk and slide show given by one of the park's rangers will give you a detailed overview of the park's history, natural resources, wildlife, and threats to its survival.

SPORTS & OUTDOOR ACTIVITIES

BIKING   The relatively flat 38-mile paved Main Park Road is excellent for bicycling, as are many park trails, including Long Pine Key. Expect to spend 2 to 3 hours along the path.

If the park isn't flooded from excess rain (which it often is, especially in spring), Shark Valley in Everglades National Park is South Florida's most scenic bicycle trail. Many locals haul their bikes out to the Glades for a relaxing day of wilderness-trail riding. You can ride the 17-mile loop with no other traffic in sight. Instead, you'll share the flat paved road only with other bikers and a menagerie of wildlife. Don't be surprised to see a gator lounging in the sun or a deer munching on some grass. Otters, turtles, alligators, and snakes are common companions in the Shark Valley area.

Those who love to mountain bike, and who prefer solitude, might check out the **Southern Glades Trail,** a 14-mile unpaved trail opened in late 1998 that is lined with native trees and teeming with wildlife like deer, alligators, and the occasional snake. The remote trail runs along the C-111 canal, off S.R. 9336 and SW 217th Street.

You can rent bikes at the Flamingo Lodge, Marina and Outpost Resort (see "Where to Stay," below) for $17 per 24 hours, $14 per full day, $8.50 per half day (any 4-hour period), and $3 per hour. A $50 deposit is required for each rental. **Bicycles are also available from Shark Valley Tram Tours,** at the park's Shark Valley entrance (☎ **305/221-8455**), for $3.25 per hour; rentals can be picked up any time after 8:30am and must be returned by 4pm.

BIRD WATCHING   More than 350 species of birds make their homes in the Everglades. Tropical birds from the Caribbean and temperate species from North America can be found here, along with exotics that have blown in from more distant regions. Eco and Mrazek ponds, located near Flamingo, are two of the best places for birding, especially in early morning or late afternoon in the dry winter months. Pick up a free birding checklist from a visitor center (see "Just the Facts," above), and ask a park ranger what's been spotted in recent days.

BOATING   Motorboating around the Everglades seems like a great way to see plants and animals in remote habitats. However, environmentalists are taking stock of the damage motorboats (especially airboats) inflict on the delicate ecosystem. If you choose to motor, remember that most of the areas near land are "no wake" zones, and for the protection of nesting birds, landing is prohibited on most of the little mangrove islands. There's a long list of restrictions and restricted areas, so get a copy of the park's boating rules from National Park Headquarters before setting out (see "Just the Facts," above).

The Everglades' only marina—accommodating about 50 boats with electric and water hookups—is the Flamingo Lodge, Marina and Outpost Resort, located in Flamingo. The well-marked channel to Flamingo is accessible to boats with a maximum 4-foot draft and is open year-round. Reservations can be made through the marina store (☎ **941/695-3101, ext. 304**). Skiffs with 15-horsepower motors are available for rent. These low-power boats cost $90 per day, $65 per half day (any 5-hour period), and $22 per hour. A $125 deposit is required.

CANOEING   The most intimate view of the Everglades comes from the humble perspective of a simple low boat. From a canoe, you'll get a closer look into the park's shallow estuaries where water birds, sea turtles, and endangered manatees make their homes.

Everglades National Park's longest "trails" are designed for boat and canoe travel, and many are marked as clearly as walking trails. The Noble Hammock Trail, a 2-mile loop, takes 1 to 2 hours, and is recommended for beginning canoers. The Hell's Bay Trail, a 3- to 6-mile course for hardier paddlers, takes 2 to 6 hours, depending on how far you choose to go. Park rangers can recommend other trails that best suit your abilities, time limitations, and interests.

You can rent a canoe at the Flamingo Lodge, Marina and Outpost Resort (see "Where to Stay," below) for $40 for 24 hours, $32 per full day, $22 per half day (any 4-hour period), and $8 per hour. They also have family canoes that rent for $12, $30, $40, and $50, respectively. A deposit is required. Skiffs, kayaks, and tandem kayaks are also available. The concessionaire will shuttle your party to the trailhead of your choice and pick you up afterward. Rental facilities are open daily from 6am to 8pm.

FISHING   About one-third of Everglades National Park is open water. Freshwater fishing is popular in brackish Nine-Mile Pond (25 miles from the main entrance) and other spots along the Main Park Road, but because of the high mercury levels found in the Everglades, freshwater fishers are warned not to eat their catch. Before casting, check in at a visitor center, as many of the park's lakes are preserved for observation only. Fishing licenses are required. See "Just the Facts," above.

Saltwater anglers will find snapper and sea trout plentiful. Charter boats and guides are available at Flamingo Lodge, Marina and Outpost Resort (see "Where to Stay," below). Phone for information and reservations.

ORGANIZED TOURS

AIRBOAT TOURS   Shallow-draft, fan-powered airboats were invented in the Everglades by frog hunters who were tired of polling through the brushes. And though it is the most efficient way to get around, airboats are not permitted in the park. Just outside the boundaries, however, you'll find a number of outfitters offering rides. These shallow-bottom runabouts tend to inflict severe damage on the animals and plants there. If you choose to ride on one, you may consider bringing earplugs; these high-speed boats are loud. Airboat rides are offered at the **Miccosukee Indian Village,** just west of the Shark Valley entrance on U.S. 41, the Tamiami Trail (☎ **305/223-8380**). Native American guides will take you through the reserve's rushes at high speed and stop along the way to point out alligators, native plants, and exotic birds. The price is just $7.

Also, the **Everglades Alligator Farm,** 4 miles south of Palm Drive/S.R. 9336 and on SW 192 Ave. (☎ **305/247-2628**), offers half-hour guided airboat tours from 9am until 6pm daily. The price, which includes admission to the park, is $12 for adults, $6 for children.

MOTORBOAT TOURS   Both Florida Bay and backcountry tours are offered at the **Flamingo Lodge, Marina and Outpost Resort** (see "Where to Stay," below). Both are available in 1½- and 2-hour versions that cost an average of $16 adults, $8 children, under 6 free. There are also charter-fishing and sightseeing boats that can be booked through the main reservation number (☎ **941/695-3101**). Florida Bay tours cruise nearby estuaries and sandbars, while six-passenger backcountry boats visit smaller sloughs. Tours depart throughout the day, and reservations are recommended.

TRAM TOURS   At the park's Shark Valley entrance, open-air tram buses take visitors on 2-hour naturalist-led tours that delve 7½ miles into the wilderness. At the trail's midsection, passengers can disembark and climb a 65-foot observation tower that offers good views of the Glades. The tour offers visitors considerable views that include plenty of wildlife and endless acres of sawgrass. Tours run November to April only, daily from 9am to 4pm, and are sometimes stalled by flooding or particularly heavy mosquito infestation. Reservations are recommended from December to March. The cost is $9.30 for adults, $5.15 for children 12 and under, and $8.25 for seniors. For further information, contact the **Shark Valley Tram Tours** at ☎ **305/221-8455.**

SHOPPING

You won't find big malls or lots of boutiques in this area, although there is an outlet center nearby, the **Keys Factory Shops** (☎ **305/248-4727**), at 250 E. Palm Dr. (where the Fla. Turnpike meets U.S. 1), in Florida City, with more than 60 stores including Nike Factory Store, Bass Co. Store, Levi's, Osh Kosh, and Izod. You can pick up a free coupon booklet from the Customer Service Center called the Come

Back Pack, which includes coupons good for discounts in the outlet. It's open Monday to Saturday until 9pm, Sunday until 6 pm.

A necessary stop and good place for a refreshment is one of Florida's best-known fruit stands, **Robert Is Here** (☎ **305/246-1592**). Robert has been selling home-grown treats for nearly 40 years at the corner of SW 344th Street (Palm Drive) and SW 192nd Avenue. You'll find the freshest pineapples, bananas, papayas, mangos, and melons anywhere as well as his famous shakes in unusual flavors like key lime, coconut, orange, and cantaloupe. Exotic fruits, bottled jellies, hot sauces, and salad dressings are also available. This is a great place to pick up culinary souvenirs and sample otherwise unavailable goodies. Open daily 8am until 7pm.

Along Tamiami Trail, there are several roadside shops hawking Indian handicrafts including one at the **Miccosukee Indian Village** (☎ **305/223-8380**), just west of the Shark Valley entrance. At nearly every one you'll find the same stock of feathered dreamcatchers, stuffed alligator heads and claws, turquoise jewelry, and other trinkets. *Tip:* Be sure to take note of the unique, colorful handmade cloth Miccosukee dolls.

WHERE TO STAY

The only lodging in the park proper is the Flamingo Lodge, a fairly priced and very recommendable option. However, here are a few hotels just outside the park that are even cheaper. As of press time, there is a $45 million casino hotel under construction adjacent to the Miccosukee bingo and gaming hall on the northern edge of the park.

Though bugs can be a major nuisance, especially in the warm months, camping is really the way to go in this very primitive environment. There are dozens of campsites and chickee platforms (see below for details) for tenters.

IN & AROUND EVERGLADES NATIONAL PARK

✪ **Flamingo Lodge, Marina and Outpost Resort.** 1 Flamingo Lodge Hwy., Flamingo, FL 33034. ☎ **800/600-3813** or 941/695-3101. Fax 941/695-3921. www.flamingolodge.com. 127 units A/C TV TEL. Winter from $95 double; from $135 cottage; $135–$150 suite. Off-season $65–$80 double; $89–$100 cottage; $99–$110 suite. Rates for cottages or suites are for one to four people. Children under 18 stay free. AE, DC, DISC, MC. Take Florida Turnpike South to Florida City; exit on U.S. 1; at 4-way intersection turn right onto Palm Dr.; continue for 3 miles and turn left at Robert Is Here fruit stand; turn right at the 3-way intersection. The park entrance is 3 miles ahead. Continue for about 35 more miles to reach lodge.

The Flamingo Lodge is the only lodging actually located within the boundaries of Everglades National Park. This woodsy, sprawling complex offers rooms overlooking the Florida Bay in either a two-story simple motel or the lodge. Either option feels very much like being at summer camp, with a few more amenities.

VCRs and videos are available for guests in the regular rooms or in the suite, but not in more primitively outfitted cottages. Still, the cottages are an especially good choice if you plan to stay more than a night or two since they come with small kitchens, equipped with dishes and flatware, but no television. They are also larger, more private, and almost romantic.

Facilities on the premises include a waterside bar and restaurant; a freshwater swimming pool; convenience store, and a gift shop; coin laundry; bike, canoe, and kayak rental; and a full-service marina. The hotel is open year-round although the restaurant (see "Where to Dine," below) closes in the summer. Reservations are accepted daily from 8am to 5pm. Guests are treated to free coffee in the lobby.

CAMPING & HOUSEBOATING IN THE EVERGLADES

Campgrounds are available in Flamingo and Long Pine Key, where there are more than 300 sites designed for tents and RVs. They have level parking pads, tables, and charcoal grills. There are no electrical hookups, and showers are cold water. Private ground fires are not permitted, but supervised campfire programs are conducted during winter months. Reservations may be made in advance through The National Park Reservations Service at ☎ **800/365-CAMP.** Campsites are $14 per night with a 14-day consecutive stay limit, 30 days a year maximum.

Camping is also available in the backcountry year-round on a first-come, first-served basis and is only accessible by boat, foot, or bicycle. Campers must register in person or by telephone no more than 24 hours before the start of their trip. Permits must be obtained at ranger stations in either Flamingo or Everglades City. Campers can use only designated campsites, which are plentiful and well marked on visitor maps.

Many backcountry sites are chickee huts—covered wooden platforms on stilts. They're accessible only by canoe and can accommodate freestanding tents (without stakes). Ground sites are located along interior bays and rivers, and beach camping is also popular. In summer especially, mosquito repellent is necessary gear.

Houseboat rentals are one of the park's best-kept secrets. Available through the Flamingo Lodge, Marina and Outpost Resort, motorized houseboats make it possible to explore some of the park's more remote regions without having to worry about being back by nightfall. You can choose from two different types of houseboats. The first, a 40-foot pontoon boat, sleeps six to eight people in a single large room that's separated by a central head (bathroom) and shower. There's a small galley (kitchen) that contains a stove, oven, and charcoal grill. Prices aren't cheap unless you are with a good-sized group. It rents for between $340 and $475 for 2 nights (there's a 2-night minimum in high season).

The newer, sleeker Gibson fiberglass boats sleep six, have a head and shower, air-conditioning, and electric stove. There's also a full rooftop sundeck. These rent for $575 for 2 nights (with a 2-night minimum). With either boat, the 7th night is free when renting for a full week.

Boating experience is helpful, but not mandatory, as the boats only cruise up to 6 miles per hour and are surprisingly easy to use. In-season reservations should be made months in advance; call ☎ **800/600-3813** or 941/695-3101.

NEARBY IN HOMESTEAD & FLORIDA CITY

Homestead and Florida City, two adjacent towns that were almost blown off the map by Hurricane Andrew in 1992, have come back better than before. Located about 10 miles from the park's main entrance, along U.S. 1, 35 miles south of Miami, these somewhat rural towns offer several budget lodging options, including a handful of chain hotels. There is a very recommendable **Days Inn** (☎ **305/ 245-1260**) in Homestead and a **Hampton Inn** (☎ **800/426-7866** or 305/ 247-8833) right off the turnpike in Florida City. The best option is the Best Western Gateway to the Keys.

✪ **Best Western Gateway to the Keys.** 1 Strano Blvd. (U.S. 1), Florida City, FL 33034. ☎ **800/528-1234** or 305/246-5100. Fax 305/242-0056. 114 units. A/C TV TEL. Winter from $89 double; from $109 suite. Off-season from $80 double; from $99 suite. Rates include continental breakfast. During races and very high season there may be a 3-night minimum. AE, DC, DISC, MC, V.

Opened in late 1994, this two-story, pink-and-white Best Western offers contemporary style and comfort about 10 miles from the park's main entrance. A decent sized pool and a small spa are especially attractive. Each identical standard room has bright, tropical bedspreads and oversize picture windows. The suites offer convenient extras like a microwave, coffeemaker, an extra sink, and a small fridge.

Overall, this business-oriented hotel is well priced and well maintained, and is the best choice in the area. The only drawback is that in season, there is often a 3-day minimum stay requirement. You'd do best to call the local reservation line instead of the toll-free number—on several occasions, the hotel made an exception to the rule while the central reservation line was not able to.

Everglades Motel. 605 S. Krome Ave., Homestead, FL 33030. ☎ **305/247-4117.** 14 units. A/C TV TEL. Winter $43 double. Off-season from $32 double. Additional person $5 extra. AE, DISC, MC, V.

This one-story hotel is probably the cheapest option you'll find in Homestead, but certainly not the greatest. There is a small swimming pool, coin laundry, and free coffee in the lobby. Though not thoroughly fluent in English, the East Indian staff is accommodating and friendly. Rooms are modest in size and decor, but could use a good scrub. Nonetheless, the place is safe, superaffordable, and perfectly fine for one or two nights. Make your local calls from here, since they are free.

WHERE TO DINE IN & AROUND THE PARK

You won't find fancy nouvelle cuisine in this suburbanized farm country, but there are plenty of fast-food chains along U.S. 1 and a few old favorites worth a taste.

Here for nearly a quarter of a century, **El Toro Taco** at 1 S. Krome Ave. (near Mowry Drive and Campbell Drive; ☎ **305/245-8182**) opens daily at 9:30am and stays crowded until at least 9pm most days. The fresh grilled meats, tacos, burritos, salsas, guacamole, and stews are mild and delicious. No matter how big your appetite, it's hard to spend more than $12 per person at this Mexican outpost. You'll have to bring your own beer or wine.

Housed in a squat, one-story, windowless stone building that looks something like a medieval fort, the **Capri Restaurant,** 935 N. Krome Ave., Florida City (☎ **305/247-1542**), has been serving hearty Italian American fare since 1958. Great pastas and salads complement a full menu of meat and fish dishes. Portions are big. They serve lunch and dinner every day (except Sunday) until 11pm.

The **Miccosukee Restaurant** (☎ **305/223-8380**), just west of the Shark Valley entrance on the Tamiami Trail (U.S. 41), serves authentic pumpkin bread, fry bread, fish, and not-so-authentic Native American interpretations of tacos and fried chicken. This interesting spot is worth a stop for brunch, lunch, or dinner.

Once inside the Everglades, you'll want to eat at the only restaurant within the boundaries of this huge park, **The Flamingo Restaurant** (☎ **941/695-3101**). Located in the Flamingo Lodge (See "Where to Stay," above), this is a very civilized and affordable restaurant. Besides the spectacular view of Florida Bay and numerous Keys from the large, airy dining room, you'll also find fresh fish, including my very favorite, mahimahi. All fish are prepared grilled, blackened, or deep-fried; and dinner entrees come with salad or conch chowder, and steamed vegetables, black beans, and rice or baked potato. The large menu has something for everyone, including basic and very tasty sandwiches, pastas, burgers, and salads. A kids menu offers standard choices like hot dogs, grilled cheese, or fried shrimp for less than $6. Prices are surprisingly moderate, with full meals starting at about $11 and going no higher than $22. You may need reservations for dinner, especially in season.

2 Biscayne National Park

35 miles S of Miami, 21 miles E of Everglades National Park

This unusual and underappreciated park celebrated its 30th birthday in 1998 when park rangers offered many free programs in order to entice more locals to visit. With only about 500,000 visitors each year (mostly boaters and divers), it is one of the least crowded parks in the country. Biscayne National Park is a little more difficult than most to access—more than 95% of its 182,00 acres are underwater.

Its significance was first formally acknowledged in 1968 when, in an unprecedented move and against intense pressure from developers, Pres. Lyndon Johnson signed a bill to conserve the barrier islands off South Florida's east coast as a national monument, a protected status that's a rung below national park. After being twice enlarged, once in 1974 and again in 1980, the waters and land surrounding the northernmost coral reef in North America became a full-fledged national park—the largest of its kind in the country

To be fully appreciated, it should be thought of more as a preserve than a destination. I suggest using your time here to explore underwater life—but most of all, to relax.

The park's greatest dry attraction is the 29-acre island known as **Boca Chita Key,** once an exclusive haven for wealthy yachters. It was closed for years after the devastating hurricane of 1992 wiped out much of the tiny park. Six years and nearly $2 million were spent to restore the quaint island which is an especially popular stopping point for boaters.

Visitors can see the island's restored historic buildings, including the county's second-largest lighthouse and a tiny chapel.

Also popular is Elliott Key, one of the park's 44 little islands, which contains a visitor center, hiking trails, and a campground. It's located about 9 miles from Convoy Point.

The park's small mainland mangrove shoreline and keys are best explored by boat. Its extensive reef system is renowned with divers and snorkelers from all over the world.

JUST THE FACTS

GETTING THERE & ACCESS POINTS   The park's mainland entrance is Convoy Point, located 9 miles east of Homestead. To reach the park from Miami, take the Florida Turnpike to the Speedway Boulevard (Exit 6). Turn left, heading south 4½ miles, then left again at North Canal Drive (SW 328th Street), and follow signs to the park. If you're coming from U.S. 1, whether you're heading north or south, turn east at North Canal Drive (SW 328th Street).

As I mentioned earlier, most of Biscayne National Park is accessible only to boaters. Mooring buoys abound, since it's illegal to anchor on coral. When no buoys are available, boaters must anchor on sand or on the new docks surrounding the small harbor off Boca Chita. Boats can dock overnight for $15. Even the most experienced boaters should carry updated nautical charts of the area, which are available at Convoy Point. The waters are often murky, making the abundant reefs and sandbars difficult to detect—and there are more interesting ways to spend a day than waiting for the tide to rise. There's a boat launch at adjacent Homestead Bayfront Park, and 66 slips on Elliott Key, available free on a first-come, first-served basis.

Transportation to and from the visitor center to the island costs $21 per person. Call for seasonal schedule (☎ **305/230-1100**).

VISITOR CENTERS & INFORMATION   For information on park activities and tours, contact **Biscayne National Underwater Park,** P.O. Box 1270, Homestead, FL 33030 (☎ **305/230-1100;** fax 230-1120; www.nps.gov/bisc; e-mail: captsaw@bellsouth.net). The center is open daily from 8:30am to 5pm and later in winter.

The **Convoy Point Visitor Center,** 9700 SW 328th St., at the park's main entrance (☎ **305/230-7275;** fax 305/230-1190), is the natural starting point for any venture into the park without a boat. In addition to providing comprehensive information on the park, rangers will show you a short video on request. Open Monday to Friday from 8:30am to 4:30pm and Saturday and Sunday from 8:30am to 5pm. The permanent visitor center opened in early 1997, and museum exhibits were installed during summer 1997 at a cost of $5 million.

ENTRANCE FEES & PERMITS   Entrance to Biscayne National Park is free. At press time, backcountry permits for campers were also free and available at the visitor center.

SEEING THE HIGHLIGHTS

Since Biscayne National Park is primarily underwater, the only way to truly experience it is with snorkel or scuba gear. You can rent a speedboat in Miami and cruise south for about an hour and a half, but a better idea would be to take one of the organized tours offered every day from the main visitor center. (See "Organized Tours," below). Beneath the surface, the aquatic universe pulses with multicolored life: Bright parrot and angelfish, gently rocking sea fans, and coral labyrinths abound. Before entering the water, be sure to apply waterproof sunblock—once you begin to explore, it's easy to lose track of time, and the Florida sun is brutal, even during winter.

Afterward, take a picnic out to Elliott Key and taste the crisp salt air blowing off the Atlantic. Or, head to Boca Chita, an intriguing island that was once the private playground of wealthy yachtsmen.

SPORTS & OUTDOOR ACTIVITIES

CANOEING & KAYAKING   Biscayne National Park offers excellent canoeing, both along the coast and across open water to nearby mangroves and artificial islands that dot the longest uninterrupted shoreline in the state of Florida. Since tides can be strong, only experienced canoeists should attempt to paddle far from shore. If you plan to go far, first obtain a tide table from the visitor center (see "Just the Facts," above) and paddle with the current. Free ranger-led canoe tours are scheduled for most weekend mornings; phone for information. You can rent a canoe at the park; rates are $8 an hour or $22 for 4 hours. Kayakers will have to bring their own boats but are welcome to explore the same quiet routes.

FISHING   Ocean fishing is excellent year-round; many people cast their lines right from the breakwater jetty at Convoy Point. A fishing license is required (see "Entrance Fees, Permits & Regulations," under "Just the Facts," in section 1, for complete information). Bait is not available in Biscayne, but is sold in adjacent Homestead Bayfront Park. Stone crabs and Florida lobsters can be found here, but you're only allowed to catch these on the ocean side when they're in season. There are strict limitations on size, season, number, and method of take (including spear fishing) for both fresh- and saltwater fishing. The latest regulations are available at most marinas, bait and tackle shops, and at the park's visitor centers. Or you can contact the **Florida Game and Fresh Water Fish Commission,** Bryant Building, 620 S. Meridian St., Tallahassee, FL 32399-1600 (☎ **904/488-1960**).

HIKING & EXPLORING   Since the majority of this park is underwater, hiking is not the main attraction here, but there are some interesting sights and trails. At Convoy Point you can walk along the 370-foot boardwalk, and along the half-mile jetty that serves as a breakwater for the park's harbor. From there you can usually see brown pelicans, little blue herons, snowy egrets, and a few exotic fish.

Elliott Key is accessible only by boat, but once you're there, you have two good trail options. True to its name, the Loop Trail makes a 1½-mile circle from the bay-side visitor center, through a hardwood hammock and mangroves, to an elevated ocean-side boardwalk. It's likely that you'll see purple and orange land crabs scurrying around the mangrove roots.

Reopened in 1998, Boca Chita Key was once the playground for wealthy tycoons; it still offers the peaceful beauty that attracted elite fishermen from cold climates. Many of the historical buildings are still in tact, including an ornamental lighthouse which was thankfully never put into use. Since it was built on the western side of the island in the path of shallow reefs, boaters would have followed the beacon only to go aground.

Take advantage of the tours, usually led by an interpretative park ranger and available every Sunday at 1pm. The tour, including the boat trip, takes about 3 hours. The price for adults is $19.95 and $9.95 for children. However, call in advance to see if the sea is calm enough for the boat trip. Rough seas often mean the boats will not be running.

SNORKELING & SCUBA DIVING   The clear, warm waters of Biscayne National Park are packed with colorful tropical fish that swim in the offshore reefs. If you don't have your own, or don't want to lug it the park, you can rent or buy snorkeling and scuba gear at the full service dive shop at Convoy Point. Rates are in line with dive shops on the mainland.

The best way to see **Biscayne National Underwater Park** (☎ **305/230-1100**) is to take a snorkel tour. Tours go out daily and last about 4 hours and cost $27.95 per person. Full gear package is only $37. They also run two-tank dives for certified divers and provide instruction for beginners. The price is $35.50 per person. The shop is open daily from 9am to 5pm. Two-tank dives depart on several days a week. Make your reservations in advance. It may sound obvious but it warrants mentioning—if you're planning to get in the water, you must know how to swim.

For a real bargain, consider a money-saving package which includes accommodations. A winter special in 1998 consisted of lodging for 1 night at a nearby (15-minute drive to the park) Hampton Inn and 2 days of diving for less than $100. Each day takes you on two different and beautiful boat dives. You'll have to rent the equipment if you don't have your own, but still this is a steal, considering that two days of diving alone would cost well over $100 at most resorts.

SWIMMING   You can swim at the protected beaches of Elliott Key, Boca Chita Key, and adjacent Homestead Bayfront Park, but none of these beaches match the width or softness of other South Florida beaches. Check the water conditions before heading into the sea. Strong currents that make this a popular destination for windsurfers and sailors, can be dangerous even for strong swimmers.

WINDSURFING & SURFING   Strong and steady winds provide an excellent venue for wind-surfers. Feel free to bring your own board and take on some of South Florida's most beautiful surf.

ORGANIZED TOURS

The best way to see the sites without getting wet is on the glass-bottom boat tour. **Biscayne National Underwater Park** (☎ **305/230-1100**) offers daily trips to view some of the country's most beautiful coral reefs and tropical fish. Boats depart year-round from Convoy Point at 10am and stay out for about 3 hours. At $19.95 for adults, $17.95 for seniors, and $9.95 for children 12 and under, the scenic and informative tours are well worth the price. Boats carry fewer than 50 passengers;

therefore, reservations are almost always necessary. The company also offers guided canoe, scuba, and snorkeling reef trips led by underwater naturalists.

WHERE TO STAY

There are no facilities available for overnight guests to this watery park. Most non-camping visitors come for an afternoon on their way to the Keys and stay overnight in nearby Homestead where there are many national chain hotels and other affordable lodgings. See "Where to Stay," in section 1 of this chapter above.

CAMPING

Although you won't find hotels or lodges in Biscayne National Park, there are some of the state's most pristine campsites. Since they are completely inaccessible by motor vehicle, you'll be sure to avoid the mass of RVs so prevalent in so many of the state's other campgrounds. Sites are on Elliott Key and Boca Chita, and can only be reached by boat. If you don't have your own, call ☎ **305/230-1100** to arrange a drop-off. Transportation to and from the visitor center costs $21 per person. The best facilities are on the northeast side of newly reopened Boca Chita where there are brand-new showers, solar-powered rest rooms, and drinking fountains, as well as barbecue grills, and picnic tables. With a backcountry permit, available from the ranger station, you can pitch your tent somewhere even more private. Ask for a map at the visitor center, and be sure to bring plenty of bug spray.

3 Cruises & Other Caribbean Getaways

Some of the most popular destinations from Miami are the Bahamian islands where gambling is a big draw, or any of the dozens of nearby Caribbean islands. Travel to Cuba is strictly prohibited from Miami for all but those who have obtained licenses from the U.S. State Department (or anywhere in the United States), although many people choose to go there from Mexico, Jamaica, or The Bahamas.

CRUISES

The Port of Miami is the world's busiest cruise-ship port, with a passenger load of close to three million annually. The popularity of these cruises shows no sign of tapering off, and the trend in ships is toward bigger, more luxurious liners. Usually all-inclusive, cruises offer value and simplicity compared to other vacation options. Most of the Caribbean-bound cruise ships sail weekly out of the Port of Miami. They are relatively inexpensive, can be booked without advance notice, and make for an excellent excursion.

All the shorter cruises are well equipped for gambling. Their casinos open as soon as the ship clears U.S. waters—typically 45 minutes after leaving port. Usually, four full-size meals are served daily, with portions so huge they're impossible to finish. Games, movies, and other on-board activities ensure you're always busy. Passengers can board up to 2 hours before departure for meals, games, and cocktails.

There are dozens of cruises from which to choose—from a 1-day excursion to a trip around the world. You can get a full list of options from the **Metro-Dade Seaport Department,** 1015 North America Way, Miami, FL 33132 (☎ **305/ 371-7678**). It's open Monday through Friday from 8am to 5pm.

The cruise lines and ships listed below offer 2- and 3-day excursions to the Caribbean, Key West, and other longer itineraries that change often. If you want more information, contact the individual line or, for Bahamas cruises, call the **Bahamas Tourist Office,** 19495 Biscayne Blvd., Suite 809, Aventura, FL 33180

(☎ **305/932-0051**). All passengers must travel with a passport or proof of citizenship for reentry into the United States.

For details on Caribbean cruises, pick up a copy of *Frommer's Caribbean Cruises* and *Frommer's Caribbean Ports of Call.*

Carnival Cruise Lines (☎ **800/327-9501** or 305/599-2200; www.carnival. com) has 3- and 4-day cruises to Key West and the Caribbean as well as 7-day excursions that include stops in Mexico and Latin America. At press time, Carnival had four ships based at the Port of Miami, including *Destiny,* the world's largest. Cruises usually depart from Miami every Friday, Saturday, Sunday, and Monday. Prices range from $400 to $3,000, not including port charges, which can be as high as $100 per person.

Cunard (☎ **800/528-6273** or 305/463-3000; www.cunardline.com), which moved here in late 1997, is the most luxurious of Miami's lines, launching some of the most elegant ships ever to take to the seas. Its Miami ships include the *Queen Elizabeth 2,* the *Royal Viking Sun,* and the *Vistafford.* Itineraries are usually at least 10 days long. Prices start at $1,300.

Norwegian Cruise Line (☎ **800/327-7030** or 305/436-0866; www.ncl.com) has four ships based in Miami during the winter months and usually one in the summer. Ships go to Key West, The Bahamas, and the Western Caribbean. Its shortest cruises are 3 days; the longest is 15 days, from Miami to France. Rates range from $349 for an inside cabin on the shortest cruises to $4,500 for the very best cabin on the transcontinental journey.

Royal Caribbean Cruise Line (☎ **800/327-6700** or 305/539-6000; www.rccl. com), one of the premier lines in Miami, has about half a dozen ships departing Miami at any given time. It mostly offers Caribbean cruises and some Bahamas destinations. The *Legend of the Seas* and the *Splendor of the Seas* offer 3- and 4-night Bahamas trips starting at $400. Longer trips can range from $1,600 per person to $7,500 for an 11-night cruise through the Caribbean.

FLIGHTS & WEEKEND PACKAGES

For those who want a quick getaway to the Caribbean without the experience of cruising, many airlines and hotels team up to offer extremely affordable weekend packages.

For example, one of the Bahamas' most elegant and family friendly resorts, The Atlantis on Paradise Island, hosts guests who like water sports or like to try their luck in its active casinos. Reasonably priced 3-day packages start at about $390, depending on departure date. It's generally cheaper to fly midweek. Flights on **Continental Airlines** (☎ **800/786-7202**) or **Paradise Airlines** (☎ **800/231-0856**) depart at least twice daily from Miami International. You can also choose to stay in the company's other luxurious resorts, The Paradise Beach Resort or the Ocean Club. Book package deals through **Paradise Island Vacations** (☎ **800/722-7466**).

Other groups that arrange competitively priced packages include **American Flyaway Vacations,** operated by American Airlines (☎ **800/321-2121**); **Bahamas Air** (☎ **800/222-4262** or 305/593-1910); **Pan Am Air Bridge** (☎ **305/371-8628**); and the slightly rundown **Princess Casino** in Freeport (☎ **305/359-9898**). Call for rates, since they vary dramatically throughout the year and also depend on what type of accommodations you choose.

12 The Keys

The Florida Keys bring to mind the raucous streets of Key West and the mellow guitar riffs of Jimmy Buffet, but listen up—there's so much more.

The islands of the Keys are strung out across the southern waters of Florida like loose beads of an exotic coral necklace, and each of the more than 400 islands that make up this 150-mile chain has a distinctive character. While some are crammed with strip malls and tacky shell shops, most are filled with unusual species of tropical plants, birds, and reptiles. All are surrounded by calm blue waters, populated by stunning sea life and graced by year-round warmth.

Despite the usually calm landscape, these rocky islands can be treacherous as the series of tropical storms, hurricanes, and tornadoes reminded residents in the summer and fall of 1998 when millions of dollars of damage was inflicted. The exposed coast has always posed dangers to those on land as well as sea.

When Spanish explorers Juan Ponce de León and Antonio de Herrera sailed amid these craggy, dangerous rocks in 1513, they and their men dubbed the string of islands "Los Martires" (The Martyrs) because they thought the rocks looked like men suffering in the surf. It wasn't until the early 1800s that the larger islands were settled by rugged and ambitious pioneers, who amassed great wealth by salvaging cargo from ships sunk nearby. Actually, legend has it that these shipwrecks were sometimes caused by the "wreckers," who occasionally removed navigational markers from the shallows to lure unwitting captains aground. At the height of the salvaging mania (in the 1830s), Key West boasted the highest per capita income in the country.

However, wars, fires, hurricanes, mosquitoes, and the Depression took their toll on these resilient islands in the early part of this century, causing wild swings between fortune and poverty. In 1938, the spectacular Overseas Highway (U.S. 1) was finally completed atop the ruins of Henry Flagler's railroad, opening the region to tourists who had never before been able to drive to this seabound destination.

These days, the highway connects more than 30 of the populated islands in the Keys. The hundreds of small, undeveloped islands that surround these "mainline" keys are known locally as the "back-country" and are home to dozens of exotic animals and plants. To get to them, you must take to the water—a vital part of any trip to the Keys. Whether you fish, snorkel, dive, or just cruise, include

The Florida Keys

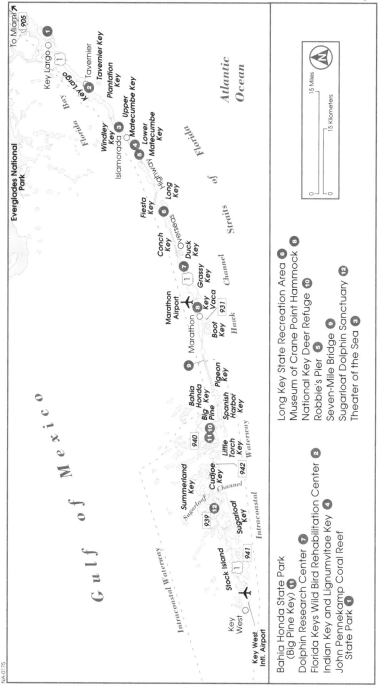

Bahia Honda State Park (Big Pine Key) **11**
Dolphin Research Center **7**
Florida Keys Wild Bird Rehabilitation Center **2**
Indian Key and Lignumvitae Key **4**
John Pennekamp Coral Reef State Park **1**

Long Key State Recreation Area **6**
Museum of Crane Point Hammock **8**
National Key Deer Refuge **10**
Robbie's Pier **5**
Seven-Mile Bridge **9**
Sugarloaf Dolphin Sanctuary **12**
Theater of the Sea **3**

some time on a boat in your itinerary; otherwise, you really haven't truly seen the Keys.

The sea and the teeming life beneath it are the main attractions here. Warm, shallow waters nurture living coral that supports a complex delicate ecosystem of plants and animals—sponges, anemones, jellyfish, crabs, rays, sharks, turtles, snails, lobsters, and thousands of types of fish. This vibrant underwater habitat thrives on one of only two living tropical reefs in the entire North American continent (the other is off the coast of Belize). As a result, anglers, divers, snorkelers, and water-sports enthusiasts of all kinds come to explore. The heavy traffic has taken its toll on this fragile ecoscape, but efforts are underway to protect it.

Although the atmosphere throughout the Keys is that of a low-key beach town, don't expect to find many impressive beaches here. Especially since the tropical storms and hurricanes in 1998, there aren't any great beaches. Beaches are mostly found in a few private resorts and some small, sandy beaches in Bahia Honda State Park and in Key West (see "The Lower Keys," below). One great exception is Sombrero Beach in Marathon (see "Beaches" in "The Upper and Middle Keys," below).

The Keys are divided into three sections, both geographically and in this chapter. The Upper and Middle Keys are closest to the Florida mainland, so they are popular with weekend warriors who come by boat or car to fish, drink, or relax in towns like Key Largo, Islamorada, and Marathon. Further on, just beyond the impressive 7-mile bridge (which actually measures only 6.4 miles), are the Lower Keys, a small unspoiled swath of islands teeming with wildlife. Here, in the protected regions of the Lower Keys is where you're most likely to catch sight of the area's many endangered animals. With patience, you may spot the rare eagle, egret, or Key deer. Also, keep an eye out for alligators, turtles, rabbits, and a huge variety of birds.

The last section of this chapter is devoted to the renowned island called Key West, literally at the end of the road. Made famous by the Nobel Prize–winning rogue Ernest Hemingway, this tiny island is the most popular destination in the Florida Keys, overrun with cruise-ship passengers and day-trippers, as well as franchises and T-shirt shops. More than 1.6 million visitors pass through each year. Still, you'll find in this "Conch Republic" a tightly knit community of permanent residents who cling fiercely to their live-and-let-live attitude—an atmosphere that has made Key West famously popular with painters, writers, and gay and lesbian travelers.

1 Exploring the Keys by Car

After you have gotten off the Florida Turnpike and landed on U.S. 1, which is also known as the Overseas Highway (see "Getting There," under "Essentials," below), you'll have no trouble negotiating these narrow islands.

The Overseas Highway is the only main road connecting the Keys. Although some find the long, straight drive from Miami to Key West tedious, it can be enjoyable if you linger and explore the diverse towns and islands along the way. If you have the time, I recommend allowing at least 3 days to work your way down to Key West and two or more days once there.

Most of U.S. 1 is a narrow, two-lane highway, with some wider passing zones along the way. The speed limit is usually 55 m.p.h. (35 to 45 m.p.h. on Big Pine Key and in some commercial areas). Despite the protestations of island residents, there has been talk of expanding the highway, but by publication date plans had not been finalized. Even on the narrow road, you can usually get from downtown Miami to Key Largo in just over an hour. If you're determined to drive straight through to Key West, allow at least 3½ hours. No matter what, avoid driving any-where in the Keys on Friday afternoons or Sunday evenings, when the roads are jammed with weekenders from the mainland.

To find an address in the Keys, don't bother looking for building numbers; most addresses (except in Key West and parts of Marathon) are delineated by mile markers (MM), small green signs on the roadside, which announce the distance from Key West. The markers start at number 127, just south of the Florida main-land. The zero marker is in Key West, at the corner of Whitehead and Fleming streets. Addresses in this chapter are accompanied by a mile marker (MM) designa-tion when appropriate.

2 The Upper & Middle Keys: Key Largo to Marathon

58 miles SW of Miami

The Upper Keys are a popular, year-round refuge for South Floridians who take advantage of the islands' proximity to the mainland. This is the fishing and diving capital of America, and the swarms of outfitters and billboards never let you forget it.

Key Largo, once called "Rock Harbor" but renamed to capitalize on the success of the 1948 Humphrey Bogart film (which wasn't actually filmed there), is the largest Key and is more developed than its neighbors to the south. Dozens of chain hotels, restaurants, and tourist information centers service the many water enthusi-asts who come to explore the nation's first underwater state park, John Pennekamp Coral Reef State Park, and its adjacent marine sanctuary. **Islamorada,** the unoffi-cial capital of the Upper Keys, offers the area's best atmosphere, food, fishing, enter-tainment, and lodging. In these "purple isles," nature-lovers can enjoy nature trails, historic explorations, and big-purse fishing tournaments. **Marathon,** smack in the middle of the chain of islands, is one of the most populated Keys. It is part fishing village, part tourist center, and part nature preserve. This area's highly developed infrastructure includes resort hotels, a commercial airport, and a highway that expands to four lanes. Thankfully, high-rises have yet to arrive.

ESSENTIALS

GETTING THERE   If you're coming from the Miami airport, take Le Jeune Road (NW 42nd Avenue) to Route 836 west. Follow signs to the Florida Turnpike South (about 7 miles). The turnpike extension connects with U.S. 1 in Florida City. Continue south on U.S. 1.

If you're coming from Florida's west coast, take Alligator Alley to the Miami exit and then turn south onto the turnpike extension. Have plenty of quarters for the tolls.

American Eagle (☎ **800/433-7300**) has daily nonstop flights from Miami to Marathon, which is near the midpoint of the chain of Keys and at the very southern end of the area referred to here as the Upper and Middle Keys. Fares range depending on the season, from $88 to $336 round-trip.

Greyhound (☎ **800/231-2222**) has buses leaving Miami for Key Largo every day. At press time, prices were $13 one way. Seats fill up in season, so come early. It's first come, first served.

VISITOR INFORMATION   Avoid the many "Tourist Information Centers" that dot the main highway. Most are private companies hired to lure visitors to spe-cific lodgings or outfitters. You're better off sticking with the official, not-for-profit centers that are extremely well located and staffed. In particular, the **Key Largo**

Chamber of Commerce, U.S. 1 at MM 106, Key Largo, FL 33037 (☎ **800/ 822-1088** or 305/451-1414; fax 305/451-4726; www.floridakeys.org) runs an excellent facility, with free direct-dial phones and plenty of brochures. Now headquartered in a handsome clapboard house, the chamber operates as an information clearinghouse for all of the Keys. It's open daily from 9am to 6pm.

The **Islamorada Chamber of Commerce,** in the Little Red Caboose, U.S. 1 at MM 82.5, P.O. Box 915, Islamorada, FL 33036 (☎ **800/322-5397** or 305/ 664-4503; fax 305/664-4289; e-mail: islacc@ix.netcom.com), also offers maps and literature on the Upper Keys.

You can't miss the big blue visitors center at MM 53.5, the **Greater Marathon Chamber of Commerce,** 12222 Overseas Hwy., Marathon, FL 33050 (☎ **800/ 842-9580** or 305/743-5417; fax 305/289-0183; www.flakeys.com).

OUTDOOR SIGHTS & ACTIVITIES
BEACHES

Anne's Beach (at MM 73.5) is really more of a picnic spot than a full-fledged beach, but die-hard suntanners still congregate on this tiny strip of coarse sand which unfortunately was damaged beyond recognition during the series of storms in 1998. There are plans to reconstruct the boardwalk and huts, but as of press time, work had not yet started.

A better choice for real beaching is **Sombrero Beach** in Marathon at the end of Sombrero Beach Road (near MM 50). This wide swath of uncluttered beachfront actually benefited from hurricane George in September 1998 with generous deposits of extra sand and a facelift courtesy of the Monroe County Tourist Development Council. More than 90 feet of sand is dotted with stands of palms, Australian Pines, and Royal Poncianas. There are some barbecue grills and clean bathrooms. A project is currently underway to add tiki huts, a pavilion, and a pier. Admission and parking at this little-known gem is free.

Indian Key and Lignumvitae Key. Off Indian Key Fill, Overseas Hwy., MM 79. ☎ **305/ 664-4815.**

If you are interested in seeing the Keys in their natural state, before modern development, you must venture off the highway and take to the water. Two backcountry islands that offer a glimpse of the "real" Keys are Indian Key and Lignumvitae Key. Visitors come to relax and enjoy the islands' colorful birds and lush hammocks (elevated pieces of land above a marsh).

Named for the lignum vitae ("wood of life") trees found there, **Lignumvitae Key** supports a virgin tropical forest, the kind that once thrived on most of the Upper Keys. Over the years, human settlers have imported "exotic" plants and animals to the Keys, irrevocably changing the botanical makeup of many backcountry islands and threatening much of the indigenous wildlife. Over the past 25 years, the Florida Department of Natural Resources has successfully removed most of the exotic vegetation, leaving this 280-acre site much as it existed in the 18th century. The island also holds a historic house built in 1919 that has survived numerous storms and major hurricanes.

Indian Key, a much smaller island on the Atlantic side of Islamorada, was occupied by Native Americans for thousands of years before European settlers arrived. The 10-acre historic site was also the original seat of Dade County before the Civil War. You can see the ruins of the previous settlement and tour the lush grounds on well-marked trails.

The 10 "Keymandments"

The Keys have always attracted independent spirits, from Ernest Hemingway and Tennessee Williams to Jimmy Buffett, Mel Fisher, and Zane Grey. Writers, artists, and free thinkers have long drifted down here to escape.

Standards do seem to be different here. In 1982, for example, when drug-enforcement agents blocked off the main highway leading into Key West, residents did what they do best—they threw a party. The festivities marked the "independence" of the newly formed "Conch Republic." The distinctive flag with its conch insignia now flies throughout the island.

Although you'll generally find a very laid-back and tolerant code of behavior in the Keys, some rules do exist. Be sure to respect the 10 "Keymandments" while you're here, or suffer the consequences.

- Don't anchor on a reef. (Reefs are Alive. Alive. A-L-I-V-E.)
- Don't feed the animals. (They'll want to follow you home, and you can't keep them.)
- Don't trash our place (or we'll send Bubba to trash yours).
- Don't touch the coral. (After all, you don't even know them.)
- Don't speed (especially on Big Pine Key, where deer reside and tar-and-feathering is still practiced).
- Don't catch more fish than you can eat. (Better yet, let them go. Some of them support schools.)
- Don't collect conch. (This species is protected by Bubba.)
- Don't disturb the bird nests. (They find it very annoying.)
- Don't damage the seagrass. (And don't even think about making a skirt out of it.)
- Don't drink and drive on land or sea. (There's absolutely nothing funny about it.)

If you want to see both islands, plan to spend at least half a day. To get there, you can rent your own boat at **Robbie's Rent-A-Boat** (U.S. 1 at MM 77.5 on the bay side). Rates range from $60 for a 14-foot boat for half a day to $155 for an 18-foot boat for a full day. It's then a $1 admission fee to each island, which includes an informative hour-long guided tour by park rangers. This is a good option if you are a confident boater.

However, I also recommend taking Robbie's **ferry service** for $15, which includes the $1 park admission. Trips to both islands cost $25 per person. (If you are planning to visit only one island, make it Lignumvitae.) Not only is the ferry more economical, but it's easier to enjoy the natural beauty of the islands when you aren't negotiating the shallow reefs along the way. The runabouts, which carry up to six people, depart from Robbie's Pier Thursday to Monday at 9am and 1pm for Indian Key, and at 10am and 2pm for Lignumvitae Key. In the busy season, you may need to book as early as 2 days before departure. Call ☎ **305/664-4815** for information from the park service or ☎ 305/664-9814 for Robbie's.

✪ **Tropical Crane Point Hammock.** 5550 Overseas Hwy. (MM 50), Marathon. ☎ **305/743-9100.** Admission $7.50 for adults; $6 for seniors over 64; $4 for students and free for children under 6. Mon–Sat 9am–5pm; Sun noon–5pm.

Crane Point Hammock is a little-known but very worthwhile stop, especially for those interested in the rich botanical and archaeological history of the Keys. This privately owned 64-acre nature area is considered one of the most important historical sites in the Keys. It contains what is probably the last virgin thatch palm hammock in North America. It also has an archaeological dig site with pre-Columbian and prehistoric Bahamian artifacts.

Now headquarters for the Florida Keys Land and Sea Trust, the hammock's impressive nature museum has simple, informative displays of the Keys' wildlife, including a walk-through replica of a coral-reef cave and life-size dioramas with tropical birds and Key deer. Kids can participate in art projects, see 6-foot-long iguanas, climb through a scaled-down pirate ship, and touch a variety of indigenous aquatic and land-lubbing creatures.

✪ **Seven-Mile Bridge.** Between MM 40 and 47 on U.S. 1. ☎ **305/289-0025.**

A stop at the Seven-Mile Bridge is a rewarding and relaxing break from the drive south. Built alongside the ruins of oil magnate Henry Flagler's incredible Overseas Railroad, the "new" bridge (between MM 40 and 47) is still considered an architectural feat. The wide arched span, completed in 1982 at a cost of more than $45 million, is impressive, its apex being the highest point in the Keys. The new bridge and especially its now-defunct neighbor provide an excellent vantage point from which to view the stunning waters of the Keys.

In the daytime, you may want to jog, walk, or bike along the scenic 4-mile stretch of old bridge, or join local fishermen, who catch barracuda, yellowtail, and dolphin on what is known as "the longest fishing pier in the world."

Pigeon Key. East end of the 7-Mile Bridge near MM 47, Marathon. ☎ **305/743-5999.** Open 9am–5pm; shuttle tours run every hour from 10am–3pm. Admission $7.50; $5 for children under 13. Price includes shuttle transportation from the Visitor's Center.

Now open to the public, Pigeon Key, at the curve of the old bridge, is an intriguing historical site that has been under renovation since late 1993. This 5-mile island was once the camp for the crew that built the old railway in the early part of the century and later served as housing for the bridge builders. From here, your vista includes both bridges, many old wooden cottages, and a truly tranquil stretch of lush foliage and sea.

If you miss the shuttle tour or would rather walk or bike to the key, it's about 2.5 miles. Either way, you may want to bring a picnic to enjoy after a brief self-guided walking tour and museum visit. There is also an informative 28-minute video of the island's history offered every hour starting at 11:15. Parking is available at the Knight's Key end of the bridge, at MM 48, or at the Visitor's Center at the old train car across the highway on the ocean side.

VISITING WITH THE ANIMALS

✪ **Dolphin Research Center.** U.S. 1 at MM 59 (on the bay side), Marathon. ☎ **305/289-1121.** Swim with the Dolphins, $110 per person. Call on the first day of the month to book for the following month. Educational walking tours five times every day: 10am, 11am, 12:30pm, 2pm, and 3:30pm. Admission $12.50 adults; $10 seniors; $7.50 children 4–12; free for children 3 and under. (Prices are scheduled to increase.) MC, V. Daily 9:30am–4pm.

Don't miss this experience. If you've always wanted to touch, swim, or play with dolphins, this is the place to do it. Of the three such centers in the continental

United States (all located in the Keys), the Dolphin Research Center is the most organized and informative. Although some people argue that training dolphins is cruel and selfish, the knowledgeable trainers at the Dolphin Research Center will tell you that the dolphins need stimulation and enjoy human contact. They certainly seem to. They nuzzle and seem to smile and kiss the lucky few who get to swim with them in the daily program. The "family" of 15 dolphins swims in a 90,000-square-foot natural saltwater pool carved out of the shoreline. If you can't get into the swim program, you can still take a walking tour of the facilities or sign up for a class in hand signals or feed the dolphins from docks. Children must be at least 12 years old to participate.

Florida Keys Wild Bird Rehabilitation Center. U.S. 1 at MM 94, Tavernier. ☎ **305/852-4486.** Donations suggested. Daily 8:30am–6pm.

Wander through lush canopies of mangroves on narrow wooden walkways to see some of the Keys' most famous residents—the large variety of native birds, including broad-wing hawks, great blue and white herons, roseate spoonbills, white ibis, cattle egrets, and a number of pelicans. This not-for-profit center operates as a hospital for the many birds that have been injured. Come at feeding time, usually about 2pm, when you can watch the dedicated staff feed the hundreds of hungry beaks.

✪ **Robbie's Pier.** U.S. 1 at MM 77.5, Islamorada. ☎ **305/664-9814.** Admission $1. Bucket of fish $2. Daily 8am–5pm. Look for the Hungry Tarpon restaurant sign on the right after the Indian Key channel.

One of the best and definitely one of the cheapest attractions in the Upper Keys is the famed Robbie's Pier. Here, the fierce steely tarpons, a prized catch for backcountry anglers, have been gathering for the past 20 years. You may recognize these prehistoric-looking giants that grow up to 200 pounds; many are displayed as trophies and mounted on local restaurant walls. To see them live, head to Robbie's Pier, where tens and sometimes hundreds of these behemoths circle the shallow waters waiting for you to feed them. New kayak tours promise an even closer glimpse.

Theater of the Sea. U.S. 1 at MM 84.5, Islamorada. ☎ **305/664-2431.** Fax 305/664-8162. Admission $16.25 adults; $9.75 children 3–12. Swim with the Dolphins and Trainer for a Day programs by reservation; $95 per person. Daily 9:30am–4pm.

Established in 1946, the Theater of the Sea is one of the world's oldest marine zoos. Although the facilities could use some sprucing up, the dolphin and sea lion shows are entertaining and informative, especially for children who can also see sharks, sea turtles, and tropical fish. If you want to swim with dolphins and you haven't booked well in advance, this is the place you may be able to get in with just a few hours, or days, notice as opposed to the more rigid Dolphin Research Center in Marathon (see above). A recently introduced program allows visitors to swim with the sea lions or with the stingrays for $65 per person. Cat lovers will be thrilled to learn that the facility also serves as a haven for dozens of stray cats that have free run of the grounds and gift shop.

TWO EXCEPTIONAL STATE PARKS

One of the best places to discover the diverse ecosystem of the Upper Keys is in its most famous park, ✪ **John Pennekamp Coral Reef State Park,** located on U.S. 1 at MM 102.5, in Key Largo (☎ **305/451-1202**). Named for a former *Miami Herald* editor and conservationist, the 188-square-mile park is the nation's first undersea preserve. It's a sanctuary for part of the only living coral reef in the continental United States. The original plans for Everglades National Park included this part of the reef within its boundaries, but opposition from local homeowners made its inclusion politically impossible.

Because the water is extremely shallow, the 40 species of coral and more than 650 species of fish here are particularly accessible to divers, snorkelers, and glass-bottomed–boat passengers. You can't see the reef from the shore. To experience this park, visitors must get in the water. Your first stop should be the visitor center, which is full of educational fish tanks and a mammoth 30,000-gallon saltwater aquarium that re-creates a reef ecosystem. At the adjacent dive shop, you can rent snorkeling and diving equipment and join one of the boat trips that depart for the reef throughout the day. Visitors can also rent motorboats, sailboats, Windsurfers, and canoes. The 2-hour glass-bottomed–boat tour is the best way to see the coral reefs if you refuse to get wet.

Canoeing around the park's narrow mangrove channels and tidal creeks is also popular. You can go on your own in a rented canoe, or in winter, sign up for a tour led by a local naturalist. Hikers have two short trails from which to choose: a boardwalk through the mangroves and a dirt trail through a tropical hardwood hammock. Ranger-led walks are usually scheduled daily from the end of November to April. Phone for schedule information and reservations.

Park admission is $2.50 per vehicle for one occupant; for two or more, it is $4 per vehicle, plus 50¢ per passenger; $1.50 per pedestrian or bicyclist. Call ☎ 305/451-1621 for information. On your way into the park, ask the ranger for a map. Glass-bottomed–boat tours cost $13 for adults and $8.50 for children 11 and under. Snorkeling tours are $23.95 for adults and $18.95 for children 17 and under, including equipment. Sailing and snorkeling tours are $28.95 for adults, $23.95 for children 17 and under, including equipment but not tax. Canoes rent for $8 per hour or $28 for 4 hours. Reef boats (powerboats) rent for $25 to $45 per hour; call ☎ 305/451-6325. Open daily from 8am to 5pm; phone for tour and dive times. Also, see below for more options on diving, fishing, and snorkeling these reefs.

Long Key State Recreation Area, U.S. 1 at MM 68, Long Key (☎ 305/664-4815), is one of the best places in the Middle Keys for hiking, camping, and canoeing. This 965-acre site is situated atop the remains of an ancient coral reef. At the entrance gate, ask for a free flyer describing the local trails and wildlife.

There are two nature trails here perfect for hiking. The Golden Orb Trail is a 1-mile loop around a lagoon that attracts a large variety of birds. Rich in West Indian vegetation, this trail leads to an observation tower that offers good views of the mangroves. Layton Trail, the only part of the park that doesn't require an admission fee, is a quarter-mile shaded loop that goes through tropical hammocks before opening onto Florida Bay. The trail is well marked with interpretive signs; you can easily walk it in about 20 minutes.

The park's excellent 1½-mile canoe trail is also short and sweet, allowing visitors to loop around the mangroves in about an hour—it couldn't be easier. You can rent canoes at the trailhead for about $4 per hour. Long Key is also a great spot to stop for a picnic if you get hungry on your way to Key West.

Railroad builder Henry Flagler created the Long Key Fishing Club here in 1906, and the waters surrounding the park are still popular with game fishers. In summer, sea turtles lumber onto the protected coast to lay their eggs.

Admission is $3.25 per car plus 50¢ per person (except for the Layton Trail, which is free). Open daily from 8am to sunset.

WATER SPORTS FROM A TO Z

There are literally hundreds of outfitters in the Keys who will set up all kinds of water activities, from cave dives to parasailing. If those recommended below are booked up or unreachable, ask the local chamber of commerce for a list of qualified members.

BOATING   In addition to the rental shops in the state parks, you will find dozens of outfitters along U.S. 1 offering a range of runabouts and skiffs for boaters of any experience level. **Captain Pip's,** U.S. 1 at MM 47.5, Marathon (☎ **800/707-1692** or 305/743-4403), rents 18.5- to 24-foot motorboats with 90 to 225 horsepower engines for $110 to $170 per day.

   Robbie's Rent-a-Boat, U.S. 1 at MM 77.5, Islamorada (☎ **305/664-9814**), rents 14- to 27-foot motorboats with engines ranging from 15 to 200 horsepower. Boats cost $60 to $205 for a half day and $80 to $295 for a whole day.

CANOEING & KAYAKING   I can think of no better way to explore the uninhabited, shallow backcountry than by kayak or canoe. You can reach places big boats just can't get to because of their large draft. Sometimes manatees will cuddle up to the boats, thinking them another friendly species.

   For a more enjoyable time, ask for a sit-inside boat—you'll stay drier. Also, a fiberglass (as opposed to plastic) boat with a rudder is generally more stable and easier to maneuver. Many area hotels rent kayaks and canoes to guests, as do the outfitters listed here. **Florida Bay Outfitters,** U.S. 1 at MM 104, Key Largo (☎ **305/451-3018**), rents canoes and sea kayaks for use in and around John Pennekamp Coral Reef State Park for $20 to $30 for a half day and $35 to $50 for a whole day. Canoes cost $25 for a half day and $35 for a whole day. At **Coral Reef Park Co.,** on U.S. 1 at MM 102.5, Key Largo (☎ **305/451-1621**), you can rent canoes and kayaks for $8 per hour, $28 for a half day; most canoes are sit-on-tops.

DIVING & SNORKELING   The **Florida Keys Dive Center,** on U.S. 1 at MM 90.5, Tavernier (☎ **305/852-4599;** fax 305/852-1293), takes snorkelers and divers to the reefs of **John Pennekamp Coral Reef State Park** and environs every day. PADI training courses are also available for the uninitiated. Tours leave at 8am and 12:30pm and cost $25 per person to snorkel (including mask, snorkels, and fins) and $40 per person to dive (plus an extra $30 if you need to rent all the gear).

   At **Hall's Dive Center & Career Institute,** U.S. 1 at MM 48.5, Marathon (☎ **305/743-5929;** fax 305/743-8168), snorkelers and divers can choose to dive at Looe Key, Sombrero Reef, Delta Shoal, Content Key, and Coffins Patch. Tours are scheduled daily at 9am and 1pm. If you mention this guide, you will get a special discounted rate of $30 per person to snorkel (including equipment) and $40 per person to dive. Choose from a wide and impressive array of equipment. Rental is extra.

   With **Snuba Tours of Key Largo** (☎ **305/451-6391**), you can dive down to 20 feet attached to a comfortable breathing apparatus that really gives you the feeling of scuba diving without having to be certified. You can tour shallow coral reefs teeming with hundreds of colorful fish and plant life, from sea turtles to moray eels. Reservations are required; call to find out where and when to meet. A 2- to 3-hour underwater tour costs $70, including all equipment. If you have never dived before, you may require a 1-hour lesson in the pool, which costs an additional $40.

FISHING   **Robbie's Partyboats & Charters,** on U.S. 1 at MM 84.5, Islamorada (☎ **305/664-8070** or 305/664-4196), located at the south end of the Holiday Isle Docks (see the Holiday Isle Resort in "Where to Stay," below), offers day and night deep-sea and reef fishing trips aboard a 65-foot party boat. Big-game–fishing charters are also available, and "splits" are arranged for solo fishers. Party-boat fishing costs $25 for a half day, $40 for a full day, and $30 at night. Charters run $400 for a half day, $600 for a full day; splits begin at $65 per person. Phone for information and reservations.

Bud n' Mary's Fishing Marina, on U.S. 1 at MM 79.8, Islamorada (☎ 800/742-7945 or 305/664-2461; fax 305/664-5592), one of the largest marinas between Miami and Key West, is packed with sailors offering guided backcountry fishing charters. This is the place to go if you want to stalk tarpon, bonefish, and snapper. If the seas are not too rough, deep-sea and coral fishing trips can be arranged. Charters cost $400 to $500 for a half day, $600 to $800 for a full day, and splits begin at $125 per person.

The Bounty Hunter, 15th Street, Marathon (☎ 305/743-2446), offers full- and half-day outings. For years, Capt. Brock Hook's huge sign has boasted no fish, no pay. You're guaranteed to catch something. Choose your prey from shark, barracuda, sailfish, or whatever else is running. Prices are $350 for a half day, $375 for three-quarters of a day, and $450 for a full day. Rates are for groups of no more than six people.

SHOPPING

On your way to the Keys, you'll find an outlet center, the **Keys Factory Shops** (☎ 305/248-4727), at 250 E. Palm Dr. (where the Fla. Turnpike meets U.S. Hwy. 1), in Florida City. The center holds more than 60 stores, including Nike Factory Store, Bass Co. Store, Levi's, Osh Kosh, and Izod. Travelers can pick up a free discount coupon booklet called the Come Back Pack from the Customer Service Center. The outlet is open daily until 9pm, except Sunday when it closes at 6pm.

The Upper and Middle Keys have no shortage of tacky tourist shops selling shells and T-shirts and other hokey souvenirs, but for real Keys-style shopping, check out the **weekend flea markets.** One of the best is held every Saturday and Sunday bayside at MM 103.5 (☎ 305/451-0677). Dozens of vendors open their stalls from 9am until 4 or 5pm selling every imaginable sort of antiques, T-shirts, plants, shoes, books, toys, and games, as well as a hearty dose of good old-fashioned junk.

A mecca for fishing and sports enthusiasts, **The World Wide Sportsman** (☎ 305/664-4615) opened in late 1997 at MM 81.5. It's not only the largest fishing store in the Keys, but also a meeting place for anglers from all over the world. Every possible gizmo and gadget, plus hundreds of T-shirts, hats, books, and gift items are displayed in its more than 25,000 square feet. The salespeople are knowledgeable and eager to help. Travel specialists can even arrange for charter trips and backcountry tours. The store is open daily from 7am until 8:30pm.

WHERE TO STAY

U.S. 1 is lined with chain hotels in all price ranges. In the Upper Keys, the best moderately priced options are the **Holiday Inn Key Largo Resort & Marina,** U.S. 1 at MM 99.7 (☎ 800/THE-KEYS or 305/451-2121), and right next door, at MM 100, the **Ramada Limited Resort & Casino** (☎ 800/THE-KEYS or 305/451-3939). Both hotels share three pools and a casino boat; however, the Ramada is cozier and offers slightly cheaper rates. Also, the **Best Western Suites at Key Largo,** 201 Ocean Dr., MM 100 (☎ 800/462-6079 or 305/451-5081), is just 3 miles from John Pennekamp Coral Reef State Park. Another good option in the Upper Keys is **Islamorada Days Inn,** U.S. 1 at MM 82.5 (☎ 800/DAYS-INN or 305/664-3681). In the Middle Keys, the **Howard Johnson** at 13351 Overseas

Hwy., MM 54 in Marathon (☎ **800/321-3496** or 305/743-8550), also offers reasonably priced ocean-side rooms.

Since the real beauty of the Keys lies mostly beyond the highways, there is no better way to see this area than by boat. Why not stay in a floating hotel? Especially if traveling with a group, houseboats can be economical. To rent a houseboat, call Ruth and Michael Sullivan at **Smilin' Island Houseboat Rentals** (MM 99.5), Key Largo, FL (☎ **305/451-1930**). Rates are from $750 to $1,350 for 3 nights. Boats accommodate up to six people.

For land options, consider these recommendations, grouped first by price, and then geographically from north to south.

VERY EXPENSIVE

Cheeca Lodge. U.S. 1 at MM 82 (P.O. Box 527), Islamorada, FL 33036. ☎ **800/327-2888** or 305/664-4651. Fax 305/664-2893. 203 units. A/C MINIBAR TV TEL. Winter $295–$650 double; $400 suite. Off-season $185–$430 double; $285 suite. AE, CB, DC, DISC, MC, V.

One of the better places to stay in the Upper Keys, Cheeca has been hosting celebrities, royalty, and politicians since its opening in 1949. Guests now enjoy the luxury of the Cheeca's freshly renovated and remodeled rooms. All of the 203 units offer all the amenities of a world-class resort in a very laid-back setting. You may not feel compelled to leave the sprawling grounds, but it's good to know the hotel is conveniently situated near the best restaurants and nightlife. Located on 27 acres of beachfront property, this rambling resort is known for its excellent sports facilities, including diving and snorkeling programs and one of the only golf courses in the Upper Keys.

All rooms are spacious and have small balconies. The nicer ones overlook the ocean and have large marble bathrooms.

Dining/Diversions: The Atlantic's Edge restaurant is one of the best in the Upper Keys (see "Where to Dine," below). A pool bar and comfortable lounge offer more casual options throughout the day and evening.

Amenities: Concierge, room service, dry-cleaning and laundry services, in-room massage, newspaper delivery, baby-sitting, express checkout, valet parking, free coffee and refreshments in lobby. Kitchenettes, VCRs and video rentals, three outdoor heated pools, kids' pool, five hot tubs, beach, access to nearby health club, Jacuzzi, bicycle rental, 9-hole, par-3 golf course, children's nature programs, conference rooms, car-rental desk, sundeck, six lighted tennis courts, water-sports equipment rental, tour desk, nature trail, boutiques.

✪ **Hawk's Cay Resort.** U.S. 1 at MM 61, Duck Key, FL 33050. ☎ **800/432-2242** or 305/743-7000. Fax 305/743-5215. 176 units. A/C TV TEL. Winter $220–$350 double; $400–$850 suite. Off-season $160–$250 double; $300–$750 suite. AE, DC, DISC, MC, V.

Located on its own 60-acre island just outside of Marathon in the Middle Keys, Hawk's Cay is a sprawling and impressive resort encompassing a marina as well as a saltwater lagoon that's home to a half dozen dolphins. It's especially popular with families, who appreciate the many activities and reasonably priced diversions. It's also more casual than other resorts, like Cheeca Lodge, which offers many of the same amenities. The manicured grounds are dotted with handsome two- and three-story flamingo-colored buildings. The guest rooms within are all quite similar—views account for the differences in price. All are large and have walk-in closets, small refrigerators, a sliding glass door opening onto a private balcony, and Caribbean-style bamboo furnishings padded with colorful fabrics. If you want to splurge, the top-floor suites have separate seating areas with pull-out sofas and large wraparound terraces with spectacular views.

Dining/Diversions: Three good restaurants and a lounge have a wide range of food, from Italian to seafood. A well-stocked ship's store has snacks and basic groceries. A lively lounge features live music every evening and most weekend afternoons.

Amenities: Concierge, room service, overnight laundry, in-room massage, express checkout, transportation to airport and golf course, free refreshments in lobby. Outdoor heated pool, a new adults-only private pool, beach, small fitness room, Jacuzzi, nearby golf course, sundeck, eight tennis courts (two lighted), watersports equipment, bicycle rental, game room, children's center or programs, self-service laundry, marina store and gift shop, conference rooms, car-rental desk.

Westin Beach Resort. U.S. 1 at MM 97, Key Largo, FL 33037. ☎ **800/728-2738,** 800/539-5274, or 305/852-5553. Fax 305/852-8669. 200 units. A/C MINIBAR TV TEL. Winter $239–$289 double; from $389 Jacuzzi suite. Off-season $139–209 double; from $289 Jacuzzi suite. AE, DC, DISC, MC, V.

Under new ownership since 1996, this resort has benefited from an extensive $3 million renovation. In addition to an overall rehab, the resort distinguishes itself by its secluded yet convenient location—it's set back on 12 private acres of gumbo-limbo and hardwood trees, making it invisible from the busy highway. Despite its hideaway location, the sprawling pink-and-blue four-story complex is surprisingly large. A three-story atrium lobby is flanked by two wings that face 1,200 feet of the Florida Bay. The large guest rooms have tasteful tropical decor and private balconies. The suites are twice the size of standard rooms and have better-quality wicker furnishings and double-size balconies. Ten suites feature private spa tubs and particularly luxurious bathrooms with adjustable showerheads, bidets, and lots of room for toiletries.

Dining/Diversions: The hotel restaurant offers terrific views of the bay and surf-and-turf dinners nightly. A casual cafe serves breakfast, lunch, and dinner both inside and outdoors. A poolside snack bar serves sandwiches, salads, and refreshments. The top-floor lounge has a dance floor and a pool table.

Amenities: Concierge, 24-hour room service, newspaper delivery, dry-cleaning and laundry service, in-room massage, twice-daily maid service, baby-sitting, secretarial services, express checkout, free morning coffee in lobby, valet parking. Two outdoor heated swimming pools, beach, small but modern fitness room with Universal equipment, Jacuzzi, nature trails, two lighted tennis courts, water-sports equipment rental, children's programs, conference rooms, hair salon.

EXPENSIVE

Jules' Undersea Lodge. 51 Shoreland Dr., Key Largo, FL 33037. ☎ **305/451-2353.** Fax 305/451-4789. 1 unit. A/C TV TEL. $225–$325 per person. Rates include breakfast and dinner as well as all equipment and unlimited scuba diving in the lagoon. AE, DISC, MC, V. From U.S. 1 south, at MM 103.2, turn left onto Transylvania Ave., across from the Central Plaza shopping mall.

Originally built as a research lab in the 1970s, this small underwater compartment now operates as a single-room hotel. As expensive as it is unusual, Jules' is most popular with diving honeymooners. The lodge rests on pillars on the ocean floor. To get inside, guests swim under the structure and pop up into the unit through a 4-by-6-foot "moon pool" that gurgles soothingly all night long. The 30-foot-deep underwater suite consists of a bedroom and galley and sleeps up to six. There is a television and VCR. Also, room service will bring breakfast, lunch, and daily newspapers in waterproof containers at no extra charge. Needless to say, this novelty is not for everyone.

Marriott Key Largo Bay Beach Resort. 103800 Overseas Hwy. (MM 103.8), Key Largo FL 33037. ☎ **800/932-9332** or 305/453-0000. Fax 305/453-0093. E-mail: baybeach@reefnet. com. 150 units. A/C MINIBAR TV TEL. Winter $209–$269 double; $500 suite. Off-season $139–$179 double; $250 suite. AE, DC, DISC, MC, V.

When this mammoth chain resort was built in 1993, many thought the sleepy little island town would be forever spoiled. On the contrary, this pristine, two-story Marriott created some major competition for the area's older resorts and the run-down 1950s motels, resulting in an overall upgrade of the neighboring accommodations. While it is hardly quaint, the amenities-laden complex built on 17 acres has everything an active or resting traveler could want, including a decent-sized beach. Guests can now enjoy the new European health spa, a nine-hole minigolf course, and new tennis courts. All guests are welcome to sail for free on a gambling cruise ship that anchors in international waters from 2pm until 2am daily. Rooms are decorated in a pleasant (if generic) tropical style and include extras such as coffeemakers, hair dryers, and safes. Most rooms (all but 22) also offer balconies overlooking the stunning Florida bay. For real pampering, consider the enormous suites, which can easily sleep a family of five. All have large wraparound terraces and large sitting areas. With its rates being slightly cheaper than the nearby Westin and Cheeca Lodge, you'll find it a good value.

Dining/Diversions: A casual bay-side grill offers casually elegant dining, and an outdoor tiki bar has snacks and cocktails throughout the afternoon and evening.

Amenities: Concierge, room service, dry-cleaning and laundry services, in-room massage, newspaper delivery, baby-sitting, express checkout. Large outdoor pool, Jacuzzi, three small beach areas, VCRs on request, gym, bicycle rental, conference rooms, sundeck, access to nearby tennis and racquetball courts, water-sports equipment rental, business center, tour desk, children's programs, game room, nature trail, boutiques.

✪ **The Moorings**. 123 Beach Rd. near MM 81.5 on the ocean side, Islamorada, FL 33036. ☎ **305/664-4708.** Fax 305/664-4242. 17 cottages. A/C TV TEL. Winter $165–$200 smaller one-bedrooms; $350 large one-bedrooms. Oceanfront two- and three-bedroom cottages $2,450–$6,300 weekly. Discounts off-season. Two-night minimum for smaller cottages; 1-week minimum for larger cottages. MC, V.

Staying at the Moorings is more like staying at your second home than at a hotel. You'll never see another soul on this 18-acre resort if you choose not to. There isn't even maid service unless you request it. The romantic whitewashed houses are spacious and modestly decorated with funky island prints, bamboo, and tropical motifs. All have full kitchens and most have washers and dryers. Some have CD players and VCRs; ask when you book. The real reason to come to this cool resort is to relax on the more than 1,000-foot beach (one of the only real beaches around). There is a simple hard tennis court, a few kayaks and Windsurfers, but absolutely no motorized water vehicles. There is no room service or restaurant (although Morada Bay across the street is excellent). This is a place for people who like each other a lot. Leave the kids at home unless they are extremely well behaved and not easily bored.

Amenities include laundry and dryers, full kitchens, some VCRs, large sandy beach, sundeck, large pool, boats, and jogging trails.

MODERATE

Banana Bay Resort & Marina. U.S. 1 at MM 49.5, Marathon, FL 33050. ☎ **800/ BANANA-1** or 305/743-3500. Fax 305/743-2670. 60 units. A/C TV TEL. Winter $95–$195 double. Off-season $75–$150 double. Rates include continental breakfast. Weekend and 3- and 7-night packages available. AE, DC, DISC, MC, V.

It doesn't look like much from the sign-cluttered Overseas Highway, but when you enter the lush grounds of Banana Bay, you will realize you're in one of the most bucolic and best-run properties in the Upper Keys. Built in the early 1950s as a fishing camp, the resort is a maze of pink-and-white two-story buildings hidden among banyans and palms. Guest rooms are very similar, but those with better views are more expensive. The rooms are moderately sized, and many have private balconies where you can enjoy complimentary coffee and newspapers every morning.

The restaurant serves breakfast, lunch, and dinner by the pool or in a kitschy old dining room. A waterfront tiki bar offers great sunset views. Head down to the marina to sign up for charter fishing, sailing, and diving. Kids will enjoy the small game room and free use of bicycles.

✪ **Conch Key Cottages.** Near U.S. 1 at MM 62.3, Marathon, FL 33050. ☎ **800/ 330-1577** or 305/289-1377. Fax 305/743-8207. wwwfloridakeys.net/conchkeycottages. 12 units. A/C TV. Winter $105 efficiency; $126 one-bedroom apt; $147 one-bedroom cottage; $194–$249 two-bedroom cottage. Off-season $74 efficiency; $115 one-bedroom apt; $132 one-bedroom cottage; $147–$215 two-bedroom cottage. DISC, MC, V.

Occupying its own private microisland just off U.S. 1, Conch Key Cottages is a unique and comfortable hideaway run by live-in owners Ron Wilson and Wayne Byrnes, who are constantly fixing and adding to their unique property. This is a place to get away from it all; the cottages aren't close to much, except maybe one or two interesting eateries. The cabins, which were built at different times over the past 40 years, overlook their own stretch of natural, but very small, private beach and have screened-in porches and cozy bedrooms and bathrooms. Each has a hammock and barbecue grill. Request one of the new two-bedroom cottages, completed in 1997—especially if you are traveling with the family. They are the most spacious and well designed, practically tailor-made for couples or families. On the other side of the pool are a handful of efficiency apartments that are similarly outfitted, but enjoy no beach frontage. All have fully equipped kitchens. There's also a small heated freshwater pool.

Faro Blanco Marine Resort. 1996 Overseas Hwy., U.S. 1 at MM 48.5, Marathon, FL 33050. ☎ **800/759-3276** or 305/743-9018. Fax 305/866-5235. 123 units, 31 houseboats with 4 units each. A/C TV TEL. Winter $65–$150 cottage; $99–$200 houseboat; $185 lighthouse; $240 condo. Off-season $55–$125 cottage; $79–$150 houseboat; $150 lighthouse; $210 condo. AE, DISC, MC, V.

Spanning both sides of the Overseas Highway and all on waterfront property, this huge, two-shore marina and hotel complex offers something for every taste. Free-standing, camp-style cottages with a small bedroom are the resort's least expensive accommodations, but are in dire need of rehabilitation. Old appliances and a musty odor also make them the least desirable units on the property.

The houseboats are the best choice and value. Permanently tethered in a tranquil marina, these white rectangular boats look like floating mobile homes and are uniformly clean, fresh, and recommendable. They have colonial American-style furnishings, fully equipped kitchenettes, front and back porches, and water, water everywhere. The boats are so tightly moored, you hardly move at all, even in the roughest weather.

Finally, there are two unusual rental units located in a lighthouse on the pier. Circular staircases, unusually shaped rooms and showers, and nautical decor make it a unique place to stay, but some guests might find it claustrophobic. Guests in any of the accommodations can enjoy the Olympic-size pool, any of the four casual restaurants, a fully equipped dive shop, barbecue and picnic areas, and a playground.

Holiday Isle Resort. U.S. 1 at MM 84, Islamorada, FL 33036. ☎ **800/327-7070** or 305/664-2321. Fax 305/664-2703. 199 units. Winter $85–$425. Off-season $65–$350. AE, CB, DISC, MC, V.

A huge resort complex encompassing five restaurants, several lounges, tiki huts, a large marina, many retail shops, and four distinct (if not distinctive) hotels, the Holiday Isle is one of the biggest resorts in the Keys. It attracts a spring-break kind of crowd year-round. Its Tiki Bar claims to have invented the rum runner drink (151-proof rum, blackberry brandy, banana liqueur, grenadine, and lime juice), and there's no reason to doubt it. Hordes of partiers are attracted to the resort's nonstop merrymaking, live music, and beachfront bars. As a result, some of the accommodations can be noisy.

Rooms can be bare-bones budget to oceanfront luxury, as the broad range of prices reflect. Even the nicest rooms could use a good cleaning. El Captain and Harbor Lights, two of the least expensive hotels on the property, are both austere. Like the other hotels here, rooms could use a thorough rehab. Howard Johnson's, another Holiday Isle property, is a little farther from the action and a tad more civilized. If you plan to be there for a few days, choose an efficiency or suite; both have kitchenettes. Guests can choose between two outdoor heated pools and a kids' pool. They also offer water-sports equipment rental, gift boutiques, and a shopping arcade.

✪ **Kona Kai Resort & Gallery.** 97802 Overseas Hwy. (U.S. 1 at MM 97.8), Key Largo, FL 33037. ☎ **800/365-7829** or 305/852-7200. Fax 305/852-4629. www.funandsun.com\konakai. 11 units. Winter $179–$209 double; $211–$559 suite. Off-season $96–$169 double; $121–$315 suite. 3- to 4-night minimum stay usually required. AE, DISC, MC, V.

Unique in the Upper Keys, this little haven is both casual and elegant—thanks to a total overhaul completed over 3 years under the supervision of owners, Joe Harris an his wife, Ronnie, former executives with NBC television. The quaint, simply furnished rooms dot the lushly landscaped 2-acre property, which boasts a large variety of native vegetation like palms, bougainvillea, and ferns, plus an impressive collection of fruit-bearing trees, such as carambola, passion fruit, banana, key lime, guava, and coconut. Lounge chairs, hammocks, a Jacuzzi, and compact artificial beach are available for those who just want to relax, while a small lighted tennis court, heated pool, Ping-Pong table, volleyball court, and all kinds of water sports are available for those who are more active. For the adventurous, Joe and Ronnie will organize excursions to the Everglades, the backcountry, or wherever. No phones in the rooms and a 4-day minimum stay requirement in the winter make relaxing imperative. All the rooms are very private and simply furnished without things like hair dryers or stereos. Smoking is not permitted on the property. An art gallery featuring work of local painters, photographers, and sculptors doubles as the property's office and lobby. Even if you are not staying here, stop in to see the artwork.

Lime Tree Bay Resort Motel. U.S. 1 at MM 68.5 in Layton, Long Key, FL 33001. ☎ **800/723-4519** or 305/664-4740. Fax 305/664-0750. 30 units. A/C TV TEL. $75–$110 motel rooms or efficiencies; $105–$125 deluxe motel rooms; $115–$150 cottages; $150–$180 one-bedroom suite; $155–$230 two-bedroom suites. AE, DC, DISC, MC, V.

The Lime Tree Bay Resort is the only hotel in the tiny town of Layton (pop. 183). Midway between Islamorada and Marathon, the hotel is only steps from Long Key State Recreation Area. Motel rooms and efficiencies have tiny bathrooms with standing showers, but are clean and well maintained. The best deal is the two-bedroom bay-view apartment. The large living area with new fixtures and furnishings leads out to a large private deck where you can enjoy a view of the gulf from your hammock. A full kitchen and two full baths make it a comfortable space for six people.

This affordable little hideaway has all the amenities you could want, including shuffleboard, tennis, a small pool, water sports, and a little cafe with a small but decent menu. It's situated on a very pretty piece of waterfront graced with hundreds of mature palm trees and lots of other tropical foliage.

INEXPENSIVE

Bay Harbor Lodge. 97702 Overseas Highway; U.S. 1 at MM 97.7 (off the southbound lane of U.S. 1), Key Largo, FL 33037. ☎ **305/852-5695.** 16 units. A/C TV TEL. Winter $65–$105 double. Off-season $78–$98 efficiency; $85–$125 cottage. MC, V.

A small, simple retreat that's big on charm, the Bay Harbor Lodge is an extraordinarily welcoming place. The lodge is far from fancy, and the wide range of accommodations are not all created equal. The motel rooms are small and ordinary in decor, but even the least expensive is recommendable. The efficiencies are larger motel rooms with fully equipped kitchenettes. The oceanfront cottages are larger still, have full kitchens, and represent one of the best values in the Keys. The vinyl-covered furnishings and old-fashioned wallpapers won't win any design awards, but elegance isn't what the "real" Keys are about. The 1½ lush acres of grounds are planted with banana trees and have an outdoor heated pool and several small barbecue grills. Guests are free to use the rowboats, paddleboats, canoes, kayaks, and snorkeling equipment. Bring your own beach towels.

✪ **Ragged Edge Resort.** 243 Treasure Harbor Rd, (near MM 86.5) Islamorada, FL 33036. ☎ **305/852-5389.** 11 units. A/C TV TEL. Winter $70–$95 motel rooms or efficiencies; $109 studio apt; $169 2-bed/2-bathroom apt. Off-season $50–$70 efficiency; $78 studio apt; $120 2-bed/2-bathroom apt. AE, MC, V.

This small, well-maintained property has only 11 units spread out along more than half a dozen gorgeous, grassy waterfront acres. All are immaculately clean and comfortable, and most are outfitted with full kitchens and tasteful furnishings. There's no bar, restaurant, or staff to speak of, but the retreat's affable owner, Jackie Barnes, is happy to lend you bicycles or good advice on the area's offerings. A large dock attracts boaters and a large variety of local and migratory birds.

CAMPING

John Pennekamp Coral Reef State Park. U.S. 1 at MM 102.5 (P.O. Box 487), Key Largo, FL 33037. ☎ **305/451-1202.** 47 campsites. Reservations can be made up to 11 months in advance by telephone or in person. $24–$26 per site. MC, V.

One of Florida's best parks (see above), Pennekamp offers 47 well-separated campsites, half available by advance reservation, the rest distributed on a first-come, first-served basis. The car-camping sites are small but well equipped with bathrooms and showers. A little lagoon nearby attracts many large wading birds. Reservations are held until 5pm, and the park must be notified of late arrival by phone on the check-in date. Pennekamp opens at 8am and closes around sundown. No pets.

Long Key State Recreation Area. U.S. 1 at MM 67.5 (P.O. Box 776), Long Key, FL 33001. ☎ **305/664-4815.** 60 campsites. $24–$26 per site for one to four people. MC, V.

The Upper Keys' other main state park is more secluded than its northern neighbor and more popular. All sites are located ocean-side and surrounded by narrow rows of trees and nearby toilet and bath facilities. Reserve well in advance, especially in winter.

WHERE TO DINE

Although not known as a culinary hot spot, the Upper and Middle Keys do offer some excellent restaurants, most of which specialize in seafood. Often, visitors (especially those who fish) take advantage of accommodations that have kitchen facilities and cook their own meals. Also, most restaurants will clean and cook your catch for a nominal charge.

VERY EXPENSIVE

✪ **Atlantic's Edge.** In the Cheeca Lodge, U.S. 1 at MM 82, Islamorada. ☎ **305/ 664-4651.** Reservations recommended. Main courses $20–$36. AE, CB, DC, DISC, MC, V. Daily 5:30–10pm. SEAFOOD/REGIONAL.

Ask for a table by the oceanfront window to feel really privileged at this, the most elegant restaurant in the Keys. Although the service and food are first class, don't get dressed up—a sport coat for men will be fine, but isn't necessary. You can choose from an innovative, varied menu, which offers several choices of fresh fish, steak, chicken, and pastas. The crab cakes, made with stone crab when in season, are the very best in the Keys; served on a warm salad of baby greens with a mild sauce of red peppers, they're the stuff cravings are made of. Other excellent dishes include a Thai-spiced fresh baby snapper and the vegetarian angel-hair pasta with mushrooms, asparagus, and peppers in a rich broth. Service can sometimes be less than efficient, but is always courteous and professional.

EXPENSIVE

Barracuda Grill. U.S. 1 at MM 49.5 (bay side), Marathon. ☎ **305/743-3314.** Reservations not accepted. Main courses $13–$30. AE, MC, V. Opened nightly 6–10pm. BISTRO/SEAFOOD.

Owned by Lance Hill and his wife, Jan (who used to be a sous chef at Little Palm Island), this casual spot serves excellent seafood, steaks, and chops. It's too bad it's open only for dinner. Some of the favorite dishes are old-fashioned meat loaf, classic beef Stroganoff, rack of lamb, and seafood stew. In addition, this small barracuda-decorated restaurant features a well-priced American wine list with a vast sampling of California vintages.

✪ **Marker 88.** U.S. 1 at MM 88 (bay side), Islamorada. ☎ **305/852-9315.** Reservations not usually required. Main courses $14–$29. AE, DC, DISC, MC, V. Tues–Sun 5–11pm. SEAFOOD/REGIONAL.

An institution in the Upper Keys, Marker 88 has been pleasing locals, visitors, and critics since it opened in the early 1970s. Chef-owner Andre Mueller has created a "gourmet" restaurant in a tropical-fish house setting. The wide range of standard fare is tinged with his take on nouvelle cuisine. Taking full advantage of his island location, Andre offers dozens of seafood selections, including Keys lobster, Bahamas conch, Everglades frogs' legs, Florida Bay stone crabs, Gulf Coast shrimp, and an impressive variety of fish from around the country. After you've figured out what kind of seafood to have, you can choose from a dozen styles of preparation. The Keys' standard is meunière, which is a subtle, tasty sauce of lemon and parsley. Although everything looks tempting, don't overorder—portions are huge. The waitresses, who are pleasant enough, require a bit of patience, but the food is worth it.

✪ **Morada Bay.** U.S. 1 at MM 81.6, Islamorada. ☎ **305/664-0604.** Reservations recommended for large groups. Main courses $16–$22; sandwiches $7–$8. AE, MC, V. Mon–Thurs 11:30am–10pm; Fri–Sun 11am–11pm. CARIBBEAN/AMERICAN.

This lovely bay-side bistro offers a great setting for its superfresh, innovative seafood, as well as some more basic offerings, such as chicken fajitas, hamburgers, and salads. Salads like the Sunshine Salad are large and generously lavished with slices of avocado, mango, and tomato. When in season, delicious raw oysters are imported from Long Island. Fish dishes are always fresh. I like mine jerked with a peppery coating and nearly black finish. If you can't decide, share a few items from the tapas menu: jumbo shrimp cocktails, fried calamari, conch fritters, smoked fish dip, or a charcuterie of sausages and hams on country bread.

MODERATE

Lazy Days Oceanfront Bar and Seafood Grill. U.S. 1 at MM 79.9, Islamorada. ☎ **305/ 664-5256.** Main courses $11–$20. AE, DISC, MC, V. Tues–Sun 11:30am–10pm. SEAFOOD/ AMERICAN.

Opened in 1992, the Lazy Days quickly became one of the most popular restaurants around, mostly because of the large portions and lively atmosphere. Meals are pricier than the casual dining room would suggest, but the food is good enough and the menu varied. Steamed clams with garlic and bell peppers make a tempting appetizer. The menu focuses on—what else?—seafood, but you can also find Italian dishes. Most main courses come with baked potato, vegetables, a tossed salad, and French bread, making appetizers redundant.

✪ **Lorelei Restaurant and Cabana Bar.** U.S. 1 at MM 82, Islamorada. ☎ **305/ 664-4656.** Reservations not usually required. Main courses $9–$22. Daily 7am–10pm. Outside bar serves lunch menu 11am–9pm. Bar closes at midnight. SEAFOOD/BAR FOOD.

Don't resist the siren call of the enormous, sparkling, roadside mermaid—you won't be dashed into the rocks. This big old fish house and bar is a great place for a snack, a meal, or a beer. Inside, a good-value menu focuses mainly on seafood. When in season, lobsters are the way to go. For $20, you can get a good-sized tail—at least a 1-pounder—prepared any way you like. Other fare includes the standard clam chowder, fried shrimp, and doughy conch fritters. Salads and soups are hearty and satisfying. For those tired of fish, the menu also offers a few beef selections. The outside bar has live music every evening, and you can order snacks and light meals from a limited menu that is satisfying and well priced. Enjoy the live entertainment every night.

INEXPENSIVE

Calypso's. 1 Seagate Blvd. (near MM 99.5), Key Largo. ☎ **305/451-0600.** Main courses $8–$16. Wed–Mon 11:30am–10pm. MC V. SEAFOOD/PASTA.

The awning still bears the name of the former restaurant "Demar's" but the food here is all Todd Lollis's. Though he looks like he might be more comfortable at a Grateful Dead concert than in a kitchen, this inspired young chef turns out inventive seafood dishes in a casual and rustic water-side setting. If it's available, try the butter pecan sauce over whatever fish is freshest. Don't miss the white wine sangria, full of tangy oranges and limes and topped with a dash of cinnamon. The prices are surprisingly reasonable, but the service can be a little more laid back than you're used to. The toughest part is finding the place. From south, turn right at the blinking yellow lights near mile marker 99.5 to Ocean Bay Drive; turn right. Look for the blue vinyl-sided building on the left.

✪ **Henry's Bakery and Gourmet Pizza Shop.** U.S. 1 at MM 82.5 (adjacent to Days Inn), 82700 Overseas Highway, Islamorada, FL ☎ **305/664-4030.** Pastas $7–$9.50; pizzas $8–$18; sandwiches and salads $4.50–$8. Mon–Sat 6am–10pm (sometimes later on weekends). No credit cards. BAKERY/PIZZERIA.

This recently expanded storefront bakery serves the best pizzas and sandwiches in town. My favorite is freshly sliced turkey on homemade warm French bread, with a splash of superbly tangy vinaigrette. Most days Henry bakes fresh multigrain, semolina, and Italian bread, too. Stop by early for delicious pastries and croissants. If you want pizza, consider the decadent Sublime Pie with lobster tail, roasted bell peppers, and sun-dried tomatoes. The crust has the perfect texture—just a bit chewy, but not too doughy.

✪ **Islamorada Fish Company.** U.S. 1 at MM 81.5 (up the street from Cheeca Lodge), Islamorada. ☎ **800/258-2559** or 305/664-9271. Reservations not accepted. Main courses $8–$20. DISC, MC, V. Mon–Sat 8am–9pm; Sun 9am–9pm. SEAFOOD.

The original Islamorada Fish Company has been selling seafood out of its roadside shack since 1948. It's still the best place to pick up a cooler of stone crab claws in season (mid-October through April). Also great are the fish sandwiches, served fried with melted American cheese, fried onions, and cole slaw. A few hundred yards up the road is the newer establishment, which looks like an average diner, but has a selection of fantastic seafood and pastas. It's also the place for breakfast. Locals gather for politics and gossip as well as delicious grits, oatmeal, omelettes, and homemade pastries. The Islamorada Fish Company Restaurant & Bakery is at MM 81.6. (☎ 305/664-8363; DISC, MC, V accepted; open Thursday to Tuesday 6am to 9pm, Wednesday 6am to 2pm).

Key Largo's Crack'd Conch. U.S. 1 at MM 105.5 (ocean side). ☎ **305/451-0732.** Reservations not accepted. Main courses $9–$15; sandwiches $5–$7. AE, MC, V, DISC, DC. Thurs–Tues noon–10pm. SEAFOOD.

This colorful little shack looks appealing from the road and isn't a bad place to stop, especially if you like beer. Over 100 imported and domestic lagers, porters, stouts, and ales are available. Food choices, on the other hand, are not as varied or as predictable. The Crack'd Conch serves decent baskets of fried clams, shrimp, chicken, and, of course, conch. Prices are higher than they ought to be, considering the quality and atmosphere, but it won't break you.

Time Out Barbecue. U.S. 1 at MM 81.5 (ocean side). ☎ **305/664-8911.** Sandwiches $3.75–$4.25; rib and chicken platters to share $9–$15. MC, V. Daily 11am–10pm. BARBECUE.

This barbecue joint serves up hot and hearty old-fashioned barbecue that is the best I've had. The secret, Steve says, is in the slow-cooking—more than 10 hours for the melt-in-your-mouth soft pork sandwich. Topped off with delicious, not too-creamy cole slaw and sweet baked beans, any of the many offerings are worth a stop. You can grab a seat at the picnic table on the grassy lawn next to the Trading Post.

THE UPPER & MIDDLE KEYS AFTER DARK

Nightlife in the Upper Keys tends to start before the sun goes down, often at noon, since most people—visitors and locals alike—are on vacation. Also, many anglers and sports-minded folk go to bed early.

Opened in the early 1990s by some young locals tired of tourist traps, **Hog Heaven,** at MM 85.3 just off the main road on the ocean side in Islamorada (☎ **305/664-9669**), is a welcome respite from the neon-colored cocktail circuit. This whitewashed biker bar offers a waterside view and diversions that include big-screen TVs and video games. The food isn't bad, either. The atmosphere is cliquish since most patrons are regulars, so start up a game of pool or skeet to break the ice.

No trip is complete without a stop at the **Tiki Bar at the Holiday Isle Resort,** U.S. 1 at MM 84, Islamorada (☎ **800/327-7070** or 305/664-2321). Hundreds of revelers visit this ocean-side spot for drinks and dancing any time of day, but the live rock music starts at 8:30pm. (See "Where to Stay" above.)

In the afternoon and early evening (when everyone is either sunburned, drunk, or just happy to be alive and dancing to live reggae), head for **Kokomo's,** just next door to the thatched-roof Tiki Bar. Kokomo's often closes at 7:30pm on weekends, so get there early. For information, call the Holiday Isle Resort.

Locals and tourists mingle at the outdoor cabana bar at **Lorelei's** (see "Where to Dine," above). Most evenings after 5pm, you'll find local bands playing on a thatched roof stage—mainly rock and roll, Caribbean, and sometimes blues.

Woody's Saloon and Restaurant, on U.S. 1 at MM 82, Islamorada (☎ **305/ 664-4335**), is a lively, wacky, raunchy place serving up mediocre pizzas and live bands almost every night. The house band, Big Dick and the Extenders, showcases a 300-pound Native American who does a lewd, rude, and crude routine of jokes and songs starting at 9pm, Tuesday through Sunday. He is a legend. By the way, don't think you're lucky if you are offered the front table: It's the target seat for Big Dick's haranguing. Avoid the lame karaoke performance on Sunday and Monday evenings. There's a small cover charge most nights. Drink specials, contests, and the legendary Big Dick keep this place packed until 4am almost every night.

For a more subdued atmosphere, try the handsome wood bar at **Zane Grey's** (on the second floor of World Wide Sportsman at MM 81.5). Outside, enjoy a view of the calm waters of the bay, or inside, soak up the history of some real old anglers. You feel like a real swell in this stained-glass, mahogany-decked club. It is open from 11am to 11pm, and later on weekends. Call to find out who is playing on weekends (☎ **305/664-4244**), when there is live entertainment and no cover charge.

3 The Lower Keys: Big Pine Key to Coppitt Key

128 miles SW of Miami

Big Pine, Sugarloaf, Summerland, and the other Lower Keys are less developed and more tranquil than the Upper Keys. If you're looking for haute cuisine and a happening nightlife, look elsewhere. If you're looking to commune with nature or adventure in solitude, you've come to the right place. Unlike their neighbors to the north and south, the Lower Keys are devoid of rowdy spring-break crowds, boast few T-shirt and trinket shops, and have almost no late-night bars. What they do offer are the very best opportunities to enjoy the vast natural resources on land and water that make the area so rich. Stay overnight in the Lower Keys, rent a boat, and explore the reefs—it might be the most memorable part of your trip.

ESSENTIALS

GETTING THERE   See "Essentials" for the Upper and Middle Keys. Continue south on U.S. 1. The Lower Keys start at the end of the Seven-Mile Bridge.

VISITOR INFORMATION   The **Lower Keys Chamber of Commerce,** ocean side of U.S. 1 at MM 31 (P.O. Box 430511), Big Pine Key, FL 33043 (☎ **800/ 872-3722** or 305/872-2411; fax 305/872-0752; e-mail: lkchamber@aol.com), is open Monday through Friday from 9am to 5pm and Saturday from 9am to 3pm. The pleasant staff will help with anything a traveler may need. Call, write, or stop in for a comprehensive, detailed information packet.

WHAT TO SEE & DO

Once the centerpiece of the Lower Keys and still a great asset is **Bahia Honda State Park,** U.S. 1 at MM 37.5, Big Pine Key (☎ **305/872-2353**), which, even after the violent storms of 1998, has one of the most beautiful coastlines in South Florida. Bahia Honda (pronounced *Bah-*ya) is a great place for hiking, bird watching, swimming, snorkeling, and fishing. The 524-acre park encompasses a wide variety of ecosystems, including coastal mangroves, beach dunes, and tropical hammocks. There are miles of trails packed with unusual plants and animals and a small white beach. Shaded seaside picnic areas are fitted with tables and grills. Although the beach is never wider than 5 feet even at low tide, this is the Lower Keys' best beach area.

True to its name (Spanish for "deep bay"), the park has relatively deep waters close to shore that are perfect for snorkeling and diving. Head to the stunning reefs at Looe Key where the coral and fish are more vibrant than anywhere in the United States. Snorkeling trips depart daily from March through September and cost $22 for adults, $18 for youths 6 to 14, and free for children 5 and under. Call ☎ **305/872-3210** for a schedule.

Admission to the park is $4 per vehicle (plus 50¢ per person), $1.50 per pedestrian or bicyclist, free for children 5 and under. If you are alone in a car, you'll only pay $2.50. Open daily from 8am to sunset.

The most famous residents of the Lower Keys are the tiny Key deer. Of the estimated 300 existing in the world, two thirds live on Big Pine Key's **National Key Deer Refuge.** To get your bearings, stop by the rangers' office at the Winn-Dixie Shopping Plaza near MM 30.5 off U.S. 1. They'll give you an informative brochure and map of the area. It is open Monday through Friday from 8am to 5pm.

If the office is closed, head out to the Blue Hole, a former rock quarry now filled with the fresh water that's vital to the deer's survival. To get there, turn right at Big Pine Key's only traffic light onto Key Deer Boulevard (take the left fork immediately after the turn), and continue 1½ miles to the observation site parking lot, on your left. The half-mile Watson Hammock Trail, about a third of a mile past the Blue Hole, is the refuge's only marked footpath. Try coming out here in the early morning or late evening to catch a glimpse of these gentle, dog-sized deer. Refuge lands are open daily from half an hour before sunrise to half an hour after sunset. Whatever you do, do not feed the deer—it will threaten their survival. Call the **park office** (☎ **305/872-2239**) to find out about the infrequent free tours of the refuge, scheduled at different times throughout the year.

The only human-made attraction in the Lower Keys is the **Sugarloaf Bat Tower,** off U.S. 1 at MM 17 (next to Sugarloaf Airport on the bay side). In a vain effort to battle the ubiquitous troublesome mosquitoes in the Lower Keys, developer Clyde Perkey built this odd structure to lure bug-eating bats. Despite his alluring design and a pungent bat aphrodisiac, his guests never showed. Since 1929, this wooden, flat-topped, 45-foot-high pyramid has stood empty and deserted, except for the occasional tourist who stops to wonder what it is. There is no sign or marker to commemorate this odd remnant of ingenuity. It's worth a 5-minute detour to see it. To get there, turn right at the Sugarloaf Airport sign, and then right again onto the dirt road that begins just before the airport gate; the tower is about 100 yards ahead.

OUTDOOR PURSUITS

BICYCLING   If you have your own bike, or your lodging offers rental (many do), the Lower Keys is a great place to get off busy U.S. 1 to explore the beautiful back roads. On Big Pine Key, cruise along Key Deer Boulevard (at MM 30). Those with fat tires can ride into the National Key Deer Refuge.

BIRD WATCHING   Bring your birding books. A stopping point for migratory birds on the Eastern Flyway, the Lower Keys are populated with many West Indian bird species, especially during spring and fall. The small vegetated islands of the

Keys are the only nesting sites in the United States for the great white heron and the white-crowned pigeon. They're also some of the very few breeding places for the reddish egret, the roseate spoonbill, the mangrove cuckoo, and the black-whiskered vireo. Look for them on Bahia Honda and the many uninhabited islands nearby.

BOATING   Dozens of shops rent powerboats for fishing and reef exploring. Most also rent tackle, sell bait, and have charter captains available. **Bud Boats,** at the Old Wooden Bride Fishing Camp and Marina, MM 30 in Big Pine Key (☎ **305/ 872-9165**), has a wide selection of well-maintained boats. Depending on the size, rentals cost between $70 and $250 for a day, between $50 and $130 for a half day. Another good option is **Jaybird's Powerboats,** U.S. 1 at MM 33, Big Pine Key (☎ **305/872-8500**). They rent for full days only. Prices start at $127 for a 19-footer.

CANOEING & KAYAKING   The Overseas Highway (U.S. 1) touches on only a few dozen of the many hundreds of islands that make up the Keys. To really see the Lower Keys, rent a kayak or canoe—perfect for these shallow waters. **Reflections Kayak Nature Tours,** operating out of Parmer's Place Resort Motel, on U.S. 1 at MM 28.5, Little Torch Key (☎ **305/872-2896**), offers fully outfitted backcountry wildlife tours, either on your own or with an expert. A former U.S. Forest Service guide, Mike Wedeking, keeps up an engaging discussion describing the area's fish, sponges, coral, osprey, hawks, eagles, alligators, raccoons, and deer. The 3-hour tours cost $45 per person and include spring water, fresh fruit, granola bars, and use of binoculars. Bring a towel and sea sandals or sneakers.

DIVING & FISHING   A day spent fishing, either in the shallow backcountry or in the deep sea, is a great way to ensure yourself a fresh fish dinner, or you can release your catch and just appreciate the challenge. Especially since the Adolphus Busch was sunk off Looe Key in 100 feet of water, the lower Keys also offers some prime diving. Whichever you choose, **Larry Threlkeld's Strike Zone Charters,** U.S. 1 at MM 29.5, Big Pine Key (☎ **305/872-9863**), is the charter service to call. Prices for fishing boats start at $250 to $400 for a half day. If you have enough anglers to share the price, it isn't too steep. They may be able to match you with other interested visitors.

To get to the Adolphus Busch Sr, a 210-foot island freighter, on your own boat, head to coordinates: 24.31.819 N 81.27.643W between Looe Key and American Shoals. Strike Zone will take you for $50 without equipment.

HIKING   You can hike throughout the flat marshy Keys, on both marked trails and meandering coastlines. The best places to trek through nature are **Bahia Honda State Park** at MM 29.5 and **National Key Deer Refuge** at MM 30 (for more information on both, see "What to See & Do," above). Bahia Honda Park has a free brochure describing an excellent self-guided tour along the Silver Palm Nature Trail. You'll traverse hammocks, mangroves, and sand dunes and cross a lagoon. You can do the walk (which is less than a mile) in under half an hour and can explore a great cross-section of the natural habitat in the Lower Keys.

SNORKELING & DIVING   Snorkelers and divers should not miss the Keys' most dramatic reefs at the **Looe Key National Marine Sanctuary.** Here, you'll see more than 150 varieties of hard and soft coral, some centuries old, as well as every type of tropical fish, including the gold and blue parrot fish, moray eels, barracudas, French angels, and tarpon. **Looe Key Dive Center,** U.S. 1 at MM 27.5, Ramrod Key (☎ **305/872-2215**), offers a mind-blowing 2½-hour tour aboard a 45-foot catamaran with two shallow 1-hour dives for snorkelers and scuba divers. Snorkelers pay $30, and divers with their own equipment pay $65. Good-quality rentals are available. (See "What to See & Do," above, for other diving options.)

SHOPPING

Certainly not known for great shopping, the Lower Keys do happen to be home to many talented visual artists, particularly those who specialize in depicting their natural surroundings. The **Artists in Paradise Gallery,** on Big Pine Key in the Winn-Dixie Shopping Plaza, near MM 30.5, 1 block north of U.S. 1 at the traffic light (☎ **305/872-1828**), displays an ever-changing selection of watercolors, oils, photos, and sculptures. This cooperative gallery displays the work of more than a dozen artists who share the task of watching the store. Usually hours are daily from 10am to 6pm.

WHERE TO STAY

There are a number of cheap fish shacks along the highway for those who want bare-bones accommodations, but so far, there are no national hotel chains in the Lower Keys. For information on lodging in cabins or trailers at local campgrounds, see "Camping," below.

VERY EXPENSIVE

✪ **Little Palm Island.** Launch is at the ocean side of U.S. 1 at MM 28.5, Little Torch Key, FL 33042. ☎ **800/343-8567** or 305/872-2524. Fax 305/872-4843. www.littlepalmisland. com. 28 bungalows, 2 deluxe suites. A/C MINIBAR. Winter $600–$850 per couple. Off-season $350–$650 including transportation to and from the island and unlimited (nonmotorized) water sports. Meal plans include two meals daily for $125 per person per day. Three meals are $140 per person. No children under 16. AE, CB, DC, DISC, MC, V.

Severely damaged in the storms of 1998, Little Palm Island was closed for reconstruction for several months. When it reopened in early 1999, it was looking even better than before. The work, at the cost of nearly $9 million, included new roofs, new furniture, a new dining room, and a thorough update of the guest rooms. Over the years this exclusive island escape—host to presidents and royalty—is not just a place to stay while in the Lower Keys; it is a resort destination all its own. Built on a private 5-acre island, it's accessible only by boat. Guests stay in thatched-roof duplexes amid lush foliage and flowering tropical plants. Many villas have ocean views and private sundecks with rope hammocks. Inside, the romantic suites have all the comforts and conveniences of a luxurious contemporary beach cottage, but without telephones, TVs, or alarm clocks. Note that on the breezeless south side of the island, you may get invaded by mosquitoes, even in the winter. Bring spray and lightweight long-sleeved clothing. Known for its innovative and pricey food, Little Palm also hosts visitors just for dinner or lunch. If you are staying on the island, opt for the full American plan, which includes three meals a day for about $140 per person. If you pay à la carte, you could spend that much just on dinner. At these prices, Little Palm appeals to those who aren't keeping track.

Dining/Diversions: The Little Palm Restaurant offers fine dining either indoors or alfresco at inflated prices. A pool bar offers refreshments and light snacks all day.

Amenities: Concierge, room service, dry cleaning, laundry, newspaper delivery, twice-daily maid service, in-room massage, courtesy van from Key West or Marathon airport, ferry service to and from the mainland. Outdoor pool with small waterfall, wide beach, in-room Jacuzzi tubs, sauna, sundeck, water-sports equipment, jogging trail, boutique.

MODERATE

Deer Run Bed and Breakfast. Long Beach Dr. (P.O. Box 431), Big Pine Key, FL 33043. ☎ **305/872-2015.** Fax 305/872-2842. E-mail: deerrunbb@aol.com. 3 units. Winter from $110 double. Off-season from $95 double. No children under 16. Rates include full American breakfast. No credit cards. From U.S. 1 south, turn left at the Big Pine Fishing Lodge (MM 33); continue for about 2 miles.

Located directly on the beach, Sue Abbott's small, homey, smoke-free B&B is a real find. One upstairs and two downstairs guest rooms are comfortably furnished with queen-size beds, good closets, and touch-sensitive lamps. Rattan and 1970s-style chairs and couches furnish the living room, along with 13 birds and three cats. Breakfast, which is served on a pretty, fenced-in porch, is cooked to order by Sue herself. The wooded area around the property is full of deer, which are often spotted on the beach as well. Ask to use one of the bikes to explore nearby nature trails. The owner prefers adults and mature children only.

INEXPENSIVE

✪ **Parmer's Place Cottages.** Barry Ave. (P.O. Box 430665), near MM 28.5, Little Torch Key, FL 33043. ☎ **305/872-2157.** Fax 305/872-2014. 41 units. Winter and during festivals, from $77 double; from $93.50 efficiency. Off-season $55–$65 double; from $75 efficiency. AE, DISC, MC, V. Turn right onto Barry Ave. Resort is a half mile down on the right.

Parmer's, a fixture here for more than 20 years, is well known for its charming hospitality and helpful staff. This downscale resort offers modest but comfortable cottages. Every unit is different. Some face the water, some are a few steps away from the water, some have small kitchenettes, and others are just a bedroom. Room 26, a one-bedroom efficiency, is especially nice, with a small sitting area that faces the water. Room 6, a small efficiency, has a little kitchenette and an especially large bathroom. The rooms all have linoleum floors, dated 1970s-style painted rattan furnishings, fake flowers, and thrift-store art. They're very clean. Many can be combined to accommodate large families. Facilities include a horseshoes court, boat ramp, and a heated swimming pool.

CAMPING

Bahia Honda State Park (☎ **305/872-2353**) offers some of the best camping in the Keys even after the devastating storms of 1998. It is as loaded with facilities and activities as it is with campers. However, don't be discouraged by its popularity—this park encompasses more than 500 acres of land. There are 80 campsites and six spacious and comfortable cabin units though some are still under reconstruction. Cabins hold up to eight guests and come complete with linens, kitchenettes, and utensils. You'll enjoy the wraparound terrace, barbecue pit, and rocking chairs.

Camping here costs about $25 per site for one to four people without electricity and $26 with electricity. Depending on the season, cabin prices change: From December 15 to September 14, it's about $125 per cabin for one to four people; from September 15 to December 14, it's $97.28 per cabin. Additional people (over four) cost $6. MasterCard and Visa are accepted.

Another excellent value can be found at the **KOA Sugarloaf Key Resort,** near MM 20. This ocean-side facility has 200 fully equipped sites that rent for about $53 a night (no-hook-up sites cost about $38). Or pitch a tent on the 5 acres of lush waterfront property. The resort also rents out travel trailers. The 22-foot Dutchman sleeps six and is equipped with eating and cooking utensils. It costs about $100 a day. More luxurious trailers go for $160 a day. All major credit cards are accepted. For details, contact P.O. Box 420469, Summerland Key, FL 33042 (☎ **800/562-7731** or 305/745-3549; fax 305/745-9889; e-mail: sugarloaf@koa.net). They lost about 80% of their trees in the big storm of 1998, but plan to replant for next season.

The Truth About Keys Cuisine

There are few world-class chefs in the Florida Keys, but that's not to say the food isn't great. Restaurants here serve very fresh fish and a few local specialties—most notably conch fritters and chowder, key lime pie, and stone crab claws and lobster when they're in season.

Although a commercial net-fishing ban has diminished the stock of once abundant fish in these parts, even the humblest of restaurants can be counted on to take full advantage of the gastronomic treasures of their own backyard. The Keys have everything a cook could want: the Atlantic and the Gulf of Mexico for impeccably fresh seafood; a tropical climate for year-round farm stand produce, including great tomatoes, beans, berries, and citrus fruit; and a freshwater swamp for rustic delicacies such as alligator, frog's legs, and hearts of palm.

Conch fritters and chowder are mainstays on most tourist-oriented menus. Because the queen conch was listed as an endangered species by the U.S. government in 1985, however, the conch in your dish was most likely shipped fresh-frozen from The Bahamas or the Caribbean.

Key lime pie consists of the juice of tiny yellow key limes (a fruit unique to South Florida), along with condensed milk, all in a graham cracker crust. Experts debate whether the true key lime pie should have a whipped cream or a meringue topping, but all agree that the filling should be yellow—never green.

Another unique offering, the **Florida lobster** is an entirely different species from the more common Maine variety, and has a sweeter meat. It's known also as the tk. You'll see only the tails on the menu because the Florida lobster has no claws.

Stone crabs are even better—succulent, sweet, tender, and very meaty. They've been written about and talked about by kings, presidents, and poets. Although you'll find them on nearly every menu in season (from October until May), consider buying a few pounds of jumbos at the fish store to take to the beach in a cooler. Don't forget to ask them to crack them for you and to get a cup of creamy mustard sauce. Topped off with a cold bottle of champagne, there is no better meal. You'll be glad to know that after their claws are harvested, the crabs grow new ones, thus ensuring a long-lasting supply of these unique delicacies.

WHERE TO DINE

There aren't many fine dining options in the Lower Keys, but the following are worth a stop for those passing through.

MODERATE

✪ **Mangrove Mama's Restaurant.** U.S. 1 at MM 20, Sugarloaf Key. ☎ **305/745-3030.** Main courses $13–$19; lunch $2–$9; brunch $5–$7. MC, V. Daily 11:30am–10pm (11am in season). SEAFOOD/CARIBBEAN.

As dedicated locals who come daily for happy hour will tell you, Mangrove Mama's is a true Lower Keys institution and a dive in the best sense of the word. The restaurant is a shack that used to have a gas pump as well as a grill. Now, guests share the property with some miniature horses (out back) and stray cats. A handful of simple tables, inside and out, are shaded by banana trees and palm fronds. Fish is, not surprisingly, the menu's mainstay, although soups, salads, sandwiches, and omelettes are also good. Grilled teriyaki chicken and club sandwiches are tasty alternatives to fish, as are meatless chef's salads and spicy barbecued baby back ribs.

✪ **Monte's.** U.S. 1 at MM 25, Summerland Key. ☎ **305/745-3731.** Main courses $10–$14; lunch $3–$8. No credit cards. Mon–Sat 9am–10pm; Sun 11am–9pm. SEAFOOD.

Monte's has survived for more than 20 years because the food is very good and incredibly fresh. Certainly nobody goes to this restaurant/fish market for its atmosphere: Plastic place settings rest on plastic-covered picnic-style tables in a screen-enclosed dining patio. The day's catch may include shark, tuna, lobster, stone crabs, or shrimp.

INEXPENSIVE

✪ **Coco's Kitchen.** 283 Key Deer Blvd. (in the Winn-Dixie Shopping Center), Big Pine Key. ☎ **305/872-4495.** Main courses $5–$12; lunch $2–$5; breakfast $1–$4.50. No credit cards. Mon–Sat 7am–7:30pm. Turn right at the traffic light near MM 30.5. Stay in the left lane. CUBAN/NICARAGUAN.

This tiny storefront has been dishing out black beans and rice and shredded beef to Cuban food fans for more than 10 years. The owners, who are actually from Nicaragua, cook not only superior Cuban food but also some local specialties, Italian food, and Caribbean food. The best bet is the daily special, which may be roasted pork or fresh grouper, served with rice and beans or salad and crispy fries. Top off the huge, cheap meal with a rich caramel-soaked flan.

No Name Pub. ¼ mile south of No Name Bridge on N. Watson Blvd., Big Pine Key. ☎ **305/872-9115.** Pizzas $8–$18; subs $5. MC, V. 11am–11pm. Turn right at Big Pine's only traffic light (near MM 30.5) onto Key Deer Blvd. Turn right on Watson Blvd. At stop sign, turn left. Look for a small wooden sign on the left marking the spot. PUB FOOD/PIZZA.

This funky old bar out in the boonies serves snacks and sandwiches until 11pm on most nights and drinks until midnight. Pizzas are tasty—thick-crusted and supercheesy. Try one topped with local shrimps, or consider a bowl of chili with all the fixings—hearty and cheap. Also decent is the smoked fish dip. Everything is served on paper plates. Locals hang out at the rustic bar, one of the Florida Keys' oldest, drinking beer and listening to a jukebox heavy with 1980s selections. The decor, if you can call it that, is basic—the walls and ceilings are plastered with thousands of autographed dollar bills.

THE LOWER KEYS AFTER DARK

Although the mellow islands of the lower Keys aren't exactly known for wild nightlife, there are some friendly bars and restaurants where locals and tourists gather to hang out and drink.

One of the most scenic is **Sandbar** (☎ **305/872-9989**), a wide-open breezy wooden house built on slender stilts and overlooking a wide channel on Barry Avenue (near MM 28.5). It attracts an odd mix of bikers and blue-hairs daily from 11am until 11pm. Pool tables are the main attraction, but there's also live music some nights. The drinks are reasonably priced and the food isn't too bad, either. For another fun bar scene, see **No Name Pub,** listed above in "Where to Dine."

4 Key West

159 miles SW of Miami

The locals, or "conchs" (pronounced "conks"), and the developers here have been at odds for years. This once low-key island has been thoroughly commercialized—

there's a Hard Rock Cafe smack in the middle of Duval Street and thousands of cruise ship passengers descending on Mallory Square each day. It's definitely not the seedy town Hemingway and his cronies once called their own.

Laid-back Key West still exists, but it's now found in different places: the backyard of a popular guest house, for example, or an art gallery, or a secret garden, or the hip hangouts of Bahama Village. And, of course, there's always the calm waters of the Atlantic and the Gulf of Mexico all around.

The heart of town offers party people a good time. Here, you'll find good restaurants, fun bars, live music, rickshaw rides, and lots of shopping. Don't bother with a watch or tie—this is the home of the perennial vacation.

ESSENTIALS

GETTING THERE   For directions by car, see "Essentials" for the Upper and Middle Keys, above. Continue south on U.S. 1. When entering Key West, stay in the far-right lane onto North Roosevelt Boulevard, which becomes Truman Avenue in Old Town. Continue for a few blocks, and you will find yourself on Duval Street, in the heart of the city. If you stay to the left, you'll also reach the city center after passing the airport and the remnants of historic houseboat row, where a motley collection of boats once made up one of Key West's most interesting neighborhoods.

Several regional airlines fly nonstop from Miami to Key West; fares are about $120 to $300 round-trip. **American Eagle** (☎ 800/443-7300) and **US Airways Express** (☎ 800/428-4322) land at **Key West International Airport,** South Roosevelt Boulevard (☎ 305/296-5439), on the southeastern corner of the island.

Greyhound (☎ 800/231-2222) has buses leaving Miami for Key West every day. At press time, prices were $30 to $32 one-way and $57 to $60 round-trip. Seats fill up in season, so come early. The ride takes about 4½ hours.

GETTING AROUND   With limited parking, narrow streets, and congested traffic, driving in Old Town Key West is more of a pain than a convenience. Unless you're staying in one of the more remote accommodations, consider trading in the car for a bicycle. The island is small and as flat as a board, which makes it easy to negotiate, especially away from the crowded downtown. Many tourists also choose to cruise by moped, an option that can make navigating the streets risky, especially since there are no helmet laws in Key West. Spend the extra few bucks and rent a helmet; hundreds of visitors are seriously injured each year.

Rates for simple one-speed cruisers start at about $8 per day (from $40 per week). Mopeds start at about $12 for two hours, $25 per day and $100 per week. The best shops include **The Bicycle Center** at 523 Truman Ave. (☎ 305/ 294-4556); the **Moped Hospital,** 601 Truman Ave. (☎ 305/296-3344); and **Tropical Bicycles & Scooter Rentals** at 1300 Duval St. (☎ 305/294-8136). **The Bike Shop,** 1110 Truman Ave. (☎ 305/294-1073), rents mountain bikes for $15 per day ($75 per week). Cruisers go for $8 per day and $40 per week.

PARKING   Note that parking in Key West's Old Town is particularly limited. There is a well-placed **municipal parking lot** at Simonton and Angela streets just behind the firehouse and police station. If you have brought a car, you may want to stash it here while you enjoy the very walkable downtown section of Key West.

VISITOR INFORMATION   The **Florida Keys and Key West Visitors Bureau,** P.O. Box 1147, Key West, FL 33041 (☎ **800/FLA-KEYS**), offers a free vacation kit packed with visitor information. The **Key West Chamber of Commerce,** 402 Wall St., Key West, FL 33040 (☎ **800/527-8539** or 305/294-2587), also offers both general and specialized information. The lobby is open daily from 8:30am to 6pm; phones are answered from 8am to 8pm. The **Key West Visitors Center** also provides information on accommodations, goings-on, and restaurants; the number is ☎ **800/LAST-KEY.** It's open weekdays from 8am to 5:30pm and weekends from 8:30am to 5pm. Gay travelers will want to call the **Key West Business Guild** (☎ **305/294-4603**), which represents more than 50 guest houses and B&Bs in town, as well as many other gay-owned businesses. Ask for its color brochure. Or try **Good Times Travel** (☎ 305/294-0980), which will set up lodging and package tours on the island.

ORIENTATION   A mere 2-by-4-mile island, Key West is simple to navigate, even though there is no real order to the arrangement of streets and avenues. As you enter town on U.S. 1 (also called Roosevelt Boulevard), you will see most of the moderately priced chain hotels and fast-food restaurants. The better restaurants, shops, and outfitters are crammed onto Duval Street, the main thoroughfare of Key West's Old Town. On surrounding streets are the many inns and lodges in picturesque Victorian/Bahamian homes. On the southern side of the island is the coral beach area and some of the larger resort hotels.

The area called Bahama Village has only recently become known to tourists. With several cool restaurants and guesthouses opened over the years, this hippie-ish neighborhood, complete with street-roaming chickens and cats, is the most urban and rough you'll find in the Keys. You might see a few seedy drug dealings on street corners, but it's nothing to be overly concerned with. Resident business owners tend to keep a vigilant eye on the neighborhood. It looks worse than it is.

SEEING THE SIGHTS

Before shelling out big bucks for any of the dozens of worthwhile attractions in Key West, I recommend getting an overview on either of the two comprehensive island tours, **The Conch Train** or the **Old Town Trolley** (See "Organized Tours" below). There are simply too many attractions to list (including a Ripley's Believe it or Not! on Duval Street) and a number of historic houses. I've highlighted my favorites below but encourage you to seek out others.

✪ **Audubon House & Tropical Gardens.** 205 Whitehead St. (between Greene and Caroline sts.). ☎ **305/294-2116.** Admission $7.50 adults; $3.50 children 6–12. Daily 9:30am–5pm (last admission at 4:45pm). Discounts for students and AAA and AARP members.

This well-preserved home dating from the early 19th century stands as a prime example of early Key West architecture. Named after the renowned painter and bird expert, John James Audubon, who was said to have visited the house in 1832, the graceful two-story home is a peaceful retreat from the bustle of Old Town. Included in the price of admission is a self-guided audiotape tour that lasts about half an hour. With voices of several characters from the house's past, the tour never gets boring—although it is at times a bit hokey. See rare Audubon prints, gorgeous antiques, historical photos, and lush tropical gardens. Even if you don't want to spend the time and money to explore the grounds and home, check out the impressive gift shop, which sells a variety of fine mementos at reasonable prices.

Ernest Hemingway Home and Museum. 907 Whitehead St. (between Truman Ave. and Olivia St.). ☎ **305/294-1575** or 305/294-1136. Admission $7.50 adults; $4.50 children. Daily 9am–5pm. Free parking.

Hemingway's particularly handsome stone Spanish Colonial house, built in 1851, was one of the first on the island to be fitted with indoor plumbing and a built-in fireplace. The author lived here from 1928 until 1940, along with about 50 six-toed cats, whose descendants still roam the premises. It was during those years that the Nobel Prize winner wrote some of his most famous works, including "For Whom

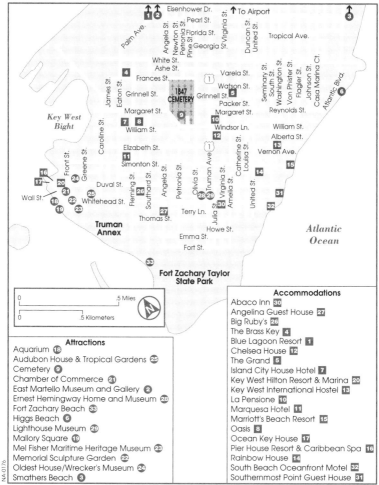

Eisenhower Dr.

↑ To Airport

Pearl St.
Palm Ave.
Angela St.
Newton St.
Petronia St.
Pine St.
Florida St.
Georgia St.
Virginia St.
Duncan St.
United St.

Tropical Ave.

White St.
Ashe St.
Frances St.

Varela St.
Watson St.

Seminary St.
South St.
Washington St.
Von Phister St.
Flagler St.
Johnson St.
Casa Marina Ct.
Atlantic Blvd.

James St.
Eaton St.
Grinnell St.

1847 CEMETERY

Grinnell St.
Packer St.

Margaret St.
Reynolds St.

Key West Bight

Margaret St.

Windsor Ln.

William St.
Alberta St.

Caroline St.

Elizabeth St.
Simonton St.

Vernon Ave.

Catherine St.
Louisa St.

Front St.
Greene St.

Duval St.

Angela St.
Petronia St.
Olivia St.
Truman Ave.
Virginia St.
Amelia St.
Julia St.

United St.

Wall St.

Whitehead St.
Fleming St.
Southard St.

Terry Ln.

Thomas St.

Truman Annex

Howe St.
Emma St.
Fort St.

Atlantic Ocean

Fort Zachary Taylor State Park

```
0                    .5 Miles
0                    .5 Kilometers
```

Attractions

Aquarium 18
Audubon House & Tropical Gardens 25
Cemetery 9
Chamber of Commerce 21
East Martello Museum and Gallery 2
Ernest Hemingway Home and Museum 28
Fort Zachary Beach 33
Higgs Beach 6
Lighthouse Museum 29
Mallory Square 19
Mel Fisher Maritime Heritage Museum 23
Memorial Sculpture Garden 22
Oldest House/Wrecker's Museum 24
Smathers Beach 3

Accommodations

Abaco Inn 30
Angelina Guest House 27
Big Ruby's 26
The Brass Key 4
Blue Lagoon Resort 1
Chelsea House 12
The Grand 5
Island City House Hotel 7
Key West Hilton Resort & Marina 20
Key West International Hostel 13
La Pensione 10
Marquesa Hotel 11
Marriott's Beach Resort 15
Oasis 8
Ocean Key House 17
Pier House Resort & Caribbean Spa 16
Rainbow House 14
South Beach Oceanfront Motel 32
Southernmost Point Guest House 31

the Bell Tolls," "A Farewell to Arms," and "The Snows of Kilimanjaro." Fans may want to take the optional half-hour tour. It's interesting and included in the price of admission.

Key West Cemetery. Entrance at Margaret and Angela sts. ☎ **305/294-WALK** for tour reservations. Free admission. Daily dawn to dusk.

This funky picturesque cemetery is the epitome of the quirky Key West image, as irreverent as it is humorous. Many tombs are stacked several high, condominium style—the rocky soil made digging 6 feet under nearly impossible for early settlers. Headstones reflect residents' lighthearted attitudes toward life and death. "I Told You I Was Sick" is one of the more famous epitaphs, as is the tongue-in-cheek widow's inscription "At Least I Know Where He's Sleeping Tonight."

East Martello Museum and Gallery. 3501 S. Roosevelt Blvd. ☎ **305/296-3913.** Admission $6 adults; $2 children 8–12; free for children 7 and under. Daily 9:30am–5pm (last admission is at 4pm).

Adjacent to the airport, the East Martello Museum is located in a Civil-War–era brick fort that itself is worth a visit. The museum contains a bizarre variety of exhibits that collectively do a thorough job interpreting the city's intriguing past. Historical artifacts include model ships, a deep-sea diver's wooden air pump, a crude raft from a Cuban "boat lift," a supposedly haunted doll, a Key West–style children's playhouse from 1918, and a horse-drawn hearse. Exhibits illustrate the Keys' history of salvaging, sponging, and cigar making. After seeing the galleries, climb a steep spiral staircase to the top of a lookout tower for good views over the island and ocean.

✪ **Key West Aquarium.** 1 Whitehead St. (at Mallory Square). ☎ **305/296-2051.** Admission $8 adults; $4 children 4–12; free for children under 4. Tickets are good for 2 consecutive days. Look for discount coupons from local hotels, at Duval St. kiosks, and from trolley and train tours. Daily 10am–6pm.

The oldest attraction on the island, the Key West Aquarium is a modest but fascinating exhibit. A long hallway of eye-level displays showcase dozens of varieties of fish and crustaceans. See delicate sea horses swaying in the backlit tanks. Kids can touch sea cucumbers and sea anemones in a shallow touch tank in the entryway. If you can, catch one of the free guided tours offered daily at 11am, 1pm, 3pm, and 4pm, when you can witness the dramatic feeding frenzy of the sharks, tarpon, barracudas, stingrays, and turtles. Tickets are good for 2 consecutive days, a bonus for kids with short attention spans.

Key West Lighthouse Museum. 938 Whitehead St. ☎ **305/294-0012.** Admission $6 adults; $2 children 7–12; free for children 6 and under. Daily 9:30am–5pm (last admission at 4:30pm).

When the Key West Lighthouse was opened in 1848, many locals mourned. Its bright warning to ships signaled the end of a profitable era for wreckers, pirate salvagers who looted reef-stricken ships. The story of this, and other Keys lighthouses, is illustrated in a small museum that was formerly the keeper's quarters. When radar and sonar made the lighthouse obsolete, it was opened to visitors as a tourist attraction. It's worth mustering the energy to climb the 88 claustrophobic steps to the top, where you'll be rewarded with magnificent panoramic views of Key West and the ocean.

Key West's Shipwreck Historeum. 1 Whitehead St. (at Mallory Square). ☎ **305/292-8990.** Admission $8 adults; $4 children 4–12. Shows daily every half hour from 9:45am–4:45pm.

You'll see more impressive artifacts at nearby Mel Fisher's museum, but the dramatic reenactments of the old shipwrecking days at this place are unique and entertaining. The interactive show is best for teens and adults and includes scenes starring Key West's wealthiest wrecker Asa Tift, plus lots of intriguing video clips and stories of the area's heyday.

✪ **Mel Fisher Maritime Heritage Museum.** 200 Greene St. ☎ **305/294-2633.** Admission $6.50 adults; $2 children 6–12; free for children 5 and under. Open daily 9:30am–5pm.

This museum honors local hero Mel Fisher, whose death in 1998 was mourned throughout South Florida, and who, along with a crew of other salvagers, found a multimillion-dollar treasure trove in 1985 aboard the wreck of the Spanish galleon *Nuestra Señora de Atocha*. The admission price is somewhat steep, but if you're into diving, pirates, and the mystery of sunken treasures, check out this small informative museum, full of doubloons, pieces of eight, emeralds, and solid-gold bars. A dated but informative film provides a good background of Fisher's incredible story.

Going, Going, Gone: Where to Catch the Famous Key West Sunset

A tradition in Key West, the Sunset Celebration can be relaxing or overwhelming, depending on your vantage point. If you're in town, you must check this ritual out at least once. Every evening, locals and visitors gather at the docks behind Mallory Square (at the westernmost end of Whitehead Street) to celebrate the day gone by. Secure a spot on the docks early to experience the carnival of portrait artists, acrobats, food vendors, and animal acts. In season the crowd can be overwhelming, especially when the cruise ships are in port.

Better yet, get a seat at the Hilton's **Sunset Deck** (☎ 305/294-4000), a luxurious bar on top of its restaurant at the intersection of Front and Greene streets. From the civilized calm of a casual bar, you can look down on the mayhem with a drink in hand.

Also near the Mallory-madness is the **Ocean Key House's bar.** This long open-air pier serves up drinks and okay bar food against a dramatic pink and yellow streaked sky. It's located at the very tip of Duval Street (☎ 800/328-9815 or 305/296-7701).

For the very best potent cocktails and great bar food on an outside patio or enclosed lounge, try **Pier House's Havana Docks** at 1 Duval St. (☎ 305/296-4600). There's usually live music and a lively gathering of visitors enjoying this island's bounty.

Memorial Sculpture Garden. Mallory Square between Whitehead and Wall sts. Free.

Installed in 1997, this impressive sculpture garden contains a large monument to the wreckers who made Key West rich more than a century ago. Also on display are 36 bronze busts of the island's most colorful leaders and characters. There's Pres. Harry Truman, Henry Flagler, and of course, Ernest Hemingway, all mounted on elegant coral columns.

Oldest House/Wrecker's Museum. 322 Duval St. ☎ **305/294-9502.** Admission $5 adults; $1 children 6–12; free for children 5 and under. Open daily 10am–4pm.

Dating from 1829, this old New England Bahama House has survived pirates, hurricanes, fires, warfare, and economic ups and downs and gives witness to a slower more easy time in the island's life. This 1½-story home was designed by a ship's carpenter and incorporates many features from maritime architecture including port holes and a ship's hatch designed for ventilation before the advent of air conditioning. Especially interesting is the detached kitchen building outfitted with a brick "beehive" oven and vintage cooking utensils. Though not a must-see on the Key West tour, history and architecture buffs will appreciate the finely preserved details.

ORGANIZED TOURS

BY TROLLEY-BUS & TRAM   Yes, it's more than a bit hokey to sit on this 60-foot tram of yellow cars, but it's worth it. The city's whole story is packed into a neat, 90-minute package on the **Conch Tour Train,** which covers the island and all its rich, raunchy history. Operating since 1958, the trains are open-air, which can make it uncomfortable in bad weather. The "train's" engine is a propane-powered

Jeep disguised as a locomotive. Tours depart from both Mallory Square and the Welcome Center, near where U.S. 1 becomes North Roosevelt Boulevard, on the other side of the island. For more information, contact the **Conch** at (☎ 305/294-5161). The cost is $18 for adults, $9 for children 4 to 12, and free for children 3 and under. Daily departures are every half hour from 9am to 4:30pm.

The **Old Town Trolley** is the choice in bad weather or if you are staying at one of the many hotels on its route. Humorous drivers maintain a running commentary as the enclosed tram loops around the island's streets past all the major sights. Trolleys depart from Mallory Square and other points around the island including many area hotels. For details, call (☎ **305/296-6688**). Tours are $18 for adults, $9 for children 4 to 12, and free for children 3 and under. Departures are daily every half hour (though not always on the hour or half hour) from 9am to 4:45pm. One or the other, these historic trivia-packed tours are well worth the price of admission.

BY AIR   Proclaimed by the mayor as "the official air force of the Conch Republic," **Island Airplane Tours,** at Key West Airport, 3469 S. Roosevelt Blvd. (☎ **305/294-8687** for reservations), offers windy rides in its open-cockpit 1940 Waco biplanes over the reefs and around the islands. Thrill seekers—and they only—will also enjoy a spin in the company's S2-B aerobatics airplane that does loops, rolls, and sideways figure-eights. Company owner Fred Cabanas was "decorated" in 1991, after he spotted a Cuban airman defecting to the United States in a Russian-built MiG fighter. Sightseeing flights cost $50 to $200, depending on the duration.

BY BOAT   The Pride of Key West, *Fireball,* at Zero Duval St. (☎ **305/296-6293;** fax 305/294-8704), is a 58-foot glass-bottomed catamaran that goes on both day and evening coral-reef tours and sunset cruises. Reef trips cost $20 per person; sunset cruises are $25 per person and include snacks, sodas, and a glass of champagne.

The Wolf, at Schooner Wharf, Key West Seaport (☎ **305/296-9653;** fax 305/294-8388), is a 44-passenger topsail schooner, equipped with a cannon, that sets sail daily for daytime and sunset cruises around the Keys. Key West Seaport is located at the end of Greene Street. Day tours cost $25 per person; sunset sails cost $30 per person and include champagne, wine, beer, soda, and live music.

OTHER TOURS   For a lively look at Key West, try a 2-hour tour of the island's five **most famous pubs.** It starts daily at 2:30pm, lasts 1½ hours, costs $21, and includes four drinks. Another fun tour, for those interested in the paranormal, is the **nightly ghost tour.** Cost is $18 for adults and $10 for children. This spooky and interesting tour gives participants insight into the many old island legends. Both tours are offered by Key West Tour Association. A new tour begun in 1998 is a cemetery tour, which leaves daily at 10:30am (☎ **305/294-WALK**).

OUTDOOR PURSUITS

BICYCLING & MOPEDING   A popular mode of transportation for locals and visitors, bikes and mopeds are available at many rental outlets in the city (see "Getting Around," above). Escape the hectic downtown scene and explore the island's scenic side streets. Head away from Duval Street to South Roosevelt Boulevard and the beachside enclaves along the way.

BEACHES   Unlike the rest of the Keys, you'll actually find a few small beaches here, although they don't compare to the state's wide natural wonders up the coast. Here are your options: **Smathers Beach,** off South Roosevelt Boulevard west of the airport; **Higgs Beach,** along Atlantic Boulevard between White Street and

Reynolds Road; and **Fort Zachary Beach,** located off the western end of Southard Boulevard.

Although there is an entrance fee ($3.75 per car, plus more for each passenger), I recommend Fort Zachary, since it also includes a great historical fort, a Civil War museum, and a large picnic area with tables, barbecue grills, bathrooms, and showers. Plus, large trees scattered across 87 acres provide shade for those who are reluctant to bake in the sun. The vulnerable point was damaged in Hurricane Georges in 1998 but replanting of native vegetation has made it even better than before. A narrow rocky beach is typical of the Key's beaches.

DIVING   One of the area's largest scuba schools, **Dive Key West Inc.,** 3128 N. Roosevelt Blvd. (☎ **800/426-0707** or 305/296-3823; fax 305/296-0609; www.divekeywest.com; e-mail: divekeywest@flakeysol.com;), offers instruction on all levels. Its dive boats take participants to scuba and snorkel sites on nearby reefs.

Wreck dives and night dives are two of the special offerings of **Lost Reef Adventures,** 261 Margaret St. (☎ **800/952-2749** or 305/296-9737). Regularly scheduled runs and private charters can be arranged. Phone for departure information.

FISHING   As any angler will tell you, there's no fishing like Keys fishing. Key West has it all: bonefish, tarpon, dolphin, tuna, grouper, cobia, and more. Sharks, too. When it comes to fishing, this is it.

Step aboard a small exposed skiff for an incredibly diverse day of fishing. In the morning, you can head offshore for sailfish or dolphin (the fish, not the mammal), and then by afternoon, get closer to land for a shot at tarpon, permit, grouper, or snapper. Here in Key West, you can probably pick up more cobia—one of the best fighting and eating fishes around—than anywhere else in the world. For a real fight, ask your skipper to go for the tarpon—the greatest fighting fish there is, famous for its dramatic "tail walk" on the water after it's hooked. Shark fishing is also popular.

You'll find plenty of competition among the charter fishing boats in and around Mallory Square. However, you should know that the bookers from the kiosks in town generally take 20% of a captain's fee in addition to an extra monthly fee. So you can usually save yourself money by booking directly with a captain or going straight to one of the docks. You can negotiate a good deal at **Charter Boat Row,** 1801 N. Roosevelt Ave. (across from the Shell station), home to more than 30 charter fishing and party boats. Just show up to arrange your outing, or call **Garrison Bite Marina** (☎ **305/292-8167**) for details.

The advantage of the smaller, more expensive charter boats is that you can call the shots. They'll take you where you want to go, to fish for what you want to catch. These "light tackles" are also easier to maneuver, which means you can go to backcountry spots for tarpon and bonefish, as well as out to the open ocean for tuna and dolphin. You'll really be able to feel the fish, and you'll get some good fights. Larger boats, for up to six or seven people, are cheaper and best for kingfish, billfish, and sailfish. Consider Jim Brienza's 27-foot *Sea Breeze,* docked at 25 Arbutus Dr. (☎ **305/294-6027**), if you want a light tackle experience. For a larger boat, try Capt. Henry Otto's 44-foot *Sunday,* docked at the Hyatt in Key West (☎ **305/294-7052**).

The huge commercial party boats are more for sightseeing than serious angling, though you can get lucky and get a few bites at one of the fishing holes. One especially good deal is the *Gulfstream III* (☎ **305/296-8494**), an all-day charter that goes out daily from 9:30am until 4pm. You'll pay $30, plus $3 for a rod and reel. This 65-foot party boat usually has at least 30 other anglers. Bring your own cooler or buy snacks on the boat. Beer and wine are allowed.

For serious anglers, nothing compares to the light tackle boats that leave from **Oceanside Marina** (☎ 305/294-4676) in Stock Island, at 5950 Peninsula Avenue, 1½ miles off U.S. 1. It's a 20-minute drive from Old Town on the Atlantic side. There are more than 30 light tackle guides, which range from flatbed, back-country skiffs to 28-foot open boats. There are also a few larger charters and a head or party boat that goes to the Dry Tortugas. Call the dockmaster for details.

For the light tackle experience of your life, call **Captain Bruce Cronin** at ☎ 305/294-4929 or **Captain Kenny Harris** at ☎ 305/294-8843, two of the more famous (and pricey) captains still working these docks. You'll pay from $550 for a full day, usually about 8am until 4pm, and from $400 for a half day.

GOLF One of the area's only courses is **Key West Golf Club** (☎ 305/294-5232), an 18-hole course located just north of the island of Key West at MM 4.5 (turn onto College Road to the course entrance). Designed by Rees Jones, the course has plenty of mangroves and water hazards on its 6,526 yards. It's open to the public and has a new pro shop. Call ahead for tee-time reservations.

KAYAKING **Mosquito Coast Outfitters,** housed in a woodsy wine bar at 1017 Duval St. (☎ 305/294-7178), operates a first-rate kayaking and snorkeling tour every day as long as the weather is mild. The tours depart at 9am sharp and cost $45 per person. Included in the price are snacks, soft drinks, and a guided tour of the mangrove-studded islands of Sugar Key or Geiger Key just north of Key West. You'll be back by about 3pm.

SHOPPING

You'll find all kinds of unique gifts and souvenirs in Key West, from coconut post-cards to Key Lime pies. On Duval Street, T-shirt shops outnumber almost any other business. If you must get a wearable memento, be careful of unscrupulous sales-people. Despite efforts to curtail the practice, many shops have been known to rip off unwitting shoppers. It pays to check the prices and the exchange rate before signing any sales slips. You are entitled to a written estimate of any T-shirt work before you pay for it.

At Mallory Square is the **Clinton Street Market,** an overair-conditioned mall of kiosks and stalls designed for the many cruise-ship passengers who never venture beyond this supercommercial zone. Amid the dreck are some delicious coffee and candy shops and some high-priced hats and shoes. There's also a free and clean rest room.

Once the main industry of Key West, cigar making is enjoying renewed success at the handful of factories that survived the slow years. Stroll through **"Cigar Alley,"** between Front and Greene streets, where you will find *viejitos* (little old men) rolling fat stogies just as they used to do in their homeland across the Florida Straits. Stop at the **Key West Cigar Factory,** at 308 Front St. (☎ 305/294-3470), for an excellent selection of imported and locally rolled smokes, including the famous El Hemingway. Remember, buying or selling Cuban-made cigars is illegal. Shops advertising "Cuban Cigars" are usually referring to domestic cigars made from tobacco grown from seeds that were brought from Cuba decades ago.

If you are looking for local or Caribbean art, you will find nearly a dozen galleries and shops clustered on Duval Street between Catherine and Fleming streets. You'll also find some excellent shops scattered on the side streets. One worth seeking out is the ✪ **Haitian Art Co.,** 600 Frances St. (☎ 305/296-8932), where you can browse through room upon room of original paintings from well-known and obscure Haitian artists in a range of prices from a few dollars to a few thousand.

Also, check out **Cuba, Cuba!** at 814 Duval St. (☎ **305/295-9442**). Here, you will find paintings, sculpture, and photos by Cuban artists and books and art from the island.

A favorite stop in the Keys is the deliciously fragrant **Key West Aloe** at 524 Front St., between Simonton and Duval streets (☎ **305/294-5592**). Since 1971, this shop has been selling a simple line of bath products, including lotions, shampoos, and soothing balms for those who want a reminder of the tropical breezes once home. At the main shop (open until 8pm), you can find great gift baskets, tropical perfumes, and candies and cookies, too. In addition to frangipani, vanilla, and hibiscus scents, sample Key West for Men, a unique and alluringly musky best-seller.

Literature and music buffs will appreciate the many bookshops and record stores on the island. **Key West Island Bookstore** (☎ **305/294-2904**) at 513 Fleming St. carries new, used, and rare books and specializes in fiction by residents of the Keys, including Hemingway, Tennessee Williams, Shel Silverstein, Ann Beattie, Richard Wilbur, and John Hersey. **Flaming Maggie's** (☎ **305/294-3931**) at 830 Fleming St. carries a wide selection of gay books. Both shops are open daily.

New in 1999 is the combination museum and gift shop called **Reworx** just behind Pandemonium and the mosaic car at 825 Duval St. (☎ **305/295-0325** or 305/294-0351). Mammoth functional art made from salvaged metal parts is on display and smaller works from recycled material are on sale. Admission to the adjacent museum is $7 for adults and $5 for children aged 5–12 and well worth it.

Also worth checking out in the newly revitalized Bahama Village section of town are the shops along Petronia Street between Thomas and Whitehead streets. Especially interesting is **Maskerville** (☎ **305/293-6937**), which sells a variety of feather-laden art work from masks to lampshades. Just next door is **Hello Gorgeous,** at 315 Petronia (☎ **305/294-1770**), which carries unique clothing, shoes, and jewelry for women and impersonators.

Off the beaten track at 814 Fleming St. (☎ **305/294-7901**) is the **Helio Gallery Store,** featuring locally made crafts and fine art.

For anything else, from bed linens to candlesticks to clothing, go to downtown's oldest and most renowned department store, **Fast Buck Freddie's,** at 500 Duval St. (☎ **305/294-2007**). For the same merchandise at reduced prices, try ✪ **Half Buck Freddie's,** 726 Caroline St. (☎ **305/294-6799**). Here you can shop for out-of-season bargains and "rejects" from the main store.

WHERE TO STAY

You'll find a wide variety of places to stay in Key West, from resorts with all the amenities to seaside motels, quaint bed-and-breakfasts, and clothing-optional guest houses. Unless you're in town during Key West's most popular holidays—Fantasy Fest (around Halloween), Hemingway Days (in July), and Christmas and New Year's—or for a big fishing tournament (many are held from October to December), you can almost always find a place to stay at the last minute. However, you may want to book early, especially in the winter, when prime properties fill up and many require 2- or 3-night minimums. Prices at these times are also extremely high. Finding a decent room for under $100 a night is a real trick.

If all my suggestions are booked, try **Vacation Key West** (☎ **800/595-5397** or 305/295-9500; www.flakeysol.com/vkw). The phones are answered weekdays from 9am to 6pm and Saturday from 11am to 2pm. This wholesaler offers discounts of 20% to 30% and can usually find last-minute deals. They represent mostly larger hotels and motels but also can place visitors in guest houses. The **Key West**

Innkeepers Association, P.O. Box 6172, Key West, FL 33041 (☎ **800/ 492-1911** or 305/292-3600), can also help find lodging in any price range from its dozens of members and affiliates.

Most major hotel chains have at least one location in Key West; most are clustered on North Roosevelt Boulevard (U.S. 1). Moderately priced options include **Howard Johnson**, 3031 N. Roosevelt Blvd. (☎ **800/942-0913** or 305/296-6595); the **Ramada Inn,** 3420 N. Roosevelt Blvd. (☎ **800/330-5541** or 305/294-5541); the **Econo Lodge,** 3820 N. Roosevelt Blvd. (☎ **800/553-2666** or 305294-5511); the **Holiday Inn Beachside,** 3841 N. Roosevelt Blvd. (☎ **800/ 292-7706** or 305/294-2571); and the **Quality Inn,** 3850 N. Roosevelt Blvd. (☎ **800/228-5151** or 305/294-6681). The Howard Johnson and the Holiday Inn are the only hotels with gulf-view rooms; the other hotels listed are just across the street. Duval Street is less than 5 minutes away by car or taxi.

A last resort should be the **Holiday Inn La Concha Hotel** at 430 Duval St. (☎ **800/745-2191**). It is centrally located, but rates are high for the mediocre rooms and rude service (from $160 in season). Also, do your best to avoid the **Best Western Hibiscus Hotel,** at 1313 Simonton St. The property is in bad shape, management is rude, and prices are high.

Gay travelers will want to call the **Key West Business Guild** (☎ **305/ 294-4603**), which represents more than 50 guest houses and B&Bs in town, as well as many other gay-owned businesses. Be advised that most gay guest houses have a clothing-optional policy. One of the most elegant and popular ones is **Big Ruby's** (☎ **800/477-7829** or 305/296-2323) at 409 Applerouth Lane (a little alley just off Duval Street). A low cluster of buildings surrounds a lushly landscaped courtyard where a hearty breakfast is served each morning and wine is poured at dusk. The mostly male guests hang out by a good-sized pool tanning in the buff. Also popular is **Oasis** at 823 Fleming St. (☎ **305/296-2131**), which is superclean and friendly, and you can enjoy the central location and a 14-seat hot tub.

Another luxurious property is **The Brass Key** at 412 Frances St. (☎ **305/ 296-4719**), which is more romantic and traditionally decorated and welcomes many lesbian travelers as well. *Out and About* gave it a five-star rating. For women only, the **Rainbow House,** 525 United St. (☎ **800/74-WOMYN** or 305/ 292-1450) is a large, fairly well-maintained guest house with lots of privacy and amenities, including two pools and two hot tubs. Rates in season range from $109 to $229.

VERY EXPENSIVE

✪ **Key West Hilton Resort and Marina.** 245 Front St. (at the end of Duval St.), Key West, FL 33040. ☎ **800/221-2424** or 305/294-4000. Fax 305/294-4086. 215 units. A/C MINIBAR TV TEL. Winter $259–$475 double; $325–$750 suite. Off-season $169–$375 double; $250–$750 suite. 37 Sunset Key Cottages, up to 4 people: winter $870–$1395; off-season $670–$925. AE, DC, DISC, MC, V.

Completed in fall 1996, this Hilton is a truly luxurious addition to downtown's hotel scene. Key West's only full-service AAA four-diamond resort is situated at the very end of Duval Street in the middle of all of Old Town's action. The sparkling new rooms are large and well appointed, with tropical decor and all the modern conveniences. Choose a suite in the main building if you want a large Jacuzzi in your living room. Otherwise, the marina building has great views. This giant will no doubt be very popular with corporate and convention visitors.

Dining/Diversions: Flagler's, the elegant indoor dining room offers ample breakfasts and a huge Sunday brunch. Lunches and dinners focus on steak and seafood. The more casual beachside tiki hut specializes in frozen drinks but also serves sandwiches, fish and chips and hearty snacks.

Amenities: Concierge, room service, laundry and dry-cleaning services, newspaper delivery, in-room massage, nightly turndown, twice-daily maid service, express checkout, valet parking, complimentary in-room coffee, secretarial services. Outdoor heated pool, offshore secluded beach, health club, Jacuzzi, sundeck, watersports equipment, full-service marina, bicycle rental, game room, business center, self-service laundry, conference rooms, gift shops, and boutiques.

Marriott's Reach Resort. 1435 Simonton St., Key West, FL 33040. ☎ **800/874-4118** or 305/296-5000. Fax 305/296-2830. 149 units. A/C MINIBAR TV TEL. Winter $309–$419 double. Off-season $170–$310 double. AE, CB, DC, DISC, MC, V. Valet parking $9.

The Reach is one of the few hotels on the island with its own strip of sandy beach. The location here can be either a highlight or a drawback; it's a 15-minute walk away from the center of the Duval Street action. Supported by stilts that leave the entire ground floor for car parking, the hotel offers four floors of rooms designed around atriums. The wonderful guest rooms are large and feature tile floors, sturdy wicker furnishings, and tropical colors. Each contains a small service bar with a sink, fridge, and tea/coffeemaker, and has a vanity area separate from the bathroom. The rooms are so nice you can easily forgive the small closets and diminutive dressers. All have sliding glass doors that open onto balconies, and some have ocean views.

Ample palm-planted grounds surround a small pool area. There's also a private pier for fishing and suntanning. The protected waters are tame and shallow.

Amenities: Concierge, room service, dry cleaning, newspaper delivery, in-room massage, baby-sitting, express checkout. Outdoor heated swimming pool, beach, health spa, Jacuzzi, sauna, bicycle rental, business center, tour desk, conference rooms, sailboats, Windsurfers, beauty salon.

✪ **Pier House Resort and Caribbean Spa.** 1 Duval St. (near Mallory Docks), Key West, FL 33040. ☎ **800/327-8340** or 305/296-4600. Fax 305/296-9085. 142 units. A/C MINIBAR TV TEL. Winter $280–$450 double; $450–$895 suite. Off-season $195–$350 double; $325–$645 suite. AE, CB, DC, DISC, MC, V.

Pier House is one of the area's best resort choices, offering luxurious rooms, top-notch service, and even a full-service spa. Its excellent location—at the foot of Duval Street and just steps from Mallory Docks—is the envy of every hotel on the island. Set back from the busy street, on a short strip of beach, this hotel is a welcome oasis of calm. The accommodations here vary tremendously, from relatively simple business-style rooms to romantic guest quarters complete with integrated stereo systems and whirlpool tubs. Their best waterfront suites and rooms have recently been renovated. Although every accommodation has either a balcony or a patio, not all overlook the water. My favorites, in the two-story spa building, don't have any view at all. But what they lack in scenery, they make up for in opulence; each well-appointed spa room has a sitting area and a huge Jacuzzi bathroom.

Dining/Diversions: The restaurant serves very respectable meals in a dark dining room or on an umbrella-covered patio overlooking the docks. Old Havana Docks is a good waterfront bar, especially at sunset.

Amenities: Concierge, room service, laundry services, newspaper delivery, in-room massage, express checkout. Heated swimming pool, beach, health club, spa treatments, two Jacuzzis, sauna, sundeck, water-sports equipment rentals, bicycle rental, tour desk, conference rooms, beauty salon.

EXPENSIVE

Island City House Hotel. 411 William St., Key West, FL 33040. ☎ **800/634-8230** or 305/294-5702. Fax 305/294-1289. 24 units. A/C TV TEL. Winter $165 studio; $195–$225 one-bedroom suite; $255–$285 two-bedroom suite. Off-season $95 studio; $125–$155 one-bedroom suite; $165–$190 two-bedroom suite. Rates include breakfast. AE, CB, DC, DISC, MC, V.

A small resort unto itself, the Island City House consists of three separate unique buildings that share a common junglelike patio and pool. The first building, unimaginatively called the Island City House building, is a historic three-story wooden structure with wraparound verandas that allow guests to walk around the entire edifice on any floor. The warmly dressed old-fashioned interiors here include wood floors and many antique furnishings. Many rooms have full-size kitchens, queen-size beds, and sumptuous floral window treatments. The tile bathrooms could use more counter space, and the room lighting isn't always perfect, but eccentricities are part of this hotel's charm.

The unpainted wooden Cigar House has particularly large bedrooms similar in ambience to those in the Island City House. Most rooms are furnished with wicker chairs and king-size beds and have big bathrooms (although lacking in counter space). As with the Island City House, rooms facing the property's interior courtyard are best. The Arch House is the least appealing of the three buildings, but still very recommendable. Built of Dade County pine, the Arch House's cozy bedrooms are furnished in wicker and rattan and come with small kitchens and baths.

Amenities: Newspaper delivery, free coffee in lobby, dry cleaning, laundry service, in-room massage, baby-sitting. Kitchenettes, VCR rental and complimentary videos, outdoor heated pool, Jacuzzi, bicycle rental, sundeck, self-service Laundromat.

✪ **Marquesa Hotel.** 600 Fleming St. (at Simonton St.), Key West, FL 33040. ☎ **800/869-4631** or 305/292-1919. Fax 305/294-2121. 27 units. A/C MINIBAR TV TEL. Winter $240–$360 double. Off-season $150–$255 double. No children under 12 allowed. AE, DC, MC, V.

One of my very favorite properties, the Marquesa offers all the charm of a small historic hotel with the amenities of a large resort. It encompasses four different buildings, two adjacent swimming pools, and a three-stage waterfall that cascades into a lily pond. Two of the hotel's houses are luxuriously restored Victorian homes with rooms outfitted with extraplush antiques and oversize contemporary furniture. The rooms in the two other, newly constructed buildings are even richer; many have four-poster wrought-iron beds with bright floral spreads. The green marble bathrooms are lush and spacious. The decor is simple, elegant, and spotless. These are the only hotel rooms I have ever seen that I would like my home to resemble.

Dining: One of Key West's most elegant and recommendable restaurants, The Cafe Marquesa serves only dinner. However, you can order breakfast to your room or poolside.

Amenities: Concierge, valet, newspaper delivery, twice-daily maid service, valet parking. Two outdoor swimming pools (one is heated), access to nearby health club.

Ocean Key House. Zero Duval St., Key West, FL 33040. ☎ **800/328-9815** or 305/296-7701. Fax 305/292-7685. www.oceankeyhouse.com. 96 units. A/C MINIBAR TV TEL. Winter from $160 double; $340–$525 one-bedroom suite; $420–$700 two-bedroom suite. Off-season $135 double; $225–$495 one-bedroom suite; $320–$600 two-bedroom suite. AE, CB, DC, DISC, MC, V.

You can't get much more central than this modern hotel, located across from the Pier House at the foot of Duval Street. Still, for the same price as the best rooms, you may do better at one of the more intimate accommodations, such as the Marquesa or the Pier House. Most of the guest rooms here are suites, ample-sized accommodations fitted with built-in couches. Many rooms have sliding glass doors that open onto small balconies, some of which enjoy unobstructed water views. All suites have Jacuzzi tubs in either the master bedroom or living room. The standard guest rooms are much less desirable. They are small and dark and have no views.

Dining: A casual dockside grill serves lunch and dinner. Breakfast is served at an indoor/outdoor cafe.

Amenities: Concierge, room service, dry-cleaning and laundry services. VCRs and video rentals, outdoor heated pool, access to nearby health club, Jacuzzi in every suite, conference rooms, sundeck, water-sports concession, tour desk.

MODERATE

Chelsea House. 707 Truman Ave., Key West, FL 33040. ☎ **800/845-8859** or 305/296-2211. Fax 305/296-4822. 20 units. A/C TV TEL. Winter $125–$205 double; $360 apt. Off-season $75–$125 double; $250 apt. Rates include breakfast. Pets $10 extra. AE, CB, DC, DISC, MC, V.

Despite its decidedly English name, the Chelsea House is "all American," a term that in Key West isn't code for "conservative." Chelsea House caters to a mixed gay/straight clientele and displays its liberal philosophy most prominently on the clothing-optional sundeck. One of only a few guest houses in Key West that offers TVs, VCRs, private bathrooms, and kitchenettes in each guest room, Chelsea House has a large number of repeat visitors. The apartments come with full kitchens and separate living areas, as well as palm-shaded balconies in back. The bathrooms and closets could be bigger, but both are adequate and serviceable.

When weather permits, which is almost always, breakfast is served outside by the pool. There is private parking. *Important note:* Children 14 and under are not accepted.

✪ **La Pensione.** 809 Truman Ave. (between Windsor and Margaret sts.), Key West, FL 33040. ☎ **800/893-1193** or 305/292-9923. Fax 305/296-6509. 9 units. A/C TEL. Winter from $158 double with Frommer's discount. Off-season from $98 double with Frommer's discount. Rates include breakfast and represent a 10% discount for readers who mention this guide. AE, DC, DISC, JCB, MC, V.

This classic bed-and-breakfast in the 1891 home of a former cigar executive distinguishes itself from other similar inns by its extreme attention to details. The friendly knowledgeable staff treat the stunning home and the guests with extraordinary care. The comfortable rooms all have air-conditioning, ceiling fans, king-size beds, and private bathrooms. Many have French doors opening onto spacious verandas. Although the rooms have no phones or televisions, the distractions of Duval Street, only steps away, should keep you adequately occupied during your visit. Breakfast, which includes made-to-order Belgian waffles, fresh fruit, and a variety of breads or muffins, can be taken on the wraparound porch or at the communal dining table. No children are allowed.

South Beach Oceanfront Motel. 508 South St. (at the Atlantic Ocean), Key West, FL 33040. ☎ **800/354-4455** or 305/296-5611. Fax 305/294-8272. 50 units. A/C TV TEL. Winter $105–$199 double. Off-season $69–$140 double. AE, MC, V.

This standard two-story motel is located directly on the ocean, within walking distance of Duval Street. Because the structure is perpendicular to the water, most of the rooms overlook a pretty Olympic-size swimming pool rather than a wide swath of beach. The best, and by far most expensive, are the lucky pair of beachfront rooms on the end (nos. 115 and 215).

All rooms share similar aging decor and include standard furnishings. The smallish bathrooms could use a makeover, and include showers but no tubs. There's a private pier, an on-site water-sports concession, and a laundry room available for guest use. When making reservations, ask for a room that's as close to the beach (and as far from the road) as possible. If you'll be there a while, ask for one of the rooms with a kitchenette; there is no restaurant on the premises.

Southernmost Point Guest House. 1327 Duval St., Key West, FL 33040. ☎ **305/294-0715.** Fax 305/296-0641. 6 units. A/C TV TEL. Winter $95–$200 double; $150 suite. Off-season $55–$135 double; $95 suite. Rates include breakfast. AE, MC, V.

One of the only inns that actually welcomes children and pets, this romantic and historic guest house is a real find. The antiseptically clean rooms are not as fancy as the house's ornate 1885 exterior. Each room has basic beds and couches and a hodgepodge of furnishings, including futon couches, high-back wicker chairs, and plenty of mismatched throw rugs. Each room is different. Room 5 is best; situated upstairs, it has a private porch, an ocean view, and windows that let in lots of light. Every room has a refrigerator and a full decanter of sherry. Mona Santiago, the hotel's kind, laid-back owner, provides chairs and towels that can be brought to the beach, which is just a block away. Plus, guests can help themselves to wine as they soak in the new 14-seat hot tub. Kids will enjoy the swings in the backyard and pet rabbits.

INEXPENSIVE

Abaco Inn. 415 Julia St. (between Truman Ave. and Virginia St.), Key West, FL 33040. ☎ **800/358-6307** or 305/296-2212. Fax 305/ 295-0349. www.abaco-inn.com. E-mail: stay@abaco-inn.com. 3 units. A/C TV TEL. Winter from $99 double. Off-season from $59 double. Three-day minimum stay in season. Additional person $15 extra. AE, DISC, MC, V.

This tidy little guest house is situated on a secluded lane just off Duval Street. Though there is no pool or view, you'll find a hair dryer, iron and ironing board, small refrigerator, microwave, and coffeemaker in each of the three simple rooms. Once the home of a cigar maker, the house dates from the early 1900s. Now, it is owned and operated by George Fontana, a friendly and knowledgeable tour guide and writer. Look for his column on local characters in the *Key West Citizen.* You can't beat the price in this superconvenient location. No smoking is allowed on the property.

Angelina Guest House. 302 Angela St. (at the corner of Thomas St.) Key West, FL 33040. ☎ **888/874-7326** or 305/294-4480. Fax 305/294-0621. E-mail: info@dolphintrvl.com. 15 units, 11 with bathroom (showers only). Winter $65–$70 double without bathroom; $79–$150 double with bathroom; suite $175 for up to six people. Off-season $39–$49 double without bathroom; $49–$79 double with bathroom; $95–$125 studio with kitchenette for up to six people. DISC, MC, V.

This youth hostel–looking guest house is well run by a bright-eyed refugee of Chicago's cold and long-time Keys resident, Robbie Byer. His two historic buildings in the middle of Bahama Village are about the cheapest in town and are conveniently located near a hot, hippie restaurant called Blue Heaven (see "Where to Dine," below) and also in a neighborhood known for occasional drug busts. Still, it is generally safe and full of character. The rooms are all furnished differently in a modest style. There are no televisions or telephones since Robbie believes guests should be out exploring Key West, and not sitting in their rooms. "I don't even put chairs in the rooms," he says. "I've even considered confiscating cell phones and beepers." Only six of the 15 rooms have air-conditioning, a real consideration in the sweltering summer days. A good cross breeze and ceiling fans do cool the rooms considerably. Though sparse, the Angelina is a good place to crash if you are on the cheap.

Blue Lagoon Resort. 3101 N. Roosevelt Blvd., Key West, FL 33040-4118. ☎ **305/ 296-1043.** Fax 305/296-6499. 72 units. A/C TV TEL. Winter $80–$240 double. Off-season $50–$110 double. MC, V.

More than half of the rooms at this funky ocean-side resort rent for less than $100 year-round—an all too unusual occurrence in Key West, especially for full-service resorts. The rooms, furnished in heavy cedar wood, are basic and a bit run-down but still decent—along the lines of a Howard Johnson or other budget accommo-dation. Second-floor rooms are generally quieter. The pricier waterfront rooms aren't really worth the extra money (although some include a jet-ski ride). Guests tend to be young college-aged kids out for a wild time. Although pretty far from Old Town, the resort is convenient by scooter and car, and it is literally surrounded by Wave Runners, boats, parasailing, and diving fun.

✪ **The Grand.** 1116 Grinnell St. (between Virginia and Catherine sts.), Key West, FL 33040. ☎ **888/947-2630** or 305/294-0590. E-mail: thegrand@flakeysol.com. 10 units. A/C TV TEL. Winter $79–$99 double; $121 suite. Off-season $39–$59 double; $79 suite. AE, DISC, MC, V.

Don't expect cabbies or locals to know about this gem. Opened in 1997, this guest house wasn't even properly listed in the phone book its first or second year. Lucky for you! It's got most everything you could want, including a very moderate price tag. It's run by another one of those happy-to-be-alive Northeastern transplants, Elizabeth Rose, who goes out of her way to provide any and all services for her appreciative guests. All rooms have private bathrooms, air-conditioning, tele-phones, and private entrances. The floors are painted in bright colors, and beds are dressed in light tropical prints. Room no. 2 on the back side of the house is the best deal; it's small, but it has a porch and the most privacy. Suites are a real steal, too. The large two-room units come with a complete kitchen. The house is in a modest residential section of Old Town, only about 5 blocks from Duval Street. This place is undoubtedly the best bargain in town.

Key West International Hostel. 718 South St., Key West, FL 33040. ☎ **800/51-HOSTEL** or 305/296-5719. Fax 305/296-0672. 100 units. A/C TV. Winter $17 for IYHF members, $20 for nonmembers dorm beds; $75–$105 motel units. Off-season from $15 for IYHF members, from $18 for nonmembers dorm beds; $50–$85 motel units. MC, V.

This well-run hostel is a 3-minute walk to the beach and to Old Town. It's not the Ritz, but it's affordable. Very busy with European backpackers, this is a great place to meet people. The dorm rooms are dark and sparse, but clean enough. The higher-priced motel rooms are a good deal, especially those equipped with full kitchens. Facilities include a pool table under a tiki-hut roof and bicycle rentals for $6 per day. There is also cheap food available for breakfast, lunch, and dinner. As in all community living arrangements, you'll want to watch your valuables; there are minisafes in each room.

WHERE TO DINE

Key West offers a vast, tempting array of food. You'll find many cuisines repre-sented: Thai, Cuban, Bahamian, Japanese, and barbecue. Plus, there are the usual drive-through fast-food franchises (mostly up on Roosevelt Boulevard). Duval Street even succumbed to the lure of a Hard Rock Cafe. Wander Old Town or the newly spruced up Bahama Village and browse menus after you have exhausted the list of my picks below.

If you don't feel like venturing out, call **We Deliver** (☎ **305/293-0078**), a service that for a small fee (between $3 and $6) will bring you anything you want from any of the area's restaurants or stores. We Deliver operates between 3 and 11pm. If you are staying in a condo or efficiency you may want to stock your fridge with groceries, beer, wine, and snacks from the area's oldest grocer, **Fausto's Food Palace.** Open since 1926, there are now two locations: 1105 White St. and 522 Fleming St. The Fleming Street location will deliver (☎ 305/294-5221 or 305/296-5663). Fausto's has a $25 minimum.

VERY EXPENSIVE

Cafe des Artistes. 1007 Simonton St. (near Truman Ave.). ☎ **305/294-7100.** Reservations recommended. Main courses $23–$39. AE, MC, V. Daily 6–11pm. FRENCH.

Open for nearly 2 decades, the Cafe des Artistes's impressive longevity is the result of its winning combination of food and atmosphere. Traditional French meals benefit from a subtle tropical twist. The food is served by uniformed waiters well versed in the virtues of fine food. Start with the duck-liver pâté made with fresh truffles and old cognac, or Maryland crabmeat served with an artichoke heart and herbed tomato confit. Nouvelle and traditional French entrees include lobster flambé with mango and basil and wine-basted lamb chops rubbed with rosemary and ginger.

Louie's Backyard. 700 Waddell Ave. ☎ **305/294-1061.** Reservations highly recommended. Main courses $25–$30; lunch $8–$15. AE, CB, DC, MC, V. Daily 11:30am–3pm and 6–10:30pm. CARIBBEAN CONTEMPORARY.

Louie's, once known as Key West's most elegant restaurant, has lost its luster. Its location, nestled amid blooming bougainvillea on a lush slice of the Gulf, remains one of the most romantic on earth. Unfortunately, the gorgeous real estate doesn't improve the uneven food, sluggish service, and sometimes snooty attitude. Try the weekend brunches, which tend to be more reliable than dinners, or, to be assured of a good time, you may just want to sit at the dockside bar and enjoy a cocktail at sunset.

EXPENSIVE

Antonia's. 615 Duval St. ☎ **305/294-6565.** Reservations suggested. Main courses $17–$24; pastas $12–$15. AE, DC, MC, V. Daily 6–11pm. REGIONAL ITALIAN.

The food is great but the atmosphere a bit fussy for Key West. If you don't have a reservation in season, don't bother. Still, if you are organized and don't mind paying high prices for dishes that elsewhere go for much less, try this old favorite. From the perfectly seasoned homemade focaccia to an exemplary crème brûlée, this elegant little standout is amazingly consistent. The menu includes a small selection of classics, such as zuppa di pesce, rack of lamb in a rosemary sauce, and veal marsala. However, the way to go is with the nightly specials. You can't go wrong with any of the handmade pastas.

✪ **Bagatelle.** 115 Duval St. ☎ **305/296-6609.** Reservations recommended. Main courses $16–$24; lunch $5–$12. AE, DC, DISC, MC, V. Daily 11:30am–3pm and 5:30–10pm. SEAFOOD/TROPICAL.

Reserve a seat at the elegant second-floor veranda overlooking Duval Street's mayhem. From the calm above, enjoy any of the selections from a large eclectic menu. You may want to start your meal with the excellent herb-and-garlic stuffed whole artichoke or the sashimi-like seared tuna rolled in black peppercorns. Also recommended is a lightly creamy garlic-herb pasta topped with gulf shrimp, Florida lobster, and mushrooms. The best chicken and beef dishes are given a tropical treatment: grilled with papaya, ginger, and soy.

✪ **Mangoes.** 700 Duval St. (at Angela St.), Key West. ☎ **305/292-4606.** Reservations recommended for parties of six or more. Main courses $12–$24; pizzas $10–$12; lunch $7–$14. AE, CB, DC, DISC, MC, V. Daily 11am–midnight; pizza until 1am. AMERICAN/REGIONAL.

This restaurant's large brick patio shaded by overgrown banyan trees, is so seductive to passersby that it's packed almost every night of the week. Appetizers include conch chowder laced with sherry, lobster dumplings with tangy key lime sauce, and grilled shrimp cocktail with spicy mango chutney. Spicy sausage with black beans and rice, crispy curried chicken, and local snapper with passion fruit sauce are typical among the entrees, but Mangoes's outstanding individual-size designer pizzas are the best menu items by far. They're baked in a Neapolitan-style oven fired by buttonwood. Even though it is right on tourist-laden Duval Street, Mangoes enjoys a good reputation among locals.

MODERATE

✪ **Blue Heaven.** 729 Thomas St. (at the corner of Petronia St.), Key West. ☎ **305/296-8666.** Main courses $9–$24; lunch $5–$13; breakfast $3–$8.50. DISC, MC, V. Mon–Sat 8am–3pm and 6–10:30pm; Sun brunch 8am–1pm and 6–10:30pm. SEAFOOD/AMERICAN/NATURAL.

This little hippie-run gallery and restaurant has become the place to be in Key West—and with good reason. Be prepared to wait in line. The food here is some of the best in town, especially for breakfast. You can enjoy homemade granola, huge tropical fruit pancakes, and seafood Benedict. Dinners are just as good and run the gamut from just-caught fish dishes to Jamaican-style jerk chicken, curried soups, and vegetarian stews. But if you're a neat freak, don't bother. Some people are put off by the dirt floors and roaming cats and birds. The building used to be a bordello, where Hemingway was said to hang out watching cockfights.

Mangia, Mangia. 900 Southard St. (at Margaret St.), Key West. ☎ **305/294-2469.** Reservations not accepted. Main courses $9–$15. AE, MC, V. Daily 5:30–10pm. ITALIAN/AMERICAN.

Mangia, Mangia is one of Key West's best values. Locals appreciate that they can get inexpensive good food here in a town of so many tourist traps. Off the beaten track, in a little corner storefront, this great Chicago-style pasta place serves some of the best Italian food in the Keys. The family run restaurant offers superb homemade pastas of every description, including one of the tastiest marinaras around. The simple grilled chicken breast brushed with olive oil and sprinkled with pepper is another good choice. You wouldn't know it from the glossy glass front room, but there's a fantastic little outdoor patio dotted with twinkling pepper lights and lots of plants. You can relax out back with a glass of one of their excellent wines or homemade beer while you wait for your table.

✪ **Pepe's.** 806 Caroline St. (between Margaret and Williams sts.), Key West. ☎ **305/294-7192.** Main courses $11–$20; lunch $5–$9; breakfast $2–$9. DISC, MC, V. Daily 6:30am–10:30pm. AMERICAN.

This old dive has been serving good, basic food for nearly a century. Steaks and Apalachicola Bay oysters are the big draw for regulars who appreciate the rustic barroom setting and historic photos on the walls. Look for original scenes of Key West in 1909, when Pepe's first opened. If the weather is nice, choose a seat on the patio under a stunning mahogany tree. Burgers, fish sandwiches, and standard chili satisfy hearty eaters. Buttery sautéed mushrooms and rich mashed potatoes are the best comfort food in Key West. Stop by early for breakfast when you can get old-fashioned chipped beef on toast and all the usual egg dishes. In the evening, there are reasonably priced cocktails on the deck.

Turtle Kraals Wildlife Grill. 213 Margaret St. (corner of Caroline St.), Key West. ☎ **305/294-2640.** Main courses $12–$20. DISC, MC, V. Mon–Thurs 11am–1am; Fri–Sat 11am–2am. SOUTHWESTERN/SEAFOOD.

You'll join lots of locals in this out-of-the-way converted warehouse with indoor and dockside seating that serves innovative seafood at great prices. Try the twin lobster tails stuffed with mango and crabmeat or any of the big quesadillas or fajitas. Kids will like the wildlife exhibits and the very cheesy menu. Blues bands play most nights.

INEXPENSIVE

✪ **Anthony's Cafe.** 1111 Duval St. (at Amelia St.) ☎ **305/296-8899.** Breakfast $2–$5; sandwiches and salads $4–$6; hot plates $4–$10. Cash only. Daily 8am–10pm. ITALIAN DELI/ROTISSERIE

Though owned and operated by a Greek import, this rustic Italian-style trattoria, is a welcome addition to an area crowded with more expensive and less delicious options. Fragrant roasted chicken and overstuffed sandwiches on fresh baked bread are the best choices. Also good are the many salads and daily specials.

The Deli. 531 Truman Ave. (corner of Truman Ave. and Simonton St.), Key West. ☎ **305/294-1464.** Full meals $5–$13; sandwiches $2–$7. DISC, MC, V. Daily 7:30am–10pm. DINER/AMERICAN.

In operation since 1950, this family owned, corner eatery has kept up with the times. It's really more of a diner than a deli and has a vast menu with all kinds of hearty options, from meat loaf to yellowtail snapper. Avoid the lobster sandwich, which is fried and a bit greasy. Other seafood options are good. A daily selection of more than a dozen vegetables includes the usual diner choices of beets, corn, and coleslaw with some distinctly Caribbean additions, such as rice and beans and fried plantains. Most dinners include a choice of two vegetables and homemade biscuits or corn bread. Breakfasts are made to order and attract a loyal following of locals. The Deli also offers ice cream sundaes and gourmet coffees.

✪ **El Siboney Restaurant.** 900 Catherine St. (at Margaret St.), Key West. ☎ **305/296-4184.** Main courses $5–$13. No credit cards. Mon–Sat 11am–9pm. CUBAN.

For good, cheap Cuban food, stop at this corner dive that looks more like a gas station than a diner. Be prepared however, to wait like the locals for succulent roast pork, Cuban sandwiches, grilled chicken, and ropa vieja, all served with heaps of rice and beans. This tiny storefront is a worthwhile, very affordable choice in a town with lots of glossy tourist traps.

PT's Late Night. 920 Caroline St. (at the corner of Margaret St.), Key West. ☎ **305/296-4245.** Main courses $5–$14; lunch $5–$12. DISC, MC, V. Daily 11am–4am. AMERICAN.

This place is worth knowing about not only because it's one of the only places in town serving food past 10pm, but it also happens to serve good food at extremely reasonable prices. The sports-bar atmosphere might make you wonder, but I've never been disappointed, although service can be a bit slow and brusque. Let's say it's 1am, you're starving, and you've just parked your bike outside: You'll be ecstatic when your heaping plate of nachos arrives. Fajitas are served sizzling hot with a huge platter of fixings, including beans, rice, lettuce, jalapeños, and tomatoes. Superfresh salads are so big they can be a meal in themselves.

KEY WEST AFTER DARK

Duval Street is the Bourbon Street of Florida. Amid the T-shirt shops and clothing boutiques, you'll find bar after bar serving neon-colored frozen drinks to revelers who bounce from one to the next from noon till dawn. Bands and crowds vary from night to night and season to season. Your best bet is to start at Truman Avenue and head up Duval to check them out for yourself. Cover charges are rare, so stop into a dozen and see which you like.

Captain Tony's. 428 Greene St. ☎ **305/294-1838.**

Just around the corner from Duval's beaten path, this smoky old wooden bar is about as authentic as you'll find. It comes complete with old-time regulars who remember the island before cruise ships docked here; they say Hemingway drank, caroused, and even wrote here. The owner, Capt. Tony Tarracino, a former controversial Key West mayor, has recently capitalized on the success of this once-quaint tavern by franchising the place.

Durty Harry's. 208 Duval St. ☎ **305/296-4890.**

This large entertainment complex features live rock bands almost every night. You can wander to one of the many outdoor bars or head up to Upstairs at Rick's, an indoor/outdoor dance club that gets going late. For the more racy singles or couples, there is the Red Garter, a pocket-size strip club popular with bachelor and divorce parties. The hawker outside reminds couples that "The family that strips together sticks together."

Epoch. 623 Duval St. ☎ **305/296-8521.**

Until an arsonist put an end to the former legend in 1995, this former gay club was the place to dance to everything from techno to house and disco to reggae. Now expanded with seven bars and an even bigger dance floor, a huge outside deck overlooking Duval Street, and a new state-of-the-art sound system, this is a better choice than ever for people of any orientation who appreciate a good time.

Jimmy Buffett's Margaritaville Cafe. 500 Duval St. ☎ **305/292-1435.**

This cafe, named after another Key West legend, is a worthwhile stop. Although Mr. Buffett moved to glitzy Palm Beach years ago, his name is still attracting large crowds. This kitschy restaurant/bar/gift shop features live bands every night—from rock to blues to reggae and everything in between. The touristy cafe is furnished with plenty of Buffett memorabilia, including gold records, photos, and drawings. The margaritas are high-priced but tasty. The cheeseburgers aren't worth singing about.

Limbo. 700 Duval St. (corner of Angela St.). ☎ **305/292-4606.**

This secret little hideaway, above the well-known restaurant Mangoes (see "Where to Dine," above), is a great bar, especially for jazz lovers. Cozy individual booths allow patrons to talk while catching a great view of the eclectic patrons who sometimes dance in the small space on the outside deck.

Sloppy Joe's. 201 Duval St. ☎ **305/294-5717.**

You'll have to stop in here just to say you did. Scholars and drunks debate whether this is the same Sloppy Joe's that Hemingway wrote about, but there's no argument that this classic bar's turn-of-the-century wooden ceiling and cracked tile floors are Key West originals. There's live music most days and nights.

THE GAY SCENE

In Key West, the best music and dancing can be found at the predominantly gay clubs. While many of the area's other hot spots are geared toward tourists who like to imbibe, the gay clubs are for those who want to rave—mostly locals (or at least, recent transplants). None of the spots mentioned here discriminate—anyone open-minded and fun is welcome. Cover varies, but is rarely more than $10.

A popular late-night spot is **One Saloon,** 524 Duval St. (☎ **305/296-8118**), featuring great drag and lots more disco. A mostly male clientele frequents this hot spot from 9pm until 4am. Another Duval Street favorite is **Diva's** at 711 Duval St. (☎ **305/292-8500**), where you might catch drag queens belting out torch songs or judges voting on the best package in the wet jockey shorts contest.

Sunday nights are fun at two local spots. **Tea by the Sea,** on the pier at the Atlantic Shores Motel, 510 South St. (☎ **305/296-2491**), attracts a faithful following of regulars and visitors alike. Show up after 7:30pm. Better known around town as La-Te-Da, **La Terraza,** at 1125 Duval St. (☎ **305/296-6706**), is a great spot to gather poolside for the best martini in town—but don't bother with the food.

5 The Dry Tortugas

70 miles W of Key West

Few people realize that the Florida Keys don't end at Key West. About 70 miles west are a chain of seven small islands known as the Dry Tortugas. As long as you have come this far, you might as well take a trip to the Dry Tortugas, especially if you're into bird watching, which is the primary draw of these seven small islands.

Ponce de León, who discovered this far-flung cluster of coral keys in 1513, named them "Las Tortugas" because of the many sea turtles, which still flock to the area during the nesting season in the warm summer months. Oceanic charts later carried the preface "dry" to warn mariners that fresh water was unavailable here. Modern intervention has made drinking water available, but little else.

These underdeveloped islands make a great day trip for travelers interested in seeing the truly natural anomalies of the Florida Keys—especially the birds. The Dry Tortugas are nesting grounds and roosting sites for thousands of tropical and subtropical oceanic birds. Visitors will also find a historical fort, good fishing, and terrific snorkeling around shallow reefs.

GETTING THERE

BY BOAT   The **Yankee Fleet,** based in Key West (☎ **800/634-0939** or 305/ 294-7009), offers day trips from Key West for sightseeing, snorkeling, or both. Cruises leave daily at 7:30am from the Land's End Marina, at Margaret Street. Breakfast is served on board. The journey takes 3 hours. Once on the island, called Garden Key, you can join a guided tour or explore it on your own. Boats return to Key West by 7pm. Tours cost $85 per person, including breakfast; $50 for children 16 and under; $75 for seniors, students, and military personnel. Snorkeling equipment rental is free. Phone for reservations.

The **Sunny Days Catamaran's "Fast Cat"** is faster than the loud Yankee fleet (☎ **305/292-6900**) and a better value. Included in the $85 round-trip adult fare is a continental breakfast and a buffet lunch with cold cuts, fresh veggies, fruits, and salads and a snorkeling excursion to a wreck in 5 to 20 feet of water. The high-speed power cat leaves Key West at 8am and returns by 6pm.

BY PLANE   **Seaplanes of Key West,** based at Key West Airport (☎ **800/ 950-2-FLY** or 305/294-0709), offers daily excursions. Weather permitting, flights depart at 8am, 10am, noon, and 2pm. The 40-minute trip at about 500 feet offers a great introduction to these little-known islets. Fares, which include snorkeling equipment and a cooler for use on the island, start at $159 for adults for a half day and $275 for a full day. Rates for kids under 12 are discounted by about 30%. Bring a bathing suit, snorkeling equipment, and some snacks to enjoy on these remote and beautiful islands.

EXPLORING THE DRY TORTUGAS

Fort Jefferson, a huge six-sided 19th-century fortress, is built almost at the water's edge of Garden Key, giving the appearance that it floats in the middle of the sea. The monumental structure is surrounded by formidable 8-foot-thick walls that rise up from the sand to nearly 50 feet. Impressive archways, stonework, and parapets make this 150-year-old monument a grand sight. With the invention of the rifled cannon, the fort's masonry construction became obsolete, and the building was never completed. For 10 years, from 1863 to 1873, Fort Jefferson served as a prison, a kind of "Alcatraz East." Among its prisoners were four of the "Lincoln Conspirators," including Samuel A. Mudd, the doctor who set the broken leg of fugitive assassin John Wilkes Booth. In 1935, Fort Jefferson became a national monument administered by the National Park Service. For more information about Fort Jefferson and the Dry Tortugas, call the **Everglades National Park Service** at ☎ **305/ 242-7700.**

OUTDOOR PURSUITS

BIRD WATCHING   Bring your binoculars and your bird books. Bird watching is the reason to visit this little cluster of tropical islands. The islands, uniquely situated in the middle of the migration flyway between North and South America, serve as an important rest stop for the more than 200 winged varieties that pass through here annually. The season peaks from mid-March to mid-May, when thousands of birds—including thrushes, orioles, boobies, swallows, black noddys, and snooty terns—show up. Many other species from the West Indies can be found year-round.

DIVING & SNORKELING   The warm, clear, shallow waters of the Dry Tortugas combine to produce optimum conditions for snorkeling and scuba diving. Four endangered species of sea turtles—the green, leatherback, Atlantic ridley, and hawksbill—can be found here, along with a myriad of marine species. The region just outside the seawall of Garden Key's Fort Jefferson is excellent for underwater touring; an abundant variety of fish, corals, and more live in just 3 or 4 feet of water.

FISHING   Fishing for snapper, tarpon, grouper, and other fish is popular. The mandatory saltwater fishing permit costs $7 for 3 days and $17 for 7 days. No bait or boating services are available in the Tortugas, but there are day docks on Garden Key as well as a cleaning table. The water is roughest in winter, but the fishing is excellent year-round. Outfitters from Key West can arrange day charters (see "Sports & Outdoor Activities," above).

CAMPING

The rustic beauty of tiny Garden Key is a camper's dream. Don't worry about sharing your site with noisy RVs or motor homes; they can't get here. The abundance of birds doesn't make it quiet, but camping here—literally a stone's throw from the water—is as picturesque as it gets. Campers are allowed to pitch tents only on Garden Key. Picnic tables, cooking grills, and toilets are provided, but there are no showers. All supplies must be packed in and out. Sites are $3 per person per night and are available on a first-come, first-served basis. With only 10 sites, they book up fast. For more information, call the **National Park Service** (☎ **305/ 242-7700**).

13 | The Gold Coast

Throughout the last decade, the cities along Florida's southeastern coast from Hallandale to the Palm Beaches have been growing at an explosive rate. Newcomers arrive by the thousands every day. While plenty have come from other countries and from the frigid cities of the Northeast, many have moved from neighboring Miami where a number of circumstances—a huge influx of immigrants from the Caribbean, a drastic increase in violent crimes, and devastating hurricanes in 1992 and 1998—caused many old-timers to head north in the hopes of escaping the densely populated regions that they once called home.

As a result, there has been a boom in building in the existing cities and westward into the swampy areas of the Everglades. More than 20 homes per day are being built in Broward County alone. Unfortunately, the area's infrastructure isn't equipped to handle this sudden surge in popularity. Over the past decade, cow pastures have given way to strip malls and dirt paths to traffic jams. A more positive by-product is the revitalization of several downtown areas, including Hollywood, Fort Lauderdale, and West Palm Beach. These once desolate urban centers have been spruced up and now attract more young travelers and families than ever before. The dozens of gorgeous beaches, of course, have always drawn a steady stream of sun worshippers and water-sports enthusiasts.

Beyond the sands, the Gold Coast offers fantastic shopping, entertainment, clubbing, boating, golfing, tennis, and plain old relaxing.

Unfortunately, like its neighbors to the south, the Gold Coast can be prohibitively hot and buggy in the summer. The good news is that bargains are plentiful in the slow months (between May and October), when many locals take advantage of package deals and uncrowded resorts.

For the purposes of this chapter, the *Gold Coast* will consist of the towns of Hallandale, Hollywood, Pompano Beach, Fort Lauderdale, Dania, Deerfield, Boca Raton, Delray Beach, Boyton Beach, and the Palm Beaches.

EXPLORING THE GOLD COAST BY CAR

Like most of the rest of South Florida, the Gold Coast consists of a mainland and an adjacent strip of barrier islands. You'll have to check the maps to keep track of the many bridges that allow access to the islands where most of the tourist activity is centered.

Interstate 95, which runs north-south, is the area's main highway. Farther west is the Florida Turnpike, a toll road that can be worth the expense since the speed limit is higher and it is often less congested than I-95. Also on the mainland is U.S. 1, which generally runs parallel to I-95 (to the east) and is a narrower thoroughfare mostly crowded with strip malls and seedy hotels.

I recommend taking Fla. A1A, a slow ocean-side road that connects the long, thin islands of Florida's whole east coast. Though the road is narrow, it is the most scenic and forces you into the ultrarelaxed atmosphere of these resort towns.

1 Broward County: Hallandale & Hollywood to Fort Lauderdale

23 miles N of Miami

With more than 23 miles of beachfront and 300 miles of navigable waterways, Broward County is a great destination for outdoor lovers. Scattered amid the tacky shopping malls, gaudy condos, and glitzy tourist areas are some impressive natural wonders, including hundreds of parks, golf courses, and tennis courts, too. With year-round temperatures averaging 77° and a growing industrial base, the area attracts more than six million visitors each year. Some 1.5 million residents call the more than 28 cities and dozens of towns that make up Broward County home.

Like many other small American towns, the quaint city of Hollywood has been working on redeveloping its downtown area for years. Finally, in the late 1990s, the efforts seemed to start paying off. A spate of redevelopment has made the pedestrian-friendly center along Hollywood Boulevard and Harrison Street east of Dixie Highway a popular destination for travelers and locals alike. Some predict Hollywood will be South Florida's next big destination—South Beach without the attitude, traffic jams, and parking nightmares. Prices are a fraction of other tourist areas, and a true artsy image is apparent in the galleries, clubs, and restaurants that dot the new "strip." Its gritty undercurrent, however, still makes it more popular with bohemians and backpackers than society-page regulars.

Fort Lauderdale and its well-known strip of beaches, restaurants, bars, and souvenir shops has also undergone a major transformation. Once especially famous (or infamous) for the annual mayhem it hosted each spring when hedonism-bent college students descended from all over the country, this area is now attracting a more affluent crowd.

In addition to beautiful wide beaches, the city includes more than 300 miles of navigable waterways and innumerable canals that permit thousands of residents to anchor boats in their backyards. Boating is not just a hobby here; it's a lifestyle. It's the reason many choose to live in this area known as the "yachting capital of the world," or the "Venice of America." Visitors can easily get on the water, too, by renting a boat, or simply by hailing a moderately priced water taxi.

Huge cruise ships also take advantage of Florida's deepest harbor, Port Everglades. It is the second-busiest cruise-ship base in Florida (after Miami) and one of the top five in the world. For further information on cruises, consult *Frommer's Caribbean Cruises* or *Frommer's Caribbean Ports of Call.*

ESSENTIALS

GETTING THERE   If you're driving up from Miami, it's a straight shot to Hollywood or Fort Lauderdale. Visitors on their way to or from Orlando should take the Florida Turnpike to Exit 53, 54, 58, or 62, depending on the location of your accommodations.

The Fort Lauderdale/Hollywood International Airport is small, easy to negotiate, and located just 15 minutes from both of the downtown areas it services.

Amtrak (☎ **800/USA-RAIL**) stations are at 200 SW 21st Terrace (Broward Boulevard and I-95), Fort Lauderdale (☎ **954/587-6692**), and 3001 Hollywood Blvd., Hollywood (☎ **954/921-4517**).

VISITOR INFORMATION The **Greater Fort Lauderdale Convention & Visitors Bureau,** 1850 Eller Dr., Suite 303 (off I-95 and I-595 east), Fort Lauderdale, FL 33316 (☎ **954/765-4466;** fax 954/765-4467; www.sunny.org), is an excellent resource in Spanish, French, or English. I highly recommend calling them in advance to request a free comprehensive guide with just about everything you could want to know about events, accommodations, and sightseeing in Broward County. In addition, once you are in town, you can call an **information line** (☎ **954/ 527-5600**) to get easy-to-follow directions, travel advice, and assistance from multilingual operators who staff a round-the-clock help line. Also available 24 hours a day are operators who can book discount scuba, cruise, or cultural packages. Call ☎ **800/22-SUNNY** for information.

The **Greater Hollywood Chamber of Commerce,** 330 N. Federal Hwy. (on the corner of U.S. 1 and Taylor Street), Hollywood, FL 33020 (☎ **954/923-4000;** fax 954/923-8737), is open Monday through Friday from 8:30am to 5pm.

HITTING THE BEACH

The southern part of the Gold Coast, Broward County, has the region's most popular and amenities-laden beaches, which stretch for more than 23 miles. Most do not charge for access, though all are well maintained. Here's a selection of some of the county's best from south to north.

Hollywood Beach, stretching from Sheridan Street to Georgia Street, is a real carnival with an odd assortment of young hipsters, big families, and sunburned French Canadians who dodge bicyclers and skaters along the rows of tacky souvenir shops, T-shirt shops, game rooms, snack bars, beer stands, hotels, and even miniature golf courses. The 3-mile-long Hollywood Beach **Broadwalk** is notable as one of the area's only beach paths where the diversions are right on the beach separated from the sand and sea by only a thin paved strip instead of a busy highway and tall buildings. Popular with runners, skaters, and cruisers, the Broadwalk is also renowned as a hangout for thousands of retirement-age snowbirds who get together for frequent dances and shows at a faded outdoor amphitheater. Despite efforts to clear out a seedy element, the area remains a haven for drunks and scammers, so keep alert.

If you tire of the hectic diversity that defines Hollywood's Broadwalk, enjoy the natural beauty of the beach itself, which is wide and clean. There are lifeguards, showers, bathroom facilities, and public areas for picnics and parties.

The **Fort Lauderdale Beach Promenade** recently underwent a $26 million renovation, and it looks fantastic. However, note that this beach is hardly pristine; it is across the street from an uninterrupted stretch of low- and high-rise hotels, bars, and retail outlets. Also nearby is a megaretail and dining complex, Beach Place, on Fla. A1A, midway between Las Olas and Sunrise boulevards (see "Shopping & Browsing," below).

Just across the road, on the sand, most days you will find hard-core volleyballers, who always welcome anyone with a good spike, and a calm ocean welcoming swimmers of any level. The unusually clear waters are under the careful watch of some of Florida's best-looking lifeguards. Freshen up afterward in any of the clean showers and rest rooms conveniently located along the strip.

Fort Lauderdale Area Attractions & Accommodations

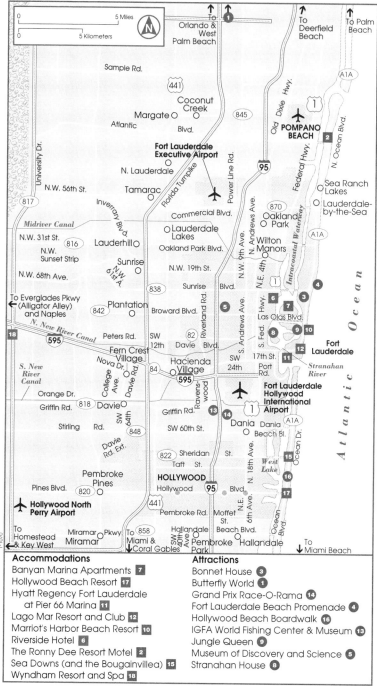

Accommodations

Banyan Marina Apartments **7**
Hollywood Beach Resort **17**
Hyatt Regency Fort Lauderdale
  at Pier 66 Marina **11**
Lago Mar Resort and Club **12**
Marriot's Harbor Beach Resort **10**
Riverside Hotel **6**
The Ronny Dee Resort Motel **2**
Sea Downs (and the Bougainvillea) **15**
Wyndham Resort and Spa **18**

Attractions

Bonnet House **3**
Butterfly World **1**
Grand Prix Race-O-Rama **14**
Fort Lauderdale Beach Promenade **4**
Hollywood Beach Boardwalk **16**
IGFA World Fishing Center & Museum **13**
Jungle Queen **9**
Museum of Discovery and Science **5**
Stranahan House **8**

Especially on weekends, parking along the ocean-side meters is nearly impossible to find. Try biking, skating, or hitching a ride on the water taxi instead. The strip is located on Fla. A1A, between SE 17th Street and Sunrise Boulevard.

ACTIVE PURSUITS

BOATING   Known as "the yachting capital of the world," Fort Lauderdale provides ample opportunity for visitors to get on the water, either along the Intracoastal Waterway or out on the open ocean. If your hotel doesn't rent boats, try **Bill's Sunrise Watersports,** 2025 E. Sunrise Blvd., Fort Lauderdale (☎ 954/462-8962). They will outfit you with a variety of watercraft, including jet-skis, Wave Runners, 13-foot Cigarette boats, 15-foot jet boats, and 8-foot powerboats, year-round. Bill's is open daily from 9am to 6pm. Rates start at about $45 an hour.

CRUISES   The **Jungle Queen,** 801 Sea Breeze Blvd. (3 blocks south of Las Olas Boulevard on Fla. A1A), in the Bahia Mar Yacht Center, Fort Lauderdale (☎ 954/462-5596), a Mississippi River–style steamer, is one of Fort Lauderdale's best-known attractions cruising up and down the New River. All-you-can-eat dinner cruises and 3-hour sightseeing tours take visitors past Millionaires' Row, Old Fort Lauderdale, and the new downtown. Cruises depart nightly at 7pm and cost $24.50 for adults and $12 for children 12 and under. Sightseeing tours are scheduled daily at 10am and 2pm and cost $11.50 for adults and $8 for children 10 and under.

If you're interested in gambling, several casino boat companies operate day cruises out of Port Everglades and offer blackjack, slots, and poker. **Discovery Cruise Lines** (☎ 800/937-4477) has daily cruises to The Bahamas where you can gamble, eat, and party for 5 to 6 hours for about $120. The price includes breakfast, lunch, and dinner, but drinks cost extra.

Sea Escape (☎ 800/327-2005 or 954/453-3333) also launches daily casino cruises. But theirs don't travel more than a few miles offshore. These trips "to nowhere" depart every day except Monday at 10am until 4pm. The party cruises offer buffet meals and full casinos for about $35 a person. I'd recommend spending an additional $20 for a cabin so you can stretch out and relax in between hands. Even though the cruises don't go far from the coast, 5 or 6 hours is a long time to spend at sea, especially if the weather is rough. Evening cruises, which leave at 7:30pm and return at 12:30 or 1:30am, cost a few dollars more and offer full buffet dinners and a Las Vegas–style show. Port charges are included, although you must pay a $3 departure tax and $2.65 passenger charge. This is one of the best deals you'll find. Sea Escape also has a new 2- and 3-night cruise option, where visitors can go to Nassau, The Bahamas, for as little as $199 per person with all meals included.

Also, see the box "More Than a Boat Tour," below, for details on the water taxi.

FISHING   Completed in 1999 at a cost of more than $32 million, the **IGFA World Fishing Center** at 300 Gulf Stream Way (☎ 954/922-4212) in Dania Beach is an anglers paradise. One of the highlights of this museum, library, and park is the virtual reality fishing simulator, which allows visitors to actually reel in their own computer generated catch. Also included in the 3-acre park are displays of antique fishing gear, record catches, famous anglers, various vessels, and a wetlands lab. To get a list of local captains and guides call **IGFA headquarters** and ask for the librarian (☎ 954-927-2628). Admission is $9 for adults, $5 for children between 3 and 12 and free for children under 3. On the grounds is also **Bass Pro Outdoor World Store,** a huge multifloor retail complex situated on a 3-acre lake.

GAME PARKS   This area seems to be the home of more megaentertainment complexes than any other region in Southeast Florida. The **Grand Prix Race-O-Rama,**

at 1801 NW 1st St., east of I-95 between Griffin and Sterling road exits, in Dania, is one of the originals and still the best for kids. With a massive video arcade, which is open 24 hours; five challenging miniature golf greens; go-carts for those over 4 feet 6 inches; and NASCAR racing for those over 5 feet tall; batting cages; and a huge sky coaster, this place is as exciting as it is exhausting. Plan to spend all day or night—or both. Call for prices and hours (☎ **954/921-1411**).

One of the newest additions to the scene is **Dave & Busters** at 3000 Oakwood Blvd. in Hollywood, just off the Sheridan Street exit of I-95 (☎ **954/923-5505**). This 50,000-square-foot complex caters primarily to adults; it features a full liquor bar and sit-down restaurant, as well as a more casual spot with table service. On weekends this place is packed with young adults on dates and rowdy groups of guys of all ages. An admission of $5 is charged only on Friday and Saturday after 10pm. D&B's opens weekdays at 11am and at 11:30am on weekends and usually closes by 1am.

Gameworks, the huge, high-tech creation of Hollywood movie mogul Steven Spielberg is located in the mammoth Sawgrass Mills outlet center (See "Shopping & Browsing," below.)

GOLF   More than 50 golf courses in all price ranges compete for players. Some of the best include **Emerald Hills** at 4100 North Hills Dr., Hollywood, just west of I-95 between Sterling Road and Sheridan Street. This beauty consistently lands on "best of" lists of golf writers throughout the country. The 18th hole on a two-tier green is the challenging course's signature; it's surrounded by water and is more than a bit rough. Greens fees start at $80. Call ☎ **954/961-4000** for tee times. For one of Broward's best municipal challenges, try the 18-holer at the **Orangebrook Golf Course** at 400 Entrada Dr. in Hollywood (☎ **954/967-GOLF**). Built in 1937, this is one of the state's oldest courses and one of the area's best bargains. Morning and noon rates range from $21 to $26. After 2pm, you can play for less than $20, including a cart.

SCUBA DIVING   In Broward County, the best wreck dive is the *Mercedes I,* a 197-foot freighter that washed up in the backyard of a Palm Beach socialite in 1984 and was sunk for divers the following year off Pompano Beach. The artificial reef, filled with colorful sponges, spiny lobsters, and barracudas, is located 97 feet below the surface, a mile offshore between Oakland Park and Sunrise boulevards. Dozens of reputable dive shops line the beach. Ask at your hotel for a nearby recommendation or contact **Lauderdale Undersea Adventures,** 2150 SE 17th St., Fort Lauderdale (☎ **954/527-0187**).

SPECTATOR SPORTS   Baseball fans can get their fix at the **Fort Lauderdale Stadium,** 5301 NW 12th Ave. (☎ **954/938-4980**), where the Baltimore Orioles play exhibition games starting in early March; call ☎ **954/776-1921** for tickets. They cost $6 for general admission, $9 for a spot in the grandstand, and $12 for box seats. During the season, the Florida Marlins play just south of Hallandale at the Pro Player Stadium near the Dade-Broward County line. Call Ticketmaster for tickets (☎ **305/358-5885**), which range from $2 to $40.

The **Pompano Harness Track,** 1800 SW 3rd St., Pompano Beach (☎ **954/972-2000**), the only one in Florida, features horse racing and betting from October to early August. Grandstand admission is free; clubhouse admission is $2. They, like many other pari-mutuel outlets in the area, opened poker rooms in 1997.

The home of the Florida Derby, **Gulfstream Park,** 901 S. Federal Hwy., Hallandale (☎ **954/454-7000**), recently underwent a revamp that has made it one of the state's biggest and best-known tracks. It has a popular clubhouse and is open January to mid-March from Wednesday to Monday starting at 11am.

A sort of Spanish-style indoor lacrosse, jai-alai was introduced to Florida in 1924 and still draws big crowds who bet on the fast-paced action. Broward's only fronton, **Dania Jai-Alai,** 301 E. Dania Beach Blvd. at the intersection of Fla. A1A and U.S. 1 (☎ **954/920-1511** or 954/426-4330), is a great place to spend an afternoon or evening.

Wrapped around an artificial lake, **Gulfstream Park,** at U.S. 1 and Hallandale Beach Boulevard, Hallandale (☎ **305/931-7223**), is both pretty and popular. Large purses and important races are commonplace at this suburban course, and the track is often crowded. Call for schedules. Admission is $3 to the grandstand, and $3 to the clubhouse. Free parking. From January 3 to March 15, post times are Wednesday to Monday at 1pm. Many weekends feature live concerts by well known musicians.

In the sport of ice hockey, the young Florida Panthers (☎ **954/835-7000**) have already made history. In the 1994–95 season, they played in the Stanley Cup finals, and the fans love them. They play in Sunrise at 2555 NW 137th Way. Call for directions and ticket information.

TENNIS   There are literally hundreds of courts in Broward County and plenty are accessible to the public. Many are at resorts and hotels. If not at yours, try one of these.

Famous as the spot where Chris Evert got in her early serves, **Holiday Park,** 701 NE 12th Ave. (off Sunrise Boulevard), Fort Lauderdale (☎ **954/761-5378**), has 18 clay and 3 hard courts (15 lighted). Her coach and father, James Evert, still teaches young players here, although he is very picky about who he'll accept. Nonresidents of Fort Lauderdale pay $3.50 to $4.50 per hour. Reservations are accepted after 2pm for the following day, but cost an extra $3. Lights are also an extra $3 per hour and are only available for the clay courts.

At the **Marina Bay Resort,** 2175 S.R. 84, west of I-95 and just behind the Ramada Inn, Fort Lauderdale (☎ **954/791-7600**), visitors can play free on any one of nine hard courts on a first-come, first-served basis. Three are lighted at night.

SEEING THE SIGHTS

For an overview of Fort Lauderdale, you may want to take an informative spin around the downtown area with **South Florida Trolley Tours** (☎ **954/946-7320**). Drivers narrate the history of the area as they loop around the city's streets past all the major (and many minor) sights. The charge for the 90-minute tour is $12 for adults, free for children 11 and under. The trolleys pick up passengers from most major hotels for six tours daily, starting at 9am. Call for current schedule.

For a tour by water, see the box below.

Anne Kolb Nature Center. 751 Sheridan St., Hollywood. ☎ **954/926-2480.** Boat tours $8 adults, $1.50 children.

A great resource in Broward county, this park offers boat tours, guided nature walks, canoe rental, bike trails, ecological exhibits, picnic shelters, and playgrounds through 1,500 acres of mangroves and lakes.

Museum of Discovery & Science. 401 SW 2nd St., Fort Lauderdale. ☎ **954/467-6637.** Museum admission $6 adults, $5 seniors, $5 children 3–12, free for children 2 and under; Exhibit and IMAX combo prices $12.50 adults, $11.50 seniors, $10.50 children. Mon–Sat 10am–5pm, Sun noon–6pm. From I-95, exit on Broward Blvd. E.; continue to SW 5th Ave.; turn right, garage on right.

Children and teenagers especially love this interactive science museum that is a model of high-tech "infotainment." During the week, school groups meander

More Than a Boat Tour

Plan to spend at least an afternoon or evening cruising Fort Lauderdale's 300 miles of waterways the only way you can: by boat. The **Water Taxi of Fort Lauderdale** (☎ **954/467-6677**) is one of the greatest innovations for water lovers since those cool Velcro sandals. A trusty fleet of old-port boats serves the dual purpose of transporting and entertaining visitors as they cruise through "The Venice of America."

Taxis operate on demand and also along a fairly regular route carrying up to 48 passengers. Choose a hotel on the route so that you can take advantage of this convenient and inexpensive system. You can be picked up at your hotel, usually within 15 minutes of calling, and then be shuttled to any of the dozens of restaurants, bars, and attractions on or near the waterfront. If you aren't sure where you want to go, ask one of the personable captains who can point out historic and fun spots along the way.

For a day cruise with the kids, pack lunch, bathing suits, sunscreen, and sunglasses and hail or call the taxi for pickup from any safe dock or seawall. Your afternoon of cruising might start with a tour of Millionaires' Row, where Lauderdale's largest yachts are dwarfed only by the homes at which they are docked. Make a stop at the Museum of Discovery and Science where you can catch an IMAX film or just enjoy the current educational exhibits. Then, if you are up for a walk, head across the 3-mile Riverwalk, a scenic palm-lined walkway along the New River where you can enjoy your picnic lunch, or try one of the restaurants dotting the way to Las Olas Boulevard and The Las Olas Riverfront. When you are ready for some shopping or a sit-down meal, reboard and head to Beach Place at Las Olas Boulevard and Cortez Street in the heart of Fort Lauderdale's most famous "strip." Stop for a refreshment at Casablanca Cafe and then hit the beach.

In the evening, the water taxi is ideal for bar-hopping—no worrying about parking or choosing a designated driver. Make your first stop at Shooters where professionals, boaters, and tourists share the large lively patio for a popular happy hour from 5 to 7pm on weekdays. Right next door is Bootlegger's, featuring more than 70 beers at an outside bar. You can eat at either spot or keep your eyes on the waterway for your ride (or call for a quicker pickup).

For those who enjoy jazz, you might want to debark in the downtown section of Las Olas Boulevard. O'Hara's (see "Where to Dine") always delivers a great mix of live jazz and blues.

Starting daily from 10am, boats usually run until midnight, and until 2am on weekends, depending on the weather. The cost is $7 per person per trip, $13 round-trip, and $15 for a full day. Children under 12 ride for half price and free on Sunday. Opt for the all-day pass; it's worth it.

---

through the cavernous two-story modern building. However, most weekend nights you'll find a diverse crowd ranging from hip high school kids to 30-somethings enjoying a rock film in the Blockbuster IMAX 3D theater, which also shows short, science-related, supersize films daily. Out front, see a 52-foot-tall "Great Gravity Clock," located in the museum's atrium, the largest kinetic-energy sculpture in the state. Exhibits vary, so call for the latest details.

Billie Swamp Safari. Big Cypress Reservation, 1½-hour drive west of Fort Lauderdale. ☎ **800/949-6101.** No admission. Boat tours $10–$20. Daily 8am–8pm. Last airboat ride 4:30pm.

Here, you can catch a glimpse of how Florida looked before developers went wild. Skimming across the shallow swamps in an airboat with native American guides you may spot alligators and rare birds. Kids especially enjoy the swamp buggy rides, which leave every hour on the hour until 5pm.

Bonnet House. 900 N. Birch Rd. (1 block west of the ocean, south of Sunrise Blvd.), Fort Lauderdale. ☎ **954/563-5393.** Admission $9 adults, $8 seniors, $7 students under 18, free for children 6 and under. Tours Wed–Fri 10am–1:30pm, Sat–Sun noon–2:30pm.

This historic 35-acre plantation home and estate survives in the middle of an otherwise highly developed beachfront condominium area and is only open by guided tour.

Built in 1921, the sprawling two-story waterfront home surrounded with formal tropical gardens is really the backdrop of a love story, which the very chatty volunteer guides will share with you if you ask. Some have actually lunched with the former resident of the house, the late Evelyn Bartlett, the wife of world-acclaimed artist Frederic Clay Bartlett. If you like quirky people, whimsical artwork, lush grounds, and very interesting details of design, you'll love this tour, which takes about 1½ hours. Inquire about literary walks and science workshops offered regularly on the grounds.

Butterfly World. Tradewinds Park South, 3600 W. Sample Rd., Coconut Creek (west of the Florida Turnpike). ☎ **954/977-4400.** Admission $11.95 adults, $6.95 children 4–12, free for children 3 and under. Mon–Sat 9am–5pm, Sun 1–5pm; last admission at 4pm.

One of the world's largest butterfly breeders, Butterfly World cultivates more than 150 species of these colorful and delicate insects. In the park's walk-through, screened-in aviary, visitors can see thousands of caterpillars and watch newborn butterflies emerge from their cocoons and flutter around as they learn to fly. Depending on how interested you are in these winged beauties, you may want to allow from 1 to 2 hours to tour the gardens and the well-stocked gift shop. Look for a new lorikeet aviary to open in the near future, where guests will be able to hand feed these birds.

Stranahan House. 335 SE 6th Ave. (Las Olas Blvd. at the New River Tunnel), Fort Lauderdale. ☎ **954/524-4736.** Admission $5 adults, $2 students and children. Wed–Sat 10am–4pm, Sun 1–4pm; last tour begins at 3:30pm. Also accessible by water taxi.

In a town whose history isn't even as old as many of its residents, visitors may want to take a minute to see Fort Lauderdale's very oldest standing structure and a prime example of classic "Florida Frontier" architecture. Built in 1901 by "the father of Fort Lauderdale," this house once served as a trading post for Seminole trappers who came here to sell pelts. It's been a post office, town hall, and general store and now is a worthwhile little museum of South Florida pioneer life, containing turn-of-the-century furnishings and historical photos of the area. It is also the site of occasional concerts and social functions. Call for details.

SHOPPING & BROWSING

Broward County has some of Florida's best malls and some fantastic boutique areas, too.

Dania is known for its antique district where hundreds of shops are clustered along U.S. 1 just south of the airport. Known as **"Antique Row,"** this area has some of South Florida's best old treasures. Although many of the more upscale shops are overpriced, many of the smaller dealers offer bargains to hagglers.

Also for bargain mavens is a strip of "fashion" stores on **Hallandale Beach Boulevard's "Schmatta Row,"** east of Dixie Highway and the railroad tracks, where off-brand shoes, bags, and jewelry are sold at deep discounts. Funky Hollywood Boulevard also offers some wild shops with everything from Indonesian artifacts to used and rare books to leather bustiers to handmade hats. Dozens of shops line the pedestrian-friendly strip just west of Young Circle. The art galleries are clustered along Harrison Street just east of Dixie Highway.

The area's only beachfront mall, **Beach Place,** is in Ft. Lauderdale on Fla. A1A just north of Las Olas Boulevard. Completed in 1997 at a cost of $23 million, this 100,000-square-foot giant sports the usual chains like Sunglass Hut, Limited Express, Banana Republic, and The Gap as well as lots of popular bars and restaurants.

Other more traditional malls include the upscale **Galleria** at Sunrise Boulevard near the Fort Lauderdale Beach, and Broward Mall, west of I-95 on Broward Boulevard, in Plantation.

If you are looking for unusual boutiques, especially art galleries, head to trendy ✪ **Las Olas Boulevard,** where there are literally hundreds of shops with alluring window decorations and intriguing merchandise. You may find kitchen utensils posing as modern art sculptures or mural-size oil paintings.

On the edge of the Arts & Science District is a new retail complex known as **Las Olas Riverfront** with 260,000 square feet of restaurants, clothing stores, arcades, and a multiplex movie theater.

The well-known department store **Lord & Taylor** has a little-known clearance center where discounts on new clothing for women, kids, and men can be as big as 75%. If you can handle open dressing rooms, overstuffed racks, and surly sales help, it's a great find at 6820 N. University Dr. in Tamarac. You may want to call (☎ **954/720-1915**) to find out about specials.

The Fort Lauderdale Swap Shop, 3291 W. Sunrise Blvd. (☎ **954/791-SWAP**), is one of the world's largest flea markets. In addition to endless acres of vendors, there's a mini amusement park, a 13-screen drive-in movie theater, weekend concerts, and even a free circus complete with elephants, horse shows, high-wire acts, and clowns.

The monster of all outlet malls is **Sawgrass Mills,** 12801 W. Sunrise Blvd., Sunrise (☎ **800-FL-MILLS** or 954/846-2350). Since the most recent expansion completed in mid-1999, which added more than 30 new designer outlet stores, this behemoth (shaped like a Florida alligator) now holds more than 300 shops, kiosks, a 24-screen movie theater, and many restaurants and bars including a Hard Rock Cafe. The enclosed area covers nearly 2.5 million square feet over 50 acres. There's no way to see it all in a day. Wear your most comfortable shoes or buy an extra pair while you're there. Stores include Donna Karan Company Store, Levi's Outlet, Sunglass Hut, Ann Taylor Loft, and Barney's New York, all selling goods at between 20% and 80% below retail. Label-conscious shoppers are especially impressed with Off Fifth, the Saks Fifth Avenue outlet store and Last Call, the Neiman-Marcus clearance center. You may want to invest in a coupon booklet ($5), which entitles you to even greater discounts at many of the mall's stores and restaurants as well as area attractions. Books are good for up to a year and can be turned in for updated books at no charge. To get there, take I-95 to I-595 west to the Flamingo Road exit, turn right, and drive 2 miles to Sunrise Boulevard; you will see the large complex on the left. From the Florida Turnpike, exit Sunrise Boulevard west. Parking is free, but don't forget where you parked; the lot holds more than 11,000 cars.

Fishing enthusiasts won't want to miss **Bass Pro Outdoor World** (☎ **954/929-7710**), a sprawling retail complex at Griffin Road and I-95 in Dania where you can buy anything from yachts to lures (see "Sports & Other Activities," above.)

WHERE TO STAY

The Fort Lauderdale beach has a hotel or motel on nearly every block, and they range from the run down to the luxurious. Both the **Howard Johnson** (☎ **800/327-8578** or 954/563-2451), at 700 N. Atlantic Blvd. (on Fla. A1A, south of Sunrise Blvd.), and the **Days Inn** (☎ **800/329-7466** or 954/462-0444), at 435 N. Atlantic Blvd. (Fla. A1A), offer clean ocean-side rooms starting at about $150.

In Hollywood, where prices are generally cheaper, the **Holiday Inn** at 101 N. Ocean Blvd. (☎ **954/921-0990**) operates a full-service hotel right on the ocean. With prices starting at around $110 in season and discounts for AAA, it's a great deal. **Howard Johnson** (☎ **800/423-9867** or 954/925-1411) has a great location right on the beach at 2501 N. Ocean Dr. (I-95 to Sheridan Street east to Fla. A1A south).

✪ **Extended Stay America/Crossland Economy Studios** (☎ **800/398-7829**) has four superclean properties in Fort Lauderdale and offers year-round rates as low as $49 a night and $159 per week. The studios are designed with business travelers in mind, Each includes free local calls, a data port, a ktchenette, a recliner, and a well-lit desk.

Especially for rentals for a few weeks or months, call **Florida Sunbreak** (☎ **800-SUNBREAK**). Or call the **South Florida Hotel Network** (☎ **800/538-3616**) for help finding small inns and lodges in any price range. Also, check out the annual list of small lodgings compiled by the **Ft. Lauderdale Convention & Visitors Bureau** (☎ **954/765-4466**). It is especially helpful for those looking for privately owned, charming, and affordable lodgings.

New hotels are going up all the time. One notable addition to the Hallandale area is the 1,000 room **Diplomat Resort & Country Club** on the site of the former landmark which closed in 1991. The $500 million project is due to open in the summer of 2000.

VERY EXPENSIVE

Hyatt Regency Fort Lauderdale at Pier 66 Marina. 2301 SE 17th St. Causeway, Fort Lauderdale, FL 33316. ☎ **800/233-1234** or 954/525-6666. Fax 954/728-3541. 380 units. A/C MINIBAR TV TEL. Winter $259 double. Off-season $209 double. Year-round from $1,000 suite. AE, CB, DC, DISC, MC, V.

The Pier 66 hotel and 142-slip marina has been hosting guests, especially boaters, since 1954. The luxurious resort attracts megayachts from all over the world, in addition to large groups and business travelers. Despite the emphasis on groups, for services and amenities this Hyatt is hard to beat.

The hotel's atrium-style lobby impresses with high ceilings and marble floors. The lushly landscaped grounds add to the exotic feel of this superconvenient locale, situated across from the beach, and within walking distance to the best shopping and dining. Every room has a balcony; the priciest have expansive panoramas of the marina, the beach across the street, and all of Fort Lauderdale beyond. The best part is that it is serviced by the convenient water taxi (see box, above). All were renovated recently.

Dining: Best known for its revolving rooftop lounge, the hotel also offers an American grill and a very popular waterfront cafe for dinner and lunch.

Amenities: Concierge, room service (24 hours), dry-cleaning and laundry services, newspaper delivery, twice-daily maid service, baby-sitting, secretarial services, express checkout, valet parking $8, courtesy car or limo. Spectravision movie channels, two swimming pools, beach, a fully equipped spa, Jacuzzi, sauna, 40-person whirlpool, jogging track, children's center or programs, business center, conference rooms, self-service Laundromat, sundeck, two lighted clay tennis courts, watersports equipment and boat rentals, 142-slip marina, tour desk, beauty salon, boutiques, shopping arcade.

Marriott's Harbor Beach Resort. 3030 Holiday Dr., Fort Lauderdale, FL 33316. ☎ **800/ 222-6543** or 954/525-4000. Fax 954/766-6193. 659 units. A/C TV TEL. Winter $349–$499 double. Off-season $169–$189 double. Year-round from $600 suite. AE, CB, DC, DISC, MC, V. From I-95, exit on I-595 east to U.S. 1 north; proceed to SE 17th St.; make a right and go over the intracoastal bridge past three traffic lights to Holiday Dr.; turn right.

Situated on 16 oceanfront acres just south of Fort Lauderdale's "strip" is the popular and predictable Marriott. From the spacious rooms and suites to the 8,000-square-foot swimming pool, everything in this very well run hotel is huge. All rooms open onto private balconies overlooking either the ocean or the Intracoastal Waterway. Return guests include many convention groups and families who enjoy the space to spread out. Service is more efficient than personal.

Dining/Diversions: A formal restaurant serves one of Fort Lauderdale's most elegant dinners and a less formal Japanese restaurant serves hibachi dinners that are prepared at your table. Three other casual restaurants serve breakfast, lunch, dinner, and late-night drinks.

Amenities: Concierge, room service, in-room massage, laundry services, newspaper delivery, baby-sitting, twice-daily maid service, express checkout, secretarial services, valet parking, courtesy car for shopping and golf, free coffee in lobby. Outdoor heated pool, beach, health club, Jacuzzi, sauna, sundeck, five clay tennis courts, water-sports equipment, bicycle rental, game room, children's center and programs, business center, self-service Laundromat, tour desk, boutiques, conference rooms, car-rental desk, beauty salon.

✪ **Wyndham Resort and Spa.** 250 Racquet Club Rd., Fort Lauderdale, FL 33326. ☎ **800/ 996-3426** or 954/389-3300. Fax 954/384-6878. 500 units. A/C TV TEL. Winter from $245 double. Off-season from $175 double. Golf and spa packages (with or without meals) $65– $305 per person based on double occupancy. AE, CB, DC, DISC, MC, V. From I-95, exit at I-595 west to I-75; exit on Arvida Pkwy.; continue west to Weston Blvd.; turn right and proceed to Saddle Club Rd.; turn left to Bonaventure Blvd. Make a right to Racquet Club Rd. From Florida Turnpike, take I-595 West, take Exit 1, SW 136th Ave., S.R. 84, and proceed to Bonaventure Blvd.

Having changed hands frequently, this unusual spa and golf resort is a bit difficult to peg down. Built in 1981 on 23 acres, this active resort quickly earned a great reputation for its world-class facilities. Unfortunately, years of mismanagement resulted in its deterioration. A $10 million renovation begun in 1996 improved things, but then the resort was sold again to Wyndham resorts, which has big plans. Though it lacks any real charm, so far the overhaul looks fantastic.

The rooms, scattered throughout nine four-story buildings, have also been thoroughly gutted and reoutfitted in a bright tropical style, with conveniences like telephone voice mail and data ports, irons, ironing boards, coffeemakers, clock radios, and hair dryers. Also, suites and deluxe rooms offer wet bars and small refrigerators.

Although it is a lengthy trek to the nearest beach, this first-class property has plenty of opportunities to sun and swim, with five pools, including separate lap pools for men and women, and a private lake.

Dining/Diversions: With four restaurants, including one serving superb Tuscan food in a formal setting and another with real spa cuisine, you'll find plenty of delicious choices. You may even want to request recipes to take home. Also on the premises are four lounges for afternoon and evening entertainment and cocktails.

Amenities: Concierge, 24-hour room service, dry-cleaning and laundry service, newspaper delivery, in-room massage, twice-daily maid service, express checkout, secretarial services, valet parking, shopping transportation. Limited kitchenettes in some suites, Spectravision movie channels, five swimming pools, full-service spa, Jacuzzi, sauna, two championship golf courses, sundeck, 15 night-lit tennis courts, children's programs, business center, tour desk, boutiques, conference rooms, car-rental desk, beauty salon, boutique, and gift shop.

EXPENSIVE

✪ **Lago Mar Resort and Club.** 1700 S. Ocean Lane, Fort Lauderdale, FL 33316. ☎ **800/ 524-6627** or 954/523-6511. Fax 954/524-6627. E-mail: reservations@lagomar.com. 212 units. A/C TV TEL. Winter $195 double; from $285 suite. Off-season $100–$135 double; from $135 suite. AE, DC, MC, V. From Federal Hwy. (U.S. 1), turn east onto SE 17th St. Causeway; turn right onto Mayan Dr.; turn right again onto S. Ocean Dr.; turn left onto Grace Dr.; then left again onto S. Ocean Lane to the hotel.

After extensive renovations, this sprawling family owned resort is even better than before. Lago Mar, a casually elegant resort, occupies its own little island between Lake Mayan and the Atlantic and is very family oriented, with lots of facilities and supervised activities for children, especially during spring break and Christmas vacations. It's also good for business travelers looking for value. Unfortunately, the word has gotten out and it has become difficult to get reservations during the season.

Most accommodations here are suites, available in a variety of configurations. The smallest suites, called "executive," are decorated in contemporary prints and are simple and comfortable. The executive suites are very large, with a king-size bed, separate dressing area, pull-out sofa, and separate tub and shower in an extralarge bathroom. Each has a private balcony and full kitchen, or at least a microwave and a refrigerator. Ask for one of the newer units since they are generally larger and have more closet space. Definitely take advantage of the hotel's waterfront location to use the convenient water taxi (see box above).

Dining/Diversions: Two full-service restaurants, a grill, soda shop, and a lounge may tempt you to never leave this top-rated resort. An outdoor cafe overlooking the sea serves grilled chicken and fish, sandwiches and salads; another more formal indoor dining room features standards like Caesar salads and filet mignon. (Note that men are required to wear jackets.) Also, in addition to a casual poolside grill, there is an old-fashioned soda shop that serves up hot dogs and milkshakes. In season, the hotel lounge features live music.

Amenities: Concierge, room service, dry-cleaning and laundry service, secretarial services, newspaper delivery, valet parking. Kitchenettes in most suites, outdoor pool and lagoon, beach, small fitness center, game rooms, children's playground, supervised children's programs during holiday periods, business center, conference rooms, sundeck, four tennis courts, miniature golf course, volleyball courts, shuffleboard, water-sports concession, men's and women's apparel shops, Laundromat, tour desk.

Riverside Hotel. 620 E. Las Olas Blvd., Fort Lauderdale, FL 33301. ☎ **800/325-3280** or 954/467-0671. Fax 954/462-2148. www.riversidehotel.com. 116 units. A/C TV TEL. Winter $179–$199 double; from $249 suite. Off-season $99–$139 double; from $139 suite. AE, DC, MC, V. From I-95, exit onto Broward Blvd.; turn right onto Federal Hwy. (U.S. 1), then left onto Las Olas Blvd.

Right in the thick of Ft. Lauderdale's hottest downtown area, the six-story Riverside Hotel is one of the oldest in South Florida. Built in 1936, it looks like a Wild West movie set, complete with a second-floor wooden terrace and an enormous mural on the front facade. You are in the middle of trendy Las Olas Boulevard and on the route of the popular water taxi. On weekends the hotel is often packed with wedding guests attending ceremonies that are held outside by the small heated swimming pool. A bit nicer than the public areas, which are outfitted in Mexican tile and wicker furnishings, the guest rooms upstairs are spacious and well maintained. Details like intricately tiled bathrooms and old-style furniture enhance the charm of the otherwise stark building. The best rooms face the New River, but it's hard to see the water past the parking lot and trees. The hotel does not have an abundance of services or facilities but the central downtown location makes almost anything you could desire just steps away.

Dining/Diversions: Do sample Indigo, a fantastic Asian/Indonesian restaurant in the hotel lobby (see "Where to Dine," below). Also on the premises is a more standard grill restaurant and a lounge.

Amenities: Room service, dry-cleaning and laundry service, secretarial services, valet parking, gift shop. Refrigerators, outdoor pool, nearby health club, conference rooms, sundeck.

MODERATE

✪ **Banyan Marina Apartments.** 111 Isle of Venice, Fort Lauderdale, FL 33301. ☎ **954/ 524-4430.** Fax 954/764-4870. www.banyanmarina.com. 10 units. A/C TV TEL. Winter $85– $190 apt. Off-season $55–$130 apt. Weekly and monthly rates available. EURO, MC, V. To get there from I-95, exit Broward Blvd. E.; cross U.S. 1 and turn right on SE 15th Ave.; at the first traffic light (Las Olas Blvd.), turn left. Turn left at the third island (Isle of Venice).

One of the best accommodation values in South Florida, this hidden treasure is built around a dramatic 75-year-old banyan tree and is located directly on the active canals halfway between Fort Lauderdale's downtown and the beach. When available, you'll choose between one- and two-bedroom apartments. All are comfortable and spacious with full kitchens and living rooms. The best part of staying here, besides your gracious and knowledgeable hosts, Peter and Dagmar Neufeldt, is that the water taxi will find you here and take you anywhere you want to be day or night. There is also a small outdoor heated pool and a marina for those with boats in tow. In 1998, the Neufeldts were honored by a local campaign to enhance the area, Broward Beautiful, winning First Place in the category of small multifamily dwellings.

✪ **Hollywood Beach Resort.** 101 N. Ocean Dr. (at Fla. A1A and Hollywood Blvd.), Hollywood, FL 33019. ☎ **954/921-0990.** Fax 954/920-9480. 400 units (approximately 200 on rental program). A/C TV TEL. Winter from $109. Off-season from $68. AE, DC, DISC, MC, V.

There is nothing cozy or quaint about this sprawling 1920s beachfront hotel, but it couldn't be better located or better priced. The two best features are that all the rooms have full kitchens and the hotel is directly on the ocean. This eight-story building actually operates as a privately held condominium where owners can elect to put their units on a rental program. So there is no telling how rooms may be furnished or outfitted (management does maintain certain standards). All the units I have seen are clean and modest. Larger units and those with views are significantly more expensive than studios. If the weather is bad, consider shopping at the adjacent Ocean Walk Mall or hit a movie at the on-site multiplex movie theater. Also on the premises is a large outdoor pool and Jacuzzi. The many conveniences of this well-situated property make it especially popular with tour groups from Europe, South America, and Canada.

INEXPENSIVE

Ronny Dee Resort Motel. 717 S. Ocean Blvd., Pompano Beach, FL 33062. ☎ **954/ 943-3020.** Fax 954/783-5112. 35 units. A/C TV. Winter from $65 double; from $475 efficiency. Off-season from $34 double; from $239 efficiency. AE, MC, V. From I-95, exit Atlantic Blvd. E. to Fla. A1A N.

The bad news is that this family owned motel is located on busy Fla. A1A; the good news is that it's just 100 yards from the beach and amazingly inexpensive. Popular with European guests, this two-story yellow motel, wrapped around a central swimming pool, contains almost three dozen suburban-style wood-paneled guest rooms filled with an eclectic mix of furniture. All contain a small refrigerator, but none have a telephone; pay phones are located in a public area, near a large game room that contains a pool table, VCR, books, and other games. Ping-Pong and shuffleboard are also available.

Sea Downs (and the Bougainvillea). 2900 N. Surf Rd., Hollywood, FL 33019. ☎ **954/ 923-4968.** Fax 954/923-8747. www.seadowns.com and www.bougainvilleahollywood.com. 14 units. A/C TV TEL. Winter $70–$86 efficiency; $98–$113 one-bedroom apt; $124 penthouse. Off-season $46–$62 efficiency; $60–$84 one-bedroom apt; $89–$92 penthouse. Special weekly and monthly rates also available. No credit cards accepted. From I-95, exit Sheridan St. E. to Fla. A1A south; drive 1/2 mile to Coolidge St.; turn left.

This bargain accommodation is often booked months in advance by returning guests who want to be directly on the beach without paying a fortune. The hosts of this superclean '50s motel, Claudia and Karl Herzog, live on the premises and keep things running smoothly. Renovations completed in 1997 have replaced bathroom fixtures, and many rooms have been redecorated here and at the Herzogs' other even less expensive property next door, the Bougainvillea. Guests at either spot can use the heated pool, barbecue grills, picnic area, laundry facilities, and sundeck.

A HOSTEL

Floyd's Youth Hostel/Crew House. Please call for address and directions in Fort Lauderdale. ☎ **954/462-0631.** Fax 954/462-6881. E-mail: FECreamer@aol.com. 20-plus beds. $12.20–$13.50 per person for a dorm bed. No credit cards. Free daytime pickup.

Although there are a number of cheap hostels operating near Fort Lauderdale's renowned strip, the best place to crash is Floyd's. While it is a few miles inland from the beach, this well-kept lodging offers what every backpacker and international traveler wants—safety and good, warm fellow travelers. Floyd himself takes care of the guests, many of whom have come looking for work on the area's yachts. In fact, we have agreed not to list the address since Floyd insists on interviewing each prospective guest by phone before booking. Rest assured, you've found one of the area's best and safest hostels with extras like a cupboard full of complimentary staples—milk, cereal, and generic-brand macaroni and cheese.

WHERE TO DINE

Having hosted visitors for so long, Fort Lauderdale, and to some extent Hollywood as well, have some of South Florida's finest restaurants. Increasingly, ethnic options are joining the legions of surf-and-turf options that dominated the area for so long.

Las Olas Boulevard has dozens of eateries (so many, in fact, that the city has disallowed any new restaurants to open on the overcrowded 2-mile street). In addition to those reviewed below, consider **Jackson's 450,** 450 E. Las Olas Blvd. (☎ **954/ 522-4450**), and **ZAN(Z)BAR,** a romantic South African restaurant decked out in zebra and leopard skin at 602 E. Las Olas Blvd. (☎ **954/767-3377**).

VERY EXPENSIVE

Cafe Arugula. 3110 N. Federal Hwy., Lighthouse Point. ☎ **954/785-7732.** Reservations recommended. Main courses $10–$25. AE, CB, DC, DISC, MC, V. Sun–Thurs 5–10pm, Fri–Sat 5–10:30pm. From I-95, take Sample Rd. E. to U.S. 1; make a right. AMERICAN CONTEMPORARY.

Even though it's a bit out of the way, loyal customers come from neighboring counties to experience one of Broward's first nouvelle restaurants. Chef/owner Dick Cingolani oversees every aspect of this elegant eatery on the very northern edge of Broward County.

The main dining room with an open kitchen and oak-burning oven as its centerpiece is elegant but not overly stuffy. Food is the main focus here. From the sautéed jumbo lump crab cakes to the handcrafted chocolate cakes, everything that comes out of the kitchen is superb. Salads and appetizers are large and beautifully displayed. One of the best is the spicy Thai shrimp "taco" served with slightly sweet and lightly spiced coconut and lemongrass sauce. For vegetable lovers, the grilled portobello mushrooms over baby greens with a crumble of herbed feta cheese also stands out. The veal chop, grilled with rosemary, is tender and aromatic and is served with a creamy mound of mashed potatoes flavored with a hint of garlic as well as a delicate stir-fry of fresh vegetables. Like all meals here, the side dishes are perfectly paired with the flavors of the main attraction.

✪ **Cafe Maxx.** 2601 E. Atlantic Blvd., Pompano Beach. ☎ **954/782-0606.** Reservations recommended. Main courses $18–$32. AE, CB, DC, DISC, MC, V. Mon–Thurs 5:30–10:30pm, Fri–Sat 5:30–11pm, Sun 5:30–10pm. From I-95, exit at Atlantic Blvd. E. The restaurant is three lights east of Federal Hwy. INTERNATIONAL.

Every one of chef/owner Oliver Saucy's restaurants has received accolades from all who bestow them in the culinary arena. This is his best. An oak-burning grill fills the contemporary and casually formal space with enticing aromas from around the globe. The pricey à la carte offerings borrow from Italian, Asian, creole, Cuban, and Caribbean kitchens to create exotic and delicious mixes like potato-encrusted softshell crab, barbecued chicken quesadilla, and pistachio-fried oysters, as well as a host of other exciting but not overwrought dishes. Reserve early on weekends when the most coveted seats, the cozy booths, book well in advance.

EXPENSIVE

East City Grill. 505 N. Atlantic Blvd. (Fla. A1A between Las Olas and Sunrise blvds.), Fort Lauderdale. ☎ **954/565-5569.** Reservations recommended well in advance. Main courses $13–$27. AE, CB, DC, DISC, MC, V. Mon–Fri 9am–3pm and 5:30–11pm, Sat 8am–3pm and 5:30pm–midnight, Sun 8am–3pm and 5:30–10pm. ASIAN AMERICAN/SEAFOOD.

This happening spot on the beach offers an ocean-side location and a killer nouvelle-style menu; it's yet another hit by the mega-Maxx group (see Cafe Maxx, above). For starters consider steamed crab and goat-cheese dumplings, lots of innovative sushi dishes, or Jamaican beer-steamed prawns. A steamer bar allows you to create your own dinner with a choice of steaming broths, sauces, and sides. You must be creative to dine here. If you are, and you love fresh, interesting seafood, you won't mind the wait at the stunning oak bar where you can look into the open kitchen. Otherwise, stick to the old-fashioned steak and fish houses in town.

Revolution 2029. 2029 Harrison St., Hollywood. ☎ **954/920-4748.** Reservations suggested. Main courses $13–$24. AE, DC, DISC, MC, V. Tues–Fri 11:30am–3pm, Sun–Thurs 5–10pm, Fri–Sat 5pm–midnight. MULTICULTURAL.

The first real fusion eatery in once dowdy Hollywood, Revolution attracts upscale hipsters looking for a dining "experience." While nearby South Beach has plenty of this kind of thing, Hollywood is just catching on. The menu is as modern as the sleek decor. With the best of everything from around the world, the menu varies both nightly and seasonally. You may want to start with gorgeous green New Zealand mussels gently flavored with coriander, coconut curry broth, and chunks of crisp apple or a rich roasted corn chowder with sweet potato and spinach corn custard. For vegetarians, there are many great options like oven-roasted portobello mushrooms, crispy vegetable egg rolls, and almond-crusted goat cheese. Innovative dishes like tamarind grilled swordfish and port marinated pork chops are interesting but not overly fussy. Except on busy weekends, service is efficient and friendly.

MODERATE

Aruba Beach Cafe. 1 E. Commercial Blvd., Lauderdale-by-the-Sea. ☎ **954/776-0001.** Reservations not accepted. Main courses $9–$16. AE, DC, DISC, MC, V. Daily 11am–11pm (bar stays open later). SEAFOOD/AMERICAN.

More recommendable as a spot to drink than to eat, Aruba is popular at all hours, especially because of its very central location, directly on the beach at the end of Commercial Boulevard. The extensive menu offers salads, sandwiches, and the requisite seafood offerings. The food is fine, but uninspired. Choose a few good appetizers like the creamy smoked fish dip served with seasoned flat bread, the fried calamari, or a selection from the raw bar.

✪ **Casablanca Cafe.** On the ocean at the corner of Fla. A1A and Alahambra St., Fort Lauderdale. ☎ **954/764-3500.** Reservations not accepted. Main courses $8–$18. AE, DISC, DC, MC, V. Daily 11:30am–11pm. CONTINENTAL/AMERICAN.

Although it may seem odd to sit next to a roaring fire while listening to live music in the warm South Florida climate, at Casablanca it's a perfect complement to the stunning architecture and stupendous cooking. Everything from the warm macadamia nut–encrusted goat-cheese salad to a filet mignon in a cognac-and-mushroom sauce served with perfectly al dente pasta is immaculately prepared and served by a friendly staff. Six or seven specials are included daily on the menu; the best are seafood creations with superfresh local fish or lobster.

Conca'D'Oro. 1833 Tyler St. (on Young Circle), Hollywood. ☎ **954/927-6704.** Reservations not accepted. Pizzas $7–$12.50. Main courses $8.95–$19.95. MC, V. Mon–Thurs 11am–11pm, Fri–Sat 11am–midnight, Sun 4–11pm. ITALIAN.

This bustling Italian restaurant is always busy. It's not that the food is so extraordinary, but that the portions are large, service is quick, and the attitude is straight from Brooklyn. The pizzas, served Neapolitan (thin crust) or Sicilian style, are large and topped with lots of cheese and a good tangy tomato sauce. Don't expect more than iceberg lettuce in the salads but do take advantage of the huge heroes and tasty house wines. If you are with a group, order one or two entrees to share. You will have leftovers. Although they are not always on the menu, ask for fresh mussels if they are in season. While other appetizers are battered and fried, the young black mussels are done to perfection in a red or white sauce. Also good is the hearty lasagna that is full of chunks of garlicky meatballs and mild sausage.

✪ **Indigo.** In the Riverside Hotel, 620 E. Las Olas Blvd. ☎ **954/467-0671.** Reservations only for groups of six or more. Main courses $11–$19. AE, DISC, DC, MC, V. Daily 7am–11pm; weekends until midnight or later. SOUTHEAST ASIAN/ECLECTIC.

This not-so-traditional Southeast Asian meal begins with a basket of pappadoms, nan, and shrimp puff bread. All are delicious and easy to fill up on, especially when spread with the tangy pineapple chutney or cucumber pickle. An impressive appetizer is a lightly peppered dusted seared tuna served in a crispy basket of udon noodles. Look underneath for a hidden dab of sweet apricot puree. It's fantastically rich and a good complement to the spicy fish. A macadamia-encrusted brie is astounding, served over baby lettuce and mixed with a citrusy basil dressing. Extra crispy crostini are scattered over the hearty dish for extra dipping advantage. Entrees run the gamut from a lean though somewhat dry Balinese lamb to a musky smoked duckling to a rosemary skewered shrimp. As to be expected in Asian cuisine, vegetarians have plenty of choices, too. In addition to a super rich grilled vegetable cassoulet au gratin and a fried rice dish with shallots, corn, and asparagus, there are pizzas baked on top of puffy nan bread covered with such toppings as onions, shiitake mushrooms, goat cheese, spinach, eggplant, garlic, curried tomato, and pine nuts. Particularly good is a meaty soy and portobello mushroom combination wrapped in fluffy puff pastry served with a delicate broccoli sauce. Ask servers for suggestions, though. Even if they are a bit harried on weekends, they tend to be knowledgeable and honest.

✪ **Sugar Reef.** 600 N. Surf Rd. (on the Boardwalk just north of Hollywood Blvd.), Hollywood. ☎ **954/922-1119.** Reservations only for groups over six. Main courses $12–$20; sandwiches and salads $5–$8.50. AE, DISC, MC, V. Mon 4–10:30pm, Tues–Thurs 11am–10:30pm, Fri–Sun 11am–11pm (sometimes later in winter). TROPICAL FRENCH.

A welcome addition to a strip of greasy fish joints, hot-dog stands, and bars, Sugar Reef has captured the attention of visitors and locals who appreciate superior and imaginative meals served for very reasonable prices. Chef/owner Patrick Farnault left a successful and formal restaurant in Fort Lauderdale to open this ocean-side bistro. Simple offerings might include a salmon BLT with dill mayonnaise or Jamaican-style pork loin or a burger and fries. Portions are generous but not huge. Escargot in a green curry sauce with lemongrass is a delicious twist on an old favorite, evoking memories of subtle and spicy Vietnamese dishes. More than half a dozen salads, some with cheese, chicken, or fish, are a perfect meal for beach-goers looking for something light and healthful as they enjoy the view. As is fitting for a beachside eatery, service is laid-back but still professional.

Sushi Blues Cafe. 1836 S. Young Circle (east on Hollywood Blvd.), Hollywood. ☎ **954/929-9560.** Reservations recommended on weekends. Main courses $11–$20; sushi $1.75–$2.75 per piece. AE, MC, V. Mon–Thurs 6pm–midnight, Fri–Sat 6pm–2am. JAPANESE.

Live loud blues and jazz combine with pretty good sushi to make an unusual pair at this small storefront eatery located on Hollywood's largest traffic circle. There are only about 12 tables and a dozen counter stools in this relatively straightforward and unadorned sushi room. In addition to raw fish, the cafe offers some inventive specials like salmon carpaccio with caper sauce, fried soft-shell crab drizzled with a spicy sesame sauce, miso-broiled eggplant, and grilled smoked sausage with Japanese mustard. The restaurant is popular with a 20-something crowd and is packed Friday and Saturday nights, when there's live music.

Topanga! 5001 N. Federal Hwy. (at Commercial Blvd.), Ft. Lauderdale. ☎ **954/771-8555.** Reservations for five or more suggested. Main courses $9–$18.95; pastas $9–$14.45. AE, DC,

DISC, MC, V. Mon–Thurs 11:30am–10pm, Fri 11:30am–11pm, Sat noon–11pm, Sun noon–10pm. CALIFORNIA-STYLE GRILL AND PIZZA BISTRO.

This bright and bustling restaurant is a perfect choice for a quick healthy lunch or dinner. Local businesspeople favor it in the afternoons since they can get in and out within 45 minutes or linger for hours in the pleasant sun-drenched eatery. There is even an outside terrace for those who don't mind the busy highway as a backdrop. With a large but not overwhelming menu featuring Italian favorites like chicken marsala, pizzas, and more than a dozen pastas, this is a place that appeals to everyone (including the kids). Salads are large (like most other entrees) and can easily be shared by three. Or, ask for a half portion, which is plenty big for one or two. My favorite is a mix of fresh baby greens with large slabs of moist and spicy dolphin (mahimahi) and chunks of feta cheese, briny Greek olives, and a slightly sweet champagne vinaigrette dressing. Pizzas, too, are fresh and filling. Try the goat cheese and basil or the unusual Acapulco chicken with tequila, lime, herbs, and a side of guacamole and salsa. The daily specials like beef and veal meat loaf, seafood quesadilla, or lemon and dill salmon are usually a good bet. An impressive selection of wines and beers plus lots of decadent desserts make this place a super value and a great find in the middle of a fast-food-glutted highway.

INEXPENSIVE

✪ **Deli Den.** 2889 Stirling Rd. (west of I-95), Hollywood. ☎ **954/961-4070.** Main courses $5–$11; bagel sandwiches $1–$7.50. AE, MC, V. Daily 8am–10pm. JEWISH-STYLE DELI.

Catering to Broward's New York crowd for nearly 3 decades, this warehouse-sized deli serves the area's finest cheese blintzes, red cabbage soup, and matzo balls. Breakfast selections include superthick French toast with bacon, sausage, or ham, plus dozens of egg specialties like minced lox, eggs and onions, or corned beef hash and eggs. All baking is done on the premises. And owners are proud to say that absolutely everything else, from coleslaw to blintzes, is also homemade. The best news is that kids under 12 eat free every Monday and Thursday.

East Coast Burrito Factory. 261 E. Commercial Blvd., Fort Lauderdale. ☎ **954/772-8007.** Tacos and burritos $3–$6; salads $4–$6. AE, CB, DC, DISC, MC, V. Mon–Sat 11am–9:45pm, Sun noon–7:45pm. FLORIDA/MEXICAN.

Just off of I-95 is an oasis. A dozen wooden benches line the counter at this super Mexican diner, which serves made-to-order soft tacos, burritos, hot dogs, and salads. For a healthier spin on a burrito, try the Florito, made with black beans instead of refried beans—a uniquely Florida invention. My favorite is the "Super Veggie," stuffed with corn, salsa, mushrooms, black olives, carrots, peppers, and hearts of palm, then doused with the restaurant's own superhot chile pepper sauce. The guacamole and various huge salads are also fantastic, especially on a sunny day on the back patio. To finish it off, try a Latin flan or an honest slice of key lime pie. There are four other locations throughout Broward and Palm Beach counties.

Flashback Diner. 220 S. Federal Highway (2 blocks south of Hallandale Beach Blvd.), Hallandale. ☎ **954/454-8300.** Main courses $9–$12; sandwiches $4–$7. DISC, MC, V. Daily 24 hours. AMERICAN/GREEK/DINER.

This classic diner serves up old-fashioned favorites like meat loaf, fried chicken, melted cheese, burgers, subs and omelets, as well as many Greek specialties including moussaka and pastitsio. Prices, especially for daily lunch specials are a real bargain. Veggies are soggy and fries greasy, but no one said this was a nouvelle cuisine. Instead, expect a true flashback complete with waitresses in thick glasses, aprons, and attitude. The place especially appeals to Broward's senior set who come for a good value and pleasant personal attention.

✪ **The Floridian Restaurant.** 1410 E Las Olas Blvd., Ft. Lauderdale. ☎ **954/463-4041.** Sandwiches $3–$7; breakfast combos $3.50–$8; hot platters $7–$14. AE, DC, MC, V. Daily 24 hours. AMERICAN/DINER.

A landmark on Las Olas, this popular spot turns out excellent diner fare around the clock. It's especially busy on weekend mornings when locals and tourists come in for huge omelets, fresh oatmeal, sausage, muffins, and biscuits. Service can be a bit brusque, but it's worth it.

Thai Spice. 1514 E. Commercial Blvd. (east of I-95), Fort Lauderdale. ☎ **954/771-4535.** Reservations recommended. Main courses $9.95–$26. AE, DC, DISC, MC, V. Mon–Thurs and Sun 11am–3pm and 5–10pm, Fri–Sat 5–11pm. THAI.

The tacky and typical decor of Thai Spice belies the authentic and delicious food turned out here. Soft-shell crab in a light and subtle chile sauce and tender shrimp cakes are fantastic and frequent specials. Regular menu items include a slightly sweet and almost buttery pad Thai with a generous serving of shrimp, chicken chunks, and scallion. Lunch specials are obscenely cheap and include all the favorites.

THE HOLLYWOOD & FORT LAUDERDALE AREA AFTER DARK

The newly hip downtown area of Hollywood is centered around **Harrison Street and Young Circle** (east of Dixie Highway at Hollywood Boulevard). A funky menagerie of bookstores, coffee shops, galleries, and a couple of live music joints are worth exploring. One of the latest and most welcome additions is **O'Hara's Pub and Jazz Cafe** at 1905 Hollywood Blvd. (☎ 954/925-2555). Kitty Ryan, who operates another club with the same name in Fort Lauderdale, has duplicated her successes here with a smoking jazz club which attracts superior acts from all over.

A funkier set hangs out at **Warehaus 57** just across the street (☎ 954/ 926-6633), where long-hairs converse over killer frozen coffee drinks or glasses of jug wine. This used bookstore, clothing store, and acoustic music venue is an inviting and happening little spot. During the week, come for a game of backgammon or a cup of joe. Folky local bands play on weekends to the delight of an eclectic crowd that comes at the generous invitation of owner Lauren Tellman (who also designs the racy and strappy leather clothing in the back). During the week she closes at 6pm. Friday and Saturday, she's there until at least midnight.

Sushi Blues was one of the first spots to offer live music in this neighborhood (see "Where to Dine," above). Live bands play jazz, blues, or world music on Friday and Saturday, and if you have dinner there you can skip the cover (usually $10).

Also in Hollywood, just west of Young Circle at Federal Highway, is **Club M** (☎ 954/925-8396), a small local blues showcase with a bit of good jazz and electric thrown in. On busy Friday and Saturday nights when live bands perform, you'll pay a small cover.

Fort Lauderdale has hundreds of bars and clubs for every taste. There are essentially four main areas that have clusters of happening scenes you can check out for yourself. To get you started, I have highlighted the best in each neighborhood. Plus, I have listed a few out-of-the-way spots for the more adventurous.

The waterfront bars and restaurants on the Intracoastal just south of Oakland Park Boulevard are especially recommendable for their outdoor patio bar scenes at all hours. Accessible by boat or car, **Bootlegger's,** at 3003 NE 32nd Ave. (☎ 954/ 563-4337), features more than 70 kinds of beers, with a featured draft of the day going for only $1. Here and next door at **Shooters**, 3033 NE 32nd Ave. (☎ **954/ 566-2855**), you'll find nautical types, families, and young professionals mixed in with a good dose of sunburned tourists enjoying the live reggae, jazz, or Jimmy Buffett–style tunes with the gorgeous backdrop of the bay and marinas all around. If you don't have your own boat, take the water taxi to really get the feel (see box above). Both are open until 2am.

The once famous "Strip" on the waterfront just north of Las Olas was overrun with spring-breakers. Now, it's been replaced with a mellower (and unfortunately more generic) scene. A newish shopping and entertainment complex called **Beach Place** is a sort of outdoor megamall modeled after Miami's hugely successful Bayside and Cocowalk. This block-long monster is the new home to a number of franchised bars and restaurants, like **Sloppy Joe's** (of Key West fame), **Howl at the Moon,** and **Hooters,** amid the requisite Gap and Banana Republic. The view, overlooking the ocean, makes it worth a stop for a drink.

Some of the college kids' old standbys remain in the neighborhood, including the **Elbo Room** at 241 S. Atlantic Blvd., on the corner of Las Olas Boulevard and Fla. A1A (☎ **954/463-4615**). It's maintained its rowdy and divey reputation by serving up frequent drink specials and live bands. A dedicated beer-drinking, football-watching crowd mingles with young tourists. This area is also accessible by water taxi.

An older crowd hangs out after dark on Las Olas Boulevard, where there are blocks and blocks of good restaurants and music clubs. One of the most happening is **O'Hara's Pub and Jazz Cafe,** at 722 E. Las Olas Blvd. (☎ **954/524-1764**). They pack 'em in until they spill onto the sidewalk of this smoky little club. Best known for presenting original jazz performers, O'Hara's also has blues and big-band music some Sunday afternoons. Call their jazz hot line (☎ **954/524-2801**) to hear the lineup for this and the newer **Hollywood Cafe.**

Most of the alternative music scene is centered in the downtown area of Fort Lauderdale. One good choice is the **Chili Pepper** (☎ **954/525-0094**) at 200 W. Broward Blvd., east of I-95. With big-name concerts as well as local band showcases, this place captures the heart and soul of the young and supercharged Wednesday through Sunday.

To find the heart of Fort Lauderdale's gay scene, head to **The Copa,** at 2800 S. Federal Hwy., east on I-595, near the airport (☎ **954/463-1507**). This big '80s-style black box has been the cornerstone of Fort Lauderdale's gay nightlife forever. Popular and updated shows are common on the many elevated stages surrounding a large and loud dance floor. **Club Cathode Ray** at 1105 E. Las Olas Blvd. (☎ **954/462-8611**) caters to a good-looking crowd and plays hot dance music every day from 4pm until 2am.

2 Boca Raton & Delray Beach

26 miles S of Palm Beach, 40 miles N of Miami

With its many mansions and waterfront condominiums, Boca Raton is the winter home to many of society's wealthy industrialists and retirees. Increasingly, the area is also attracting young families from other areas in the state who have tired of crime, corruption, and overcrowding. This planned city, known simply as "Boca," is a bit overmanicured and glitzy for my taste, although there are certainly some great restaurants and resorts worth exploring.

Delray, named after a suburb of Detroit, grew up completely separate from its southern neighbor. This community was founded in 1894 by a Midwestern postmaster who sold off 5-acre lots through Michigan newspaper ads. Because of their close proximity, Boca and Delray can easily be explored together. Budget-conscious travelers would do well to eat and sleep in Delray and dip into Boca for sightseeing and beaching only.

ESSENTIALS

GETTING THERE   Like the rest of the cities on the Gold Coast, Boca Raton and Delray are easily reached from I-95 or the Turnpike. both the Fort Lauderdale/Hollywood International Airport and the Palm Beach International Airport (at Congress Avenue and Belvedere Road) are convenient. Amtrak (☎ 800/USA-RAIL) trains make stops in Delray Beach at an unattended station at 345 S. Congress Ave.

VISITOR INFORMATION   Before your trip, call or write the **Palm Beach County Convention and Visitors Bureau,** 1555 Palm Beach Lakes Blvd., Suite 204, West Palm Beach, FL 33401 (☎ **800/554-PALM** or 561/471-3995; fax 561/471-3990). On weekdays from 8:30am until at least 4pm, stop by the **Boca Raton Chamber of Commerce** at 1800 N. Dixie Hwy., 4 blocks north of Glades Road (☎ **561/395-4433;** fax 561/392-3780; www.bocaratonchamber.com), Boca Raton, FL 33432, for information on attractions, accommodations, and events in the area. Also, try the **Delray Beach Chamber of Commerce** (☎ **561/278-0424;** fax 561/278-0555; e-mail: chamber@delraybeach.com), at 64 SE 5th Ave., half a block south of Atlantic Avenue on U.S. 1, Delray Beach, FL 33483.

WHERE TO PLAY, ON & OFF THE BEACH

BEACHES   Thankfully, Florida had the foresight to set aside some of its most beautiful coastal areas for the public's enjoyment. Many of the area's best beaches are located in state parks and are free to pedestrians and bikers. Most do charge for parking.

The **Delray Beach Public Beach,** on Ocean Boulevard at the east end of Atlantic Avenue, is one of the area's most popular hangouts. Weekends especially attract a young and good-looking crowd of active locals and tourists. Regular volleyball, Frisbee, and paddleball games make for good entertainment. For refreshments, a number of snack shops, bars, and restaurants are just across the street. Families enjoy the protection of lifeguards on the clean, wide beach. Gentle waters make it a good swimming beach, too. There's limited parking at meters along Ocean Boulevard.

Spanish River Park, on North Ocean Boulevard (Fla. A1A), 2 miles north of Palmetto Park Road in Boca Raton, is a huge oceanfront park with a large grassy area, making it one of the best choices for picnicking. Facilities include picnic tables, grills, rest rooms, and a bilevel 40-foot observation tower. You can walk through tunnels under the highway to nature trails that wind through fertile grasslands. Volleyball nets are ocean-side and always have at least one serious game going on. The park is open from 8am until 8pm. Also, read below about Red Reef Park.

GOLF   This area has plenty of good courses. Unfortunately, most of the best are private or are in the very expensive resorts. However, from May to October or November, about a dozen private courses open their greens to visitors staying in Palm Beach County hotels. This "Golf-A-Round" program is free or severely discounted (carts are additional), and reservations can be made through most major hotels. Ask at your hotel, or contact the **Palm Beach County Convention and Visitors Bureau** (☎ **561/471-3995**) for information on which clubs are available for play.

The semiprivate, 18-hole, par-61 course at the **Boca Raton Executive Country Club,** 7601 E. Country Club Blvd. (☎ 561/997-9410), is usually open to the public. A driving range is also on the property as well as a pro shop and a restaurant. A PGA professional gives lessons, and rental clubs are available. From Yamato Road East, turn left onto Old Dixie Highway; after about a mile, turn left onto Hidden Valley Boulevard and continue straight to the club. Greens fees are $11 to $27.

The **Boca Raton Municipal Golf Course,** 8111 Golf Course Rd. (☎ 561/483-6100), is located just north of Glades Road, half a mile west of the Florida Turnpike. This public 18-hole, par-72 course covers approximately 6,200 yards. There's a snack bar and a pro shop where clubs can be rented. Greens fees are $11 to $14 for 9 holes and $19 to $25 for 18 holes. Ask for special summer discount fees.

SCUBA DIVING & SNORKELING   Moray Bend, a 58-foot dive spot located about ¾ mile off Boca Inlet, is the area's most popular. It's home to three moray eels that are used to being fed by scuba divers. The reef is accessible by boat from **Force E Dive Center,** 877 E. Palmetto Park Rd., Boca Raton (☎ **561/368-0555**). Phone for dive times. Dives cost $38 to $45 per person.

Red Reef Park, 1400 N. Ocean Park Blvd. (☎ **561/393-7974**), a fully developed 67-acre oceanfront park in Boca Raton, has year-round lifeguard protection. There's good snorkeling for beginners around the rocks and reefs that lie just off the beach in 2 to 6 feet of water. There's also good swimming and a small picnic area with grills, tables, and rest rooms. The park, located a half mile north of Palmetto Park Road, is open daily from 8am to 10pm. You only pay if you drive in. It's $8 per car during the week or $10 on weekends.

TENNIS   The snazzy **Delray Beach Tennis Center, 201 W. Atlantic Ave. (☎ **561/243-7360**), has 14 lighted clay courts and 5 hard courts available by the hour. Phone for rates and reservations.

The 17 public lighted hard courts at **Patch Reef Park,** 2000 NW 51st St. (☎ **561/997-0881**), are available by reservation. The fee for nonresidents is $5.75 per person per hour. Courts are available Monday to Saturday from 7:30am to10pm and Sunday from 7:30am to dusk; you can phone ahead to see if a court is available. To reach the park from I-95, exit at Yamato Road West and continue past Military Trail to the park.

SEEING THE SIGHTS

Boca Raton Museum of Art. 801 W. Palmetto Park Rd. (1 mile east of I-95), Boca Raton. ☎ **561/392-2500.** Admission $3 adults, $2 seniors, $1 students. Tues–Wed and Sat–Sun 10am–6pm, Thurs–Fri 10am–9pm. Closed Mon. Free admission Wed.

In addition to a relatively small but well-chosen permanent collection that's strongest in 19th-century European oils, the museum stages a wide variety of temporary exhibitions by local and international artists. Lectures and films are offered on a fairly regular basis, so call ahead for details.

Gumbo Limbo Environmental Complex. 1801 N. Ocean Blvd. (on Fla. A1A between Spanish River Blvd. and Palmetto Park), Boca Raton. ☎ **561/338-1473.** Free admission. Mon–Sat 9am–4pm, Sun noon–4pm.

Named for an indigenous hardwood tree with continuously shedding bronze bark, the 20-acre complex protects one of the few surviving coastal hammocks, or forest islands, in South Florida. Visitors can walk through the hammock, on a ½-mile-long elevated boardwalk that ends at a 40-foot observation tower, from which you can see the Atlantic Ocean, the Intracoastal Waterway, and much of Boca Raton.

From mid-April to September, sea turtles come ashore here to lay their eggs. During this time, the center conducts turtle-watching tours and sea-turtle lectures. If you haven't seen turtles doing their thing, definitely stop in for a memorable experience.

In the museum is an impressive array of local flora and fauna, including live snakes, fish, crabs, sea turtles, and scorpions. Even city kids seem to like touching all the strange creatures here.

International Museum of Cartoon Art. 201 Plaza Real at Mizner Park, Boca Raton. ☎ **561/391-2200.** Admission $6 adults, $5 seniors, $4 students, $3 children 6–12 years old, under 5 free as well as members. Tues–Sat 10am–6pm, Sun noon–6pm. Closed Mon.

Reborn and hugely expanded after nearly 20 years of life in New York City, this extensive collection of cartoon art spans the decades and styles in its glitzy home in Mizner Park. In a gorgeous 52,000-square-foot gallery space, cartoon fans can see prints, frames, moving pictures, and books by some of the world's greatest cartoonists, including many by the museum's founder, Mort Walker (of *Beetle Bailey* fame). A fantastic gift shop offers posters, books, and lots of memorabilia.

✪ **Morikami Museum and Japanese Gardens.** 16869 Jog Rd., Delray Beach. ☎ **561/495-0233.** Museum $4.25 adults, $3.75 seniors, $2 children 6–18, free for children 5 and under, free for everyone Sun 10am–noon; gardens free. Museum Tues–Sun 10am–5pm; gardens Tues–Sat 10am–5pm. Closed major holidays.

Slip off your shoes and into a serene Japanese garden community that dates from 1905, when an entrepreneurial farmer, Jo Sakai, came to Boca Raton to build a tropical agricultural community. The Yamato Colony, as it was known, was short-lived; by the 1920s only one tenacious colonist remained: George Sukeji Morikami. But Morikami was quite successful, eventually holding one of the largest pineapple plantations in the area. The 200-acre Morikami Museum and Japanese Gardens, which opened to the public in 1977, was Morikami's gift to Palm Beach County and the State of Florida. The park section, dedicated to the preservation of Japanese culture, is constructed to appeal to all the senses. An artificial waterfall that cascades into a koi- and carp-filled moat, a small rock garden for meditation, and a large bonsai collection that includes miniature maple, buttonwood, juniper, and Australian pine trees are all worth contemplation—and it's free. There is also a great Asian restaurant on the premises worth checking out for lunch.

SHOPPING & BROWSING

Famous in New York City for its upscale antiques and gorgeous rugs, **ABC Carpet & Home** also has an outlet store in Delray Beach just off I-95 at 777 S. Congress (between Linton and Atlantic). Look for deep discounts (usually at least 30%) on very high-priced furnishings and flooring.

Mizner Park, on Federal Highway (between Palmetto Park and Glades roads) in Boca Raton (☎ **561/362-0606**), is the town square of this tiny enclave, complete with clothing shops, shoe stores, restaurants, live performances, and lots of beautiful landscaping. It's really an outdoor mall, with 45 specialty shops, seven good restaurants, and a multiscreen movie house. Each shop front faces a grassy island with blue and green gazebos, potted plants, and garden benches. It's extremely popular with folks who come here just to stroll, often until late in the evening.

Town Center Mall of Boca Raton has six huge department stores including Bloomingdale's, Burdines, Lord & Taylor, and Saks Fifth Avenue. Add to that hundreds of specialty shops, an extensive food court, and a range of other restaurants, and you have got the area's most comprehensive and beautiful shopping opportunity. The mall is located on the south side of Glades Road just west of I-95.

Another great area for a stroll is in the more artsy community of **Delray Beach,** known by many as Pineapple Grove. Here, along Atlantic Avenue, especially east of Swinton Avenue, you'll find a fantastic array of antique shops, clothing stores, and art galleries shaded by palm trees and colorful awnings. A lively cafe culture and many celebrations take place on this quaint old-style main street. Pick up the "Downtown Delray Beach" map and guide at almost any of the stores on this strip, or call ☎ **561/278-0424** for more information.

WHERE TO STAY

If you choose to stay in Boca or the surrounding areas, you will find some very luxurious lodgings, epitomized by the famous and often photographed pink **Boca Raton Hotel and Country Club,** where deluxe suites have gone for up to $6,000 per night. But don't worry, there are plenty of other choices on and near the beach.

A number of national chain hotels worth considering include a moderately priced **Holiday Inn Highland Beach Oceanside** at 2809 S. Ocean Blvd., on Fla. A1A southeast of Linton Boulevard (☎ **800/234-6835** or 561/278-6241). **The Radisson Bridge Resort,** at 999 E. Camino Real (☎ **800/333-3333** or 561/368-9500), operates a particularly popular and affordable resort on the Intracoastal Waterway just a few blocks from the Boca Raton Resort. *Beware:* It books up well in advance.

Although you won't find the rows and rows of cheap hotels as in Fort Lauderdale and Hollywood, a handful of mom-and-pop motels have survived along Fla. A1A between the towering condos of Delray Beach. Look along the beach just south of Atlantic Boulevard. Especially noteworthy is a pleasant little two-story, shingle-roofed **Bermuda Inn** at 64 S. Ocean Blvd. (☎ **561/276-5288**).

Even more economical options can be found in Deerfield Beach, Boca's neighbor, south of the county line. A number of beachfront efficiencies offer great deals, even in the winter months. Try the **Panther Motel and Apartments**, at 715 S. A1A (☎ **954/427-0700**). This clean and convenient motel has rates starting as low as $40. Although in season, you may find you have to book for a week at a time. Weekly rates in season start at $457.

If you are looking for something more private or for longer than just a few days, you may want to call a reservations service for help. Especially for rentals for a few weeks or months, call **Palm Beach Accommodations** (☎ **800/543-SWIM**).

VERY EXPENSIVE

✪ **Boca Raton Resort and Club.** 501 E. Camino Real (P.O. Box 5025), Boca Raton, FL 33431. ☎ **800/327-0101** or 561/395-3000. Fax 561/447-3183. 1,000 units. A/C MINIBAR TV TEL. Winter $200–$450 double; $450 golf villa apt; $420–$6,000 suite. Off-season $135–$410 double; $375 golf villa apt; $285–$6,000 suite. Very reasonable seasonal packages available. AE, DC, DISC, MC, V. From I-95 N., exit onto Palmetto Park Rd. E.; turn right onto Federal Hwy. (U.S. 1), and then left onto Camino Real to the resort.

Boca's most historical and romantic resort straddles both sides of the Intracoastal Waterway and encompasses more than 350 acres of land, with extensive and outstanding facilities for tennis, golf, and anything else an active family or individual could want, including three fitness centers with brand-new equipment, more than 30 tennis courts, and two 18-hole golf courses. Since 1926, this palatial hotel has been hosting the most discriminating international guests. Now, with a sizable population of local sports enthusiasts who have joined the country club, and lots of conferences going on, the place is still pleasing demanding visitors. Don't worry:

Palm Beach & Boca Raton

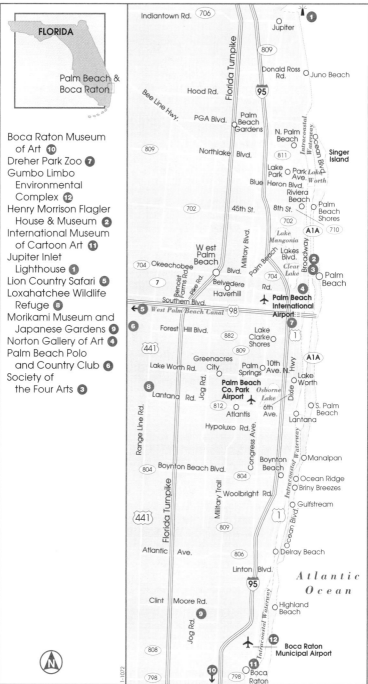

FLORIDA

Palm Beach & Boca Raton

Boca Raton Museum of Art ⑩
Dreher Park Zoo ⑦
Gumbo Limbo Environmental Complex ⑫
Henry Morrison Flagler House & Museum ②
International Museum of Cartoon Art ⑪
Jupiter Inlet Lighthouse ①
Lion Country Safari ⑤
Loxahatchee Wildlife Refuge ⑧
Morikami Museum and Japanese Gardens ⑨
Norton Gallery of Art ④
Palm Beach Polo and Country Club ⑥
Society of the Four Arts ③

271

The huge proportions of the Spanish-Moorish architecture and the sprawling grounds will ensure that you will never feel crowded or processed. And yearly renovations guarantee that you won't feel as if you are staying in a musty museum.

Compared to other destination resorts on Florida's east coast, this superior facility is a great value with all the amenities and elegance but none of the stuffiness. Everything is easy once you have decided which type of room you'll stay in. There are several options. Those in the original Cloisters building have exquisite architectural details, like arched doorways, high-beamed ceilings, a mix of reproduction antiques, and the most charm. The best part is that, although they are more modest in size than newer rooms, they are also the least expensive. The Boca Beach Club building, just a 5-minute drive and accessible by free shuttle or your own car, offers spacious cabana-style rooms on the ocean with sliding glass doors that open to beach breezes. Dressed with dark woods and rich colors, the rooms in the modern 27-story tower adjacent to the Cloisters are the most formal and enjoy sweeping views of this idyllic coast. Golf villas overlook the perfectly manicured greens. All are outfitted with two phones, large bathrooms, fluffy robes, and first-class furnishings.

Dining/Diversions: There are nine restaurants and three lounges to satisfy all tastes and budgets. A formal Italian restaurant on the top floor of the main building offers extraordinary views over Boca Raton. A seafood restaurant at the Boca Beach Club is known for its excellent and diverse menu. A coffee bar in the Cloister building is particularly popular in mornings and afternoons.

Amenities: Concierge, room service (24 hours), fitness classes, evening turndown, laundry, overnight shoe shine. An impressive array of children's programs. Three fitness centers, 5 swimming pools, 2 golf courses, 34 tennis courts (9 lighted), water-sports and bicycle rentals, snorkeling and scuba instruction, croquet, volleyball, basketball court, 2-mile jogging course, business center, well-priced boutiques and gift shops, racquetball.

MODERATE

Colony Hotel & Cabana Club. 525 E. Atlantic Ave. (P.O. Box 970), Delray Beach, FL 33483. ☎ **800/552-2363** or 561/276-4123. Fax 561/276-0123. www.thecolonyhotel.com/florida/. E-mail: info-fla@thecolonyhotel.com. 66 units. A/C TV TEL. Winter $145–$190 double. Off-season $90–$140 double. AE, MC, V.

This lovely three-story hotel is located right on Delray's main commercial thoroughfare about a mile from the hotel's private beach and club. The Colony benefited from a 1996 refurbishment that brought back some of its original 1926 details, including hardwood floors and authentic furnishings. Still, the rooms are modest in size and style but comfortable and clean. The hotel is popular with families who appreciate the many planned activities at the hotel's beachfront club 1 mile away, which offers a heated saltwater swimming pool, a private beach, as well as putting and shuffleboard tournaments. All facilities are free for guests.

Seagate Hotel & Beach Club. 400 S. Ocean Blvd., Delray Beach, FL 33483. ☎ **800/233-3581** or 561/276-2421. Fax 561/243-4714. 70 units. A/C TV TEL. Winter $179–$299 suite; $339–$369 two-bedroom suite. Off-season $74–$105 suite; $136–$152 two-bedroom suite. AE, CB, DC, MC, V. From I-95, exit onto Atlantic Ave. E., turn right onto Ocean Blvd. (Fla. A1A), and continue ½ mile to the hotel.

This modest, well-located hotel features generously sized rooms located in two buildings directly across the street from the beach. To make your stay more affordable and convenient, the hotel furnishes coffeemakers, fully stocked kitchens or kitchenettes, irons, large closets, and safes in each room. A recent redecorating replaced the quaint Old Florida furnishings with industrial Formica, plain blond wood, and commercial-grade carpeting. Also regretful are the tiny bathrooms with little or no counter space.

The Beach Club is located across the street, directly on the sand, where you can relax on a chaise lounge or dip into one of the heated pools. A moderately priced restaurant and bar will deliver snacks and cocktails to the beach. There's 400 feet of private beach, and special children's programs are offered during the high season. Overall, the resort is pleasant and extremely practical, especially for families. Little extras like newspapers and refreshments in the lobby make this an especially appealing option.

Spanish River Resort. 1111 E. Atlantic Ave., Delray Beach, Fl 33483. ☎ **800/543-SWIM** or 561-243-7946. Fax 561/276-9634. www.pbai.com. 75 units. A/C TV TEL. Winter $150–$250 studio or 1-bedroom; $315–$350 2-bedroom. Off-season from $85 studio or 1-bedroom; from $200 2-bedroom. Free 6th and 7th nights with weekly booking. DISC, MC, V.

An especially good value for those staying longer than a few days, this pleasant family oriented property offers fully furnished condominiums half a block from a popular beach and walking distance to Delray's best shops, restaurants, and galleries. The 11-story Mediterranean-style building has free lighted tennis courts, a large outdoor pool, and lovely ocean-view balconies. Apartments are spacious and outfitted with fully equipped kitchens. All units also have pullout queen-size sofa beds. The best part is there is no additional charge for extra guests. A one-bedroom unit can comfortably fit four or five people; a two-bedroom unit can easily accommodate six. Cots and rollaway beds are available at a minimum charge. Compared with many of the run-down 1950s motels in the area, this moderately priced, well-maintained tower is a real find.

INEXPENSIVE

Ocean Lodge. 531 N. Ocean Blvd. (just north of Palmetto Park Rd. on Fla. A1A), Boca Raton, FL 33432. ☎ **800/STAY-BOCA** or 561/395-7772. Fax 561/395-0554. 18 units. A/C TV TEL. Winter $95–$100 double; $105–$115 efficiency. Off-season $55–$60 double; $55–$75 efficiency. AE, MC, V.

Situated around a small heated pool and sundeck, this two-story motel is a particularly well-kept accommodation in an area of run-down or overpriced options. The large rooms offer furnishings and decor that are clean but a bit impersonal. A recent do-over that added modern Formica and floral wallpaper makes this a notch above a basic motel. Ask for a room in the back since the street noise can be a bit loud, especially in season. The bonus is that you are across the street from the ocean and in one of Florida's most upscale resort towns.

Shore Edge Motel. 425 N. Ocean Blvd. (on Fla. A1A, north of Palmetto Park Rd.), Boca Raton, FL 33432. ☎ **561/395-4491.** Fax 561/347-8759. 16 units. A/C TV TEL. Winter $75–$85 double; $95–$115 efficiency. Off-season from $45 double; from $55 efficiency. AE, MC, V.

Another relic of the '50s recently spiffed up with new landscaping and some redecorating, this motel is a good choice, especially because of its location—across the street from a public beach, just north of downtown Boca Raton. It's the quintessential South Florida motel: a small, pink, single-story structure surrounding a modest swimming pool and courtyard. Although the rooms are a bit on the small side, they're very neat and clean. The higher-priced accommodations are larger and come with full kitchens.

WHERE TO DINE

The Boca Raton and Delray areas have more than their fair share of expensive fish and steak houses. Thankfully, too, there are more and more innovative and health-conscious places moving in. Mizner Park has nearly a dozen eateries including a fantastic oyster bar, serving microbrew beers, called **Gigi's** (☎ **561/368-4488**). The area's other great options are highlighted below.

VERY EXPENSIVE

La Vieille Maison. 770 E. Palmetto Park Rd., Boca Raton. ☎ **561/391-6701** or 561/737-5677. Reservations recommended. Main courses $17–$40; fixed-price dinners $40 and $64. AE, CB, DC, DISC, MC, V. Daily 6–9:30pm (call for seating times). FRENCH.

The luxurious setting, a Mediterranean-inspired home filled with a variety of antique French furnishings and paintings, gives you the feeling of walking into a friend's country manor. Begin with lobster bisque, gratin of escargots with fennel and pistachio nuts, or pan-seared foie gras—each is equally delectable. It's difficult to choose from the many enticing entrees, which range from red snapper in black-and green-olive potato crust to medallions of beef, lamb, and venison over three sauces. You'll surely have to try at least a few of the gorgeous cheeses the server offers after your main course—the most extensive selection I've ever seen in this country. The lemon crepe soufflé with raspberry sauce is the dessert of choice—remember to order it early.

✪ **New York Prime.** 2350 Executive Center Dr. (west of I-95, exit Glades Rd.), Boca Raton. ☎ **561/998-3881.** Reservations suggested. Main courses $20–$60. AE, CB, DC, DISC, MC, V. Daily 5–11pm. STEAK HOUSE.

This ultraformal steak house is rivaled only by New York's famous few for its excellent meat, fish, and lobster dinners—and for the price. A professional staff of uniformed waiters knows the small but selective menu intimately and can recommend the appropriate cut of steak, the restaurant's signature dish. The sparkling atmosphere of the dining room allows for great people-watching and quiet conversation. Ask for a seat in the cozy booths. Unless you are a smoker, avoid the bar area. Cigar and cigarette smoking are encouraged in this den of excess. The expensive filtering system does a decent job of clearing stale smoke, but the aroma of freshly lighted cigars does waft far.

EXPENSIVE

Fifth Avenue Grill. 821 S. Federal Hwy., Delray Beach. ☎ **561/265-0122.** Additional location 4650 N. Federal Hwy., Lighthouse Point. ☎ 954/782-4433. Reservations accepted only for large parties. Main courses $16–$29. AE, DC, MC, V. Sun–Mon 11:30am–4pm and 5–11pm. STEAK HOUSE.

The old-world Fifth Avenue Grill is very popular with well-dressed seniors who come for the superb steaks, reliable service, and classic selections—onion soup, shrimp scampi, London broil, Caesar salad, and broiled local fish. This is the kind of place where they still remember to offer a touch of sherry for your conch chowder. Every main course includes unlimited house salad and is accompanied by a cheese-stuffed baked potato, fried shoestrings, or brown rice. Add to that a huge and varied wine list, and you've got a perfect night out in Delray. Everything on the predictable menu is well prepared and presented by professional servers in a dark and woodsy dining room.

Max's Grille. 404 Plaza Real, in Mizner Park, Boca Raton. ☎ **561/368-0080.** Reservations accepted only for six or more. Main courses $14–$26; pastas $10.95–$16.95. AE, CB, DC,

DISC, MC, V. Daily 11:30am–3pm, Mon–Thurs 5–10:30pm, Fri–Sat 5–11pm, Sun 5–10pm. AMERICAN.

One of the most popular choices in restaurant-crowded Mizner Park, Max's Grille is part of the growing chain of Unique Restaurants that have been wowing critics for years. With a large exhibition kitchen that occupies the entire back wall of the restaurant, patrons can watch as their yellowfin tuna steak or filet mignon is seared on a flaming oak grill. A large selection of chicken, meat loaf, pastas, and main-course salads provide healthful and delicious choices for sophisticated palates. A stunning bar serves trendy martinis in more than 15 varieties. For a more economical option, try Max's coffee shop next door at 402 Plaza Real for good old-fashioned comfort food in a real diner atmosphere.

Nick and Max's. 5050 Town Center Circle (in the Boca Center west off Palmetto Park Rd.), Boca Raton. ☎ **561/391-7177.** Reservations recommended. Main courses $16 and $30. AE, DC, DISC, MC, V. Mon–Fri 11:30am–2:30pm; Mon–Thurs 6–10:30pm; Fri–Sat until 11pm and Sun until 10pm. AMERICAN/MEDITERRANEAN.

Formerly Maxaluna, this hot spot in Boca Raton is another successful eatery in the Dennis Max empire. Serving creative Mediterranean inspired food like oak-grilled pork chops with mushroom lasagna with cherries and sage, marinated tuna with pasta, couscous paella with shrimp, calamari, and pearl onions, the chef and co-owner Nick Morfugen lets his Greek heritage shine. A well-heeled clientele crowds the sleek, art deco dining room every night and are happy to pay steep prices for food that is utterly decadent.

MODERATE

Splendid Blendeds. 432 E. Atlantic Ave., Delray. ☎ **561/265-1035.** Reservations recommended. Main courses $10.95–$19.95; sandwiches and salads $3.50–$8.95. AE, DC, MC, V. Mon–Fri 11:30am–2:30pm; Mon–Sat 5:30–10pm. Closed Sun. ECLECTIC.

Loyal regulars would like to keep this storefront bistro a secret so that the lines won't get even longer on weekends. The draw here is fresh, uncomplicated seafood and pastas that are interesting without being overly ambitious. The Southwestern-inspired chicken Santa Cruz is tender and juicy, served with a black-bean sauce and tangy pico de gallo. Many seafood specialties, like tuna, snapper, and shrimp dishes, are slight departures from classic recipes and seem to work most of the time. The drawback of this otherwise superb spot is the staff; they're well-meaning but easily flustered.

INEXPENSIVE

The Tin Muffin Cafe. 364 E. Palmetto Park Rd. (between Federal Hwy. and the Intercoastal Bridge). ☎ **561/392-9446.** Sandwiches and salads $5.95–$8.95. No credit cards. Mon–Fri 11am–5pm, Sat 11am–4pm. BAKERY/SANDWICH SHOP.

Popular with the downtown lunch crowd, this excellent storefront bakery keeps them lining up for big fresh sandwiches on fresh bread, muffins, quiches, and good homemade soups like split pea or lentil. The curried chicken sandwich is stuffed with oversized chunks of only white meat doused in a creamy curry dressing and fruit. There are a few cafe tables inside and even one outside on a tiny patio. Be warned, however, that service is forgivably slow and parking is a nightmare. Try parking a few blocks away at a meter on the street.

Tom's Place. 7251 N. Federal Hwy., Boca Raton. ☎ **561/997-0920.** Reservations not accepted. Main courses $8–$15; sandwiches $5–$6; early bird special $6.95. AE, MC, V. Tues–Fri 11:30am–10pm, Sat noon–10pm. Closed Mon. BARBECUE.

There are two important factors in a successful barbecue: the cooking and the sauce. Tom and Helen Wright's no-nonsense shack wins on both counts, offering flawlessly grilled meats paired with well-spiced sauces. Beef, chicken, pork, and fish are served soul-food style, with your choice of two sides like rice with gravy, collard greens, black-eyed peas, coleslaw, or mashed potatoes. Decoration is limited to signed celebrity photographs and plastic tablecloths.

BOCA RATON & DELRAY AFTER DARK
THE BAR, CLUB & MUSIC SCENE

The best variety of entertainment is offered in Delray Beach where a younger and funkier set makes its home. Atlantic Avenue now boasts several venues for live music, including **The Back Room,** 909 W. Atlantic Ave. near the corner of Swinton Avenue (☎ **561/243-9110**). A reasonable cover, usually between $2 and $6, depends on who is playing. A funky decor, eclectic crowd, and excellent music almost every night make this old standby another good option for live music from jazz to big band to classic rock. Only beer and wine are served (in plastic glasses). It's open Tuesday to Saturday until 3am.

Boston's on the Beach, at 40 S. Ocean Blvd. (☎ **561/278-3364**), is always a good choice for happy hour, Monday to Friday from 4 to 8pm, or for live reggae on Monday. A lively bar scene and good seafood on a deck overlooking the beach keep this place packed almost every night.

Boca Raton's most famous dance spot, **Club Boca** at 7000 W. Palmetto Park Rd. (☎ **561/368-3333**), which you'll hear advertised on obnoxious radio commercials, is a big, noisy warehouse out west of the highway that attracts a range of big-haired girls and macho guys. It's a fun diversion in otherwise sterile Boca and is open Thursday to Sunday until 5am.

True to her word, Gloria Gaynor has survived, and she is in Boca at **Polly Esther's,** 99 SE 1st Ave. (☎ **561/447-8955**). She and other disco divas can be heard blasting from the enormous sound system as the mixed young and 30-something set dances like it's Saturday night and they have the fever. Open Wednesday to Saturday. Take Palmetto Park Road East to Federal Highway; turn left onto SE 1st Avenue, where you'll see the club on the left.

THE PERFORMING ARTS

For details on upcoming events, check the *Boca News, Sun-Sentinel,* or call the **Palm Beach County Cultural Council** information line at ☎ **800/882-ARTS.** During business hours, a staffer can give details on current performances. After hours, a recorded message describes the week's events. The *Sun-Sentinel* also hosts a comprehensive "Source Line" for information on everything from weather to garage sales. Detailed arts information is included.

The **Florida Symphonic Pops,** a 70-piece professional orchestra, performs jazz, swing, rock, big band, and classical music throughout Boca Raton. For nearly 50 years this ever-growing musical force has entertained audiences of every age. Call ☎ **561/393-7677** for a schedule of concerts.

Boca's best theater company is the **Caldwell Theatre,** and it's worth checking out. Located in a strip shopping center at 7873 N. Federal Hwy., this equity showcase does well-known dramas, comedies, classics, Off-Broadway hits, and new works throughout the year. Prices are reasonable (usually between $29 and $38). Full-time students will be especially interested in the little-advertised "Student Rush." When available, tickets are sold for $5 to those who arrive at least an hour in advance. Call ☎ **561/241-7432** for details.

3 Palm Beach & West Palm Beach

65 miles N of Miami, 193 miles E of Tampa

Palm Beach County encompasses cities including Boca Raton in the south to Jupiter and Tequesta in the north. But it is Palm Beach, the small island town across the Intracoastal Waterway, that has been the traditional winter home of America's aristocracy—the Kennedys, the Rockefellers, the Pulitzers, the Trumps, and plenty of CEOs.

The island holds the distinction of being the only continental destination with three resorts that have earned the prestigious AAA Five-Diamonds rating.

And beyond the upscale resorts and chic boutiques, it holds some surprises too, from a world-class art museum to one of the top bird-watching areas in the state.

By contrast, West Palm Beach is a grittier workaday city. Recent renovations have made the metropolitan area a lively and affordable place to dine, shop, and hang out.

In addition to good beaching, boating, and diving, you'll find great golf and tennis throughout the county.

Note: For a general map of Palm Beach and West Palm Beach, see the map on page 271.

ESSENTIALS

GETTING THERE   If you're driving up or down the Florida coast, you'll probably reach the Palm Beach area by I-95. Exit at Belvedere Road or Okeechobee Boulevard and head east to reach the most central part of Palm Beach.

Visitors on their way to or from Orlando or Miami should take the Florida Turnpike, a toll road with a speed limit of 65 m.p.h. If you are watching your budget, avoid the Turnpike—tolls are high. You may pay upward of $9 from Orlando and $4 from Miami. Finally, if you're coming from Florida's west coast, you can take either S.R. 70, which runs north of Lake Okeechobee to Fort Pierce, or S.R. 80, which runs south of the lake to Palm Beach.

Among the airlines serving **Palm Beach International Airport,** at Congress Avenue and Belvedere Road (☎ **561/471-7400**), are **American** (☎ 800/433-7300), **Continental** (☎ 800/525-0280), **Delta** (☎ 800/221-1212), **Kiwi** (☎ 800/538-5494), **Northwest** (☎ 800/225-2525), **TWA** (☎ 800/221-2000), **United** (☎ 800/241-6522), and **US Airways** (☎ 800/428-4322).

Amtrak (☎ **800/USA-RAIL**) has a terminal in West Palm Beach, at 201 S. Tamarind Ave. (☎ 561/832-6169).

GETTING AROUND   Although a car is almost a necessity in this area, a recently revamped public transportation system is extremely convenient for getting to some attractions. Palm Tran underwent a major expansion in late 1996, increasing service to 32 routes and more than 140 buses. The fare is $1 for adults, 50¢ for children ages 3 to 18, as well as for the elderly and disabled. Free route maps are available by calling ☎ **561/233-4-BUS.** Information operators are available from 6am to 7pm, except Sunday.

In downtown West Palm, free shuttles operate Monday through Friday from 9am until 4pm with plans to expand operations to evenings and weekends too. Look for the bubble-gum-pink minibuses throughout downtown. Call ☎ **561/833-8873** for more details.

For a more nostalgic route, consider the stately wicker chariots that run in the downtown area especially on weekends and during special events. Rates vary according to the time of day but average $1 to $2 per block, plus a per person charge of $1. Call ☎ **561/835-8922** for pickup or information.

VISITOR INFORMATION   The **Palm Beach County Convention and Visitors Bureau,** 1555 Palm Beach Lakes Blvd., Suite 204, West Palm Beach, FL 33401 (☎ **800/554-PALM** or 561/471-3995), distributes an informative brochure and will answer questions about visiting the Palm Beaches. Ask for a map as well as a copy of its Arts and Attractions Calendar, a day-to-day guide to art, music, stage, and other events in the county.

FUN ON & OFF THE BEACH

BEACHES   Public beaches are a rare commodity here in Palm Beach. Most of the island's best beaches are fronted by private estates and inaccessible to the general public. However, there are a few notable exceptions, including the newly renourished Midtown Beach on Ocean Boulevard, between Royal Palm Way and Gulfstream Road, which boasts more than 100 feet of undeveloped beach. There are no rest rooms or concessions here, although a lifeguard is on duty until sundown. This newly widened sandy coast is now a centerpiece and a natural oasis in a town dominated by commercial glitz. Also, about 1½ miles north near Dunbar Street is a popular hangout for locals who enjoy the relaxed atmosphere. Parking is available at meters along Fla. A1A. To the south is a less popular but better equipped beach at Phipps Ocean Park. On Ocean Boulevard, between the Southern Boulevard and Lake Avenue causeways, is a large and lively public beach encompassing over 1,300 feet of groomed and guarded oceanfront. With picnic and recreation areas as well as plenty of parking, the area is especially good for families.

BICYCLING   Rent anything from an English single-speed to a full-tilt mountain bike at the **Palm Beach Bicycle Trail Shop,** 223 Sunrise Ave. (☎ **561/659-4583**). The rates—$7 an hour, $18 a half day (9am to 5pm), or $24 for 24 hours—include a basket and lock (not that it's necessary in this fortress of a town). The most scenic route is called the Lake Trail, running the length of the island along the Intracoastal Waterway. On it you'll see some of the most magnificent mansions and grounds. Enjoy the views of downtown West Palm Beach and some great wildlife.

CRUISES   **Atlantic Coastal Cruises,** 900 E. Blue Heron Blvd., Singer Island (☎ **561/848-7827**), runs regularly scheduled tours along the Intracoastal Waterway, offering visitors unobstructed views of the area's grand mansions. Daily sightseeing as well as lunch, dinner, and theme cruises are offered, some with live entertainment. They cost $14 to $38. Phone for more information and reservations.

The *Palm Beach Princess* (☎ 800/841-7447 or 561/845-7447), a small cruise ship (421 feet), offers reasonably priced casino gambling cruises out of the Port of Palm Beach (U.S. 1 between 45th Street and Blue Heron Boulevard) every day and evening. Evening cruises usually leave at 7pm and cost $20 to $25; they include a large buffet with average food like spaghetti and meatballs, chicken, shrimp, Greek salad, and vegetables. Best is the prime rib at the carving board. Day trips cost the same and offer slightly less food. Sunday brunch trips cost $25. A popular monthly Bahamas voyage costs $95. Call during business hours for details. Choose from craps, roulette, poker, blackjack, and slots.

GOLF   There's good golfing here, but many of the private club courses are maintained exclusively for the use of their members. Ask at your hotel, or contact the **Palm Beach County Convention and Visitors Bureau** (☎ **561/471-3995**) for information on which clubs are currently available for play. In the off-season, some private courses open their greens to visitors staying in a Palm Beach County hotel.

This "Golf-A-Round" program offers free greens fees (carts are additional); reservations can be made through most major hotels.

One of the state's best courses that is open to the public is ✪ **Emerald Dunes Golf Course,** 2100 Emerald Dunes Dr. in West Palm Beach (☎ 561/687-1700). Designed by Tom Fazio, this dramatic 7,006-yard, par-72 course was voted "One of the Best 10 You Can Play" by *Golf* magazine. It is located just off the Florida Turnpike at Okeechobee Boulevard. Bookings are taken up to 30 days ahead. Fees start at $125.

The **Palm Beach Public Golf Course,** 2345 S. Ocean Blvd. (☎ 561/547-0598), a popular public 18-hole course, is a par-54 and is open at 8am; the course is run on a first-come, first-served basis. Club rentals are available. Greens fees start at $19 per person.

POLO What's Palm Beach without polo? See the box on the next page for details.

SCUBA DIVING Year-round warm waters, barrier reefs, and plenty of wrecks make South Florida one of the world's most popular places for diving. One of the best-known artificial reefs in this area is a vintage Rolls-Royce Silver Shadow, which was sunk offshore in 1985. Mother Nature has taken her toll, however, and divers can no longer sit in the car ravaged by time and saltwater.

Call any of the following outfitters for gear and excursions: **Dixie Divers,** 1401 S. Military Trail, West Palm Beach (☎ 561/969-6688); and **Ocean Sports Scuba Center,** 1736 S. Congress Ave., West Palm Beach (☎ 561/641-1144).

TENNIS There are literally hundreds of tennis courts in Palm Beach County. Wherever you are staying, you are bound to be within walking distance of one. In addition to the many hotel tennis courts (see "Where to Stay," below), you can play at **Currie Park,** 2400 N. Flagler Dr., West Palm Beach (☎ 561/835-7025), a public park with three lighted hard courts. They are free and available on a first-come, first-served basis.

WATER SPORTS Call the **Seaside Activities Station** (☎ 561/835-8922) to arrange sailboat, jet-ski, bicycle, kayak, water ski, and parasail rentals.

SEEING THE SIGHTS

Flagler Museum. 1 Whitehall Way (at Cocoanut Row), Palm Beach. ☎ **561/655-2833.** Admission $7 adults, $3 children. Tues–Sat 10am–5pm, Sun noon–5pm.

Known as the "Taj Mahal of North America," this luxurious mansion was commissioned as a gift to his third wife by the renowned Henry Flagler, a cofounder of the Standard Oil Company and builder of the Florida East Coast Railroad. The classically columned Edwardian-style mansion contains 55 rooms that include a Louis XIV music room and art gallery, a Louis XV ballroom, and 14 guest suites outfitted with original antique European furnishings. Out back, climb aboard "The Rambler," Mr. Flagler's recently revamped railroad car. Allow at least 1½ hours to tour the stunning grounds and interior.

Norton Museum of Art. 1451 S. Olive Ave., West Palm Beach. ☎ **561/832-5196.** Admission $5 adults, $2 students, free for children 12 and under. Tues–Sat 10am–5pm, Sun 1–5pm. From I-95, take Belvedere Rd. (Exit 51) east to the end; then, turn left onto S. Olive Ave. to the museum.

Since a 1997 expansion doubled the Norton's space, the museum has gained even more prominence in the art world. It is world famous for its prestigious permanent collection and top temporary exhibitions. The museum's major collections are divided geographically. The American galleries contain major works by Edward Hopper, Georgia O'Keefe, and Jackson Pollack. The French collection contains

The Sport of Kings

The annual ritual of the ponies is played out each season at the posh Palm Beach Polo and Country Club. It is one of the world's premier polo grounds and hosts some of the sport's top-rated players.

Even if you're not a sports fan, you absolutely must attend a match. Although the field is actually on the mainland in an area called Wellington, rest assured, the spectators, and many of the players, are pure Palm Beach. After all, a day at the pony grounds is one of the only good reasons to leave Palm Beach proper.

Don't worry, though—you need not be a Vanderbilt or a Kennedy to attend. Matches are open to the public and are surprisingly affordable.

Even if you haven't a clue how the game is played, you can spend your time people-watching. Star-gazers have spotted Prince Charles, the duchess of York, Sylvester Stallone, and Ivana Trump in recent years, among others. Dozens of lesser-known royalty, and just plain old characters, keep box seats or chalets right on the grounds.

The general admission seats will land you a spot on metal bleachers across the field from the boxes, where celebrity spotting during a match is a bit difficult. If you want to mingle with the elite, splurge on the more expensive boxes for a chance to overhear great tidbits, like the one I caught recently—"Oh, I know I should be rooting for the Coca-Cola team. That's how I made all my money," whined one flamboyant heiress dressed all in gold as she cheered for the opposing team. "Still, I just can't help cheering for my friends."

Good eavesdropping is possible even with a ticket from the bleachers, since you can wander the grounds and see the whole show. Between chukkers, head to the Polo Club, a covered tent where you can enjoy snacks like popcorn, hot dogs, ice cream, pretzels, and a cocktail from the full bar while listening to live music. Or on a Sunday afternoon, enjoy brunch in the Polo House or Players Club restaurant on the north end of field no. 1.

Incidentally, the point of polo is to keep the other team from getting the ball through your goal. The fast-paced game is divided into six chukkers—like an inning in baseball—each 7 minutes long. There are 3-minute breaks between chukkers except at half-time, which lasts 10 minutes. The whole thing is narrated by a British chap who sounds as though he has walked off a Monty Python set.

Oh dear, whatever will you wear? Unless it is an opening game or some other special event, dress is casual. A navy or tweed blazer over jeans or khakis is a standard for men, while neat-looking jeans or a pantsuit is the norm for ladies. On warmer days, shorts and, of course, a polo shirt are fine, too.

General admission is $6 to $10; box seats cost $10 to $36. Matches are held throughout the week. Schedules vary, but the big names usually compete on Sunday at 3:30pm from January to April.

The fields are located at 11809 Polo Club Rd., Wellington, 10 miles west of the Forest Hill Boulevard exit of I-95. Call ☎ **561/798-7000** for a detailed schedule of events.

Impressionist and post-Impressionist paintings by Cézanne, Degas, Gauguin, Matisse, Monet, Picasso, Pissarro, and Renoir. And the Chinese collection contains more then 200 bronzes, jades, and ceramics as well as a collection of monumental Buddhist sculptures.

✪ **Playmobil Fun Park.** 8031 N. Military Trail, Palm Beach Gardens. ☎ **800/351/8697.** Admission is free. Tues–Sun 10am–6pm. I-95 North to Palm Beach Lakes Blvd west to Military Trail. Turn left, and the park is about a mile down on the right side.

This monstrous retail outlet and play park is one of only two such parks in the world (the other one is in Germany, the company's headquarters). Housed in a replica of a castle, this indoor fantasy world is even better than FAO Schwarz. You could spend hours here and not spend a penny. The 17,000 square foot play floor is divided into age-specific play areas and theme areas, including a water zone for kids to play with boats and a Victorian area with elaborately constructed doll houses.

Society for the Four Arts. 2 Four Arts Plaza (off Royal Palm Way), Palm Beach. ☎ **561/ 655-7226.** Admission varies depending on program. Gardens, library, Sunday-afternoon films, art exhibitions, and gallery talks free to the public. Movies, concerts, and lectures $3–$25. Call for schedule.

Great for kids who are bored with the beach, this Palm Beach institution is a place to hang out and absorb some culture. The society was founded more than 60 years ago to encourage appreciation of art, music, drama, and literature—it does a stellar job with at least three of the four (there hasn't been much drama lately). Call for the schedule of concerts, art exhibitions, and weekly lectures given by big names like John Updike, Gregory Hines, David Frost, and Colin Powell. The excellent and little-known children's library includes an enormous collection of books, videos, and games for the little ones.

NATURE PRESERVES & ATTRACTIONS

Lion Country Safari. Southern Blvd. W. at S. R. 80, West Palm Beach. ☎ **561/793-1084,** or 561/793-9797 for camping reservations. Admission $14.95 adults, $9.95 seniors and children 3–9, free for children under 3. Daily 9:30am–5:30pm (last vehicle admitted at 4:30pm). From I-95, exit on Southern Blvd. Go west for about 18 miles.

More than 1,300 animals are divided into their indigenous regions, from the East African preserve of the Serengeti to the American West. On this 500-acre preserve you can see elephants, wildebeest, ostriches, American bison, buffalo, watusi, pink flamingos, and many other more unusual species. Even the lions and elephants roam the huge grassy landscape without a cage in sight. In fact, you're the one who's confined, in your own car without an escort (no convertibles allowed). You're given a detailed informational pamphlet with photos and descriptions and are instructed to obey the 15-m.p.h. speed limit—unless you see the rhinos charge, in which case you're encouraged to floor it. To drive the loop takes just over an hour, though you could make a day of just watching the chimpanzees play on their secluded islands. Included in the admission price is Safari World, an amusement park with paddleboats, a carousel, and a nursery for baby animals born in the preserve. Picnics are encouraged and camping is available (call for reservations). Don't miss this incredible experience.

Palm Beach Zoo at Dreher Park. 1301 Summit Blvd. (east of I-95 between Southern and Forest Hill blvds.). ☎ **561/547-WILD.** Admission $6, $5 senior citizens, $4 children 3–12, children under 3 free. Daily 9am–5pm.

Unlike big city zoos, this intimate 23-acre park is more like a stroll in the park than an all-day excursion. It features about 500 animals representing more than 100 different species. A special monkey exhibit and petting zoo are favorites with kids. Stroller and wagon rental available.

SHOPPING & BROWSING

From thrift to jewels, Palm Beach has it all.

Known as "the Rodeo Drive of the south," Worth Avenue is a window-shopper's dream. No matter what your budget, don't miss the Worth Avenue experience. To look like you belong you might want to dress as if you were going to an elegant luncheon, not to the mall down the street. The 4 blocks between South Ocean Boulevard and Cocoanut Row—a stretch of more than 200 boutiques, posh shops, art galleries, and upscale restaurants—are home to the stores of Armani, Louis Vuitton, Cartier, Polo Ralph Lauren, and Chanel, among like company.

Victoria's Secret, Limited Express, and several other chains have snuck in here too, but so have a good number of unique boutiques. Stop into **Paper Treasures,** at 217 Worth Ave.; it's an autograph gallery with a priceless collection of John Hancocks like those of Joe DiMaggio, Mickey Mantle, Andrew Jackson, Abe Lincoln, Howard Hughes, and hundreds more, all displayed in beautiful frames. At **Myer's Luggage**, 313 Worth Ave., Richard Myers is happy to demonstrate his impressive assortment of toys and gifts, including a vast collection of amusing alarm clocks, spy equipment, gorilla masks, and gag gifts, along with pricey leather bags and English picnic baskets. Just off Worth Avenue, at 374 S. County Rd., is the **Church Mouse** (☎ **561/659-2154**), a great consignment/thrift shop with antique furnishings and tableware. Lots of good castaway clothing and shoes are reasonably priced. This shop usually closes for 2 months during the summer. Call to be sure.

The **Palm Beach Outlet Center,** at 5700 Okeechobee Blvd. (3 miles west of I-95), West Palm Beach, is the most elegant outlet mall I have ever seen. Upscale clothing, luggage, and shoes at bargain prices are offered in lushly decorated surroundings. The fully enclosed mall also sports a food court.

Downtown West Palm Beach has a number of interesting boutiques along Clematis Street. In addition to a large and well-organized bookstore, Clematis Street Books, at 206 Clematis (☎ **561/832-2302**), there are used-record stores, clothing shops, and a few interesting art galleries.

WHERE TO STAY

The island of Palm Beach is perhaps the most exclusive destination in the country. Royalty and celebrities come to winter here, and there are plenty of royally priced options to accommodate them. It's no accident that the only three hotels in the state to receive five stars from AAA are all located in Palm Beach County. Happily, there exist a few special little inns that offer reasonably priced rooms in elegant settings. Surrounding the island are many more modest places to lay your straw hat.

A few of the larger hotel chains operating in Palm Beach include the **Howard Johnson Palm Beach,** at 2870 S. Ocean Blvd. (☎ **800/654-2000** or 561/582-2581), which is across the street from the beach. Also beachside is the pricey **Palm Beach Hilton,** at 2842 S. Ocean Blvd. (☎ **800/433-1718** or 561/586-6542).

An excellent and affordable alternative right in the middle of Palm Beach's commercial section is a condo that operates as a hotel, too: the **Palm Beach Hotel,** at 235 Sunrise Ave. (between County Road and Bradley Place, across the street from Publix; ☎ **561/659-7794**). With winter prices starting at about $105, this clean and comfortable accommodation is a great option for those looking for the rarely available bargain in Palm Beach.

In West Palm Beach, the chain hotels are mostly located on the main arteries close to the highways and a short drive to the activities in downtown. They include a **Best Western,** 1800 Palm Beach Lakes Blvd. (☎ **800/331-9569** or 561/683-8810), and, just down the road, a **Comfort Inn,** 1901 Palm Lakes Blvd.

(☎ **800/221-2222** or 561/689-6100). Further south is the **Parkview Motor Lodge,** 4710 S. Dixie Hwy. just south of Southern Boulevard (☎ **561/833-4644**). This 28-room, single-story motel is the best of the many motels along Dixie Highway (U.S. 1). With rates starting at $50 for a room with television, air-conditioning, and telephone, you can't ask for more.

For other options, try Palm Beach Accommodations (☎ **800/543-SWIM**).

VERY EXPENSIVE

✪ **The Breakers.** 1 S. County Rd., Palm Beach, FL 33480. ☎ **800/833-3141,** 888/ BREAKERS, or 561/655-6611. Fax 561/659-8403. www.thebreakers.com. 572 units. A/C MINIBAR TV TEL. Winter $360–$675 double; $540 club double; from $600 suite. Off-season $180–$395 double; $295 club double; from $360 suite. Special packages available. AE, CB, DC, DISC, MC, V. From I-95, exit Okeechobee Blvd. E., and head east to S. County Rd.; turn left.

The biggest and grandest of all of this area's resorts, this five-star historic beauty epitomizes Palm Beach luxury. It's one of only two Florida properties to win five stars from the Mobil guide and five diamonds from AAA. From the expansive manicured lawns to the elegant marble lobby, The Breakers is the place to be in Palm Beach if you want to be on the beach, but within walking distance from all the area's most exclusive shopping and dining. The lush 130-acre grounds also sport one of the island's only 18-hole golf courses.

The attentive staff is as accustomed to handling steamer trunks and fur wraps as they are to sending faxes and programming VCRs. Though this 1926 palace was built for the world's most elite, it now handles more corporate clients and families with ease. While the Gatsby-esque grounds of Palm Beach's first hotel reveal a sense of history, the newly reconstructed rooms are equipped with all the modern conveniences. A $75 million renovation completed in time for the behemoth's 100th birthday has increased the size of the smaller rooms and spruced up the fading common areas.

There are more than a dozen categories of rooms from which to choose, with the traditional and superior being the smallest and least expensive. Even these tiny rooms are luxuriously appointed and include all the amenities you could desire. Ask for one of the few corner rooms, which tend to be larger and have more windows for the same price. Oceanfront suites offer huge sitting areas, closets, and sleeping quarters.

The Breakers is great for families, though the formality of the lobbies and restaurants may put some off. Jackets are suggested (but not required) in the formal restaurants and lounge.

Dining/Diversions: Five restaurants and three bars offer a delicious range of meals and snacks from an elegant European dining room to a beach bar with burgers and fries. A romantic oceanfront bar (Palm Beach's only) is reserved for hotel guests.

Amenities: Concierge, 24-hour room service, dry-cleaning and laundry service, overnight shoe shine, newspaper delivery, in-room massage, evening turndown, twice-daily maid service, baby-sitting, secretarial services, express checkout, valet parking $15. VCR and video rentals, four outdoor pools, private beach, bicycle rental, two golf courses (one, the Ocean Course, ca. 1897, is Florida's oldest 18-hole course), putting green, game rooms, supervised children's activities, children's playground, business center, car-rental desk, 14 tennis courts (11 of which are lighted), water-sports concession (including scuba and sailing), croquet, shuffleboard, beach volleyball courts, beauty salon, boutiques and shopping arcade, full-service spa/fitness center.

⚙ **Four Seasons Resort Palm Beach.** 2800 S. Ocean Blvd., Palm Beach, FL 33480.
☎ **800/332-3442** or 561/582-2800. Fax 561/547-1557. 210 units. A/C MINIBAR TV TEL.
Winter $350–$625 double; from $1,200 suite. Off-season $255–$475 double; $775 suite. AE,
CB, DC, DISC, EURO, ER, JCB, MC, V. From I-95, take 6th Ave. exit east and turn left onto Dixie
Hwy.; then, turn east onto Lake Ave. and north onto S. Ocean Blvd., and the hotel is just ahead
on your right.

For over-the-top pampering in a perfect location, the Four Seasons is my favorite in
an area filled with fantastic resorts. Built in 1989 at the edge of Palm Beach's downtown district, this elegant resort has quickly gained accolades from around the
world. The incredibly hospitable staff works hard to be sure this beachfront gem
lives up to its reputation. The elegant marble lobby is replete with hand-carved
European furnishings, grand oil paintings, tapestries, and dramatic flower arrangements.

The ambience of the common areas extends to the guest rooms as well. All are
exceptionally spacious and thoughtfully appointed with extras like a small color TV
in the bathroom. Club-floor rooms include access to a special lounge where continental breakfast, afternoon refreshments, and evening cocktails are served gratis.
One-bedroom suites include an additional sitting room, a CD/stereo, oversize balconies, and two bathrooms.

Dining/Diversions: The main dining room for dinner serves one of the best
meals in Palm Beach. An impeccable menu of Southeastern regional cuisine
includes daily fish, meat, and pasta specials served in white-glove elegance. Two
other less formal restaurants, including a pool bar and grill, round out the dining
options. The lobby lounge is one of the best places in town for an intimate cocktail. Weekend evenings promise excellent live jazz.

Amenities: Concierge, room service (24 hours), evening turndown, dry-cleaning
and laundry services, overnight shoe shine, complimentary newspaper delivery, in-
room massage, twice-daily maid service, baby-sitting and a wide range of other baby
and child amenities, pet amenities (including special water, biscuits, and dog
walking), secretarial services, express checkout, valet parking. VCRs and complimentary video rental, movie channels and video games, outdoor heated pool, beach,
whirlpool, jogging track, bicycle rentals, supervised activities for children 3 to 12,
conference rooms, weekly cooking classes, sundeck, three tennis courts, water-
sports rentals, beauty salon, gift shop, spa shop. The 6,000-square-foot spa contains
cardiovascular equipment, free weights, and saunas and offers classes, massages, and
body wraps.

⚙ **Ritz-Carlton Palm Beach.** 100 S. Ocean Blvd., Manalpan, FL 33462. ☎ **800
/241-3333** or 561/533-6000. Fax 561/540-4999. E-mail: ritzpalmbch@earthlink.net. 270
units. A/C MINIBAR TV TEL. Winter $350–$625 double; $705–$775 club-level double; from
$1,095–$3,200 suite. Off-season $175–$265 double; $325–$375 club-level double; from
$325–$2,700 suite. AE, CB, DISC, MC, V, EURO, JCB. From I-95, take Exit 45 east; after a mile,
turn left onto Federal Hwy. (U.S. 1), continue north for about a mile, and turn right onto
Ocean Ave.; cross the Intracoastal Waterway, turn right onto Fla. A1A.

As is to be expected from any member of this upscale chain, the Palm Beach Ritz-
Carlton is superluxurious. In this case, it is on a beautiful beach in a tiny town
about 8 miles from Palm Beach's shopping and dining area—a plus for those who
want privacy and a drawback for those interested in the activity of "town."

The hotel's elegant and dramatic lobby is dominated by a huge, double-sided
pink-marble fireplace, and French 18th- and 19th-century antique furnishings give
no hint that the property is not yet 10 years old. The ambience and attention to
detail here is rivaled by no other hotel in the area.

Each room has a private balcony and at least a glimpse of the ocean below. All are spacious and decorated in lush contemporary design. Thoughtful details include plush bathrobes and telephones in the large marble bathrooms. Club-level accommodations come with dedicated concierge service and a private lounge where complimentary continental breakfasts, afternoon snacks, and evening cordials are served.

Dining/Diversions: The elegant dining room serves continental-style dinners in ornate surroundings. Other restaurants on the property include a grill, for dinner only; a casual restaurant, which serves all day; and a poolside cafe and bar. Cocktails are also served in the lobby lounge, where you can often find live entertainment. Afternoon tea is served daily but is best Wednesday to Saturday when a jazz trio entertains.

Amenities: Concierge, 24-hour room service, dry-cleaning and laundry services, overnight shoe shine, newspaper delivery, in-room massage, evening turndown, twice-daily maid service, baby-sitting, secretarial services, express checkout, valet parking, airport transportation, free coffee or refreshments in lobby. VCR rentals, Spectravision movie channels, outdoor pool, beach, health club, Jacuzzi, sauna, bicycle rental, children's center and programs, business center, conference rooms, car-rental desk, seven night-lit tennis courts, scuba and snorkeling concessions, beauty salon, gift shop.

EXPENSIVE

Chesterfield Hotel. 363 Cocoanut Row, Palm Beach, FL 33480. ☎ **800/243-7871** or 561/659-5800. Fax 561/659-6707. E-mail: chesterpb@aol.com. 65 units. A/C TV TEL. Winter $269–$389 double; from $529 suite. Off-season $89–$219 double; from $219 suite. Rollaway bed $15 extra. AE, CB, DC, DISC, MC, V. From I-95, exit onto Okeechobee Blvd. E., cross the Intracoastal Waterway, and turn right onto Cocoanut Row.

With more charm than its more expensive rivals, the intimate Chesterfield, located just a block from Worth Avenue, has been popular with visitors in the know since the 1920s. Behind its light stucco facade, arched windows, and colorful flags is an overly designed interior with Laura Ashley prints battling Ralph Lauren. It all creates a wonderfully authentic country-manor feel.

Guest rooms also have formal chintz and taffeta prints. Heavy wooden furniture and plush carpets give each room a warm but dark feel. Although most rooms have no view to speak of, they are comfortable and attractive. A stunning lobby library provides a quiet nook for those who may want to read at the large oak desk or borrow a book for the beach. Afternoon tea completes the illusion of being in a well-run country inn across the Atlantic.

Dining/Diversions: The Leopard Room serves fantastic English, French, and continental favorites all day; reservations are essential for dinner and Sunday brunch. The Leopard Lounge is an area hangout in the evenings when there is usually live music and no cover charge (see "The Palm Beaches After Dark," below).

Amenities: Concierge, room service, newspaper delivery, in-room massage, dry cleaning, twice-daily maid service, baby-sitting, valet parking, secretarial services, express checkout. Swimming pool, access to nearby health club, Jacuzzi, nature trails, bicycle rental, video rentals, conference rooms, business center, car-rental desk, tour desk.

Plaza Inn. 215 Brazilian Ave., Palm Beach, FL 33480. ☎ **800/233-2632** or 561/832-8666. Fax 561/835-8776. www.plazainnpalmbeach.com. 49 units. A/C TV TEL. Winter $160–$235 double; $275 suite. Off-season $95–$145 double; $165 suite. Rates include breakfast. AE, MC, V. From I-95, exit onto Okeechobee Blvd. E., cross the Intracoastal Waterway, turn right onto Cocoanut Row, then left onto Brazilian Ave.

This ever-improving bed-and-breakfast–style inn is as understated and luxurious as the guests it hosts. Nothing is flashy here. From the simple and elegant flower arrangements in the marble lobby to the well-worn period antiques haphazardly strewn throughout, the Plaza Inn has the look of studied nonchalance. A small staff, including owner Ajit Asrani, is remarkably hospitable and knowledgeable about the island's inner workings.

Each uniquely decorated room is dressed with quality furnishings, several with carved four-poster beds, hand-crocheted spreads, and lace curtains. The bathrooms are lovely if quite small, and the wall-mounted air conditioners can be noisy when they are needed in the warm months. Choose a corner room or one overlooking the small pool deck for the best light.

In any room, you are sure to appreciate the convenient location: less than 2 blocks from the ocean and all of the best shopping. For those who appreciate the fine hospitality of a small lodging without the sometimes invasive feel of a bed-and-breakfast, this is the island's number-one choice.

Dining/Diversions: A full cooked-to-order breakfast that includes fresh fruit, breakfast breads, and hot main dishes is served each morning in a charming, English country–style dining room. The cozy Stray Fox Pub, a comfortable little bar with mahogany tables, serves cocktails throughout the evening and sometimes has live piano music on the weekends.

Amenities: Concierge, dry-cleaning and laundry services, newspaper delivery, in-room massage, baby-sitting, secretarial services. VCRs, heated outdoor pool, Jacuzzi and small workout room, access to nearby health club.

MODERATE

Heart of Palm Beach Hotel. 160 Royal Palm Way, Palm Beach, FL 33480. ☎ **800/ 523-5377** or 561/655-5600. Fax 561/832-1201. 90 units. A/C TV TEL. Winter $149–$259 double; $275 suite. Off-season $69–$149 double; $175 suite. AE, DC, MC, V. From I-95, exit onto Okeechobee Blvd. E. and continue over the Royal Palm Bridge onto Royal Palm Way.

The centrally located Heart of Palm Beach Hotel is within walking distance of Worth Avenue's shops and just half a block from the beach. Ongoing renovations since the 1990s have improved the patio space as well as the rooms in the hotel's two buildings. Most are decorated with modest but new furnishings and fittings in a colorful contemporary style. The tiled bathrooms are small, clean, and functional. Besides the great location, another plus here is that each accommodation comes with a private balcony or patio. Choose a room on a higher floor, as those on the ground floor tend to be a bit dark. The staff is particularly outgoing and will help guests plan outings and itineraries.

There's a heated swimming pool and complimentary covered parking. A clubby restaurant serves a selection of salads, sandwiches, pastas, and cocktails. Breakfast is served in a bright dining room overlooking the gardens.

Palm Beach Historic Inn. 365 S. County Rd., Palm Beach, FL 33480. ☎ **561/832-4009.** Fax 561/832-6255. 13 units. A/C TV TEL. Winter $150–$170 double; from $200 suite. Off-season $75–$95 double; from $100 suite. Rates include continental breakfast. Children stay free in parents' room. AE, CB, DC, DISC, MC, V.

Despite a rather abandoned look, this bed-and-breakfast is a cozy and comfortable place to stay in Palm Beach. Built in 1923, the Palm Beach Historic Inn is an area landmark located within walking distance of Worth Avenue, the beach, and several good restaurants. The small lobby is filled with antiques, books, magazines, and an old-fashioned umbrella stand, all of which add to the homey feel of this intimate bed-and-breakfast. All the rooms are on the second floor, and each is uniquely decorated and full of frills. Floral prints, sheer curtains, and the plethora of lace can sometimes be overwhelming, masking rather than complementing beautiful antique writing desks and dressers. Happily, there are also fluffy bathrobes, an abundance of towels, and plenty of good-smelling toiletries.

MODERATE/INEXPENSIVE

✪ **Beachcomber Apartment Motel.** 3024 S. Ocean Blvd., Palm Beach, FL 33480. ☎ **800/833-7122** or 561/585-4646. Fax 561/547-9438. 45 units. A/C TV TEL. Winter $85–$155 motel room; from $105–$210 apt. Off-season $45–$80 motel room; from $60–$125 apt. AE, DISC, MC, V. From I-95, exit 10th Ave. N., head east to Federal Hwy., and turn right. Continue to Lake Ave. and turn left. Go over bridge and turn right at first traffic light (S. Ocean Dr.).

It's not just the bright-pink building that makes this two-story motel stand out. For more than 35 years the Beachcomber has been bringing sanity to pricey Palm Beach by offering a good standard of accommodation at reasonable prices. Squeezed between beachfront high-rises, the motel is located oceanfront, adjacent to Lake Worth Beach and a short drive from Worth Avenue shops and local attractions. Every room has two double beds, large closets, and distinctive green-and-white tropical-style furnishings; some have kitchenettes. The most expensive have balconies overlooking the ocean. The bathrooms are basic, and amenities are limited to towels and soap. Facilities at the motel include a coin-operated laundry, shuffleboard, a large pool, and a sundeck overlooking the Atlantic.

Hibiscus House. 501 30th St., West Palm Beach, FL 33407. ☎ **800/203-4927** or 561/ 863-5633. Fax 561/863-5633. www.hibiscushouse.com. 8 units. A/C TV TEL. Winter $95–$175 double. Off-season $65–$130 double. Rates include breakfast. AE, DC, MC, V. From I-95, exit onto Palm Beach Lakes Blvd. E. and continue 4 mi.; turn left onto Flagler Dr., continue for about 20 blocks, then turn left onto 30th St.

Inexpensive bed-and-breakfasts are rare in Southeast Florida, making the Hibiscus House one of the area's firsts, a true find. Located a few miles from the coast in a quiet residential neighborhood, this 1920s-era B&B is filled with handsome antiques and tapestried in luxurious fabrics. Every room has its own private terrace or balcony. The backyard, a peaceful retreat, has been transformed into a tropical garden with a heated swimming pool and lounge chairs. Also, there are plenty of pretty areas for guests to enjoy inside; one little sitting room is wrapped in glass and is stocked with playing cards and board games. *Beware:* Breakfast portions are enormous. The gourmet creations are as filling as they are beautiful. Ask for any special requests in advance; owners Raleigh Hill and Colin Rayer will be happy to oblige.

WHERE TO DINE

Palm Beach has some of the area's finest restaurants, with many classical and elegant options as well as a few more innovative choices. Dress here is slightly more formal than in most other areas of Florida: Men wear blazers, and women generally put on modest dresses when they dine out, even in the dog days of summer.

EXPENSIVE

✪ **Amici.** 288 S. County Rd. (at Royal Palm Way), Palm Beach. ☎ **561/832-0201.** Fax 561/659-3540. Reservations strongly recommended on weekends. Main courses $18–$29; pastas and pizzas $8–$19. AE, DC, MC, V. Mon–Thurs 11:30am–3pm and 5:30–10:30pm, Fri–Sat 11:30am–3pm and 5:30–11pm, Sun 5:30–10:30pm. ITALIAN.

You'd think that there would be a dozen good Italian restaurants in Palm Beach. There are plenty of decent ones, but Amici tops them all, with homemade pastas, a vast array of innovative antipasti, and a variety of lighter fare,. They come dressed in blazers and ties at lunch, though the atmosphere here is fairly casual, with simple decor and lots of window space to let in light. The food is nothing unusual—grilled sandwiches, pastas with rustic sauces, pizzas, grilled shrimp, and fish—but the execution is flawless. You could argue that the prices don't match the simple food, but where else in Palm Beach can you get broccoli rabe, fresh roasted peppers loaded with garlic, and pizzas with escarole, homemade sausage, and pine nuts.

Cafe l'Europe. 331 S. County Rd. (at the corner of Brazilian Ave.), Palm Beach. ☎ **561/ 655-4020.** Reservations recommended. Main courses $18–$32. AE, CB, DC, DISC, MC, V. Tues–Sat noon–2:30pm and 5:45–10:30pm, Fri–Sat open until 1am. Sun 6–10:30pm. FRENCH/CONTINENTAL.

One of Palm Beach's very finest, this award-winning formal restaurant is located on the upper level of the Esplanade, a Spanish-style shopping arcade. The interior is made romantic and luxurious by the tapestried cafe chairs and linen-topped tables set with crystal and china. The enticing appetizers served by a superb staff might include Chinese spring rolls, baked goat-cheese salad with raspberry-walnut dressing, poached salmon, or chilled gazpacho with avocado. Main courses run the gamut from sautéed potato-crusted Florida snapper to lamb chops to roast Cornish game hen. Seafood dishes and steaks in sumptuous but light sauces are always exceptional.

Chuck & Harold's Cafe. 207 Royal Poinciana Way (corner of S. County Rd.), Palm Beach. ☎ **561/659-1440.** Reservations recommended. Main courses $16–$33. AE, DC, DISC, MC, V. Mon–Thurs 7:30am–midnight, Fri–Sat 7:30am–1am, Sun 8am–11pm. AMERICAN.

For predictable American fare, this old standby delivers. Chuck & Harold's serves good food at inflated prices. Remember, you are paying for one of the area's best people-watching perches. Sit outside and enjoy the view. Main dishes include fresh grilled or broiled fish, boiled lobster, and a small variety of straightforward homemade pasta and chicken dishes. If you happen to visit during stone crab season, order them here. The crab claws are steamed or chilled and served with a traditional honey-mustard sauce.

MODERATE

✪ **Aquaterra.** 230 Sunrise Ave. (between Sunrise and Park aves.), Palm Beach. ☎ **561/ 366-4000.** Reservations recommended, especially on weekends. Main courses $15–$18.50. Fixed-price menu 5–6pm $19. AE, MC, V. Tues–Sun 5–11pm. INNOVATIVE AMERICAN.

New York's Charlie Palmer, James Beard winner for best chef in 1997, has taken his spatula south and opened a stunning new lunch and dinner spot in Palm Beach. Slightly off the beaten track on Sunrise Avenue (across the street from the Palm Beach Hotel), this fantastic restaurant is bound to please even the pickiest eaters. With nearly 20 options for bar snacks and appetizers including crispy fried oysters, beef skewers with peanut sauce, vegetable spring rolls, eggplant fritters, and rock shrimp pillows, the menu is simple yet diverse. A more limited selection of entrees, as the name suggests, is from the sea or land. The best choices are waterborne. Depending on the season there is mahimahi (dolphin), salmon, swordfish, snapper, or tuna, all of which can be prepared grilled, roasted, or sautéed with a complimentary array of herbs and seasonings. I favor the clean-tasting snapper grilled with caramelized lemon, olive oil, and fresh parsley. Likewise, you can choose how you'd like your meats or chicken cooked. A delicate filet mignon sautéed with wild mushroom ragout is memorable. Don't skip the architecturally striking and delicious desserts. Especially good are the double caramelized banana parfait and the bittersweet chocolate torte with homemade mint ice cream.

Rhythm Cafe. 3800 S. Dixie Hwy., West Palm Beach. ☎ **561/833-3406.** Reservations recommended on weekends. Main courses $10–$24. AE, DISC, MC, V. Tues–Sat 6–10pm; Sun 10am–2pm and 6–10pm during winter. Sometimes earlier on Sun. From I-95, exit east on Southern Blvd., 1 block north of Southern Blvd., on the right. ECLECTIC AMERICAN.

This hole-in-the-wall is where those in the know come to eat some of West Palm Beach's most laid-back gourmet food. On the handwritten, photocopied menu, you'll always find a fish specialty with a hefty dose of greens and garnishes. Also reliably outstanding is the sautéed medallion of beef tenderloin served on a bed of arugula with a tangy rosemary vinaigrette. Salads and soups are a great bargain since portions are relatively large and the display usually spectacular. The kitschy decor of this tiny cafe comes complete with vinyl tablecloths and paintings by local amateurs. Young, handsome waiters are attentive but not solicitous. The old drugstore where the restaurant recently relocated features an original '50s lunch counter and stools.

Taboo. 221 Worth Ave., Palm Beach. ☎ **561/835-3500.** Reservations recommended. Main courses $14–$22. AE, DC, MC, V. Sun–Thurs 11:30am–11pm, Fri–Sat 11:30am–1am. AMERICAN BISTRO.

Taboo is a snazzy Worth Avenue eatery that successfully combines the classic and the trendy. Lots of greenery, a fireplace, and a contemporary Southwestern charm make it comfortable and inviting. Variety is always the chef's special, with extensive lunch and dinner offerings that are often calorie- and cholesterol-conscious. For lunch, the kitchen creates California-style individual-size pizzas topped with delicacies like barbecued chicken, goat and mozzarella cheeses, and sweet roasted red peppers. Other choices include a delicious sandwich of sweet peppers and goat cheese. The best dinner starter is fresh tuna marinated in ginger and lime. Dinner choices change nightly and may include grilled swordfish topped with olive-caper sauce or grilled veal served on the bone.

INEXPENSIVE

Green's Pharmacy. 151 N. County Rd., Palm Beach. ☎ **561/832-0304.** Breakfast $2–$5; burgers and sandwiches $3–$6. AE, MC, V. Mon–Sat 7am–6pm, Sun 7am–5pm. AMERICAN.

This neighborhood corner pharmacy offers one of the best meal deals in Palm Beach. Both breakfast and lunch are served coffee-shop style at either a Formica bar or plain tables above a black-and-white checkerboard floor. Breakfast specials include eggs and omelettes served with home fries and bacon, sausage, or corned-beef hash. At lunch, the grill serves burgers and sandwiches, as well as ice-cream sodas and milkshakes, to a loyal crowd of pastel-clad Palm Beachers.

✪ **John G's.** 10 S. Ocean Blvd., Lake Worth. ☎ **561/585-9860.** Reservations not accepted. Breakfast $3–$8.50; lunch $5–$14. No credit cards. Daily 7am–3pm. Off Florida Turnpike, take the Lake Worth exit and head toward the ocean. AMERICAN.

This coffee shop is the most popular in the county. For decades, John G's has been attracting huge breakfast crowds; lines run out the door (on weekends, all the way down the block). Stop in for some good, greasy-spoon-style food served in heaping portions right on the beachfront. This place is known for fresh and tasty fish-and-chips and its selection of creative omelettes and grill specials.

TooJay's. 313 Royal Poinciana Plaza (3 miles east of I-95 off Exit 52A), Palm Beach. ☎ **561/659-7232.** Reservations not accepted. Main courses $7–$12. CB, DC, MC, V. Daily 8am–9pm. DELICATESSEN.

This simple and predictable restaurant and take-out deli is a favorite with locals and out-of-towners who want good old-fashioned deli food. So popular, in fact, that

TooJay's now has more than a dozen outlets. For good cover while people-watching, choose a booth surrounded by a jungle of potted plants. The food is excellent and could hardly be fresher. All the classic sandwiches are available: hot pastrami, roast beef, turkey, chicken, chopped liver, egg salad, and more. Comfort food in the form of huge portions of stuffed cabbage, chicken pot pie, beef brisket, and sautéed onions and chicken livers is sure to satisfy.

THE PALM BEACHES AFTER DARK
THE BAR, CAFE & MUSIC SCENE: DOWNTOWN WEST PALM BEACH

A decade-old project to revitalize downtown West Palm Beach has finally become a reality, with ✪ **Clematis Street** at the heart. Artist lofts, sidewalk cafes, bars, restaurants, consignment shops, and galleries dot the street from Flagler Drive to Rosemary Avenue, creating a hot spot for a night out, especially on weekends when yuppies mingle with stylish Euros and disheveled artists. Every Thursday night is a popular night out called *Clematis by Night.* Each week features a different rock, blues, or reggae band plus an art show. Vendors sell food and drinks and the street's bars and restaurants are packed. It is a bit raucous at times, but fun. Note that minors unaccompanied by their guardians are not permitted in the downtown area around Clematis Street after 10pm on weeknights and after 11pm on weekend nights.

Some highlights of the Strip include **Sforza,** at 223 Clematis St.—it's the only Italian restaurant I've seen that needs a bouncer at the door. On weekends this place draws crowds of yuppies and well-dressed Euros who wait to be picked to get in the elegant dining room to dance and sip expensive martinis (☎ **561/832-8819**).

If you are looking for a more casual scene, stop by **Ray's,** at 519 Clematis St. (☎ **561/835-1577**), on a Thursday, Friday, or Saturday for free blues and mediocre drinks. This dusty little bar hosts homegrown blues bands who give it all up for the few patrons who appreciate the rough stuff.

Across the street is a longtime favorite, **Respectable Street café,** at 518 Clematis St. (☎ **561/832-9999**). The cafe's plain storefront exterior belies its funky high-ceilinged interior decorated with large black booths, psychedelic wall murals, and a large checkerboard-tile dance floor where young hipsters dance to both live and recorded alternative music.

Over the bridge in Palm Beach is ✪ **E. R. Bradley's Saloon,** at 111 Bradley Place, between Royal Poinciana Way and Sunset Avenue (☎ **561/833-3520**). Bradley's, as it is known, is about as wild as the "island" allows. Most nights a crowd of young professionals share the old wooden tavern with hard-drinking regulars in blue blazers. Check out the happy-hour buffets in the late afternoon.

A more sophisticated crowd gathers nightly at the **Leopard Lounge** in the **Chesterfield Hotel** (see "Where to Stay," above). Live piano music, good conversation, and a comfortable sofa make this a perfect place to spend an evening.

THE PERFORMING ARTS

With a number of dedicated patrons and enthusiastic supporters of the arts, this area happily boasts many good venues for those craving culture. Check the *Palm Beach Post* or the *Palm Beach Daily News,* known as "the shiny sheet," for up-to-date listings and reviews. Call ☎ **800/882-ARTS** for a recorded announcement of the week's events.

The **Raymond F. Kravis Center for the Performing Arts,** 701 Okeechobee Blvd., West Palm Beach (☎ **561/832-7469**), is the area's largest and most active performance space. With a huge curved-glass facade and more than 2,500 seats in two lushly decorated indoor spaces, and a new outdoor amphitheater, The Kravis, as it is known, stages more than 300 performances each year. Phone for a current schedule of Palm Beach's best music, dance, and theater.

4 Jupiter & Northern Palm Beach County

20 miles N of Palm Beach, 81 miles N of Miami

Northern Palm Beach County and its main town, Jupiter, are known primarily for pristine beaches and expansive tracts of land. The surrounding towns of Tequesta, Jupiter, Juno Beach, North Palm Beach, Palm Beach Gardens, and Singer Island are inviting for tourists who want to enjoy the many outdoor activities that make this area so popular with retirees, snowbirds, and families. Beaches and parks are clean, large, and easily accessible to the public.

ESSENTIALS

GETTING THERE   The quickest route from West Palm Beach to Jupiter is on the Florida Turnpike or the sometimes congested I-95. You can also take a slower but more scenic coastal route, U.S. 1 or Fla. A1A.

Since Jupiter is so close to Palm Beach, it's easy to fly into the **Palm Beach International Airport** (☎ **561/471-7420**) and rent a car there. The drive should take less than half an hour.

VISITOR INFORMATION   A **Visitor Information Center** is located between I-95 and the Florida Turnpike at 8020 Indiantown Rd. in Jupiter (☎ **561/575-4636**) and is open from 9am to 6pm daily.

BEACHES & OUTDOOR PURSUITS

BASEBALL   The **Roger Dean Stadium,** 4751 Main St. (☎ **561/775-1818**), hosts spring training for both the St. Louis Cardinals and the Montreal Expos, along with minor-league action from Florida's state league, The Hammerheads. Tickets range in price from $5 to $15. Baseball aficionados should call for schedules and specific ticket information.

BEACHES   The farther north you head from populated Palm Beach, the more peaceful and pristine the coast becomes. Just a few miles north of the bustle, castles and condominiums give way to wide open space and public parkland. There are dozens of recommendable spots. Following are a few of the best.

John D. MacArthur Beach, a state park, dominates a large portion of Singer Island, the barrier island just north of Palm Beach. Straddling the island from shore to shore, the park has lengthy frontage on both the Atlantic Ocean and Lake Worth Cove. The beach is great for hiking, swimming, and sunning. To reach the park from the mainland, cross the Intracoastal Waterway on Blue Heron Boulevard and turn north on Ocean Boulevard.

Jupiter Inlet meets the ocean at **Dubois Park,** a 29-acre beach that is popular with families. The shallow waters and sandy shore are perfect for kids, while adults can play in the rougher swells of the lifeguarded inlet. A footbridge leads to **Ocean Beach,** an area popular with windsurfers and surfers. There's a short fishing pier, and plenty of trees shading barbecue grills and picnic tables. Visitors can also explore the Dubois Pioneer Home, a small house situated atop a shell mound built by the Jaega Indians. The park entrance is on Dubois Road, about a mile south of the junction of U.S. 1 and Fla. A1A.

BICYCLING   Bring your own, get one from your hotel, or rent one from **Raleigh Bicycles of Jupiter,** at 103 US1, Unit F1 (☎ **561/746-0585**). Bicycle enthusiasts will enjoy exploring this flat and uncluttered area. North Palm Beach has hundreds of miles of smooth paved roads. Loggerhead Park in Juno Beach or Fla. A1A along the ocean has great trails for starters. You'll find many more scenic routes over the bridges and west of the highway.

BOATING & CANOEING　You can rent a boat at several outlets throughout northern Palm Beach County, including **Canoe Outfitters,** 8900 W. Indiantown Rd. (west of I-95), North Jupiter (☎ **561/746-7053**), which provides access to one of the area's most beautiful natural waterways. Canoers start at Riverbend Park along an 8-mile stretch of Intracoastal Waterway where the lush foliage supports dozens of exotic birds and reptiles. Keep your eyes open for gators who love to sunbathe on the shallow shores of the river. You'll end up tired and thoroughly wide-eyed at Jonathan Dickinson Park about 5 or 6 hours later. Eric Bailey, a local who runs the concession, will sell the environmentally minded a pamphlet for $1 that describes local flora and fauna. Trips run Wednesday to Sunday and cost $16 per person, including park charges.

CRUISES　Several sightseeing cruises offer scenic tours of the magnificent waterways that make up northern Palm Beach County. Several water taxis conduct daily narrated tours through the scenic waters. One interesting excursion departs from **Panama Hatties** at PGA Boulevard and the Intracoastal Waterway. Prices are $15 per person for the 1½-hour ride. Call ☎ **561/775-2628.** The *Manatee Queen,* 1065 N. Ocean Blvd. (at the Crab House), Jupiter (☎ **561/744-2191**), a 40-foot catamaran with bench seating for up to 49 people, offers 2-hour tours of Jupiter Island departing daily at 2:30pm that pass Burt Reynolds's and Perry Como's mansions, among other historical and natural spots of interest. Reservations are highly recommended, especially in season; call for the current schedule of offerings. The cruise is wheelchair-accessible. Prices start at $14 for adults and $10 for children and can range up to $15 for special tours. Bring your own lunch or purchase chips and sodas at the minisnack bar.

FISHING　Before you leave, send for an information-packed fishing kit with details on fish camps, charters, tournament, and tide schedules, distributed by the **West Palm Beach Fishing Club,** c/o Fish Finder, P.O. Box 468, West Palm Beach, FL 33402. The cost is $10 and is well worth it. Allow at least 4 weeks for delivery.

Once in town, several outfitters along U.S. 1 and Fla. A1A have vessels and equipment for rent if your hotel doesn't. One of the most complete facilities is the **Sailfish Marina & Resort,** 98 Lake Dr. (off Blue Heron Boulevard), Palm Beach Shores (☎ **561/844-1724**). Call for equipment, bait, guided trips, or boat rentals.

GOLF　Even if you're not lucky enough to be staying at the PGA National Resort, you may still be able to play on their award-winning courses. If you or someone in your group is a member of another golf or country club, have the head pro write a note on club letterhead to **Jackie Rogers at PGA** (see "Where to Stay," below) to request a play date. Be sure the pro includes his PGA number and contact information. Allow at least 2 weeks for a response. Also, ask about the Golf-A-Round program, where selected private clubs open to nonmembers for free or discounted rates. Contact the **Palm Beach County Convention and Visitors Bureau** (☎ **561/471-3995**) for details.

Plenty of other great courses dot the area, including the **Golf Club of Jupiter,** 1800 Central Blvd., Jupiter (☎ **561/747-6262**). A well-respected 18-hole, par-70 course is situated on over 6,200 yards featuring narrow fairways and fast greens. Fees are $27 to $60, depending on the season, and include a mandatory cart. The course borders I-95.

Discovering a Remarkable Natural World

North Palm Beach is well known for the giant sea turtles that lay their eggs on the county's beaches from May to August. These endangered marine animals return here annually, from as far as South America, to lay their clutch of about 115 eggs each. Nurtured by the warm sand, but preyed upon by birds and other predators, only about one or two babies from each nest survive to maturity.

Many environmentalists recommend that visitors take part in an organized turtle-watching program (rather than going on their own) to minimize disturbance to the turtles. The Jupiter Beach Resort (see "Where to Stay," below) and the Marinelife Center of Juno Beach (see below) both sponsor free guided expeditions to the egg-laying sites from May to August. Phone for times and reservations.

Just south of Jupiter, in Juno Beach, is the **Marinelife Center of Juno Beach,** in Loggerhead Park, 14200 U.S. 1, Juno Beach (☎ **561/627-8280**). A small combination science museum and nature trail, the Marinelife Center is dedicated to the coastal ecology of northern Palm Beach County. Hands-on exhibits teach visitors about wetlands and beach areas, as well as offshore coral reefs and the local sea life. Visitors are encouraged to walk the center's sand dune nature trails, all of which are marked with interpretive signs. This is one place that you're guaranteed to see live sea turtles year-round, and during high breeding season (June and July) the center conducts narrative walks along a nearby beach. Reservations are a must. The book opens on May 1 and is usually full by mid-month. Admission to the center is free, though donations are accepted. Open Tuesday to Saturday from 10am to 4pm and Sunday from noon to 3pm.

HIKING   In an area that's not particularly known for extraordinary natural diversity, **Blowing Rocks Preserve** has a terrific hiking trail along a dramatic limestone outcropping. You won't find hills or scenic vistas, but you will see Florida's unique and varied tropical ecosystem. The well-marked mile-long trail passes oceanfront dunes, coastal strands, mangrove wetlands, and a coastal hammock. The preserve, owned and managed by the Nature Conservancy, also protects an important habitat for West Indian manatees and loggerhead turtles. The preserve is located along South Beach Drive (Fla. A1A), north of the Jupiter inlet, about a 10-minute drive from Jupiter. From U.S. 1, head east on S.R. 707 and cross the Intracoastal Waterway to the park. Admission is free, but a $3 per person donation is requested. For more information, contact the Preserve Manager, Blowing Rocks Preserve, P.O. Box 3795, Tequesta, FL 33469 (☎ **561/575-2297**).

SCUBA DIVING & SNORKELING   Year-round, warm, clear waters make northern Palm Beach County great for both diving and snorkeling. The closest coral reef is located a quarter-mile from shore and can easily be reached by boat. Three popular wrecks are clustered near each other less than a mile off shore of the Lake Worth Inlet at about 90 feet. If your hotel doesn't offer dive trips, call the **South Florida Dive Headquarters,** 23141 Lyons Rd., Boca Raton (☎ **800/771-DIVE** or 561/627-9558); or **Seafari Dive and Surf,** 75 E. Indiantown Rd., Suite 603, Jupiter (☎ **561/747-6115**).

TENNIS   In addition to the many hotel tennis courts (see "Where to Stay," below), you can swing a racquet at a number of local clubs. The **Jupiter Bay Tennis Club,** 353 U.S. 1, Jupiter (☎ **561/744-9424**), has seven clay courts (three lighted) and charges $12 per person per day. Reservations are highly recommended.

More economical options are available at relatively well-maintained municipal courts. Call for locations and hours (☎ **561/966-6600**). Many are available free on a first-come, first-served basis.

A HISTORIC LIGHTHOUSE

Jupiter Inlet Lighthouse. U.S. 1 and Alt. Fla. A1A, Jupiter. ☎ **561/747-8380.** Admission $5. Sun–Wed 10am–4pm (last tour departs at 3:15pm). Children must be 4 feet or taller to climb.

Completed in 1860, this redbrick structure is the oldest extant building in Palm Beach County. Still owned and maintained by the U.S. Coast Guard, the lighthouse is now home to a small historical museum, located at its base. The Florida History Museum sponsors tours of the lighthouse, enabling visitors to explore the cramped interior, which is filled with artifacts and photographs illustrating the rich history of the area. First, a 15-minute video explains the various shipwrecks, Indian wars, and other events that helped shape this region. Helpful volunteers are eager to tell colorful stories to highlight the 1-hour tour.

SHOPPING

Northern Palm Beach County may not have the glitzy boutiques of Worth Avenue, but it does have an impressive indoor mall, the **Gardens of the Palm Beaches,** at 3101 PGA Blvd., where you can find large department stores including Bloomingdale's, Burdines, Macy's, and Saks Fifth Avenue, as well as more than 100 specialty shops. A large and diverse food court and fine sit-down restaurants in this 1.3 million-square-foot facility make this shopping excursion an all-day affair. Call ☎ **561/775-7750** for store information.

WHERE TO STAY

The northern part of Palm Beach County is much more laid-back and less touristy than the rest of the Gold Coast. Here, there are relatively few fancy hotels or attractions. In addition to several Holiday Inns, there is a reasonably priced and recently renovated **Wellesley Inn,** at 34 Fisherman's Wharf (I-95, exit east on Indian Town Road; turn left before the bridge), in Jupiter (☎ **800/444-8888**). Suites include sofa beds, refrigerators, and microwave ovens. Though not within walking distance of the beach, the inn is located near shops and restaurants and Fla. A1A.

VERY EXPENSIVE

Jupiter Beach Resort. 5 N. Fla. A1A, Jupiter, FL 33477. ☎ **800 228-8810** or 561/746-2511. Fax 561/747-3304. 176 units. A/C MINIBAR TV TEL. Winter $200–$340 double; $310–$450 suite; $750–$1,000 penthouse. Off-season $115–$205 double; $135–$205 suite; $400–$600 penthouse. AE, DC, DISC, MC, V. From I-95, take Exit 59A east to the end of Indiantown Rd. at A1A. Jupiter Beach Resort is at this intersection on the ocean.

The only resort located directly on Jupiter's beach, this unpretentious retreat is a world away from the more luxurious resorts just a few miles to the south. The lobby and public areas have a formal Caribbean motif, accented with green marble, arched doorways, and chandeliers. The simple and elegant guest rooms are furnished in a comfortable island style, and every room has a private balcony with ocean or sunset views looking out over the uncluttered beachfront. A thorough refurbishing in the mid-1990s has made this resort very popular with conventions and large groups. In fact, it is so popular that it is being gradually converted into a time-share property. Excursions are available to top-rated golf courses in the area.

Dining/Diversions: A popular and well-run lobby restaurant serves an eclectic mix of continental, Southwestern, and Caribbean cuisine. Three other pool and beach bars serve snacks and refreshments throughout the day. The lounge features live music several nights a week.

Amenities: Concierge, room service, dry-cleaning and laundry services, overnight shoe shine, newspaper delivery, in-room massage, daily maid service, baby-sitting, express checkout, valet parking for $5, free coffee in room. Kitchenettes and VCRs in suites, VCR rentals, Spectravision movie channels, outdoor heated swimming pool, beach, exercise room, bicycle rental, supervised children's programs, conference rooms, self-service Laundromat, car-rental desk, night-lit tennis court, water-sports equipment rentals, boutique, dive shop, summer turtle-watch program.

✪ **PGA National Resort & Spa.** 400 Avenue of the Champions, Palm Beach Gardens, FL 33418. ☎ **800/633-9150** or 561/627-2000. Fax 561/622-0261. 339 units. A/C MINIBAR TV TEL. Winter $309–$369 double; from $469 suite. Off-season $119–$149 double; from $229 suite. Children 16 and under stay free in parents' room. Special packages available. AE, DC, DISC, MC, V. From I-95, take Exit 57B (PGA Blvd.) west and continue for approximately 2 miles to the resort entrance on the left.

This rambling resort, built in 1981, is known primarily as a golf destination. With five 18-hole courses on more than 2,300 acres, golfers and other sports-minded travelers will find plenty to keep them occupied—croquet, tennis, sailing, a health and fitness center, and a top-rated Mediterranean-style spa. Constant updating has kept the grounds and buildings in like-new condition. The par-72 Champion Course, redesigned in 1990 by Jack Nicklaus, is the resort's most valuable asset. More than 100 sand bunkers and plenty of water on 6,400-square-foot greens keep golfers of all levels alert. Watch out for hole 16.

When you are ready to rest, you will enjoy the comfortable and spacious accommodations and good food. Ample-size guest rooms are furnished with tasteful modern furnishings and tropical prints. Bathrooms are large and thoughtfully outfitted with cushy robes, good light, and magnifying mirrors. Although you are miles from the beach, the resort has nine pools and a private lake where you can ski or sail. As for views, the best you will get is the golf course or gardens.

Dining/Diversions: Six restaurants and lounges include Don Shula's award-winning steak house, a poolside grill, and another with spa cuisine.

Amenities: Concierge, room service, evening turndown, overnight shoe shine, laundry, baby-sitting. This is the national headquarters of the PGA, so it's no surprise that there are five 18-hole tournament courses, plus the PGA National's Academy of Golf. There are also 19 clay tennis courts (12 lighted), nine swimming pools, a private beach on a 26-acre lake, water-sports equipment rentals, five tournament croquet lawns, five indoor racquetball courts, a full-service Mediterranean spa, aerobics studio, salon, and car rental.

MODERATE/INEXPENSIVE

Baron's Landing Motel & Apartments. 18125 Ocean Blvd. (Fla. A1A at the corner of Love St.), Jupiter, FL 33477. ☎ **561/746-8757.** 8 units. A/C TV TEL. Winter from $90 double. Off-season from $50 double. No credit cards.

This charming family run inn is a perfect little beach getaway. It's not elegant, but it's cozy. A single-story motel fronting the Intracoastal Waterway is often full in winter with snowbirds, who dock their boats at the hotel's marina for weeks or months at a time. Nearly all rooms, which are situated around a small pool, have small kitchenettes. Each unit has a hodgepodge of used furniture, and some have pull-out sofas. Considering that you're a few blocks from some of the most expensive real estate in the country, this is a good deal.

Cologne Motel. 220 U.S. 1, Tequesta/Jupiter, FL 33469. ☎ **561/746-0616.** 9 units. A/C TV. Winter $50–$60 double. Off-season $45 double. Weekly rates available. AE, DC, MC, V.

A pleasant Hungarian couple runs this modest roadside motel that is always busy. After they finish the landscaping and pool, they hope to add more rooms to this nine-room, one-story little gem. The small rooms have just been updated with modest but bright bedspreads and curtains, and the newly retiled bathrooms are small but clean. The area is safe if not scenic and only about a 5-minute drive to the beach. A more direct route by foot gets you there in about 15 minutes.

WHERE TO DINE

In addition to all the national fast-food joints that line Indiantown Road and U.S. 1, you'll find a number of touristy fish restaurants serving battered and fried everything. There are only a few really exceptional eateries in North Palm Beach and Jupiter. Try these listed below for guaranteed good food at reasonable prices.

Athenian Cafe. In the Chasewood Shopping Center, 6350 Indiantown Rd., Suite 7, Jupiter. ☎ **561/744-8327.** Main courses $5–$16. AE, MC, V. Mon–Sat 11am–9pm. Sun 4–9pm during season. GREEK.

Peter Papadelis and his family have been running this pleasant storefront cafe for more than a decade. Tucked in the corner of a strip mall, this place is a favorite with businesspeople, who stop in for a heaping portion of rich and meaty moussaka or a flaky spinach pie made fresh by Peter himself. You could make a meal of the thick and lemony Greek soup and the large fresh antipasto. In a town replete with tourist-priced fish joints, this is a welcome alternative. Early bird specials, served until 7pm, include many Greek favorites and broiled local fish with soup or salad, rice, vegetables, pita, dessert, and coffee or tea.

✪ **Capt. Charlie's Reef Grill.** 12846 U.S. 1 (behind O'Brian's and French Connection), Juno Beach. ☎ **561/624-9924.** Reservations not accepted. Main courses $9.95–$18.95. MC, V. Mon–Sat 11:30am–2pm, daily 5–10pm. Tapas/dessert Mon–Thurs 3–11pm, Fri–Sat 3pm–midnight. SEAFOOD/CARIBBEAN.

The trick here is to arrive early, ahead of the crowd of local foodies who come for more than a dozen daily local-catch specials prepared in dozens of styles. Imaginative appetizers include Caribbean chili, a rich chunky stew filled with fresh seafood; or a tuna spring roll big enough for two. The enormous Cuban crab cake is moist and perfectly browned without tasting fried and is served with homemade mango chutney and black beans and rice. Sit at the bar to watch the hectic kitchen turn out perfect dishes on the 14-burner stove. Somehow the pleasant waitresses keep their cool even when the place is packed. In addition to the terrific seafood, this little dive offers an extensive, affordable wine and beer selection—more than 30 of each from around the world.

Nick's Tomato Pie. 1697 W. Indiantown Rd. (1 mile east of I-95, Exit 59A), Jupiter. ☎ **561/744-8935.** Reservations accepted only for parties of six or more. Main courses $11–$19; pastas $9–$14. AE, CB, DC, DISC, MC, V. Mon–Thurs 5–10pm, Fri–Sat 4:30–11pm, Sun 4:30–10pm. ITALIAN.

A Bennigan's-style family restaurant, Nick's is a popular attraction in otherwise food-poor Jupiter. With a huge menu of pastas, pizzas, fish, chicken, and beef, this cheery (and noisy) spot has something for everyone. On Saturday night you'll see lots of couples on dates and some families leaving with take-out bags left over from the impossibly generous portions. The homemade sausage is a delicious treat, served with sautéed onions and peppers. The *pollo marsala,* too, is good and authentic.

No Anchovies! 2650 PGA Blvd., Palm Beach Gardens. ☎ **561/622-7855.** Pizza and pasta $7–$13; main courses $10–$17. AE, DC, MC, V. Mon–Thurs 11:30am–2:30pm and 4:30–10:30pm, Fri–Sat 11:30am–2:30pm and 4:30–11pm, Sun 4:30–10:30pm. ITALIAN.

This large and colorful restaurant is popular with families that appreciate the large portions and reasonably priced children's specials. An equally colorful menu offers a large variety of pastas, pizzas, salads, and meat and fish specials. Mix and match your pasta with half a dozen sauces. My favorite is the thick and simple *fillete de tomato* over fusilli. You may also want to try some of the delicious chicken or meats prepared on the oak-burning grill.

JUPITER & NORTHERN PALM BEACH COUNTY AFTER DARK

With one notable exception, there just isn't much going on here after dark. **Club Safari,** 4000 PGA Blvd. (just east of I-95), in Palm Beach Garden's Marriott Hotel (☎ **561/622-8888**), is more hip than any hotel dance club I have ever seen, although the safari theme is a bit much. The huge, sunken dance floor is surrounded by vines and lanky, potted trees. Nearby, a large Buddha statue blows steam and smoke while waving its burly arms in front of a young gyrating crowd. There is deejay music, a large video screen, and a modest cover charge on the weekends.

Appendix: Useful Toll-Free Numbers & Web Sites

AIRLINES

Air Canada
☎ 800/776-3000
www.aircanada.ca

America West Airlines
☎ 800/235-9292
www.americawest.com

American Airlines
☎ 800/433-7300
www.americanair.com

British Airlines
☎ 800/247-9297
☎ 0345/222-111 in Britian
www.british-airways.com

Canadian Airlines International
☎ 800/426-7000
www.cdnair.ca

Continental Airlines
☎ 800/525-0280
www.flycontinental.com

Delta Air Lines
☎ 800/221-1212
www.delta-air.com

Midway Airlines
☎ 800/446-4392

Northwest Airlines
☎ 800/225-2525
www.nwa.com

Southwest Airlines
☎ 800/435-9792
www.iflyswa.com

Tower Air
☎ 800/34-TOWER (800/348-6937) outside New York
☎ 718/553-8500 in New York
www.towerair.com

Trans World Airlines (TWA)
☎ 800/221-2000
www.twa.com

United Airlines
☎ 800/241-6522
www.ual.com

US Airways
☎ 800/428-4322
www.usairways.com

Virgin Atlantic Airways
☎ 800/862-8621
in the continental U.S.
☎ 0293/747-747 in Britain
www.fly.virgin.com

CAR RENTAL AGENCIES

Advantage
☎ 800/777-5500
www.arac.com

Alamo
☎ 800/327-9633
www.goalamo.com

Avis
☎ 800/331-1212 in continental U.S.
☎ 800/TRY-AVIS in Canada
www.avis.com

Budget
☎ 800/527-0700
www.budgetrentacar.com

Dollar
☎ 800/800-4000
www.dollarcar.com

Enterprise
☎ 800/325-8007
www.pickenterprise.com

Hertz
☎ 800/654-3131
www.hertz.com

National
☎ 800/CAR-RENT
www.nationalcar.com

Payless
☎ 800/PAYLESS
www.paylesscar.com

Rent-A-Wreck
☎ 800/535-1391
rent-a-wreck.com

Thrifty
☎ 800/367-2277
www.thrifty.com

Value
☎ 800/327-2501
www.go-value.com

MAJOR HOTEL & MOTEL CHAINS

Best Western International
☎ 800/528-1234
www.bestwestern.com

Clarion Hotels
☎ 800/CLARION
www.hotelchoice.com/cgi-bin/res/webres?clarion.html

Comfort Inns
☎ 800/228-5150
www.hotelchoice.com/cgi-bin/res/webres?comfort.html

Courtyard by Marriott
☎ 800/321-2211
www.courtyard.com

Days Inn
☎ 800/325-2525
www.daysinn.com

Doubletree Hotels
☎ 800/222-TREE
www.doubletreehotels.com

Econo Lodges
☎ 800/55-ECONO
www.hotelchoice.com/cgi-bin/res/webres?econo.html

Fairfield Inn by Marriott
☎ 800/228-2800
www.fairfieldinn.com

Hampton Inn
☎ 800/HAMPTON
www.hampton-inn.com

Hilton Hotels
☎ 800/HILTONS
www.hilton.com

Holiday Inn
☎ 800/HOLIDAY
www.holiday-inn.com

Howard Johnson
☎ 800/654-2000
www.hojo.com/hojo.html

Hyatt Hotels & Resorts
☎ 800/228-9000
www.hyatt.com

ITT Sheraton
☎ 800/325-3535
www.sheraton.com

Marriott Hotels
☎ 800/228-9290
www.marriott.com

Motel 6
☎ 800/4-MOTEL6 (800/466-8536)

Quality Inns
☎ 800/228-5151
www.hotelchoice.com/cgi-bin/res/webres?quality.html

Radisson Hotels International
☎ 800/333-3333
www.radisson.com

Ramada Inns
☎ 800/2-RAMADA
www.ramada.com

Red Carpet Inns
☎ 800/251-1962

Red Lion Hotels & Inns
☎ 800/547-8010
www.travelweb.com

Red Roof Inns
☎ 800/843-7663
www.redroof.com

Residence Inn by Marriott
☎ 800/331-3131
www.residenceinn.com

Rodeway Inns
☎ 800/228-2000
www.hotelchoice.com/cgi-bin/res/webres?rodeway.html

Super 8 Motels
☎ 800/800-8000
www.super8motels.com

Travelodge
☎ 800/255-3050

Vagabond Inns
☎ 800/522-1555
www.vagabondinns.com

Wyndham Hotels and Resorts
☎ 800/822-4200 in Continental
U.S. and Canada
www.wyndham.com

Frommer's Online Directory

By Michael Shapiro
Michael Shapiro is the author of *Internet Travel 101:*
How to Plan Trips and Save Money Online (The Globe Pequot Press).

Frommer's Online Directory is a new feature designed to help you take advantage of the Internet to better plan your trip. Section 1 lists some general Internet resources that can make any trip easier, such as sites for booking airline tickets. Please keep in mind that this is not a comprehensive list, but rather a discriminating selection of useful sites to get you started. In Section 2 you'll find some top online guides for Miami. Throughout this directory, you'll find tips about when to use the Net, and when it's best to go a more traditional route and talk to a trained travel professional.

1 The Top Travel-Planning Web Sites

Among the most popular travel sites are online travel agencies. The top agencies, including Expedia, Preview Travel, and Travelocity, offer an array of tools that are valuable even if you don't book online. You can check flight schedules, hotel availability, car rental prices, or even get paged if your flight is delayed.

While online agencies have come a long way over the past few years, they don't always yield the best price. Unlike a travel agent, for example, they're unlikely to tell you that you can save money by flying a day earlier or a day later. On the other hand, if you're looking for a bargain fare, you might find something online that an agent wouldn't take the time to dig up. Because airline commissions have been cut, a travel agent may not find it worthwhile spending half an hour trying to find you the best deal. On the Net you can be your own agent and take all the time you want.

Online booking sites aren't the only places to book airline tickets—all major airlines have their own Web sites and often offer incentives, such as bonus frequent flyer miles or Net-only discounts, for buying online. These incentives have helped airlines capture the majority of the online booking market. According to Jupiter Communications, online agencies such as Travelocity booked about 80 percent of tickets purchased online in 1996, but by 1999 airline sites (such as **www.ual. com**) were projected to own about 60 percent of the online market, with online agencies' share of the pie dwindling each year.

Note: See the appendix on page 298 for toll-free numbers and Web addresses for airlines, hotels, and rental car companies.

Far more people look online than book online, partly due to fear of putting their credit cards through on the Net. Though secure encryption has made this fear less justified, there's no reason why you can't find a flight online and then book it by calling a toll-free number or through your local travel agent. To be sure you're in secure mode when you book online, look for a little icon of a key (in Netscape) or a padlock (Internet Explorer) at the bottom of your Web browser.

WHEN SHOULD YOU BOOK ONLINE?

Online booking is not for everyone. If you prefer to let others handle your travel arrangements, one call to an experienced travel agent should suffice. But if you want to know as much as possible about your options, the Net is a good place to start, especially for bargain hunters.

The most compelling reason to use online booking is to take advantage of last-minute specials, such as American Airlines' weekend deals or other Internet-only fares that must be purchased online. Another advantage is that you can cash in on incentives for booking online, such as rebates or bonus frequent flyer miles. Online booking works best for trips within North America—for international tickets, it's usually cheaper and easier to use a travel agent or consolidator.

Online booking is certainly not for those with a complex international itinerary. If you require follow-up services, such as itinerary changes, use a travel agent. Though Expedia and some other online agencies employ travel agents available by phone, these sites are geared primarily for self-service.

LEADING BOOKING SITES

Below are listings for the top travel booking sites. The starred selections are the most useful and best-designed sites.

Cheap Tickets. **www.cheaptickets.com**
Essentials: This site offers discounted rates on domestic and international airline tickets and hotel rooms.

Sometimes, discounters such as Cheap Tickets have exclusive deals that aren't available through more mainstream channels. Registration at Cheap Tickets requires inputting a credit-card number before getting started, which is one reason many people elect to call the company's toll-free number rather than booking online. Cheap Tickets actually regards this policy as a selling point, arguing that "lookers" who don't intend to buy will be scared off by its "credit card first" approach and won't bog down the site with their queries. If Cheap Tickets is serious about getting people to use its online booking service, it should abolish this credit card-first approach. That being said, Cheap Tickets is worth the effort because its fares can be substantially lower than those offered by its competitors.

✪ Expedia. **expedia.com**
Essentials: Domestic and international flight, hotel, and rental car booking; late-breaking travel news, destination features and commentary from travel experts; deals on cruises and vacation packages. Free registration is required for booking.

Expedia makes it easy to handle flight, hotel, and car booking on one itinerary, so it's a good place for one-stop shopping. Expedia's hotel search offers crisp, zoomable maps to pinpoint most properties; click on the camera icon to see images of the rooms and facilities. But like many online databases, Expedia focuses on the major chains, such as Hilton and Hyatt, so don't expect to find too many one-of-a-kind resorts or B&Bs here.

What You'll Find at Frommer's Site

We highly recommend Arthur Frommer's Budget Travel Online (**www.frommers.com**) as an excellent travel planning resource. Of course, we're a little biased, but you will find indispensable travel tips, reviews, monthly vacation giveaways, and online booking.

Subscribe to Arthur Frommer's Daily Newsletter (**www.frommers.com/newsletters**) to receive the latest travel bargains and inside travel secrets in your mailbox every day. You'll read daily headlines and articles from the dean of travel himself, highlighting last-minute deals for airfares, accommodations, cruises, and package vacations. You'll also find great travel advice by checking our Tip of the Day or Hot Spot of the Month.

Search our Destinations archive (**www.frommers.com/destinations**) of more than 200 domestic and international destinations for great places to stay, tips for traveling there, and what to do while you're there. Once you've researched your trip, you might try our online reservation system (**www.frommers.com/booktravelnow**) to book your dream vacation at affordable prices.

Once you're registered (it's only necessary to do this once from each computer you use), you can start booking with the Roundtrip Fare Finder box on the home page, which expedites the process. After selecting a flight, you can hold it until midnight the following day or purchase online. If you think you might do better through a travel agent, you'll have time to try to get a lower price. And you may do better with a travel agent because Expedia's computer reservation system does not include all airlines. Most notably absent are some leading budget carriers, such as Southwest Airlines. (*Note:* At press time, Travelocity was the only major booking service that includes Southwest.)

Expedia's World Guide, offering destination information, is a glaring weakness—it takes a lot of page views to get very little information. However, Expedia compensates by linking to other Microsoft Network services, such as its Sidewalk city guides, which offer entertainment and dining advice for many of the cities it covers.

Preview Travel. www.previewtravel.com

Essentials: Domestic and international flight, hotel, and rental car booking; Travel Newswire lists fare sales; deals on cruises and vacation packages. Free (one-time) registration is required for booking. Preview offers express booking for members but at press time this feature was buried below the fold on Preview's reservation page.

Preview features the most inviting interface for booking trips, though the wealth of graphics involved can make the site somewhat slow to load. Use Farefinder to quickly find the lowest current fares on flights to dozens of major cities. Carfinder offers a similar service for rental cars, but you can only search airport locations, not city pick-up sites. To see the lowest fare for your itinerary, input the dates and times for your route and see what Preview comes up with.

In recent years, Preview and other leading booking services have added features, such as Best Fare Finder. After Preview searches for the best deal on your itinerary, it will check flights that are a bit later or earlier to see if it might be cheaper to fly at a different time. While these searches have become quite sophisticated, they still occasionally overlook deals that might be uncovered by a top-notch travel agent. If you have the time, see what you can find online and then call an agent to see if you can get a better price.

With Preview's Fare Alert feature, you can set fares for up to three routes and you'll receive e-mail notices when the fare drops below your target amount. For example, you could tell Preview to alert you when the fare from New York to Miami drops below $200. If it does, you'll get an e-mail telling you the current fare.

Minor quibbles: When you search for a fare, hotel or car—at least when we went to press—Preview launched an annoying little "Please Wait" window which gets in the way of the main browser window, so when your results begin to appear, the small window obstructs what you want to see. The hotel search feature is intuitive, but the images and maps aren't as crisp as those at Expedia. Also: All sorts of other extraneous information (such as NYC public school locations) is listed on maps, which is irrelevant to most travelers.

Priceline.com. www.priceline.com
Essentials: Even people who aren't familiar with too many Web sites have heard about Priceline.com. Launched in 1998 with a $10 million ad campaign featuring William Shatner, Priceline lets you "name your price" for domestic and international airline tickets. In other words, you select a route and dates, guarantee with a credit card, and make a bid for what you're willing to pay. If one of the airlines in Priceline's database has a fare that's lower than your bid, your credit card will automatically be charged for a ticket.

Furthermore, you can't say when you want to fly—you have to accept any flight leaving between 6 a.m. and 10 p.m., and you may have to make a stopover. No frequent flyer miles are awarded, and tickets are non-refundable and can't be exchanged for another flight. So if your plans change, you're out of luck. Priceline can be good for travelers who have to take off on short notice (and who are thus unable to qualify for advance purchase discounts). But be sure to shop around first—if you overbid, you'll be required to purchase the ticket and Priceline will pocket the difference.

Travelocity. www.travelocity.com
Essentials: Domestic and international flight, hotel, and rental car booking; deals on cruises and vacation packages. Travel Headlines spotlights latest bargain airfares. Free (one-time) registration is required for booking.

Travelocity almost got it right. Its Express Booking feature enables travelers to complete the booking process more quickly than they could at Expedia or Preview, but Travelocity gums up the works with a page called "Featured Airlines." Big placards of several featured airlines compete for your attention—if you want to see the fares for all available airlines, click the much smaller box at the bottom of the page labeled "Book a Flight."

Some have worried that Travelocity, which is owned by American Airlines' parent company AMR, directs bookings to American. This doesn't seem to be the case—I've booked here dozens of times and have always been directed to the cheapest listed flight, often on Tower or ATA. But this "Featured Airlines" page seems to be Travelocity's way of trying to cash in with ads and incentives for booking certain airlines. (*Note:* It's hard to blame these booking services for trying to generate some revenue—many airlines have slashed commissions to $10 per domestic booking for online transactions so these virtual agencies are groping for revenue streams.) There are rewards for choosing one of the featured airlines. You'll get 1,500 bonus frequent flyer miles if you book through United's site, for example, but the site doesn't tell you about other airlines that might be cheaper. If the United flight costs $150 more than the best deal on another airline, it's not worth spending the extra money for a relatively small number of bonus miles.

On the plus side, Travelocity has some high-tech tools for modern travelers. Exhibit A is Fare Watcher Email, an "intelligent agent" that keeps you informed of the best fares offered for the city pairs (round-trips) of your choice. Whenever the fare changes by $25 or more, Fare Watcher will alert you by e-mail. Exhibit B is Flight Paging—if you own an alphanumeric pager with national access that can receive e-mail, Travelocity's paging system can alert you if your flight is delayed.

Finally, though Travelocity doesn't include every budget airline, it does include Southwest, the leading U.S. budget carrier.

FINDING LODGINGS ONLINE

While the services above offer hotel booking, it can be best to use a site devoted primarily to lodging because you may find properties that aren't listed on more general online travel agencies. Some lodging sites specialize in a particular type of accommodations, such as bed and breakfast inns, which you won't find on the more mainstream booking services. Other services, such as TravelWeb, offer weekend deals on major chain properties, which cater to business travelers and have more empty rooms on weekends.

Note: See the appendix on page 298 for toll-free numbers and Web addresses for airlines, hotels, and rental car companies.

All Hotels on the Web. www.all-hotels.com
Well, this site doesn't include all the hotels on the Web, but it does have tens of thousands of listings throughout the world. Bear in mind that each hotel listed has paid a small fee of ($25 and up) for placement, so it's not as much an objective list as a book of online brochures.

Hotel Reservations Network. www.180096hotel.com
This site features bargain hotel room rates in more than two dozen U.S. cities. The cool thing is that HRN pre-books blocks of rooms in advance, so sometimes it has rooms—at discount rates—at hotels that are "sold out." Select a city, input your dates, and you'll get a list of best prices for a selection of hotels. Descriptions include an image of the property and a locator map—to book online click the "Book Now" button. HRN is notable for some deep discounts, even in cities where hotel rooms are expensive. The toll-free number is printed all over this site; call it if you want more options than are listed online.

InnSite. www.innsite.com
B&B listings for inns in all 50 U.S. states and dozens of countries around the globe. Find an inn at your destination, have a look at images of the rooms, check prices and availability, and then send e-mail to the innkeeper if you have further questions. This is an extensive directory of bed and breakfast inns but only includes listings if the proprietor submitted one. (*Note:* It's free to get an inn listed.) The descriptions are written by the innkeepers and many listings link to the inn's own Web sites, where you can find more information and images.

Places to Stay. www.placestostay.com
Mostly one-of-a-kind places in the U.S. and abroad that you might not find in other directories, with a focus on resort accommodations. Again, listing is selective—this

isn't a comprehensive directory, but can give you a sense of what's available at different destinations.

✪ **TravelWeb. www.travelweb.com**

TravelWeb lists more than 16,000 hotels worldwide, focusing on chains such as Hyatt and Hilton, and you can book almost 90 percent of these online. TravelWeb's Click-It Weekends, updated each Monday, offers weekend deals at many leading hotel chains. TravelWeb is the online home for Pegasus Systems, which provides transaction processing systems for the hotel industry.

LAST-MINUTE DEALS & OTHER ONLINE BARGAINS

There's nothing airlines hate more than flying with lots of empty seats (except maybe the competition). The Net has enabled airlines to offer last-minute bargains to entice travelers to fill those seats. Most of these are announced on Tuesday or Wednesday and are valid for travel the following weekend, but some can be booked weeks or months in advance. You can sign up for weekly e-mail alerts at airlines' sites (for airline's Web site addresses, see the appendix on airlines, hotels, and car rental companies) or check sites such as WebFlyer (see below) that compile lists of these bargains. To make it easier, visit a site (see below) that will round up all the deals and send them in one convenient weekly e-mail. But last-minute deals aren't the only online bargains—other sites can help you find value even if you can't wait until the eleventh hour.

✪ **1travel.com. www.1travel.com**

Deals on domestic and international flights, cruises, hotels, and all-inclusive resorts such as Club Med. 1travel.com's Saving Alert compiles last-minute air deals so you don't have to scroll through multiple e-mail alerts. A feature called "Drive a little using low-fare airlines" helps map out strategies for using alternate airports to find lower fares. And Farebeater searches a database that includes published fares, consolidator bargains and special deals exclusive to 1travel.com. *Note:* The travel agencies listed by 1travel.com have paid for placement.

BestFares. www.bestfares.com

Budget seeker Tom Parsons lists some great bargains on airfares, hotels, rental cars and cruises, but the site is poorly organized. News Desk is a long list of hundreds of bargains but they're not broken down into cities or even countries, so it's not easy trying to find what you're looking for. If you have time to wade through it, you might find a good deal. Some material is available only to paid subscribers.

Go4less.com. www.go4less.com

Specializing in last-minute cruise and package deals, Go4less has some eye-popping offers, such as off-peak Caribbean cruises for under $100 per day. The site has a clean design but the bargains aren't organized by destination. However, you avoid sifting through all this material by using the Search box and entering vacation type, destination, month, and price.

Moment's Notice. www.moments-notice.com

As the name suggests, Moment's Notice specializes in last-minute vacation and cruise deals. You can browse for free, but if you want to purchase a trip you have to join Moment's Notice, which costs $25.

Smarter Living www.smarterliving.com

Best known for its e-mail dispatch of weekend deals on 20 airlines, Smarter Living also keeps you posted about last-minute bargains on everything from Windjammer Cruises to flights to Iceland.

Handy Tip ───

While most people learn about last-minute weekend deals from e-mail dispatches, it can be best to find out precisely when these deals become available and check airlines' Web sites at this time. To find out when deals become available, check the pages devoted to these deals on airlines' Web pages. Because these deals are limited, they can vanish within hours, sometimes even minutes, so it pays to log on as soon as they're available. An example: Southwest's specials are posted at 12:01am Tuesdays (Central time). So if you're looking for a cheap flight, stay up late and check Southwest's site (www.iflyswa.com) at that time to grab the best new deals.

───

✪ **WebFlyer. www.webflyer.com**
WebFlyer is the ultimate online resource for frequent flyers and also has an excellent listing of last-minute air deals. Click on "Deal Watch" for a round-up of weekend deals on flights, hotels, and rental cars from domestic and international suppliers.

TRAVELER'S TOOLKIT

Seasoned travelers always carry some essential items to make their trips easier. Following is a selection of online tools to smooth your journey.

ATM LOCATORS
Visa. (www.visa.com/pd/atm/)
MasterCard. (www.mastercard.com/atm)
Find ATMs in hundreds of cities in the U.S. and around the world. Both include maps for some locations and both list airport ATM locations, some with maps. Remarkably, MasterCard lists ATMs on all seven continents (there's one at Antarctica's McMurdo Station). *Tip:* You'll usually get a better exchange rate using ATMs than exchanging traveler's checks at banks.

✪ **CultureFinder. www.culturefinder.com**
Up-to-date listings for plays, opera, classical music, dance, film, and other cultural events in more than 1,300 U.S. cities. Enter the dates you'll be in a city and get a list of events happening then—you can also purchase tickets online. Also see FestivalFinder (**www.festivalfinder.com**) for the latest on more than 1,500 rock, folk, reggae, blues, and bluegrass festivals throughout North America.

Intellicast. www.intellicast.com
Weather forecasts for all 50 states and cities around the world. Note that temperatures are in Celsius for many international destinations, so check carefully before you pack that winter coat for your trip to Athens.

✪ **MapQuest. www.mapquest.com**
Specializing in U.S. maps, MapQuest enables you to zoom in on a destination, calculate step-by-step driving directions between any two U.S. points, and locate restaurants, hotels, and other attractions on maps.

✪ **Net Café. Guide www.netcafeguide.com**
Locate Internet cafés at hundreds of locations around the globe. Catch up on your e-mail, log on to the Web, and stay in touch with the home front, usually for just a few dollars per hour.

The Travelite FAQ. www.travelite.org
Tips on packing light, choosing luggage, and selecting appropriate travel wear.

Check E-Mail At Internet Cafés While Traveling

Until a few years ago, most travelers who checked their e-mail while traveling carried a laptop, but this posed some problems. Not only are laptops expensive, but they can be difficult to configure, incur expensive connection charges, and are attractive to thieves. Thankfully, Web-based free e-mail programs have made it much easier to check your mail.

Just open an account at a freemail provider, such as Hotmail (hotmail.com) or Yahoo! Mail (mail.yahoo.com) and all you'll need to check your mail is a Web connection, easily available at Net cafés and copy shops around the world. After logging on, just point the browser to www.hotmail.com, enter your username and password and you'll have access to your mail.

Internet cafés have become ubiquitous, so for a few dollars an hour you'll be able to check your mail and send messages back to colleagues, friends, and family. If you already have a primary e-mail account, you can set it to forward mail to your freemail account while you're away. Freemail programs have become enormously popular (Hotmail claims more than 10 million members), because they enable everyone, even those who don't own a computer, to have an e-mail address they can check wherever they log on to the Web.

TheTrip: Airport Maps and Flight Status. www.thetrip.com
A business travel site where you can find out when an airborne flight is scheduled to arrive. Click on "Guides and Tools" to peruse airport maps for more than 40 domestic cities.

2 The Top Web Sites for Miami

CITY GUIDES & ENTERTAINMENT SITES

City guides are a good way to get acquainted with what's going on in Miami. While some are geared toward residents, they are still excellent resources for travelers who want to get the local scoop on nightlife, restaurants, and places to shop.

About.com: Miami for Visitors. gomiami.about.com
Primarily a collection of Web sites for travelers to Miami, the Mining Co. includes sections on culture, fishing, and shopping, among many others. While you won't find in-depth stories here, the site does include some short features on Miami, such as one on what to do if it's too cold for the beach. All these features are rich with links to other relevant Web sites.

✪ **CitySearch: Miami. miami.citysearch.com**
This site offers listings and reviews for Miami arts and entertainment, restaurants, shopping, and attractions. CitySearch is part of a national network of city guides, and has editorial reviews as well as paid Web pages from restaurants and other businesses. CitySearch clearly labels its pages "editorial profile" and "advertiser's Web site." Click on the calendar for events recommended by the editors. The extensive shopping listings range from clothing to specialty stores and include updates on sales. Along with Sidewalk, CitySearch is a leading directory for arts and dining in Miami.

Digital City South Florida on AOL. Keyword: South Florida
Click on here for entertainment, dining, sports, and festivals produced in cooperation with the *Sun-Sentinel.* This site includes a lively forum, where you can read comments

from others or post a question of your own. Digital City is also available on the Web at southflorida.digitalcity.com.

Just Go: South Florida. www.justgo.com/southflorida
Dining, music, theater, and movies are listed and reviewed on this site. Just Go does a nice job in spotlighting upcoming concerts and makes it easy to find restaurants by cuisine and neighborhood.

Metroguide: Miami. miami.metroguide.net
This site offers listings for arts and entertainment, restaurants, shopping, and attractions. Wading through Metroguide after visiting CitySearch or Sidewalk is like watching home movies after seeing the latest Star Wars epic. But it's still worth visiting for its relatively deep events listings (though you'll have to click down three pages to get these). The dining, hotel, and shopping listings appear to include solely businesses that have paid for pages on Metroguide. These can still be valuable as long as you realize you're not getting the whole enchilada.

South Florida Sidewalk. southflorida.sidewalk.msn.com
Reviews and listings for entertainment, restaurants, shopping, and attractions. There are two types of Sidewalk sites—those with local city staffs and those that rely heavily on content from Sidewalk's national edition. At press time, South Florida Sidewalk had begun to add more local content and was hiring local staffers. Sidewalk also includes Yellow Pages for local businesses and features on what to do around town, such as HispanicFest. Like CitySearch, Sidewalk is geared for locals but is an excellent guide for travelers who want to do more than lie on a beach.

Time Out: Miami. www.timeout.com/miami
This site offers reviews and listings for attractions, entertainment, restaurants, hotels and shopping, and includes categories for kids and gay/lesbian. Time Out is a lively guide with a youthful approach but has features for everyone, such as festival previews. Unlike some other city guides, Time Out Miami makes a concerted effort to cater to tourists as well as locals. The listings appear uninfluenced by ads, because there are no ads visible here. Plus, the site's clean design makes it a pleasure to navigate.

Tropicool Miami (Miami Convention & Visitors Bureau).
www.miamiandbeaches.com
This is a nice site to get an overview of Miami and its beckoning beaches. Sure, the content is a bit salesy, but it's still informative. You won't find detailed listings for restaurants and hotels, but there is general information about Miami's dining and arts scene, as well as advice about shopping and lodging in various districts. If you want more, you can order the print guide through the Web site or by calling a toll-free number.

NEWSPAPERS & MAGAZINES

One of the best ways to take a city's pulse is to browse through the virtual pages of its newspapers and magazines. Now, you no longer have to go to a newsstand to browse through Miami's news sources, which also contain entertainment information.

Miami Herald. www.herald.com
Miami's leading news source can give you a sense of what's going on in the city, but don't expect extensive entertainment listings.

Miami New Times. www.miaminewtimes.com
Miami's leading alternative weekly includes features and listings for music, theater, film, and more. Click on Music and then Concerts This Week to see listings ranging from the Florida Philharmonic to the Blues Festival.

Sun-Sentinel: Showtime. **www.sun-sentinel.com/showtime**
A nice round-up of music, theater, sports, and dining choices for South Florida with coverage of local festivals and events. For hard news and weather, see www.sun-sentinel.com.

DINING GUIDES
Get a taste of Miami's restaurants with online reviews. You can also find extensive restaurant listings at Sidewalk, CitySearch, and some other city guides (see above).

CuisineNet. **www.cuisinenet.com**
Listings and reviews for Miami and 15 other U.S. cities. Each restaurant has a capsule review compiled by CuisineNet and ratings based on surveys received from site users. For many restaurants, only two or three people have bothered to submit ratings, so they may not be statistically significant. However, comments can be instructive, as CuisineNet's readers discuss service, parking, free birthday desserts, and a host of other insightful observations.

Zagat Restaurant Survey. **cgi.pathfinder.com/cgi-bin/zagat/homepage**
Reviews of top restaurants for Miami and many other U.S. cities. Zagat has made a name for itself as the people's choice, as its listings are based on extensive surveys. As this book went to press, Zagat, after several years on Pathfinder's site, was launching its own site at a more friendly Web address: **www.zagat.com.**

ATTRACTIONS
Though there's absolutely nothing wrong with just lying on a beach, Miami offers much more for visitors. Here's a sampling.

Bayside Waterfront. **www.baysidemarketplace.com**
Tourism information, a searchable directory and calendar of events for this downtown shopping, dining, and entertainment complex. There's even a coupon on the Web site that you can print and redeem at Bayside.

Biltmore Hotel. **www.biltmorehotel.com**
Even if you don't stay at the Biltmore, you can enjoy its opulence and events, which include historic tours, opera nights, and afternoon tea.

Biscayne National Park. **www.nps.gov/bisc**
Just a hop, skip, and jump across Biscayne Bay, this park is a terrific place for recreation and is home to mangrove shorelines, a shallow bay, undeveloped islands, and living coral reefs. The site includes basic information on activities, attractions, and nearby lodgings.

✪ Everglades National Park. **www.nps.gov/ever**
This fairly comprehensive guide from the National Park Service includes everything you'd expect—information on attractions, activities, lodging, camping, fishing, and climate for this remarkable park. You'll also find superb features on the Everglades at GORP—visit **www.gorp.com** and search for "Everglades."

Fairchild Tropical Garden. **www.ftg.org**
Visitor information, events, and history for this lush botanical garden of rare tropical plants, flowering trees, and vines.

Historical Museum of Southern Florida. **www.historical-museum.org**
Tracing human history in South Florida back 10,000 years, the Historical Museum site lets you preview the exhibition online. Perhaps most interesting to tourists are the Historic Tours—by foot, bus, boat, metrorail, and bicycle. A schedule is available at the site.

Jungle Queen. www.junglequeen.com
Schedule, fares, and online reservations for this riverboat that cruises between Miami and Fort Lauderdale.

Miami-Dade County Online. www.co.miami-dade.fl.us
At Dade County's official government site, you'll find up-to-date information on county parks, sports, attractions such as Miami Metro Zoo, and cultural events.

Miami Film Festival. www.miamifilmfestival.com
If you'll be in Miami during the latter half of February, the film festival could be just the thing to wake up your mind. The site offers information about the films, events, and show times.

Miami International Boat Show. www.boatshows.com/miami99/home.html
One of the largest boat shows anywhere. Check this site for a schedule, overview, exhibitors, and tickets. *Note:* The Web address above was for the 1999 show—if it doesn't roll over to the current site, try replacing the "99" with "00" or "2000."

Miami Museum of Science. www.miamisci.org
Visitor information, exhibit previews, and a look inside the museum's Space Transit Planetarium, where you can lean back and search the night sky during the brightest Miami day.

Miami Seaquarium. miamiseaquarium.com
Featuring dolphins, whales, manatees, and alligators, Seaquarium is fascinating for the entire family. The site includes general park information (admission prices, hours, etc.), and a virtual tour of the attractions.

Parrot Jungle. www.parrotjungle.com
Homo sapiens isn't the only species that goes to Florida to retire—some colorful parrots and macaws spend their golden years at this south Miami park. The site includes park information, a $2 coupon, and audio samples of a park tour. *Note:* RealAudio software is required to hear this audio sample—the software is available for free from **www.real.com.**

Venetian Pool. www.venetianpool.com
From humble beginnings as a rock quarry, the 820,000-gallon Venetian Pool today features two waterfalls, coral caves, and grottoes. The site includes a tour, maps, photos, history, programs, and other visitor information.

LOCAL SPORTS TEAMS

Miami is home to some of the best professional and college teams in the country. You can learn more about them and make plans to catch a game during your next trip.

Florida Marlins. www.flamarlins.com
In only their fifth year, the Marlins stunned the baseball world by winning the World Series. However, the glory of bringing a world championship to south Florida wasn't enough for mega-millionaire Wayne Huizenga, who claimed the team wasn't profitable and traded its well-paid stars. Despite the fire sale, the Marlins are rebuilding under new ownership and can be entertaining at times. You'll find schedules, tickets, and game coverage here.

Florida Panthers. www.flpanthers.com
Though hockey seems like a sport more suited to northern climes, tropical South Florida has caught hockey fever. The Panthers' site includes arena and ticket information, schedules, and player profiles.

Miami Dolphins. www.miamidolphins.com/home.html
Tickets, schedules, and news for the NFL team that spawned legends such as Bob Griese, Larry Csonka, and coach Don Shula.

Miami Heat. www.nba.com/heat
Scores and schedules, player profiles, and tickets for this NBA team that has become a perennial playoff contender.

University of Miami Hurricanes. www.miami.edu/athletics/football
Schedule, tickets and arena information, and game stories for the 'Canes, who are usually at or near the top of college football polls.

TICKETS

If you want to purchase tickets for concerts, theater, or sporting events, try the following online services.

TicketMaster. events.ticketmaster.com
A national outlet, TicketMaster sells tickets for sports, theater, and concerts—all with a hefty service charge. Remember, you can buy tickets through Culturefinder.com and you can also reach TicketMaster through CitySearch.

TicketWeb. www.ticketweb.com
TicketWeb sells theater and concert tickets, usually with a much lower service charge than TicketMaster. TicketWeb is best for events at smaller venues—many of the larger arenas and halls are locked into exclusive deals with large ticket sellers and do not sell through other outlets.

GETTING AROUND

Get acquainted with the airport, check options for getting from the airport to your hotel, and learn how the locals get around at a fraction of the cost of a cab.

Miami-Dade Transit. www.co.miami-dade.fl.us/mdta/
Though this is a terribly slow-loading site, it does have basic information on bus and rail lines in and around Miami.

Miami International Airport. www.miami-airport.com
Terminal map, airline counter locations, car rental information, taxi and van advice, and other services to help you get around this labyrinthine airport.

Supershuttle: Miami. www.supershuttle.com/mia.htm
For single travelers this shuttle can be considerably cheaper than taking a cab. The site includes sample fares and toll-free reservations lines.

Index

See also Accommodations and Restaurant indexes, below.
Page numbers in *italics* refer to maps.

General Index

ACCOMMODATIONS

RESTAURANTS

FROMMER'S® COMPLETE TRAVEL GUIDES

Alaska
Amsterdam
Arizona
Atlanta
Australia
Austria
Bahamas
Barcelona, Madrid & Seville
Beijing
Belgium, Holland & Luxembourg
Bermuda
Boston
Budapest & the Best of Hungary
California
Canada
Cancún, Cozumel &
   the Yucatán
Cape Cod, Nantucket & Martha's Vineyard
Caribbean
Caribbean Cruises & Ports of Call
Caribbean Ports of Call
Carolinas & Georgia
Chicago
China
Colorado
Costa Rica
Denmark
Denver, Boulder & Colorado Springs
England
Europe
Florida
France
Germany
Greece
Greek Islands
Hawaii
Hong Kong
Honolulu, Waikiki & Oahu
Ireland
Israel
Italy
Jamaica & Barbados
Japan
Las Vegas
London
Los Angeles
Maryland & Delaware
Maui
Mexico
Miami & the Keys

Montana & Wyoming
Montréal & Québec City
Munich & the Bavarian Alps
Nashville & Memphis
Nepal
New England
New Mexico
New Orleans
New York City
Nova Scotia, New Brunswick &
   Prince Edward Island
Oregon
Paris
Philadelphia & the
   Amish Country
Portugal
Prague & the Best of the Czech Republic
Provence & the Riviera
Puerto Rico
Rome
San Antonio & Austin
San Diego
San Francisco
Santa Fe, Taos &
   Albuquerque
Scandinavia
Scotland
Seattle & Portland
Singapore & Malaysia
South Africa
Southeast Asia
South Pacific
Spain
Sweden
Switzerland
Thailand
Tokyo
Toronto
Tuscany & Umbria
USA
Utah
Vancouver & Victoria
Vermont, New Hampshire
   & Maine
Vienna & the Danube Valley
Virgin Islands
Virginia
Walt Disney World & Orlando
Washington, D.C.
Washington State

FROMMER'S® DOLLAR-A-DAY GUIDES

Australia from $50 a Day	Hawaii from $70 a Day	New Zealand from $50 a Day
California from $60 a Day	Ireland from $50 a Day	Paris from $85 a Day
Caribbean from $70 a Day	Israel from $45 a Day	San Francisco from $60 a Day
England from $70 a Day	Italy from $70 a Day	Washington, D.C.,
Europe from $60 a Day	London from $85 a Day	from $60 a Day
Florida from $60 a Day	New York from $80 a Day	

FROMMER'S® PORTABLE GUIDES

Acapulco, Ixtapa & Zihuatanejo	Dublin	Puerto Vallarta, Manzanillo & Guadalajara
Alaska Cruises & Ports of Call	Hawaii: The Big Island	San Diego
Bahamas	Las Vegas	San Francisco
Baja & Los Cabos	London	Sydney
Berlin	Maine Coast	Tampa & St. Petersburg
California Wine Country	Maui	Venice
Charleston & Savannah	New Orleans	Washington, D.C.
Chicago	New York City	
	Paris	

FROMMER'S® NATIONAL PARK GUIDES

Family Vacations in the National Parks	National Parks of the American West	Yellowstone & Grand Teton
Grand Canyon	Rocky Mountain	Yosemite & Sequoia/ Kings Canyon
		Zion & Bryce Canyon

FROMMER'S® GREAT OUTDOOR GUIDES

New England	Southern California & Baja
Northern California	Washington & Oregon

FROMMER'S® MEMORABLE WALKS

Chicago	New York	San Francisco
London	Paris	Washington D.C.

FROMMER'S® IRREVERENT GUIDES

Amsterdam	London	New Orleans	Seattle & Portland
Boston	Los Angeles	Paris	Vancouver
Chicago	Manhattan	San Francisco	Walt Disney World
Las Vegas			Washington, D.C.

FROMMER'S® BEST-LOVED DRIVING TOURS

America	Florida	Ireland	Scotland
Britain	France	Italy	Spain
California	Germany	New England	Western Europe

THE COMPLETE IDIOT'S TRAVEL GUIDES

Boston	Ireland	Paris
Chicago	Las Vegas	San Francisco
Cruise Vacations	London	Spain
Planning Your Trip to Europe	Mexico's Beach Resorts	Walt Disney World
Florida	New Orleans	Washington, D.C.
Hawaii	New York City	

THE UNOFFICIAL GUIDES®

SPECIAL-INTEREST TITLES

WHEREVER YOU TRAVEL, *H*ELP IS NEVER FAR AWAY.

From planning your trip to providing travel assistance along the way, American Express® Travel Service Offices are always there to help you do more.

Miami and The Keys

American Express Travel Service
330 Biscayne Blvd.
305/358-7350

Corporate International Travel (R)
7901 N.W. 53rd St.
305/477-7070

Travel is Fun (R)
7760 S.W. 88th St.
305/271-0010

Zmax Travel & Tours (R)
420 Lincoln Rd.
Suite 239
305/532-0111

Travelwise, Inc.
100 Westwood Dr.
305/888-1601

do more

Travel

www.americanexpress.com/travel

American Express Travel Service Offices are located throughout the United States. For the office nearest you, call 1-800-AXP-3429.